Quantitative Methods for Business

DONALD WATERS

D1513005

Quantitative Methods for Business

DONALD WATERS
UNIVERSITY OF CALGARY

ADDISON-WESLEY PUBLISHING COMPANY

Harlow, England • Reading, Massachusetts • Menlo Park, California • New York
Don Mills, Ontario • Amsterdam • Bonn • Sydney • Singapore
Tokyo • Madrid • San Juan • Milan • Paris • Mexico City • Seoul • Taipei

© 1994 Addison-Wesley Publishers Ltd.
© 1994 Addison-Wesley Publishing Company Inc.

All rights reserved. No part of this publication may be reproduced, stored in a retrieval system, or transmitted in any form or by any means, electronic, mechanical, photocopying, recording or otherwise, without prior written permission of the publisher.

The programs in this book have been included for their instructional value. They have been tested with care but are not guaranteed for any particular purpose. The publisher does not offer any warranties or representations nor does it accept any liabilities with respect to the programs.

Many of the designations used by manufacturers and sellers to distinguish their products are claimed as trademarks. Addison-Wesley has made every attempt to supply trademark information about manufacturers and their products mentioned in this book.

Cover designed by Viva Design Limited, Henley-on-Thames.

Printed and bound in Great Britain by Bookcraft Ltd, Midsomer Norton, Somerset

First printed 1993. Reprinted 1995 and 1996.

ISBN 0-201-62752-3

British Library Cataloguing-in-Publication Data
A catalogue record for this book is available from the British Library.

Library of Congress Cataloguing-in-Publication Data is available

Dedication:

To Charles

Preface

Introduction

This is a textbook on **quantitative methods for business**. Its main features are:

- it is an introductory text and assumes no previous knowledge of management or quantitative methods
- it can be used by students doing a wide range of business courses, or individuals studying by themselves
- it covers a lot of material, concentrating on methods that have proved useful in practice
- it illustrates principles by examples, rather than theoretical discussion
- proofs and derivations are largely omitted, but some are put into appendices
- it uses computer output to illustrate calculations
- it lists objectives for each chapter, and includes summaries, self-assessment questions, worked examples, reviews, additional problems, computer exercises and case studies
- there is a logical development of material through the book

Audience

A growing number of students are taking courses in management. Some of these courses give a broad description of business, while others specialize in accountancy, marketing, or some other function. The courses are run by colleges, universities, professional organizations and companies.

It is generally agreed that managers need some understanding of quantitative methods, so despite the diversity of courses, most business students will attend a course with a title like 'Quantitative Methods'. This book describes a range of methods that have proved useful to managers, and which are included in most business courses. It can be used widely: for example, as a source book over two years for BTEC courses; in the early years of an undergraduate business studies course; in a one-term course for MBA students; or in a short professional course. It can also be used by people who are not attending a specific course, but want to develop their quantitative abilities.

Management students have diverse backgrounds and interests. A single course might contain some students with backgrounds in science or engineering, and others with backgrounds in arts or humanities. A textbook cannot, therefore, assume much common knowledge. This book starts with the assumption that students have no previous knowledge of management or quantitative methods. It works from basic principles and develops ideas in a logical sequence.

Management students often find quantitative ideas difficult. They are not usually interested in elegant mathematical proofs and derivations, but are more concerned with how useful a result is, and where it can be applied in their work. For this reason the contents of this book are practical rather than theoretical. A deliberate decision has been made to avoid rigorous (and often tedious) mathematics and concentrate on applications rather than theory. Formal mathematical proofs are avoided and methods are described by examples rather than theoretical argument.

Format

Each chapter uses a consistent format which has:

- a list of contents for the chapter
- an outline of the material to be covered and list of things that a reader should be able to do by the end of the chapter
- the main material of the chapter divided into coherent sections
- worked examples to illustrate methods described
- a summary of the main points at the end of each section
- self-assessment questions throughout the text to ensure that the material is being understood
- a review at the end of each chapter listing the material that has been covered
- additional problems
- computer exercises
- a case study where appropriate
- derivations where appropriate

Solutions to self-assessment questions and numerical problems are given in appendices, together with suggestions for further reading.

Many people have access to computers, so there is little point in doing intricate calculations by hand. The book does not assume access to a computer, but there are many points where results from a computer package are shown, or it is suggested that calculations can be done using standard software. Spreadsheets are particularly useful for a variety of applications.

Contents

Almost any topic in mathematics might be useful to managers in some circumstances. There is, therefore, a wide range of material that could be put into a book of this type. To keep the book to a reasonable length, only the most widely used methods have been included. Thankfully, there is increasing agreement about which methods these are.

The book covers the material that is generally included in quantitative methods courses for managers. Some traditional topics have been omitted because they are becoming less widely used. All textbooks must limit their material, and in this case a line has been drawn that omits topics whose complexity seems excessive in relation to their practical use.

This book attempts to take a balanced view and does not emphasize some topics at the expense of others. In general, a broad approach is taken, describing many topics rather than concentrating on the details of a few.

The book is divided into five sections which develop the subject in a logical sequence.

- Section One gives an introduction to the subject. The first chapter outlines the importance of quantitative methods in management, says why they are used, describes quantitative data, and so on. The second chapter gives a review of basic mathematical principles.

- Section Two describes the collection and description of data. All quantitative methods need reliable data, so these chapters show how such data are collected, presented and summarized.

- Section Three illustrates some application of these quantitative ideas in finance, regression, forecasting, solving sets of equations, linear programming and calculus.

- Section Four describes some statistical methods, including calculation of probabilities, probability distributions and statistical inference.

- Section Five illustrates some applications of these ideas in decision analysis, inventory control, project network analysis, queues and simulation.

Students often find probabilistic ideas much more difficult than deterministic ones. For this reason there is a clear separation of deterministic methods (described in Section Two with examples in Section Three) and probabilistic methods (described in Section Four with examples in Section Five).

The whole book provides students with a solid foundation for understanding quantitative methods and their use in business.

Contents

Chapter 6
Describing changes with index numbers

SECTION THREE
SOLVING BUSINESS PROBLEMS

Chapter 7
Calculations with money

Chapter 8
Relating variables by regression

SECTION FIVE
BUSINESS PROBLEMS WITH UNCERTAINTY   **563**

Chapter 18
Controlling stocks

Chapter 19
Planning projects with networks

Chapter 20
Queues and simulation

SECTION ONE

Background to quantitative methods

This book is divided into five sections, each of which covers a different aspect of quantitative methods in business. This first section gives the background and context for the rest of the book. The second section discusses some aspects of data and information, while the third section looks at ways of solving specific types of problem. The last two sections describe various statistical analyses.

There are two chapters in this first section. Chapter 1 describes how we are surrounded by numbers, which we use in a variety of ways. This means that we all need some appreciation of quantitative analyses. Such appreciation is particularly important in business where managers rely on a range of numerical information to support their decision making.

A number of quantitative models are described in later chapters. Before we can discuss these in detail you should be familiar with some basic mathematical tools. Chapter 2 outlines these tools, emphasizing:

- basic numerical skills
- drawing graphs
- use of algebra, particularly for solving equations

Numbers and managers | 1 |

CHAPTER OUTLINE

This chapter gives a general introduction to quantitative methods. It lays the foundation for the rest of the book by outlining the importance of numerical information, particularly to business. Then it describes the use of quantitative models for solving problems.

After reading this chapter and doing the exercises you should be able to:

- appreciate the importance of quantitative analyses
- say why these are particularly relevant to business
- understand the use of models
- describe a general approach to solving problems

1.1 ‖ Who needs numbers?

We are surrounded by numbers. On a typical day we might find that the temperature is 17° C, petrol costs 62 pence a litre, 2.3 million people are unemployed, a group of employees want a pay rise of £1.50 an hour, the local cricket team scored 274 runs in their last innings, 78% of people questioned want shops to open on Sunday, and so on. Numbers are so common that we all need some appreciation of their use. Without this appreciation, a normal life would be almost impossible.

We use numbers in a variety of calculations. If we buy three bars of chocolate costing 30 pence each, we know that the total cost is 90 pence; if we pay for these with a £5 note we expect to get £4.10 in change. Often such calculations are done roughly to get an impression of the results. If, for example, you are going on a journey of 230 miles and travel at 50 miles an hour you know the journey will take around 5 hours. If you see a car being sold, you might not know exactly how much it would cost to run, but a rough calculation will show if you can afford it; if you get a bill from a tradesman you can tell fairly quickly if it seems reasonable, and so on. This kind of calculation is so common that we do it routinely without much thought. The clear implication is that calculations in one form or another are a central part of our lives.

The main advantage of numbers is that they give an objective measure. When we can measure something and express it in numbers, we can describe it exactly: when we cannot measure it our understanding is much less clear. A bank manager, for example, can tell exactly how wealthy you are by counting your assets. Suppose, though, you develop a pain in your stomach and go to the doctor. You immediately have a problem with describing what kind of pain you have, how bad it is, or how it makes you feel.

The use of numbers considerably enhances our understanding of a situation. This does not, of course, mean that we need to be expert mathematicians to live effectively. It does mean that we should be able to appreciate quantitative arguments and do some numerical analyses. Consider the following worked example.

WORKED EXAMPLE 1.1

A jukebox has a notice which says, 'This machine only accepts 10p coins'. The number of plays given are:

10p – 1 play, 20p – 3 plays, 30p – 4 plays, 40p – 5 plays, 50p – 7 plays.

What is the best way for a customer to use the machine?

Solution

From the customers' point of view the best use of the jukebox is the one which gives the lowest cost per play. The costs per play for each amount are:

10p: $10/1 = 10$p a play   20p: $20/3 = 6.7$p a play   30p: $30/4 = 7.5$p a play
40p: $40/5 = 8$p a play   50p: $50/7 = 7.1$p a play

The best option for customers is to buy 3 plays for 20p.

This ability to look at problems quantitatively is particularly important in business. Managers want to run their businesses as efficiently as possible, and to achieve this they make a series of decisions. Most of these decisions have a quantitative aspect which is phrased in terms of 'improving productivity', 'increasing return on investment', 'scheduling production', 'increasing numbers served', and so on. Taking a broader view, the overall performance of an organization is summarized by its accounts, which are largely numerical. This sets the tone for many decisions, and it is difficult to find a management decision which does not involve some quantitative analysis.

You should not be surprised that managers rely on quantitative analyses, as these are accepted practice in many circumstances. Civil engineers, for example, are expected to do calculations when they design bridges; doctors prescribe measured quantities of drugs; accountants give quantitative views of a company's performance. In the past, many people took the view that managers did not need such formal analyses, but were expected to guess the right decisions using only their intuition. Here we are trying to overcome this view by illustrating the benefits of quantitative methods in a number of areas.

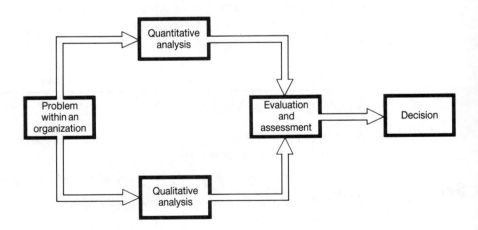

Figure 1.1   Quantitative and qualitative aspects of decision-making.

Many problems have a numerical element, but it would be misleading to say that quantitative methods can always identify the best answers. It is difficult to apply quantitative methods in some areas, such as industrial relations, negotiations, recruitment, identification of objectives, personal relations, or pattern recognition. Other problems need experience, creative thinking or intuition. Overall, the best approach to decision making is shown in Figure 1.1. Here both quantitative and qualitative analyses are done, but ultimately it is managers who make the decisions. They assess all available information, both quantitative and qualitative, and on the basis of their skills, knowledge and experience make final decisions.

WORKED EXAMPLE 1.2

A firm of consultants aims to have 10 clients on its books for each consultant employed. Last month there were 125 clients on their books. How many consultants should they employ?

Solution

A purely quantitative analysis would suggest employing $125/10 = 12.5$ consultants. This could be rounded to either 12 or 13. Now a range of qualitative factors should be included (such as expected changes in business, attitudes of consultants, type of business, planned staff departures and arrivals, and so on). When all available information has been reviewed the management should make their final decision.

IN SUMMARY

We are surrounded by numerical information, and routinely use it in calculations. Problems in business often contain quantitative elements, so it is important for managers to do numerical analyses and to appreciate quantitative arguments.

Self-assessment questions

1.1   What are the benefits of quantitative methods?

1.2   Are all management decisions based on mathematics?

1.3 Do quantitative analyses make the best decisions?

1.4 Why has the use of quantitative methods by managers increased in the past 20 years?

1.2 | Using models

Most of this book looks at ways of solving particular types of problem. A common feature, however, is the use of **models**. Here we are defining a 'model' as any simplified representation of reality, and not its common meaning of a toy. Thus the main characteristics of a model are:

- it is a representation of reality
- it is simplified, with only relevant details included, and
- properties in reality are represented by other properties in the model

Three distinct types of model are used in business:

- iconic
- analogue
- symbolic

Iconic models have things in reality represented by the same things in the model, but on a different scale. A model car is an example of an iconic model as it has small wheels to represent real wheels, a small engine to represent a real engine, and so on. A manufacturer's prototype for a new product would be an iconic model.

Analogue models have properties in reality represented by other properties in the model. The time of day can be represented by the position of hands on a clock, temperature can be represented by the height of a column of mercury, speed can be represented by the position of a speedometer needle, and so on. The control room in a power station would have many analogue models.

Most quantitative analyses are concerned with **symbolic** models where real properties are represented by some kind of symbol. A symbolic model in business may be a graph or chart, but is more likely to consist of numerical expressions. If a company makes a product for £200 a unit and sells it for £300 a unit, a symbolic model of the profit would be:

Profit = number made × (selling price – cost)

or

$$P = N \times (300 - 200) = N \times 100$$

This gives a symbolic model with P representing the profit and N the number of units produced. You should not be intimidated by this use of symbols to represent real things: it is simply a useful notation which describes a given situation accurately and concisely.

The main purpose of a model is to allow experiments without changing the real system. In the illustration above we looked at the relationship between profit and production. We could, of course, find the profit for various production levels by experimenting with the real system. In other words, we could change the production and observe the corresponding profit. This has obvious disadvantages: it is time-consuming, difficult to implement, expensive, and could possibly cause permanent damage to the company. It would be much easier to experiment with the symbolic model, $P = N \times 100$, substituting different values for N and calculating the consequent values for P.

Experimenting with real operations can be damaging, but it may also be impossible. The best location for a factory, for example, could be found by experimentally trying different locations and keeping the best, but this would be prohibitively expensive and disruptive. A company deciding which new product to make cannot start making all possible products and then scrap those that it finds unsuitable. As experiments with reality are, at best, expensive the only feasible alternative is to build a model of the situation and experiment with this.

IN SUMMARY

Quantitative analyses are based on symbolic models. These are simplified representations of reality where real features are depicted by symbols. In business the symbols used most commonly are variables in equations.

Self-assessment questions

1.5   What is a model?

1.6   Why are models used in business?

1.7   What type of model will we use most frequently in this book?

1.3 | Stages in solving a problem

A wide variety of quantitative models are used in business. Some of these are very simple and easy to work with: others are very complex and take years to develop. Some situations are so complex that realistic models have not yet been built, and in other cases models have been built but they are too difficult to solve. Despite this diversity there is a useful general approach to business problems. This has four distinct stages:

1 **observation stage**, where the problem is examined, data are collected, details of the problem are identified, objectives are set, context is considered, various ideas are discussed, and so on

2 **modelling stage**, where data are analysed, a model is built and tested, and initial solutions are obtained

3 **experimental stage**, where solutions are tested to see if they match predictions, optimal solutions are searched for, movements away from optimal solutions are examined, alternative values for variables are considered, other data are collected, and recommendations are made

4 **implementation stage**, where final decisions are made, values for variables are set, these decisions are implemented, actual performance is monitored, feedback is given to management, and models are kept updated.

The length and complexity of each stage depend on the type of problem tackled. An oil company with a complex production policy might take years to go through all this process, while a small company with a minor decision could finish it in a few minutes.

In business most decisions are not isolated, but are part of a continuing management process. Then it becomes important for the consequences of earlier decisions to be reviewed, so that good decisions are repeated, but poor ones are not. This is the basis of **feedback**. Suppose a decision maker supplies inputs to a model, obtains results, makes decisions and implements these. Feedback ensures that the consequences of the decisions are fed back to the decision maker who can use them to modify the model. This process is shown in Figure 1.2. This

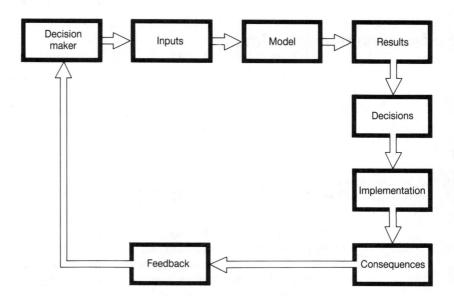

Figure 1.2 Feedback in decision-making.

reinforces the view that management does not consist of a series of disconnected decisions, but is a continuous process which must be performed throughout the life of an organization.

> ## IN SUMMARY

Although models vary considerably, they share common features. Four distinct stages can be identified in the development of a model: observation, modelling, experimentation and implementation.

Self-assessment questions

1.8   What are the major stages in the development of a quantitative model?

1.9   Is there only one correct way to tackle a problem?

CHAPTER REVIEW

This chapter introduced the ideas of quantitative analysis. In particular it described:

- how we are surrounded by numerical information and constantly do calculations based on this
- how quantitative analyses are particularly important in business
- the use of symbolic models
- an approach to solving business problems, based on observation, modelling, experimentation and implementation

---

Problems

1.1   Last year at the Southern Florida Amateur Tennis Championships there were 1947 entries in the women's singles. If this was a standard knockout tournament, how many matches were needed to find the champion?

1.2   What is the smallest number of coins needed to pay a bill of £127.87 exactly?

1.3   A family of three is having grilled steak for dinner. The steaks will be grilled for 10 minutes on each side. Unfortunately, the family's grill pan is only big enough to grill one side of two steaks at a time. How long will it take to cook dinner?

1.4 A shopkeeper buys an article for £25. A customer buys it for £35 and pays with a £50 note. The shopkeeper does not have enough change, so he goes to a neighbour and changes the £50 note. A week later he is told that the £50 note was a forgery, so he immediately repays his neighbour the £50. How much does the shopkeeper lose in this transaction?

1.5 Devise a scheme for doctors to see how bad a stomach pain is.

1.6 Describe a problem in business which has absolutely no quantitative elements.

1.7 Devise a fair system for electing parliamentary candidates.

Computer exercises

1.1 Computer programs can be used throughout this book. See what computers you have access to. Make sure you know how these work. Find out what programs there are (perhaps including word processors, spreadsheets, databases, graphics, statistics packages and various languages). Practise using these programs.

1.2 Table 1.1 shows the number of units of a product sold each month by a shop, the amount the shop paid for each unit, and the selling price. Use a spreadsheet to find the total values of sales, costs, income and profit.

Table 1.1

Month	Units sold	Cost to the shop	Selling price
January	56	120	135
February	58	122	138
March	55	121	145
April	60	117	145
May	54	110	140
June	62	106	135
July	70	98	130
August	72	110	132
September	43	119	149
October	36	127	155
November	21	133	161
December	22	130	161

Use a word processor to write a brief report on your findings. This report may include outputs from graphics and statistics packages.

Tools for quantitative methods

| 2 |

CHAPTER OUTLINE

Chapter 1 outlined the reasons why managers need an appreciation of quantitative ideas. The rest of this book describes some quantitative methods which have proved especially useful in business. Before we look at these in detail, however, we need to revise some basic mathematical tools. You may find that these are all familiar, in which case the chapter will be fairly straightforward. Alternatively, some of the material may be new and you will need to spend more time on it. The tools lay the foundations for other chapters, so it is important that you understand them. If you have difficulties with any material it is worth spending the time to study it until you understand it thoroughly. If you want to read additional material, some useful references are listed in Appendix A.

After reading this chapter and doing the exercises you should be able to:

- view quantitative methods as the application of mathematics to business
- do arithmetic using integers, fractions, decimals and percentages
- appreciate the use of algebra to describe and solve problems
- solve simultaneous equations
- solve quadratic equations
- use arithmetic and geometric series
- draw graphs to show relationships between variables
- use graphs to solve simultaneous and quadratic equations

‖ 2.1 ‖ Working with numbers

‖ 2.1.1 ‖ Introduction

Chapter 1 discussed the reasons why managers should be familiar with a range of quantitative ideas. The main argument was that managers are concerned with decisions about costs, profit, demand, productivity, output, and other factors, all of which are numerical. It follows that good decisions can only be made if the numerical aspects of a problem are analysed properly. The rest of this book describes a range of widely used quantitative analyses. Before we look at these in detail, however, we must revise some basic mathematical tools.

It is important to remember that this book describes the **use** of quantitative methods in business. Its approach is practical, and it describes methods which give valuable, and even essential, results. It is certainly not a book on pure mathematics; it does not describe ideas for their own sake, and does not get bogged down in the details of proofs, analyses or computation. Concepts are illustrated by examples rather than theoretical derivations.

In case you are worried, we should emphasize that this approach does not need a high level of mathematical ability. Business students come from a variety of backgrounds, so it would be wrong to assume that they share a common body of mathematical knowledge. Some of you will be strong mathematicians who are looking forward to applying your knowledge in a new area. Others will view the prospect of doing any mathematics with horror. Most of you will be in between these extremes, will remember some quantitative ideas, and will have forgotten or be unsure about a lot more.

This chapter describes the basic tools of quantitative methods which are used throughout the rest of the book. You may find that these ideas are familiar, in which case the chapter will be fairly straightforward, so you can skip over sections and move to newer material. Conversely, some of the material may be new and you will need to spend more time over it. These tools lay the foundations for other chapters, so it is important that you understand them. If there is any part you find difficult, it is worth spending enough time working through the material until you thoroughly understand it. You might also want to look at a more detailed text, some of which are listed in Appendix A.

IN SUMMARY

This book describes some quantitative methods which have proved useful in business. These methods do not rely on a high level of mathematical ability. Nonetheless, it is important to understand the basic tools which are described in this chapter.

2.1.2 | Numbers and arithmetic

The main assumption in this book is that you are familiar with numbers and arithmetic operations. You can use these to do various calculations, and know that:

- if you buy 10 loaves of bread at 72 pence a loaf the bill will be £7.20
- if you drive at an average speed of 80 kilometres an hour it will take you 5 hours to complete a 400 kilometre journey
- if you spend £300 a month on housing, £100 a month on food and entertainment, and £200 a month on other things, your net income must be at least £600 a month, which is the same as £7,200 a year or £138.46 a week
- if a company has a gross income of £1 million a year and costs of £0.8 million a year, it makes a profit of £200,000 a year
- and so on.

In practice, calculators and computers are widely available. These save a lot of effort (and a lot of mistakes) and should be used whenever possible. In this book we shall assume that a calculator is used for any complicated arithmetic, and will mention specific places where a computer would be beneficial. If you do not have a calculator, this may be the time to buy one and practise using it.

There are four basic operations in arithmetic: addition, subtraction, multiplication and division. To describe these we use the following notation:

- $+$ addition   e.g. $2 + 7 = 9$
- $-$ subtraction   e.g. $15 - 7 = 8$
- $\times$ multiplication   e.g. $4 \times 5 = 20$
- $/$ division   e.g. $12/4 = 3$

There are several variations on this notation. Division is sometimes shown as $12 \div 4 = 3$ or $\frac{12}{4} = 3$, while multiplication can be shown as $3 \times 2 = 6$, $3 \cdot 2 = 6$, $3.2 = 6$ or $3(2) = 6$.

We must be careful when using these operators to describe arithmetic. Does $3 + 4 \times 5$, for example, mean $7 \times 5 = 35$ (with the addition done first) or $3 + 20 = 23$ (with the multiplication done first)? By convention, the second of these is correct and multiplication is done before addition. Whenever there is any doubt about the order of arithmetic, brackets can be put around parts of the calculation which are done together.

Then

$$(3 + 4) \times 5 = 7 \times 5 = 35$$

while

$$3 + (4 \times 5) = 3 + 20 = 23$$

All calculations in brackets must be done first, so the general order of calculations becomes:

---

1   all operations inside brackets
2   raising to powers (which we mention later in the chapter)
3   multiplication and division in the order they appear
4   addition and subtraction in the order they appear

This means that brackets can be used to change the order in which calculations are done.

For example:

$$12 \times 2 + 4 + 2 = 24 + 4 + 2 = 30$$

while

$$12 \times (2 + 4 + 2) = 12 \times 8 = 96$$

and

$$12 \times (2 + 4) + 4 = 12 \times 6 + 4 = 72 + 4 = 76$$

Similarly

$$4 \times 5 - 3 \times 4/4 - 2 = 20 - 3 - 2 = 15$$

while

$$(4 \times 5) - (3 \times 4)/(4 - 2) = 20 - 12/2 = 20 - 6 = 14$$

and

$$4 \times (5 - 3) \times (4/4) - 2 = 4 \times 2 \times 1 - 2 = 8 - 2 = 6$$

If one set of brackets is not enough, we can use several sets inside others. Then operations are done from the inside set of brackets and working outwards.

For example:

$$[(32/2) + (6/3)] - 1 = (16 + 2) - 1 = 17$$

while

$$[32/(2 + 6)]/(3 - 1) = (32/8)/2 = 4/2 = 2$$

Sometimes calculations with a lot of brackets appear rather messy, but you should have no difficulty in understanding them if you follow the order given above.

WORKED EXAMPLE 2.1

Find the value of:

(a) 120/6   (b) –120/6   (c) –120/(–6)   (d) $[(-2 \times 4) \times (15 - 17)] \times (-2)$
(e) $(10+20) - (3 \times 7)$ (f) $(15 - 5) + [(20 - 3) \times 7)]$ (g) $[(20 - 5) \times [30/(2 + 1)]]$

Solution

Using the standard rules gives:

(a) $120/6 = 20$

(b) $-120/6 = -20$

(c) $-120/(-6) = 20$ (Notice that the minus signs cancel each other.)

(d) $[(-2 \times 4) \times (15 - 17)] \times (-2) = [(-8) \times (-2)] \times (-2) = 16 \times (-2) = -32$

(Remember that multiplying two negative numbers together gives a positive number, while multiplying a positive number by a negative number gives a negative number.)

(e) $(10 + 20) - (3 \times 7) = 30 - 21 = 9$

(f) $(15 - 5) + [(20 - 3) \times 7)] = 10 + (17 \times 7) = 10 + 119 = 129$

(g) $[(20 - 5) \times [30/(2+1)]] = 15 \times (30/3) = 15 \times 10 = 150$

The numbers used in Worked Example 2.1 are integers. In other words they are whole numbers, such as 20, 9 or 150. Integers can be positive (such as 3, 100, 257) or negative (such as −2, −157, −356). To improve clarity, long numbers are often divided into groups of three digits by commas (like 1,247,822), but some people prefer spaces (like 1 247 822).

Often we need to divide integers into smaller parts. When, for example, two people share a bar of chocolate they get $^1\!/_2$ each. Parts of integers are expressed either as **common fractions** (like $^1\!/_2$ or $^3\!/_4$) or **decimal fractions** (like 0.5 or 0.25). As metric units are replacing imperial units, and calculators are used almost universally, decimal fractions have become more common. Nonetheless, common fractions (which are invariably abbreviated to 'fractions') are very important, particularly when dealing with ratios or probabilities. You should be familiar with the rules for manipulating these, which are illustrated in the following examples.

WORKED EXAMPLE 2.2

Find the value of the following as decimal fractions:

(a) 6/8   (b) 36/8   (c) 1/2 + 4/5   (d) 3/4 − 1/6   (e) −1/2 − 1/4

(f) 1/4 × 2/3   (g) −1/4 × 2/3 × 1/2

(h) (3/5) ÷ (4/5)   (i) 3/6 × 2/5 ÷ 3/4

Solution

Common fractions can be transformed into decimal fractions by straightforward division. This is done most easily using a calculator.

(a) $6/8 = 0.75$

(b) $36/8 = 4.5$

For addition and subtraction of fractions, all numbers below the lines (called the **denominators**) are made the same, and then numbers above the line (called the **numerators**) are added or subtracted.

(c) $1/2 + 4/5 = 5/10 + 8/10 = 13/10 = 1.3$

(d) $3/4 - 1/6 = 9/12 - 2/12 = 7/12 = 0.583$

(e) $-1/2 - 1/4 = -2/4 - 1/4 = -3/4 = -0.75$

For multiplication of fractions, all the denominators are multiplied together, and all the numerators are multiplied together.

(f) $1/4 \times 2/3 = (1 \times 2)/(4 \times 3) = 2/12 = 1/6 = 0.167$

(g) $-1/4 \times 2/3 \times 1/2 = (-1 \times 2 \times 1)/(4 \times 3 \times 2) = -2/24 = -1/12 = -0.083$

For division of fractions, the fraction which is dividing is inverted and then used for multiplication.

(h) $(3/5) \div (4/5) = 3/5 \times 5/4 = (3 \times 5)/(5 \times 4) = 0.75$

(i) $3/6 \times 2/5 \div 3/4 = 3/6 \times 2/5 \times 4/3 = (3 \times 2 \times 4)/(6 \times 5 \times 3) = 0.267$

WORKED EXAMPLE 2.3

A Canadian visitor to Britain wants to change $250 into pounds. The exchange rate is $2.15 to the pound and banks charge a fee of £5 for the conversion. How many pounds does the visitor get?

Solution

$250 is equivalent to $250/2.15 = £116.28$. The bank then takes its fee of £5 to give the visitor £111.28.

WORKED EXAMPLE 2.4

If 1 km is about 5/8 miles, how far is 2.4 miles in km?

Solution

5/8 miles = 1 km

so

1 mile = 8/5 km

and

2.4 miles = 2.4 × 8/5 km = (2.4 × 8)/5 = 3.84 km

An alternative way of describing fractions is to use **percentages**. These are fractions where the bottom line is 100, and the '/100' has been replaced by the abbreviation '%'. Then if we hear '20% of the electorate did not vote in the last election' we know that 20 people out of each 100 did not vote. This ratio can be represented as any of:

- common fraction: 20/100 = 1/5
- decimal fraction: 0.2
- percentage: 20%

If a company made a net profit of £12m last year and £3m of this came from overseas, we can make the equivalent statements:

- fraction of profit from overseas = 3/12 = 1/4
- decimal fraction of profit from overseas = 0.25
- percentage of profit from overseas = 25%

Calculations with percentages can be done in the same way as other fractions.

WORKED EXAMPLE 2.5

(a) What is 17/20 as a percentage?

(b) What is 80% as a fraction?

(c) What is 35% as a decimal fraction?

(d) What is 40% of 120?

(e) If 20% of 50 is multiplied by ½ of 60 and the result is divided by 0.25 of 60, what is the result?

Solution

(a) $17/20 = 85/100 = 85\%$

(b) $80\% = 80/100 = 4/5$

(c) $35\% = 35/100 = 0.35$

(d) 40% of $120 = 0.4 \times 120 = 48$

(e) 20% of $50 = 20/100 \times 50 = 0.2 \times 50 = 10$: $\frac{1}{2} \times 60 = 30$; $0.25 \times 60 = 15$

The calculation is: $(10 \times 30)/15 = 300/15 = 20$

WORKED EXAMPLE 2.6

A shop sells dining room tables for £400 each. At one time it was difficult to get supplies of the table, so the shop raised the price by 20%. When supplies returned to normal the shop reduced the higher price by 20%. What was the final selling price? What percentage reduction from the higher price would have returned the price to £400?

Solution

- The normal price was £400. During the shortage the shop raised this by 20% to 120% of £400, which is $(120/100) \times 400 = 1.2 \times 400 = £480$.

- At the end of the shortage the shop reduced the higher price by 20% to give a final selling price of 80% of £480 which is $(80/100) \times 480 = 0.8 \times 480 = £384$.

- To return the price from £480 to £400 the price would be reduce by a proportion 80/480, which equals 16.667/100 or 16.667%.

The last answer above was given as 16.667%. The exact answer is 16.666 6666...% (where ... signifies an unending row of sixes). We have rounded the answer to:

- three decimal places (showing only three digits after the decimal point) and
- five significant figures (showing only the five most important digits)

Rounding of this kind is widely used to ensure that we get enough information, but are not overwhelmed by too much detail. There is no general rule for the number of decimal points or significant figures that should be used, except the vague advice to use the number which best suits the purpose. We can give two more specific suggestions.

- Only give the number of decimal points or significant figures which is useful. Avoid answers like £120.347 826 59 and quote the figure as £120.35, or even £120.

- Results from calculation are only as accurate as the data used. When multiplying a forecast demand of 32.63 units by a unit cost of £17.19 we should not describe the projected total cost as 32.63 × 17.19 = £560.9097. A more reasonable answer would be £560.91 (or £561, £560 or £600 depending on the use of the data).

Remember the convention that when rounding to, say, two decimal places and the digit in the third decimal place is 0, 1, 2, 3 or 4 the result is rounded **down**, and when it is 5, 6, 7, 8 or 9 the result is rounded **up**. Then 11.111 become 11.11 to two decimal places, but 11.119 becomes 11.12; 1.364 becomes 1.36, while 1.365 becomes 1.37.

WORKED EXAMPLE 2.7

What is to 1374.341 481 2 to:
  (a) two decimal places   (b) four significant figures
  (c) two significant figures?

What is 3/7 as a decimal to three places?

Solution

(a) 1374.341 481 2 is 1374.34 when rounded to two decimal places, and

(b) 1374 when rounded to 4 significant figures

(c) 1400 when rounded to 2 significant figures

   3/7 is 0.428 57... which is 0.429 when rounded to three decimal places.

IN SUMMARY

There are some standard rules for doing calculations. These can be used for integers, decimals and fractions. Percentages are a useful form of fraction. Results can be rounded to a specified number of decimal places or significant figures.

Self-assessment questions

2.1   Is it true that quantitative methods are widely used in business?

2.2   What is the value of:
(a) $(-12)/(-3)$ (b) $(24/5) \div (3/7)$ (c) $[(2-4) \times (3-6)]/(7-5)$?

2.3   What is the difference between 75%, 3/4, 15/20 and 0.75? Which of these gives the best representation?

2.4   What is 1 745 800.362 37 rounded to three decimal places and three significant figures?

| 2.2 | Changing numbers to letters

| 2.2.1 | Forming equations

Suppose we want to find the cost of running a car. This is normally related to the distance travelled, so we might find during one period that we drove 6000 km and had total costs of £2400. Then we could say

$$\text{cost per km} = \frac{2400}{6000} = £0.40 \text{ per km}$$

We calculated this specific result from the general equation

$$\text{cost per km} = \frac{\text{total cost}}{\text{number of km travelled}}$$

Rather than writing this equation in full, we could save time by using some abbreviations. We could, for example, abbreviate the total cost to T, which is simple and easy to remember. Similarly, we could define

$$C = \text{cost per km}$$

$$K = \text{number of km travelled}$$

Then the cost per km can be written as

$$C = \frac{T}{K} = T/K$$

Now we have an equation which shows the relationship between three quantities: C, K and T. This has the advantages of being general, concise and accurate. The only difference from the original equation is that we have used letters to represent numbers or quantities. This is the basis of algebra.

We chose the abbreviations C, T and K to remind us of what they stood for. We could equally have chosen other names. For example:

$$C = \frac{T}{K}$$

$$c = \frac{t}{k}$$

$$y = \frac{x}{z}$$

$$\text{COST} = \frac{\text{TOTAL}}{\text{KILOM}}$$

$$\text{COSTPERKM} = \frac{\text{TOTALCOST}}{\text{KILOMETRES}}$$

Provided the meaning is clear, the names are not important. Some names, however, like T^2, should be treated with caution. These make it difficult to describe the square of T, which cannot now be written as T^2, or the square of T^2, which cannot be written as T^{22}. Similarly, the multiplication sign in equations is often implicit, so that $2 \times a$ is written as $2a$, $4 \times a \times b \times c$ is written as $4abc$, and so on. This causes no problems when single-letter abbreviations are used, but can be misleading with longer names. If the total unit cost is abbreviated to *TUC*, it would make no sense to write an equation

$$TUC = NTUC$$

when we really mean

$$TUC = N \times T \times UC$$

Provided common sense is used in the selection of names and presentation of equations, algebra gives a concise and accurate way of describing situations.

Our basic equation

$$C = T/K$$

can be rearranged to give two equivalent forms. If we multiply both sides of the equation by K, we get:

$$C \times K = \frac{T}{K} \times K \qquad \text{or} \qquad T = C \times K$$

Now if we divide both sides of this equation by C, we get

$$T/C = C \times K/C \qquad \text{or} \qquad K = T/C$$

These three are different representations of the same situation. They are simple rearrangements of the first equation, and we should remember that an equation remains true if we perform the same operations to both sides. Thus we could multiply both sides by 2 to get

$$2C = 2T/K$$

and add 10 to get

$$2C + 10 = 2T/K + 10$$

and divide by 3A, where A is a known constant, to give

$$(2C + 10)/3A = (2T/K + 10)/3A$$

and so on. Provided we do the same operations on both sides of the equation, it is still true.

This kind of manipulation allows us to define some general laws of algebra. Because algebra simply replaces numbers by letters, these rules are the same as those used for calculations, so we can define the basic operations using two variables a and b, as follows:

- \+   addition   e.g. $a + b$
- \−   subtraction   e.g. $a - b$
- ×   multiplication   e.g. $a \times b$
- /   division   e.g. a/b

One important point in algebra is that two adjacent variables are assumed to be multiplied together. Thus:

$a \times b$	is usually written as	ab
$l \times m \times n$	is usually written as	lmn
$a \times (b + c)$	is usually written as	$a\,(b + c)$

The order of evaluation remains the same, so we have:

1. all operations inside brackets
2. raising to powers (which we mention later in the chapter)
3. multiplication and division in the order they appear
4. addition and subtraction in the order they appear

When discussing algebra we should add explicitly three simple rules which are used implicitly in most arithmetic.

- The **commutative law** for multiplication and addition means that the order in which two numbers are multiplied or added is not important. Then:

$$a + b = b + a$$

and

$$ab = ba$$

- The **associative law** for addition and multiplication extends this idea to more numbers, so that:

$$a + b + c = (a + b) + c = a + (b + c) = b + (a + c)$$

and

$$abc = (ab)\, c = a\, (bc) = b\, (ac)$$

- The **distributive law** of multiplication and addition says that:

$$a\, (b + c) = ab + ac$$

You can check that these laws work by replacing a, b and c by any numbers, as illustrated in the following example.

WORKED EXAMPLE 2.8

Confirm the commutative, associative and distributive laws when $a = 5$, $b = 2$ and $c = 6$.

Solution

We can confirm these laws by repeating the calculations and showing that the same result is given.

- The commutative law has:

for addition: $a + b = b + a$

so $5 + 2 = 2 + 5 = 7$, which is true

for multiplication: $ab = ba$

so $5 \times 2 = 2 \times 5 = 10$, which is true

- The associative law has:

for addition: $a + b + c = (a + b) + c = a + (b + c) = b + (a + c)$

so $5 + 2 + 6 = (7) + 6 = 5 + (8) = 2 + (11) = 13$

for multiplication: $abc = (ab)\, c = a\, (bc) = b\, (ac)$

so $5 \times 2 \times 6 = (10) \times 6 = 5 \times (12) = 2 \times 30 = 60$

- The distributive law has:

$$a\, (b + c) = ab + ac$$

so $5\,(2 + 6) = 5 \times 2 + 5 \times 6 = 40$

Short names can be used to identify constants and variables. The manipulation of these is the basis of algebra. Algebra gives a precise way of describing situations. There are a number of rules for algebra which are based on the rules for calculations with numbers.

2.2.2 | Solving simple equations

We saw above that the cost of running a car can be described by the equation $C = T/K$. Here the cost per km, C, is fixed and a driver cannot change it, so in any particular circumstances C is a constant. The number of kilometres travelled, K, and the total cost, T, are both variables which are related through the equation. Thus we have:

- **constants**, which take fixed values for the circumstances considered
- **variables**, which can take any one of a range of values

The purpose of an equation is to show the relationship between constants and variables. Then the value of a previously unknown constant or variable can be found by relating it to other known constants and variables. This is called **solving an equation**.

The easiest way of solving an equation is to arrange it so that the unknown value is on one side of the equals sign, and all known values are on the other side.

Suppose, for example, a survey of managers found that they spend an average of 15.2 hours a week attending meetings and that their time is valued at £22.40 an hour. The total cost of attending meetings a year for a typical manager can be found from

> total annual cost = hours attending meetings a year × cost per hour

which can be abbreviated to

$$T = H \times C$$
$$= (15.2 \times 52) \times 22.4$$
$$= £17,704.96 \text{ a year}$$

Here we have solved the equation by using the known values of H and C to find a previously unknown value, T.

This example highlights a number of points about equations.

- A single equation can only give the value of **one** unknown. If there are several unknowns, more equations must be used (as described in the following section).
- An equation can be solved by arranging it so that the unknown value is on one side of the equals sign and all the known values are on the other side.

- The units in the equation must be consistent. The equation above worked with hours and pounds for all values. Provided the units are consistent, any convenient ones can be used.

- The answer can be rounded to an appropriate number of significant figures. It is important to remember that results cannot be more accurate than the known values. In this case values are quoted to three significant figures, so we could not reasonably say more than 'the annual cost of managers attending meetings is about £17,700'.

Now we can use these observations to solve some problems. This involves three steps:

- define the constants and variables to be used
- develop an equation to describe the relationship between the constants and variables
- solve the equation

Use of these steps is one of the most important parts of quantitative methods. We can illustrate it by the following examples, where we should remember that equations are manipulated by making the same changes to both sides.

WORKED EXAMPLE 2.9

A hotel paid £1200 for heat and power in July. It was found that heating costs were £200 short of three times the cost of power. How much did power cost?

Solution

Let the cost of power in the month be x. Then the cost of heat is $3x - 200$. This gives a total cost of $x + (3x - 200)$. But we know that the total cost was £1200, so

$$x + (3x - 200) = 1200$$

Adding 200 to both sides of the equation gives

$$x + 3x = 1400$$

or

$$4x = 1400$$

$$x = £350$$

WORKED EXAMPLE 2.10

A company employing 10 people has total costs of £250,000 a year. These costs include a fixed cost of £50,000 for overheads, and a variable cost for each person employed. What is this variable cost? What would be the total cost if the company expanded to employ 45 people?

Solution

Suppose we let:

t = total cost

o = overheads

v = variable cost per employee

n = number employed

The total cost can be described by:

$$\text{total cost} = \text{overheads} + (\text{variable cost} \times \text{number employed})$$

or

$$t = o + nv$$

We know current values for t, o and n, and so we can find the variable cost v by rearranging the equation. If we subtract o from both sides and divide by n we get

$$v = \frac{t - o}{n}$$

Substituting the known values gives

$$v = \frac{250\,000 - 50\,000}{10} = £20,000 \text{ a year for each employee}$$

If the company expands we can find the new total cost t by substituting known values for v, o and n in the original equation:

$$t = o + nv$$

$$= 50\,000 + 45 \times 20\,000$$

$$= £950,000 \text{ a year}$$

WORKED EXAMPLE 2.11

1200 parts arrive from a manufacturer in two batches. Each unit of the first batch costs £35, while each unit of the second batch costs £37. If the total cost was £43,600 how many units were in each batch?

Solution

Let f be the number of units in the first batch, and $(1200 - f)$ be the number in the second batch. Then the total cost is given by:

$$35f + 37(1200 - f) = 43\ 600$$

So

$$35f + 44\ 400 - 37f = 43\ 600$$

$$35f - 37f = 43\ 600 - 44\ 400$$

$$-2f = -800$$

$$f = 400$$

So the first batch had 400 units while the second batch had 800 units.

WORKED EXAMPLE 2.12

Rearrange the following equations so that the unknown variable y can be found:

    (a) $(2a - 7)/6y = (3b - 5)/2c$ (b) $3 - 4y + 2a = (3b - 5)/(2c + 1)$

What are the values of y when $a = 2$, $b = 3$ and $c = 4$?

Solution

With both of these equations we need to manipulate them until the unknown variable y is on one side and the known values are on the other side. We do this, as usual, by treating both sides of the equation in the same way.

(a) $(2a - 7)/6y = (3b - 5)/2c$

    If we multiply throughout by $(6y \times 2c)$ we get

$$\frac{(2a - 7)(6y \times 2c)}{6y} = \frac{(3b - 5)(6y \times 2c)}{2c}$$

or

$$(2a - 7) \times 2c = (3b - 5) \times 6y$$

Then dividing both sides by $(3b - 5)$ gives:

$$2c(2a - 7)/(3b - 5) = 6y$$

or

$$y = \frac{2c(2a - 7)}{6(3b - 5)}$$

When $a = 2$, $b = 3$ and $c = 4$:

$$y = \frac{(2 \times 4)(2 \times 2 - 7)}{6(3 \times 3 - 5)} = \frac{8 \times (-3)}{24} = -1$$

(b) $3 - 4y + 2a = \dfrac{3b - 5}{2c + 1}$

Subtracting $3 + 2a$ from both sides gives

$$-4y = \frac{3b - 5}{2c + 1} - 3 + 2a$$

Then dividing throughout by -4 gives:

$$y = \frac{-\left(\dfrac{3b - 5}{2c + 1}\right) - 3 + 2a}{4}$$

When $a = 2$, $b = 3$ and $c = 4$:

$$y = \frac{-\left(\dfrac{3 \times 3 - 5}{2 \times 4 + 1}\right) - (3 + 2 \times 2)}{4} = \frac{-\left(\dfrac{4}{9} - 7\right)}{4} = 1.64$$

IN SUMMARY

Equations show the relationships between variables and constants. These equations can be solved to find previously unknown values. This is done by rearranging the equation until the unknown variable is on one side, and all the known values are on the other side.

2.2.3 | Solving simultaneous equations

An equation can be solved to find one previously unknown value. If we want to find more than one unknown variable we must have more than one independent equation. In particular, to find n values, we need n independent equations relating them. With two unknowns, for example, we need two independent equations to find a solution. If we only knew that $x + y = 3$ it would be impossible to find values for both x and y. If we also knew that $y - x = 1$ we would have two independent equations and could find values for both x and y (in fact $x = 1$ and $y = 2$).

In this sense **independent** means the two equations are not simply different ways of saying the same thing. For example:

$$x + y = 10$$

and

$$x - 10 = y$$

are not independent as they are different forms of the same equation. Similarly:

$$x + y = 10$$

and

$$2x + 2y = 20$$

are not independent as, again, they are simply different forms of the same equation.

Sets of independent equations of this type are called **simultaneous equations**, and they are solved when values are found for all the unknowns.

We can start by considering two simultaneous equations with two unknown variables. The method of solving these is to multiply one equation by a number which allows the two equations to be added or subtracted to eliminate one of the variables. Then when one variable has been eliminated, we are left with a single equation with one variable, which can then be found. Substituting this value into one of the original equations allows the value of the second variable to be found. This process can best be illustrated by an example.

WORKED EXAMPLE 2.13

Two variables, x and y, are related by the following equations. What are the values of the variables?

$$3y = 4x + 2 \tag{1}$$

$$y = -x + 10 \tag{2}$$

Solution

If we multiply equation (2) by 3, we get the revised equations:

$$3y = 4x + 2 \text{ as before} \tag{1}$$

and

$$3y = -3x + 30 \tag{2}$$

Subtracting equation (2) from equation (1):

$$3y - 3y = 4x - (-3x) + 2 - 30$$

or

$$0 = 7x - 28$$

so that

$$x = 4$$

This gives a value for one variable, which can be substituted in one of the original equations, say (1), to give the value for the other variable:

$$3y = 4x + 2$$

so

$$3y = 4 \times 4 + 2$$

or

$$y = 6$$

These answers can be checked in equation (2):

$$y = -x + 10$$

or

$$6 = -4 + 10$$

which is correct and confirms the solution.

WORKED EXAMPLE 2.14

Two variables are related by the following equations. What are the values of the variables?

$$x + 2y = 7 \tag{1}$$

$$2x + y = 5 \tag{2}$$

Solution

If we multiply equation (1) by 2, we get the revised equations:

$$2x + 4y = 14 \tag{1}$$

and

$$2x + y = 5 \text{ as before} \tag{2}$$

Subtracting equation (2) from equation (1) gives

$$3y = 9$$

so

$$y = 3$$

This gives a value for one variable, which can be substituted in one of the original equations, say (1), to give the value for the other variable:

$$x + 2y = 7$$

so

$$x + 6 = 7$$

or

$$x = 1$$

These answers can be checked in equation (2):

$$2x + y = 5$$

or

$$2 + 3 = 5$$

which is correct and confirms the solution.

This method of elimination can be used with any number of variables. If, for example, we have three variables, these can be manipulated until we get two equations with two variables, and then further manipulation gives one equation with one variable. This can be solved, and substitution allows the other variables to be found.

WORKED EXAMPLE 2.15

Solve the simultaneous equations:

$$2x + y + 2z = 10 \tag{1}$$

$$x - 2y + 3z = 2 \tag{2}$$

$$-x + y + z = 0 \tag{3}$$

Solution

We can start by using equations (2) and (3) to eliminate the variable x from equation (1). Multiplying equation (2) by 2 gives

$$2x - 4y + 6z = 4$$

Subtracting this from equation (1) gives

$$5y - 4z = 6 \tag{4}$$

Multiplying equation (3) by 2 gives

$$-2x + 2y + 2z = 0$$

Adding this to equation (1) gives

$$3y + 4z = 10 \tag{5}$$

Now we have two equations, (4) and (5), with two unknowns, y and z. Adding these together gives $8y = 16$ or $y = 2$

Now we can substitute this value for y in equation (4) to give $10 - 4z = 6$ or $z = 1$. The values for y and z can be substituted in equation (1) to give $2x + 2 + 2 = 10$ or $x = 3$.

These values can be confirmed by substitution in equations (2) and (3):

$$3 - 4 + 3 = 2 \tag{2}$$

$$-3 + 2 + 1 = 0 \tag{3}$$

WORKED EXAMPLE 2.16

Solve the following simultaneous equations:

$$2x + 2y + 4z = 24 \tag{1}$$

$$6x + 3y = 15 \tag{2}$$

$$y + 2z = 11 \tag{3}$$

Solution

Multiplying equation (3) by 2 gives

$$2y + 4z = 22$$

Subtracting this from equation (1) gives

$$2x = 2 \text{ or } x = 1$$

Substituting this value, $x = 1$, in equation (2) gives

$$6 \times 1 + 3y = 15 \text{ or } 3y = 9 \text{ or } y = 3$$

Substituting this value, $y = 3$, in equation (3) gives

$$3 + 2z = 11 \text{ or } 2z = 8 \text{ or } z = 4.$$

Thus the solution is $x = 1$, $y = 3$ and $z = 4$. This can be checked by substitution in any of the equations.

$$2 \times 1 + 2 \times 3 + 4 \times 4 = 24 \tag{1}$$

$$6 \times 1 + 3 \times 3 = 15 \tag{2}$$

$$3 + 2 \times 4 = 11 \tag{3}$$

There are two circumstances in which this elimination method of solving simultaneous equations does not work. In the first, the equations are not independent. If, for example, we have the following two equations:

$$2x + 3y = 6 \tag{1}$$

$$6x + 9y = 18 \tag{2}$$

Multiplying equation (1) by 3 immediately gives equation (2), so we really have only one equation and cannot find the two unknowns.

The second circumstance in which the method does not work occurs when there is a contradiction. Suppose we are told:

$$x + y = 7$$

$$2x + 2y = 12$$

Multiplying the first equation by 2 gives $2x + 2y = 14$ which contradicts the second equation. In these circumstances there is no feasible solution and we have to assume that there is an error in one of the equations.

The method of eliminating variables can be used for larger sets of simultaneous equations, but a more compact approach is based on matrices. We shall describe this in more detail in Chapter 10. At this point, however, we should note that computers can easily solve large sets of simultaneous equations, and a typical dialogue with a program solving four equations is shown in Figure 2.1.

```
=>  SIMULTANEOUS
*   Ready to Solve Simultaneous Linear Equations
=>  VARIABLES 4
*   Number of variables is 4
=>  SET DATA
Data =>    1    1    1    1    10
Data =>    2    0   -4   -1    2
Data =>    0    1    2   -1    3
Data =>    0    1    0    1    5
*   Data complete
=>  SHOW
        1 X1 + 1 X2 + 1 X3 + 1 X4 = 10
        2 X1 + 0 X2 - 4 X3 - 1 X4 =  2
        0 X1 + 1 X2 + 2 X3 - 1 X4 =  3
        0 X1 + 1 X2 + 0 X3 + 1 X4 =  5
=>  SOLVE
        X1  =  4
        X2  =  3
        X3  =  1
        X4  =  2
=>  QUIT
```

Figure 2.1   Computer dialogue for solving simultaneous equations.

IN SUMMARY

Values for n unknown variables can be found using n independent simultaneous equations. The equations can be solved by a process of elimination and substitution.

2.2.4 | Powers and roots

If a number is multiplied by itself several times the convention is to describe this by a superscript. Then if the variable b is multiplied by itself the result is 'b to the power 2' or 'b squared', which is written as b^2. So if 3 is multiplied by itself the result is 3 squared, which is written as 3^2 which equals 3×3 or 9.

Similarly:

$$b \text{ squared} = b \times b = b^2$$

$$b \text{ cubed} = b \times b \times b = b^3$$

$$b \text{ to the fourth} = b \times b \times b \times b = b^4$$

and in general

$$b \text{ to the power } n = b \times b \times b \times ... (n \text{ times}) = b^n$$

If $b = 2$ we have:

$$2 \text{ squared} = 2 \times 2 = 2^2 = 4$$

$$2 \text{ cubed} = 2 \times 2 \times 2 = 2^3 = 8$$

$$2 \text{ to the fourth} = 2 \times 2 \times 2 \times 2 = 2^4 = 16$$

and in general

$$2 \text{ to the power } n = 2 \times 2 \times 2 \times ... (n \text{ times}) = 2^n$$

In this notation, the single variable b could equally be written as b^1, but this is unnecessary and is seldom done.

Suppose we want to multiply two variables which are raised to powers, perhaps multiplying b^2 by b^3. We can write this out in full as $b^2 \times b^3$ but this is $(b \times b) \times (b \times b \times b)$ or $b \times b \times b \times b \times b$ and this in turn is b^5. Thus $b^2 \times b^3 = b^5$. This observation leads to the general rule that multiplying a variable raised to one power by the same variable raised to another power results in the variable raised to the sum of the two powers:

$$b^m \times b^n = b^{m+n}$$

Thus $3^2 \times 3^3 = 3^5$, which can be confirmed by expanding the calculation to $3^2 \times 3^3 = 9 \times 27 = 243 = 3^5$. In passing we should note two common errors, and emphasize that:

$$b^m + b^n \text{ does } \textbf{not} \text{ equal } b^{m+n}$$

$$a^n + b^n \text{ does } \textbf{not} \text{ equal } (a + b)^n$$

You can confirm this by substituting any values such as $a = 1$, $b = 2$, $m = 1$ and $n = 3$.

Now we know how to multiply a variable raised to powers, we can extend this and look at division in the same way. If we want to divide b^3 by b^2 this can be written as

$$\frac{b^3}{b^2} \quad \text{which is} \quad \frac{b \times b \times b}{b \times b} = b$$

We know that another way of writing b is b^1, so we now have $b^3/b^2 = b^1$. This leads to the general rule that a variable raised to one power divided by the same variable raised to another power results in the variable raised to the difference of the two powers:

$$\frac{b^m}{b^n} = b^{m-n}$$

Thus $5^4/5^2 = 5^{4-2} = 5^2$. We can confirm this by expanding the calculation to show that $5^4/5^2 = 625/25 = 25 = 5^2$. One interesting result from this occurs when $m = n$. Suppose, for example, $m = n = 3$. Then with division we get

$$\frac{b^3}{b^3} = \frac{b \times b \times b}{b \times b \times b} = 1$$

but

$$\frac{b^3}{b^3} = b^{3-3} = b^0$$

So $b^0 = 1$. This is a general result, that anything raised to the power 0 equals 1.

WORKED EXAMPLE 2.17

What is the value of: (a) $b^4 \times b^2$ (b) $b^6 \div b^2$ (c) $b^6 - b^3$ (d) $2^3 \times 2^2$ (e) $3^4 \div 3^2$ (f) $(4^{23} \times 4^{17})/(2+2)^{38}$ (g) $(1+b)^2$ (h) $(1-b)^4/(1-b)^2$

Solution

Using the rules above gives:

(a) $b^4 \times b^2 = b^{4+2} = b^6$

(b) $b^6 \div b^2 = b^{6-2} = b^4$

(c) $b^6 - b^3$ cannot be simplified and is **not** b^{6-3}

(d) $2^3 \times 2^2 = 2^{3+2} = 2^5 = 32$

(e) $3^4 \div 3^2 = 3^{4-2} = 3^2 = 9$

(f) $(4^{23} \times 4^{17})/(2+2)^{38} = 4^{(23+17)}/4^{38} = 4^{(40-38)} = 4^2 = 16$

Values in brackets can be treated in the same way as other values.

(g) $(1 + b)^2 = (1 + b) \times (1 + b)$

This can be expanded to:

$$1 \times (1 + b) + b \times (1 + b)$$
$$= (1 + b) + (b + b^2) = 1 + 2b + b^2$$

(h) $(1 - b)^4/(1 - b)^2 = (1 - b)^{4-2} = (1 - b)^2$

Again, this can be expanded to:

$$(1 - b) \times (1 - b)$$
$$= 1 \times (1 - b) - b \times (1 - b)$$
$$= (1 - b) - (b - b^2) = 1 - 2b + b^2$$

Parts (g) and (h) in the last worked example showed two important results, which we shall use frequently:

$$(1 + b)^2 = 1 + 2b + b^2$$
$$(1 - b)^2 = 1 - 2b + b^2$$

Suppose we now apply the rule for division when n is larger than m with, say, $n = 3$ and $m = 2$. Then

$$b^m/b^n = b^2/b^3 = b^{2-3} = b^{-1}$$

But how do we interpret a value raised to a negative power? The answer is found by expanding the calculation:

$$\frac{b^2}{b^3} = \frac{b \times b}{b \times b \times b} = \frac{1}{b}$$

Then $b^{-1} = 1/b$, and we have the general rule

$$b^{-n} = \frac{1}{b^n}$$

There is one other aspect of this notation that we need to consider: raising values to fractional powers. The meaning of these can be found from the work we have already done. Take, for example, $b^{0.5}$. If we square this, we know that

$$b^{0.5} \times b^{0.5} = b^{0.5 + 0.5} = b^1 = b$$

Now the number which multiplied by itself gives b is the square root of b, so we can infer that:

$$b^{0.5} = b^{1/2} = \sqrt{b}$$

Remember that $\sqrt{}$ is the standard sign for the square root, so $\sqrt{9} = 3$.
We could show similarly that:

$$b^{0.33} = b^{1/3} \text{ which is the cube root of } b$$

$$b^{0.25} = b^{1/4} \text{ which is the fourth root of } b$$

$$b^{0.2} = b^{1/5} \text{ which is the fifth root of } b$$

and so on.
This idea can be extended to other fractional powers. For example:

$$b^{1.5} = b^{3/2} = (b^{1/2})^3 = (\sqrt{b})^3$$

$$b^{2.5} = b^{5/2} = (b^{1/2})^5 = (\sqrt{b})^5$$

and so on.

WORKED EXAMPLE 2.18

What are the values of: (a) $1/b^4$ (b) $b^{6/2}$ (c) $b^5 \times b^{1/2}$ (d) $(b^3 \times b^2)/\sqrt{b}$
(e) $25^{1/2}$ (f) $9^{1.5}$ (g) $8^{0.67}$ (h) $243^{0.4}$

Solution

Using the rules defined above:

(a) $1/b^4 = b^{-4}$

(b) $b^{6/2} = b^3$

(c) $b^5 \times b^{1/2} = b^{5+1/2} = b^{5.5} = (\sqrt{b})^{11}$

(d) $(b^3 \times b^2)/\sqrt{b} = b^{3+2}/b^{0.5} = b^5 \times b^{-0.5} = b^{4.5} = (\sqrt{b})^9$

(e) $25^{1/2} = \sqrt{25} = 5$

(f) $9^{1.5} = 9^{3/2} = (\sqrt{9})^3 = 3^3 = 27$

(g) $8^{0.67} = 8^{2/3} = (8^{1/3})^2 = 2^2 = 4$

(h) $243^{0.4} = 243^{(0.2 + 0.2)} = 243^{0.2} \times 243^{0.2} = 3 \times 3 = 9$

This use of powers leads to a convenient notation for very large or very small numbers. **Scientific notation** is used to represent any number in the format

$$a \times 10^b$$

where a is a number between 0 and 10, and b is the appropriate power of 10.

This notation is based on the fact that $10^1 = 10$, $10^2 = 100$, $10^3 = 1000$, and so on. Then:

- 12 can be written as 1.2×10^1 (that is, 1.2×10)
- 1200 as 1.2×10^3 (that is, 1.2×1000)
- 1 380 197.892 as about 1.38×10^6
- the United Kingdom's annual exports as about £1.1×10^{11}

and so on.

Similarly, $10^{-1} = 0.1$, $10^{-3} = 0.001$ and $10^{-6} = 0.000\ 001$, so:

- 0.12 can be written as 1.2×10^{-1} (that is, 1.2×0.1)
- 0.0012 as 1.2×10^{-3} (that is, 1.2×0.001)
- 0.000 004 29 as 4.29×10^{-6}

We shall not use this notation often, but remember that it gives a compact format for describing very large or very small numbers.

IN SUMMARY

Superscripts are used to show when values are raised to powers. There are several rules for manipulating powers, including:

- multiplication involves adding powers ($a^m \times a^n = a^{m+n}$)
- division involves subtracting powers ($a^m/a^n = a^{m-n}$)
- $a^{-n} = 1/a^n$

2.2.5 | Solving quadratic equations

In the last section we did some calculations which involved raising variables to powers. Now we can try solving equations which contain such powers. Unfortunately, these equations are usually difficult to solve and there are almost no general methods. One exception is an equation of the form

$$ax^2 + bx + c = 0$$

where a, b and c are constants, and x is the variable to be found. This is called a **quadratic equation.**

If we look at a very simple quadratic equation, where $a = 1$, $b = 0$ and $c = -4$, we have

$$x^2 - 4 = 0 \quad \text{or} \quad x^2 = 4$$

There are two solutions to this equation

$$x = 2 \quad \text{and} \quad x = -2$$

and this illustrates the general rule, that a quadratic equation has two solutions. These are called the **roots**, which can be found from the standard formula:

$$x = \frac{-b \pm \sqrt{b^2 - 4ac}}{2a}$$

where $\pm$ means 'plus or minus'.

In other words, the two roots of a quadratic equation are given by:

$$x = \frac{-b + \sqrt{b^2 - 4ac}}{2a} \quad \text{and} \quad x = \frac{-b - \sqrt{b^2 - 4ac}}{2a}$$

If we substitute the values used above, where $x^2 - 4 = 0$, we have $a = 1$, $b = 0$ and $c = -4$. Then the roots are:

$$x = \frac{-0 + \sqrt{0^2 + 4 \times 1 \times 4}}{2 \times 1} \quad \text{and} \quad x = \frac{-0 - \sqrt{0^2 + 4 \times 1 \times 4}}{2 \times 1}$$

$$= \ 4/2 \qquad\qquad\qquad = \ -4/2$$

$$= \ 2 \qquad\qquad\qquad\quad = \ -2$$

This confirms our initial result.

In this text we are going to avoid rigorous proofs. Nonetheless, some people like to see how results are derived, so a number of proofs are given in appendices. The derivation of the roots of a quadratic equation is given at the end of this chapter, while its use is shown in the following worked example.

WORKED EXAMPLE 2.19

What are the roots of the equation

$$2x^2 + 3x - 2 = 0$$

Solution

This is in the general form $ax^2 + bx + c = 0$, with $a = 2$, $b = 3$ and $c = -2$. The two roots are found by substitution in the equations

$$x = \frac{-b + \sqrt{b^2 - 4ac}}{2a} \quad \text{and} \quad x = \frac{-b - \sqrt{b^2 - 4ac}}{2a}$$

to give

$$x = \frac{-3 + \sqrt{3^2 + 4 \times 2 \times 2}}{2 \times 2} \quad \text{and} \quad x = \frac{-3 - \sqrt{3^2 + 4 \times 2 \times 2}}{2 \times 2}$$

Notice that the calculation of $-4ac$ has been simplified from $-4 \times 2 \times (-2)$ to $+4 \times 2 \times 2$.

Then

$$x = \frac{-3 + \sqrt{25}}{4} \quad \text{and} \quad x = \frac{-3 - \sqrt{25}}{4}$$

or

$$x = 2/4 \quad \text{and} \quad x = -8/4$$

$$= 0.5 \qquad\qquad = -2$$

These values can be checked by substitution in the original equation.

$$2 \times 0.5^2 + 3 \times 0.5 - 2 = 0 \quad \text{and} \quad 2 \times 2^2 - 3 \times 2 - 2 = 0$$

The only problem with this approach occurs when $4ac$ is greater than b^2. Then $b^2 - 4ac$ is negative and we have to find the square root of a negative number. This is not defined in real arithmetic, so we conclude that there are no real roots and they are both imaginary.

One example of the use of quadratic equations in business occurs when the cost per unit varies with the number of units produced. Suppose, for example, a workshop has fixed overheads of £2000 a week, and the basic cost of making a unit of product is £200, but this declines by £5 for every unit of weekly production. Then the unit cost can be written as $200 - 5x$, where x is the weekly production. So:

$$\text{total weekly cost} = \text{overheads} + (\text{unit cost} \times \text{number made in week})$$

$$= 2000 + (200 - 5x) \times x$$

$$= 2000 + 200x - 5x^2$$

WORKED EXAMPLE 2.20

The basic income generated by a product is £12 a unit, but this increases by £2 for every unit made. If there are fixed costs of £1000 for the process, how many units must be sold to cover costs?

Solution

The income generated by each unit is $12 + 2x$, where x is the number of units sold. Therefore the total income is $12x + 2x^2$. Then the profit is $2x^2 + 2x - 1000$. When this is equal to zero the income just covers costs. This happens when:

$$x = \frac{-b + \sqrt{b^2 - 4ac}}{2a} \qquad \text{and} \qquad x = \frac{-b - \sqrt{b^2 - 4ac}}{2a}$$

$$x = \frac{-2 + \sqrt{(2^2 + 4 \times 2 \times 1000)}}{2 \times 2} \qquad \text{and} \qquad x = \frac{-2 - \sqrt{(2^2 + 4 \times 2 \times 1000)}}{2 \times 2}$$

$$= 21.87 \qquad\qquad\qquad\qquad = -22.87$$

Obviously, the company cannot sell a negative number of units, so the answer must be 21.87 units.

IN SUMMARY

Equations containing variables raised to powers are difficult to solve. The only equations of this type which are easy to solve are quadratic equations of the form

$$ax^2 + bx + c = 0$$

2.2.6 | Arithmetic and geometric series

Sometimes we are concerned not with a single number, but with a series of observations. We might, for example, be interested in how the profit made by a company has changed over some period. Then the monthly profit figures (in thousands of pounds) would form a sequence of numbers, like:

$$10, 15, 21, 22, 25, 30, 35, 36, 40$$

This is a **sequence** of numbers. If the numbers in the sequence follow a distinct pattern, they are referred to as a **series**. There are two main types of series:

- **arithmetic series**, in which each number is larger than the previous number by a fixed amount, such as 1, 4, 7, 10, 13, 16, and 19. If the initial number is a and the common difference between terms is d, an arithmetic series is described by $a, a + d, a + 2d, a + 3d, a + 4d$, so the nth term is $a + (n-1)d$.
- **geometric series**, in which each number is found by multiplying the previous number by a fixed amount, such as 5, 15, 45, 135, 405 and 1215. If the initial number is a and the common ratio is r, a geometric series is described by a, ar, ar^2, ar^3, ar^4, so the nth term is $ar^{(n-1)}$.

These series have the useful property that their sums are easy to calculate. In particular, the sum of the first n terms of an arithmetic series is given by

$$S = \frac{n[2a + (n-1)d]}{2}$$

while the sum of the first n terms of a geometric series is given by

$$S = \frac{a(r^n - 1)}{(r-1)}$$

For those who are interested, the derivations of these results are given at the end of this chapter.

WORKED EXAMPLE 2.21

(a) What are the next three terms of the arithmetic series which starts 10, 12? What is the sum of the first ten terms of this series?

(b) What are the next three terms of the geometric series which starts 3, 9? What is the sum of the first ten terms of this series?

Solution

(a) The series has $a = 10$ and $d = 2$, so the next three terms are 14, 16 and 18. The sum of the first ten terms is given by

$$\frac{n[2a + (n-1)d]}{2} = \frac{10 \times [2 \times 10 + (10-1) \times 2]}{2} = \frac{380}{2} = 190$$

(b) The series has $a = 3$ and $r = 3$, so the next three terms are 27, 81 and 243. The sum of the first ten terms is given by

$$\frac{a(r^n - 1)}{(r-1)} = \frac{3 \times (3^{10} - 1)}{(3-1)} = \frac{177\,144}{2} = 88\,572$$

WORKED EXAMPLE 2.22

A company offers an employee the choice of two contracts. The first contract gives an initial salary of £15,000 a year rising by £1000 every year. The second contract gives an initial salary of £14,000 a year rising by 10% each year. Which contract will give the higher total income over five years?

Solution

The salary in the first contract is an arithmetic series with $a = 15\,000$ and $d = 1000$. The total salary over five years is

$$S = \frac{n[2a + (n-1)d]}{2} = \frac{5[2 \times 15\,000 + 4 \times 1000]}{2} = £85,000$$

The salary in the second contract is a geometric series with $a = 14\,000$ and $r = 1.1$. The total salary over five years is:

$$S = \frac{a(r^n - 1)}{(r-1)} = \frac{14\,000(1.1^5 - 1)}{(1.1 - 1)} = £85,471$$

The higher total salary clearly comes with the second contract.

IN SUMMARY

A series is a sequence of numbers with a distinct relationship between consecutive numbers. This may be a fixed difference (for arithmetic series) or a fixed ratio (for geometric series). The sums of series can be calculated easily.

| **2.2.7** | # Logarithms and the exponential function

Earlier in the chapter we showed how to evaluate numbers raised to powers. Then:

$$2^4 = 16$$

$$3^2 = 9$$

$$10^3 = 1000$$

and so on.

In other words we can represent one number (say 16) by a second number (say 2) raised to a power (4). In this representation the second number is called a **base** and the power it is raised to is called a **logarithm**. Thus the logarithm of a number is the power to which the base must be raised to give the number.

- $16 = 2^4$, so we can say that the logarithm to the base 2 of 16 is 4 (that is, the base 2 must be raised to the power 4 to give 16). This relationship is written as $\log_2 16 = 4$

- $9 = 3^2$, so we can say that the logarithm to the base 3 of 9 is 2, which is written as $\log_3 9 = 2$

- $10^3 = 1000$, so we can say that the logarithm to the base 10 of 1000 is 3, which is written $\log_{10} 1000 = 3$

These are specific examples of the general notation:

$$\text{If:} \quad n = b^y$$

$$\text{then:} \quad y = \log_b n$$

In the past this notation was widely used for calculation. In recent years its use has markedly declined with the arrival of calculators and computers. It is, however, still useful for simplifying some calculations.

In practice, the only two types of logarithm used are **common logarithms** which use the base 10, and **natural logarithms** which use the base e. Now e is a number, called the **exponential constant**, which is found in a surprisingly large number of applications. It can be calculated from $(1 + 1/n)^n$, where n is a large number, and it has a value about 2.718 281 8. At first glance this may seem a strange number, but it is actually very useful, and we shall meet it several times in this book. Here, though, we shall simply consider it as a useful base for natural logarithms.

Now we have:

- common logarithms, which are always written as:

$$y = \log x \qquad \text{which implies that} \qquad x = 10^y$$

  Notice that we do not need to specify the base of the log, and this is understood.

- natural logarithms, which are always written as:

$$y = \ln x \qquad \text{which implies that} \qquad x = e^y$$

  Again we do not need to specify the base of the log, as this is understood.

  Values for logarithms can be found in tables, but these are seldom used as most calculators automatically give the values.

WORKED EXAMPLE 2.23

Find the value of:

(a) $\log_2 32$ (b) $\log 1000$ (c) $\log 10$ (d) $\ln 2$ (e) $\ln 200$

What do these values mean?

Solution

(a) $\log_2 32$ is the power to which 2 must be raised to equal 32. This is 5, as $2^5 = 32$.

(b) $\log 1000$ is the power to which 10 must be raised to equal 1000. This is 3, as $10^3 = 1000$.

(c) $\log 10$ is the power to which 10 must be raised to equal 10. This is 1, as $10^1 = 10$.

(d) $\ln 2$ is the power to which e must be raised to equal 2. This can be found using a calculator to be 0.6931.

(e) $\ln 200$ is the power to which e must be raised to equal 200. This can be found using a calculator to be 5.2983.

IN SUMMARY

Logarithms are defined as the power to which a base must be raised to equal a number. The most common types are common logarithms (using the base 10) and natural logarithms (using the base e).

Self–assessment questions

2.5 Why is algebra useful in business?

2.6 Is the order of doing calculations in equations always the same?

2.7 Could you solve an equation of the form $y = 4x + 3$, where both x and y are unknown?

2.8 Would it be better to write an equation in the form:
    (a)   speed = distance/time
    (b) $S = D/T$
    (c)   SPD = DST/TME
    (d) $s = dt^{-1}$

2.9 What is the value of $((((1 + 3)/(4 - 2))/2) - 1)$?

2.10 If you knew values for p, q and r, how would you solve the equations:
    (a) $4r/(33 - 3x) = q/2p$ (b) $(q - 4x)/2q - 7p/r = 0$

2.11 How many simultaneous equations would be needed to find values for 7 unknown variables?

2.12 What is the value of $x^{1.5}/y^{2.5}$ when $x = 9$ and $y = 4$?

2.13 What is the value of 41.1635°?

2.14 Write 1 230 000 000 and 0.000 000 253 in scientific notation.

2.15 What can you say about the roots of the equation $x^2 + 2x + 3 = 0$?

2.16 Having shown how to solve quadratic equations, why do we not describe formulae for solving other equations with variables raised to powers?

2.17 It is suggested that the total weekly cost of making x units of a product is $2000 + 200x - 5x^2$. What inference can you make about the production quantities?

2.18 What is the difference between an arithmetic series and a geometric series?

2.19 If $\log a = 2$ and $\log b = 3$, what is $\log (ab)$?

‖ 2.3 ‖ Drawing graphs

‖ 2.3.1 ‖ Cartesian coordinates

Algebra gives a precise way of describing many situations. Unfortunately, most people find it difficult to follow arguments by looking only at a set of equations. It is much easier to understand information which is presented as some form of diagram. We shall discuss the use of diagrams in Chapter 4, but we shall introduce one widely used type now. This is a **line graph**, which shows the relationship between two variables.

The most common type of graph is drawn with two rectangular (or Cartesian) axes. The horizontal axis is traditionally labelled x and the vertical axis is labelled y (as shown in Figure 2.2). Then x is the **independent variable**, which is the one that we can control, and y is the **dependent variable**, whose value is determined by x. Thus x might be the expenditure on advertising which we can control, while y is the resulting sales which we cannot control; x might be the interest rate for loans which can be fixed, while y is the amount borrowed from banks; x might be the price charged for a service and y the resulting demand, and so on.

One thing we should say straight away when discussing dependent and independent variables is that we do not assume any cause and effect. Although there might be a clear relationship, this is no evidence that change in one variable actually **causes** changes in the other. A shopkeeper, for example, might find that in one period he reduced the price of overcoats and sales of ice cream increased. There might be a clear relationship between these two, but one does not cause the other, and they are both likely to be consequences of the prevailing hot weather. This theme is discussed in more detail in Chapter 10.

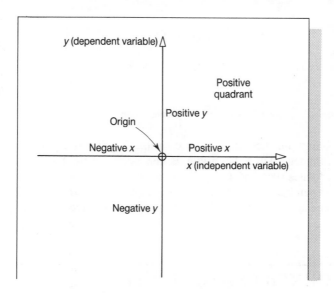

Figure 2.2 Cartesian axes.

The point where the two axes cross is called the **origin**, and corresponds to the point where both x and y have the value zero. At any point above the origin, y is positive, while at any point below it, y is negative: at any point to the left of the origin x is negative, while at any point to the right of it x is positive.

Having drawn the axes, any point on a graph can be specified by two numbers called **coordinates**. The first number specifies the distance along the x axis from the origin, while the second number specifies the distance up the y axis. The point $x = 3$, $y = 4$, for example, is three units along the x axis and four units up the y axis. A standard notation describes coordinates as (x,y), so this point can be described as $(3,4)$. The only thing we have to be careful about is that $(3,4)$ is not the same as $(4,3)$, as shown in Figure 2.3.

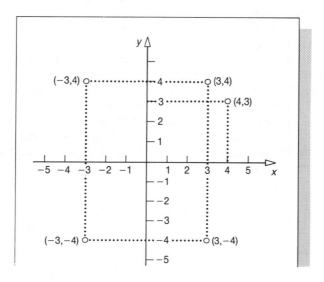

Figure 2.3 Use of coordinates to locate points.

Points on the x axis have coordinates $(x,0)$ and points on the y axis have coordinates $(0,y)$. The origin is the point where the axes cross, which has coordinates $(0,0)$. Many applications are only concerned with areas where both the dependent and independent variables are positive (for example, a graph of income against sales) so they only show the positive quadrant.

WORKED EXAMPLE 2.24

Plot the following points on a graph.

x	2	5	7	10	15
y	7	18	22	30	46

Draw a line graph to emphasize the relationship between x and y.

Solution

Only positive numbers are given so we need draw only the positive quadrant of the graph. Then the first point, (2,7), is 2 units along the *x* axis and 7 units up the *y* axis, and is shown as point A in Figure 2.4. The second point, (5,18), is five units along the *x* axis and 18 units up the *y* axis, and is shown by point B. The other points are plotted in the same way.

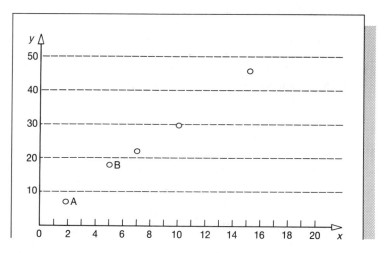

Figure 2.4 Graph of points for Worked Example 2.24.

There seems to be a fairly strong relationship between *x* and *y*, so we can emphasize this by joining the points by a line. This line can either go through all the points to show detailed changes, or else it can ignore the details and show general trends. Figure 2.5 shows both the detailed line and a superimposed straight line of the general trend.

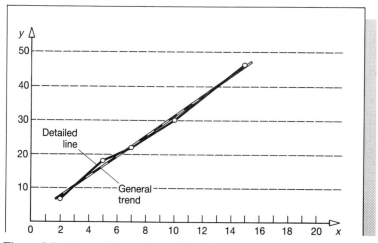

Figure 2.5 Line graph for Worked Example 2.24.

IN SUMMARY

Graphs using rectangular coordinates give a useful means of showing a relationship between two variables; an independent one, x, and a dependent one, y.

2.3.2 | Drawing straight-line graphs

If two variables x and y are related, the relationship is described by an equation. We might find, for example, that $y = 4x + 10$. Then for every value of the independent variable x there is a corresponding value of the dependent variable y. An alternative way of saying 'there is a relationship' is to describe y **as a function of** x, or

$$y = f(x) = 4x + 10$$

Here $f(x)$ is simply a shorthand way of saying that the dependent variable y is a function of the independent variable x. It might be that y depends on two variables, say x and z, so we can extend the notation to say that y is a function of both x and z, or $y = f(x, z)$. Again, we could have $y = f(p, q, r, s)$ which means that the value of the dependent variable y is determined by the values of the independent variables p, q, r and s.

Now we can describe how to draw graphs of functions. We shall start with a simple function, for which y does not vary with x. In other words, $y = c$, where c is a constant. In this case we get a straight line which is parallel to the x axis (see Figure 2.6). If, for example, $y = 10$, the graph of this is a straight line 10 units up the y axis and parallel to the x axis.

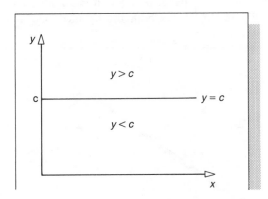

Figure 2.6   Graph of $y = c$.

Such lines divide the area of the graph into three zones:

- at any point **on** the line y is equal to c (so we have $y = c$)
- at any point **above** the line y is greater than c, which is written $y > c$
- at any point **below** the line y is less than c, which is written $y < c$

We could equally say:

- at any point **on or above** the line y is greater than or equal to c, which is written $y \geqslant c$
- at any point **on or below** the line y is less than or equal to c, which is written $y \leqslant c$

The graph of $y = c$ is an example of a linear function, for which the graph relating two variables is a straight line. In general, such linear relationships have the form

$$y = ax + b$$

where x and y are the independent and dependent variables, and a and b are constants.

One benefit of straight-line graphs is that only two points need be specified to draw them, as you can see in the following example.

WORKED EXAMPLE 2.25

Draw a graph of $y = 10x + 2$.

Solution

This is a straight-line graph of the standard form $y = ax + b$, with $a = 10$ and $b = 2$. We need only take two points to draw the line, so will take two convenient ones. We shall arbitrarily take $x = 0$ and $x = 20$.
Then:

- when $x = 0$, $y = 10x + 2$ $\quad = 10 \times 0 + 2$ $\quad = 2$, which defines the point (0,2)
- when $x = 20$, $y = 10x + 2$ $\quad = 10 \times 20 + 2 = 202$, which defines the point (20, 202)

Plotting these points and the connecting line gives the graph shown in Figure 2.7.

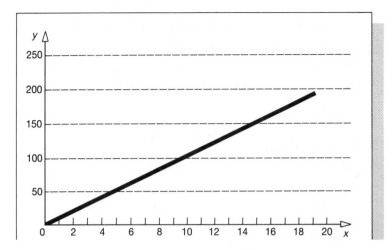

Figure 2.7 Graph of $y = 10x + 2$ for Worked Example 2.25.

If you look at a straight-line graph, two features are obvious. These are:

- **intercept**, which shows where the line crosses the y axis
- **gradient**, which shows how steep the line is

Now a line crosses the y axis when x has the value 0, so the intercept is the value of y when $x = 0$. If we substitute $x = 0$ into the general equation $y = ax + b$, we find that this gives $y = b$. In other words, b is the intercept of the line.

The gradient shows how quickly the line is rising, so it can be defined as the increase in y for a unit increase in x. Now if we look at the graph of $y = 10x + 2$ shown in Figure 2.7 we can find the change in y when x rises between, say 10 and 11. (These numbers are chosen arbitrarily, as a straight line will have the same gradient at any point.)

Substitution gives

$$\text{when } x = 10, y = 10x + 2 = 10 \times 10 + 2 = 102$$

and

$$\text{when } x = 11, y = 10x + 2 = 10 \times 11 + 2 = 112$$

So the gradient is $(112 - 102) = 10$. But you can see that this is the value of a. This is no coincidence, and in general the gradient of a straight-line graph is always given by the value of a.

WORKED EXAMPLE 2.26

Describe the graph of the equation $y = 4x + 20$.

Solution

This is a straight-line graph with intercept of 20 and gradient of 4, as shown in Figure 2.8.

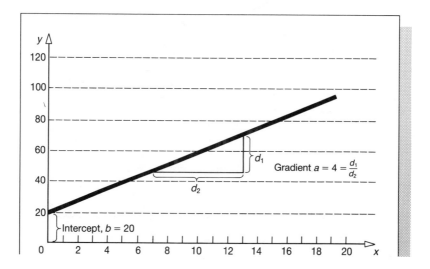

Figure 2.8 Graph of $y = 4x + 20$ for Worked Example 2.26.

WORKED EXAMPLE 2.27

Plot the graph of $y = 100 - 5x$.

Solution

This is a straight-line graph with $a = -5$ and $b = 100$. We only need to find two points to draw the line, so we shall take two convenient ones, such as $x = 0$ and $x = 10$. Then:

- when $x = 0$, $y = 100 - 5x = 100 - 5 \times 0 = 100$

and

- when $x = 10$, $y = 100 - 5x = 100 - 5 \times 10 = 50$

Plotting the two points (0,100) and (10,50) and drawing the connecting line gives the result shown in Figure 2.9. In this example the gradient is negative, implying that y decreases when x increases.

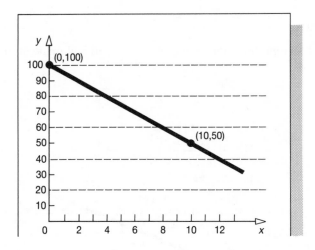

Figure 2.9 Graph of $y = 100 - 5x$ for Worked Example 2.27.

IN SUMMARY

Line graphs are used to give a diagrammatic view of a function. Straight-line graphs have the form $y = ax + b$, where a is the gradient and b is the intercept. Such graphs can be drawn by plotting any two points and drawing the straight line through them.

2.3.3 | Drawing graphs of other equations

Now that we have seen how straight-line graphs can be drawn, we can extend these ideas to other functions. The easiest way of drawing a graph of a function is to take a series of convenient values for the independent variable x, and substitute these into the equation to find corresponding values for the dependent variable y. This gives a series points for (x,y). These points can be joined by a line to show the graph of the relationship. Straight-line graphs can be drawn from only two points, but more complex functions give curves which can only be drawn accurately if more points are known. This principle is shown in the following worked example, which draws a graph of a quadratic equation.

WORKED EXAMPLE 2.28

Draw the graph of the quadratic equation $y = 2x^2 + 3x - 3$, between $x = -6$ and $x = 5$
Where does this curve cross the x axis?

Solution

The shape of this graph is not obvious from the equation, but as we are
interested in values of y for x between -6 and $+5$ we can calculate the following
coordinates by substitution.

$$\text{When } x = -6, \quad y = 2x^2 + 3x - 3 = 2 \times (-6)^2 + 3 \times (-6) - 3 = 51$$

$$\text{when } x = -5, \quad y = 2x^2 + 3x - 3 = 2 \times (-5)^2 + 3 \times (-5) - 3 = 32$$

and so on, to give the following table:

x	-6	-5	-4	-3	-2	-1	0	1	2	3	4	5
y	51	32	17	6	-1	-4	-3	2	11	24	41	62

When these points are plotted on rectangular axes and joined together the
graph in Figure 2.10 is given. We can see that the curve crosses the x axis at
roughly the points $x = -2$ and $x = 1$.

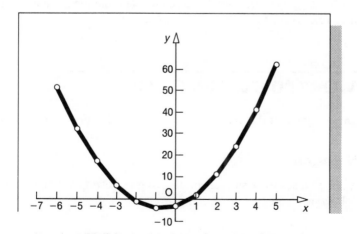

Figure 2.10   Graph of $y = 2x^2 + 3x - 3$ for Worked Example 2.28.

Quadratic equations always give this kind of U-shaped curve, which has one turning point (where the graph changes direction and the gradient changes sign). If the x^2 term in a quadratic equation is negative the graph is inverted, so it looks like a hill rather than a valley. Now we can relate this graph back to Section 2.2.5, which described the solution of quadratic equations. The two roots of a quadratic were defined as the points where $ax^2 + bx + c = 0$. In other words, they are the two points where $y = 0$ and the graph crosses the x axis. For the worked example above, we can calculate the roots of the equation as:

$$x = \frac{-b + \sqrt{b^2 - 4ac}}{2a} \quad \text{and} \quad x = \frac{-b - \sqrt{b^2 - 4ac}}{2a}$$

$$= \frac{-3 + \sqrt{(9 + 24)}}{4} \qquad\qquad = \frac{-3 - \sqrt{(9 + 24)}}{4}$$

$$= 0.686 \qquad \text{and} \qquad = -2.186$$

This is a more accurate value for our observations from the graph, and means that the curve crosses the x axis at the points (0.686, 0) and (–2.186, 0).

We have now drawn graphs of straight lines (where $y = ax + b$) and quadratic equations (where $y = ax^2 + bx + c$). These are two examples of **polynomials**, which are equations containing a variable, x, raised to some power (1 for straight lines and 2 for quadratics). Sometimes we need to look at polynomials where x is raised to a higher power. Cubic equations, for example, contain x raised to the power 3, with the form

$$y = ax^3 + bx^2 + cx + d$$

These graphs are slightly more complex, but the method of drawing them is the same, as shown in the following example.

WORKED EXAMPLE 2.29

Draw a graph of the function $y = x^3 - 1.5x^2 - 18x$ between $x = -5$ and $x = +6$.

Solution

Taking values for x and substituting to give corresponding values for y gives the following results:

x	-5	-4	-3	-2	-1	0	1	2	3	4	5	6
y	-72.5	-16	13.5	22	15.5	0	-18.5	-34	-40.5	-32	-2.5	54

The resulting graph is shown in Figure 2.11.

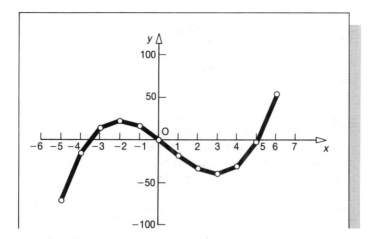

Figure 2.11   Graph of $y = x^3 - 1.5x^2 - 18x$ for Worked Example 2.29.

The graph in Figure 2.11 has two turning points where the gradient changes sign. These are located around $x = -2$ and $x = 3$. Most cubic equations have this general shape, but they vary a little in detail: some are the other way around, some have the two turning points merged into one, and so on. Figure 2.11 also illustrates the general point that more complex polynomials give more complex graphs. When drawing these we must be careful to

- plot enough points to show the true shape of the curve, and
- draw a smooth curve through the points (rather than a series of straight lines between points).

The method of drawing graphs of polynomials can be extended to any other functions. We mentioned earlier that many functions are based on the exponential constant, e, which is defined as e = 2.718 281 8... Although this may seem a strange number, there are sound theoretical reasons for its use. It is particularly well suited to functions which rise at an accelerating rate, and you have probably heard of this referred to as 'exponential growth'. We shall return to exponential functions at several points in the book, but at the moment shall limit ourselves to drawing typical graphs.

WORKED EXAMPLE 2.30

Draw graphs of $y = e^x$ for values of x between 0 and 10 and $y = e^{2x}$ for values of x between 0 and 5.

Solution

Following the usual procedure, we can build a table of values and transfer these to a graph. For this kind of calculation you need, at least, a calculator which can automatically calculate exponential values.

x	0	1	2	3	4	5	6	7	8	9	10
e^x	1	2.7	7.4	20.1	54.6	148.4	403.4	1096.6	2981.0	8103.1	22026.5
e^{2x}	1	7.4	54.6	403.4	2981.0	22026.5					

The results of this are drawn in Figure 2.12, which shows a characteristic exponential growth curve. As you can see, the graph of $y = e^{2x}$ rises much more steeply than the graph of $y = e^x$. These curves are examples of the general exponential form

$$y = ne^{mx}$$

where the exact shape of the curve is determined by the values of n and m.

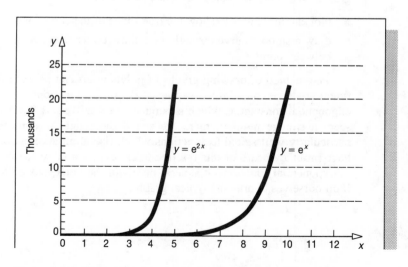

Figure 2.12   Exponential curves for Worked Example 2.30.

WORKED EXAMPLE 2.31

Draw the graph of $y = e^{-x}$ between $x = 0$ and $x = 8$.

Solution

Following the usual procedure, we can build the table of values shown below.

x	0	1	2	3	4	5	6	7	8
e^{-x}	1	0.368	0.135	0.050	0.018	0.007	0.002	0.001	0.000

These points are plotted in Figure 2.13, which shows a standard exponential decline, which is generally described by the equation $y = ne^{-mx}$.

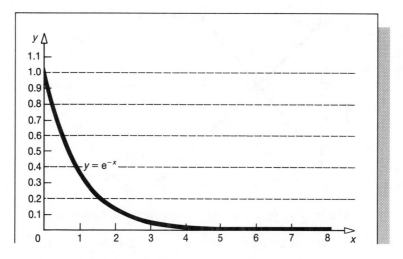

Figure 2.13   Negative exponential curve for Worked Example 2.31.

IN SUMMARY

Line graphs can be used to give a diagrammatic view of any function. They are drawn most easily by plotting a series of separate points (x,y) and joining them with a line. This approach can be illustrated using polynomials and exponential functions.

2.3.4 | Using graphs to solve simultaneous equations

Earlier in the chapter we described how to find the roots of a quadratic equation algebraically, and then we showed a graphical interpretation of the solution. We also showed how to solve simultaneous equations algebraically, so we can now show how these solutions are derived from graphs. Suppose, for example, we have two unknown variables x and y related by the simultaneous equations

$$3y = 4x + 2 \tag{1}$$

$$y = -x + 10 \tag{2}$$

One way of finding a solution would be to draw a graph of each equation. This gives a graph with two straight lines. The first equation is true at any point on the first line, and the second equation is true at any point on the second line. It follows that the point where the lines cross is the point where both equations are true. Figure 2.14 shows that the lines cross at about the point where $x = 4$ and $y = 6$.

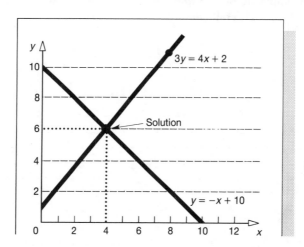

Figure 2.14   Graphical solution of simultaneous equations.

We can also tackle the problem algebraically to give

$$3y = 4x + 2 \tag{1}$$

$$y = -x + 10 \tag{2}$$

Multiply equation (2) by 3 and subtract it from equation (1):

$$0 = 7x - 28$$

$$x = 4$$

Substituting in equation (1):

$$3y = 4 \times 4 + 2$$

$$y = 6$$

This confirms the graphical solution.

The main problem with using graphs to solve equations is accuracy. It is difficult to draw graphs exactly, so with complicated curves or small scales the results are not likely to be very accurate. Much more accurate results can be found by solving equations algebraically, but graphs have the important advantage of giving a clear picture of the problem.

We can use a graph to see where any two curves intersect. We can, for example, see where a quadratic equation with the general form $y = ax^2 + bx + c$ crosses a straight line with the general form $y = ax + b$, as illustrated in the following example.

WORKED EXAMPLE 2.32

Use a graphical method to find the roots of the quadratic equation

$$2x^2 + 3x - 2 = 0$$

At what points are both this equation and $y = 2x + 10$ satisfied?

Solution

Taking a range of values from, say, $x = -5$ to $x = +4$ and substituting into the original equation gives

x	-5	-4	-3	-2	-1	0	1	2	3	4
y	33	18	7	0	-3	-2	3	12	25	42

These points are plotted in Figure 2.15. The roots are the points where the

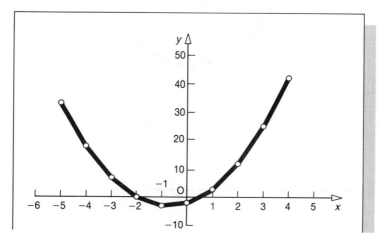

Figure 2.15 Graph of $y = 2x^2 + 3x - 2$ for Worked Example 2.32.

curve crosses the x axis, and these are about -2 and 0.5. These values can be calculated more accurately as $x = -2.186$ and $x = 0.686$.

If we superimpose the straight-line graph of $y = 2x + 10$ (Figure 2.16), we can see that both equations are satisfied at the points where the graphs cross, which is about $x = -3$ and $x = 2$. These values can be calculated more accurately by saying that both equations are satisfied when

$$y = 2x^2 + 3x - 2 \qquad \text{and} \qquad y = 2x + 10$$

so

$$(y =) \, 2x^2 + 3x - 2 = 2x + 10$$

Rearranging this equation gives

$$2x^2 + x - 12 = 0$$

which can be solved to find x in the usual way, giving the solutions $x = 2.21$ and $x = -2.71$. Substituting these two values for x into one of the original equations, say $y = 2x + 10$, gives the corresponding values for y:

$$x = 2.21 \qquad y = 2x + 10 = 2 \times 2.21 + 10 = 14.42$$

$$x = -2.71 \qquad y = 2x + 10 = 2 \times (-2.71) + 10 = 4.59$$

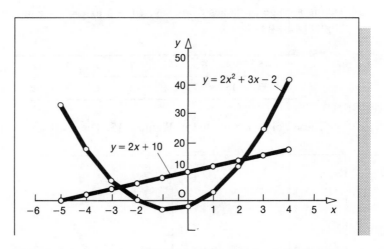

Figure 2.16   Graph of $y = 2x^2 + 3x - 2$ and $y = 2x + 10$ for Worked Example 2.32.

IN SUMMARY

Graphs can be used to solve simultaneous equations of several types. In practice, the results are not very accurate, so it is better to draw graphs to get an overall view of the problem, and then find the solutions algebraically.

Self-assessment questions

2.20 What is meant by a 'dependent variable'?

2.21 What does '$y = f(x, z)$' mean?

2.22 What are the coordinates of the origin of a graph?

2.23 Describe the graph of the equation $y = 2x + 4$.

2.24 What are the gradients of the lines

    (a) $y = 10$ (b) $y = x$ (c) $x = 10$

2.25 Where are the solutions of a quadratic equation found on a graph?

2.26 What is a turning point of a graph?

2.27 Why is it generally preferable to use algebraic rather than graphical methods to solve equations?

2.28 What does it mean when two graphs cross each other?

CHAPTER REVIEW

The remaining chapters in this book describe some quantitative analyses which are widely used in business. This chapter described the basic tools which are used in these analyses. In particular, it described:

- the overall approach to quantitative methods used in the book
- calculations using integers, decimals, fractions and percentages
- the use of algebra
- the solution of simple, simultaneous and quadratic equations
- use of powers, roots, logarithms and exponential functions
- arithmetic and geometric series
- drawing of graphs on Cartesian coordinates
- use of graphs to solve equations

If you want more information about any point mentioned in this chapter it might be worth looking at a more detailed book on mathematics. Many of these are available and some useful ones are listed in Appendix A.

Problems

2.1 What are the values of: (a) -12×8 (b) $-35/(-7)$ (c) $(24-8) \times (4+5)$ (d) $(18-4)/(3+9-5)$ (e) $(22/11) \times (-18+3)/(12/4)$

2.2 Simplify the common fractions: (a) $3/5 + 1/2$ (b) $3/4 \times 1/6$ (c) $3/4 - 1/8$ (d) $-18/5 \div 6/25$ (e) $(3/8 - 1/6) \div 4/7$

2.3 What are the answers to Problem 2.2 as decimal fractions?

2.4 (a) What is $23/40$ as a percentage? (b) What is 65% as a fraction? (c) What is 17% as a decimal?

2.5 What is $1037/14$ to (a) three decimal places; (b) one decimal place; (c) two significant figures; (d) one significant figure?

2.6 In one exam 64 people passed and 23 failed; in a second exam 163 people passed and 43 failed. Which exam was the more difficult to pass?

2.7 A car travels 180 miles in 3 hours. What is its average speed? What is the equation for the average speed of a car on any journey?

2.8 A shopkeeper buys an item from a wholesaler and sells it to customers. If he sells n units a day, what is his profit?

2.9 A school has £1515 to spend on footballs. Match balls cost £35 each while practice balls cost £22 each. The school must buy 60 balls each year, so how many of each type should be bought to exactly match the budget?

2.10 A company finds that 30% of its costs are direct labour. Each week raw materials cost £1000 more than twice this amount, and there is an overhead of 20% of direct labour costs. What are the weekly costs to the company?

2.11 Solve the following simultaneous equations:

(a) $a + b = 3$ and $a - b = 5$

(b) $2x + 3y = 27$ and $3x + 2y = 23$

(c) $x + y - 2z = -2$ and $2x - y + z = 9$ and $x + 3y + 2z = 4$

(d) $4r - 2s + 3t = 12$ and $r + 2s + t = -1$ and $3r - s - t = -5$

2.12 A company finds that one of its productivity measures is related to the number of employees e and the production n by the following equations:

$$10n + 3e = 45 \quad \text{and} \quad 2n + 5e = 31$$

What are the current values for e and n?

2.13 What are the values of: (a) $x^{1/2} \times x^{1/4}$ (b) $(x^{1/3})^3$ (c) $9^{0.5}$ (d) $4^{2.5}$ (e) $7^{3.2}$ (f) $4^{1.5} \times 6^{3.7}/6^{1.7}$

2.14 What are the roots of: (a) $x^2 - 6x + 8 = 0$; (b) $3x^2 - 2x - 5 = 0$ (c) $x^2 + x + 1 = 0$?

2.15 The basic income generated by a product is £10 a unit, but this increases by £1 for every unit made. If there are fixed costs of £100 for the process how many units must be sold to cover costs?

2.16 (a) What is the sum of the first ten terms of the series 7, 12, 17, 22...?
(b) What is the sum of the first ten terms of the series 3, 9, 27, 81...?

2.17 The income of a company is £20,000 a month and rising by 10% a month. How long will it take for the total income generated to exceed £400,000?

2.18 If $\log a = 0.3010$, $\log b = 0.4771$ and $\log c = 0.6021$, find the value of $\log (ab/c)$. Use this result to find some general relationships for logarithms. What would be the answer if natural logarithms were used?

2.19 If $3000 = 1500 \times 1.1^n$, what is the value of n?

2.20 Draw a graph showing the following points: (2, 12), (4, 16), (7, 22), (10, 28), (15, 38). How would you describe this function?

2.21 The number of people employed in a chain of shops is related to the size (in consistent units) by the equation

$$\text{employees} = \text{size}/1000 + 3$$

Draw a graph of this function and use it to find the number of employees in a shop of size 50 000 units.

2.22 Draw a graph of   (a) $y = 10$ (b) $y = x + 10$ (c) $y = x^2 + x + 10$
(d) $y = x^3 + x^2 + x + 10$

2.23 Draw appropriate graphs to confirm the results of Problem 2.11.

2.24 The output y from an assembly line is related to one of the settings x by the equation

$$y = -5x^2 + 2500x - 12\,500$$

What is the maximum output from the line, and the corresponding value for x?

2.25 The unit cost of operating some production equipment is given by the equation

$$\text{cost} = 1.5x^2 - 120x + 4000$$

where x is the number of units produced. Draw a graph to find the minimum unit cost. What production level does this correspond to?

2.26 Where does the line $y = 20x + 15$ cross the line $y = 2x^2 - 4x + 1$?

2.27 Where do the curves $y = x^2 + 4$ and $y = -x^2 + 2x + 20$ intersect?

Computer exercises

2.1 Figure 2.17 shows a section of a spreadsheet and the formulae which produced it. What calculations are being done?

Design a similar spreadsheet to calculate the sum of the first 60 terms of the series:

(a) 1, 3, 5, 7...   (b) 1, 1.1, 1.21, 1.331...

	A	B	C
1	**Term**	**Arithmetic**	**Geometric**
2		**Series**	**Series**
3			
4	1	100	100
5	=+A4+1	=+B4+10	=+C4*1.1
6	=+A5+1	=+B5+10	=+C5*1.1
7	=+A6+1	=+B6+10	=+C6*1.1
8	=+A7+1	=+B7+10	=+C7*1.1
9	=+A8+1	=+B8+10	=+C8*1.1
10	=+A9+1	=+B9+10	=+C9*1.1
11	=+A10+1	=+B10+10	=+C10*1.1
12	=+A11+1	=+B11+10	=+C11*1.1
13	=+A12+1	=+B12+10	=+C12*1.1
14			
15	**Totals**	=SUM(B4:B13)	=SUM(C4:C13)

(a)

	A	B	C
1	**Term**	**Arithmetic**	**Geometric**
2		**Series**	**Series**
3			
4	1	100	100
5	2	110	110
6	3	120	121
7	4	130	133.1
8	5	140	146.41
9	6	150	161.051
10	7	160	177.1561
11	8	170	194.87171
12	9	180	214.35888
13	10	190	235.79477
14			
15	**Totals**	1450	1593.7425

(b)

Figure 2.17   Spreadsheet results for Computer Exercise 2.1: (a) calculations; (b) results.

2.2   Use a spreadsheet to calculate $x^3 - 3x^2 - 4x + 10$ for values of x from 1 to 50. Draw a graph of this function using both a spreadsheet and a graphics package. Which package is easier to use?

2.3   Use a suitable package to draw the graphs of $y = 22 - 3x$ and $y = x + 4$. Where do these lines cross?

2.4   Use a graphics package to draw the functions $y = e^{2x}$ and $y = x^2 + 10$. Where do these lines cross?

2.5   Figure 2.18 shows a dialogue with Minitab. What does this show?

```
MTB   > SET INTO C1
DATA  > 1 2 3 4 5 6 7 8 END
MTB   > SET INTO C2
DATA  > 11 23 29 38 52 61 69 81 END
MTB   > PRINT C1 C2

        ROW     C1      C2
         1       1      11
         2       2      23
         3       3      29
         4       4      38
         5       5      52
         6       6      61
         7       7      69
         8       8      81
```

MTB > PLOT C2 C1

MTB > STOP

Figure 2.18   Dialogue with Minitab for Computer Exercise 2.5.

2.6 Use a statistics package to plot the following points:

x	1	3	6	8	9	10	13	14	17	18	21	25	26	29
y	22	24	31	38	41	44	52	55	61	64	69	76	81	83

Derivation 2.1 Solution of quadratic equations

We know that

$$ax^2 + bx + c = 0$$

so

$$x^2 + \frac{bx}{a} + \frac{c}{a} = 0$$

or

$$x^2 + \frac{bx}{a} = -\frac{c}{a}$$

Adding $b^2/4a^2$ to both sides gives

$$x^2 + \frac{bx}{a} + \frac{b^2}{4a^2} = \frac{b^2}{4a^2} - \frac{c}{a}$$

or

$$\left[x + \frac{b}{2a}\right]^2 = \frac{b^2 - 4ac}{4a^2}$$

Taking the square root of both sides gives

$$x + \frac{b}{2a} = \pm \frac{\sqrt{b^2 - 4ac}}{2a}$$

or

$$x = \frac{-b \pm \sqrt{b^2 - 4ac}}{2a}$$

Derivation 2.2 Sum of an arithmetic series

The sum of the first n terms of an arithmetic series is:

$$S = a + [a + d] + [a + 2d] + ... + [a + (n - 2)d] + [a + (n - 1)d]$$

If we reverse this series we get

$$S = [a + (n - 1)d] + [a + (n - 2)d] + ... [a + 2d] + [a + d] + a$$

Adding these two versions together term by term gives the result

$$2S = [2a + (n - 1)d] + [2a + (n - 1)d] + [2a + (n - 1)d] ... + [2a + (n - 1)d]$$

In other words there are n identical terms. The sum of these is then

$$2S = n[2a + (n - 1)d]$$

or

$$S = \frac{a[2a + (n - 1)d]}{2}$$

Derivation 2.3 Sum of a geometric series

The sum of the first n terms of a geometric series is

$$S = a + ar + ar^2 + ar^3 + ... + ar^{n-2} + ar^{n-1}$$

Multiplying this by r gives

$$Sr = ar + ar^2 + ar^3 + ar^4 .... + ar^{n-1}n + ar^n$$

If the first of these is subtracted from the second almost all the terms cancel to give

$$Sr - S = ar^n - a$$

or

$$S(r - 1) = a(r^n - 1)$$

so

$$S = \frac{a(r^n - 1)}{(r - 1)}$$

SECTION TWO

Data collection and description

This book is divided into five sections, each of which covers a different aspect of quantitative methods in business. The first section gave the background and context for the rest of the book. This second section discusses data collection and description. The third section looks at methods of solving specific types of problem, while the last two sections describe various statistical analyses.

There are four chapters in this section. The first chapter discusses data collection, while the next three chapters cover aspects of data presentation and description.

Chapter 3 discusses data collection. Managers can only make good decisions if they have reliable information, and this is provided by collecting data and processing them. The implication is that information, and hence data collection, is an essential function in every organization. The chapter describes different types of data and how they are collected, primarily through sampling.

The raw data collected often have too much detail, so they must be summarized and presented in forms which emphasize the important features. The purpose of data presentation is to show the main patterns of the data in a format which is both accurate and easy to understand. Chapter 4 describes how this can be done using diagrams.

Chapter 5 continues the theme of summarizing data by looking at numerical descriptions. In particular, it describes measures for the location and dispersion of data.

Chapter 6 looks at index numbers. A lot of analysis is concerned with the way that a variable changes over time, and one way of describing these changes is to use index numbers.

Collecting data

3

CHAPTER OUTLINE

In Chapter 1 we suggested that managers should assess all available information before making their decisions. The necessary information has to be gathered from a number of sources. In this chapter we discuss the principles of data collection.

The chapter starts by outlining the importance of data collection and relating it to management decisions. There are several types of data and some useful classifications are described. These are important, because data of different types are collected, presented and analysed in different ways.

Most data collection relies on sampling, where data are only collected from a proportion of possible suppliers. Available methods of selecting a sample are outlined. When an appropriate sample has been identified, actual data must be collected. This often relies on a questionnaire, and some guidelines are given for their design.

After reading the chapter and doing the exercises you should be able to:

- appreciate the importance of data collection

- discuss the timing and amount of data to be collected

- classify data in several ways

- appreciate the purpose of sampling

- select samples in different ways

- collect data in a number of ways

- design questionnaires

71

3.1 | Introduction

3.1.1 | Why collect data?

There is a difference between data and information. Essentially, data are the raw numbers or facts which must be processed to give useful information (Figure 3.1). Thus 78, 64, 36, 70 and 52 are data which could be processed to give the information that the average mark of five students in an exam was 60%; data about new business performance could be collected as a large set of numbers, and this could be processed to give the information that two thirds of new companies cease trading within two years of opening; the ten-year government census has individual returns providing data, which are processed to give information about the population as a whole; entries in a company's transaction records give data which are consolidated into accounting information; and so on.

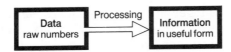

Figure 3.1 Relating data and information.

In this book we emphasize quantitative data, and these appear as sets of numbers. We should recognize, though, that data can be any collection of facts, observations, measurements, opinions, or anything else which gives details about a situation.

In business, data are collected and transformed into the information which allows managers to make their decisions. There are several implications in this statement:

- managers need information before they can make decisions
- they should examine all available information before making decisions
- they should have enough information to allow good decisions
- this information should be reliable
- the information is provided by data collection and analysis

It is clear, then, that data collection is an important, and even vital, function in any organization. Without data collection, managers do not have access to reliable information and cannot make reasoned decisions. The rest of this chapter discusses ways in which data can be collected.

| *IN SUMMARY* |

Managers need reliable information to make decisions about the running of their organizations. This information is provided by data collection and processing.

3.1.2 | Timing and quantity of data collection

You can see that we are discussing the collection of data before discussing their presentation (which is covered in Chapter 4). This seems a sensible approach, as you have to collect data before presenting them. However, data are collected for a specific purpose and the way they are used should have an effect on the way they are collected. If, for example, we want to decide how many beds a hospital should set aside for road accident victims, we could collect data from local accident statistics; if we want to know how retired people spend their leisure time, we could enclose a questionnaire with information which is routinely posted to pensioners; if we want to find how many people will buy a new product, we could run a market survey; if we want to see how many people wear car seat belts, we could stand by a road and observe passing cars. In other words, the way data will be used has an effect on the way they are collected. We should, therefore, design data collection to meet its specific purpose, and not the other way around.

> Data collection should be designed
> **after** deciding the use of the data.

One problem with data collection is knowing how much to collect. In many circumstances there is an almost limitless amount of data which could be collected and might be useful. We should resist the temptation to collect data simply because they are available, and limit ourselves to those which are relevant and useful. The reason for this is that data collection and processing inevitably costs money and collecting unnecessary data is wasteful.

In principle there is an optimal amount of data which should be collected for any purpose. If we consider the marginal cost of data as the cost of collecting the last 'unit', then the marginal cost increases with the amount of data collected. We could find some general data about, say, British Rail very easily (it operates trains and stations, employs staff, and so on); more detailed data would need a trip to a specialized library (to find exactly how many trains of different types are operated or staff of different grades employed); yet more detailed data would need a search of British Rail's own records (to find the wage bill for each grade of employee in each region); yet more detailed data would need a special survey (to ask what each grade of employee felt about their conditions), and so on.

More detailed data are clearly more difficult and more expensive to collect. Conversely, the marginal benefit of data (which is the benefit of the last 'unit' of data collected) is likely to fall. Using the above illustration, the fact that British Rail runs a rail service is a very useful item of data, but most people would find the views of different grades of employees about their conditions less useful. We could use this observation to suggest the relationship shown in Figure 3.2.

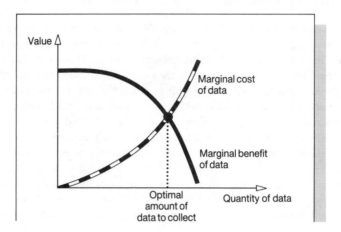

Figure 3.2   Finding the optimal quantity of data to collect.

An optimal amount of data collection can be defined by the point at which the marginal cost becomes greater than the marginal benefit. In other words, the cost of collecting another bit of data is greater than the benefit. Collecting more data would be wasteful, but collecting less would lose some potential benefit. In practice, of course, the problem with this analysis lies in the difficulty of defining the costs and benefits of the data collected. This means that the optimal amount of data is not usually calculated, but is suggested in the light of previous experience.

Another factor which is important in data collection is the time available. Some methods of collection, such as reviewing published statistics, can be done very quickly; others, such as running consumer surveys, need a lot of time. The time available can limit both the type of data that can be collected and the amount. If a company decides to launch a new product next year, this automatically sets a limit to the amount of consumer advice that can be collected. Similarly, government-funded research projects are often limited to three years, so any project which aims to follow economic progress over, say, ten years automatically becomes infeasible.

A long period of data collection may also make the results either irrelevant or out of date before they can be properly analysed. It is often said that the 1851 census in America was not properly analysed before the 1861 census was taken.

On a smaller scale it would be pointless to spend so long collecting data about the sales of a product that it was withdrawn from the market before the analysis could be completed.

If there are pressures on the time available for collecting data, or if proper planning is not done, there is a possibility that mistakes might be made. It is a common view that some data, even if they are slightly inaccurate, are better than no data at all. In some circumstances this is certainly a valid opinion. If we are buying a car it is better to ask a salesman for some details, even though we know that the replies may not be entirely accurate. In many circumstances, however, wrong data can be worse than no data at all. A car salesman might mistakenly persuade us that an expensive car is cheap to run, and we might end up being unable to meet the payments. More broadly, inaccurate data may be so misleading that managers make decisions which are not the correct ones and which might actually harm an organization rather than give benefits. The obvious conclusion is that we must ensure data collected are as accurate as possible.

IN SUMMARY

Data collection is expensive, so it is sensible to decide what the data will be used for before they are collected. In principle, there is an optimal amount of data which should be collected. These data should be as accurate as possible.

Self-assessment questions

3.1 What is the difference between data and information?

3.2 Why is data collection important for an organization?

3.3 'It is always best to collect as much data as possible about a situation.' Is this statement true or false?

3.2 | Types of data

Data of different types are collected in different ways. The weights of packages coming off an assembly line can be measured directly; the number of customers in a shop can be found by observation; the efficiency of a service can be found by giving customers a questionnaire; the age of a population can be found in statistics published by the government; and so on. We should, then, start by describing different types of data.

Data can be classified in several ways. One classification we have already discussed defines data as either qualitative or quantitative. The collection, presentation and analysis of quantitative data is much easier and more precise so we should, wherever possible, use them in preference to qualitative data. Even data which are essentially qualitative can be given a quantitative form. Everybody has some opinion about a range of political questions, for example, and although it is impossible to **measure** each of these opinions, we can say '70% of people generally agree with this policy' or '60% support the policies of this party'. Sometimes a scale can be added. Doctors, for example, may want to know how bad a patient's pain is. This is impossible to measure, but the patient can be asked to rank it on a scale of 0 to 10, where 0 corresponds to no pain at all and 10 is the worst pain it is possible to imagine. Then if a patient says they have a pain of about 8 a doctor will know that it is serious and needs immediate attention.

Unfortunately, the use of numbers to express qualitative ideas needs considerable care. When we hear 'Eight out of ten dogs prefer' a particular kind of dog food we should think carefully about what this means and compare it with the less positive statement, 'In a limited test eight out of ten owners who expressed an opinion said their dog seemed to prefer this dog food to an alternative.'

Even so, not all data can be transformed into a convincing quantitative form. When we hear a poet ask, 'How do I love thee? Let me count the ways...' we know that this is more for effect than for realism.

An extension of this basic classification of data describes how well they can be measured. This describes data according to:

- nominal
- ordinal
- cardinal

3.2.1 | Nominal data

This is the kind of data which really cannot be quantified with any meaningful units. They are sometimes referred to as categorical data. The fact that a company is a manufacturer, or a country operates a centrally planned economy, or a cake has cream in it, are examples of nominal data.

A common analysis for nominal data defines a number of different categories and says how many observations fall into each. Thus a survey of companies in a particular area might show that there are 7 manufacturers, 16 service companies and 5 in primary industries. This says nothing about companies' sizes, profits, owners and so on, and it does not matter in which order the categories are taken. A common example of nominal data comes from political polls, which typically show that 40% of respondents would vote for political party X, 35% for party Y, 20% for party Z, and 5% do not know.

3.2.2 | Ordinal data

Ordinal data are one step more quantitative, in that the categories into which observations are divided can be ranked in some order. Sweaters, for example, may be described as extra large, large, medium, small or extra small. Describing a sweater as 'medium' tells us something, but really gives little quantifiable information. In essence we are told, 'A medium sweater is smaller than a large one but larger than a small one'. Similarly, consumer surveys often collect ordinal data by asking questions like, 'Say how strongly you agree with this statement on a scale of 1 to 5 where 1 means strongly agree and 5 means strongly disagree', while sociologists classify people according to A, B, C1, C2 and D. The essential characteristic is that data can be put into different categories, and that the order of these categories is important.

Sometimes, when there are few observations, they can all be ranked individually rather than put into ranked categories. Thus horses are ranked in a race, as are applicants for jobs, students' performance in courses, consumers' preferences between competing products, and so on.

3.2.3 | Cardinal data

Cardinal data have some attribute which can be directly measured. Thus we can weigh a bag of chocolates, measure the time to perform a task, find the temperature in an office, and so on. These measures give a precise description of a particular characteristic.

Sometimes it is useful to group observations which are similar, and then a common analysis for cardinal data defines different categories according to direct measurements. Thus a sample of basketball players might have twelve who are between 6 ft and 6 ft 2 in tall, eight who are 6 ft 2 in to 6 ft 4 in tall, and three who are 6 ft 4 in to 6 ft 6 in tall.

Cardinal data are generally the easiest to analyse and are the most relevant to quantitative methods. Cardinal data can be divided into two types depending on whether they are discrete or continuous.

Discrete data

Data are discrete if they can only take integer values. When asking the number of children in families, the answer will be 0, 1, 2 or some other integer number. Similarly, the number of cars owned, machines operated, shops opened and people employed are discrete data which can only come in integer quantities.

Continuous data

Those measures which can take any value and are not restricted to integers are called continuous. Thus the weight of a bag of biscuits is continuous as it can be any value, such as 256.312 grams. Similarly, the time taken to perform a task, the length of metal bars, the area covered by a carpet and the height of flagpoles are continuous data.

Sometimes there is a mismatch in data types. The circumferences of men's necks, for example, are continuous data, but shirt collars use a discrete measure; feet come in any size, but shoes come in a range of discrete sizes which are good enough for most needs; heights are continuous but most people describe their height to the nearest inch or centimetre. If the units of measurement are small, the distinction between discrete and continuous data begins to vanish. Salaries, for example, are really discrete as they must be multiples of a penny. Normally, however, they can be considered continuous because the units are small in relation to the values measured.

Finally, there is one more classification of data which is directly related to the method of collection. If an organization wants to use some data for a particular purpose, it may use either primary or secondary data:

- **primary data** are collected by the organization itself for the particular purpose
- **secondary data** are collected by other organizations or for other purposes

Any data which are not collected by the organization for the specified purpose are secondary data. These may be published by other organizations, available from research studies, published by the government, and so on. They may also be collected by the organization itself for another purpose.

The benefit of primary data is that they fit the needs exactly, are up to date and are reliable. Secondary data have the advantages of being much cheaper and faster to collect. They also have the benefit of using sources which are not generally available: companies will, for example, respond to a survey by the government, the Confederation of British Industry, or a group of students, but they would not answer questions from another company.

If adequate secondary data are available they should be used. Unfortunately, there is often not enough appropriate, up-to-date secondary data for a particular purpose. Then a balance must be drawn between the benefits of primary data and the cost of obtaining them. If a company is about to launch a new product it will run a market survey to collect primary data and gauge customer reactions; if it wants to evaluate general economic activity in an area it will use secondary data prepared by the government. Sometimes a combination of primary and secondary data is used, perhaps using secondary data to give the overall picture, and then adding details from primary data. In any case, it is sensible to survey secondary data first, and then consider primary data for extensions and clarifications.

IN SUMMARY

Data of different types can be collected in different ways. There are several classifications of data, including quantitative/qualitative, nominal/ordinal/cardinal, discrete/continuous and primary/secondary.

Self-assessment questions

3.4 Why is it useful to classify data?

3.5 How might data be classified?

3.6 What is the difference between discrete and continuous data?

3.7 Give examples of nominal, ordinal and cardinal data.

3.3 | Sampling methods

3.3.1 | Purpose of sampling

If appropriate secondary data are not available, an organization must use primary data. Then there are several ways of collecting them. Most are based on the assumption that data will be collected by sampling. In other words, data are collected from a representative sample of items or people, and these are used to infer characteristics about all items or people. Suppose, for example, a company is about to launch a new product and wants some data about likely sales. There are two ways of finding this:

- it could ask every person in the country who might buy the product whether they actually will buy it, and if so how much they would buy
- it could take a sample of people, ask them how much of the product they will buy, and then estimate the likely demand from the population as a whole

The first of these approaches (which is called a **census**) has the obvious disadvantage of being time-consuming and expensive. The second approach (which uses **sampling**) has a number of advantages, the most obvious being the reduced cost and time. Another consideration is the practicality of collecting data from an entire population. How, for example, could you find the views of everyone living in southeast England when at any time some people are sick, others are on holiday or travelling, some will refuse to answer questions, and so on?

The purpose of sampling is to get reliable results using only a sample of the whole population. Notice that we are using **population** in its statistical sense of a set of items which share some common characteristics. For data collection the population is the set of all items or people which could supply data. Suppose the Post Office want to find how long it takes to deliver first-class letters; then the population is all letters which are posted first-class. Similarly, a toy manufacturer getting reactions to a particular game might define the population of potential customers as all girls between the ages of 10 and 14; a consumer organization wanting to test the quality of a product would define the population as all units of the product which have been made; a bus company testing the reliability of a bus service would define the population as all journeys that their buses make.

When collecting data it is important to identify the proper population which could supply the data. This is not always as easy as it seems. The toy manufacturer above, for example, may find its population should also include boys aged 10 to 14. A survey of student opinion about a particular government policy would have a population which is clearly students, but does this mean full-time students only, or does it include part-time, day-release and distance-learning students? What about students doing block-release courses during their period of work, school students and those studying but not enrolled in courses? Care must be taken in identifying the correct population, because a mistake at this stage will make the remaining analysis useless.

Even when a population can be identified in principle there may be difficulties in practice. If a population is identified as all people who bought a foreign car within the last five years, or all people who use a particular supermarket, how could a list of such people actually be found? In some cases this is relatively straightforward. If the population is houses with telephones, they are easy to identify from entries in telephone directories. Such lists of the population are called **sampling frames**, and are often given by electoral registers, association membership lists (such as the Automobile Association), credit rating agencies, or specialized companies who prepare lists of people with specified characteristics. Unfortunately, sampling frames are often not available and then some other method of identifying a sample must be used.

We have said that the purpose of sampling is to take a sample of units from the population, collect data about the desired property and use this to estimate data for the population as a whole. Then the population is all items or people which **could** give data, while the sample is those items or people which **actually** give data. What we need to discuss now are:

- a means of determining a suitable sample size (large enough to be representative of the population but small enough to be practical and cost effective)
- a method of selecting this sample

The problem of determining a sample size is considered in detail in Chapter 15, but the next section describes some methods of selecting the sample.

$\boxed{IN\ SUMMARY}$

Data collection often uses sampling, where data from a sample are used to estimate data for the population. This is done when data collection from the entire population would be too expensive, time-consuming or impractical.

3.3.2 | Types of sample

Samples can be selected in several ways and we can classify these according to:

- census
- random sample
- systematic sample
- quota sample
- stratified sample
- multi-stage sample
- cluster sample

Census

If the population is small and the results are important it may be worth doing a census, where data are collected from every member of the population. Then the sample is the same as the population. The UK Government carries out a population census of this kind every ten years.

The benefit of a census is that very accurate data can be obtained. Although the data may not be completely accurate (as there will still be errors and omissions), they are as accurate as possible. Unfortunately, the cost and time needed for a census are prohibitive in all but a few investigations and this means that a smaller sample is usually used.

Random sample

If a census is not taken we have to find a sample which accurately represents the population as a whole. The easiest way of arranging this is to take a **random sample**. The essential characteristic here is that every member of the population has exactly the same chance of being selected for data collection. We should emphasize that if a sample is random it does not mean that it is disorganized or haphazard. If we were collecting data about the contents of tinned soup, we could simply go to a supermarket and buy the first dozen tins of soup that we saw. This would be haphazard, but it would certainly not be random.

There are several ways of selecting random members of a population. A small club could ask each member to write their name on a piece of paper and put this in a hat. Then picking one piece of paper from the hat would give a random selection. Most random sampling is more complicated than this and needs a more formal approach, but this must still ensure that every member of the population has an equal chance of being picked. A common way of organizing this is to use random numbers.

Random numbers are simply a string of random digits, as shown in Appendix D. Traditionally these have been prepared in tables but now they are almost invariably generated by computer. Most computer languages have a function such as RND or RAND, which automatically generates random digits.

Suppose we want to collect data from a random sample of people visiting an office. It might be too disruptive and impractical to take a census of visitors, so we could take a sample which is selected using random numbers. If we generate a series of random digits, 5 4 6 1 5 3 1, we could stand by the office door and interview the fifth person to pass, then the fourth person after that, then the sixth after that, then the first after that, and so on.

Random numbers can give totally random samples. This has a major benefit when using statistical analyses, most of which are only valid if the sample is genuinely random. Unfortunately, some samples which appear to be random are not. Suppose we decide to save time and simply write down a series of numbers which looks random. The series will probably not really be random, as most people have preferences – perhaps for even numbers, or for sequences which are easy to type on numerical keyboards. Similarly, if interviewers are asked to select people at random they will inevitably give a biased sample; they are more likely to approach people they find attractive, and to avoid people they find unattractive, or very tall people, people in an obvious hurry, or people in groups.

A well-organized random sample will ensure that, in the long run, the sample is representative of the population as a whole. If a sample does not exactly reflect the population, it is said to be **biased** in favour of one section. Unfortunately, random samples must be fairly large, as small samples can contain atypical results and show bias. Exactly how large a random sample should be is discussed in Chapter 15. Even so, a well-organized and relatively large sample could, by chance, give atypical data. This can be avoided by using some form of structured or non-random sample. These try to find results of equivalent accuracy but with a smaller sample.

WORKED EXAMPLE 3.1

A company receives 10 000 invoices in a financial year. An auditor does not have time to examine each of these, so takes a random sample of 200. How might this sample be organized?

Solution

The first thing to do is to form the sampling frame by listing the invoices and numbering them 0000 to 9999. Then we generate a set of 200 random numbers, each with four digits. One set is:

4271 6845 2246 9715 4415 0330 8837 and so on

Then we select invoices numbered 4271, 6845, 2246, and so on, as a completely random sample.

Systematic sample

Perhaps the easiest way to organize a non-random sample is to collect data at regular intervals. Then every tenth unit from a production line might be weighed, or every twentieth person using a service. The essence of a random sample is that every member of the population has the same chance of being chosen. If, say, every tenth member is chosen, this means that members 11, 12, 13 and so on have no chance of being selected and the sample is not random. In practice, a systematic sample is almost always acceptable as being random, or at least 'pseudo-random'. There are, however, occasions when the regularity introduces bias. Checking the contents of every twentieth bottle filled in a bottling plant may be invalid if every twentieth bottle is filled by the same head on the filling machine; collecting data from every thirtieth person leaving a bus station may introduce bias as buses hold an average of about 30 people, so we may always be interviewing the older and slower people, who get off a bus last.

WORKED EXAMPLE 3.2

A production line produces 5000 units a day. Quality control checks are needed on 2% of these. How could a systematic sample identify these?

Solution

The number of samples a day is 2% of 5000, which is 100. A systematic sample would check every hundredth unit.

Quota samples

An alternative way of applying some structure to samples is to ensure that the overall sample has the same characteristics as the population. Suppose, for example, we want to find how people would vote in an election. We could take a large random sample, and this would certainly reflect the views of the population. Unfortunately, the sample would have to be very large to ensure the right mix of people. An alternative would be to look at population figures (where the population is those people who are eligible to vote) and see what proportions have various characteristics. Then the sample is chosen so that it contains the same proportions with these characteristics. If the population consists of 47% men and 32% who are over 50 years old, then the sample will also have 47% men and 32% over 50 years old. Political opinion polls are generally based on samples of around 1200 people, so 564 of the sample would be men and 384 would be over 50 years old.

This approach is known as quota sampling. Each interviewer is given a quota of people with different characteristics to interview: perhaps 12 women who are single, between 20 and 30 years old, have full-time professional jobs, and so on. Although each interviewer is given a quota of each type to fill, the actual choice of people is left to their discretion, so there is still a significant random element. However, the process is not truly random, as an interviewer who has already filled the quota of one category of people does not interview any others in the category, so they have no chance of selection.

WORKED EXAMPLE 3.3

56 300 people are eligible to vote in an electoral constituency. Census records suggest the following mix of characteristics:

Age	18 to 25	16%
	26 to 35	27%
	36 to 45	22%
	46 to 55	18%
	56 to 65	12%
	66 and over	5%
Sex	Female	53%
	Male	47%
Social class	A	13%
	B	27%
	C1	22%
	C2	15%
	D	23%

A poll of 1200 people is to be taken to assess their probable voting behaviour. How many people should be in each category?

Solution

The sample should contain exactly the same proportion in each category as the population. 16%, or 192 people, should be aged 18 to 25. Of these 192 people, 53% or 102, should be women. Of these 102 women, 13% or 13 should be in social class A. Similarly, 5%, or 60 people, should be over 66 years old, 47%, or 28 of these should be male, and 23% of these, or 6 people, should be in social class D. Repeating these calculations for all other combinations gives the quotas shown in Table 3.1.

Table 3.1

Age		18 to 25	26 to 35	36 to 45	46 to 55	56 to 65	66 and over
Female	A	13	22	18	15	10	4
	B	27	46	38	31	21	9
	C1	22	38	31	25	17	7
	C2	15	26	21	17	11	5
	D	23	40	32	26	18	7
Male	A	12	20	16	13	9	4
	B	24	41	34	27	18	8
	C1	20	34	27	22	15	6
	C2	14	23	19	15	10	4
	D	21	35	29	23	16	6

The only problem with such calculations is that rounding to integers may sometimes cause small errors in the quotas. Provided the sample size is fairly large, these errors are small enough to be ignored.

Stratified samples

An extension to quota sampling can be used when there are distinct groups or strata in the population. Then it may be desirable to have some representatives from each stratum in the sample. Before any samples are taken, the population is divided into strata and a random sample is selected from each stratum. This randomness is the main difference from quota sampling. If, for example, we wanted to find the views of various companies, we might want views from manufacturers, transport operators, retailers, wholesalers, and so on. In a particular area there might not be many transport operators, but it would still be important to get their views. Then a stratified sample would specify that certain numbers of each type of company be approached, even if this meant that small groups were over-represented. Any conclusions drawn from the results would, of course, have to bear this in mind.

Multistage samples

Suppose an organization wants to take a sample of people who share certain characteristics – perhaps the fact that they subscribe to a certain magazine. The organization could simply take a random sample of the population (that is, the people who share this characteristic). Unfortunately, they would then incur a lot of expense in travelling to meet these people and collecting their views. A cheaper solution would be to use multistage sampling. In this, the country is divided into a number of geographical regions (independent television regions, for example). Some of these regions are chosen at random, and then subdivisions are considered, perhaps parliamentary constituencies or local authority areas. Some of these are again selected at random and then divided into smaller areas (perhaps towns or parliamentary wards). This process is continued until, say, streets are identified and then appropriate individuals in these streets are identified as the sample.

The benefit of this multistage approach is that samples are found which are concentrated in a few geographical areas. This dramatically reduces the amount of travelling needed by interviewers and reduces the costs.

Cluster sampling

This chooses the items in a sample not individually, but in clusters. If, for example, we wanted views from people living in a town it would be more convenient to visit a sample which was clustered in a single area than to visit a sample spread over the whole town. Thus the population is divided into a number of groups or clusters, and a number of these clusters are chosen at random to be the sample. Then one cluster might be everybody who lives in a particular road.

Cluster sampling has the benefits of reducing costs and being convenient to organize. It is especially useful when surveying people working in a particular industry. Then individual companies can form the clusters. In other words, companies are selected at random and the sample is made up of all people who work in these random companies. This method works best if the clusters are somewhat dissimilar so that a representative sample can be found.

IN SUMMARY

There are several ways of sampling. These can be classified according to census, random, systematic, quota, stratified, multistage and cluster samples.

Self-assessment questions

3.8 Why is sampling used to collect data?

3.9 Why is it important to identify the correct population for a survey?

3.10 What types of sampling might be used?

3.11 What is the key feature of random sampling?

3.12 What is the difference between quota sampling and stratified sampling?

3.13 Where could you find data about UK exports and imports?

3.4 Ways of collecting data

3.4.1 Types of survey

When an appropriate sample has been selected (and for simplicity we shall assume that this is a sample of people), the next stage is to approach them and actually collect data. In many cases this involves observation (including measurement, counting, recording, and so on). In other cases data are collected by asking people relevant questions, in which case we often use a series of related questions presented in a questionnaire.

The Gallup organization suggests five possible objectives for a survey of this type:

- to find if a respondent is aware of an issue ('Do you know of any plans to develop...')
- to get general feelings about an issue ('Do you think this development is beneficial...')
- to get views about specific points in an issue ('Do you think this development will affect...')
- to get reasons for a respondent's views ('Are you against this development because...')
- to find out how strongly these views are held ('On a scale of 1 to 5 how strong are your feelings about this development...')

There are other ways of collecting data, and the best one depends on a combination of use and type of sample. One classification of methods is as follows:

- observation
- personal interview
- telephone interview
- postal survey
- panel survey
- longitudinal survey

Observation

If the population to be sampled consists of machines, animals, files or other inanimate objects the only feasible way of collecting data is direct observation. Even when the population is people, there are many circumstances in which the most reliable results come from direct observation. This is because people often give the answer they feel they ought to give or the answer the interviewer wants, rather than the true answer. Studies have shown, for example, that more people say they use their car seat belts than are shown by direct observation. Similarly, more people say they wash their hands after going to the toilet than is found from observation.

The reliability of observation depends largely on the observer and the circumstances, so it is best for counting, but less good for data which require some judgement. This is particularly true when there is personal involvement. Asking people who are leaving a restaurant what they thought of the meal would give replies based on the whole experience (including who they were with, how they felt, or what the weather was like) rather than a valid opinion of the food. Asking motorway police to give data on accidents would give biased results, because their involvement with the consequences of accidents would lead to emotional rather than factual replies.

Personal interview

Personal interviews are the most reliable way of getting accurate information from people. They have the benefit of ensuring a high response rate, with only 10% of people generally refusing to answer questions. They also allow interviewers to help with questions which are unclear. In some situations, such as quota sampling, some assessment of people is needed before they are questioned, so personal interviews are the only feasible method.

In principle, collecting data by personal interviews is easy; it needs someone to pose questions and listen to the answers. The reality is more complicated, and interviewers need training to ensure that they get reliable replies. Without training, some interviewers might, for example, explain the questions to people, or help those having trouble with an answer (hence introducing the interviewer's bias to the answer). Similarly, interviewers should be careful not to direct respondents to a particular answer by their expression, tone of voice or additional comments. If an interviewer listens to an answer and then says, 'How strange – not many people give that answer!' the respondent is likely to reconsider the answer and change it.

One of the main drawbacks of personal interviews is the cost. Each interviewer must be transported to the right place and given meals, accommodation, and so on. Typically, 40% of an interviewer's time is spent in travel, while only 35% is available for asking questions (the rest is spent on preparation and administration).

Telephone interview

About 90% of houses have a telephone, so this provides a popular way of organizing surveys. It has the advantages of being cheap and easy to organize, it involves no travel for interviewers and gets a high response rate. Conversely, it has the disadvantages of introducing bias (as only those with telephones can be contacted), allowing no personal observation of respondents, and annoying people who object to the intrusion of their homes.

A common procedure for telephone interviews is for a computer to select a telephone number at random from a directory listing. Then an interviewer asks the questions presented on a computer screen and record answers directly into the computer. This prevents any errors from being introduced during the transfer of answers from paper forms to the analysing computer.

Postal survey

Sending a printed questionnaire through the post has the advantage of being very cheap and easy to organize, so that very large samples can be used. Postal surveys work best when a series of short questions asks for factual (preferably numerical) data. Major drawbacks are the lack of opportunity to observe respondents and clarify points which respondents do not understand. Perhaps the main disadvantage of postal surveys is the lack of response. Generally, a survey can be expected to generate replies from about 20% of questionnaires. This response can be increased by ensuring the questionnaire is short and easy to complete and is sent to the correct, named individual, by enclosing a pre-paid return envelope, by promising anonymity of replies, by using a follow-up letter or telephone call if replies are slow, by promising a summary of results, or by offering some reward for completion. Unfortunately, a reward for completion (which is typically a small gift or discount on a future purchase) introduces bias, since respondents feel more kindly disposed towards the questionnaire.

One common problem with postal questionnaires is bias. When people are asked for their views on, say, a holiday more people who have had bad experiences will write to complain, than those who have had good experiences. This is an extension of the principle of book reviews, which are always written by 'critics' rather than by 'supporters'.

Panel survey

Panel surveys are generally concerned with monitoring changes over time. A panel of respondents are selected, and they are asked a series of questions on different occasions. Thus the political views of a panel can be monitored during the lifetime of a government, or awareness of a product can be monitored during an advertising campaign. Panel surveys are expensive and difficult to administer, so they must rely on small samples.

One interesting problem with panel surveys is that respondents often become so involved in the issues raised that they change their views and behaviour. A panel which is looking at the effects of an anti-smoking advertising campaign might be encouraged to look more deeply into the question of smoking and change their own habits. Another problem is that panel members inevitably leave for some reason and the remainder of the panel become less representative of the population.

Longitudinal survey

This is an extension of a panel survey that involves the monitoring of a group of respondents over a long period. One television company has, for example, been monitoring the progress of a group of children for the past 35 years. The obvious problem with this approach is that considerable resources are needed to sustain an extended survey, and even then a small initial sample must be used. These small samples become vulnerable when some members leave during a long investigation. Longitudinal surveys are generally limited to studies of sociological, health and physical changes.

IN SUMMARY

When a sample has been identified, data can be collected by several means, including observation, personal interview, telephone interview, postal survey, panel survey or longitudinal survey.

3.4.2 | Design of questionnaires

Most data collection uses a questionnaire. Even observers are generally asked to record their observations on a sheet of questions. It is important, therefore, that questionnaires are designed carefully and after a great deal of thought. There are many examples of surveys which have failed because they asked the wrong questions, or asked the right questions in the wrong way.

Although it may seem easy, the design of a good questionnaire is difficult. An enormous amount of work has been done on questionnaire design and this allows us to give some guidelines for good practice. The following comments are by no means complete, and although most of them are common sense, they are often overlooked.

- A questionnaire should ask a series of related questions. These should be short, simple questions phrased in everyday terms, and should follow a logical sequence.

- Make questions simple and easy to understand; if people do not understand the question they will give any convenient answer rather than the true one.

- Make questions brief, unambiguous, and without too many conditional clauses.

- Be very careful with the phrasing of questions. Even simple changes in phrasing can give different results, so that, for example, a medical treatment which gives a 60% success rate is viewed differently from one which gives a 40% failure rate. Similarly, a phrase such as 'four out of five people' is viewed differently from '16 out of 20 people' or '80% of people'.

- Avoid leading questions such as 'Do you agree with the common view that BBC television programmes are of a higher quality than IBA television programmes?' Such questions will encourage conformity rather than truthful answers.

- Use phrases which are as neutral as possible. Then, 'Do you like this cake?' would be rephrased as 'Say how you feel about the taste of this cake on a scale of 1 to 5'.

- Remember that respondents are not always objective, so the question 'Do you think prison sentences should be used to deter speeding drivers?' will get a different response from 'If you were caught speeding do you think you should go to prison?'

- Phrase all personal questions carefully. 'Have you retired from paid work?' might receive better responses and be just as useful as the more sensitive 'How old are you?'

- Do not start questions with warning clauses. A question which starts 'We hope you do not mind answering this question, but will understand if you do not want to...' will discourage everyone from answering.

- Avoid vague questions such as 'Do you usually buy more meat than vegetables?' This raises questions about 'What is usual?', 'What is more?', 'Should frozen meals be counted as meat or vegetables?' and so on.

- Ask positive questions such as 'Did you buy a Sunday newspaper last week?' rather than the less definite 'How has the number of Sunday newspapers you read changed in the past few years?'

- Avoid hypothetical questions such as 'How much would you spend on life insurance if you suddenly won £500,000 on the football pools?' This does not give useful data, because the answer is speculative and has probably not been thought out in any detail.

- Avoid asking two or more questions in one, such as 'Do you think this development should go ahead because it will increase employment in the area and improve facilities?' This will get confused answers from people who think the development should not go ahead, or those who think it will increase employment but not improve facilities, and so on.
- Make the questionnaire as short as possible, consistent with its purpose. A poorly presented questionnaire, or a long one, will frequently not be answered.
- Do not ask irrelevant questions. There are a lot of data which could be collected and might be useful. As a questionnaire is being used, it is tempting to assume that an extra question or two could be added with little effect. In reality this costs more to collect and analyse and discourages people from completing the questionnaire.

1 Will you be joining an evening class this term? YES/NO

2 How many children do you have? (please circle answer)

0 1 2 3 4 more

3 Do you have a computer in your office? (please tick a box)

Yes ☐ No ☐ Do not know ☐

4 Do you think the government should spend more on education? (please tick a box)

Strongly agree	Agree	Do not know	Disagree	Strongly disagree

5 A proposal has been made to ban all traffic from the town centre. Please circle the number which most accurately reflects your view on this.

Strongly approve 1 2 3 4 (neutral) 5 6 7 Strongly disapprove

6 Why are you taking this course? (please circle any appropriate answers)

(a) out of interest
(b) to get a qualification
(c) to help in work
(d) friends are taking it
(e) to resit a course failed last year
(f) other reason, please specify ....

7 How old are you? (please tick one answer)

(a) less than 18
(b) 18 to 35
(c) 35 to 50
(d) 50 to 70
(e) more than 70

Figure 3.3 Examples of precoded questions.

- Open questions (such as 'Have you any other comments to make?') allow general comments, but they favour the articulate and quick-thinking.

- Ask questions which allow precoded answers, so that respondents are offered a series of choices and have to select the most appropriate. There are many formats for these, some of which are illustrated in Figure 3.3.

- Address postal surveys to a named person (or at least a title), enclose a covering letter to explain the purpose of the survey, benefits to the respondent, guarantee of anonymity, contact to discuss any difficulties, etc, and include a stamped, addressed return envelope.

- Be prepared for unexpected effects, such as sensitivity to the colour and format of the questionnaire, or different types of interviewer getting different responses.

- Always run a pilot survey before starting the whole survey. This will highlight any poor questions or other difficulties, and allow improvements to be made to the questionnaire design.

IN SUMMARY

Getting a good design for a questionnaire is difficult and needs a lot of thought. A number of guidelines can be given, but a pilot survey is essential to sort out any problems.

3.4.3 | Non-responses

We have already mentioned that around 80% of questionnaires sent by post and 10% of personal interviews can expect to generate no response. There are a number of reasons for non-response, including the following:

- people are unable to answer the questions (perhaps because of language difficulties or ill health)

- they were out when the interviewer called (this problem can be reduced by careful timing of calls and making revisits as necessary)

- they were away for some longer period (holiday or business commitments make surveys during summer more difficult)

- they have moved house and are no longer at the given address (it is rarely worth following up a new address)

- they refuse to answer (probably only 10% of people refuse to answer on principle, but nothing can be done about these)

There is an obvious temptation to simply ignore non-responses and assume that the data collected are typical of the sample: in other words, that the respondents properly represent the sample which in turn properly represents the population. This is not necessarily true. In an extreme case a postal questionnaire might be used to see how fluently people can read and write (in the same way that people who have reading difficulties are told that they can pick up packages of information when visiting their local library, or write to a central address for more information). Biased replies can also be found when, for example, a survey asks companies how they use computers, with an initial question, 'Does your company use a computer?' Those companies which would answer 'No' to this question are unlikely to be interested enough to complete the rest of the questionnaire, so the responses are biased towards companies which actually use computers.

To avoid this kind of bias, there should be follow-up of non-respondents, with perhaps another visit, telephone call or letter. Initially this should encourage non-respondents to reply, and surveys often increase their response rate by over 20% with a well-timed telephone call or letter. This does not always work and then non-respondents should be examined closely to make sure that they do not share some common characteristic which is absent in respondents.

IN SUMMARY

Most surveys can be expected to yield some non-respondents. These should be carefully examined to ensure that they do not introduce bias to the data collected.

Self-assessment questions

3.14 What method of data collection is appropriate for:
   (a) asking how much different companies use computers
   (b) asking colleagues for their views on a proposed change in working conditions
   (c) testing the effect of exercise on heart disease
   (d) testing the accuracy of invoices

3.15 What is wrong with the following questions in a survey:
   (a) 'Most people want higher retirement pensions. Do you agree with them?'
   (b) 'Does watching too much television affect children's school work?'
   (c) 'Should the United Kingdom destroy its nuclear arms, reduce spending on conventional arms and increase expenditure on education?'
   (d) 'What is the most likely effect of a single European currency on pensions?'

3.16 What should be done about non-responses in a postal survey?

3.17 Why are non-responses irrelevant for quota sampling?

CHAPTER REVIEW

This chapter considered the collection of data. In particular it:

- reviewed the need for information and explained how this relied on data collection
- considered the amount and timing of data collection
- classified data according to qualitative/quantitative, nominal/ordinal/cardinal, discrete/continuous and primary/secondary
- described how data collection relies on taking samples from appropriate populations
- discussed sampling methods, including census, random, systematic, quota, stratified, multistage and cluster samples
- classified alternative ways of collecting data from the sample (including observation, personal interview, telephone interview, postal survey, panel survey and longitudinal survey)
- gave some guidelines for questionnaire design
- mentioned non-responses

From these discussions it is clear that the stages in data collection can be summarized as follows:

- set the objectives and type of data needed
- check available secondary data
- define the relevant population to give primary data
- determine the best sampling method and sample size
- identify an appropriate sample
- design a questionnaire or other method of collection
- train any interviewers, observers or experimenters needed
- run a pilot study
- do the main study
- do any necessary follow-up, such as contacting non-respondents
- analyse and present the results

Problems

3.1 How would you describe the following data:
   (a) weights of books posted to a bookshop
   (b) numbers of pages in books
   (c) positions of football teams in the leagues
   (d) opinions about a new novel

3.2 Use government statistics to find how the Gross National Product has changed over the past 20 years.

3.3 What is the appropriate population to give data on:
   (a) likely sales of a computer game
   (b) problems facing small shopkeepers
   (c) parking near a new shopping mall
   (d) proposals to close a shopping area to all vehicles

3.4 Describe a sampling procedure which would find reliable data about house values around the country.

3.5 An auditor wants to select a sample of 300 invoices from 9000 available. How might this be done?

3.6 The readership of a Sunday newspaper is felt to have the following characteristics:

Age	16 to 25	12%
	26 to 35	22%
	36 to 45	24%
	46 to 55	18%
	56 to 65	12%
	66 to 75	8%
	76 and over	4%
Sex	Female	38%
	Male	62%
Social class	A	24%
	B	36%
	C1	24%
	C2	12%
	D	4%

What would be the quotas for a sample of size 2000?

3.7 Describe how you would collect data from a sample of shops selling postage stamps in a particular area.

3.8 Give five examples of poor questions used in a survey.

3.9 Give five examples where non-respondents could introduce bias to data.

3.10 Run a survey to find the opinions of your colleagues on proposed restrictions on smoking in public places.

3.11 Design a questionnaire to collect data on the closure of a shopping area to all vehicles.

3.12 Find a copy of a recent survey by the Consumers' Association (or any equivalent organization). Describe the data collection used.

Computer exercises

3.1 Use a computer to generate a set of random numbers. Now use these numbers to design a sampling scheme for finding the views of passengers using a local bus service.

3.2 Problem 3.6 gives some characteristics of the readers of a Sunday newspaper. Design a spreadsheet to find the quotas in each category automatically for different sample sizes.

3.3 Conduct a survey into the use of computers by companies operating in your area. How would you select a sample of companies for this? Now use a word processor to design a questionnaire to collect information from the companies. The combination of sample and questionnaire should be good enough to give a reliable view of computer use. Design a spreadsheet to record the data collected by your questionnaire. Now analyse the results and use a word processor to write a report on your findings.

3.4 Design a questionnaire to find the views of a sample of your colleagues on a topical issue. Now use this questionnaire to collect actual data. Use a statistical package to record views and see how the results can be presented. Discuss the relative advantages of using a statistical package and a spreadsheet to record results. Write a report on your findings.

Case study

Natural Biscuits

Natural Biscuits make a range of foods which are sold to health food shops around the country. They divide the UK into 13 geographical regions based around major cities. The populations, number of shops stocking their goods and annual sales in each region last year are shown in Table 3.2.

Table 3.2

Region	Population (millions)	Shops (£'000s)	Sales
Greater London	8130	94	240
Birmingham	1205	18	51
Glasgow	870	8	24
Leeds	853	9	18
Sheffield	641	7	23
Liverpool	580	12	35
Bradford	556	8	17
Manchester	541	6	8
Edinburgh	526	5	4
Bristol	470	17	66
Coventry	372	8	32
Belfast	365	4	15
Cardiff	336	4	25

Natural Biscuits are about to introduce a Vegan Veggie Bar which is made from a combination of nuts, seeds and dried fruit, and is guaranteed to contain no animal products. The company want to assess likely sales of the bar and are considering a market survey.

Natural Biscuits already sell 300 000 similar bars a year at an average price of 40 pence, and with an average profit of 7.5 pence. An initial survey of 120 customers in three shops earlier this year gave the characteristics of customers for these bars shown in Table 3.3.

Experience suggests that it costs £10 to interview a customer personally, while a postal or telephone survey would cost £5 a response. The analysis of information can be done relatively cheaply by the Management Information Group at Natural Biscuits.

The problem is to help Natural Biscuits to collect information about the potential sales of their Vegan Veggie Bar. They want as much information as possible, but obviously want to limit costs to reasonable levels.

Table 3.3

Sex	Female	64%
	Male	36%
Age	Less than 20	16%
	20 to 30	43%
	30 to 40	28%
	40 to 60	9%
	More than 60	4%
Social class	A	6%
	B	48%
	C1	33%
	C2	10%
	D	3%
Vegetarian	Yes	36%
		(5% vegan)
	No	60%
	Other response	4%
Reason for buying	Like the taste	35%
	For fibre content	17%
	Never tried before	11%
	Help diet	8%
	Other response	29%
Regular buyer of bar	Yes	32%
	No	31%
	Other response	37%

Your problem is to design a data-collection project. Full details should be given of all aspects of the project, including timing and costs. You can use any relevant secondary information and make valid assumptions where appropriate.

Using diagrams to present data

4

CHAPTER OUTLINE

In the last chapter we saw how data could be collected. Now we are going to show how these data can be summarized and presented to an audience. There are essentially two ways of summarizing data, either using diagrams or numbers. This chapter discusses the use of diagrams, while Chapter 5 continues the theme by looking at numerical summaries.

Raw data often give so much detail that it is impossible to see the overall patterns. Data reduction clears away the detail and highlights the underlying patterns: it presents summarized results which are concise, but still give an accurate view of the original data. The reduction can be done in several ways, and in this chapter we describe alternative types of diagram.

After reading this chapter and doing the exercises you should be able to:

- outline the purpose of data reduction
- design tables of numerical data
- draw graphs to show the relationship between variables
- design pie charts
- draw a variety of bar charts
- draw pictograms and recognize their limitations
- use frequency distributions and tables
- draw histograms
- draw ogives and Lorenz curves for cumulative data

4.1 | Summarizing data

4.1.1 | Introduction

This chapter is based on the principle that there is a difference between data and information. Data are the raw numbers or facts which must be processed to give useful information. Thus 78, 64, 36, 70 and 52 are data which could be processed to give the information that the average mark of five students sitting an exam is 60%.

Imagine that you have spent a lot of effort collecting data and now want to communicate your findings to other people. This is done by **data presentation**. The purpose of data presentation is to show the characteristics of a set of data and highlight any important patterns. This can either be done numerically, or by using diagrams. The remainder of this chapter describes methods of presentation based on diagrams, while the next chapter discusses numerical presentations.

If you look around, there are countless examples of information presented in diagrams. Typically, newspaper articles describe a situation, and add summary diagrams to accompany the text. People find these diagrams attractive and are more likely to look at them than read the article (hence the saying, 'One picture is worth a thousand words'). The main benefit of diagrams is that people are good at recognizing patterns and can extract a lot of information in a short time.

In general, then, the success of a presentation can be judged by how easy it is to understand. A good presentation should make information clearer and allow us to see the overall picture, which would be missed if data were presented in any other form. Unfortunately, good presentations do not happen by chance but need careful planning. If you look at a diagram and cannot understand it, it is safe to assume that the presentation is poor; the fault is with the presenter rather than the viewer.

Sometimes, even when a presentation appears clear, closer examination may show that it does not give a true picture of the data. This may be a result of poor presentation, but sometimes results from a deliberate decision to present data in a form that is both misleading and dishonest. Advertisements are notorious for presenting data in a way that gives the desired impression, rather than accurately reflecting a situation. Likewise, politicians may be concerned with appearance rather than truth. The problem is that diagrams are a powerful means of presenting data, but they only give a summary. This summary can easily be misleading, either intentionally or by mistake. In this chapter we shall demonstrate good practice in data presentation and shall be rigorous in presenting results that are fair and honest.

IN SUMMARY

The aim of data presentation is to give an accurate summary of data. Here we concentrate on diagrammatic presentations. These have considerable impact, but need careful planning.

4.1.2 | Data reduction

Provided they come in small quantities, most people can deal with numerical data. We can happily say, 'This building is 60 metres tall', 'A car can travel 40 miles on a gallon of petrol', 'An opinion poll shows one political party has 6% more support than another', and so on. Problems begin when there are a lot of data and we are swamped with detail. Suppose, for example, we know that weekly sales of a product in a shop over the past year are:

51 60 58 56 62 69 58 76 80 82 68 90 72

84 91 82 78 76 75 66 57 78 65 50 61 54

49 44 41 45 38 28 37 40 42 22 25 26 21

30 32 30 32 31 29 30 41 45 44 47 53 54

If these data were given in a report, people would find it, at best, boring and would skip to more interesting material. They would ignore the figures, despite the fact that they could be important. To make the figures less daunting we could try including them in the text, but when there are a lot of numerical data this does not work. The figures above could only be described in the text of a report by saying, 'In the first week sales were 51 units, and then they rose by nine units in the second week, but in the third week they fell back to 58 units, and fell another two units in the fourth week...'. We need a more convenient way of presenting data.

The problem is that the raw data do not really tell us very much; we are simply swamped with detail and cannot see the wood for the trees. In most cases we are not interested in the small detail, but really want the overall picture. What we need, then, is a way of identifying general patterns in data and presenting a summary which allows these to be seen. This is the purpose of **data reduction**.

> The aim of data reduction is to give a simplified and accurate view of the data which shows the underlying patterns but does not overwhelm us with detail.

Thus the sequence of activities concerned with analysing data starts with data collection, then moves to data reduction, and finally to data presentation.

In practice, the distinction between data reduction and data presentation is not clear, and they are usually combined into a single activity.

Data reduction has a number of clear advantages:

- results are shown in a compact form
- results are easy to understand
- graphical or pictorial representations can be used
- overall patterns can be seen
- comparisons can be made between different sets of data
- quantitative measures can be used

Conversely, it has the disadvantages that:

- details of the original data are lost
- the process is irreversible

We mentioned in the last chapter that we are discussing the presentation of data after discussing their collection. We should say again that this is often the way things are organized in practice, but the way data will be presented should have an effect on the way they are collected. If, for example, results of a survey are to be shown as a graph, appropriate data could not be collected by asking an open-ended question like, 'Please give your comments on...'. If we want to present a summary of a company's financial position we need not collect data about every transaction that it made in the past few years.

It should also be clear that if you have a large quantity of data, processing them will always be done on a computer. However, the computer only manipulates the data and it plays no part in making decisions about the best analyses or how to present results. These decisions must be made by the person presenting the results.

IN SUMMARY

The detail given in raw data can be overwhelming and can obscure overall patterns. Data reduction simplifies the data and presents them so that underlying patterns can be seen.

Self-assessment questions

4.1 What is the difference between data and information?

4.2 Give five examples of misleading data presentation.

4.3 Why is data reduction necessary?

4.4 'Data reduction always gives a clear, detailed and accurate picture of the initial data.' Is this statement true?

4.2 | Diagrams for presenting data

4.2.1 | Introduction

The purpose of data presentation is to summarize data and present them in a form which is more precise, but still gives an accurate view of the raw data. There are several ways in which data can be summarized in diagrams, and we shall classify the most important of these as:

- tables of numerical data
- graphs to show relationships between variables
- pie charts, bar charts and pictograms showing relative frequencies
- histograms which show relative frequencies of continuous data

The choice of best format is essentially a matter of personal judgement. There are, however, some guidelines that are largely common sense and include, where appropriate:

- select the most suitable format for the purpose
- present data fairly and honestly
- make sure any diagram is clear and easy to understand
- give each diagram a title
- state the source of data
- use consistent units and say what these units are
- label axes clearly and accurately
- put a clear scale on axes
- include totals, subtotals and any other useful summaries
- add notes to highlight reasons for unusual or atypical values.

It is worth mentioning that drawing diagrams for data presentation used to be quite time-consuming, but business graphics packages (such as Harvard Graphics, DrawPerfect, Corel Draw, Aldus FreeHand, Dr Halo and a whole range of equivalent packages) have made this task much simpler.

IN SUMMARY

Data can be presented in several ways, but the final choice is often a matter of opinion. Some guidelines for good practice can be given.

4.2.2 | Tables

The easiest way of presenting numerical data is in a table. This is 'perhaps the most widely used method of data presentation (and has already been used several times in this book). Whenever you pick up a newspaper, magazine or report you are likely to see a number of tables. This is one of the easiest, and most effective, ways of presenting a lot of information, and spreadsheet packages make the design and manipulation of tables very easy.

The general features of a table can be seen in Table 4.1, which is a presentation of the data for sales given above.

Table 4.1

Week	Quarter 1	Quarter 2	Quarter 3	Quarter 4	Total
1	51	84	49	30	214
2	60	91	44	32	227
3	58	82	41	30	211
4	56	78	45	32	211
5	62	76	38	31	207
6	69	75	28	29	201
7	58	66	37	30	191
8	76	57	40	41	214
9	80	78	42	45	245
10	82	65	22	44	213
11	68	50	25	47	190
12	90	61	26	53	230
13	72	54	21	54	201
Totals	882	917	458	498	2 755

This gives some idea of the overall patterns so we can see, for example, that demand is higher in the first two quarters and lower in the second two. In this format, though, the table is still really a presentation of the raw data and it is difficult to get a feel for a typical week's sales; there is no indication of minimum or maximum sales; and so on. These defects would be even more noticeable if there were hundreds or thousands of observations. It would be useful to reduce the data and emphasize the patterns. The minimum sales are 21, so we might start by seeing how many weeks had sales in a range of, say, 20 to 29. If we count these, there are six weeks. Then we could count the number of observations in other ranges, as follows:

Range of sales	Number of weeks
20 to 29	6
30 to 39	8
40 to 49	10
50 to 59	9
60 to 69	7
70 to 79	6
80 to 89	4
90 to 99	2

This table shows how many values are in each range, and is called a **frequency table** (we shall return to these later in the chapter). The 'ranges' are usually referred to as **classes**. Then we can talk about the 'class of 20 to 29', where 20 is the lower class limit and 29 is the upper class limit and the class width is $29 - 20 = 9$. We arbitrarily chose classes of 20 to 29, 30 to 39, and so on, but could have used any appropriate classes. It might be useful, for example, to choose the classes 17 to 32, 33 to 48, or any other convenient ones. The only constraint is that there should be enough classes to make any patterns clear, but not so many that they are obscured. If we felt that the eight classes used above were too many, we could redefine the classes to, say, the four shown in the following table. This table has also been given a title and a statement about the source of data.

Table 4.2 Weekly sales of product

Range	Number of weeks
20 to 39	14
40 to 59	19
60 to 79	13
80 to 99	6

Source: Company weekly sales reports

These tables show one inevitable effect of data reduction: the more data are summarized, the more detail is lost. The last table, for example, shows the frequency of sales, but it gives no idea of the seasonal variations. Such loss of detail is acceptable if the table is easier to understand and still shows the required information, but is not acceptable if we need to know more detail.

Drawing tables needs a compromise between making them too long (where lots of details can be seen, but they are complicated with underlying patterns hidden) and too short (where underlying patterns are clear, but most details are lost). The number of classes, in particular, must be a subjective decision based on the use of the presentation, but a guideline would set a maximum number at about ten.

There is an almost limitless number of ways of drawing tables. Sometimes they are very simple, like a review of answers to the survey question, 'Did you read a Sunday newspaper last week?':

	Percentage of replies
Yes	76%
No	14%
Don't know	10%

Sometimes tables are very complex. They can show a lot of information and may be the only realistic means of presentation. The example in Table 4.3 shows figures for crops grown in the UK during the 1980s.

Table 4.3 Main cereal crops grown in the United Kingdom

	1975–1977 average	1984	1985	1986 forecast
Wheat				
Area ('000 hectares)	1115 (30.6)	1939 (48.2)	1902 (47.5)	1997 (49.8)
Harvest ('000 tonnes)	4 834 (33.3)	14 958 (56.4)	12 050 (53.8)	13 910 (56.9)
Yield (tonnes per hectare)	4.32	7.71	6.33	6.96
Barley				
Area ('000 hectares)	2313 (63.4)	1979 (49.2)	1966 (49.1)	1917 (47.8)
Harvest ('000 tonnes)	8897 (61.3)	11 064 (41.7)	9740 (43.5)	10 010 (41.0)
Yield (tonnes per hectare)	3.85	5.59	4.95	5.22
Oats				
Area ('000 hectares)	221 (6.1)	106 (2.6)	134 (3.3)	97 (2.4)
Harvest ('000 tonnes)	783 (5.4)	517 (1.9)	615 (2.7)	505 (2.1)
Yield (tonnes per hectare)	3.54	4.89	4.59	5.16
Totals				
Area ('000 hectares)	3649	4024	4002	4011
Harvest ('000 tonnes)	14 514	26 539	22 405	24 425

Source: *Annual Review of Agriculture*, HMSO
Notes: Figures in brackets are percentages of annual totals
        Rounding may make percentages not add to 100%
        Droughts in the summers of 1975 and 1976 had an effect on yields in these years.

In common with most tables there are several ways in which this information could be presented and the format given is only one suggestion. If you are repeatedly presenting data over some period, it is a good idea to keep the same format so that direct comparisons can be made. Useful examples of this are given in government publications, such as *Annual Abstract of Statistics, Monthly Digest of Statistics, Social Trends* and *Economic Trends* which are published by the Central Statistical Office.

Unfortunately, complex tables need more interpretation and do not easily show patterns. This could be avoided by splitting the table into smaller self-contained tables. An alternative is to use a table of values as the first step in data reduction and then give summaries in some other form. Alternatives for this are described in the following sections.

| *IN SUMMARY* |

Tables are a widely used method of presenting numerical data. A well-designed table can show a lot of information and can be tailored to specific needs. A poorly designed table can obscure underlying patterns and lose details of the data.

4.2.3 | Graphs

Tables are good at presenting a lot of information, but they do not necessarily highlight underlying patterns. These can be seen more clearly with some form of pictorial representation. Perhaps the most widely used of these are graphs, which we described in Chapter 2.

In essence, a graph shows the relationship between two variables on a pair of rectangular (or Cartesian) axes, where:

- the horizontal or x axis shows the variable that is responsible for a change (the independent variable)
- the vertical or y axis shows the variable that we are trying to explain (the dependent variable)

In some cases it is not obvious which is the dependent and which the independent variable. If we are plotting sales of ice cream against temperature, then clearly there is an independent variable (temperature) and a dependent variable (sales of ice cream). However, if we are plotting sales of ice cream against sales of sausages, then there is no such clear relationship. Then it is a matter of choice as to which way round to plot the axes.

Graphs summarizing a set of raw data can be drawn in a number of ways. Returning to the weekly sales described earlier, we could start by plotting sales (the dependent variable that we are trying to explain) against the week (the independent variable that causes the changes). The simplest graph of this would just show the individual points in a **scatter diagram**, as illustrated in Figure 4.1.

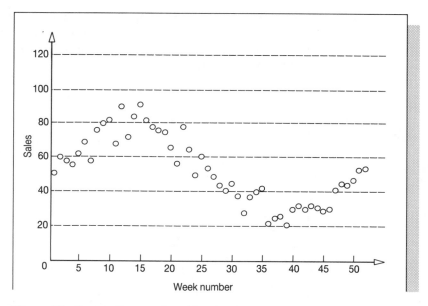

Figure 4.1 Scatter diagram of weekly sales.

This graph shows the general pattern, but this is made clearer if the points are joined, as shown in Figure 4.2. The sales clearly follow a seasonal cycle with peak sales around week 12 and lowest sales around week 38. There are small

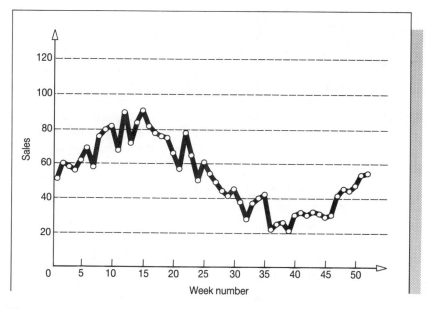

Figure 4.2 Graph of weekly sales.

random variations away from this overall pattern, so the graph is not a smooth curve. Usually we are more interested in the smooth trend than the random variations, so we should emphasize this. Figure 4.3 shows individual points plotted around the smooth trend line.

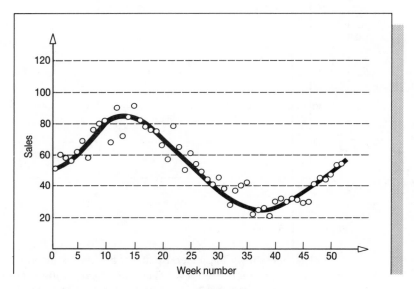

Figure 4.3   Smoothed graph of weekly sales.

The most common difficulty with graphs is the choice of scale for the *y* axis. We could redraw the graphs in Figures 4.1 – 4.3 with changed scales for the *y* axis, and the shape of the graph would vary considerably. Figure 4.4 shows a very stable pattern with only small variations from a low constant value. Figure 4.5 shows widely varying values, which are consistently high in the first half, and then almost zero in the second half. These two graphs actually show the same data as Figures 4.1 – 4.3, but with changed scales for the *y* axis.

As graphs give a very strong initial impact, the choice of scale for the axes is clearly important, with a bad choice giving a false view of the data. Although the choice of scale is largely subjective, some guidelines for good practice can be given:

● always label the axes clearly and accurately

● show the scales on both axes

● the maximum of the scale should be slightly above the maximum observation

● wherever possible the scale on axes should start at zero: if this cannot be done the scale must be shown clearly, perhaps with a zig-zag on the axis to indicate a break

● where appropriate, give the source of data

● where appropriate, give the graph a title

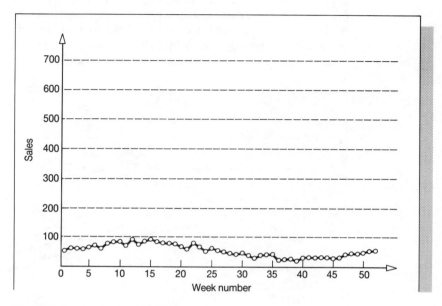

Figure 4.4 Graph of stable weekly sales.

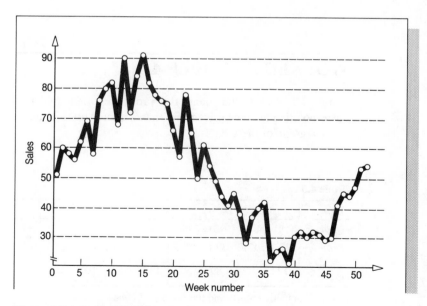

Figure 4.5 Graph of variable weekly sales.

One of the benefits of graphs is their ability to compare data by plotting several graphs on the same axes. Figure 4.6, for example, shows how the unit price of a basic commodity has varied each month over the past five years. Notice that the price axis does not go down to zero. The price differences are small and can be highlighted by using a narrower range for the y axis. This means, of course, that the axis must be clearly labelled.

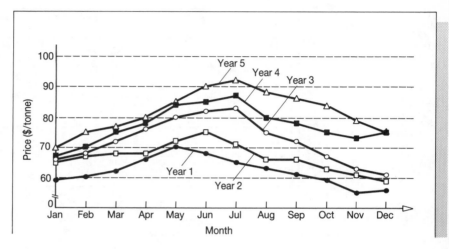

Figure 4.6 Price in $ per tonne of commodity by month. (Source: UN Digest)

WORKED EXAMPLE 4.1

Table 4.3 shows the quarterly profit reported by a company and the corresponding average price of its shares quoted on the London Stock Exchange. Draw a graph of these data.

Table 4.3

Year	1				2				3			
Quarter	1	2	3	4	1	2	3	4	1	2	3	4
Profit	12.1	12.2	11.6	10.8	13.0	13.6	11.9	11.7	14.2	14.5	12.5	13.0
Share price	122	129	89	92	132	135	101	104	154	156	125	136

Source: company reports and the *Financial Times*
Note: profits are in millions of pounds and share prices are in pence

Solution

The independent variable is the one that is responsible for changes; in this example it is the company profit. The dependent variable is the one that we are trying to explain; in this example it is the share price. A graph of these results is shown in Figure 4.7. The chosen scale highlights the linear relationship between profit and share price. As always, information must be carefully examined, and in this case inflation might have a significant effect on the results. If it is important to show the cyclical nature of the data, graphs could also be drawn of profit and share price against quarter.

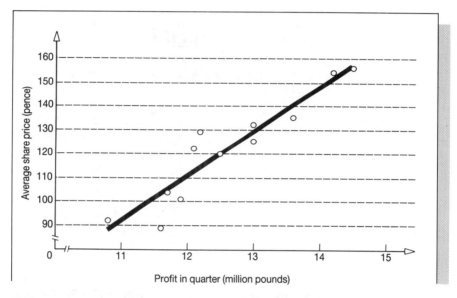

Figure 4.7   Graph of share price against sales for Worked Example 4.1.

IN SUMMARY

Graphs show clear relationships between two variables. Underlying patterns are easily identified and different sets of data can be compared. Care must be taken in choosing appropriate scales for the axes.

4.2.4 | Pie charts

Graphs are good at showing relationships between two variables, but other methods of presenting data rely more directly on pictures. Pie charts are simple diagrams that are used for comparisons of limited amounts of information.

To draw a pie chart the data are first classified into distinct categories. Then a circle is drawn (the pie) which is divided into sectors, each of which represents one category. The area of each sector (and hence the angle at the centre of the circle) is proportional to the number of observations in the category.

WORKED EXAMPLE 4.2

Sales in four regions are given in the following table. Draw a pie chart to represent these.

Region	Sales
North	25
South	10
East	45
West	25
Total	105

Solution

There are 360° in a circle, and these represent 100 observations. Therefore each observation is represented by an angle of $360/100 = 3.6°$ at the centre of the circle. Then the sales in the North region are represented by a sector with an angle of $25 \times 3.6 = 90°$ at the centre of the circle; sales in the South region are represented by a sector with an angle of $10 \times 3.6 = 36°$ at the centre, and so on. A basic pie chart for this is shown in Figure 4.8(a). The appearance of pie charts can be improved in several ways, and Figure 4.8(b) shows the same results with slices in the pie sorted into order, percentages calculated and a three-dimensional effect added.

Sometimes two pies can be linked, so Figure 4.8(c) shows the sales and profits from each region, with the results for the West region pulled out for emphasis.

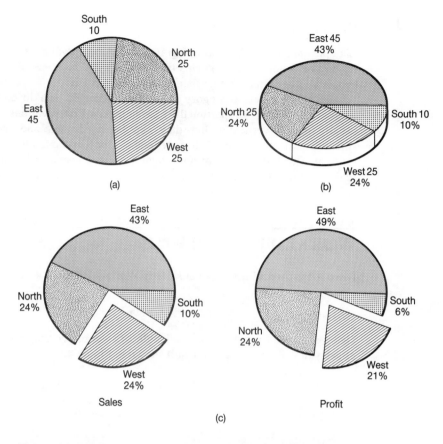

Figure 4.8 (a) Basic pie chart of sales for Worked Example 4.2
(b) Fuller pie chart of sales. (c) Associated pie charts.

Pie charts compare the relative number of observations in different categories. They can be used for percentages, but really have little other use. They are certainly only useful when there are a few categories, say four to eight, as beyond this they become too complicated and lose their impact.

IN SUMMARY

Pie charts represent the relative frequency of observations by the sectors of a circle. They can give considerable impact, but are only useful for small quantities of data.

4.1.1 | Bar charts

Like pie charts, bar charts are diagrams that show the number of observations in different categories of data. This time, though, the numbers of observations are shown by lines or bars rather than sectors of a circle.

In a bar chart, each category of data is represented by a different bar, and the length of the bar is proportional to the number of observations. Bar charts are usually drawn vertically, but they can be horizontal, and there are many adjustments that enhance their appearance. One constant rule, however, is that the scale must start at zero; any attempt to save space or expand the vertical scale by omitting the lower parts of bars is simply confusing.

WORKED EXAMPLE 4.3

Draw a bar chart of the regional sales in Worked Example 4.2.

Solution

Using a simple format, where the length of each bar corresponds to the number of sales in a region, gives the result shown in Figure 4.9.

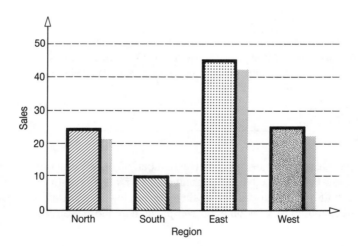

Figure 4.9 Bar chart of sales for Worked Example 4.3.

There are several different types of bar chart and the most appropriate is, again, a matter of choice. We should, however, remember that the purpose of diagrams is to present the characteristics of the data clearly; it is not necessarily to draw the prettiest picture. One particularly useful type of bar chart compares several sets of data, as illustrated in the following example.

WORKED EXAMPLE 4.4

There are five hospitals in a Health District, and they classify the number of beds in each hospital as follows.

	Hospital				
	Foothills	General	Southern	Heathview	St John
Maternity	24	38	6	0	0
Surgical	86	85	45	30	24
Medical	82	55	30	30	35
Psychiatric	25	22	30	65	76

Draw a bar chart to represent these data.

Solution

There are many possible formats for bar charts. Figure 4.10 shows a vertical form which has an added three-dimensional effect. This chart emphasizes the number of beds of each type, but if we wanted to highlight the relative sizes of the hospitals, we could 'stack' the bars to give the single bars shown in Figure 4.11.

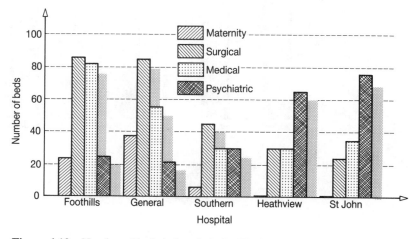

Figure 4.10 Number of beds in hospitals for Worked Example 4.4.

We could also represent these as percentages, as shown in Figure 4.12. There is an almost limitless variety of bar charts, and the most appropriate one to choose depends on the circumstances.

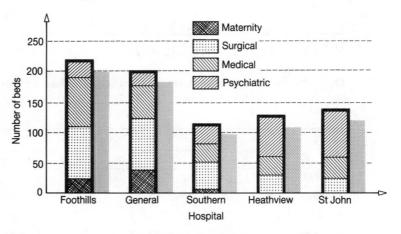

Figure 4.11 Emphasizing the number of beds in each hospital.

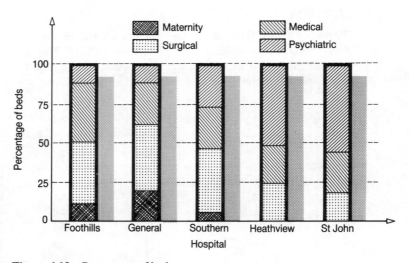

Figure 4.12 Percentage of beds.

Bar charts can give flexible presentations. They use bars to represent categories, with the length of each bar proportional to the number of observations in the category.

4.2.6 | Pictograms

These are similar to bar charts, except that the bars are replaced by sketches of the things being described. Thus the percentage of people owning cars might be represented as in Figure 4.13. In this pictogram, each 10% of people are represented by one car.

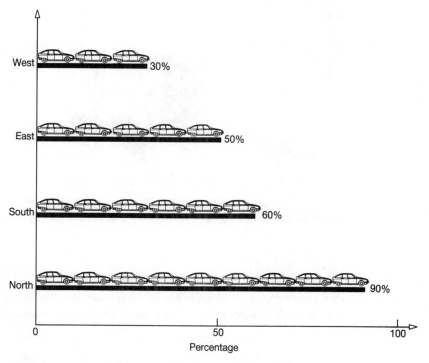

Figure 4.13 Pictogram showing percentage of people with cars.

Pictograms are very eye-catching and are, therefore, widely used in newspapers and magazines. They are not very accurate, but they are effective in giving general impressions. A problem arises with fractional values, such as 53% of people owning cars in Figure 4.13. This would be shown by a stack of 5.3 cars, and the 0.3 of a car clearly has little meaning. Nonetheless, the diagram would give the general impression of 'just over 50%'.

Pictograms should show different numbers of observations by different numbers of sketches, as shown in Figure 4.13. The wrong way to draw them is to make a single sketch bigger, as shown in Figure 4.14. The problem here is that we should be concentrating on the height of the sketches, but it is the area that has the immediate impact. If the number of observations is doubled, the sketch should also be doubled in height. Unfortunately, it is the area of the sketch that is noticed and this is increased by a factor of four. Figure 4.14 shows (as nuclear bomb mushroom clouds) the number of nuclear missiles built by 'Us' and 'Them'. All the figures are put on the graph to show that 'They' have just over twice as many missiles as 'Us', but it is the area of the graph that makes the impact, and this suggests a considerably greater difference.

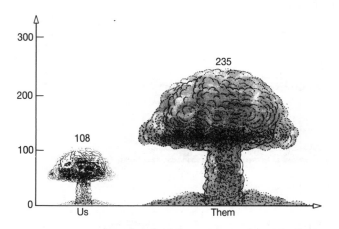

Figure 4.14   Poor pictogram showing the number of nuclear missiles.

> ### IN SUMMARY

Pictograms replace the bars in bar charts by sketches. These can attract attention, but the results are not very accurate and need careful interpretation.

Self-assessment questions

4.5   What are the two main methods of presenting statistical data?

4.6   What are the advantages of using tables of data?

4.7   Why is it necessary to label the axes of graphs?

4.8   If you had a large quantity of numerical data what formats would you consider for their presentation?

4.9 'When using bar charts there is only one format that can be used for any set of data.' Is this statement true? Is it true of other methods of presenting data?

4.10 What are the main problems with pictograms?

4.3 Frequency distributions

Earlier in the chapter we showed that the number of observations in different classes could be drawn as a frequency table. In this section we are going to look at this idea in more detail.

4.3.1 Frequency tables

We have already met a frequency table of the form shown below. This divides weekly sales into a number of distinct classes and shows the number of weeks where demand fell in each class. The result is called a **frequency distribution**.

Class	Number of weeks
20 to 39	14
40 to 59	19
60 to 79	13
80 to 99	6

There are six observations in the highest class of sales, 80 to 99. Sometimes it is better to be less specific when defining classes, particularly if there are odd outlying values. If, for example, the data had included one observation of 120 it would be better to include this in the highest class, than create an additional class some distance from the others. Then we might define a class as '80 or more'. Similarly, it could be better to replace the precise '20 to 39' by the less precise '39 or fewer'.

When defining the boundaries between classes we must be sure there is no doubt about which class an observation is in. We would not, for example, have adjacent classes of '20 to 30' and '30 to 40', as a value of 30 could be in either one. To overcome this the classes are defined as '20 to 29' and '30 to 39'. This solution works if data are discrete (such as the number of sales) but is more difficult with continuous data. If, for example, we were classifying people by age we could not use classes '20 to 29' and '30 to 39', as this would leave no place for people who were 29.5. We must, therefore, describe the classes clearly and unambiguously, so that ages might be '20 or more and less than 30', and so on.

Most of the data described so far in this chapter have been discrete, but we should now move on and discuss continuous data in more detail. This is not a major step, as the comments we have made apply equally to discrete and continuous data. We can demonstrate this by drawing a frequency table of continuous data. The only thing we have to be careful about is defining the classes so that any observation can fall into one, and only one, class.

WORKED EXAMPLE 4.5

During a particular period the wages (in pounds) paid to 30 people have been recorded as follows:

202 457 310 176 480 277 87 391 325 120 554 94 362 221 274

145 240 437 404 398 361 144 429 216 282 153 470 303 338 209

Draw a frequency table of these data.

Solution

The first decision concerns the number of classes. Although this is largely a subjective decision, the number should be carefully chosen. Too few classes (say, three) does not allow patterns to be highlighted; too many classes (say, 20) is confusing and too detailed. In this example we shall look for about six classes.

Now we have to define ranges for our six classes. The range of wages is £87 to £554, and a suitable set of classes is:

'Less than £100', '£100 or more and less than £200', '£200 or more and less than £300', and so on

Notice that we are careful not to say 'more than £100 and less than £200', as someone might earn exactly £100 and would then not appear in any class.

Adding the number of observations in each class gives the following frequency table:

Class	Frequency
Less than £100	2
£100 or more, but less than £200	5
£200 or more, but less than £300	8
£300 or more, but less than £400	9
£400 or more, but less than £500	5
£500 or more, but less than £600	1

This clearly shows the frequency distribution of wages, with more than half of people earning between £200 and £400.

Frequency distributions show the actual number of observations in each class. A useful extension is a **percentage frequency distribution**, which shows the percentage of observations in each class. The results are presented in exactly the same way as in standard frequency tables. The data in Worked Example 4.5 can be shown in the following percentage frequency distribution:

Class	Frequency	Percentage frequency
Less than £100	2	6.7
£100 or more, but less than £200	5	16.7
£200 or more, but less than £300	8	26.7
£300 or more, but less than £400	9	30.0
£400 or more, but less than £500	5	16.7
£500 or more, but less than £600	1	3.3

Another useful extension of frequency distributions looks at **cumulative frequencies**. Instead of recording the number of observations in a class, cumulative frequency distributions add all observations in lower classes. In the last table there were 2 observations in the first class, 5 in the second class and 8 in the third. The cumulative frequency distribution would show 2 observations in the first class, $2 + 5 = 7$ in the second class and $2 + 5 + 8 = 15$ in the third. We could also extend this into a **cumulative percentage frequency distribution**, as shown in Table 4.4.

Table 4.4

Class	Frequency	Cumulative frequency	Percentage frequency	Cumulative percentage frequency
Less than £100	2	2	6.7	6.7
£100 or more, but less than £200	5	7	16.7	23.3
£200 or more, but less than £300	8	15	26.7	50.0
£300 or more, but less than £400	9	24	30.0	80.0
£400 or more, but less than £500	5	29	16.7	96.7
£500 or more, but less than £600	1	30	3.3	100.0

The calculations for such tables are best done in the order:

- frequency distribution
- percentage frequency distribution
- cumulative frequency distribution
- cumulative percentage frequency distribution

We should also note that spreadsheets make such calculations very easy.

WORKED EXAMPLE 4.6

Construct a table showing the frequency, cumulative frequency, percentage frequency and cumulative percentage frequency for the following discrete data:

150 141 158 147 132 153 176 162 180 165

174 133 129 119 103 188 190 165 157 146

161 130 122 169 159 152 173 148 154 171

Solution

We start by defining suitable classes, and as we do not know the purpose of the data, any suitable ones can be suggested. We shall note that the data are discrete and arbitrarily use 100 to 109, 110 to 119, 120 to 129, and so on. The results are shown in Table 4.5. The cumulative percentage frequency distribution does not add up to 100% because of rounding.

Table 4.4

Class	Frequency	Cumulative frequency	Percentage frequency	Cumulative percentage frequency
100 to 109	1	1	3.3	3.3
110 to 119	1	2	3.3	6.6
120 to 129	2	4	6.7	13.3
130 to 139	3	7	10.0	23.3
140 to 149	4	11	13.3	36.6
150 to 159	7	18	23.3	59.9
160 to 169	5	23	16.7	76.6
170 to 179	4	27	13.3	89.9
180 to 189	2	29	6.7	96.6
190 to 199	1	30	3.3	99.9

IN SUMMARY

Frequency tables show the number of observations that fall into different classes. They can be used for both continuous and discrete data, and can be extended to show percentage frequency distributions and cumulative distributions.

4.3.2 | Histograms

Histograms are diagrams of frequency distribution for continuous data. In appearance they are similar to bar charts, but there are some important differences. The most important difference is that histograms are only used for continuous data, so the horizontal axis has a continuous scale. Bars are drawn on this scale, so their width, as well as their height, has a definite meaning. This is an important point: in bar charts it is only the height of the bar that is important, but in histograms it is both the width and the height, or in effect the area. We can show this by drawing a histogram of the continuous data for wages shown above.

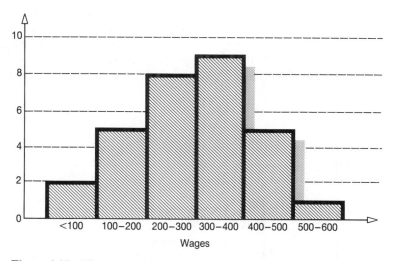

Figure 4.15 Histogram of wages.

In Figure 4.15 each class is the same width, so the areas are determined by the height of the bars. In effect, this is the same as a bar chart. Suppose, though, that the classes were of different widths. If we doubled the width of one class, we would have to halve its height to maintain the same area. This is demonstrated in the following worked example.

WORKED EXAMPLE 4.7

Draw a histogram of the following data:

Class	Frequency
Less than 10	8
10 or more, but less than 20	10
20 or more, but less than 30	16
30 or more, but less than 40	15
40 or more, but less than 50	11
50 or more, but less than 60	4
60 or more, but less than 70	2
70 or more, but less than 80	1
80 or more, but less than 90	1

Solution

Using the classes given we can draw the histogram shown in Figure 4.16. Because this diagram has a long tail with only eight observations in the last four classes, we might be tempted to combine these into one class with eight observations and then draw the histogram in Figure 4.17. This would be wrong, however. We cannot change the horizontal scale, so the single class would be

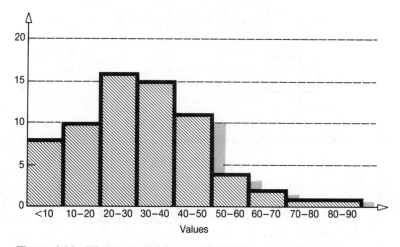

Figure 4.16 Histogram of value for Worked Example 4.7.

four times as wide as the other classes. Making the last bar four units wide and eight units high would imply that it represents 32 observations instead of eight. As the area represents the number of observations the single last box should be four units wide and, therefore, two units high, as shown in Figure 4.18.

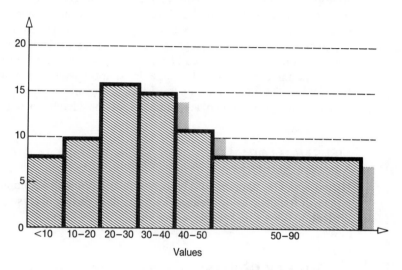

Figure 4.17 Incorrect histogram combining last few classes.

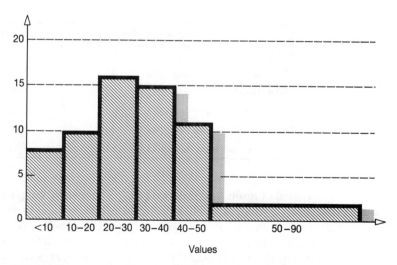

Figure 4.18 Correct histogram combining last few classes.

One problem with histograms occurs with open-ended categories. How, for example, do we deal with classes containing values 'greater than 20'? The answer (apart from avoiding such definitions wherever possible) is to make assumptions about the upper limit. By examining the data we can suggest an appropriate upper limit whereby 'greater than 20' might be interpreted as 'greater than 20 and less than 22'. Another consistent problem is that the shape of a histogram depends to a large extent on the way that classes are defined.

Overall, the use of histograms can be quite difficult. This is especially relevant as the less precise bar charts often give better-looking results with less effort, so there is some advantage in simply using bar charts rather than histograms. The main point in favour of histograms is that they allow further statistical analyses and they are, therefore, of considerable practical use.

IN SUMMARY

Histograms are diagrams of frequency distributions for continuous data. They represent frequencies by areas and are useful in further analyses. It is sometimes difficult to draw a reasonable histogram.

4.3.3 | Summary charts

Earlier in this section we described how tables can be drawn to show cumulative frequency distributions, like the one below:

Class	Frequency	Cumulative frequency
100 or less	22	22
150 or less, but more than 100	44	66
200 or less, but more than 150	79	145
250 or less, but more than 200	96	241
300 or less, but more than 250	44	285
350 or less, but more than 300	15	300

This kind of result can be drawn on a graph relating cumulative frequency to class. The resulting curve has the scale of classes across the x axis and the cumulative frequency up the y axis and is called an **ogive.** We can start drawing an ogive of the data above by plotting the point (100,22) to show that 22 observations are in the class '100 or less'. The next point is (150,66) which shows that 66 observations are 150 or less, then the point (200,145) shows 145 observations are 150 or less, and so on. Plotting these points and joining them gives the result shown in Figure 4.19. We should note that ogives are always drawn vertically, and they are usually an elongated S shape.

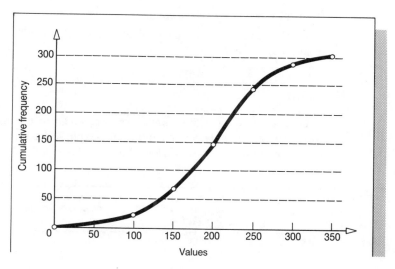

Figure 4.19   Ogive of observations.

A specific extension to ogives is a **Lorenz curve**. This is primarily used to describe the distribution of income or wealth among a population. It is a graph of cumulative percentage wealth, income or some other appropriate measure against cumulative percentage of the population.

WORKED EXAMPLE 4.8

Annual tax returns suggest that the percentages of a country's total wealth owned by various percentages of the population are as shown in the following table:

Percentage of population	Percentage of wealth before tax	Percentage of wealth after tax
45	5	15
20	10	15
15	15	15
10	10	15
5	15	15
3	25	15
2	20	10

(a) Draw a Lorenz curve of the wealth before tax.

(b) Draw a Lorenz curve of the wealth after tax. What conclusion can be drawn from these curves?

Solution

(a) A Lorenz curve plots the cumulative percentage of population against the corresponding cumulative percentage of wealth, so we first have to find these values, as shown in the following table:

Percentage of population	Cumulative percentage of population	Percentage of wealth before tax	Cumulative percentage of wealth
45	45	5	5
20	65	10	15
15	80	15	30
10	90	10	40
5	95	15	55
3	98	25	80
2	100	20	100

Now we plot these cumulative figures on a graph. The first point is (45,5), the second point is (65,15) and so on, as shown in Figure 4.20. A diagonal line has also been added to emphasize the shape of the Lorenz curve.

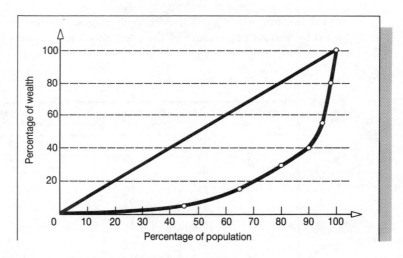

Figure 4.20 Lorenz curve for wealth before tax.

(b) Repeating the calculations for the after-tax wealth gives the following values:

Percentage of population	Cumulative percentage of population	Percentage of wealth before tax	Cumulative percentage of wealth
45	45	15	15
20	65	15	30
15	80	15	45
10	90	15	60
5	95	15	75
3	98	15	90
2	100	10	100

This gives the Lorenz curve shown in Figure 4.21.

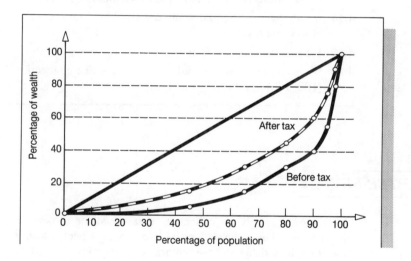

Figure 4.21   Lorenz curve for wealth after tax.

If the distribution of wealth is perfectly fair, we would get the diagonal straight line connecting the origin to the point (100, 100). If the graph is significantly below this, the distribution of wealth is unequal, and the further from the straight line the less equal is the distribution. The Lorenz curve for after-tax wealth is considerably closer to the straight line, and this shows that taxes have had an effect in redistributing wealth.

IN SUMMARY

Ogives are graphs of cumulative frequency against class. One extension of these is the Lorenz curve, which shows the distribution of income or wealth among a population. It can also be used for related measures, such as the effect of taxation.

Self-assessment questions

4.11 What is a frequency distribution?

4.12 What is the difference between a frequency distribution, a percentage frequency distribution, a cumulative distribution and a cumulative percentage distribution?

4.13 'In bar charts and histograms the height of the bar shows the number of observations in each class.' Is this statement correct?

4.14 If two classes of equal width are combined into one for a histogram, how high is the resulting bar?

4.15 What is the purpose of an ogive?

4.16 'A fair Lorenz curve should be a straight line connecting points (0, 0) and (100, 100).' Is this statement true?

CHAPTER REVIEW

Once they have been collected, data must be processed to give useful information. This chapter considered one aspect of this processing, by describing how data can be summarized in diagrams. In particular it:

● discussed the purpose of data reduction as showing the overall pattern of data without getting bogged down in the details

● described alternative formats for data presentation, and suggested that the best depends on the purpose of the presentation, but is largely a matter of personal judgement

● designed tables of numerical data (which can show a lot of information but do not emphasize overall patterns)

● drew graphs to show relationships between variables

● drew pie charts, bar charts and pictograms to show relative frequencies

- described frequency tables and distributions, including percentage and cumulative distributions
- drew histograms for continuous data
- drew ogives and Lorenz graphs

Problems

4.1 Find some recent trade statistics published by the government and present these in different ways to emphasize different features. Discuss which formats are fairest and which are most misleading.

4.2 A question in a survey gets the answer 'Yes' from 47% of men and 38% of women, 'No' from 32% of men and 53% of women, and 'Do not know' from the remainder. How could you present this result effectively?

4.3 The number of students taking a course in the past ten years is summarized in the following table:

Year	1	2	3	4	5	6	7	8	9	10
Male	21	22	20	18	28	26	29	30	32	29
Female	4	6	3	5	12	16	14	19	17	25

Use a selection of graphical methods to summarize these data. Which do you think is the best?

4.4 Table 4.6 shows the quarterly profit reported by a company and the corresponding average price of its shares quoted on the London Stock Exchange. Devise suitable formats for presenting these data.

Table 4.6

Year	1				2				3			
Quarter	1	2	3	4	1	2	3	4	1	2	3	4
Profit	36	45	56	55	48	55	62	68	65	65	69	74
Share price	137	145	160	162	160	163	166	172	165	170	175	182

Source: company reports and the *Financial Times*
Note: profits are in millions of pounds; share prices are in pence

4.5 The number of people employed by Testel Electronics over the past ten years is as follows:

Year	1	2	3	4	5	6	7	8	9	10
Number	24	27	29	34	38	42	46	51	60	67

Design suitable ways of presenting these data.

4.6 Four regions of Yorkshire classify companies according to primary, manufacturing, transport, retail and service. The number of companies operating in each region in each category is shown below. Draw a number of bar charts to represent these data. Are bar charts the most appropriate format here?

	Industry type				
	Primary	Manufacturing	Transport	Retail	Service
Daleside	143	38	10	87	46
Twendale	134	89	15	73	39
Underhill	72	67	11	165	55
Perithorp	54	41	23	287	89

4.7 The average wages of 45 people have been recorded as follows:

221 254 83 320 367 450 292 161 216 410 380 355 502 144 362

112 387 324 576 156 295 77 391 324 126 154 94 350 239 263

276 232 467 413 472 361 132 429 310 272 408 480 253 338 217

Draw a frequency table, percentage frequency and cumulative frequency table of these data. How could the data be presented in charts?

4.8 Draw a histogram of the following data:

Class	Frequency
Less than 100	120
100 or more, but less than 200	185
200 or more, but less than 300	285
300 or more, but less than 400	260
400 or more, but less than 500	205
500 or more, but less than 600	150
600 or more, but less than 700	75
700 or more, but less than 800	35
800 or more, but less than 900	15

How could the last (a) two (b) three classes be combined?

4.9 Draw an ogive of the data in Problem 4.8.

4.10 Present the following data in a number of appropriate formats:

Class	Frequency
Less than 2.5	0
2.5 or more, but less than 4.5	26
4.5 or more, but less than 6.5	40
6.5 or more, but less than 8.5	61
8.5 or more, but less than 10.5	75
10.5 or more, but less than 12.5	69
12.5 or more, but less than 14.5	55
14.5 or more, but less than 16.5	38
16.5 or more, but less than 18.5	15
18.5 or more	0

4.11 The wealth of a population is described in the following frequency distribution. Draw Lorenz curves to represent this. Draw other appropriate graphs to represent the data.

Percentage of people	5	10	15	20	20	15	10	5
Percentage of wealth before tax	1	3	6	15	20	20	15	20
Percentage of wealth after tax	3	6	10	16	20	20	10	15

Computer exercises

4.1 The following table shows last year's total production and profits (in consistent units) from six factories:

Factory	A	B	C	D	E	F
Production	125	53	227	36	215	163
Profit	202	93	501	57	413	296

Use a graphics package to present this data in a number of formats.

(Note: The most appropriate software for this is some form of business graphics package, but alternatives include word processing, desktop publishing, statistical analysis packages and spreadsheets.)

4.2 The following data have been collected by a company. Put them into a spreadsheet, and hence reduce, manipulate and present them.

245 487 123 012 159 751 222 035 487 655 197 655 458 766 123 453 493 444 123 537

254 514 324 215 367 557 330 204 506 804 941 354 226 870 652 458 425 248 560 510

234 542 671 874 710 702 701 540 360 654 323 410 405 531 489 695 409 375 521 624

357 678 809 901 567 481 246 027 310 679 548 227 150 600 845 521 777 304 286 220

667 111 485 266 472 700 705 466 591 398 367 331 458 466 571 489 257 100 874 577

Now pass the data to a graphics package and describe them using suitable diagrams. Write a report on your findings.

4.3 The printout in Figure 4.22 uses Minitab to present a set of data (C1). This gives a simplified version of a histogram and a frequency distribution. Use a statistical package to get equivalent results.

4.4 Figure 4.23 shows part of a spreadsheet. In this, a frequency table is drawn for a block of data. Use a spreadsheet to duplicate the results given and extend the analysis.

4.5 You are asked to prepare a report on the distance that people travel to get to work. Design a questionnaire to collect expected travel times for a large group of people. Now use this questionnaire to collect a set of real data. Use appropriate software to reduce and analyse the data. Now prepare your report in two formats:

● a written report

● the overhead slides to accompany a presentation to clients

```
MTB   > SET C1
DATA  > 12 13 18 24 28 17 25 18 14 30
DATA  > 29 15 15 16 19 20 20 21 22 23
DATA  > 24 26 22 19 25 24 23 27 END
MTB   > HISTOGRAM C1
```

Histogram of C1   N = 28

Midpoint	Count	
12	1	*
14	2	* *
16	3	* * *
18	3	* * *
20	4	* * * *
22	3	* * *
24	5	* * * * *
26	3	* * *
28	2	* *
30	2	* *

MTB > DOTPLOT C1

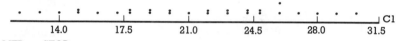

```
MTB > STOP
```

Figure 4.22   Example of Minitab printout.

	A	B	C	D	E	F	G	H
1	**DATA**							
2	5	4	1	2				
3	4	5	5	2				
4	6	7	6	4				
5	7	1	4	8				
6	1	5	3	7				
7	1	4	8	6				
8	2	8	7	6				
9	4	2	4	3				
10	5	4	2	4				
11	7	8	6	4				
12	8	6	4	5				
13	8	4	3	1				
14	9	8	7	2				
15	4	1	9	9		**CLASS FREQUENCY**		
16	5	2	5	7		0	0	
17	4	7	1	6		2	16	
18	5	9	2	4		4	22	
19	5	5	5	5		6	22	
20	4	1	8	3		8	16	
21	5	3	4	5		10	4	

Figure 4.23   Frequency table drawn using a spreadsheet.

Case study

High Acclaim Importers

The finance director of High Acclaim Importers was giving a summary of company business to a selected group of shareholders. He asked Jim Bowlers to collect some data from company records for his presentation.

At first Jim had been worried by the amount of detail available. The company seemed to keep enormous amounts of data on all aspects of its operations. These data ranged from transaction records in a computerized data base, to subjective management views which were never written down. The finance director had told Jim to give him some concise figure that could be used on overhead slides.

Jim did a conscientious job of collecting data and he looked pleased as he approached the finance director. As he handed over the results (Table 4.7), Jim explained: 'Some of our most important trading results are shown in this table. We trade in four regions, so for movements between each of these I have recorded seven key facts. The following table shows the number of units shipped (in hundreds), the average income per unit (in pounds sterling), the percentage gross profit, the percentage return on investment, a measure (between 1 and 5) of trading difficulty, the number of finance administrators employed in each area, and the number of agents. I thought you could make a slide of this and use it as a focus during your presentation.'

Table 4.7

From	To			
	Africa	America	Asia	Europe
Africa	105, 45, 12, 4, 4, 15, 4	85, 75, 14, 7, 3, 20, 3	25, 60, 15, 8, 3, 12, 2	160, 80, 13, 7, 2, 25, 4
America	45, 75, 12, 3, 4, 15, 3	255, 120, 15, 9, 1, 45, 5	60, 95, 8, 2, 2, 35, 6	345, 115, 10, 7, 1, 65, 5
Asia	85, 70, 8, 4, 5, 20, 4	334, 145, 10, 5, 2, 55, 6	265, 85, 8, 3, 2, 65, 7	405, 125, 8, 3, 2, 70, 8
Europe	100, 80, 10, 5, 4, 30, 3	425, 120, 12, 8, 1, 70, 7	380, 105, 9, 4, 2, 45, 5	555, 140, 10, 6, 110, 8

The finance director looked at the figures for a few minutes and then asked for some details on how trade had changed over the past ten years. Jim replied that in general terms the volume of trade had risen by 1.5, 3, 2.5, 2.5, 1, 1, 2.5, 3.5, 3 and 2.5% respectively in each of the last ten years, while the average price had risen by 4, 4.5, 5.5, 7, 3.5, 4.5, 6, 5.5, 5 and 5% respectively.

The finance director looked up from his figures and said: 'I am not sure these figures will have much impact on our shareholders. I was hoping for something a bit briefer and with a bit more impact. Could you give me the figures in a revised format by this afternoon?'

Your problem is to help Jim Bowlers to put the figures into a suitable format for presentation to shareholders.

Using numbers to describe data

5

CHAPTER OUTLINE

Chapter 3 discussed data collection. Once a set of data has been collected it must be processed to give useful information. Chapter 4 discussed ways of summarizing data and presenting it in diagrams. This chapter continues the theme of data presentation by looking at numerical descriptions. The chapter concentrates on measures of average and spread.

After reading this chapter and doing the exercises you should be able to:

- appreciate the need for measures of data
- calculate arithmetic means for grouped and ungrouped data
- identify medians and modes for grouped and ungrouped data
- discuss the benefits and drawbacks of these measures
- calculate ranges and quartile deviations
- calculate mean absolute deviations
- calculate variances and standard deviations
- understand coefficients of variation and skewness

5.1 | Measures for business data

Chapter 3 discussed some aspects of data collection. Unfortunately, large quantities of raw data tend to overwhelm us with detail so that overall patterns are obscured: we cannot see the wood for the trees. This means that the data must be processed to give useful information. The process of summarizing data and highlighting general patterns is called **data reduction**. Chapter 4 discussed ways in which data could be reduced and presented in diagrams. In this chapter we are going to extend this idea by looking at numerical ways of summarizing data.

The benefit of diagrams is that they give powerful presentations which show patterns clearly. However, they concentrate on overall impressions, giving a 'feel' for the data but not necessarily giving any objective measures. A pie chart, for example, shows patterns very clearly but relies on visual impact rather than accurate measures; a pictogram relies even more on impact. What we really need are some objective measures to describe data. These are provided by the numerical measures described in this chapter.

Suppose we have the following set of data.

32 33 36 38 37 35 35 34 33 35 34 36 35 34 36 35 37 34 35 33

There are 20 observations, but what measures could we devise to describe these data and differentiate them from the following set?

2 8 21 10 17 24 18 12 1 16 12 3 7 8 9 10 9 21 19 6

```
MTB  > SET C1
DATA > 32 33 36 38 37 35 35 34 33 35
DATA > 34 36 35 34 36 35 37 34 35 33
DATA > END
MTB  > SET C2
DATA > 2 8 21 10 17 24 18 12 1 16
DATA > 12 3 7 8 9 10 9 21 19 6
DATA > END

MTB  > DOTPLOT C1;
SUBC > START 0 END 40.
```

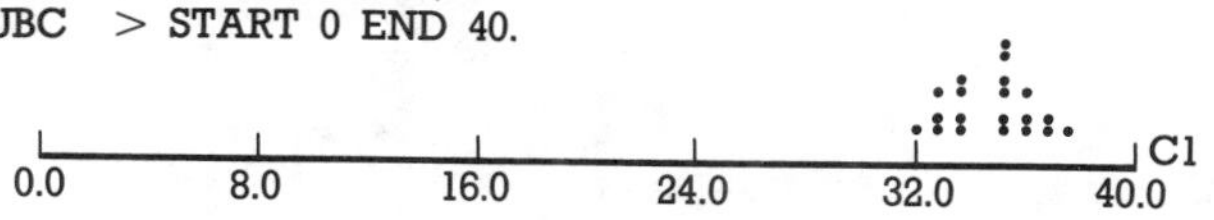

```
MTB  > DOTPLOT C2;
SUBC > START 0 END 40.
```

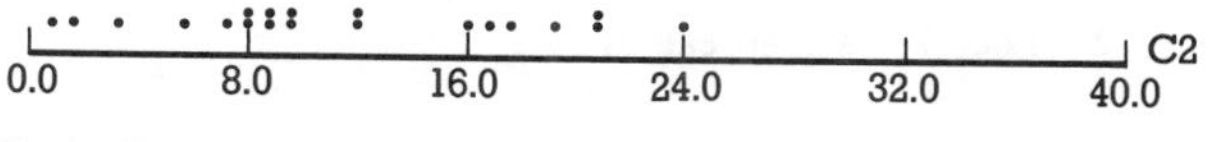

```
MTB  > STOP
```

Figure 5.1 Minitab diagrams of two data sets.

We could start by drawing frequency diagrams. Figure 5.1 shows a Minitab printout which draws frequency diagrams (in a form which Minitab calls 'dotplots') of the two sets of data. Each set of data has 20 observations, but there are two clear distinctions:

● the second set of data is lower than the first set, with its centre around 12 rather than around 35

● the second set of data is more spread out than the first set, ranging from 1 to 24 rather than 32 to 38

This suggests two measures for data:

> ● a **measure of location** to show where the centre of the data is: one suggestion for this would be an average value
> ● a **measure of spread** to show how spread out the data is around the centre: one suggestion for this would be the range of values

Then, if we take a histogram of observations, as shown in Figure 5.2, a measure of location would show where this histogram lies on the x axis, while a measure of spread would show how dispersed the data are along the axis.

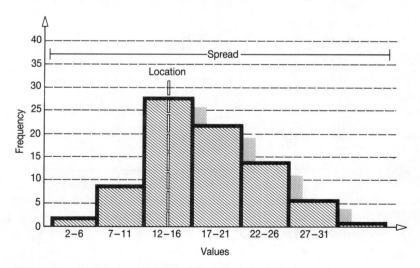

Figure 5.2 Location and spread of data.

In practice, these two measures are the most important, but others are used to a lesser extent. We could, for example, measure the spread of data in relation to frequency, but we will return to this later in the chapter.

$\boxed{IN\ SUMMARY}$

Raw data must be summarized to give useful information. Diagrams are useful for this, but they emphasize the overall impression and do not give objective measures. Numerical measures are needed to describe data more accurately. Two important measures give the location and spread.

Self-assessment questions

5.1 What is the main problem with using diagrams to describe data?

5.2 What is meant by the location of data?

5.3 'To fully describe a set of data we only need to measure its location and spread.' Is this statement true?

Finding the average

Introduction

Most people are familiar with the average as some sort of 'typical' value. If we know that the average age of students in a night class is 45, this gives some feel for what the class looks like; if the average income of a group of people is £50,000 a year we know they are prosperous; if houses in a village have an average of six bedrooms we know they are large; and so on. These are, however, largely intuitive feelings and we really need to discuss what is meant by an 'average' value. We can start by saying that it can be misleading. The group of people with an average income of £50,000 a year might consist of ten people, nine of whom have an income of £10,000 a year and one of whom has an income of £410,000 a year. The village where houses have an average of six bedrooms might have 99 houses with two bedrooms each, and a stately home with 402 bedrooms. In both of these cases the quoted average is accurate, but does not represent a typical value. To get around this problem, we can define different types of average for different purposes. There are several alternatives and we will concentrate on the three most important for business applications:

- **arithmetic mean**, which finds the centre of gravity of a set of data
- **median**, which is the middle value
- **mode**, which is the most frequent value

Each of these is useful in different circumstances, as outlined in the following sections.

| *IN SUMMARY* |

There are several measures for the location of data. We will concentrate on the most useful of these, being arithmetic mean, median and mode.

| **5.2.2** | ## Arithmetic mean

If you ask a group of people to find the average of 2, 4 and 6, they will usually say 4. This is the most widely used measure of location, which is called the **arithmetic mean**. It is usually abbreviated to the **mean**, and is sometimes called the arithmetic average, simple average, or average.

The method of calculating the (arithmetic) mean is:

- add all observations together

- divide this sum by the number of observations.

In the illustration above we added all the observations to give $2 + 4 + 6 = 12$ and divided this by the number of observations, 3, to calculate the mean as $12/3 = 4$. We can now make some general comments about means, but shall first introduce a notation which describes the calculations more efficiently. This is based on the use of subscripts.

Suppose we have a set of n observations. We could call them a, b, c, d ... until we reached the nth observation. This is, of course, difficult if we have more than 26 observations as we would run out of letters and would have to start using other names. An easier notation is to call the set of data x, and identify each observation by a subscript. Thus x_1 is the first observation, x_2 is the second observation, x_3 is the third observation, and so on. The nth observation now becomes x_n.

One advantage of this notation is that we can refer to a general observation as x_i. Then when $i = 5$, x_i is x_5. At first sight this may not seem very useful, but in practice it saves a lot of effort. Suppose, for example, we wanted to add x_1, x_2, x_3 and x_4. We could write an expression like:

$$y = x_1 + x_2 + x_3 + x_4$$

where y is the sum we want. Alternatively we could write:

$$y = \text{sum of } x_i \text{ when } i = 1, 2, 3 \text{ and } 4$$

There is a standard abbreviation for this calculation which replaces 'the sum of' by the Greek letter $\sum$, which is a capital sigma. Then we get:

$$y = \sum x_i \qquad \text{when } i = 1, 2, 3 \text{ and } 4$$

Ordinarily the values of i are put on top of and below the $\sum$ to give:

$$y = \sum_{i=1}^{4} x_i$$

The '$i = 1$' below the $\sum$ gives the name of the variable, i, and the initial value, 1. The '4' above the $\sum$ gives the final value. The steps between the initial and final values are always assumed to be 1.

WORKED EXAMPLE 5.1

(a) If you have a set of observations, x, how would you describe the sum of the first 10 observations?

(b) If you have a set of observations, a, how would you describe the sum of the observations numbered 18 to 35?

(c) If a set of data, v, consists of the even numbers starting with 2, what is the value of

$$\sum_{i=4}^{7} v_i$$

(d) With the following set of data, p, what is the value of

$$\sum_{i=3}^{9} p_i$$

5 14 13 6 8 10 3 0 5 1 15 8 0

Solution

(a) We want the sum of x_i when $i = 1$ to 10. This is written as:

$$\sum_{i=1}^{10} x_i$$

(b) We want the sum of a_i from $i = 18$ to 35. This is written as:

$$\sum_{i=18}^{35} a_i$$

(c) This calculates the sum of v_i from $i = 4$ to $i = 7$, which is $v_4 + v_5 + v_6 + v_7$. Now $v_1 = 2$, $v_2 = 4$, $v_3 = 6$, and so on, so we want to calculate $8 + 10 + 12 + 14$, which equals 44.

(d) This calculates $p_3 + p_4 + p_5 + p_6 + p_7 + p_8 + p_9$. Reading the list of data we see that p_3 is the third number, 13, p_4 is the fourth number, 6, and so on. Then the calculation becomes

$$13 + 6 + 8 + 10 + 3 + 0 + 5 = 45$$

Now we can use this subscript notation to define the mean of a set of data. A common abbreviation is to call the mean $\bar{x}$ which is pronounced 'x bar'. Then the definition of the mean is:

$$\text{Mean} = \bar{x} = \frac{x_1 + x_2 + x_3 + \ldots x_n}{n} = \frac{\sum_{i=i}^{n} x_i}{n}$$

WORKED EXAMPLE 5.2

The times taken to inspect five units coming from a production line are recorded as 3, 4, 1, 7 and 1 minutes. What is the mean?

Solution

The mean is found by adding the observations, x_i, and dividing by the number of observations, n:

$$\text{mean} = \frac{\sum x}{n} = \frac{3 + 4 + 1 + 7 + 1}{5} = \frac{16}{5} = 3.2 \text{ minutes}$$

Notice that in this worked example we used the abbreviation $\sum x$ for the summation. When there can be no misunderstanding it is common to replace the rather cumbersome:

$$\sum_{i=1}^{n} x_i$$

by the simpler

$$\sum x$$

Then it is assumed that all values of x_i are summed from $i = 1$ to n. The fuller notation is more precise, but it makes even simple equations appear rather daunting. Wherever possible we shall use the simpler notation.

Notice also that the mean of a set of integers is often a real number. This leads to the well known result that the average number of children in a family is 2.1. The mean clearly does not give a typical result, as no family can actually have 2.1 children. It does, however, give a calculated measure for the location of data, and this is often good enough for our purpose.

Occasionally, the arithmetic mean does not give a reasonable value. Suppose, for example, a company has three owner/directors who are voting on the percentage of profits which should be retained for future investment. If the directors suggest 5%, 7% and 9% then the mean is 7%, and this might represent an acceptable value. Suppose, though, that the directors hold 10, 10 and 1000 shares respectively in the company. The views of the third director should carry more weight than the others. In such cases we can define a **weighted mean** where each observation is assigned a weight. In particular:

$$\text{Weighted mean} = \frac{\sum w_i x_i}{\sum w_i}$$

where:

x_i = observation i

w_i = weight given to observation i

In the example above we could assign weights to opinions in proportion to the number of shares held. Then the weighted mean becomes:

$$\text{Weighted mean} = \frac{10 \times 5 + 10 \times 7 + 1000 \times 9}{10 + 10 + 1000} = 8.94$$

Often the weights are so not so clear as in the illustration, and then they have to be agreed after discussions.

WORKED EXAMPLE 5.3

It is decided that six observations, 12, 20, 17, 5, 9 and 22, should be given the weights 10, 4, 6, 18, 16 and 3 respectively. What is the weighted mean?

Solution

The weighted mean is calculated from:

$$\frac{\sum wx}{\sum w} = \frac{(10 \times 12) + (4 \times 20) + (6 \times 17) + (18 \times 5) + (16 \times 9) + (3 \times 22)}{(10 + 4 + 6 + 18 + 16 + 3)}$$

$$= \frac{602}{57} = 10.6$$

This compares with an arithmetic mean of $(12 + 20 + 17 + 5 + 9 + 22)/6 = 14.2$. The weighted mean has clearly put more emphasis on the lower observations.

This idea of weighted means can be extended to find the mean of data which have already had some processing. Suppose, for example, a set of raw data has been summarized in a frequency table. Then we have a set of **grouped data** where we do not know the actual observations, but we know the number of observations in each class. As we do not have the actual observations we cannot find the true mean, but we can find an approximate value. For this we assume that all observations in a class lie at the midpoint of the class. If, for example, we have ten observations in a class 20 to 29, we assume that all ten observations have the value $(20 + 29)/2 = 24.5$. The mean is then calculated in the usual way. The errors in this approximation should be reasonably small.

Suppose we have a frequency distribution for n observations, with:

$$f_i \text{ as the number of observations in class } i$$

and

$$x_i \text{ as the midpoint of class } i$$

The sum of all observations is $\Sigma f_i x_i$ but this is usually abbreviated to Σfx. Then the mean of grouped data is given by:

$$\text{For grouped data, mean} = \bar{x} = \frac{\Sigma fx}{\Sigma f} = \frac{\Sigma fx}{n}$$

The top line in this equation is the sum of all observations, while the bottom line is the number of observations. This calculation is illustrated for discrete and continuous values in the following worked examples.

WORKED EXAMPLE 5.4

Find the mean of the following discrete frequency distribution.

Class	1–3	4–6	7–9	10–12	13–15	16–18
Frequency	1	4	8	6	3	1

Solution

The important thing to remember is that the value of x_i is taken as the midpoint of the class. The midpoint of the first class, x_1, is $(1 + 3)/2 = 2$, the midpoint of the second class, x_2, is $(4 + 6)/2 = 5$, and so on. Then the easiest way of doing the calculation is in a table, and with any reasonable amount of data this is best organized on a spreadsheet. Figure 5.3 shows the result from a typical spreadsheet. The first table (Figure 5.3a) shows the actual figures, while the second table (Figure 5.3b) shows the calculations to get these results. The calculated mean value is 9.17.

	A	B	C	D
1	**Frequency Distribution**			
2				
3	**Class**	**Midpoint**	**Frequency**	
4		x	f	xf
5				
6	1 – 3	2	1	2
7	4 – 6	5	4	20
8	7 – 9	8	8	64
9	10 – 12	11	6	66
10	13 – 15	14	3	42
11	16 – 18	17	1	17
12				
13	**Totals**		23	211
14	**Mean**			9.17

(a)

	A	B	C	D
1	**Frequency Distribution**			
2				
3	**Class**	**Midpoint**	**Frequency**	
4		x	f	xf
5				
6	1 – 3	2	1	=+B6*C6
7	4 – 6	5	4	=+B7*C7
8	7 – 9	8	8	=+B8*C8
9	10 – 12	11	6	=+B9*C9
10	13 – 15	14	3	=+B10*C10
11	16 – 18	17	1	=+B11*C11
12				
13	**Totals**		=SUM(C6:C11)	=SUM(D6:D11)
14	**Mean**			=+D13/C13

(b)

Figure 5.3 Calculation of the mean for discrete data:
(a) values on a spreadsheet; (b) calculations.

WORKED EXAMPLE 5.5

Find the mean of the following continuous frequency distribution.

Class	0–0.99	1.00–1.99	2.00–2.99	3.00–3.99	4.00–4.99	5.00–5.99
Frequency	1	4	8	6	3	1

Solution

The midpoint of the first class, x_1, is $(0+0.99)/2 = 0.5$; the midpoint of the second class, x_2, is $(1.00+1.99)/2 = 1.50$, and so on. Again these calculations can be done on a spreadsheet, as shown in Figure 5.4.

	A	B	C	D
1	Frequency Distribution			
2				
3	Class	x	f	xf
4				
5	0 – 0.99	0.5	1	0.5
6	1.00 – 1.99	1.5	4	6
7	2.00 – 2.99	2.5	8	20
8	3.00 – 3.99	3.5	6	21
9	4.00 – 4.99	4.5	3	13.5
10	5.00 – 5.99	5.5	1	5.5
11				
12	Totals		23	66.5
13	Mean			2.89

Figure 5.4 Calculation of the mean for continuous data.

The arithmetic mean usually gives a reasonable measure for location and has the advantages of:

- being easy to calculate
- being familiar and easy to understand
- using all the data
- being useful in a number of other analyses
- being objective

However, it also has some weaknesses. Suppose seven people enter a shop during a 10 minute spell. The mean number of people entering each minute is

0.7, so we are left asking, 'What does 0.7 people mean?' The problem is that means can take any value, even when dealing with discrete data.

Another problem is that the mean may be misleading. If we know that five students get a mean mark of 50% in an exam, we would expect this to represent a typical value. It might be, though, that the students' marks are 100%, 40%, 40%, 35% and 35%, so that four results are below the mean while only one is above.

A specific problem with grouped data occurs with open classes such as 'more than 100'. For these we have to make some assumptions about the limits before doing the calculation. If, for example, we are running a survey of pupils in schools, we might have a distribution of age which has a class '5 and younger'. It would be reasonable to suggest a lower limit on this class of 4. The only guidance for determining suitable limits is to examine the data and use common sense.

In general, then, we can suggest that the mean has the following disadvantages. It:

- only really works with cardinal data
- can be misleading
- may be some distance from the majority of observations
- is affected by outlying results
- can give fractional values, even for discrete data
- is approximated for grouped data

Alternative measures for location are needed to overcome these disadvantages. The two most common alternatives are median and mode.

IN SUMMARY

The most commonly used measure of location is the arithmetic mean, which is calculated by $\sum x/n$ for ungrouped data and $\sum fx/\sum f$ for grouped data.

5.2.3 | Median

If a set of data is arranged in order of increasing magnitude, the **median** is defined as the middle value. Thus the median of 10, 20 and 30 is 20. This measure does not really need any calculation, but can be found by observation using the procedure:

- arrange the observations in order of size
- find the number of observations and hence the middle observation
- identify the median as this middle value

With n observations the median is the value of observation $(n + 1)/2$ when they are sorted into order.

WORKED EXAMPLE 5.6

The times taken to inspect five units coming from a production line are recorded as 13, 14, 11, 17 and 11 minutes. What is the median?

Solution

The median is found by arranging the values in order and selecting the middle one. There are five observations so the median is number $(5 + 1)/2 = 3$.

$$11, 11, \mathbf{13}, 14, 17 \qquad \text{median} = 13$$

One obvious problem occurs if there is an even number of observations. Suppose the last worked example had one more observation of 16 minutes to give values of:

$$11, 11, 13, 14, 16, 17$$

With six observations the middle one is number $(6 + 1)/2 = 3.5$, so its value is somewhere between 13 and 14. The usual convention is to take the mean of these two values, to give the median as $(13 + 14)/2 = 13.5$. This gives a value which did not actually occur, but is the best estimate we can get.

If data are presented as a frequency distribution, identification of the median is slightly more complicated. We have to start by seeing which class the median is in, and then find how far up this class it is. This is demonstrated in the following worked example.

WORKED EXAMPLE 5.7

Find the median of the following continuous frequency distribution.

Class	0–0.99	1.00–1.99	2.00–2.99	3.00–3.99	4.00–4.99	5.00–5.99
Frequency	1	4	8	6	3	1

Solution

There are 23 observations, so when these are sorted into order the median is observation number $(n + 1)/2 = (23 + 1)/2 = 12$. There is one observation in the first class (0–0.99) and four in the second class (1.00–1.99), so the median is the seventh observation in the third class (2.00–2.99). As there are eight observations in this class, it is reasonable to assume that the median is 7/8th of the way up the class. In other words:

$$\text{Median} = \text{lower limit of third class} + \frac{7}{8} \times \text{width of third class}$$

$$= 2.00 + \frac{7}{8} \times (2.99 - 2.00) = 2.87$$

This calculation is equivalent to drawing an ogive (which plots cumulative number of observations against value) and finding the value on the x axis which corresponds to the 12th point on the y axis, as shown in Figure 5.5.

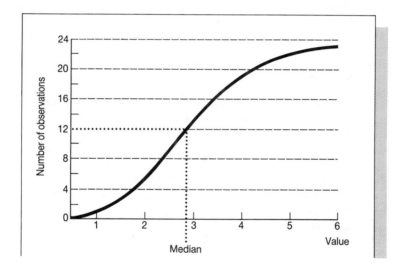

Figure 5.5 Finding the median from the ogive for Worked Example 5.7.

Because it is difficult to get accurate results from graphs it is generally better to calculate the median rather than estimating it from an ogive.

The median is quite widely used and understood. Its main advantages are that it:

- is easy to understand
- usually gives a value which actually occurred
- does not give fractional or impossible values (except with grouped data)
- can be used when the mean would be misleading

- is not affected by outlying values
- needs no calculation (for ungrouped data)

Conversely it has disadvantages, including that it:

- can only be used with cardinal data
- can give values which have not actually occurred (for grouped data)
- is not so easy to use in other analyses

IN SUMMARY

The median is the middle value, when observations are ranked in order of size. This sometimes gives a more typical result than the mean.

5.2.4 | Mode

The **mode** is the value which occurs most frequently. If we have four values 5, 7, 7 and 9, the value which occurs most frequently is 7, so this is the mode. Like the median, the mode relies more on observation than calculation. The way to find it is:

- draw a frequency table for the data
- identify the mode as the most frequent value

WORKED EXAMPLE 5.8

The times taken to serve 12 customers in a shop have been recorded as 3, 4, 3, 1, 5, 2, 3, 3, 2, 4, 3 and 2 minutes. What is the mode of the times?

Solution

Translating the data into a frequency table gives the following result.

Class	Frequency
1	1
2	3
3	5
4	2
5	1

The most frequent value is 3, so this is the mode. This compares with a mean of 2.7 minutes and a median of 3 minutes.

Sometimes there are several modes to a set of data. Consider the following observations:

$$3, 5, 3, 7, 6, 7, 4, 3, 7, 6, 7, 3, 2, 3, 2, 4, 6, 7, 8$$

A frequency table of these would show that the most frequent values are 3 and 7, which both appear five times. Then we say the data has two modes (that is, it is bimodal) at 3 and 7, as illustrated in Figure 5.6. It is common for data to have several modes (that is, to be multimodal).

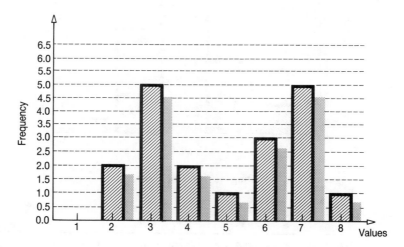

Figure 5.6   Frequency distribution for bimodal data.

When data are grouped in a frequency distribution, finding the mode is slightly more difficult. We have to start by identifying the modal class, which is the class with most observations. This gives the range within which the mode lies, but we still have to identify an actual value. This depends on the density of observations around the modal class. The easiest way of finding this is to draw the two crossing lines, shown in the histogram in Figure 5.7. The point where these two lines cross identifies the mode. It is difficult to get accurate values from graphs, so we can calculate the point where these lines cross using the rather messy equation:

$$\text{Mode} = L + \frac{H - H_b}{(H - H_b) + (H - H_a)} \times (U - L)$$

where:

> L = lower boundary of the modal class
>
> U = upper boundary of the modal class
>
> H = height of the modal class
>
> H_b = height of the class below the modal class
>
> H_a = height of the class above the modal class

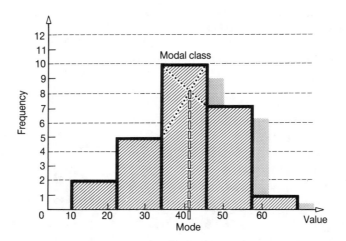

Figure 5.7 Calculating the mode for grouped data.

WORKED EXAMPLE 5.9

Find the mode of the following frequency distribution.

Value	10–19.9	20–29.9	30–39.9	40–49.9	50–59.9	60–69.9
Frequency	2	6	10	8	3	1

Solution

The modal class is the class with most observations, which is clearly 30–39.9. The actual mode is somewhere in this class. The data are drawn in the histogram in Figure 5.8, and the lines drawn cross at around 37, so this gives an approximate value for the mode. A more accurate value can be found by the calculation above.

Substituting known values:

$$L = \text{lower boundary} = 30.0$$

$$U = \text{upper boundary} = 39.9$$

$$H = \text{height of modal class} = 10$$

$$H_b = \text{height of class below} = 6$$

$$H_a = \text{height of class above} = 8$$

$$\text{Mode} = L + \frac{H - H_b}{(H - H_b) + (H - H_a)} \times (U - L)$$

$$= 30 + \frac{10 - 6}{(10 - 6) + (10 - 8)} \times (39.9 - 30)$$

$$= 36.6$$

This value reflects the fact that there are more observations in the class above the modal class, than the class below, so the mode is likely to be closer to the higher limit.

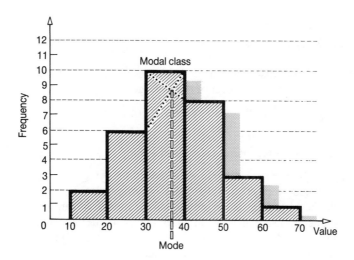

Figure 5.8   Calculating the mode for Worked Example 5.9.

The mode has several advantages including that it:

- is an actual value (except for grouped data)
- shows the most frequent value
- requires no calculation (except for grouped data)
- can be used with non-numerical data

Conversely the disadvantages are:

- there can be several modes
- it cannot be used in further analyses
- it ignores all data which are not at the mode

IN SUMMARY

The mode is the most frequently occurring value in a set of data. Although useful in some circumstances, this is probably the least widely used measure of location.

5.2.5 | Choice of measure

We have now discussed three measures for the location of data, each of which describes a different aspect of the average:

- the mean gives the centre of gravity of the data
- the median finds the middle observation
- the mode finds the most frequent value

Figure 5.9 shows a histogram of data and the typical relationship between mean, median and mode. If the histogram is symmetrical the three measures coincide, but if the histogram is asymmetrical the measures can differ considerably. The best one to use depends on both the type of data and the purpose of the information. As with graphical summaries of data, the choice of best in any circumstances is often a matter of opinion.

One consideration which is not very important is the difficulty of calculating the measures. They are all fairly simple, but for problems of any size it is best to use a computer. Spreadsheet packages usually have a number of statistical functions, but a more specialized package can give fuller analyses. Figure 5.10 shows a Minitab printout illustrating some calculations of the average.

We can, perhaps, get more feel for the alternative measures of location from the following worked example.

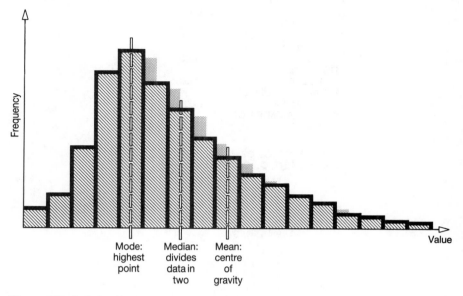

Figure 5.9 Relating the mean, median and mode.

WORKED EXAMPLE 5.10

Two doctors and three receptionists work in a village health centre. Last year the gross annual salaries earned by these five were £52,000, £48,000, £14,000 £8000 and £8000. How could you describe the pay? Which is the most useful measure?

Solution

The mean pay is £26,000 a year, the median is £14,000 and the mode is £8000. Here the mean gives a value which is not close to any observation, and the mode shows the lowest income. Although none is perfect, the median is probably the best measure.

IN SUMMARY

The mean, median and mode all have distinct meanings and uses. Care should be taken to use the most appropriate measure.

```
MTB   > SET C1
DATA  > 4 7 6 9 1 3 2 5 8 3 4 2
DATA  > END

MTB > MEAN C1
      MEAN   =              4.5000
MTB > MEDIAN C1
      MEDIAN   =            4.0000
MTB > MINIMUM C1
      MINIMUM   =           1.0000
MTB > MAXIMUM C1
      MAXIMUM   =           9.0000


MTB > SORT C1 C2
MTB > PRINT C1 C2

ROW        C1      C2
  1         4       1
  2         7       2
  3         6       2
  4         9       3
  5         1       3
  6         3       4
  7         2       4
  8         5       5
  9         8       6
 10         3       7
 11         4       8
 12         2       9

MTB > HISTOGRAM C1

Histogram of C1    N = 12

Midpoint        Count
       1          1     *
       2          2     * *
       3          2     * *
       4          2     * *
       5          1     *
       6          1     *
       7          1     *
       8          1     *
       9          1     *
```

Figure 5.10   Minitab listing to give the mean, median, etc. of a set of data.

Self-assessment questions

5.4   The average of a set of data has a clear meaning which accurately describes the data. Is this statement true?

5.5   Define three measures for the average of a set of data.

5.6   Why is the mean so widely used?

5.7 If the mean of ten observations is 34, and the mean of an additional five observations is 37, what is the mean of all 15 observations?

5.8 Why are we not really concerned about the difficulty of calculating measures of location?

5.3 | Measuring the spread of data

5.3.1 | Initial measures

Averages give a measure for the location of a set of data, but they give no indication of the spread or dispersion. The average age of students in a night class might be 45 but this does not tell us if they are all around the same age, or if the ages range from 5 to 95. The dispersion is often important. A local authority may find that the mean number of people visiting a mobile library is 500 a week. This is useful information, but it would be even more useful if they knew how the numbers fluctuated. They might show little variation from, say, 490 on quiet weeks to 510 on busy weeks: alternatively they might show large variations between 0 and 2000. It would clearly be easier to organize the library to deal with a steady demand than to cope with a widely fluctuating one.

The simplest measure of spread is the **range**, which is the difference between the largest and smallest values.

$$\text{Range} = \text{Maximum value} - \text{Minimum value}$$

This calculation is easy for ungrouped data. It is, however, more difficult for grouped data, when taking the range as the top of the largest class to the bottom of the smallest class would give a result which depended more on how the classes are defined than on the range of actual observations.

The range can also be affected by one or two extreme values. A convenient way of overcoming bias introduced by a few extreme results is to ignore outlying observations which are a distance from the mean. This can be done using **quartiles**. Quartiles are defined as values which are a quarter of the way through the data. Then we can define:

- Q_1 as the first quartile, which is the value below which 25% of observations are found

- Q_2 as the second quartile, which is halfway through the data and is, therefore, the median

- Q_3 as the third quartile, below which 75% of observations are found

We can use these quartiles to find a narrower range Q_3–Q_1 which contains 50% of observations. Then the **quartile deviation** or **semi-interquartile range** is calculated as:

$$Quartile\ deviation = QD = \frac{Q_3 - Q_1}{2}$$

It follows that data with a high quartile deviation are widely spread out, while data with a low quartile deviation are more compact. In practice, the quartile deviation is usually found for grouped data, with quartiles identified in the same way as the median.

WORKED EXAMPLE 5.11

Find the quartile deviation for the following data.

Class	0–9.9	10–19.9	20–29.9	30–39.9	40–49.9	50–59.9	60–69.9
Observations	5	19	38	43	34	17	4

Solution

There are a total of 160 observations, or 40 in each quarter. When the observations are ranked, the first quartile, Q_1, is the 40th and the third quartile, Q_3, is the 120th.

- Q_1 is the 16th observation out of 38 in the class $20 - 29.9$, so a reasonable value is:

$$20 + (16/38) \times (29.9 - 20) = 24.2$$

- Q_3 is the 15th observation out of 34 in the class of $40 - 49.9$, so a reasonable value is:

$$40 + (15/34) \times (49.9 - 40) = 44.4$$

Then the quartile deviation is:

$$\frac{Q_3 - Q_1}{2} = \frac{44.4 - 24.2}{2} = 10.1$$

This is shown graphically in the ogive in Figure 5.11.

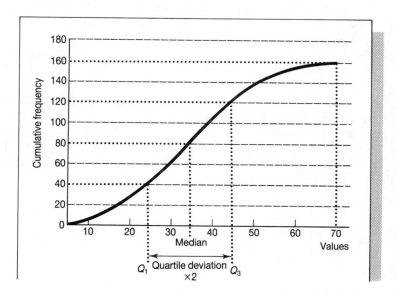

Figure 5.11   Finding the quartile deviation from the ogive for Worked Example 5.11.

There are several extensions to the calculation of quartile deviation which are usually based on various percentiles. The 5th percentile, for example, is defined as the value with 5% of observations below it, while the 95th percentile is defined as the value with 95% of observations below it. Then a frequent measure finds the range between the 5th and 95th percentile. This type of measure is useful for ignoring extreme values but, conversely, it ignores data which may be highly relevant.

IN SUMMARY

Two common measures of spread are range and quartile deviation. These are simple measures which describe the amount of dispersion in data.

5.3.2 | Mean absolute deviation

The quartile deviation is clearly related to the median. Other measures of spread are more closely related to the mean. In particular, they are based on the amount by which each observation is away from the mean, which is called the **deviation**.

$$\text{deviation} = (\text{value} - \text{mean value}) = (x_i - \bar{x})$$

Each observation has a deviation, so the mean of these deviations would give a measure of spread. The larger the mean deviation, the more dispersed the data.

Unfortunately, this approach has the major disadvantage of allowing positive and negative deviations to cancel. If we have observations of 3, 4 and 8 the mean is 5, and the mean deviation is:

$$\text{mean deviation} = \frac{(3-5)+(4-5)+(8-5)}{3} = 0$$

Thus a set of dispersed data could have a mean deviation of zero. The measure is clearly unreliable and is, therefore, never used. A more useful alternative is the **mean absolute deviation** (MAD), which simply takes the absolute values of deviations from the mean. In other words it ignores negative signs and adds all deviations as if they are positive. This gives a measure of the average distance of observations from the mean.

$$\text{Mean absolute deviation} = \frac{\Sigma\,ABS[x - \bar{x}]}{n}$$

$$MAD = \frac{\Sigma\,|x - \bar{x}|}{n}$$

Where

x = the observations

$\bar{x}$ = mean value of observations

n = number of observations

$ABS[x - \bar{x}]$ = the absolute value of $x - \bar{x}$
(that is, ignoring sign): this is also written as $|x - \bar{x}|$

The steps in calculating the mean absolute deviation are:

- calculate the mean value
- find the deviation of each observation from this mean
- take the absolute values of these deviations
- add the absolute values
- divide this sum by the number of observations to give the MAD

It is worth mentioning that many people refer to the mean absolute deviation as the mean deviation, so you should be careful to find exactly which measure is being used.

WORKED EXAMPLE 5.12

What is the mean absolute deviation of 4, 7, 6, 10 and 8?

Solution

The mean of the numbers is:

$$\bar{x} = \frac{4 + 7 + 6 + 10 + 8}{5} = 7$$

Then the mean absolute deviation is calculated as:

$$\text{MAD} = \frac{4 - 7 + 7 - 7 + 6 - 7 + 10 - 7 + 8 - 7}{5}$$

$$= \frac{-3 + 0 + -1 + 3 + 1}{5} = \frac{3 + 0 + 1 + 3 + 1}{5} = 1.6$$

This tells us that on average the observations are 1.6 units away from the mean.

The calculation of MAD for grouped data is a little longer. We saw that the mean of a set of grouped data was found by taking the midpoint of each class and multiplying this by the number of observations in the class. The same approach can be used for calculating mean absolute deviations. The absolute deviation of each class is found as the difference between the midpoint of the class and the mean, and this is multiplied by the class size. Thus for grouped data the mean absolute deviation is defined as:

$$\text{Mean absolute deviation} = \frac{\sum |x - \bar{x}| f}{\sum f} = \frac{\sum |x - \bar{x}| f}{n}$$

where:

x = midpoint of a class

f = number of observations in the class

$\bar{x}$ = mean value of all observations

n = total number of observations

WORKED EXAMPLE 5.13

Find the mean absolute deviation of the following data.

Class	0–4.9	5–9.9	10–14.9	15–19.9	20–24.9
Frequency	3	5	7	6	2

Solution

The arithmetic in this kind of calculation soon gets tedious unless it is done on a computer. Figure 5.12 shows the calculation on a spreadsheet. There are 23 observations with a mean of 12.28. This is used to find the deviation of each class. The calculated mean absolute deviation is 4.63, implying that observations are, on average, 4.63 from the mean.

	A	B	C	D	E	F	G
1				Mean Absolute Deviation			
2							
3	Class	x	f	f*x	Deviation	Abs. Dev.	f* Abs. Dev.
4							
5	0-4.9	2.5	3	7.5	-9.78	9.78	29.35
6	5-9.9	7.5	5	37.5	-4.78	4.78	23.91
7	10-14.9	12.5	7	87.5	0.22	0.22	1.52
8	15-19.9	17.5	6	105	5.22	5.22	31.30
9	20-24.9	22.5	2	45	10.22	10.22	20.43
10							
11	Sums		23.00	282.50			106.52
12	Means			12.28			4.63

Figure 5.12 Spreadsheet for calculating the MAD in Worked Example 5.13.

Taking absolute values ensures that positive and negative deviations do not cancel. The result is a measure which is easy to calculate and which is based on all observations. It also has a clear meaning: if the MAD is 2 units, observation are an average of 2 units away from the mean. It follows that larger MADs indicates a wider dispersion of data.

One drawback with the mean absolute deviation is that it can be affected by a few extreme values. A more important problem, however, is the difficulty of using it in further statistical analyses. This tends to limit its use and an alternative, the variance, is more widely used.

| *IN SUMMARY* |

The absolute deviation is the difference between an observation and the mean. This can be used to calculate the mean absolute deviation for a set of data, which gives a clear measure of spread.

5.3.3 | Variance and standard deviation

The mean absolute deviation stopped positive and negative deviations from cancelling by taking absolute values. An alternative, which is equally simple, would be to square the deviations. This is the basis of the **variance.** This gives a measure of the mean squared error, which has all the advantages of MAD, but overcomes some of its limitations.

$$Variance = \frac{\sum (x - \bar{x})^2}{n}$$

An obvious problem with the variance is that the units are the square of the units of the original observations. If, for example, the observations are measured in tonnes the variance will have the meaningless units of tonnes^2. To return the units to normal, the square root of the variance can be taken. This gives the most widely used measure of spread, which is called the **standard deviation.**

$$\text{Standard deviation} = s = \sqrt{\frac{\sum (x - \bar{x})^2}{n}} = \sqrt{\text{variance}}$$

The calculation of variance, and hence standard deviation, is very similar to the calculation of the mean absolute deviation, and consists of the following steps:

- calculate the mean value
- find the deviation of each observation from this mean
- take the square of these deviations
- add the squares
- divide this sum by the number of observations to give variance
- take the square root of the variance to give the standard deviation

WORKED EXAMPLE 5.14

Find the variance and standard deviation of 2, 3, 7, 8 and 10.

Solution

The mean of these numbers is $(2 + 3 + 7 + 8 + 10)/5 = 6$.
   Then the deviations, defined as $(x - \bar{x})$, are:

$$2 - 6 = -4, \qquad 3 - 6 = -3, \qquad 7 - 6 = 1, \qquad 8 - 6 = 2 \qquad \text{and} \qquad 10 - 6 = 4$$

The variance is found by squaring these deviations, adding them and dividing by the number of observations to get the mean squared deviation:

$$\text{variance} = \frac{\sum(x - \bar{x})^2}{n}$$

$$= \frac{(-4)^2 + (-3)^2 + (1)^2 + (2)^2 + (4)^2}{5} = \frac{46}{5} = 9.2$$

Then the standard deviation is found by taking the square root of the variance.

$$\text{standard deviation} = s = \sqrt{9.2} = 3.03$$

The standard deviation is the most widely used measure of dispersion. Obviously, the bigger its value, the more spread out are the data. However, its main strength is that we can develop a rule for the number of observations we expect to find within, say, 2 standard deviations of the mean. This analysis was first done by Chebyshev, who found that for any sample:

- it is possible that no observations will fall within 1 standard deviation of the mean, i.e. in the range $(\bar{x} + s)$ to $(\bar{x} - s)$
- at least 3/4 of observations will fall within 2 standard deviations of the mean, i.e. in the range $(\bar{x} + 2s)$ to $(\bar{x} - 2s)$
- at least 8/9 of observations will fall within 3 standard deviations of the mean, i.e. in the range $(\bar{x} + 3s)$ to $(\bar{x} - 3s)$
- in general, at least $(1 - 1/k^2)$ observations will fall within k standard deviations of the mean, i.e. in the range $(\bar{x} + ks)$ to $(\bar{x} - ks)$

This rule is actually quite conservative, and empirical evidence suggests that for a frequency distribution with a single mode, 68% of observations will usually fall within one standard deviation of the mean, 95% of observations within 2 standard deviations and almost all observations within 3 standard deviations.

WORKED EXAMPLE 5.15

Find the mean and standard deviation of the following 20 numbers. How many observations fall within 1, 2 and 3 standard deviations of the mean?

10.8 17.4 8.3 9.1 4.7 2.9 12.0 11.8 14.1 9.0

7.3 6.2 8.4 14.7 12.0 5.0 7.7 10.1 6.9 7.8

Solution

The mean is $(\sum x)/n = 9.31$

The variance is

$$\frac{\sum(x - \bar{x})^2}{n} = 12.30$$

so the standard deviation is $\sqrt{12.30} = 3.52$

- the range within one standard deviation of the mean is:

$$9.31 - 3.52 \quad \text{to} \quad 9.31 + 3.52$$

or

$$5.79 \quad \text{to} \quad 12.83$$

There are 16 observations (80% of the total) within this range.

- the range within two standard deviations of the mean is:

$$9.31 - (2 \times 3.52) \quad \text{to} \quad 9.31 + (2 \times 3.52)$$

or

$$2.27 \quad \text{to} \quad 16.35$$

There are 19 observations (95% of the total) within this range.

- the range within three standard deviations of the mean is:

$$9.31 - (3 \times 3.52) \quad \text{to} \quad 9.31 + (3 \times 3.52)$$

or

$$-1.25 \quad \text{to} \quad 19.87$$

There are 20 observations (100% of the total) within this range.

We can now extend the calculations for variance and standard deviation to grouped data. As with the mean, the actual observations are approximated by the midpoint of the classes. When these are multiplied by the frequency of each class, we get:

$$Variance = \frac{\sum (x - \bar{x})^2 f}{\sum f} = \frac{\sum (x - \bar{x})^2 f}{n}$$

$$\text{Standard deviation} = \sqrt{\text{variance}}$$

$$s = \sqrt{\frac{\sum (x - \bar{x})^2 f}{\sum f}} = \sqrt{\frac{\sum (x - \bar{x})^2 f}{n}}$$

WORKED EXAMPLE 5.16

Find the variance and standard deviation of the following data.

Class	0–4.9	5–9.9	10–14.9	15–19.9	20–24.9
Frequency	3	5	7	6	2

Solution

These calculations can be done in a table, but for any reasonable amount of data a computer should be used. Figure 5.13 shows the result on a spreadsheet. The mean of the 23 observations is 12.28 and this is used to find the deviations. Then the variance is calculated as 33.65, so the standard deviation is $\sqrt{33.65} = 5.8$.

	A	B	C	D	E	F	G
1	**Variance**						
2							
3	**Class**	**x**	**f**	**f*x**	**Deviation**	**Dev.Sqrd.**	**f*Dev.Sqrd**
4							
5	**0-4.9**	2.5	3	7.5	-9.78	95.70	287.10
6	**5-9.9**	7.5	5	37.5	-4.78	22.87	114.37
7	**10-14.9**	12.5	7	87.5	0.22	0.05	0.33
8	**15-19.9**	17.5	6	105	5.22	27.22	163.33
9	**20-24.9**	22.5	2	45	10.22	104.40	208.79
10							
11	**Sums**		23.00	282.50			773.91
12	**Means**			12.28			33.65

Figure 5.13   Calculation of variance and standard deviation for grouped data.

A spreadsheet was used for the calculations in the last worked example. Sometimes, though, a problem is small enough to be solved with a calculator. Then the form of the equations given above is rather awkward, as values have to be entered to find the mean, and then entered again to find the variance (assuming your calculator does not have built-in statistical functions.) To overcome this the standard equations can be rewritten in the more convenient form:

$$\text{For ungrouped data: } variance = \frac{\sum x^2}{n} - \left(\frac{\sum x}{n}\right)^2$$

$$\text{For grouped data: } variance = \frac{\sum x^2 f}{\sum f} - \left(\frac{\sum x f}{\sum f}\right)^2$$

If you are interested, the derivation of the first of these is given at the end of this chapter.

One problem with variance and standard deviation is that they do not have a direct meaning like mean absolute deviation. A large variance indicates more spread than a smaller one, so we know that data with a variance of 22.5 are less spread out than equivalent data with a variance of 42.5, but the figures do not have any real meaning. Perhaps their most important property is that they can be used in a variety of other analyses. Because of this they are the most widely used measures of dispersion.

One important feature of variances is that they can sometimes be added. Provided two sets of observations are completely unrelated (which is technically described as their covariance being zero) the variance of the sum of data is equal to the sum of the variances of each set. If, for example, the daily demand for an item has a variance of 4, while the daily demand for a second item has a variance of 5, the variance of total demand for both items is 4 + 5 = 9. Standard deviations can never be added in this way.

WORKED EXAMPLE 5.17

The mean weight and standard deviation of airline passengers are known to be 72 kg and 6 kg respectively. What is the mean weight and standard deviation of total passenger weight in a 200 seat aeroplane?

Solution

The mean weight of 200 passengers is found by multiplying the mean weight of each passenger by the number of passengers:

$$\text{mean} = 200 \times 72 = 14\ 400 \text{ kg}$$

Standard deviations cannot be added, but variances can. Then the variance in weight of 200 passengers is found by multiplying the variance in weight of each passenger by the number of passengers:

$$\text{variance} = 200 \times 6^2 = 7200 \text{ kg}^2$$

The standard deviation in total weight is $\sqrt{7200} = 84.85$ kg

---

IN SUMMARY

The most widely used measure of data spread is the variance, which is the mean squared deviation. The square root of this is the standard deviation.

5.3.4 | Other measures for data

In the last section we said that the standard deviation was important because it could be used for other analyses. Here we will mention two of these. The first calculates a coefficient of variation, while the second deals with the skewness of a frequency distribution.

The measures of dispersion described so far can describe a set of data, but cannot be used to compare different sets. The standard deviation, for example, calculates the dispersion of data around its mean, so unless two sets of data have the same mean we cannot really use the standard deviation to compare their relative dispersions. What we need is some means of relating dispersion and location. One measure for this is the **coefficient of variation**, which is defined as the ratio of standard deviation over mean.

$$\text{Coefficient of variation} = \frac{\text{Standard deviation}}{\text{Mean}}$$

The higher the coefficient of variation, the more dispersed are the data. We might, for example, look at the costs of operating various facilities in one year and find a coefficient of variation of 0.8. If the coefficient rises to 0.9 in the following year it shows that there is more variation in costs, regardless of how these costs have changes in absolute terms.

A second measure based on the standard deviation is the **coefficient of skewness**. Frequency distributions may be symmetrical about their mean, or they may be skewed, as shown in Figure 5.14.

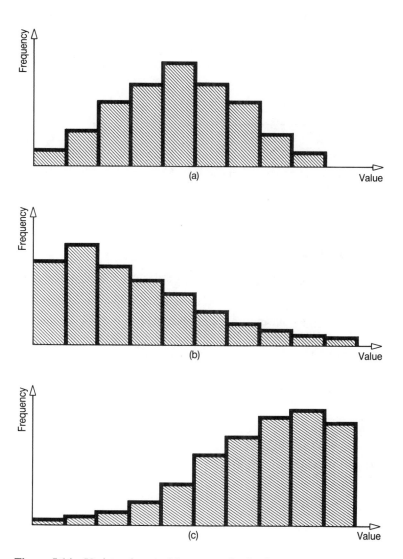

Figure 5.14 Various shapes of frequency distributions:
(a) symmetrical; (b) positive skew; (c) negative skew.

We might look at a frequency distribution and see that it is skewed, but we really need some measure of skewness. For this we can use Pearson's coefficient of skewness, which is defined as:

$$\text{Coefficient of skewness} = \frac{3 \times (\text{mean} - \text{median})}{\text{standard deviation}}$$

This automatically gives the correct sign of the skew. Its precise interpretation is somewhat difficult, but values around +1 or −1 are generally considered highly skewed.

IN SUMMARY

The standard deviation can be used for other analyses, including the coefficients of variation and skewness.

Self-assessment questions

5.9 List four measures for data spread. Are any other measures available?

5.10 Why is the mean deviation not used to measure data dispersion?

5.11 If the mean of a set of observations is 10.37 metres, what are the units of the variance?

5.12 Why is the standard deviation so widely used, when its practical meaning is unclear?

5.13 Two sets of data have means of 10.2 and 33.4 and variances of 4.3 and 18.2. What does this tell you?

CHAPTER REVIEW

This chapter discussed ways in which sets of data can be described numerically. It concentrated on measures for location and spread. In particular it:

- discussed the need for numerical descriptions of data
- described measures for the location of data
- calculated the arithmetic mean, median and mode

- considered measures for the spread of data, starting with the range and quartile deviation
- calculated mean absolute deviation, variance and standard deviation
- mentioned the coefficients of variation and skewness

Problems

5.1 The number of visitors received by a hospital patient in five consecutive days were 4, 2, 1, 7 and 1. What are the mean, median and mode of numbers visiting?

5.2 Find the mean, median and mode of the following numbers.

24 26 23 24 23 24 27 26 28 25 21 22 25 23 26 29 27 24 25 24 24 25

5.3 Find the mean, median and mode of the following discrete frequency distribution.

Class	0–5	6–10	11–15	16–20	21–25
Frequency	1	5	10	8	2

5.4 Find the mean, median and mode of the frequency distribution shown in the following table.

Class	1.00–2.99	3.00–4.99	5.00–6.99	7.00–8.99	9.00–10.99	11.00–12.99
Frequency	2	6	15	22	12	4

5.5 Find the mean, median and mode of the frequency distribution shown in the following table.

Class	0–9.9	10–19.9	20–29.9	30–39.9	40–49.9	50–59.9	60–69.9	70–79.9	80–89.9
Frequency	2	15	27	32	25	19	12	7	1

5.6 Find the mean absolute deviation, variance and standard deviation of 27, 32, 34, 28, 35, 30.

5.7 Find the variance and standard deviation of the following data.

3   45   28   83   62   44   60   18   73   44   59   67   78   32   74
28   67   97   34   44   23   66   25   12   58   9   34   58   29   45   37
91   73   50   10   71   72   19   18   27   41   91   90   23   23   33

5.8 Measure the spread of the ungrouped data described in Problems 5.1 and 5.2.

5.9 Measure the spread of the grouped data described in Problems 5.3 to 5.5.

5.10 How would you summarize the following data?

121 148 167 101 205 192 105 118 146 97 133 160 194 185 151

130 167 159 147 203 99 109 137 165 171 182 144 186 108 170

5.11 A hotel is concerned about the number of people who book rooms by telephone but do not actually turn up. Over the past few weeks it has kept records of the number of people who do this, as shown below. How can these data be summarized?

Day	1	2	3	4	5	6	7	8	9	10	11	12	13	14	15
No-shows	4	5	2	3	3	2	1	4	7	2	0	3	1	4	5
Day	16	17	18	19	20	21	22	23	24	25	26	27	28	29	30
No-shows	2	6	2	3	3	4	2	5	5	2	4	3	3	1	4
Day	31	32	33	34	35	36	37	38	39	40	41	42	43	44	45
No-shows	5	3	6	4	3	1	4	5	6	3	3	2	4	3	4

Computer exercises

5.1 There are many programs available for describing data numerically. Most of these (such as Minitab) do several other statistical analyses, while some spreadsheets also include statistical features. Figure 5.15 shows a spreadsheet calculation. Design your own spreadsheet to give an improved version of these results.

5.2 Minitab, in common with other statistical programs, has several functions to describe a set of data. Figure 5.16 shows a printout from a typical session. Make sure you understand what is happening here. Use a statistical package to get equivalent results, and extend the analysis. Two features are particularly interesting in Figure 5.16. The 'describe' function includes a value TRMEAN, which is a 'trimmed mean' calculated by ignoring the largest and smallest 5% of observations. Second, 'boxplot' function draws a 'box and whisker' diagram. These are not widely used but give a concise picture of the spread of data. A box represents the middle half of the data, extended by dashed lines to represent the largest and smallest 25% of values. The median is marked by a '+'.

	A	B	C	D	E	F	G
1			MEASURES OF DISPERSION				
2							
3		Class				Sums	Means
4		0-9.99	10-19.99	20-29.99	30-39.99		
5							
6	x	5	15	25	35		
7	f	4	17	22	7	50	
8							
9	f*x	20	255	550	245	1070	21.4
10							
11	deviation	-16.4	-6.4	3.6	13.6		
12							
13	dev.sqrd	268.96	40.96	12.96	184.96		
14	f*dev.sqrd	1075.84	696.32	285.12	1294.72	3352	67.04
15							
16	abs.dev.	16.4	6.4	3.6	13.6		
17	f*abs.dev.	65.6	108.8	79.2	95.2	348.8	6.976

(a)

	A	B	C	D	E	F	G
1			MEASURES OF DISPERSION				
2							
3		Class				Sums	Means
4		0-9.99	10-19.99	20-29.99	30-39.99		
5							
6	x	5	15	25	35		
7	f	4	17	22	7	=SUM(B7:E7)	
8							
9	f*x	=+B7*B6	=+C7*C6	=+D7*D6	=+E7*E6	=SUM(B9:E9)	=+F9/F7
10							
11	deviation	=+B6-G9	=+C6-G9	=+D6-G9	=+E6-G9		
12							
13	dev.sqrd.	=+B11^2	=+C11^2	=+D11^2	=+E11^2		
14	f*dev.sqrd.	=+B13*B7	=+C13*C7	=+D13*D7	=+E13*E7	=SUM(B14:E14)	=+F14/F7
15							
16	abs.dev.	=ABS(B11)	=ABS(C11)	=ABS(D11)	=ABS(E11)		
17	f*abs.dev.	=+B16*B7	=+C16*C7	=+D16*D7	=+E16*E7	=SUM(B17:E17)	=+F17/F7

(b)

Figure 5.15 Spreadsheet calculations for statistics: (a) values; (b) calculations.

```
MTB    > SET C1
DATA   > 25 32 27 29 30 28 31 29 30 26 30 29 31 30 28
DATA   > END
MTB    > HISTOGRAM OF C1
```

Histogram of C1   N = 15

Midpoint	Count	
25	1	*
26	1	*
27	1	*
28	2	* *
29	3	* * *
30	4	* * * *
31	2	* *
32	1	*

MTB > DESCRIBE C1

C1	N	MEAN	MEDIAN	TRMEAN	STDEV	SEMEAN
	15	29.000	29.000	29.077	1.927	0.498

C1	MIN	MAX	Q1	Q3
	25.000	32.000	28.000	30.000

MTB > BOXPLOT C1

```
                          -I    +    I-
      ------------------------|   |--------------
          ┴         ┴        ┴        ┴        ┴      -C1
        25.5      27.0     28.5     30.0     31.5
```

Figure 5.16   Minitab listing to describe a set of data.

5.3   The following data has been collected by a company. See how you can reduce, manipulate and present it.

245	487	123	012	159	751	222	035	487	655	197	655
458	766	123	453	493	444	123	537	254	514	324	215
367	557	330	204	506	804	941	354	226	870	652	458
425	248	560	510	234	542	671	874	710	702	701	540
360	654	323	410	405	531	489	695	409	375	521	624
357	678	809	901	567	481	246	027	310	679	548	227
150	600	845	521	777	304	286	220	667	111	485	266
472	700	705	466	591	398	367	331	458	466	571	489
257	100	874	577								

Write a report about your findings.

5.4   Find a set of data about the performance of some sports teams (for example, last year's results from football leagues). Describe the performance of the teams, both numerically and graphically. Write a report about your findings.

Case study
Consumer advice office

When people buy things they have a number of statutory rights. A fundamental one is that the products should be of an adequate quality and fit for the purpose intended. When someone thinks these rights have been infringed there are a number of things they can do. One of the easiest and most effective is to contact their local authority's trading standards service.

Mary Smith has been working in the local authority as a consumer advice officer for the past 14 months. Her job is to advise people who have complaints against traders. She listens to the complaints, assesses the problem and then takes any necessary follow-up action. Often her clients can be dealt with quickly, but sometimes there is a deal of follow-up including legal work and appearances in court.

The local authority is always looking for ways to reduce costs and improve their service. It is important, then, for Mary to show that she is doing a good job. She is particularly keen to show that her increasing experience and response to pressures for improved efficiency have allowed her to deal with more clients.

Mary has kept records of the number of clients she dealt with during her first eight weeks at work, and during the same eight weeks this year.

Number of customers dealt with each working day in the first eight weeks:

6 18 22 9 10 14 22 15 28 9 30 26 17 9 11 25 31 17 25 30

32 17 27 34 15 9 7 10 28 10 31 12 16 26 21 37 25 7 36 29

Number of customers dealt with each working day in the last eight weeks:

30 26 40 19 26 31 28 41 18 27 29 30 33 43 19 20 44 37 29 22

41 39 15 9 22 26 30 35 38 26 19 25 33 39 31 30 20 34 43 45

During the past year she estimates that her working hours have increased by an average of two hours a week, which is unpaid overtime. Her wages increased by 3% after allowing for inflation. What she needs is a way of presenting these figures to her employers in a form that they will understand.

Derivation 5.1 Calculation of variance

In the chapter we used two statements for the variance:

$$\text{variance} = \frac{\sum (x - \bar{x})^2}{n} = \frac{\sum x^2}{n} - \left(\frac{\sum x}{n}\right)^2$$

We can show these are equivalent by expanding the first form. Now:

$$\sum (x - \bar{x})^2 = \sum x^2 - \sum 2x\bar{x} + \sum \bar{x}^2$$

But

$$\sum x = n\bar{x} \text{ and } \sum \bar{x}^2 = n\bar{x}^2$$

so

$$\sum (x - \bar{x})^2 = \sum x^2 - 2n\bar{x}^2 + n\bar{x}^2$$
$$= \sum x^2 - n\bar{x}^2$$
$$= \sum x^2 - n \left(\frac{\sum x}{n}\right)^2$$

When this is divided by n it gives the second form of the equation.

Describing changes with index numbers | 6

CHAPTER OUTLINE

Managers are often concerned with the way in which a variable changes over time. Prices, for example, tend to increase with inflation; sales vary from month to month; the number of people employed changes each week; and so on. It would be useful to have a means of monitoring these changes. This is provided by index numbers.

Index numbers measure the changing value of a variable over time in relation to its value at some fixed point. Several different types of index can be used, and the main ones are discussed in this chapter.

After reading this chapter and doing the exercises you should be able to:

- appreciate the use of index numbers
- calculate indices for changes in the value of a variable
- change the base of an index
- find simple aggregate and mean price relative indices
- calculate base weighting and current period weighting for aggregate indices
- appreciate the use of the Retail Price Index

6.1 │ Index numbers for describing changes

6.1.1 │ Introduction

The last two chapters have discussed graphical and numerical ways of describing data. These have taken a snapshot of data and have described the values at a specific time. In business, however, the values of most variables change over time. The prices paid for material, number of people employed, annual income and profit, company contributions to charities, number of customers, tax rates, and so on, all change over time. It would be useful to have a way of describing these changes. This chapter continues the theme of data presentation by using index numbers to describe the way in which a variable changes over time.

Consider, as an example of changing values, the number of crimes committed in a particular area. Suppose there were 127 crimes of a particular type in one year, 142 crimes in the second year and 116 crimes in the third year. We could say that the number of crimes had risen by 11.8% between years 1 and 2, and had then declined by 18.3% between years 2 and 3. Although accurate, this is a rather messy description and has the disadvantage of not directly comparing the number of crimes in years 1 and 3. We could plot a graph of the number of crimes each year and this would certainly show any trends. Unfortunately, it would not give a **measure** for the changes. What we really need is a numerical measure for monitoring the changes, and this is provided by an **index** or **index number**.

An index is a number which compares the value of a variable at any time with its value at another fixed time, called the **base period**. Then we can define:

$$\text{index for period} = \frac{\text{value in period}}{\text{value in base period}}$$

With the crime figures above we could use the first year as a base period. Then the index for the second year is 142/127 = 1.12, as shown in the following table:

Year	Value	Calculation	Index
1	127	127/127	1.00
2	142	142/127	1.12
3	116	116/127	0.91

The index in the base period will always be 1.00. The index of 1.12 in the second year tells us that crime is 12% higher than the **base value** (which is the value in the base period), while the index of 0.91 in the third period tells us that crime is 9% lower than the base value.

We chose the first year as the base period, but this was an arbitrary choice and any other year could be used. The choice depends on the information needed. If a comparison of crimes in the third year is being made with previous years, we could take year 3 as the base year. Then the base value is 116, the index in year 1 is 127/116 = 1.09, and so on, as shown in the following table:

Year	Value	Calculation	Index
1	127	127/116	1.0
2	142	142/116	1.22
3	116	116/116	1.00

IN SUMMARY

In business, the value of most variables changes over time. An index can be used to measure these changes, by calculating the ratio of the current value over a base value.

6.1.2 | Price indices

One of the most important use of indices is to show how the price of a product changes over time. This change might be a result of:

- changing costs of raw materials
- changes in the production process
- variable supply (such as seasonal vegetables)
- variable demand (such as holidays)
- changing financial objectives of suppliers (perhaps aiming for higher profits)
- general inflation which causes prices to drift upwards

and so on.

The index we used above was based on a value of 1.00 in the base period. For convenience, indices are usually multiplied by 100 to define an index with a base figure of 100. Then subsequent price indices are defined as the ratio of the current price to the base price, multiplied by 100.

$$\text{price index in period } N = \frac{\text{price in period } N}{\text{base price}} \times 100$$

If the base price of a product is £5 and this rises to £7 the price index is $7/5 \times 100 = 140$. This immediately shows that the price has risen by 40% since the base period. If the price in the next period is £8 the index rises to $8/5 \times 100 = 160$, which is an increase of 60% since the base period: if the price is £4 the index is $4/5 \times 100 = 80$, which is a decrease of 20% since the base period. As well as showing changes in one product's price, indices can be used for comparisons between different products. If the price indices of two products are 125 and 150 we know that the second product has risen in price twice as quickly as the first (assuming that the same base period is used).

WORKED EXAMPLE 6.1

If the price of an item is £20 in January, £22 in February, £25 in March, £26 in April and £27 in May, what is the price index in each month using January as the base month?

Solution

Taking January as the base month, the base price is £20. Then the price indices for each month are:

January: $\dfrac{20}{20} \times 100 = 100$ (as expected in the base period)

February: $\dfrac{22}{20} \times 100 = 110$

March: $\dfrac{25}{20} \times 100 = 125$

April: $\dfrac{26}{20} \times 100 = 130$

May: $\dfrac{27}{20} \times 100 = 135$

In the last worked example, we saw that the index of 110 in February shows the price has risen by 10% over the base level, while an index of 125 in March shows a rise of 25% over the base level, and so on. Changes in indices between periods are referred to as **percentage point** changes. Thus between February and March the index shows an increase of $125 - 110 = 15$ percentage points (compared with a percentage increase of $15/110 \times 100 = 13.6\%$). It is important to remember that percentage point changes refer back to the base price and not the current price.

WORKED EXAMPLE 6.2

A car showroom is giving a special offer on one type of car. The advertised price of this car in four consecutive quarters was £10,450, £10,800, £11,450 and £9,999. Find the price indices based on the final quarter's price. What are the quarterly changes in price in terms of percentage points and percentages?

Solution

Taking indices based on the fourth quarter gives:

$$\text{first quarter price index} = \frac{10\ 450}{9999} \times 100 = 104.5$$

$$\text{second quarter price index} = \frac{10\ 800}{9999} \times 100 = 108.0$$

$$\text{third quarter price index} = \frac{11\ 450}{9999} \times 100 = 114.5$$

$$\text{fourth quarter price index} = \frac{9999}{9999} \times 100 = 100.0$$

The percentage price rise in each quarter is found from:

$$\text{percentage price rise} = \frac{\text{price this quarter} - \text{price last quarter}}{\text{price last quarter}} \times 100$$

The percentage point rise is found from the indices as:

percentage point price rise = index this quarter − index last quarter

Then the rise in price between the first and second quarter is:

£350 which is $350/10\ 450 \times 100 = 3.3\%$

or

$108 - 104.5 = 3.5$ percentage points

The rise in price between the second and third quarter is:

£650 which is $650/10\ 800 \times 100 = 6.0\%$

or
$$114.5 - 108 = 6.5 \text{ percentage points}$$

The fall in price between the third and fourth quarter is:
$$£1451 \text{ which is } 1451/11\,450 \times 100 = 12.7\%$$

or
$$114.5 - 100 = 14.5 \text{ percentage points}$$

So far we have discussed indices largely in terms of price indices, but we should make a number of general points.

- Although we have concentrated on price indices, an index can be used to measure the way any variable changes over time, such as unemployment numbers, car registrations, or gross national product.

- We chose a base value of 100 for the index, but this is only for convenience and any other value could be used.

- The choice of base period can be any convenient time; it is usual to take a typical value during a period when there are no unusual circumstances.

- The index can be calculated with any convenient frequency. Unemployment figures are updated monthly, stock market prices daily, GNP annually and so on.

WORKED EXAMPLE 6.3

The following table shows the monthly price index for an item:

Month	1	2	3	4	5	6	7	8	9	10	11	12
Index	121	112	98	81	63	57	89	109	131	147	132	126

(a) If the price in month 3 is £240 what is the price in month 8?
(b) If the price in month 10 is £1200 what is the price in month 2?

Solution

(a) In month 3 the price is £240 and the price index is 98, so

$$\text{base price} = \frac{240}{98} \times 100 = 244.90$$

Then in month 8 the price index is 109 so the price is

$$\text{price} = 244.90 \times \frac{109}{100} = 266.94$$

We could have found this directly by taking the ratio of the price indices to give

$$\text{price} = 240 \times \frac{109}{98} = 266.94$$

(b) The ratio of the price indices in periods 2 and 10 is 112/147, so the price in period 2 is

$$\text{price} = 1200 \times \frac{112}{147} = £914.29$$

IN SUMMARY

Indices are often used to monitor price changes. They are commonly based on a value of 100, in which case percentage point changes are easy to monitor.

6.1.3 | Changing the base period

When calculating an index the base period can be chosen as any convenient time. However, rather than keep the same base period for a long time, it is usual to update it continually. There are two reasons for this:

- **changing circumstances.** It is advisable to reset the index whenever there are significant changes in circumstances, which would make comparisons with earlier periods meaningless. A manufacturer, for example, who calculates an index for production will return the base value to 100 whenever the product range is changed.

- **an index becomes too large.** It is advisable to reset the index when its value becomes too high. If the index rises to, say, 1000 a 10% increase in a period will raise the index to 1100, and this may appear a more significant change than, say, 100 to 110.

When the base period is changed, we should know how to convert an existing, old index to a new one. Suppose we have an old index whose base value was set in period N_1. Then the old index for period M is:

$$\text{old index} = \frac{\text{value in period } M}{\text{value in period } N_1} \times 100$$

If we want to reset the index to a base value set in period N_2 we have a new index defined by:

$$\text{new index} = \frac{\text{value in period } M}{\text{value in period } N_2} \times 100$$

Rearranging these equations gives the result

$$\text{value in period } M \times 100 = \text{new index} \times \text{value in period } N_2$$

and

$$\text{value in period } M \times 100 = \text{old index} \times \text{value in period } N_1$$

So

$$\text{new index} = \text{old index} \times \frac{\text{value in period } N_1}{\text{value in period } N_2}$$

As the values in both periods N_1 and N_2 are fixed, the new index is found by multiplying the old index by a constant amount. If we know, for example, that the old index for a period is 250 and a new index is 100, the value of the constant is 100/250. The new index for any period can then be found by multiplying the old index by 100/250; conversely, the old index for any period is found by multiplying the new index by 250/100.

WORKED EXAMPLE 6.4

The number of units produced each year in a factory is described by the following indices:

Year	1	2	3	4	5	6	7	8
Index 1	100	138	162	196	220			
Index 2					100	125	140	165

(a) What are the base years for the indices?

(b) If the factory had not changed to index 2, what values would index 1 have in years 6 to 8?

(c) What values would index 2 have in years 1 to 4?

(d) If the factory made 4860 units in year 3, how many did it make in year 5? How many did it make in year 7?

Solution

(a) Indices take the value 100 in base periods, so index 1 uses the base year 1 and index 2 uses the base year 5.

(b) Index 1 is found by multiplying index 2 by a constant amount. This constant can be found from year 5 as 220/100. Then the values for index 1 are

$$\text{year 6:} \quad 125 \times 220/100 = 275$$

$$\text{year 7:} \quad 140 \times 220/100 = 308$$

$$\text{year 8:} \quad 165 \times 220/100 = 363$$

(c) Index 2 is found by multiplying index 1 by a constant amount. Again this is found from year 5 as 100/220. Then the values for index 2 are

$$\text{year 4:} \quad 196 \times 100/220 = 89.09$$

$$\text{year 3:} \quad 162 \times 100/220 = 73.64$$

$$\text{year 2:} \quad 138 \times 100/220 = 62.73$$

$$\text{year 1:} \quad 100 \times 100/220 = 45.45$$

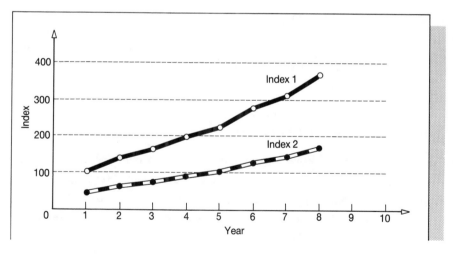

Figure 6.1

(d) If the factory made 4860 units in year 3 the production in the base year (year 1) was

$$\text{base production} = \frac{4860}{162} \times 100 = 3000 \text{ units}$$

Each percentage point of production in the base year corresponds to 3000/100 = 30 units, so production in year 5 is 30 × 220 = 6600 units. This result could also be found directly from the index numbers for years 3 and 5:

$$\frac{4860}{162} \times 220 = 6600 \text{ units}$$

Production in year 7 can be found using either of the indices. Using index 1, each percentage point of production in the base year is 4860/162, so production in year 7 is given by

$$\frac{4860}{162} \times 308 = 9240 \text{ units}$$

This result can be confirmed using index 2, which has each percentage point of production in the base year as 4860/73.64. Then production in year 7 is given by

$$\frac{4860}{73.64} \times 140 = 9240 \text{ units}$$

IN SUMMARY

Base periods for index numbers should be revised periodically. A new index number can be calculated by multiplying the old index by a constant.

Self-assessment questions

6.1 What is the purpose of an index number?

6.2 'Indices always use a base value of 100.' Is this statement true or false?

6.3 When should the base period be changed?

6.4 What is the difference between a percentage rise of 10% and a percentage point rise of 10?

6.5 In one period the old price index for a product is 345 while the new price index is 125. In the following period the new price index is 132. What is the old index for this period?

6.2 | Indices for more than one variable

6.2.1 | Average indices

We have seen how an index can measure the changes in a variable over time. Sometimes, however, we are not interested in the changes in a single variable but in a combination of different variables. The Retail Price Index, for example, shows how the aggregate price of a range of goods varies over time; a shop is interested in changes in sales of all items it sells rather than a single item; a local authority is interested in changes in the number of people of all types it employs; and so on. Indices which measure changes in a number of variables are called aggregate indices, and in this section we shall show how these can be defined. For simplicity we shall phrase the discussion in terms of a price index, but the same reasoning can be used for any other type of index.

Two obvious ways of defining an aggregate price index are:

- add all prices and calculate an index based on the total price. This is called the **simple aggregate index** or **simple composite index**

$$\text{Simple aggregate index for period } n = \frac{\text{sum of prices in period } n}{\text{sum of prices in base period}} \times 100$$

- calculate the mean value of separate indices for all items. The price of an item at any time divided by the base price is called the **price relative**, so the index based on mean values is called the **mean price relative index**.

$$\text{Mean price relative index for period } n = \frac{\text{sum of all price relatives for period } n}{\text{number of indices}} \times 100$$

WORKED EXAMPLE 6.5

Last year the prices of bread, milk and tea in a shop were 55 pence, 28 pence and 72 pence respectively. This year the same items cost 62 pence, 32 pence and 74 pence respectively. What are the simple aggregate index and the mean price relative index for this year, using last year as the base year?

Solution

The simple aggregate index is found by adding all prices and taking the ratio of total price:

$$\text{base price} = 55 + 28 + 72 = 155$$

$$\text{current price} = 62 + 32 + 74 = 168$$

So the simple aggregate index = 168/155 × 100 = 108.4.

To find the mean price relative index we calculate the price relative for each item and find the mean of these. The individual price relatives are

bread:　　62/55 = 1.127

milk:　　32/28 = 1.143

tea:　　　74/72 = 1.028

The mean price relative index is the mean of these multiplied by 100, which is

$$100 \times \frac{112.7 + 114.3 + 102.8}{3} = 109.9$$

These two indices are easy to define and use, but they do not really give good measures. One obvious criticism, particularly of the simple aggregate index, is that it depends on the units used for each index. An aggregate index including the price of tea per kilogram would give a different index from one based on the price per pound. If the index used the price of tea per tonne, it would be so high as to swamp the other costs and effectively ignore them. In the worked example above the price of a ton of tea rose from 2240 × 0.72 = £1612.80 to 2240 × 0.74 = £1657.60. The simple aggregate index based on these figures would be

$$\text{index} = 100 \times \frac{1657.60 + 0.65 + 0.32}{1612.80 + 0.55 + 0.28} = 102.8$$

Another weakness of the two indices is that they do not consider the relative importance of each product. If people used more milk than tea, then the index should reflect this. Taking a broader example, a service company might have spent £1000 on raw materials and £1 million on wages in the base year, and this year it spends £2000 on raw materials and £1 million on wages. It would make little sense to say that the aggregate index of costs is 150, which is the mean price relative index calculated from the separate indices for raw materials (200) and wages (100).

A reasonable aggregate index must take into account two factors:

● the price paid for each unit of product
● the quantity of each product used

There are several ways of combining these into a reasonable weighted index. The two most common methods use base-period weighting and current-period weighting, as discussed in the following sections.

IN SUMMARY

An aggregate index shows changes in a combination of variables. A simple aggregate index or mean price relative index can be used, but these both have weaknesses.

6.2.2 | Weighted indices

Weighted indices take into account the relative importance of each variable. If, for example, we are looking at the changing amount that a family pays for food, the easiest way of doing this is to look at each week's shopping basket and find the total cost. This total cost depends both on the price of each item and on the number of items bought, so we could define a weighted price index as

$$\text{weighted price index} = \frac{\text{current cost of week's shopping basket}}{\text{cost of shopping basket in base period}}$$

This approach seems reasonable, but in practice there is an immediate problem. If some prices change, the amount that a family buys will also change. Suppose, for example, the price of cake increases with respect to the price of biscuits; then a family may reduce the quantity of cakes bought and increase the quantity of biscuits. The index we use should take such changes into account, but still emphasize changes in price. In practice, there are two widely used methods of doing this:

- **base-weighted index** assumes that the quantities purchased do not change from the base period
- **current-weighted index** assumes that the current shopping basket was used in the base period

Base-weighted index

Suppose that in the base period the shopping basket contained quantities Q_0 at prices P_0; then the total cost is the sum of all quantities multiplied by the prices.

$$\text{total cost in base period} = \text{sum of quantities} \times \text{price}$$

$$= \sum Q_0 P_0$$

In another period, n, the prices changed to P_n, but we assume that the quantities bought remained unchanged, so the total cost is $\sum Q_0 P_n$. Then we can calculate a base-weighted index as the ratio of these two costs base-weighted index

$$= \frac{\text{cost of base period quantities at current prices}}{\text{cost of base period quantities at base period prices}}$$

This index is usually multiplied by 100, giving

$$\text{base-weighted index} = \frac{\sum Q_0 P_n}{\sum Q_0 P_0} \times 100$$

This is sometimes called the Laspeyre index, after its inventor. It has the advantage of giving a direct comparison of costs and reacting to actual price rises. Conversely, it has the disadvantage of assuming that amounts bought do not change over time. In practice, purchases do change and, in particular, the quantities are affected by price; a product with rapidly increasing price may well be replaced by one with lower price. The result is that base-weighted indices tend to give values which are too high. However, by updating the base period at suitable intervals (and particularly by adjusting the list of purchases) the errors can be kept small.

Current-period weighting

If prices in a period n are P_n, and a family buys a shopping basket with quantities Q_n, the total cost is $\sum Q_n P_n$. A reasonable price index would compare this cost with the cost of the same products in the base period, which would have been $\sum Q_n P_0$. Then the current-period weighted index is the ratio of these costs:

current-period weighted index

$$= \frac{\text{cost of current quantities at current prices}}{\text{cost of current quantities at base period prices}}$$

Again, this index is usually multiplied by 100, giving:

$$\text{current-period weighted index} = \frac{\sum Q_n P_n}{\sum Q_n P_0} \times 100$$

This index is sometimes called the Paasche index. It has the advantage of giving an accurate measure of changes in the costs of current purchases. Conversely, it has the disadvantage of changing the basis of calculation each period, so that it does not give a direct comparison of prices over time. Moreover, by allowing substitution of products which are relatively cheaper than they were in the base period, it gives an index which tends to be too low. This index also takes more effort to update, primarily because of the data collection needed to continually monitor quantities purchased. For these reasons, current-period weighting is less widely used than base-period weighting.

WORKED EXAMPLE 6.6

A company buys four products with the following characteristics:

Items	Number of units bought Year 1	Year 2	Price paid per unit Year 1	Year 2
A	20	24	10	11
B	55	51	23	25
C	63	84	17	17
D	28	34	19	20

(a) Find the price indices for each product in year 2 using year 1 as the base year.

(b) Calculate a base-weighted index for the products.

(c) Calculate a current-period weighted index.

Solution

(a) Simple price indices do not take into account usage of a product, so we have

Product A: $11/10 \times 100 = 110$

Product B: $25/23 \times 100 = 108.7$

Product C: $17/17 \times 100 = 100$

Product D: $20/19 \times 100 = 105.3$

(b) A base-weighted index shows the price that would be paid later for the basket of items bought in the base period:

$$\text{base-weighted index} = \frac{\sum Q_0 P_n}{\sum Q_0 P_0} \times 100$$

$$= \frac{11 \times 20 + 25 \times 55 + 17 \times 63 + 20 \times 28}{10 \times 20 + 23 \times 55 + 17 \times 63 + 19 \times 28} = \frac{3226}{3068}$$

$$= 105.15$$

(c) A current-period weighted index shows how the price of the basket of items bought in a later period has changed since the base period.

$$\text{current-period weighted index} = \frac{\sum Q_n P_n}{\sum Q_n P_0} \times 100$$

$$= \frac{11 \times 24 + 25 \times 51 + 17 \times 84 + 20 \times 34}{10 \times 24 + 23 \times 51 + 17 \times 84 + 19 \times 34} = \frac{3647}{3487}$$

$$= 104.59$$

Other weighted indices

Base-weighted and current-period weighted indices both assign weights to prices according to the quantities bought. There are circumstances in which other weights would be more useful. Suppose, for example, we are looking at the price of journeys on public transport. The two indices described so far would weight the prices by the number of journeys. In some circumstances, however, it might be more sensible to weight them by the total distance travelled. In general, when a different weighting is preferred, we can define a weight w to multiply each price by and then divide the index by the sum of these weights:

$$\text{weighted index} = \frac{\sum wP_n / P_0}{\sum w} \times 100$$

In principle, the weights can take any values, but they are usually related to total expenditure, time, typical value, general importance, and so on. It may clearly be difficult to define an appropriate set of weights, and this is usually done by discussion and agreement. Despite this problem, weighted indices are widely used in applications such as the Retail Price Index (RPI).

WORKED EXAMPLE 6.7

The weights used in a price index, and the relevant prices are shown in the following table:

Item	Weight	Base price	Current price
One	20	25	31
Two	35	24	28
Three	25	120	140
Four	50	65	85
Five	70	75	100

What is the weighted price index?

Solution

The calculation for this is

$$\text{weighted index} = \frac{\sum w\, P_n/P_0}{\sum w} \times 100$$

$$= \frac{(20 \times 31/25) + (35 \times 28/24) + (25 \times 140/120) + (50 \times 85/65) + (70 \times 100/75)}{(20 + 35 + 25 + 50 + 70)} \times 100$$

$$= \frac{24.8 + 40.8 + 29.2 + 65.4 + 93.3}{200} \times 100$$

$$= 126.8$$

IN SUMMARY

Aggregate price indices should reflect changes in both price and quantities bought. The two most common aggregate indices use base weighting and current-period weighting. Other weighting can be used.

6.2.3 | Retail price indices

Each month the government publishes figures for the annual rate of inflation. Several indices are used to monitor this, but the most important is the Retail Price Index (RPI). This shows changes in the amount spent by a typical household. It is an aggregate index based on the price of a representative selection of 350 products and services in 14 main groups (listed in Problem 6.10). Details of current prices are collected on the Tuesday nearest the middle of the month, with a total of 150 000 prices collected. Some of these are collected centrally, but accurate figures need to reflect price variations around the country, so some prices are collected by people from the Department of Employment who visit representative shops.

The index is used for a number of purposes, including wage bargaining, calculating index-linked benefits, and raising insurance values. It can be criticized as not properly representing the inflation felt by certain sectors of the community. For example, people who do not have a mortgage are not affected when mortgage interest rates change. The government, when publishing the RPI, does attempt to take into account some of these factors, by publishing special indices for households which consist of, for example, only one or two pensioners. It also publishes specific indices for each group of items (such as food or transport). In practice, these effects are surprisingly small, and the RPI is widely accepted as giving a reasonable measure of changing prices.

The RPI shows price changes clearly, and it has important practical implications, particularly when considering inflation. If someone's pay doubled between 1974 and 1979 they would expect to be much better off. Unfortunately, this was a period of high inflation and the index of prices in 1979, with 1974 as the base year, was 206. Thus wages would have to more than double just to keep up with prices. It seems reasonable for people to expect an index of their pay to be comparable with the RPI, so that their real pay does not decline over time. Similarly, investors should look at the future value of their investment and compare this with likely values for the RPI. This theme is discussed in more detail in Chapter 7.

WORKED EXAMPLE 6.8

Table 6.1 shows the price index of manufactured products from 1970 to 1990.

(a) What is the approximate rate of inflation in each year?

(b) If an item cost £1400 in 1970 how much would you expect it to cost in 1990?

(c) Which is the cheapest real price of £1000 in 1970: £1500 in 1980 or £2000 in 1990?

Table 6.1

Year	Index	Year	Index	Year	Index
1970	120	1977	310	1984	566
1971	131	1978	339	1985	597
1972	138	1979	376	1986	623
1973	149	1980	428	1987	646
1974	181	1981	469	1988	676
1975	223	1982	505	1989	710
1976	260	1983	533	1990	752

Solution

(a) The annual rate of inflation shows the percentage increase in prices. This can be found directly from the price index:

Between 1970 and 1971 the price index rose by

$$\frac{131 - 120}{120} \times 100 = 9.2\%$$

which gives the annual rate of inflation.

Between 1972 and 1971 the price index rose by

$$\frac{138 - 131}{131} \times 100 = 5.3\%$$

and so on.

(b) A price would be raised by the ratio of the indices in 1990 and 1970 to give

price in 1990 = 1400 × 752/120 = £8773

(c) The prices can be compared by finding their values in the base year. This is done by dividing the amounts by the price index:

£1000 in 1970 is worth 1000/120 × 100 in the base year = £833.33

£1500 in 1980 is worth 1500/428 × 100 in the base year = £350.47

£2000 in 1990 is worth 2000/752 × 100 in the base year = £265.96

It is clear that inflation has made the highest actual cost of £2000 in 1990 the cheapest real cost.

IN SUMMARY

The Retail Price Index is a widely accepted measure of price increase based on the expenditure of a typical family.

Self-assessment questions

6.6 How are the mean price relative index and the simple aggregate index defined?

6.7 What are the weaknesses of the mean price relative index and the simple aggregate index?

6.8 What is the difference between base-period weighting and current-period weighting for aggregate indices?

6.9 Base-period weighting often gives a higher index than current-period weighting. Why?

6.10 Is it possible to use a weighting other than base period or current period?

6.11 'The Retail Price Index gives an accurate measure of the cost of living?' Is this statement true?

CHAPTER REVIEW

This chapter discussed the use of index numbers to describe changing values over time. In particular it:

- discussed the need to monitor changing values
- calculated index numbers for prices and other variables
- changed the base of indices
- described the use of aggregate indices including base weighting and current-period weighting
- commented on the Retail Price Index.

Problems

6.1 The price of an item in consecutive months has been £106, £108, £111, £112, £118, £125, £130 and £132. Use an index based on the first month to describe these changes. How would this compare with an index based on the last month?

6.2 The number of fishing boats operating from a harbour over the past ten years has been recorded as follows:

> 325 321 316 294 263 241 197 148 102 70

Describe these changes by indices based on the first and last year's observations.

6.3 The number of people employed in a factory over the past 12 months is as follows. Use an index to describe these figures.

Month	1	2	3	4	5	9	7	8	9	10	11	12
Number	121	115	97	112	127	135	152	155	161	147	133	131

6.4 The annual output of a company is described by the following indices:

Year	1	2	3	4	5	6	7	8
Index 1	100	125	153	167				
Index 2				100	109	125	140	165

If the factory made 23 850 units in year 2, how many did it make in the other years? What is the percentage increase in output each year?

6.5 An insurance company uses an index to describe the number of agents working for it. This index was revised five years ago, and had the following values over the past ten years:

Year	1	2	3	4	5	6	7	8	9	10
Index 1	106	129	154	173	195	231				
Index 2						100	113	126	153	172

If the company had not changed to index 2, what values would index 1 have in years 7 to 10? What values would index 2 have in years 1 to 5? If the company had 645 agents in year 4, how many did it have in each other year?

6.6 Employees in a company are put into four wage groups. During a three-year period the number employed in each group and the average weekly wage are as follows:

Group	Year 1		Year 2		Year 3	
	Number	Wage	Number	Wage	Number	Wage
1	45	125	55	133	60	143
2	122	205	125	211	132	224
3	63	245	66	268	71	293
4	7	408	9	473	13	521

Use a number of different indices to describe changes in wages paid and numbers employed.

6.7 The following table shows the price of drinks served in a pub. Find the simple aggregate index and mean price relative index for each year.

	Beer	Lager	Cider	Soft drinks
Year 1	91	95	78	35
Year 1	97	105	85	39
Year 3	102	112	88	42
Year 4	107	125	93	47

6.8 A company buys four products with the following characteristics:

Products	Number of units bought		Price paid per unit	
	Year 1	Year 2	Year 1	Year 2
A	121	141	9	10
B	149	163	21	23
C	173	182	26	27
D	194	103	31	33

Calculate a base-weighted index and a current-period weighted index for the products.

6.9 The average prices for four items over four years are as follows:

Item	Year 1	Year 2	Year 3	Year 4
A	25	26	30	32
B	56	61	67	74
C	20	25	30	36
D	110	115	130	150

The number of units of each item bought by a company are approximately 400, 300, 800 and 200 respectively. Calculate weighted price indices for years 2 to 4, taking year 1 as the base year.

6.10 The Retail Price Index currently uses the following weights:

Food	158	Household goods	71
Catering	47	Household services	40
Alcoholic drink	77	Clothing and footwear	69
Tobacco	34	Personal goods and services	39
Housing	185	Fares and travel costs	21
Fuel and light	50	Leisure goods	48
Motoring expenditure	131	Leisure services	30

How are these weights used in calculating the RPI? What are the most important categories of expenditure? What would be the effect on the RPI of a 10% increase in the cost of housing? What would be the effect of a 10% increase in fares and travel costs?

Computer exercises

6.1 Figure 6.2 shows part of a spreadsheet for calculating aggregate indices. Analyse the results and make sure they are correct. Design a spreadsheet to do these calculations. Extend the analysis to calculate other indices.

	A	B	C	D	E	F	G
1			CALCULATION OF INDICES				
2							
3		Year 0		Year n			
4	Item	Quantity	Price	Quantity	Price	PoQo	PnQo
5	Shoes	4	25	5	28	100	112
6	Shirts	10	8	8	10	80	100
7	Trousers	5	28	4	32	140	160
8	Dresses	8	45	8	48	360	384
9	Gloves	4	5	6	6	20	24
10	Hats	3	12	3	12	36	36
11	Coats	2	95	3	120	190	240
12							
13	Sums					926	1056
14							
15				Ratio		Index	
16	Base weighted			1.14		114.04	
17							

Figure 6.2

6.2   Use a spreadsheet to calculate indices for the data in Table 6.2.

Table 6.2

Item	Year 1		Year 2		Year 3		Year 4	
	Price	Quantity	Price	Quantity	Price	Quantity	Price	Quantity
AL403	142	27	147	26	155	32	165	32
ML127	54	284	58	295	65	306	75	285
FE872	1026	5	1026	8	1250	2	1250	3
KP332	687	25	699	25	749	20	735	55
KP333	29	1045	31	1024	32	1125	36	1254
CG196	58	754	64	788	72	798	81	801
CG197	529	102	599	110	675	120	750	108
CG404	254	306	275	310	289	305	329	299
CG405	109	58	115	62	130	59	140	57
NA112	86	257	83	350	85	366	90	360
QF016	220	86	220	86	225	86	225	86
QT195	850	10	899	9	949	12	999	16
LJ878	336	29	359	38	499	11	499	25

6.3   The government publishes many statistics in its *Monthly Digest of Statistics*. Take an appropriate set of figures (such as the annual inflation rate) and see how indices have been used to monitor changes over the past 20 years. Use a spreadsheet to check the published indices.

6.4   Figure 6.3 shows a dialogue with a statistical package (Minitab) which puts two sets of prices in columns C1 and C2 and a set of demands in C3. It then finds the total price paid with each price range and hence calculates an index. Check these figures and make sure they are correct. Use a statistical package to generate other price indices. What is the benefit of using a spreadsheet rather than a statistical package?

6.5   Run a survey to find the contents of a typical week's purchases for a sample of people. Find the cost of these purchases. Now find government figures for inflation over the past 30 years. Find the cost of the purchases at different times. Write a report about your findings, being sure to mention any specific problems, the generality of results, and so on.

```
MTB    > SET C1
DATA   > 26 10 17 21 15 22 30 END
MTB    > SET C2
DATA   > 28 11 18 23 17 24 34 END
MTB    > SET C3
DATA   > 125 36 21 45 109 82 17 END

MTB    > LET C4 = C1 * C3
MTB    > LET C5 = C2 * C3

MTB    > PRINT C1 C2 C3 C4 C5
```

ROW	C1	C2	C3	C4	C5
1	26	28	125	3250	3500
2	10	11	36	360	396
3	17	18	21	357	378
4	21	23	45	945	1035
5	15	17	109	1635	1853
6	22	24	82	1804	1968
7	30	34	17	510	578

```
MTB > LET K1 = SUM (C4)
MTB > LET K2 = SUM (C5)
MTB > LET K3 = K2 / K1 * 100

MTB > PRINT K1 K2 K3

K1      8861.00
K2      9708.00
K3      109.559

MTB > STOP
```

Figure 6.3

Case study

Macleod Engines

In the 1970s Macleod Engineering had a poor record of industrial relations. In the early 1980s it tried hard to overcome these and made a series of major changes in the way employees were involved in decision making and rewarded. Some of these changes included profit sharing, reducing the number of layers of management from 13 to 6, introducing more flexible working practices, improved communications between different grades of employees, and using the same basic pay rise for all grades of employees.

Part of these changes included an annual negotiation of a basic pay rise for all employees. This pay rise was proposed by a committee with representatives from all parts of the company, and which included a number of independent members. The purpose of the independent members was to give a disinterested view in a process which, by its nature, generates strong feelings from those involved. John Burns was one of these independent members. This meant that he could not work for Macleod Engines, be a shareholder or be connected in any other way with the company operations. John was an accountant working at the head office of a major building society, and his employers had no connection at all with Macleod or with engineering work.

John was preparing for the first meeting to set this year's annual wage rise. His aim was to make suggestions about a fair settlement and he was collecting initial ideas. He had already collected some data about Macleod for the past ten years, as shown in Table 6.3. Unfortunately, John did not know how well the company was doing at the moment, nor how well it was likely to do next year. He had to work out some initial ideas, based only on the limited data he had. How would you suggest he tackle this problem?

Table 6.3

Year	Average weekly earnings	Average hours worked	Company revenue £ million	Gross company profit (£000)	Index of industry wages	Retail Price Index
1	80.45	44	12.0	1210	85.5	84.5
2	104.32	43	15.1	1450	100.0	100.0
3	124.21	45	17.3	1650	115.6	113.5
4	140.56	46	20.8	1920	130.2	126.4
5	152.80	46	21.6	2150	141.1	139.8
6	182.90	45	22.3	2290	158.3	156.2
7	214.033	44	29.3	2950	168.1	168.8
8	242.75	43	34.5	2210	182.5	185.6
9	254.16	43	42.6	2890	190.7	198.9
10	264.34	42	44.5	3870	201.3	218.4

SECTION THREE

Solving business problems

This book is divided into five sections, each of which covers a different aspect of quantitative methods in business. The first section gave the background and context for the rest of the book. The second section discussed data collection and description. This is the third section, which looks at methods of solving specific types of business problem. The problems tackled here are essentially deterministic, which means that they do not involve any probabilities. The next section introduces probabilities and statistical methods. The final section shows how these ideas can be applied in probabilistic models.

There are six chapters in this section.

Chapter 7 describes some financial calculations, starting with break-even points and economies of scale. Then it looks at the changing value of money over time. These calculations are based on compound interest rates, with applications including investment decisions, project comparison, depreciation and mortgages.

Chapter 8 describes linear regression. This is a method of relating variables so that the value of one can be predicted from the value of another. The demand for a product may, for example, be predicted from the price charged. Linear regression may be used for forecasting, and this theme is continued in the following chapter.

Chapter 9 describes some standard methods of forecasting. It starts by looking at different types of forecast and classifies these in different ways. Perhaps the most common type of forecast is based on judgement. A more reliable method is projective forecasting, which examines past patterns of observations and projects these into the future.

Chapter 10 shows how some problems can be described as matrices. These provide a notation that is particularly useful for solving sets of simultaneous equations. They are also used in linear programming, which is described in the following chapter.

Chapter 11 describes linear programming. This is a method of solving problems of constrained optimization, where an optimal solution is needed for a problem, but there are constraints on the values that can be used. Linear programming is widely used in business and has proved particularly useful for planning decisions.

Chapter 12 looks at calculus. This is used to describe situations of change, and can again find optimal solutions to certain types of problem. The two main parts to calculus are differentiation and integration.

Calculations with money | **7** |

CHAPTER OUTLINE

Every organization is concerned with its finances. For this reason, many quantitative models have been developed to help managers make financial decisions. This chapter looks at some of the most important of these analyses. It starts by calculating a break-even point, which ensures that an organization makes enough products to cover its fixed costs.

The rest of the chapter looks at the value of money over time. Money invested earns interest, so its value increases over time. This has important consequences for many business decisions, such as the evaluation of alternative investments, project funding, depreciation allowances, and mortgage repayments.

After reading the chapter and doing the exercises you should be able to:

- calculate break-even points
- appreciate the reasons for economies of scale
- calculate investment values with simple and compound interest
- calculate present values and internal rates of return
- depreciate the value of assets
- use continuous discounting
- calculate payments for sinking funds, mortgages and annuities

7.1 | Financial measures

The performance of every organization is measured by its finances, whether it is a company wanting to make a profit, a charity wanting to collect and disperse as much money as possible, a hospital wanting to treat all patients at acceptable cost, a local authority wanting to provide a good service within a fixed budget, or a school wanting to provide education from limited resources. Sometimes the financial measure of performance is obvious, such as a company wanting to improve its return on investment. At other times the measure is less clear, as in a social club. In practice, however, the performance of a social club may be measured by the entertainment it provides, but this costs money that the club must generate, so its performance is also judged in financial terms.

Most decisions in finance are quantitative, and are based on some measure of money. There are, however, many ways in which these financial measures can be used to judge the performance of an organization. Perhaps the most common measure is **return on assets**, which is defined as the ratio of income to total assets. This can be expanded to link the profit margin and ratio of sales to assets:

$$\text{return on assets} = \frac{\text{income}}{\text{assets}} = \frac{\text{income}}{\text{sales}} \times \frac{\text{sales}}{\text{assets}}$$

From a purely financial point of view, the return on assets should be as high as possible, so 15% is considerably better than 10%. Other commonly used financial measures include:

- $\text{debt ratio} = \dfrac{\text{long-term debt} + \text{value of leases}}{\text{long-term debt} + \text{value of leases} + \text{shareholders' equity}}$

- $\text{current ratio} = \dfrac{\text{current assets}}{\text{current liabilities}}$

- $\text{quick (or acid-test) ratio} = \dfrac{\text{current assets} - \text{inventories}}{\text{current liabilities}}$

- $\text{net profit margin} = \dfrac{\text{earnings before interest and taxes} - \text{tax}}{\text{sales}}$

- $\text{price-earnings ratio} = \dfrac{\text{stock price}}{\text{earnings per share}}$

These, and many other measures, are useful in describing various aspects of the performance of an organization. In the rest of this chapter, we shall look at some useful financial measures, starting with break-even points and moving on to calculations for the value of money over time.

$\boxed{IN\ SUMMARY}$

Finances are important for all organizations. Many quantitative models have been developed to help with financial decisions. This chapter concentrates on break-even points and the changing value of money over time.

7.2 | Break-even point

7.2.1 | Making enough for a profit

Organizations usually aim at making a profit, where **profit** is defined as the difference between revenue and total cost:

$$\text{profit} = \text{revenue} - \text{total cost}$$

Most organizations offer a range of different products (both services and goods) and it is important to know how much profit or loss is made on each one. This can be found from break-even analyses. Although we shall describe these in terms of companies making products, they can be used in a variety of different circumstances.

When a company sells a product for a fixed price, the revenue is found from

$$\text{revenue} = \text{price per unit} \times \text{number of units sold}$$

$$= PN$$

where:

$$P = \text{price charged for unit}$$

$$N = \text{number of units sold}$$

The costs associated with the product are a little more awkward as some are fixed regardless of the number of units made, while others vary with the output. If, for example, a machine is leased to make a certain product, the cost of leasing may be fixed regardless of the number of units made, but the cost of raw materials will vary. Another example of this separation is the cost of running a car, which can be divided into a fixed cost (repayment of purchase loan, road tax, insurance, etc) and a variable cost for each mile travelled (petrol, oil, tyres, depreciation, etc). This leads to a general separation of costs into

$$\text{total cost} = \text{fixed cost} + \text{variable cost}$$

$$= \text{fixed cost} + (\text{cost per unit} \times \text{number of units made})$$

$$= F + CN$$

where:

F = fixed cost

C = cost per unit

N = number of units made

Comparing the total cost of producing N units of a product with the revenue generated from selling them leads to the important concept of a **break-even point**. This is the number of units that must be sold before a profit is made. Suppose a new product needs £200,000 spent on research, development, tooling and other preparations before production can start. During normal production each unit costs £20 to make and is sold for £30. The company will only start to make a profit when the original £200,000 has been recovered. The point when this occurs is the break-even point. In this example each unit sold contributes £30 − £20 = £10 to the company and therefore 200 000/10 = 20 000 units must be sold to cover the original investment. After this point the excess of revenue over expenditure is profit.

The break-even point is defined as the point where

$$\text{revenue} = \text{total cost}$$

$$\begin{array}{c}\text{price per} \\ \text{unit}\end{array} \times \begin{array}{c}\text{number of} \\ \text{units sold}\end{array} = \text{fixed cost} + \begin{array}{c}\text{cost per} \\ \text{unit}\end{array} \times \begin{array}{c}\text{number of} \\ \text{units made}\end{array}$$

Assuming that all production is sold, this gives:

$$PN = F + CN$$

so

$$N(P - C) = F$$

or

$$\text{Break-even point} = N = \frac{F}{P - C}$$

Both the revenue and total cost rise linearly with the number of units, so we can plot the relationships on the graph in Figure 7.1.

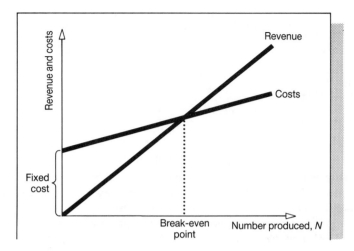

Figure 7.1   Illustrating the break-even point.

We can see from this graph that:

● if the number of units sold is higher than the break-even point, fixed costs are recovered and a profit is made:

$$\text{profit} = N(P - C) - F$$

The difference between price and unit cost, $P - C$, is called the **contribution to profit** of each unit sold.

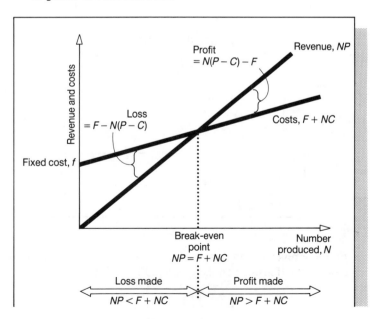

Figure 7.2   Profit and loss around the break-even point.

- if the number of units sold is equal to the break-even point, revenue equals total cost:

$$N(P - C) = F$$

- if the number of units sold is less than the break-even point, fixed costs are not recovered and a loss is made:

$$\text{loss} = F - N(P - C)$$

WORKED EXAMPLE 7.1

A company makes and sells 200 units of a product every week; associated fixed costs for buildings, machines and employees amount to £12,000 a week, while raw material and other variable costs amount to £50 a unit.

(a) What is the profit if the selling price is £130 a unit?

(b) What is the profit if the selling price is £80 a unit?

(c) What is the profit if the selling price is fixed at £80 but sales rise to 450 units a week?

Solution

(a) We know that:

$$N = 200 \text{ units} = \text{number of units sold each week}$$

$$F = £12,000 \text{ a week} = \text{fixed cost each week}$$

$$C = £50 \text{ a unit} = \text{variable cost per unit}$$

If the selling price P is set at £130, the break-even point is

$$N = \frac{F}{P - C} = \frac{12\,000}{130 - 50} = 150 \text{ units}$$

Actual sales are more than this, so the product makes a profit of

$$\text{profit} = N(P - C) - F = 200 \times (130 - 50) - 12\,000$$

$$= £4000 \text{ a week}$$

(b) If the selling price P is set at £80, the break-even point is

$$N = \frac{F}{P - C} = \frac{12\,000}{80 - 50} = 400 \text{ units}$$

Actual sales are less than this, so the product makes a loss of

$$\text{loss} = F - N(P - C) = 12\,000 - 200 \times (80 - 50)$$

$$= £6000 \text{ a week}$$

In these circumstances some thought should be given to reducing the costs of production, increasing the selling price or stopping production of the item.

(c) With the selling price set at £80 a unit, the break-even point is 400 units. If sales increase to 450 units a week a profit is made of

$$\text{profit} = N(P - C) - F = 450 \times (80 - 50) - 12\,000$$

$$= £1500 \text{ a week}$$

This shows that a profit can still be made with a low selling price provided sales are high enough.

WORKED EXAMPLE 7.2

A local electricity board offers two alternative prices for domestic consumers. The normal rate has standing charges of £18.20 a quarter, with each unit of electricity used costing £0.142. A special economy rate has standing charges of £22.70 a quarter, with each unit of electricity during the day costing £0.162, but each unit used during the night costing only £0.082. What consumption pattern would make it cheaper to use the economy rate?

Solution

If a consumer uses an average of D units per quarter during the day and N units a quarter during the night, their costs would be

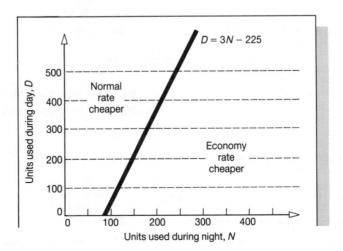

Figure 7.3 Cost of electricity for Worked Example 7.2.

normal rate: $18.20 + 0.142 \times (D + N)$

economy rate: $22.70 + 0.162 \times D + 0.082 \times N$

It would be cheaper to use the economy rate when

$$22.7 + 0.162 \times D + 0.082 \times N < 18.2 + 0.142 \times (D + N)$$

$$4.5 < 0.06 \times N - 0.02 \times D$$

$$D < 3 \times N - 225$$

If consumption during the day is less than three times consumption during the night minus 225 units, it is cheaper to use the economy rate; otherwise it is cheaper to use the standard rate. This is illustrated in Figure 7.3.

A break-even analysis is useful for the obvious purpose of seeing how many units must be sold to make a profit, but it also helps with other types of decision, such as the choice between buying or leasing equipment, ensuring adequate capacity when buying new equipment, whether to buy an item or make it within the company, or the choice of competitive tenders for services.

It is also worth mentioning the most common difficulty in calculating break-even points, which is assigning a reasonable proportion of overheads to the fixed cost of each product. This depends on the accounting conventions used within the organization. The problem is made worse if the product mix is constantly changing. Then accounting practices will allocate a changing amount of overheads to each product. In other words, the costs of making a particular product, and hence its profit, can change even though there has been no change in the product itself or the way it is made.

IN SUMMARY

Costs can be classified as either fixed or variable and revenue must cover both of these before a profit is made. The number of units at which revenue equals total cost is called the break-even point.

7.2.2 | Economies of scale

The break-even analysis shows one reason why organizations can get **economies of scale**, where the average unit cost declines as the number of units sold increases. We know that

total cost = fixed cost + variable cost

$$T = F + NC$$

Now the average cost per unit can be found by dividing the total cost by the number of units, N:

$$\text{average total cost per unit} = T/N = F/N + C$$

As N increases, the average cost per unit will decline, because the proportion of fixed cost to be recovered by each unit sold is reduced. If sales are increased to N' units the average cost per unit reduces to $F/N' + C$, which gives a reduction of

$$(F/N + C) - (F/N' - C) = \frac{F(N' - N)}{N \times N'}$$

as shown in Figure 7.4

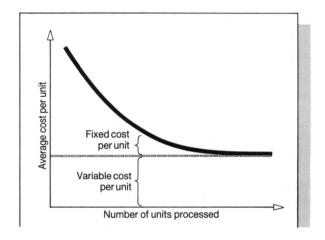

Figure 7.4 Changes in the average cost per unit with production quantity.

WORKED EXAMPLE 7.3

A restaurant serves 200 meals a day at an average price of £20. The variable cost of each meal is £10 and there are fixed costs of running the restaurant of £1750 a day.

(a) What profit is made by the restaurant?

(b) What is the average total cost of a meal?

(c) By how much would the average cost of a meal fall if the number served rose to 250 a day?

(d) How many meals should be served to make a profit of 10% of income?

Solution

(a) The break-even point is

$$N = \frac{F}{P-C} = \frac{1750}{20-10} = 175$$

Actual sales are above this so a profit is made:

$$\text{profit} = N(P-C) - F = 200 \times (20-10) - 1750$$

$$= £250 \text{ a day}$$

(b) The average total cost of a meal is

$$\text{average cost} = \text{total cost} / \text{number of meals}$$

$$= \frac{1750 + 200 \times 10}{200}$$

$$= £18.75 \text{ a meal}$$

(c) Serving 250 meals a day would give:

$$\text{average cost} = \frac{1750 + 250 \times 10}{250}$$

$$= £17 \text{ a meal}$$

(d) When the restaurant serves N meals its income is $20N$, so a profit of 10% of this is $2N$. But the profit is $N(P-C) - F$. This means we want

$$2N = N(P-C) - F$$

$$2N = N(20-10) - 1750$$

or

$$N = 218.75$$

If the restaurant serves 219 meals a day it will make a profit of 10% of income.

The distribution of fixed costs to more units is only one reason for economies of scale. In many situations economies of scale exist even when fixed costs are ignored. Then cost reductions occur because people become more familiar with the operations and take less time, machine operators become more practised, problems are sorted out, or disruptions are eliminated.

Economies of scale are often suggested as a reason for making facilities as large as possible. This is certainly the reason why, say, oil tankers have become increasingly large. In many circumstances, however, there are also **diseconomies of scale**. Here the advantage of reduced fixed cost per unit is more than offset by increased bureaucracy, difficulties of communication, more complex management hierarchies, increased costs of supervision, and perceived reduction in the importance of individuals. This usually leads to economies of scale up to an optimal size, and then diseconomies of scale, as illustrated in Figure 7.5.

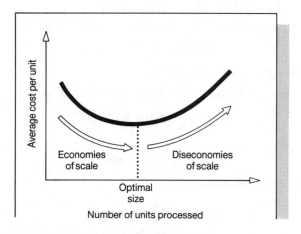

Figure 7.5   Economies and diseconomies of scale.

$\boxed{IN\ SUMMARY}$

Economies of scale may be achieved by spreading fixed costs over a larger number of units processed. There may also be diseconomies of scale.

Self-assessment questions

7.1   'Only companies aiming to make a profit are interested in financial analyses.' Is this statement true?

7.2   What is meant by the 'return on assets'?

7.3   What does the 'variable cost' vary with?

7.4   What is the 'break-even point'?

7.5   The break-even point for a product is calculated as 1500 units a week. If actual sales are 1200 units a week, what does this mean?

7.6   'Because of economies of scale it is always better to have a single large factory than a number of smaller ones.' Is this statement true or false?

7.3 | Value of money over time

When somebody wants to buy a house, there are a number of ways of paying for it. One option is to save enough money and then pay cash. Unfortunately, experience suggests that house prices rise faster than savings, so a more attractive option is to save a deposit and then borrow the remainder of the money as a mortgage. This is repaid over a long period, and even though the total repayments are two or three times the original amount borrowed, it is still considered a good investment.

Anyone borrowing money must pay the lender **interest**. The amount borrowed is called the **principal** and the time for which it is borrowed is called the **duration of the loan**. The amount of interest is usually quoted as an annual percentage of the principal, so a typical interest rate might be 15% a year.

7.3.1 | Interest rates

If money is put into a bank account it earns interest. If £1000 is left in an account offering interest of 10% a year it will attract $1000 \times 10/100 = £100$ interest at the end of the year. If the interest earned is removed from the account, the initial deposit will remain unchanged at £1000. This is the principle of **simple interest**, where interest is only paid on the initial deposit. Each year the same amount of interest is paid. If the original amount invested is A_0 and the interest rate is I, the amount of interest paid each year is $A_0 I$. Then after n periods:

- total interest paid:

$$\frac{A_0 In}{100}$$

- value of investment:

$$A_n = A_0 + \frac{A_0 In}{100} = A_0 \times \left(1 + \frac{In}{100}\right)$$

where: A_0 = original amount invested

A_n = amount of money after n periods

I = percentage interest rate earned each period

n = number of periods considered

It is generally easier to consider the interest rate as a decimal fraction or proportion, i, than as a percentage, I. This means that an interest rate of 10% is represented by $i = 0.1$, an interest rate of 15% by $i = 0.15$, and so on. Then with simple interest, the interest paid is:

$$\text{amount of principal} \times \text{interest rate} \times \text{duration} = A_0 in$$

and the value of A_0 after n periods is

For simple interest $\quad A_n = A_0 \times (1 + in)$

Simple interest assumes that no additional interest is paid on interest that has already been earned, even if it is left in the account. This would be a good deal for borrowers, but most lenders of money would find it unacceptable. For this reason, most loans are based on **compound interest**, which pays interest both on the original investment and on interest earned previously and left in the account.

If an amount of money A_0 is put into a bank account and is left untouched for a year earning interest at an annual rate i, at the end of the year there will be an amount A_1, where

$$A_1 = A_0 \times (1 + i)$$

If the amount A_1 is left untouched for a second year it will earn interest not only on the initial amount deposited, but also on the interest earned in the first year. This amounts to

$$A_2 = A_1 \times (1 + i)$$

or, substituting the value of A_1:

$$= [A_0 \times (1 + i)] \times (1 + i)$$

$$= A_0 \times (1 + i)^2$$

The amount of money will increase in this compound way, so that at the end of three years there will be $A_0 \times (1 + i)^3$ in the account, and at any time n years in the future the account will contain A_n, where:

For compound interest $\quad A_n = A_0 \times (1 + i)^n$

The variation in A_n over time is shown in Figure 7.6. This shows how an initial investment of £1 increases with a range of interest rates between 3% and 25%. Although interest rates are usually quoted as annual figures, any consistent units can be used, such as 1% a month or 0.03% a day.

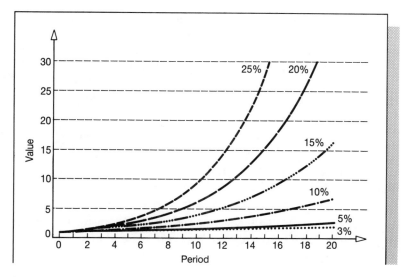

Figure 7.6 Increasing value with varying interest rates.

WORKED EXAMPLE 7.4

If £1000 is left in a bank account earning 5% compound interest a year, how much will be in the account at the end of 5 years? How much will there be at the end of 20 years?

Solution

We know that

$$A_0 = \text{£}1000$$

$$i = 0.05$$

With compound interest the amount in the account is

$$A_n = A_0 \times (1 + i)^n$$

At the end of five years there will be

$$A_5 = 1000 \times (1 + 0.05)^5 = 1000 \times 1.2763 = \text{£}1276$$

At the end of 20 years there will be:

$$A_{20} = 1000 \times (1 + 0.05)^{20} = 1000 \times 2.6533 = \text{£}2653$$

Interest rates are usually quoted annually, but there are several ways in which they can be calculated. To avoid confusion, there is often a legal requirement to quote an APR, or **annual percentage rate**, which is the true cost of borrowing. Suppose you borrow £100 with interest payable of 2% at the end of each month. A quick calculation would suggest that this is equal to $2 \times 12 = 24\%$ a year. In fact, this is the **notional interest rate**, but it is not the APR. We can demonstrate this as follows:

- Borrowing £100 at 24% APR would raise the debt to $100 \times (1 + 0.24) =$ £124 by the end of the year.

- Borrowing £100 at 2% a month, and using compound interest to calculate the debt at the end of 12 months gives

$$A_n = A_0 \times (1 + i)^n = 100 \times (1 + 0.02)^{12} = £126.82$$

This means that interest of £26.82 will be charged, giving an APR of 26.82%. The lesson from this is that comparisons of interest rates are a little more complicated than they seem, and need some care.

| *IN SUMMARY* |

The value of money varies over time, and a given amount at present can generate a larger amount in the future. Any money invested with compound interest increases over time, so that $A_n = A_0 \times (1 + i)^n$.

| 7.3.2 | Present value of money

In the last section we saw that an amount of money A_0 invested now will have a value of $A_0(1 + i)^n$ at a time n periods in the future. Turning this the other way round, we could say that an amount A_n, n periods in the future, has a present value of A_0, where

$$A_0 = \frac{A_n}{(1 + i)^n}$$

$$= A_n \times (1 + i)^{-n}$$

The process of calculating the present value of an amount in the future is called **discounting to present value** or finding the discounted value. This can be used to compare amounts of money that become available at different times.

WORKED EXAMPLE 7.5

A company is considering the introduction of a new product. There are two alternatives available. The returns from these are phased over many years, but they can be summarized as:

- product 1 returns £300,000 in five years' time
- product 2 returns £500,000 in ten years' time.

Which product should the company introduce if it uses a discounting rate of 20% a year for future revenues?

Solution

This problem needs a comparison of money generated at different times. The way to make such comparisons is to find the value of both amounts at the same time. Any convenient time can be used, but the obvious one is to reduce amounts to their present value.

Product 1

$$A_0 = A_n \times (1 + i)^{-n}$$
$$= 300\ 000 \times (1 + 0.2)^{-5}$$
$$= £120{,}563$$

Product 2

$$A_0 = A_n \times (1 + i)^{-n}$$
$$= 500{,}000 \times (1 + 0.2)^{-10}$$
$$= £80{,}753$$

Now we have the present values of both products, and the better one is clearly the one with the higher value. Based on this information, product 1 is the better alternative.

For many purposes the use of a straightforward interest rate for discounting would be an over-simplification, as it ignores the effects of inflation, opportunity costs, taxes and other factors. There is also the problem that interest rates vary over time. For these reasons it becomes difficult to set a discount rate that takes all influences into account. One step towards this would calculate a real interest rate from

real interest rate = actual interest rate − inflation

If the rate of inflation is low, the real interest rate is positive and the value of money invested will grow; if the rate of inflation is high, the real interest rate is negative and any money invested will decrease in value.

Discounting to present value gives a useful means of comparing amounts of money available at different times. This is particularly useful with large projects that have payments and incomes spread over varying time periods. Then we can discount all amounts to their present values, and subtracting the present value of all costs from the present value of all revenues gives a **net present value**:

$$\begin{array}{ccc} \text{net present} \\ \text{value} \end{array} = \begin{array}{ccc} \text{sum of discounted} \\ \text{revenues} \end{array} - \begin{array}{ccc} \text{sum of discounted} \\ \text{costs} \end{array}$$

If the net present value is negative, a project will make a loss and it should not be undertaken. If alternative projects each have a positive net present value, the best is the one with the highest net present value.

WORKED EXAMPLE 7.6

Three alternative projects have been proposed with initial costs and projected revenues (each in thousands of pounds) for the next five years as shown below:

| Project | Initial cost | Net revenue generated in each year | | | | |
		1	2	3	4	5
A	1000	500	400	300	200	100
B	1000	200	200	300	400	400
C	500	50	200	200	100	50

If the company has enough resources to start only one project, use a discounting rate of 10% to suggest the best.

Solution

Conventional accounting often takes an **average rate of return**, which is the average annual revenue as a percentage of initial investment. In this example the average rates of return are:

	Project A	Project B	Project C
Initial cost	1000	1000	500
Total revenue	1500	1500	600
Average annual revenue	300	300	120
Average rate of return	30%	30%	24%

Projects A and B have the same average rate of return, but project C offers a lower rate and would only be considered if the company could not afford the initial investment of £1 million, if 24% were considered an acceptable rate of return, or if some other factor made projects A and B less acceptable.

Looking in more detail at the money flows for projects A and B, we can see that the revenues vary over time and, in particular, A offers more in early years while B offers more in later years. To give a valid comparison between these we can transform all amounts to present values and compare the net present value of each project. So, for project A:

$$500 \text{ in year 1 has a present value of } 500/1.1^1 = 454.545$$

$$400 \text{ in year 2 has a present value of } 400/1.1^2 = 330.579$$

$$300 \text{ in year 3 has a present value of } 300/1.1^3 = 225.394$$

and so on. Such calculations are easily done by specialized computer software or a spreadsheet. Figure 7.7 shows a spreadsheet of results for this example.

	A	B	C	D	E	F	G	H
1			**Project A**		**Project B**		**Project C**	
2	**Year**	**Discount**	**revenue**	**Present**	**revenue**	**Present**	**revenue**	**Present**
3		**factor**		**value**		**value**		**value**
4	1	1.1	500.00	454.55	200.00	181.82	50.00	45.45
5	2	1.21	400.00	330.58	200.00	165.29	200.00	165.29
6	3	1.331	300.00	225.39	300.00	225.39	200.00	150.26
7	4	1.4641	200.00	136.60	400.00	273.21	100.00	68.30
8	5	1.61051	100.00	62.09	400.00	248.37	50.00	31.05
9	**Totals**		**1500.00**	**1209.21**	**1500.00**	**1094.08**	**600.00**	**460.35**

Figure 7.7 Net present values for Worked Example 7.6.

Subtracting the present values of costs (in this case the single initial project costs) from the present values of revenues gives net present values of:

	Project A	Project B	Project C
Present value of revenue	1209.21	1094.08	460.35
Present value of costs	1000.00	1000.00	500.00
Net present value	209.21	94.08	− 39.65

Project A has the highest net present value and should, all other things being equal, be the one adopted. Project C has a negative net present value, indicating a loss, and this alternative should clearly be avoided. One other consideration that might be important is that the revenues from A are declining, implying that the project has a limited life span of around five years, while revenues from project B are rising, implying a longer potential life. Considerations of this kind must be taken into account before any final decisions are made.

IN SUMMARY

Discounting amounts to present values allows direct comparison of revenues and payments made at different times. The difference between these is the net present value.

7.3.3 | Internal rate of return

To compare the three projects in Worked Example 7.6 we assumed that the discounting rate was fixed, and calculated three net present values. It is frequently difficult to find a suitable discounting rate that takes into account interest rates, inflation, taxes, opportunity costs, exchange rates, risk and everything else. An alternative would be to find the discounting rate that would lead to a specified net present value: in other words, keep the same net present value for each project and calculate three different discounting rates. The usual approach is to calculate the discounting rate that will lead to a net present value of zero; this is called the **internal rate of return**:

> The internal rate of return is the discounting rate
> that leads to a net present value of zero

Projects can be compared by calculating the internal rate of return (IRR) for each, and adopting the one with the highest value. We should add one note of caution here: if the internal rate of return is less than the current discounting rate, a project should not be started, as it will generate a net loss. In other words, we select the project with the highest IRR, provided this is greater than the current discounting rate.

One small difficulty with internal rates of return is that there is no straightforward formula for calculating them. This means that we have to try one of two approaches.

Draw a graph of project net present value against discount rate

This gives a straight-line graph, and the internal rate of return is the point where this has the value zero: in other words the point where it crosses the *x* axis. Figure 7.8 shows a graph of net present value against discounting rate for project B of Worked Example 7.6. The internal rate of return is just over 13%. This approach can be rather tedious, as it needs several calculations to draw the graph and even then the result may not be very accurate.

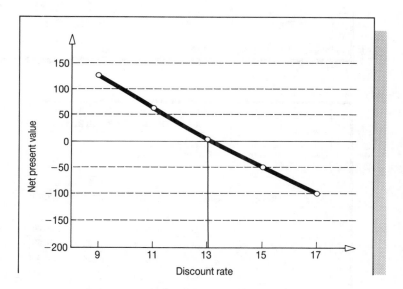

Figure 7.8 Graph to find the internal rate of return.

Use iterative calculations

In project B of Worked Example 7.6 a discounting rate of 10% gave a net present value of £94,080. If a discounting rate of 15% is used, the net present value is – £50,030. In other words, a discounting rate of 10% gives a positive net present value while a discounting rate of 15% gives a negative value, so the internal rate of return (which gives a net present value of zero) must lie between these two. By doing more calculations the internal rate of return can be found more accurately. A spreadsheet is a convenient way of doing such calculations and Figure 7.9 shows some results for project B. The first part of the diagram shows initial calculations to find an approximate value for the internal rate of return, while the second part homes in on a more accurate value. The actual internal rate of return is between 13.1% and 13.2%.

	A	B	C	D	E	F	G	H
1			CALCULATION OF INTERNAL RATE OF RETURN					
2								
3	Discount rate step		0.0200					
4								
5				-------	Discount	rates	-------	-------
6	Year	Revenue	Costs	0.0900	0.1100	0.1300	0.1500	0.1700
7								
8	0	0	1000	-1000.00	-1000.00	-1000.00	-1000.00	-1000.00
9	1	200	0	183.49	180.18	176.99	173.91	170.94
10	2	200	0	168.34	162.32	156.63	151.23	146.10
11	3	300	0	231.66	219.36	207.92	197.25	187.31
12	4	400	0	283.37	263.49	245.33	228.70	213.46
13	5	400	0	259.97	237.38	217.10	198.87	182.44
14	Totals	1500	1000	126.82	62.74	3.97	-50.03	-99.74

(a)

	A	B	C	D	E	F	G	H
1			CALCULATION OF INTERNAL RATE OF RETURN					
2								
3	Discount rate step		0.0010					
4								
5				-------	Discount	rates	-------	-------
6	Year	Revenue	Costs	0.1300	0.1310	0.1320	0.1330	0.1340
7								
8	0	0	1000	-1000.00	-1000.00	-1000.00	-1000.00	-1000.00
9	1	200	0	176.99	176.83	176.68	176.52	176.37
10	2	200	0	156.63	156.35	156.08	155.80	155.53
11	3	300	0	207.92	207.36	206.81	206.27	205.72
12	4	400	0	245.33	244.46	243.60	242.74	241.88
13	5	400	0	217.10	216.15	215.19	214.24	213.30
14	Totals	1500	1000	3.97	1.16	-1.64	-4.42	-7.20

(b)

Figure 7.9 Spreadsheet calculations for the internal rate of return:
(a) approximate values; (b) homing in on more accurate values.

WORKED EXAMPLE 7.7

What is the internal rate of return for an investment that gives the following net cash flow?

Year	0	1	2	3	4	5	6	7	8
Net cash flow	− 2000	− 5000	− 200	800	1800	1600	1500	200	100

Solution

To find the internal rate of return we calculate the net present value for a number of discounting rates until we get a result that is close to zero. Then we refine the discounting rate until the value is sufficiently accurate. In this case the internal rate of return is 20% as shown in Table 7.1 (the slightly negative value is caused by rounding).

Table 7.1

Year	Net cash flow	Discounting factor	Discounted value
0	– 2000	1.0	– 2000.00
1	– 500	1.2	– 416.67
2	– 200	1.44	– 138.89
3	800	1.728	462.96
4	1800	2.074	868.06
5	1600	2.488	643.00
6	1500	2.986	502.35
7	200	3.583	55.82
8	100	4.300	23.26
Total	3300		– 0.11

IN SUMMARY

The internal rate of return is the discounting rate that gives a net present value of zero. The best investment is the one with the highest internal rate of return.

| 7.3.4 | Depreciation

When people buy a car, they expect to drive it for a few years and then replace it. This is because maintenance and repair costs rise, there are more frequent breakdowns, new cars are more efficient and comfortable, and so on. The implication is that the value of a car decreases as it gets older. Similarly, when a company buys a piece of equipment, it is used for some period and then replaced. One problem for companies, however, is that equipment forms part of the assets, and must have an accurate valuation at any time. The value will obviously reduce over time, and the allowance for this is known as **depreciation.**

Most organizations **write down** the value of their assets each year. This means that they reduce the book value that they put on assets. Depreciation is then recorded as a loss that can be counted against profits, so the company can replace equipment when necessary.

There are several ways of calculating depreciation, but the two most widely used are:

- straight-line method
- reducing-balance method

Both of these assume that equipment is bought, operated for its expected life, and then sold for a scrap value. This scrap value would normally be the resale value and does not imply that the equipment is actually scrapped. Perhaps a better term would be residual value.

Straight-line method

This reduces the equipment's value by the same amount every year. Then:

$$\text{annual depreciation} = \frac{\text{cost of equipment} - \text{scrap value}}{\text{estimated life of equipment}}$$

A machine costing £20,000 with an estimated scrap value of £5000 and a useful life of 10 years would have annual depreciation of:

$$\text{annual depreciation} = \frac{20\,000 - 5000}{10} = £1500$$

Straight-line depreciation is easy to calculate, but it does not reflect actual values. Most equipment will lose a lot of value in the first year of operation, and will actually be worth less than its depreciated value.

Reducing-balance method

In the reducing-balance method, a fixed percentage of the value of equipment is written off each year. Typically, a piece of equipment has its book value reduced by 20% a year. This has the benefit of giving more depreciation in the first few years, and more accurately reflecting the real value of equipment.

With the reducing-balance method, the calculation of an asset's value is a simple extension of compound interest. We know that an amount A_0 which increases at a fixed percentage, i, in each period has a value after n periods of

$$A_n = A_0 \times (1 + i)^n$$

If the amount is decreasing at a fixed percentage, as it does with depreciation, we simply subtract i instead of adding it. Then for a depreciation rate of i, equipment whose cost is A_0 has a depreciated value after n periods of

$$A_n = A_0 \times (1 - i)^n$$

WORKED EXAMPLE 7.8

A company buys an asset for £10,000 and now has to consider its depreciation.

(a) Use the straight-line method to find the annual depreciation if the asset has an expected life of five years and a scrap value of £1000.

(b) If the reducing-balance method is used with a depreciation rate of 30%, what is the value of the asset after five years?

(c) With the reducing-balance method, what depreciation rate would reduce an asset's value to £2000 after three years?

Solution

(a) For straight-line depreciation we know that

$$\text{annual depreciation} = \frac{\text{cost of equipment} - \text{scrap value}}{\text{estimated life of equipment}}$$

so

$$\text{annual depreciation} = \frac{10\,000 - 1000}{5} = £1800$$

(b) For reducing-balance depreciation:

$$A_n = A_0 \times (1 - i)^n$$

or

$$A_5 = 10\,000 \times (1 - 0.3)^5 = £1681$$

① Year = Price × $\left(1 - \dfrac{\%}{\text{Dep}^a}\right)^{\text{next Yrs.}}$

② Year = new price × $\left(1 - \dfrac{\%}{\text{Dep}}\right)^{\text{no ot Yrs.}}$

(c) We want A_n to be £2000 when n is 3, so

$$A_n = A_0 \times (1 - i)^n$$

or

$$2000 = 10\,000 \times (1 - i)^3$$

$$0.2 = (1 - i)^3$$

$$0.585 = 1 - i$$

or

$$i = 0.415$$

giving a depreciation rate of 41.5%.

| *IN SUMMARY* |

The value of equipment decreases with its age. There are several methods for calculating depreciated values, with the straight-line and reducing-balance methods being widely used.

7.3.5 | Continuous discounting

If interest is paid frequently, say every week or even every day, the calculation of compound interest becomes rather messy as n becomes large. If we pay interest daily, for example, the value in a year's time becomes

$$A_n = A_0 \times (1 + i)^{365}$$

In these circumstances we can use an approximation to make the arithmetic easier. This is based on the exponential constant, e, which has a value of 2.71828..., and the standard result that if n is large, the discrete function $(1 + i)^n$ can be approximated by the continuous function e^{in} . This is the basis of continuous discounting.

The calculations for continuous discounting are exactly the same as for discrete discounting except that $(1 + i)^n$ is replaced by e^{in}, so

$$A_n = A_0 \times (1 + i)^n$$

becomes

$$A_n = A_0 \times e^{in}$$

WORKED EXAMPLE 7.9

How much will an initial investment of £1000 earning interest of 8% a year be worth at the end of 20 years?

Solution

Using discrete compounding:

$$A_{20} = A_0 \times (1 + i)^{20}$$

$$= 1000 \times 1.08^{20}$$

$$= £4661$$

Using continuous compounding:

$$A_{20} = A_0 \times e^{in}$$

$$= 1000 \times e^{(0.08 \times 20)}$$

$$= £4953$$

These answers are slightly different and the 'correct' one will depend on whether interest is actually calculated annually or is compounded more frequently. Generally the latter is true and continuous compounding will be more reliable.

WORKED EXAMPLE 7.10

Part of a major project is to be done by subcontractors. Two firms submit tenders for the work with projected cash flows as follows (with negative figures representing payments and positive figures revenues):

	Year 1	Year 2	Year 3
Firm A	– 50 000	20 000	60 000
Firm B	– 80 000	10 000	100 000

	A	B	C	D	E	F
1			Firm A		Firm B	
2	Year	Discount	Revenue	Present	Revenue	Present
3		factor		value		value
4	1	1.08	-50000	-46296.3	-80000	-74074.07
5	2	1.1664	20000	17146.78	10000	8573.388
6	3	1.259712	60000	47629.93	100000	79383.22
7	Totals		30000	18480.41	30000	13882.54

(a)

	A	B	C	D	E	F
1			Firm A		Firm B	
2	Year	Discount	Revenue	Present	Revenue	Present
3		factor		value		value
4	1	1.083287	-50000	-46155.82	-80000	-73849.31
5	2	1.173511	20000	17042.88	10000	8521.438
6	3	1.271249	60000	47197.67	100000	78662.79
7	Totals		30000	18084.73	30000	13334.92
8						
9						
10						

(b)

Figure 7.10 Comparing (a) discrete discounting and (b) continuous discounting for Worked Example 7.10.

If inflation and opportunity costs suggest a discounting rate of 8% a year, which firm should get the contract?

Solution

These two tenders can be compared by calculating the net present value of each. We shall start by using discrete discounting and follow this by continuous discounting to see if there is much difference. The results are shown in the spreadsheet in Figure 7.10, where:

- with discrete discounting Firm A gives a better net present value of £18,480.
- with continuous discounting Firm A again gives a better net present value of £18,085.

These results are very similar and show that the two approaches give comparable results.

IN SUMMARY

When interest is calculated frequently it may be more convenient to use continuous rather than discrete discounting.

Self-assessment questions

7.7 Is £1000 now worth
   (a) more than £1000 in five years' time
   (b) less than £1000 in five years' time
   (c) the same as £1000 in five years' time?

7.8 Is an interest rate of 12% a year the same as 1% a month?

7.9 How could you compare the net benefits of two projects, one of which lasts for five years and the other for seven years?

7.10 What is a discounting rate?

7.11 What is the difference between the straight-line and the reducing-balance methods of calculating depreciation?

7.12 What is meant by 'continuous discounting'?

7.4 | Mortgages, annuities and sinking funds

In the last section we saw how the value of money changed over time, and in particular how it could attract interest and grow at a compound rate. In this section we shall look at an extension to this, where regular savings are also added. This happens in a variety of circumstances including mortgages, annuities and sinking funds.

Suppose we have an initial amount to invest, A_0, which earns interest at a rate i, and we add an additional investment F at the end of each period. It can be shown that the amount invested after n periods is

$$A_n = A_0 \times (1 + i)^n + \frac{F \times (1 + i)^n - F}{i}$$

The first part of this equation shows the income generated by the original investment, while the second part shows the amount accumulated by regular payments. If you are interested, the derivation of this result is given at the end of the chapter.

WORKED EXAMPLE 7.11

An investor puts £1000 into a building society account that earns 10% interest a year. If the investor adds an additional £500 at the end of each year, how much will there be in the account at the end of five years?

Solution

The variables we are given are:

$$A_0 = £1000$$

$$i = 0.1$$

$$F = £500$$

$$n = 5$$

and we want the value of A_5, which can be found from substitution as

$$A_n = A_0 \times (1 + i)^n + \frac{F \times (1 + i)^n - F}{i}$$

so

$$A_5 = 1000 \times 1.1^5 + \frac{500 \times 1.1^5 - 500}{0.1} = \pounds4663$$

This kind of calculation is used by businesses that want to set aside regular payments to accumulate a certain amount of money at the end of some period. This is called a **sinking fund** and is typically set up to allow for replacement of equipment or vehicles. Sinking funds usually do not have an initial payment (so $A_0 = 0$), but have equal payments in every period.

WORKED EXAMPLE 7.12

How much should be invested each year to ensure that a sinking fund has £20,000 at the end of ten years with expected interest rates of 15%?

Solution

The variables are:

$$A_n = \pounds20{,}000$$

$$A_0 = \pounds0$$

$$i = 0.15$$

$$n = 10$$

$$A_n = A_0 \times (1 + i)^n + \frac{F \times (1 + i)^n - F}{i}$$

So substitution gives:

$$20\,000 = 0 + \frac{F \times (1 + 0.15)^{10} - F}{0.15}$$

$$3000 = F \times 4.046 - F$$

or

$$F = \pounds985.04$$

The company should put £985.04 into the fund each year.

Many people have an aversion to debts, but although they are usually expensive they can have benefits. Given a choice between £100 now or £100 in a year's time we should take the money now because it has a higher value. This reasoning can be used as a justification for some debts: they allow us to receive money now and then make repayments in the future using money that has a lower value. From a financial point of view, whether debts are beneficial or not depends on the purpose to which the money is being put, real interest rates, the inflation rate, and so on. The most widely used purpose of private borrowing is to buy a house. This is usually financed by a mortgage, which uses the kind of regular payments described above. The initial investment A_0 is then negative, and the investment after n periods must be zero, signifying that the debt has been repaid.

WORKED EXAMPLE 7.13

A mortgage of £30,000 is borrowed over 25 years at 12% interest. This loan is repaid by regular instalments at the end of every year. How much should each instalment be?

Solution

We know that:

$$A_0 = -\pounds30,000$$

$$A_{25} = \pounds0$$

$$i = 0.12$$

$$n = 25$$

and want to find F. Substitution gives:

$$A_n = A_0 \times (1 + i)^n + \frac{F \times (1 + i)^n - F}{i}$$

$$0 = -30\,000 \times 1.12^{25} + \frac{F \times 1.12^{25} - F}{0.12}$$

Then

$$30\,000 \times 17 \times 0.12 = F \times 17 - F$$

or

$$F = \pounds3825$$

After 25 payments of £3825 the original debt will be repaid. Notice that the total payment here is £95,625. It is quite common for total mortgage repayments to be several times the original loan, especially when interest rates are high.

An annuity is the reverse of a mortgage. In other words, someone who has a lump sum can invest it and in return be given regular payments for some period in the future. This scheme is usually run by finance companies and appeals to retired people who are able to convert their savings into a regular income.

WORKED EXAMPLE 7.14

If interest rates are 12%, how much would an annuity cost that gave £10,000 a year for the next 10 years?

Solution

If we take the position of the person paying the annuity, this can be seen in the same way as a mortgage, with:

$$A_n = 0$$

$$F = £10,000$$

$$n = 10$$

$$i = 0.12$$

and we want to find A_0.

Now

$$A_n = A_0 \times (1 + i)^n + \frac{F \times (1 + i)^n - F}{i}$$

so

$$0 = A_0 \times (1 + 0.12)^{10} + \frac{10\,000 \times (1 + 0.12)^{10} - 10\,000}{0.12}$$

$$= A_0 \times 3.11 + 175\,487.35$$

or

$$A_0 = -£56,502$$

The negative sign here signifies that the original payment is made to the borrower.

IN SUMMARY

The value of an investment with regular additional payments is given by

$$A_n = A_0(1 + i)^n + \frac{F(1 + i)^n - F}{i}$$

This equation has several applications in finance.

Self-assessment questions

7.13 What is a sinking fund?

7.14 How would you calculate the payment worth making for an annuity?

7.15 'The value of i is always the current interest rate.' Is this statement true?

CHAPTER REVIEW

Every organization is concerned with its finances. Many quantitative models are available to help with these, and this chapter has described some of the most important. In particular it described:

● calculation of break-even points and the reason for economies of scale

● the value of money over time with simple and compound interest

● discounting to present values and internal rates of return

● depreciation of assets

● continuous discounting

● payments of sinking funds, mortgages and annuities

Problems

7.1 A firm of taxi operators has an average fixed cost of £4500 a year for each car. Each kilometre driven costs 20 pence with fares averaging 30 pence. How many kilometres a year does each car need to travel before making a profit? Last year each car drove 160 000 kilometres. What were the total and net incomes?

7.2 An airline is considering a new service between Aberdeen and Calgary. Its existing aeroplanes, each of which has a capacity of 240 passengers, could be used for one flight a week with fixed costs of £30,000 and variable costs amounting to 50% of ticket price. If the airline plans to sell tickets at £200 each, how many passengers will be needed to break even on the proposed route? Does this seem a reasonable number

7.3 A company is planning the introduction of a new product. It must select one product from three available and has estimated the following data:

	Product A	Product B	Product C
Annual sales	600	900	1200
Unit cost	680	900	1200
Fixed cost	200 000	350 000	500 000
Product life	3 years	5 years	8 years
Selling price	760	1000	1290

Which product would you recommend?

7.4 How much will an initial investment of £1000 earning interest of 8% a year be worth at the end of 20 years?

7.5 Several years ago a couple bought an endowment insurance policy that has recently matured. They have the option of receiving £20,000 now or £40,000 in ten years' time. Because they have retired and pay no income tax, they could invest the money with a real interest rate expected to remain at 10% a year for the foreseeable future. Which option should they take?

7.6 Given the cash flows for three projects shown in Table 7.2, calculate the net present values using a discounting rate of 12% a year.

Table 7.2

	Project A		Project B		Project C	
Year	Income	Expenditure	Income	Expenditure	Income	Expenditure
0	0	18 000	0	24 000	0	21 000
1	2 500	0	2 000	10 000	0	12 000
2	13 500	6 000	10 000	6 000	20 000	5 000
3	18 000	0	20 000	2 000	20 000	1 000
4	6 000	2 000	30 000	2 000	30 000	0
5	1 000	0	30 000	2 000	30 000	0

7.7 What is the internal rate of return for the data in problem 7.6?

7.8 What is the internal rate of return for a product that gives the following net cash flow?

Year	1	2	3	4	5	6	7	8	9
Net cash flow	− 6000	− 1500	− 500	600	1800	2000	1400	300	100

7.9 A company buys new vehicles for £15,000. If these have an expected life of six years, and a scrap value of £2000, use a straight-line method to find annual depreciation. If the reducing-balance method is used with a depreciation rate of 25%, what is the value of the vehicles after six years? What depreciation rate would be needed to reduce the vehicles' value to £1000 after four years?

7.10 Use continuous discounting on the data for problem 7.6 to see if there is much difference. Which of the two answers is more reliable?

7.11 A company makes fixed annual payments to a sinking fund to replace equipment in five years' time. The equipment is valued at £100,000 and interest rates are 12%. How much should each payment be?

7.12 How much are monthly payments on a mortgage of £25,000 taken out for 25 years at an interest rate of 1% a month?

7.13 A couple are about to buy a new car. They have decided on the model, which costs £12,000. The supplier gives them an option of either a five-year car loan at a reduced APR of 7%, or £1250 in cash and a five-year car loan with an APR of 10%. Which choice is the better? If the couple depreciate the car at 20% a year, what will its value be in ten years' time?

Computer exercises

7.1 The fixed cost of a product is £100,000 and the variable cost is £50. If the product sells for £100, use a spreadsheet to calculate the break-even point. Use the figures to draw a graph of the profit and loss. Extend the spreadsheet to deal with other values.

7.2 Figure 7.11 shows the printout from a package that calculates the net present value for a project, taking into account a number of features such as depreciation and tax. The investment, revenue and expenses are given for each year. Make sure you understand what is happening in this printout. See what packages you have to do financial calculations. Use them to confirm the results given.

7.3 Figure 7.12 shows (a) a spreadsheet of results for calculating the internal rate of return and (b) the results drawn on a graph. Look at the spreadsheet and see what improvements you can make. Then design a spreadsheet for

Financial Analysis – Net Present Value
Straight Line Depreciation

Data Entered

Number of time periods	:	4
Initial investment	:	20000
Estimated salvage value	:	2000
Tax rate	:	0.3000
Discount rate	:	0.2000
Investment threshold	:	0

Financial Analysis – Net Present Value
Straight Line Depreciation

Solution

	Year0	Year1	Year2	Year3	Year4
Investment	20000	10000	2000	0	0
Revenue	0	5000	10000	20000	20000
Expenses	0	5000	5000	5000	5000
Before tax cash flow	0	0	5000	15000	15000
Depreciation	0	4500	7833.3330	8833.3330	8833.3330
Taxable cash flow	0	-4500	-7333.3330	-1166.6660	5000.0010
Taxes	0	0	0	0	1500.0004
After tax cash flow	0	0	5000	15000	13500
PV cash flow	0	0	3472.2222	8680.5547	6510.4160

Salvage

Investment	0
Revenue	2000
Expenses	0
Before tax cash flow	2000
Depreciation	0
Taxable cash flow	2000
Taxes	0
After tax cash flow	2000
PV cash flow	964.5062

Financial Summary

NPV of total investment	:	29722.2227
Total PV cash flows	:	19627.6992
Investment threshold	:	0
Discount rate	:	0.2000
Project NVP	:	-10094.5225

Conclusion = DO NOT FUND PROJECT

Figure 7.11 A package for calculating net present value.

your improved version. Use this with a graphics package to draw a graph of results and confirm the results in Figure 7.12.

7.4 Imagine that you are about to take out a mortgage. Find the current interest rates quoted by a number of financial institutions. Use a suitable program to calculate the monthly payments. Hence find the payments, interest, principal repaid and debt outstanding at the end of each month. Prepare a report of your findings.

	A	B	C	D	E	F	G	H
1			CALCULATION OF INTERNAL RATE OF RETURN					
2								
3	Discount rate step		0.001					
4								
5				-------	Discount	rates	-------	-------
6	Year	Revenue	Costs	0.137	0.138	0.139	0.14	0.141
7								
8	0	0	5000	-4397.54	-4393.67	-4389.82	-4385.96	-4382.12
9	1	1000	3000	-1759.01	-1757.47	-1755.93	-1754.39	-1752.85
10	2	2000	1000	773.5334	772.1745	770.8192	769.4675	768.1194
11	3	4000	1000	2040.985	2035.609	2030.253	2024.915	2019.595
12	4	4000	1000	1795.062	1788.761	1782.487	1776.241	1770.022
13	5	4000	1000	1578.77	1571.846	1564.958	1558.106	1551.29
14	Totals	15000	12000	31.7983	17.24804	2.774764	-11.622	-25.9426

(a)

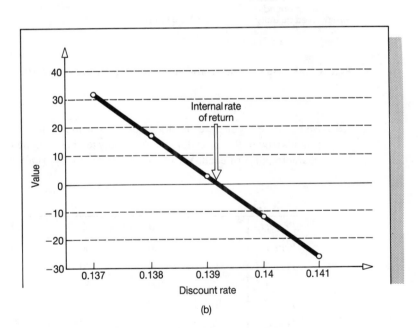

(b)

Figure 7.12   Spreadsheet for calculating the internal rate of return:
(a) table of results;   (b) graph of results.

7.5 Figure 7.13 shows the results from a specialized program that does break-even analyses. Use an appropriate program to check these results.

Program: Break-even analysis

Problem title: Break-even

Input data

Total fixed cost :	120000.00
Unit variable cost :	45.00
Unit selling price :	65.00
Expected sales units :	0.00

Program output

Total fixed cost :	120000.00
Unit variable cost :	45.00
Unit selling price :	65.00
Expected sales units :	Unknown

Break-even pounds :	390000.00
Break-even quantity :	6000.00

End of output

Figure 7.13 Output from a program calculating break-even values.

7.6 Five projects generate the incomes shown in Table 7.3 (in thousands of pounds) over the next ten years. Analyse these figures and discuss the characteristics of each. Write a well-presented report about your findings.

Table 7.3

Project	A	B	C	D	E
Year 1	− 120	− 200	− 60	0	− 500
Year 2	− 60	0	30	10	− 200
Year 3	5	100	30	20	− 100
Year 4	30	80	30	30	50
Year 5	45	60	30	30	100
Year 6	55	50	− 40	20	200
Year 7	65	40	30	− 100	300
Year 8	65	40	30	50	350
Year 9	60	35	30	40	400
Year 10	50	35	30	30	450

Case study

Mrs Hamilton's retirement saving

Mrs Hamilton has just had her 55th birthday. For many years she has been investing in endowment insurance policies and some of these have now matured to give her a lump sum of around £50,000. She is self-employed and plans to continue working until she is 65. This means that Mrs Hamilton is looking for an investment that will increase in value over the next ten years.

Mrs Hamilton went to her bank manager for some advice. When she suggested that she could add an additional £2000 a year to her savings the manager did some sums, and made several suggestions:

- a Saving Account that would give a return of 7.5% a year
- a Gold Account for the fixed sum. This would give her a return of 9% but would leave the money tied up for at least a year. The additional savings could go into a Saving Account
- a Personal Accumulator that gives 5% interest on a minimum of £30,000, but 15% on any additional savings that are made

Mrs Hamilton also visited a building society manager who gave her similar advice, but gave an additional option: 'The most secure investment is to put the money in our Inflation Fighter. This has an interest rate that is linked to the Retail Price Index, and is guaranteed to give a return that is 1% above inflation.'

The building society manager also discussed the possibility of buying a house as an investment: 'The housing market has been very unsettled lately. If you take a long-term view, house prices have risen by an average of 10% to 15% a year for the past decade. During this time inflation has averaged 6.5%, so houses have been a good investment. They can also generate income from rent. Usually you could expect to get about 0.5% of the value of the house a month. Something like a quarter of this is needed for repairs and maintenance. Some of my customers take out a mortgage with interest of 11% a year to add to their savings and buy a bigger house.'

Mrs Hamilton went home and did some thinking. She could calculate how much each of the investments would be worth at the end of ten years. Perhaps, though, she should decide how much she wants to have when she retires, and add to her savings to achieve this amount. She thought that £150,000 would be enough, but perhaps she should aim for a larger amount. She wants a reasonable income over the next 20 years, even when taking inflation into account. She thought that perhaps an annuity would suit her.

Mrs Hamilton has to decide what to do with her savings. She would like some advice on the schemes she has considered, and any other alternatives.

Derivation 7.1: Value of additional payments

Suppose we invest an initial amount A_0, and then add to this investment a fixed amount F at the end of every period. At the end of the first period we have interest on A_0 plus an additional investment of F, giving a total of A_1:

$$A_1 = A_0(1 + i) + F$$

At the end of the second period we have interest on A_1 and an additional investment of F, giving a total of A_2:

$$A_2 = A_0(1 + i)^2 + F(1 + i) + F$$

Similarly, at the end of three periods we have a total of A_3 invested:

$$A_3 = A_0(1 + i)^3 + F(1 + i)^2 + F(1 + i) + F$$

and after n periods:

$$A_n = A_0(1 + i)^n + F(1 + i)^{n-1} + F(1 + i)^{n-2} + F(1 + i)^{n-3} \ldots + F$$

The multipliers of F form a geometric series, and we saw in Chapter 2 that the sum of a geometric series is:

$$\frac{a(r^n - 1)}{(r - 1)}$$

Here $a = 1$ and $r = (1 + i)$, so substitution gives

$$A_n = A_0(1 + i)^n + \frac{F[(1 + i)^n - 1]}{(1 + i) - 1}$$

$$= A_0 \times (1 + i)^n + \frac{F \times [(1 + i)^n - 1]}{i}$$

$$= A_0 \times (1 + i)^n + \frac{F \times (1 + i)^n - F}{i}$$

Relating variables by regression | 8 |

CHAPTER OUTLINE

Chapter 2 showed how the relationship between two variables can be plotted as a graph. In this chapter we look in more detail at such relationships and their use in business. The chapter begins by suggesting that observations often follow an underlying pattern, but with some unpredictable variations. The size of these variations can be used to measure the strength of a relationship.

The chapter then describes linear regression, which draws the straight line of best fit through a set of data. The closeness of this fit is measured by the coefficients of determination and correlation.

After reading this chapter and doing the exercises you should be able to:

- appreciate the need for measuring the strength of a relationship
- calculate mean errors, mean absolute deviations and mean squared errors
- find the straight line of best fit using linear regression
- use linear regression to forecast values
- calculate coefficients of determination and correlation for cardinal data
- calculate Spearman's coefficient of rank correlation
- appreciate the use of computers in regression

247

8.1 | Measuring relationships

8.1.1 | Noise and errors

Chapter 2 showed how the relationship between two variables can be plotted as a graph. At the time we said that any relationship will be shown clearly on a graph, but we made no attempt to **measure** the strength of a relationship. In this chapter we are going to develop a measure for this. We shall approach this in two stages:

● find the best relationship (which is called **regression**)
● find how well this relationship fits the data

Both these calculations are based on the errors that are found in actual observations. We have already discussed these in connection with data spread in Chapter 5, so this section starts by revising some important results.

Suppose we have collected data about the consumption of electricity in a region and the corresponding average daily temperature. We might get the data shown below (where some consistent units are used):

Observation	1	2	3	4	5	6
Temperature	5	7	10	12	15	17
Electricity	15	19	25	29	35	39

Generally, if you have a set of data like this, the first step in analysing it is to draw a graph. A simple scatter diagram shows any underlying pattern, and in this case there is a linear relationship, as shown in Figure 8.1. This shows a

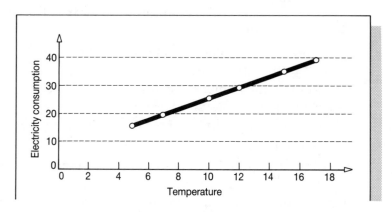

Figure 8.1 Graph of electricity consumption against temperature.

perfect relationship, with the dependent variable being determined exactly by the independent variable. To be precise:

consumption of electricity = 2 × average temperature + 5

In practice, the relationship between variables will rarely be this exact, and there is usually some fluctuation about expected values. It would, for example, be more common to find figures relating electricity consumption to average daily temperature like the following:

Observation	1	2	3	4	5	6
Temperature	5	7	10	12	15	17
Electricity	17	21	24	26	32	40

There is still a clear linear relationship, but superimposed on this underlying pattern is a random variation called **noise.** Then the relationship becomes:

> actual value = underlying pattern + random noise

There might be even more noise, with observations like the following:

Observation	1	2	3	4	5	6
Temperature	5	7	10	12	15	17
Electricity	20	25	23	22	40	35

These three sets of figures are plotted in Figure 8.2.

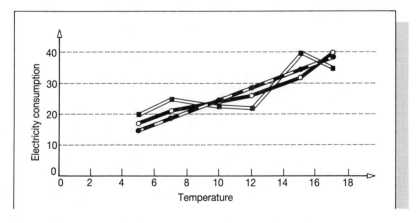

Figure 8.2   Graphs of electricity consumption with more noise.

The amount of random noise determines how strong a relationship is:

- If there is no noise, as in the first set of figures above, the relationship is perfect.
- If there is some noise, the relationship is weaker.
- If there is a lot of noise, the relationship becomes so weak that it hardly exists.

What we need is a way of measuring the noise and hence the strength of the relationship.

The noise in an observation can be viewed as an error, which is the difference between the value expected from the relationship and the actual value:

> E_i = actual value of observation i
>   – value predicted from relationship

Now we need to combine all the errors from separate observations into a single measure for the strength of the relationship. Building on the results in Chapter 5, we could combine the errors into:

- mean error
- mean absolute deviation
- mean squared error

These are described again in the following section.

IN SUMMARY

In practice there is usually some noise in the relationship between two variables. The amount of noise determines the strength of a relationship. We need some measure of the strength, and this can be based on individual errors.

8.1.2 | Combining individual errors

The following discussion is based on a linear relationship, but this is just for convenience and the same principles apply to any other type.

Suppose two variables have a linear relationship, but there is superimposed noise. A graph of observations will show variations about a straight line, as shown in Figure 8.3. Each observation has an error, which is the vertical distance from the line. In other words, the error in observation i is defined as E_i, where:

E_i = actual value of y_i – value of y_i suggested by underlying relationship

$$= y_i - \hat{y}_i$$

where

y_i = actual value

$\hat{y}_i$ (which is pronounced 'y hat') = value suggested by the underlying relationship

This error is often called the **residual.** Repeating the calculation for each observation allows us to find a mean error, where:

$$\text{Mean error} = \frac{\sum E_i}{n} = \frac{\sum (y_i - \hat{y}_i)}{n}$$

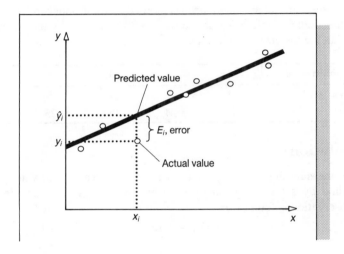

Figure 8.3   Showing noise as an error in y_i.

The mean error has a major drawback, which we have already met when discussing the variance. It allows positive and negative errors to cancel each other, and data with very large errors can have zero mean error. We really need an alternative measure, and the two most common ones take the absolute values of errors (and calculate the mean absolute deviation), and the squares of errors (and calculate the mean squared error):

$$\text{mean absolute deviation} = \frac{\sum |E_i|}{n} = \frac{\sum |y_i - \hat{y}_i|}{n}$$

$$\text{mean squared error} = \frac{\sum (E_i)^2}{n} = \frac{\sum (y_i - \hat{y}_i)^2}{n}$$

The mean absolute deviation has an obvious meaning; when it takes a value of 1.5 the actual value is on average 1.5 away from the predicted value. The mean squared error has a less clear meaning, but is useful for other statistical analyses. Whichever measure is used, smaller values show that there is less noise in the observations and therefore a stronger relationship between variables.

WORKED EXAMPLE 8.1

Six sets of values have been recorded for an independent variable x and dependent variable y. These are thought to be related by the equation $y = 3x + 3$. What are the errors in the actual observations?

Observation	1	2	3	4	5	6
x	3	6	10	8	4	1
y	10	24	29	25	12	5

Solution

To measure the errors, we first have to find the calculated values of y. These are found by substituting values for x into $y = 3x + 3$. Then the error for each observation is found from

$$E_i = \text{actual } y_i - \text{calculated } y_i \quad = y_i - \hat{y}$$

Observation	1	2	3	4	5	6
x	3	6	10	8	4	1
Actual y	10	24	29	25	12	5
Calculated y	9	21	33	27	15	6
Error, E	1	3	-4	-2	-3	-1

Then the errors become:

● mean error = $\dfrac{1 + 3 - 4 - 2 - 3 - 1}{6} = -1$

● mean absolute error = $\dfrac{1 + 3 + 4 + 2 + 3 + 1}{6} = 2.33$

● mean squared error = $\dfrac{1 + 9 + 16 + 4 + 9 + 1}{6} = 6.67$

IN SUMMARY

The noise found in most relationships can be considered as errors or deviations from expected values. These can be measured by the mean error, mean absolute deviation and mean squared error. The mean squared error is particularly useful for other analyses.

Self-assessment questions

8.1 What is meant by the 'noise' in a relationship?

8.2 Why do almost all relationships contain errors?

8.3 What is the mean error and why is it of limited value?

8.4 Define two other measures of error.

8.5 It is suggested that two equations might be used to fit a set of data. How could you tell which gives the stronger relationship?

8.2 | Linear relationships

8.2.1 | Finding the line of best fit

In the last section we suggested that many relationships could be viewed as an underlying pattern with superimposed noise. We illustrated this by the noise around a linear relationship. In this section we continue this theme, concentrating on examples where the underlying pattern is a straight line. The sales of a product, for example, might rise linearly with the price being charged, demand for a service might depend on advertising expenditure, productivity might depend on bonus payments, borrowings might depend on interest rates, crop size might depend on the amount of fertilizer used. These are examples of causal relationships where changes in the first (dependent) variable are actually caused by changes in the second (independent) variable. However, relationships between variables need not be causal. Sales of ice cream are directly related to sales of sunglasses, but there is no cause and effect here, and the way to increase sales of ice cream is not to increase the sales of sunglasses. Obviously, both variables are affected by a third factor: the weather.

People commonly assume that because a relationship exists there must be some cause and effect. It is easy to spot ridiculous examples of this mistaken assumption. The number of lamp posts is related to prosecutions for drunken driving; the number of storks nesting in Sweden is related to the birth rate in the United Kingdom; the number of people in higher education is related to life expectancy; and in the nineteenth century there was a direct link between the number of asses and the number of PhD graduates in America. Unfortunately, not all mistakes of this kind are as easy to spot. The productivity of a coalmine, for example, may decline while investment increases (because of the age of the mine and the increasing difficulty of extracting coal); a common view in macroeconomics is that price inflation is caused by high wages (ignoring the fact that countries with the highest wage rates often have the lowest inflation); and the income generated by a bus company is directly related to the fares charged (but increasing fares deter passengers and will reduce long-term income)

In this section, then, we shall look at relationships between variables without implying any cause and effect. In particular, we shall use available data to find a linear relationship between two variables; in other words, we are looking for the straight line that best fits the data. This process is called **linear regression**, and we can illustrate the overall approach by the following example.

WORKED EXAMPLE 8.2

A factory records the number of shifts worked each month and the resulting output, as shown in the following table. If 30 shifts are planned for next month, what is the expected output?

Month	1	2	3	4	5	6	7	8	9
Shifts worked	50	70	25	55	20	60	40	25	35
Output	352	555	207	508	48	498	310	153	264

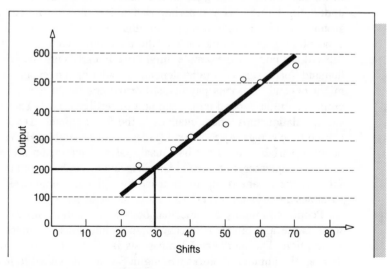

Figure 8.4 Linear relationship on a scatter diagram.

Solution

The best thing to do with a set of data is to draw a graph of it. A scatter diagram of shifts worked (the independent variable, x) and units made (the dependent variable, y) shows a clear linear relationship (Figure 8.4). A reasonable straight line can be drawn by eye through the data. This line shows that with 30 shifts worked, the output will be around 200 units.

In the worked example above we drew a scatter diagram, noticed a linear relationship and then drew a line of best fit by eye. Although this informal approach can work quite well, it is not very reliable. It would be useful to have a more formal way of defining a **line of best fit** through the data. This is the purpose of linear regression.

The equation of a straight line is:

$$y = a + b \times x$$

where: x = independent variable

y = dependent variable

a = point where the line intersects the y axis

b = gradient of the line

Linear regression looks for the values of the constants a and b that define the line of best fit through a set of points. We can approach this by looking at the errors. Even the best line will not usually fit the data perfectly, so there will be an error at each point, x_i. In other words, at each point i:

$$y_i = a + bx_i + E_i$$

The line of best fit is defined as the line that minimizes some measure of this error. We saw earlier that simply adding the errors and finding the mean allows positive and negative errors to cancel. Better alternatives would be to minimize the mean absolute deviation or the mean squared error. Because it allows other statistical analyses, the mean squared error is generally preferred for regression. Then deriving the equation for the line of best fit is quite straightforward and gives the following standard result:

$$b = \frac{n \sum xy - \sum x \sum y}{n \sum x^2 - (\sum x)^2}$$

$$a = \bar{y} - b\bar{x}$$

If you are interested, a summary of this derivation is given at the end of the chapter.

WORKED EXAMPLE 8.3

Calculate the line of best fit through the following data for advertising budget (in thousands of pounds) and units sold. Hence forecast the number of units sold if the advertising budget is £30,000.

Month	1	2	3
Advertising budget	20	40	60
Units sold	110	170	230

Solution

There is a clear linear relationship here, as shown in Figure 8.5, with

units sold, $y = a + b \times$ advertising budget, x

The calculations can easily be done in a table. Substituting the data and calculated values for xy and x^2 gives the following results:

Month	x	y	xy	x^2
1	20	110	2 200	400
2	40	170	6 800	1 600
3	60	230	13 800	3 600
Totals	120	510	22 800	5 600

The number of observations, n, is equal to 3, and substitution gives

$$\bar{x} = 120/3 = 40$$

$$\bar{y} = 510/3 = 170$$

$$b = \frac{n \sum (xy) - \sum x \sum y}{n \sum x^2 - (\sum x)^2}$$

$$= \frac{3 \times 22\,800 - 120 \times 510}{3 \times 5600 - 120 \times 120}$$

$$= 3$$

$$a = \bar{y} - b\bar{x}$$

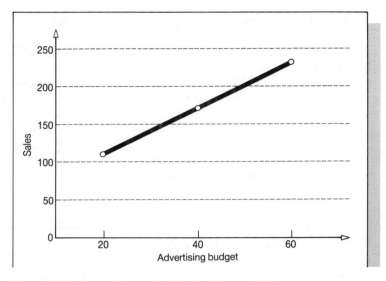

Figure 8.5 Scatter diagram for Worked Example 8.3.

$$= 170 - 3 \times 40$$

$$= 50$$

The line of best fit is

$$y = a + bx$$

units sold = 50 + 3 × advertising budget

With an advertising budget of £30,000, $x = 30$, so

units sold = 50 + 3 × 30

$$= 140$$

IN SUMMARY

Linear regression can be used to find the line of best fit through a set of data. Standard calculations find the line of best fit, which is defined as the one line that minimizes the sum of squared errors.

8.2.2 | Using linear regression to forecast

The main purpose of linear regression is to predict the value that a dependent variable will take when an independent variable has a particular value. Thus in Worked Example 8.3 we found a relationship between advertising budget and sales. This relationship can now be used to forecast expected sales when the advertising budget is set at any particular value. Similarly, in the following worked example the expected number of defects can be forecast when the number of inspections is set at a particular value. This approach is known as **causal forecasting**, even though changes in the independent variable may not actually cause changes in the dependent variable.

WORKED EXAMPLE 8.4

A company is about to change the way it inspects a product. Experiments were done with differing numbers of inspections, and figures are now available to show how the average number of defects varies with the number of inspections:

Inspections	0	1	2	3	4	5	6	7	8	9	10
Defects	92	86	81	72	67	59	53	43	32	24	12

If the company adopts six inspections, how many defects would they expect? What would be the effect of doing 20 inspections?

Solution

The independent variable x is the number of inspections, and the dependent variable y is the consequent defects. There is a clear linear relationship between these (Figure 8.6) and Table 8.1 lists the data and calculations.

With $n = 11$, substitution gives

$$b = \frac{n \Sigma (xy) - \Sigma x \Sigma y}{n \Sigma x^2 - (\Sigma x)^2}$$

$$= \frac{11 \times 2238 - 55 \times 621}{11 \times 385 - 55 \times 55} = -7.88$$

$$a = \bar{y} - b\bar{x} = 621/11 + 7.88 \times 55/11 = 95.85$$

The line of best fit is

$$y = 95.85 - 7.88x$$

or

Table 8.1

x	y	xy	x^2
0	92	0	0
1	86	86	1
2	81	162	4
3	72	216	9
4	67	268	16
5	59	295	25
6	53	318	36
7	43	301	49
8	32	256	64
9	24	216	81
10	12	120	100
Totals 55	621	2238	385

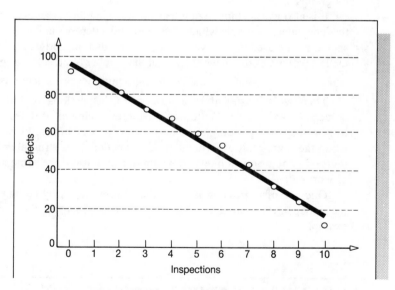

Figure 8.6   Scatter diagram for Worked Example 8.4.

defects = 95.85 − 7.88 × number of inspections

With six inspections the company could forecast

95.85 − 7.88 × 6 = 48.57 defects.

With 20 inspections we have to be a little more careful, as substitution gives 95.85 − 7.88 × 20 = − 61.75. It is clearly impossible to have a negative number of defects, so we would simply forecast zero defects. This would be the result for any number of inspections above 95.85/7.88 = 12.16.

This last example shows how the line of best fit is only really valid within the range of x used to find it. A value of x within this range can be substituted into the regression equation to find a corresponding value of y; this is known as **interpolation**. However, there is no evidence that the same relationship holds outside the range of x. Using a value of x outside the specified range to find a corresponding value of y is called **extrapolation**, and the results cannot be guaranteed. In practice, of course, it is often necessary to extrapolate values, and provided the values of x are not too far outside the range, the errors should not be too large. These results should, however, be used with caution and supported by graphs of the function.

It is also worth emphasizing that we are using the regression of y on x: then x is the independent variable which is used to find a dependent variable y. This equation should not be used to set a value for y and predict the corresponding value for x. In the last worked example we found that the number of defects was given by

defects = 95.85 − 7.88 × number of inspections

Then we can substitute a number of inspections to find the number of defects. However, we should **not** substitute a number of defects and expect this to give the corresponding number of inspections. This could, however, be found using the regression of x (number of inspections) on y (number of defects). The regression of x on y is likely to be similar to, but not the same as, the regression of y on x.

One use of regression is to predict future values by setting time periods as the independent variable. We can illustrate this by the following worked example.

WORKED EXAMPLE 8.5

Demand for a product in each of the last eight weeks has been 17, 23, 41, 38, 42, 47, 51 and 56. Use linear regression to forecast demand for next week.

Solution

In this example we can use time (that is, week number) as the independent variable and demand as the dependent variable. Then we get:

Week, x	1	2	3	4	5	6	7	8
Demand, y	17	23	41	38	42	47	51	56

Using the regression equations in the usual way gives the line of best fit as:

$$\text{demand} = 16.07 + 5.18 \times \text{week}$$

Substituting week = 9 gives the demand as $16.07 + 5.18 \times 9 = 62.69$. This has, of course, used extrapolation, but the figures suggest that in this case the results will be reasonably good.

IN SUMMARY

The main purpose of linear regression is to predict the value of a dependent variable for a known value of an independent variable. Care should be taken when interpreting the results.

Self-assessment questions

8.6 What is the main purpose of linear regression?

8.7 Define each of the terms in the linear regression equation $y_i = a + b \times x_i + E_i$.

8.8 What is meant by the regression of x on y? Is this the same as the regression of y on x?

8.3 ‖ Measuring the strength of a relationship

8.3.1 ‖ Coefficient of determination

We can now find the line of best fit through a set of data, but still need some way of measuring how good this line is. If the errors are small the line is a good fit, but if the errors are large even the best line is not very good. To measure the goodness of fit we shall use a measure called the **coefficient of determination**.

We defined the line of best fit as the one that minimizes the sum of squared errors. If we look carefully at the errors, we can separate this sum of squared errors (SSE) into different components. Suppose we take a number of observations of y_i and calculate the mean, $\bar{y}$. Actual values will vary around this mean, and we can define the total sum of squared errors as

$$\text{total SSE} = \Sigma\, (y_i - \bar{y})^2$$

When we build a regression model, we estimate values, $\hat{y}_i$, which show what the observations would be if all noise was eliminated. Thus the regression model explains some of the variation from the mean:

$$\text{explained SSE} = \Sigma\, (\hat{y}_i - \bar{y})^2$$

Because of random noise, the regression model does not explain all the variation, and there is some residual left unexplained:

$$\text{unexplained SSE} = \Sigma\, (y_i - \hat{y}_i)^2$$

With a little algebra it can be shown that:

$$\text{total SSE} = \text{explained SSE} + \text{unexplained SSE}$$

as shown in Figure 8.7. The coefficient of determination is defined as the proportion of total SSE explained by the regression model:

$$\text{coefficient of determination} = \frac{\text{explained SSE}}{\text{total SSE}}$$

This measure has a value between zero and one. If it is near to one, most of the variation is explained by the regression and the line is a good fit for the data. Conversely, if the value is near to zero, most of the variation is unexplained and the line is not a good fit.

The easiest way of calculating the coefficient of determination is the following rather messy-looking equation:

coefficient of determination =

$$\left[\frac{n \sum xy - \sum x \sum y}{\sqrt{[n \sum x^2 - (\sum x)^2] \times [n \sum y^2 - (\sum y)^2]}} \right]^2$$

All the values in this, except Σy^2, have already been calculated to find the regression line. However, the arithmetic is messy, and such calculations are best done using a computer.

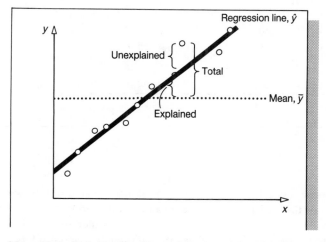

Figure 8.7   Relationships between total, explained and unexplained variations.

WORKED EXAMPLE 8.6

Calculate the coefficient of determination for the data in Worked Example 8.4.

Solution

Drawing the table of results as before, and adding values for Σy^2 gives Table 8.2. We already know that the line of best fit through this data is $y = 95.85 - 7.88x$, but we are now checking to see how good this line is. The coefficient of determination is calculated as follows:

coefficient of determination = $\left[\dfrac{n \sum xy - \sum x \sum y}{\sqrt{[n \sum x^2 - (\sum x)^2] \times [n \sum y^2 - (\sum y)^2]}} \right]^2$

$$= \left[\frac{11 \times 2238 - 55 \times 621}{\sqrt{[11 \times 385 - 55 \times 55] \times [11 \times 41\,977 - 621 \times 621]}} \right]^2$$

$$= [-0.9938]^2$$

$$= 0.9877$$

This shows that 99% of the variation can be explained by the regression model and only 1% is unexplained. This is evidence of a very good fit.

Table 8.2

x	0	1	2	3	4	5	6	7	8	9	10	Totals 55
y	92	86	81	72	67	59	53	43	32	24	12	621
xy	0	86	162	216	268	295	318	301	256	216	120	2238
x^2	0	1	4	9	16	25	36	49	64	81	100	385
y^2	8464	7396	6561	5184	4489	3481	2809	1849	1024	576	144	41\,977

Suppose a coefficient of determination had a value of 0.9; we would know that 90% of the variation from the mean is explained by the regression, and 10% is unexplained (owing to random effects or other explanations). Normally any value for the coefficient of determination above about 0.5 is considered a good fit. If the coefficient of determination is low at, say, 0.2, then 80% of the variation is not explained by the regression and some other factors should be considered.

IN SUMMARY

The coefficient of determination measures the proportion of the total variation explained by the regression line. A value close to 1 shows a good fit of the regression line, while a value close to 0 shows a poor fit.

8.3.2 | Coefficient of correlation

A second useful measure in regression is the coefficient of correlation which answers the basic question 'are x and y linearly related?'. The coefficients of correlation and determination answer very similar questions, and a straightforward calculation (which we need not describe) shows:

$$\text{coefficient of correlation} = \sqrt{\text{coefficient of determination}}$$

The coefficient of determination is usually referred to as r^2 and the coefficient of correlation as r.

This correlation coefficient is often called Pearson's coefficient and, as you can see, has a value between +1 and −1:

- a value of $r = 1$ shows that the two variables have a perfect linear relationship with no noise at all, and as one increases so does the other.

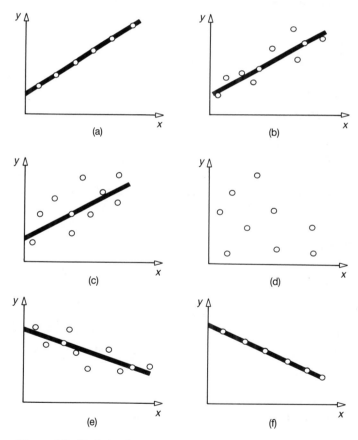

Figure 8.8 Variation in coefficient of correlation:
(a) $r = +1$ (perfect positive correlation); (b) r is close to + 1 (line is good fit);
(c) r is decreasing (line is poor fit); (d) $r = 0$ (random points);
(e) r is close to −1 (line is good fit); (f) $r = -1$ (perfect negative correlation).

- a lower positive value of r shows that the linear relationship is getting weaker.
- a value of $r = 0$ shows that there is no correlation at all between the two variables and no linear relationship.
- a lower negative value of r shows that the linear relationship is getting stronger.
- a value of $r = -1$ shows that the two variables have a perfect linear relationship and as one increases the other decreases.

With a correlation coefficient r, near to $+1$ or -1 there is a strong linear relationship between the two variables. When r is between 0.7 and -0.7 the coefficient of determination, r^2, is less than 0.49 and less than half the sum of squared errors is explained by the regression model. Thus values of r between 0.7 and -0.7 suggest that a linear regression line is not very reliable. These results are depicted graphically in Figure 8.8.

WORKED EXAMPLE 8.7

Calculate the coefficients of correlation and determination for the following data. What conclusions can be drawn from these? What is the line of best fit?

x	4	17	3	21	10	8	4	9	13	12	2	6	15	8	19
y	13	47	24	41	29	33	28	38	46	32	14	22	26	21	50

Solution

The data are tabulated in Table 8.3. First, we can see if there is a linear relationship by calculating the coefficient of correlation:

$$r = \left[\frac{n \sum (xy) - \sum x \sum y}{\sqrt{[n \sum x^2 - (\sum x)^2] \times [n \sum y^2 - (\sum y)^2]}} \right]$$

$$= \left[\frac{15 \times 5442 - 151 \times 464}{\sqrt{[15 \times 2019 - 151 \times 151] \times [15 \times 16\,230 - 464 \times 464]}} \right]$$

$$= 0.797$$

This indicates quite a strong linear relationship. If we square this we get the coefficient of determination:

$$r^2 = 0.635$$

This shows that 63.5% of the variation is explained by the linear relationship, and only 26.5% is unexplained.

Table 8.3

x	y	xy	x^2	y^2
4	13	52	16	169
17	47	799	289	2 209
3	24	72	9	576
21	41	861	441	1 681
10	29	290	100	841
8	33	264	64	1 089
4	28	112	16	784
9	38	342	81	1 444
13	46	598	169	2 116
12	32	384	144	1 024
2	14	28	4	196
6	22	132	36	484
15	26	390	225	676
8	21	168	64	441
19	50	950	361	2 500
Total 151	464	5 442	2 019	16 230

As there is a fairly strong linear relationship, it is worth calculating the line of best fit:

$$\bar{x} = 151/15 = 10.07$$

$$\bar{y} = 464/15 = 30.93$$

So:

← Gradient of the line.

$$b = \frac{n\sum xy - \sum x \sum y}{n\sum x^2 - (\sum x)^2}$$

$$= \frac{15 \times 5442 - 151 \times 464}{15 \times 2019 - 151 \times 151}$$

$$= 1.55$$

and:

$$a = \bar{y} - b\bar{x}$$

$$= 30.93 - 1.55 \times 10.07$$

$$= 15.32$$

So the line of best fit is:

$$y = 15.32 + 1.55 \times x$$

IN SUMMARY

The correlation coefficient shows how strong the linear relationship is between two variables. A value close to 1 or −1 shows a strong relationship, while a value close to zero shows a weak one.

8.3.3 | Rank correlation

Pearson's correlation coefficient can only be used for cardinal data (that is, data that have known, numerical values). Sometimes we need to measure the strength of a relationship between ordinal data (that is data that are ranked, but the values are not known). This is common with market surveys, where respondents are asked to put their choices into an order of preference. If we have two sets of ranked data it would be useful to see if there is a linear relationship between them. We could then see, for example, if people who prefer one newspaper also prefer a particular type of television programme. The way of doing this is to use a correlation coefficient based on rankings, which is called **Spearman's coefficient of rank correlation**.

Suppose we have five products (V to Z) which are ranked in some order of preference, 1 to 5, according to two characteristics, *a* and *b*. We might get the following results:

		Product				
		V	*W*	*X*	*Y*	*Z*
Characteristic	*a*	2	5	1	3	4
for ranking	*b*	1	3	2	4	5

We can see if there is a linear relationship between the ranks of *a* and *b* by using Spearman's rank correlation coefficient. This is based on the differences between ranking, so we define:

$$D = \text{ranking of } a - \text{ranking of } b$$

Then Spearman's coefficient, which is usually called r_s, is calculated as:

$$\text{Spearman's coefficient} = r_s = 1 - \frac{6 \sum D^2}{n(n^2 - 1)}$$

where *n* is the number of pairs of observations.

In this case there are five rankings, so $n = 5$. The sum of D^2 is:

$$(2-1)^2 + (5-3)^2 + (1-2)^2 + (3-4)^2 + (4-5)^2 = 1 + 4 + 1 + 1 + 1 = 8$$

So Spearman's coefficient of correlation is:

$$r_s = 1 - \frac{6 \times 8}{5 \times (25-1)} = 1 - \frac{48}{120} = 0.6$$

This suggests quite a strong linear relationship.

Spearman's coefficient is not really a separate measure, but is derived from Pearson's coefficient. This means that the interpretation of values is exactly the same. The only difference is that Spearman's coefficient is based on ranks, and the calculation is easier.

It is worth remembering that ordinal data are less precise than cardinal, so an item ranked first may be slightly better than the item ranked second, or it may be considerably better. It follows that the results of regressions are also less precise and they should be interpreted with caution. Wherever possible Pearson's coefficient should be used.

WORKED EXAMPLE 8.8

Seven trainees are employed in a factory. Their performance is judged by a combination of interviews and job performance. In the last year they have been ranked as follows:

Trainee	A	B	C	D	E	F	G
Interview	3	2	6	4	1	7	5
Job performance	1	3	5	2	4	6	7

Calculate Spearman's coefficient for these data.

Solution

There are seven rankings, so $n = 7$. The differences are:

Trainee	A	B	C	D	E	F	G
Interview	3	2	6	4	1	7	5
Job performance	1	3	5	2	4	6	7
Difference	2	-1	1	2	-3	1	-2
Difference^2	4	1	1	4	9	1	4

The sum of squared differences is $4 + 1 + 1 + 4 + 9 + 1 + 4 = 24$. Then Spearman's coefficient is

$$r_s = 1 - \frac{6\sum D^2}{n(n^2 - 1)} = 1 - \frac{6 \times 24}{7(49 - 1)} = 0.57$$

This shows a reasonably strong relationship.

IN SUMMARY

Spearman's coefficient of correlation can be used for ranked data. It is based on Pearson's coefficient of correlation, and is interpreted in the same way.

Self Assessment questions

8.9 What is measured by the coefficient of determination?

8.10 What values can be taken by the coefficient of correlation, and how is it related to the coefficient of determination?

8.11 What is the difference between Pearson's and Spearman's coefficients of correlation?

8.12 'A coefficient of determination of 0.9 shows that 90% of variation in the dependent variable is caused by change in the independent variable.' Is this statement true?

| 8.4 | Practical aspects of linear regression

| 8.4.1 | Extensions to linear regression

Linear regression finds the straight line of best fit through a set of data. There are several extensions to this analysis. An obvious one is to fit a more complex function through the data. Rather than a straight line, we could do regressions to find the quadratic of best fit:

$$y = ax^2 + bx + c$$

For this we need to solve three simultaneous equations and find the best values for the constants a, b and c.

There are many occasions when higher polynomials, or other functions, could be fitted through a set of data. This is called **non-linear regression**, and is exactly the same in principle as linear regression. However, the arithmetic is somewhat more complicated and computers are almost inevitably used.

Sometimes, rather than fit a more complicated function directly, it is easier to transform complex relationships into linear ones. It might be, for example, that one variable is rising exponentially with respect to another, so that $y = ae^{bx}$. The exponential line of best fit through the data is found by determining the best values for a and b. It is quite difficult to find the exponential curve of best fit, but if we take logarithms we get $\ln y = \ln a + bx$. Then there is a linear relationship between $\ln y$ and x, and we could easily find the straight line of best fit in terms of $\ln a$ and b.

In addition to non-linear regression, another common extension to linear regression is **multiple regression**. This is done when a dependent variable is related to not just one, but a series of independent variables. The sales of a product, for example, may depend on the price, income levels, unemployment rates, advertising budget, competition, and so on. Then multiple regression (which is almost always considered in terms of multiple linear regression) assumes a relationship between a dependent variable and several independent ones of the form

$$y = a + b_1 \times x_1 + b_2 \times x_2 + b_3 \times x_3 + b_4 \times x_4 \ldots$$

The arithmetic in multiple regression would be very tedious by hand, and it should only be tackled with a computer. Some examples of computer use for regression are given in the following section.

IN SUMMARY

There are several possible extensions to regression. The two most common ones are non-linear regression and multiple linear regression.

8.4.2 | Use of computers

Linear regression is one of the most widely used analyses in business. It is fairly simple to do, is widely understood, and the results can be used in a wide range of applications. Unfortunately, it is often used badly: false causal relationships are suggested, random patterns are said to show linear trends, or low coefficients of determination are ignored. This is, of course, more the fault of the person doing the analysis than of the method.

In the past, another common problem was the amount of arithmetic needed: for situations of any reasonable size there are a lot of calculations and simple mistakes were common. This is no longer true, as calculations are inevitably done by computer. Many specialized programs are available and general-purpose programs (such as spreadsheets) often include regression. Minitab has the following useful commands:

- CORRELATE, which finds coefficients of correlation
- REGRESS, which is a more powerful command to calculate related values.

An example of a Minitab printout is given in Figure 8.9. In this the y values were put into a column c1, and the x values were put into c2. As you can see, the program gives the basic information on coefficient of correlation and the regression equation, and follows this with some other statistics. We are not interested in these at the moment, but can return to them if needed. By specifying more sets of x data, such as c3 in Figure 8.9, Minitab can also be used for multiple regression.

IN SUMMARY

Because of the amount of arithmetic, calculations for regression are inevitably done on a computer. There are many packages, both specialized and general-purpose, which can do this.

Self-assessment questions

8.13 What are the most common extensions to linear regression?

8.14 'Multiple regression always considers linear relationships.' Is this statement true?

8.15 'The amount of computation makes linear regression very difficult to use with real problems.' Is this statement true?

8.16 'In practice multiple non-linear regression will often give the best relationships.' Is this statement true?

CHAPTER REVIEW

This chapter described the relationship between variables. It concentrated on linear regression, which finds the straight line of best fit through a set of data. The goodness of fit is judged by the coefficients of determination and correlation. In particular the chapter:

- outlined the need to measure the strength of relationships
- measured errors, including mean error, mean absolute deviation and mean squared error
- used linear regression to find the line of best fit through data

```
MTB   > set cl
DATA > 8 12 18 23 22 31
DATA > end

MTB   > set c2
DATA > 2 4 5 6 8 11
DATA > end

MTB   > correlate cl c2
```

Correlation of C2 and C1 = 0.959

```
MTB   > regress cl 1 c2
```

The regression equation is
C1 = 4.00 + 2.50 C2

Predictor	Coef	Stdev	t-ratio	p
Constant	4.000	2.469	1.62	0.181
C2	2.5000	0.3708	6.74	0.003

s = 2.622   R-sq = 91.9%   R-sq(adj) = 89.9%

Analysis of Variance

SOURCE	DF	SS	MS	F	p
Regression	1	312.50	312.50	45.45	0.003
Error	4	27.50	6.87		
Total	5	340.00			

```
MTB   > set c3
DATA > 120 133 147 162 189 196
DATA > end

MTB   > correlate cl c2 c3
```

	C1	C2
C2	0.959	
C3	0.934	0.968

```
MTB   > regress cl 2 c2 c3
```

The regression equation is
C1 = 1.7 + 2.29 C2 + 0.023 C3

Predictor	Coef	Stdev	t-ratio	p
Constant	1.68	18.43	0.09	0.933
C2	2.289	1.714	1.34	0.274
C3	0.0227	0.1784	0.13	0.907

s = 3.020   R-sq = 92.0%   R-sq(adj) = 86.6%

Analysis of variance

SOURCE	DF	SS	MS	F	p
Regression	2	312.65	156.32	17.15	0.023
Error	3	27.35	9.12		
Total	5	340.00			

SOURCE	DF	SEQ SS
C2	1	312.50
C3	1	0.15

Figure 8.9   Minitab printout for regression.

- showed how linear regression can be used for forecasting
- used the coefficients of determination and correlation to measure the goodness of fit
- mentioned extensions to linear regression
- outlined the use of computers for regression

Problems

8.1 The productivity of a factory has been recorded over a ten-month period, together with forecasts made the previous month by the production manager, the foreman and the management services department (Table 8.4). Compare the three sets of forecasts in terms of bias and accuracy.

Table 8.4

Month	1	2	3	4	5	6	7	8	9	10
Productivity	22	24	28	27	23	24	20	18	20	23
Production manager	23	26	32	28	20	26	24	16	21	23
Foreman	22	28	29	29	24	26	21	21	24	25
Management services	21	25	26	27	24	23	20	20	19	24

8.2 Find the line of best fit through the following data. How good is this fit?

x	10	19	29	42	51	60	73	79	90	101
y	69	114	163	231	272	299	361	411	483	522

8.3 A local amateur dramatic society is staging a play and wants to know how much to spend on advertising. Its objective is to attract as many people as possible, up to the hall capacity. For the past 11 productions the spending on advertising (in hundreds of pounds) and subsequent audience is shown in the following table. If the hall capacity is now 300 people how much should be spent on advertising?

Spending	3	5	1	7	2	4	4	2	6	6	4
Audience	200	250	75	425	125	300	225	200	300	400	275

8.4 Ten experiments were done to assess the effects of bonus rates paid to salesmen on sales, with the following results:

% Bonus	0	1	2	3	4	5	6	7	8	9
Sales ('00s)	3	4	8	10	15	18	20	22	27	28

What is the line of best fit through this data? How good is this line?

8.5 Sales of a product for the past ten months are shown below. Use linear regression to forecast sales for the next six months. How reliable are these figures?

Month	1	2	3	4	5	6	7	8	9	10
Sales	6	21	41	75	98	132	153	189	211	243

8.6 A company records sales of four products for a ten-month period. What can you say about these figures?

Month	1	2	3	4	5	6	7	8	9	10
p	24	36	45	52	61	72	80	94	105	110
q	2 500	2 437	2 301	2 290	2 101	2 001	1 995	1 847	1 732	1 695
r	150	204	167	254	167	241	203	224	167	219
s	102	168	205	221	301	302	310	459	519	527

8.7 A company's staff appraisal scheme uses the views of two managers. In one department the two managers rank staff as follows. How reliable does this scheme seem?

Person	A	B	C	D	E	F	G	H	I	J	K	L
Rank 1	5	10	12	4	9	1	3	7	2	11	8	6
Rank 2	8	7	10	1	12	2	4	6	5	9	11	3

8.8 A panel of tasters ranked eight foods as follows:

Food	A	B	C	D	E	F	G	H
Rank	3	2	8	5	7	1	4	6

The amount of a taste enhancer added to each food was also known:

Food	A	B	C	D	E	F	G	H
Amount	22	17	67	35	68	10	37	50

Use a ranking method to see if the flavour enhancer works.

Computer exercises

8.1 Figure 8.10 shows the printout from a session using Minitab. Make sure you can understand the basic functions here, but do not worry about the statistical details. Use a statistical package to check the results.

8.2 Figure 8.11 shows the printout from a session using a specialized forecasting program to do regression. As you can see, the amount of detail which some programs give is quite daunting (especially as this is only part of the printout). Make sure you can understand the basic operations, but again do not worry about the statistical detail. Use an equivalent program to check the results.

8.3 Figure 8.12 shows a spreadsheet that has been used for regression. Design a spreadsheet that will do linear regression and check these results. Examine the spreadsheet and improve the presentation of results.

8.4 The average number of flights from a small airport has been recorded over a typical period as follows.

24 23 25 24 27 29 32 30 35 34 34 39 41 40
38 46 41 51 48 46 41 57 56 62 61 62 68

Use a statistics package to analyse these figures and forecast future numbers of flights. Present your results in a report, including graphs of the figures.

```
MTB   > set c2
DATA  > 17 23 41 38 42 47 51 56
DATA  > end
MTB   > set c1
DATA  > 8 7 6 5 4 3 2 1
DATA  > end
MTB   > correlate c2 c1
```

Correlation of C2 and C1 = -0.949

```
MTB   > regress c2 1 c1 c20 c21;
SUBC  > coefficients c22;
SUBC  > residuals c23.
```

The regression equation is
C2 = 62.7 − 5.18 C1

Predictor	Coef	Stdev	t-ratio	p
Constant	62.679	3.536	17.73	0.000
C1	-5.1786	0.7002	-7.40	0.000

s = 4.538   R-sq = 90.1%   R-sq(adj) = 88.5%

Analysis of Variance

SOURCE	DF	SS	MS	F	p
Regression	1	1126.3	1126.3	54.71	0.000
Error	6	123.5	20.6		
Total	7	1249.9			

Unusual Observations

Obs.	C1	C2	Fit	Stdev.Fit	Residual	St.Resid
3	6.00	41.00	31.61	1.92	9.39	2.28R

R denotes an obs. with a large st. resid.

MTB   > print c1 c2 c20−c23

ROW	C1	C2	C20	C21	C22	C23
1	8	17	-1.22634	21.2500	62.6786	-4.25000
2	7	23	-0.88668	26.4286	-5.1786	-3.42857
3	6	41	2.28398	31.6071		9.39286
4	5	38	0.28706	36.7857		1.21429
5	4	42	0.00844	41.9643		0.03571
6	3	47	-0.03474	47.1429		-0.14286
7	2	51	-0.34174	52.3214		-1.32143
8	1	56	-0.43282	57.5000		-1.50000

Figure 8.10   Printout from a Minitab session.

Forecasting – Linear Regression

Data Entered

Number of Variables	:	2
Number of time periods	:	10
Critical T Value	:	0
Critical F Value	:	0
Column number of Dependent Variable	:	1

	x	y		x	y		x	y
Jan	24	95	May	17	65	Sep	45	155
Feb	11	49	Jun	29	105	Oct	26	92
Mar	32	125	Jul	37	141			
Apr	41	152	Aug	21	79			

Forecasting – Linear Regression

Solution

Variable	B-Coeff	Beta	T-Value
y	0.2900	0.9910	20.9642

B0 Intercept	:	-2.3778
Critical T Value	:	0
Mean Square Regression	:	1015.6133
Mean Square Residual	:	2.3108
Coefficient of Determination	:	0.9821
Adjusted C.O.D.	:	0.9799
Multiple Correlation Coefficient	:	0.9910
Standard Error Estimate	:	1.5201
Degrees of Freedom – Regression	:	1
Degrees of Freedom – Error	:	8
Computed F Score	:	439.4984
Critical F Score	:	0
Average x	:	28.3000
Mean Square Error	:	1.8486
Mean Absolute Deviation	:	1.2137

Correlation Coefficients

	x	y
y	1	0.991
x	0.991	1

	Mean Value	Standard Deviation
y	105.8000	36.6357
x	28.3000	10.7191

Residual Analysis

Period	x	Computed	Difference
Jan	24	25.1684	-1.1684
Feb	11	11.8303	-0.8303
Mar	32	33.8672	-1.8672
Apr	41	41.6961	-0.6961
May	17	16.4696	0.5304
Jun	29	28.0680	0.9320
Jul	37	38.5066	-1.5066
Aug	21	20.5291	0.4709
Sep	45	42.5660	2.4340
Oct	26	24.2986	1.7014

Figure 8.11 Printout from a forecasting program.

x	y		Regression Output:		
10	89		Constant			5.745961
19	201		St Err of Y Est			19.08293
29	294		R Squared			0.991783
42	389		No. of Observations			6
55	512		Degrees of Freedom			4
59	587					
			X Coeffient(s)		9.521141	
			Std Err of Coef.		0.43333	
			x	y	Predictions	Residuals
			10	89	100.96	-11.96
			19	201	186.65	14.35
			29	294	281.86	12.14
			42	389	405.63	-16.63
			55	512	529.41	-17.41
			59	587	567.49	19.51

Figure 8.12   Using a spreadsheet for regression.

8.5 A manufacturing company records the following data.

Table 8.6

Period	Output	Shifts	Advertising	Bonuses	Faults
1	1120	10	1056	0	241
2	131	10	1050	0	236
3	144	11	1200	0	233
4	152	11	1250	10	228
5	166	11	1290	15	210
6	174	12	1400	20	209
7	180	12	1510	20	225
8	189	12	1690	20	167
9	201	12	1610	25	210
10	225	12	1802	30	128
11	236	13	1806	35	201
12	245	13	1988	40	165
13	261	13	1968	40	132
14	266	13	2045	40	108
15	270	14	2163	45	98
16	289	15	2138	50	134
17	291	16	2431	50	158
18	300	16	2560	55	109
19	314	16	2570	55	65

Use appropriate packages to analyse that data. Write a report about your findings.

8.6 Find a set of government figures for variables that you think should be related. You might start with, say, inflation and unemployment over the past 25 years. See if there is a strong relationship between these. Extend your analysis to related figures, such as gross national product and interest rates. What conclusions can you reach from these results?

Case study

Western General Hospital

Each term the Western General Hospital accepts a batch of 50 new student nurses. Their training lasts for several years before they become state registered or state enrolled.

It is very expensive to train nurses and hospital administrators want to ensure that the training is cost-effective. A continuing problem is the number of nurses who fail exams and do not complete their training. If the hospital could reduce the number of these nurses leaving they could make substantial savings.

It has been suggested that the recruitment procedure is deficient in some way, and administrators should take more care in selecting students who are likely to complete the course. One way of doing this could be to relate the nurses' likely performance in exams to their performance in school exams. Unfortunately, nurses come from a variety of backgrounds and start training at different ages, so their performance at school may not be relevant. Other possible factors are age and number of previous jobs.

Table 8.7 shows results for last term's nurses. Grades in exams have been converted to numbers ($A = 5$, $B = 4$ and so on), and average marks are given.

When the hospital collected data on the number of nurses who did not finish training in the past ten terms, they got the following results:

Term	1	2	3	4	5	6	7	8	9	10
Number	4	7	3	6	9	11	10	15	13	17

The hospital is looking for three things:
- a presentation of the data in a form that is easy to understand
- a discussion of which, if any, of the factors listed can be used to predict nurses' grades
- a discussion of other factors to consider in future analyses.

Table 8.7

Nurse	Year of birth	Nursing grade	School grade	Number of jobs	Nurse	Year of birth	Nursing grade	School grade	Number of jobs
1	72	2.3	3.2	0	26	60	4.1	3.7	4
2	65	3.2	4.5	1	27	74	2.6	2.3	1
3	72	2.8	2.1	1	28	74	2.3	2.7	1
4	62	4.1	1.6	4	29	72	1.8	1.9	2
5	70	4.0	3.7	2	30	71	3.1	1.0	0
6	73	3.7	2.0	1	31	62	4.8	1.2	3
7	65	3.5	1.5	0	32	68	2.3	3.0	1
8	63	4.8	3.6	0	33	70	3.1	2.1	5
9	73	2.8	3.4	2	34	71	2.2	4.0	2
10	74	1.9	1.2	1	35	72	3.0	4.5	3
11	74	2.3	4.8	2	36	62	4.3	3.3	0
12	73	2.5	4.5	0	37	72	2.4	3.1	1
13	66	2.8	1.0	0	38	68	3.2	2.9	0
14	59	4.5	2.2	3	39	74	1.1	2.5	0
16	70	3.4	4.0	0	41	68	2.0	1.2	1
17	68	3.0	3.9	2	42	74	1.0	4.1	0
18	68	2.5	2.9	2	43	67	3.0	3.0	0
19	69	2.8	2.0	1	44	70	2.0	2.2	0
20	71	2.8	2.1	1	45	66	2.3	2.0	2
21	68	2.7	3.8	0	46	66	3.7	3.7	4
22	61	4.5	1.4	3	47	58	4.7	4.0	5
23	65	3.7	1.8	2	48	65	4.0	1.9	2
24	70	3.0	2.4	6	49	65	3.8	3.1	0
25	71	2.9	3.0	0	50	69	2.5	4.6	1

Derivation 8.1: Line of best fit

Note: This derivation uses differentiation which is discussed in Chapter 12.
A set of data consists of n values of y_i. The regression line of best fit is

$$\hat{y}_i = a + bx_i$$

Then the error at each point is:

$$E_i = y_i - \hat{y}_i = y_i - a - bx_i$$

and the sum of squared errors is:

$$\text{SSE} = \sum E_i^2 = \sum (y_i - a - bx_i)^2$$

For any particular problem the values of x_i and y_i are fixed, so the variables are a and b. Then to find the minimum of SSE we differentiate with respect to both a and b and set the results to zero:

$$\frac{\partial \text{SSE}}{\partial a} = -2 \sum (y_i - a - bx_i) = 0 \qquad \text{or} \qquad na = \sum y - b \sum x$$

$$\frac{\partial \text{SSE}}{\partial b} = -2 \sum x_i(y_i - a - bx_i) = 0 \qquad \text{or} \qquad a\sum x = \sum xy - b \sum x^2 \qquad (1)$$

The first of these can be rearranged to give

$$a = \sum y/n - b \sum x/n = \bar{y} - b\bar{x} \qquad (2)$$

Multiplying equation (2) by $\sum x$ and equating the result to equation (1) gives

$$\sum x \sum y/n - b \sum x \sum x/n = \sum xy - b \sum x^2$$

or

$$b[n \sum x^2 - (\sum x)^2] = n \sum xy - \sum x \sum y$$

or

$$b = \frac{n \sum xy - \sum x \sum y}{n \sum x^2 - (\sum x)^2}$$

Business
forecasting

9

CHAPTER OUTLINE

All decisions become effective at some point in the future. Managers should, therefore, make decisions that are not based on present circumstances, but on circumstances as they will be when the decisions become effective. These circumstances must be forecast. It is clear, then, that forecasting must be a central part of any organization.

Despite the importance of forecasting, progress in many areas has been limited. There are many methods of forecasting, but none is obviously better than the rest in all circumstances. Even the best forecasts are not entirely accurate, so there are differences between forecast and actual observations. If this were not true we could rely on weather forecasts, predict the winner of a horse race, become rich by speculating on the price of shares, or not buy too much food for a dinner party. There are, however, many circumstances in which good forecasts can be found and this chapter looks at some methods of making them.

After reading this chapter and doing the exercises you should be able to:

- appreciate the importance of forecasting in organizations
- list different types of forecasting
- discuss the characteristics of judgemental forecasting
- describe a variety of judgemental forecasting methods
- describe the characteristics of projective forecasting

- appreciate the importance of time series
- calculate errors in forecasts
- forecast using simple averages, moving averages and exponential smoothing
- forecast for time series with seasonality and trend

9.1 | Forecasting in organizations

In Chapter 7 we described a break-even analysis. This finds the number of units of a product that must be sold to recover fixed costs and begin contributing to profit. If a new product is proposed, but its sales are unlikely to reach the break-even point, the product will make a loss and it should not be introduced. This analysis clearly depends on forecast demand, and there are many similar examples that show the importance of forecasting. In practice, all decisions become effective at some point in the future, so they should be based on circumstances not as they are at present, but as they will be when the decision becomes effective. It is clear, then, that any decision depends on forecasts of future circumstances. This means that forecasting is of central importance to all organizations. If you have any doubts about this you might try to think of a decision that does not involve some form of forecasting.

We should say that much of the following discussion talks of 'forecasting demand', but this is only for convenience, and does not limit the areas of application.

It would be convenient to say that 'a lot of work has been done on forecasting and the best method is...'. Unfortunately, this is not possible. Because of the diversity of things to be forecast and the different situations in which forecasts are needed, there is no single best method. In this chapter we shall describe a variety of methods and suggest the circumstances in which each can be used.

Forecasting methods can be classified in several ways. One classification concerns the time in the future covered by forecasts. In particular:

- **long-term forecasts** look ahead several years (the time typically needed to build a new factory)
- **medium-term forecasts** look ahead between three months and two years (the time typically needed to replace an old product by a new one)
- **short-term forecasts** cover the next few weeks (describing the continuing demand for a product)

The time horizon affects the choice of forecasting method because of the availability and relevance of historical data, time available to make the forecast, cost involved, consequences if errors are made, effort considered worth while, and so on.

Another classification of forecasting methods draws a distinction between qualitative and quantitative approaches (as shown in Figure 9.1).

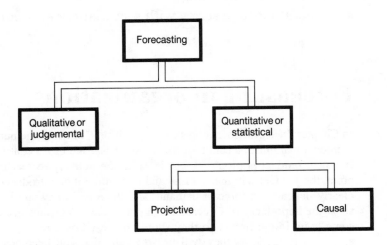

Figure 9.1   Classification of forecasting methods.

If a company is already making a product, it will probably have records of past demand and know the factors that affect this. Then it could use a quantitative method to forecast future demand. There are two alternatives for this:

- **projective methods**, which examine the pattern of past demand and extend this into the future. If demand in the past four weeks has been 100, 120, 140 and 160, it would be reasonable to project this pattern and suggest that demand in the following week will be around 180

- **causal methods**, which analyse the effects of outside influences and use these to produce forecasts. Productivity of a factory might depend on the bonus rates paid to employees, so it would be sensible to use the current bonus rate to forecast productivity. This approach has been described by linear regression in Chapter 8

Both of these approaches rely on the availability of accurate, quantified data. Suppose, though, that a company is introducing an entirely new product. There are no past demand figures that can be projected forwards, and the factors that affect demand are unknown. In such circumstances there are no quantitative data and a qualitative method must be used. Such methods are generally referred to as **judgemental**, and they rely on subjective assessments and opinions.

We have discussed causal forecasting in relation to linear regression in the last chapter, so the rest of this chapter looks at other forecasting methods, starting with qualitative or judgemental methods.

IN SUMMARY

Forecasting is an essential part of all planning and decision making. There are several ways of classifying forecasts, with two useful ones describing the time they look ahead, and the overall approach used.

Self-assessment questions

9.1 Why is forecasting used in organizations?

9.2 'Forecasting is a specialized function that uses mathematical techniques to project historical data.' Is this statement true?

9.3 List three fundamentally different approaches to forecasting.

9.4 What factors should be considered when choosing a forecasting method?

9.2 | Judgemental forecasting

Suppose a company is about to market an entirely new product, or a medical team is considering a new organ transplant, or a board of directors is considering plans for 25 years in the future. In these circumstances, there are no appropriate historical data on which to base a quantitative forecast. Sometimes there is a complete absence of data, and at other times the data available are unreliable or irrelevant to the future. As quantitative forecasts cannot be used, a judgemental method is the only alternative. These methods use subjective assessments from various informed sources. Five widely used methods are:

- personal insight
- panel consensus
- market surveys
- historical analogy
- Delphi method

9.2.1 | Personal insight

This has a single expert who is familiar with the situation and produces a forecast based on their own judgement. This is the most widely used forecasting method, and is the one that managers should try to avoid. It relies entirely on one person's judgement (opinions, prejudices and ignorance). It can give good forecasts, but often gives very bad ones, and there are countless examples of experts being totally wrong. Perhaps the major weakness of the method is its unreliability. This may not matter for minor decisions, but when the consequences of errors are large some more reliable method should be used.

Comparisons of forecasting methods clearly show that someone who is familiar with a situation, using experience and subjective opinions to forecast, will consistently produce **worse** forecasts than someone who knows nothing about the situation but uses a more formal method.

9.2.2 | Panel consensus

A single expert can easily make a mistake, but collecting together several experts and allowing them to talk freely to each other should lead to a consensus that is more reliable. If there is no secrecy and the panel are encouraged to talk openly, a genuine consensus may be found. Conversely, there may be difficulties in combining the views of different experts when a consensus cannot be found.

Although it is more reliable than one person's insight, panel consensus still has the major weakness that all experts can make mistakes. There are also problems of group working, where 'he who shouts loudest gets his way', everyone tries to please the boss, some people do not speak well in groups, and so on. Overall, panel consensus is an improvement on personal insight, but results from either method should be viewed with caution.

9.2.3 | Market surveys

Sometimes, even groups of experts do not have enough knowledge to make a satisfactory forecast. This frequently happens with the proposed launch of a new product. Experts may give their views, but more useful information is found by talking directly to potential customers. Market surveys collect data from a representative sample of customers. Their views are analysed, with inferences drawn about the population at large (as described in Chapter 3).

Market surveys can give useful information, but they tend to be expensive and time-consuming. They are also prone to errors as they rely on:

- a sample of customers that is representative
- useful, unbiased questions
- reliable analyses of the replies
- valid conclusions drawn from the analyses

9.2.4 | Historical analogy

If a new product is being introduced, it may be possible to find a similar product that was launched recently, and assume that demand for the new product will follow the same pattern. If, for example, a publisher is introducing a new book, it could forecast likely demand from the actual demand for the last, similar book it published.

Historical analogy relies on the availability of similar products that were introduced in the recent past. In practice, it is often difficult to find products that are similar enough to give reliable results.

9.2.5 | Delphi method

This is the most formal of the judgemental methods and has a well-defined procedure. A number of experts are contacted by post and each is given a questionnaire to complete. The replies from these questionnaires are analysed and summaries are passed back to the experts. Each expert is then asked to reconsider their original reply in the light of the summarized replies from others. Each reply is anonymous so that undue influences of status and the pressures of face-to-face discussions are avoided. This process of modifying responses in the light of replies made by the rest of the group is repeated several times (often between three and six). By this time, the range of opinions should have narrowed enough to help with decisions.

We can illustrate this process by an example from offshore oil fields. A company may want to know when underwater inspections on platforms will be done entirely by robots rather than by divers. A number of experts would be contacted to start the Delphi forecast. These experts would come from various backgrounds, including divers, technical staff from oil companies, ships' captains, maintenance engineers and robot designers. The overall problem would then be explained, and each of the experts would be asked when they thought robots would replace divers. The initial returns would probably give a wide range of dates from, say, 1995 to 2050 and these would be summarized and passed back. Each person would then be asked if they would like to reassess their answer in the light of other replies. After repeating this several times, views might converge so that 80% of replies suggest a date between 2005 and 2015, and this would be enough to help planning.

IN SUMMARY

Judgemental forecasts are typically used when there are no relevant historical data. They rely on subjective views and opinions, as demonstrated by personal insight, panel consensus, market surveys, historical analogy and the Delphi method.

Self-assessment questions

9.5 What are judgemental forecasts?

9.6 List five types of judgemental forecast.

9.7 What are the main problems with judgemental forecasts?

9.3 | Projective forecasting

Projective forecasting examines historical observations and uses these to forecast future values. It ignores any external influences and only looks at past values of, say, demand to suggest future demand. We shall describe four methods of this type:

- simple averages
- moving averages
- exponential smoothing
- models for seasonality and trend

These methods are most commonly used with time series, which are described in the following section.

9.3.1 | Time series

A lot of data occur as **time series**, which are series of observations taken at regular intervals of time. Monthly unemployment figures, daily rainfall, weekly demand, and annual population statistics are examples of time series.

Like many other sets of data, if you have a time series the first step in analysing it is to draw a graph, and a simple scatter diagram will show clearly any underlying patterns. The three most common patterns in time series are:

- **constant series**, in which observations take roughly the same value over time, such as annual rainfall
- **series with a trend**, which either rise or fall steadily, such as the gross national product per capita
- **seasonal series**, which have a cyclical component, such as the weekly sales of soft drinks

These three patterns are shown in Figure 9.2.

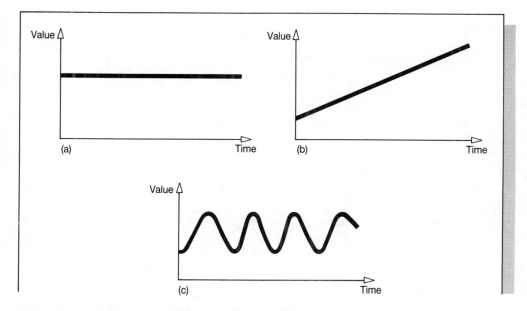

Figure 9.2   Common patterns in time series:
(a) constant series;   (b) series with time trend;   (c) series with seasonality.

If observations followed such simple patterns there would be no problems with forecasting. Unfortunately, there are nearly always differences between actual observations and the underlying pattern. A random noise is superimposed on the underlying pattern so that a constant series, for example, does not always take exactly the same value, but is somewhere close. Thus:

200 205 194 195 208 203 200 193 201 198

is a constant series of 200 with superimposed noise (see Figure 9.3).

It is the random noise that makes forecasting so difficult. If the noise is relatively small it is easy to get good forecasts, but if there is a lot of noise it obscures the underlying pattern and forecasting becomes more difficult.

actual value = underlying pattern + random noise

This kind of noise has been discussed in Chapter 8, where we showed that the difference between an actual observation and the value predicted by the underlying pattern could be seen as an error. If, for example, the underlying pattern in a set of data is a linear trend, a graph of observations will show variations about a straight line, as shown in Figure 9.4. Each observation has an error, which is its vertical distance from the line. Then the error in period t is defined as E_t:

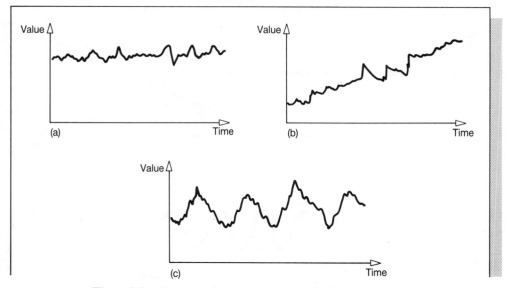

Figure 9.3 Common patterns in time series including noise:
(a) constant series; (b) series with time trend; (c) series with seasonality.

$$E_t = \text{observation in period } t$$
$$\quad - \text{value forecast from underlying pattern}$$
$$= y_t - F_t$$

where:

y_t = the actual observation

F_t = the value forecast from the underlying pattern

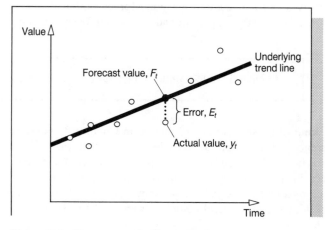

Figure 9.4 Errors around a linear trend.

This error is often called the **residual.** Repeating this calculation for each period allows us to find a mean error, where:

$$\text{mean error} = \frac{\Sigma E_t}{n} = \frac{\Sigma (y_t - F_t)}{n}$$

As we have seen before, the mean error has the major drawback of allowing positive and negative errors to cancel each other, and data with very large errors can have zero mean error. Consider, for example, the following values for demand and forecast:

t	1	2	3	4
y_t	100	200	300	400
F_t	0	0	0	1000

The demand pattern is clear and forecasting should be easy. The forecasts are obviously very poor, but the mean error is zero. This shows that the mean error is not a reliable measure of forecast accuracy, but measures bias. If the mean error has a positive value, the forecast is consistently too low; if the mean error has a negative value, the forecast is consistently too high.

The two most common alternatives to the mean error are the mean absolute deviation (MAD) and the mean squared error (MSE):

$$\text{mean absolute deviation} = \frac{\Sigma | E_t |}{n} = \frac{\Sigma | y_t - F_t |}{n}$$

$$\text{mean squared error} = \frac{\Sigma (E_t)^2}{n} = \frac{\Sigma (y_t - F_t)^2}{n}$$

WORKED EXAMPLE 9.1

Two forecasting methods have been used to give the following results for a time series. Which method is better?

t	1	2	3	4	5
y_t	20	22	26	19	14
F_t with method 1	17	23	24	22	17
F_t with method 2	15	20	22	24	19

Solution

Method 1 gives forecasts that are always nearer to actual demand than method 2, so in this case the decision is easy. This can be confirmed by calculating the errors.

Method 1

t	1	2	3	4	5
y_t	20	22	26	19	14
F_t with method 1	17	23	24	22	17
E_t	3	− 1	2	− 3	− 3
$|E_t|$	3	1	2	3	3
$[E_t]^2$	9	1	4	9	9

- mean error = $(3 - 1 + 2 - 3 - 3)/5 = -0.4$ (so each forecast is slightly biased, being an average of 0.4 too high)
- mean absolute deviation = $(3 + 1 + 2 + 3 + 3)/5 = 2.4$ (so each forecast is, on average, 2.4 away from actual demand)
- mean squared error = $(9 + 1 + 4 + 9 + 9)/5 = 6.4$

Method 2

t	1	2	3	4	5
y_t	20	22	26	19	14
F_t with method 2	15	20	22	24	19
E_t	5	2	4	− 5	− 5
$|E_t|$	5	2	4	5	5
$[E_t]^2$	25	4	16	25	25

- mean error = $(5 + 2 + 4 - 5 - 5)/5 = 0.2$ (so each forecast is slightly biased, being an average of 0.2 too low)
- mean absolute deviation = $(5 + 2 + 4 + 5 + 5)/5 = 4.2$ (so each forecast is, on average, 4.2 away from actual demand)
- mean squared error = $(25 + 4 + 16 + 25 + 25)/5 = 19.0$

The first forecasting method has lower mean absolute deviation and mean squared error, and is the better choice. The second method has slightly less bias, measured by the mean error.

| IN SUMMARY |

Projective forecasts only look at historical observations to forecast future values. There are several methods of projective forecasting. The most common use of these is for time series. These are observations taken at regular intervals that generally follow an underlying pattern with superimposed noise.

9.3.2 | Simple averages

Suppose you are going away on holiday and want to know the expected temperature at your destination. The easiest way of finding this is to look up records for previous years and take an average. With a holiday due to start on 1st July you could find the average temperature on 1st July over, say, the past 20 years. This is an example of forecasting using simple averages:

$$F_{t+1} = \frac{\sum y_t}{n} \qquad \text{actual averages forecast}$$

where:

n = number of periods of historical data

t = time period

y_t = observation at time t

F_{t+1} = forecast for time $t + 1$

WORKED EXAMPLE 9.2

Use simple averages to forecast values for period 6 of the following two time series. How accurate are the forecasts? What are the forecasts for period 24?

Period	1	2	3	4	5
Series 1	98	100	98	104	100
Series 2	140	66	152	58	84

Solution

Series 1: $F_6 = 1/n \times \sum y_t = 1/5 \times 500 = 100$

Series 2: $F_6 = 1/5 \times 500 = 100$

Although the forecasts are the same, there is clearly less noise in the first series than the second. Consequently we would be more confident in the first forecast and expect the error to be less. This could be confirmed by calculating the errors.

Simple averages assume that the underlying pattern is constant. Therefore, the forecasts for period 24 are the same as the forecasts for period 6 (that is 100).

Using simple averages to forecast is easy and can work well for constant values. Unfortunately, it does not work so well if the pattern changes. Older data tend to swamp the latest figures and the forecast is very unresponsive to the change. Suppose, for example, demand for an item has been constant at 100 units a week for the past two years. Simple averages would give a forecast demand for week 105 of 100 units. If the actual demand in week 105 suddenly rises to 200 units, simple averages would give a forecast for week 106 of

$$F_{106} = \frac{104 \times 100 + 200}{105} = 100.95$$

A rise in demand of 100 gives an increase of 0.95 in the forecast. If demand continues at 200 units a week subsequent forecasts are

$$F_{107} = 101.89 \qquad F_{108} = 102.80 \qquad F_{109} = 103.70, \text{ and so on.}$$

The forecasts are rising but the response is very slow.

Very few time series are stable over long periods, and the restriction that simple averages can only be used for constant series makes this approach of limited value. The problem is that old data, which may be out of date, tend to swamp newer, more relevant data. One way round this is to ignore old data and only use a number of the most recent observations. This is the principle of **moving averages**, which is described in the following section.

IN SUMMARY

Using simple averages can give reasonable results if observations are constant. For any other patterns some alternative method should be used.

9.3.3 | Moving averages

The patterns in observations often vary over time, and only a certain quantity of historical data are relevant to future forecasts. The implication is that all observations older than some specified time can be ignored. This suggests a forecasting method where the average weekly value over, say, the past six weeks is used as a forecast, and any data older than this are ignored. This is the basis of moving averages, where instead of taking the average of all historical data, only the latest n periods of data are used. As new data become available the oldest data are ignored. n-period moving average forecasts are found from:

$$F_{t+1} = \text{average of n most recent pieces of data}$$

$$= \frac{\text{latest demand} + \text{next latest} + \ldots n\text{th latest}}{n}$$

$$= \frac{y_t + y_{t-1} + \ldots y_{t-n+1}}{n}$$

WORKED EXAMPLE 9.3

The number of employee grievances dealt with by a large company has been recorded each month as follows:

t	1	2	3	4	5	6	7	8
y_t	135	130	125	135	115	80	105	100

Continuously changing conditions within the company mean that any data over three months old are no longer valid. Use a moving average to forecast the number of grievances in the future.

Solution

Only data more recent than three months are valid, so we can use a three-month moving average for the forecast. If we consider the situation at the end of period 3, the forecast for period 4 is

$$F_4 = \frac{y_1 + y_2 + y_3}{3} = \frac{135 + 130 + 125}{3} = 130$$

At the end of period 4, when actual numbers are known to be 135, this forecast can be updated to give

$$F_5 = \frac{y_2 + y_3 + y_4}{3} = \frac{130 + 125 + 135}{3} = 130$$

Similarly:

$$F6 = \frac{y_3 + y_4 + y_5}{3} = \frac{125 + 135 + 115}{3} = 125$$

$$F7 = \frac{y_4 + y_5 + y_6}{3} = \frac{135 + 115 + 80}{3} = 110$$

$$F8 = \frac{y_5 + y_6 + y_7}{3} = \frac{115 + 80 + 105}{3} = 100$$

$$F9 = \frac{y_6 + y_7 + y_8}{3} = \frac{80 + 105 + 100}{3} = 95$$

In this example, the error at each stage can be calculated to see how the forecast is performing. It is clearly responding to changes, with a high number of grievances moving the forecast upwards and vice versa. This ability of a forecast to respond to changing demand is important, and most forecasting methods allow the speed of response, or sensitivity, to be adjusted. The sensitivity of a moving average can be adjusted by altering the period, which means changing the value of n. A large value of n takes the average of a large number of observations and the forecast will be unresponsive: the forecast will smooth out random variations, but may not follow genuine changes in patterns. Conversely, a small value for n will give a responsive forecast that will follow genuine changes, but may be too sensitive to random fluctuations. A compromise value of n is needed to give reasonable results and typically a value around six periods is used.

WORKED EXAMPLE 9.4

The following table shows monthly demand for a product over the past year. Use moving averages with $n = 3$, $n = 6$ and $n = 9$ to produce one period ahead forecasts.

Month	1	2	3	4	5	6	7	8	9	10	11	12
Demand	16	14	12	15	18	21	23	24	25	26	37	38

Solution

The earliest forecast that can be made using a three-period moving average
(i.e. $n = 3$) is

$$F_4 = \frac{y_1 + y_2 + y_3}{3}$$

Similarly, the earliest forecasts for a six- and nine-period moving average
are F_7 and F_{10} respectively. Then the forecasts are as shown in Table 9.1.
Plotting a graph of these forecasts shows a rising trend, which the three-month
moving average is following quite quickly, while the nine-month moving
average is less responsive (Figure 9.5).

Table 9.1

Month	Demand	Forecasts $n = 3$	$n = 6$	$n = 9$
1	16	-	-	-
2	14	-	-	-
3	12	-	-	-
4	15	14	-	-
5	18	13.7	-	-
6	21	15	-	-
7	23	18	16	-
8	24	20.7	17.2	-
9	25	22.7	18.8	-
10	26	24	21	18.7
11	37	25	22.8	19.8
12	38	29.3	26	22.3
13		33.7	28.8	25.2

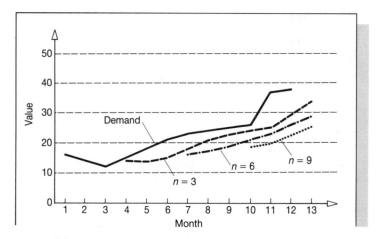

Figure 9.5   Moving averages for Worked Example 9.4.

Moving averages are particularly useful for data that have strong seasonal variations. If n is chosen to equal the number of periods in a season, a moving average will completely deseasonalize the data. This is illustrated in the following example.

WORKED EXAMPLE 9.5

Use a moving average with two, four and six periods to calculate the one-month-ahead forecasts for the following data:

Month	1	2	3	4	5	6	7	8	9	10	11	12
Demand	100	50	20	150	110	55	25	140	95	45	30	145

Solution

These data have a clear seasonal pattern, with a peak every fourth month. Calculating the moving averages gives the results shown in Table 9.2. The patterns can be seen clearly in a graph, as shown in Figure 9.6. The moving averages with both $n = 2$ and $n = 6$ have responded to the peaks and troughs of demand, but neither has got the timing right: both forecasts lag behind demand. As expected, the two-period moving average is much more responsive than the six-period one. The most interesting result is the four-period moving average which has completely deseasonalized the data.

Table 9.2

Month	Demand	Forecasts		
		$n = 2$	$n = 4$	$n = 6$
1	100	-	-	-
2	50	-	-	-
3	20	75	-	-
4	150	35	-	-
5	110	85	80	-
6	55	130	82.5	-
7	25	82.5	83.75	80.8
8	140	40	85	68.3
9	95	82.5	82.5	83.3
10	45	117.5	78.75	95.8
11	30	70	76.25	78.3
12	145	37.5	77.5	65
13		87.5	78.75	80

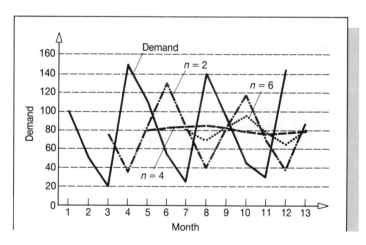

Figure 9.6 Moving averages for Worked Example 9.5.

Although moving averages overcome some of the problems with simple averages, the method still has a number of defects, including:

● all observations are given the same weight
● the method only works well with constant time series (as we have seen,

it either removes seasonal factors or gets the timing wrong)

- a large volume of historical data must be stored to allow forecast updates
- the choice of n is often arbitrary.

The first of these defects can be overcome by assigning different weights to observations. A three-period moving average, for example, gives equal weight to the last three observations, so each is given a of weight of 0.33. These weights could be changed to put more emphasis on later results, perhaps using

$$F_4 = 0.2 \times y_1 + 0.3 \times y_2 + 0.5 \times y_3$$

In practice, a more convenient way of changing the weights is to use exponential smoothing, which is described in the following section.

IN SUMMARY

Moving averages give forecasts based on the latest n observations and ignore all older values. The sensitivity can be changed by altering the value of n. Time series can be deseasonalized by setting n to the number of periods in the season.

9.3.4 | Exponential smoothing

Exponential smoothing is currently the most widely used forecasting method. It is based on the idea that as data get older they becomes less relevant and should be given less weight. In particular, exponential smoothing gives a declining weight to observations, as shown in Figure 9.7. This declining weight can be achieved using only the latest observation and the previous forecast. In particular, a new forecast is calculated by taking a proportion, α, of the latest observation and adding a proportion, $1 - \alpha$, of the previous forecast:

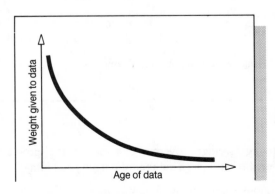

Figure 9.7 Weight given to data with exponential smoothing.

new forecast = $\alpha \times$ latest observation

$+ (1 - \alpha) \times$ last forecast

or $\qquad F_{t+1} = \alpha y_t + (1 - \alpha)F_t$

In this equation, α is the smoothing constant, which usually takes a value between 0.1 and 0.2.

We can illustrate the way in which exponential smoothing adapts to changes in observations with a simple example. Suppose a forecast was optimistic and suggested a value of 200 for an observation that actually turns out to be 180. Taking a value of $\alpha = 0.2$, the forecast for the next period is

$$F_{t+1} = \alpha y_t + (1 - \alpha)F_t$$

$$= 0.2 \times 180 + (1 - 0.2) \times 200$$

$$= 196$$

The optimistic forecast is noted and the value for the next period is adjusted downwards. The reason for this adjustment is clear if we rearrange the exponential smoothing formula:

$$F_{t+1} = \alpha y_t + (1 - \alpha)F_t$$

$$= F_t + \alpha(y_t - F_t)$$

but

$$E_t = y_t - F_t$$

so

$$F_{t+1} = F_t + \alpha E_t$$

The error in each forecast is noted and a proportion is added to adjust the next forecast. The larger the error in the last forecast, the greater is the adjustment for the next forecast.

WORKED EXAMPLE 9.6

Use exponential smoothing with $\alpha = 0.2$ and an initial value of $F_1 = 170$ to produce one-period-ahead forecasts for the following time series:

Month	1	2	3	4	5	6	7	8
Demand	178	180	156	150	162	158	154	132

Solution

We know that $F_1 = 170$ and $\alpha = 0.2$. Substitution then gives:

$$F_2 = \alpha y_1 + (1 - \alpha)F_1 = 0.2 \times 178 + 0.8 \times 170 = 171.6$$

$$F_3 = \alpha y_2 + (1 - \alpha)F_2 = 0.2 \times 180 + 0.8 \times 171.6 = 173.3$$

$$F_4 = \alpha y_3 + (1 - \alpha)F_3 = 0.2 \times 156 + 0.8 \times 173.3 = 169.8$$

and so on, as shown in the following table:

t	1	2	3	4	5	6	7	8	9
y_t	178	180	156	150	162	158	154	132	
F_t	170	171.6	173.3	169.8	165.8	165	163.6	161.7	155.8

Although we have described how exponential smoothing works, it may not be obvious that it actually does give less weight to data as they get older. We can demonstrate this by taking an arbitrary value for α, say 0.2. Then:

$$F_{t+1} = 0.2y_t + 0.8F_t$$

But substituting $t - 1$ for t gives:

$$F_t = 0.2y_{t-1} + 0.8F_{t-1}$$

and using this in the equation above gives

$$F_{t+1} = 0.2y_t + 0.8 \times (0.2y_{t-1} + 0.8F_{t-1})$$

$$= 0.2y_t + 0.16y_{t-1} + 0.64F_{t-1}$$

But

$$F_{t-1} = 0.2y_{t-2} + 0.8F_{t-2}$$

so

$$F_{t+1} = 0.2y_t + 0.16y_{t-1} + 0.64 \times (0.2y_{t-2} + 0.8F_{t-2})$$

$$= 0.2y_t + 0.16y_{t-1} + 0.128y_{t-2} + 0.512F_{t-2}$$

You can see that in this equation the weight put on older data is getting progressively less (0.2, then 0.16, then 0.128). This calculation could be continued to give the weights shown in Table 9.3. If you plot these values they form an exponential curve of the type shown in Figure 9.7. In this calculation we took an arbitrary value of $\alpha = 0.2$, but repeating the calculations with other values would lead to similar results.

The value given to the smoothing constant α is important in setting the sensitivity of the forecasts. α determines the balance between the last forecast and the latest observation. To give responsive forecasts, a high value of α is used (say 0.3 to 0.35): to give less responsive forecasts a lower value is used

Table 9.3

Age of Data	Weight
0	0.2
1	0.16
2	0.128
3	0.1024
4	0.08192
5	0.065536
6	0.0524288
etc	etc

(say 0.05 to 0.1). Again, a compromise is needed between having a responsive forecast (which might follow random fluctuations) and an unresponsive one (which might not follow real patterns).

WORKED EXAMPLE 9.7

The following time series has a clear step upwards in demand in month 3. Use an initial forecast of 500 to compare exponential smoothing forecasts with varying values of α.

Month	1	2	3	4	5	6	7	8	9	10	11
Demand	480	500	1 500	1 450	1 550	1 500	1 480	1 520	1 500	1 490	1 500

Solution

Taking values of $\alpha = 0.1, 0.2, 0.3$ and 0.4 gives the results shown in Table 9.4. All these forecasts would eventually follow the sharp step and raise forecasts to around 1500. Higher values of α make this adjustment more quickly and give a more responsive forecast, as shown in Figure 9.8.

Table 9.4

		Forecast			
Period	Demand	$\alpha = 0.1$	$\alpha = 0.2$	$\alpha = 0.3$	$\alpha = 0.4$
1	480	500.00	500.00	500.00	500.00
2	500	498.00	496.00	494.00	492.00
3	1 500	498.20	496.80	495.80	495.20
4	1 450	598.38	697.44	797.06	897.12

Table 9.4 (continued)

Period	Demand	Forecast			
		$\alpha = 0.1$	$\alpha = 0.2$	$\alpha = 0.3$	$\alpha = 0.4$
5	1 550	683.54	847.95	992.94	1 118.27
6	1 500	770.19	988.36	1 160.06	1 290.96
7	1 480	843.17	1 090.69	1 262.04	1 374.58
8	1 520	906.85	1 168.55	1 327.43	1 416.75
9	1 500	968.17	1 238.84	1 385.20	1 458.05
10	1 490	1 021.35	1 291.07	1 419.64	1 474.83
11	1 500	1 068.22	1 330.86	1 440.75	1 480.90
12		1 111.39	1 364.69	1 458.52	1 488.54

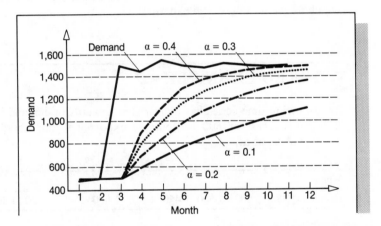

Figure 9.8 Exponential smoothing with different smoothing constants.

Although higher values of α give more responsive forecasts, they do not necessarily give more accurate ones. Observations always contain noise, and very sensitive forecasts tend to follow these random fluctuations. One way of selecting an appropriate value for α is to test several values over a trial period, and select the one that gives the smallest errors. This value is then used for all future forecasts.

IN SUMMARY

Exponential smoothing produces forecasts by adding portions of the last forecast and the latest observation. This reduces the weight given to data as their age increases. The smoothing constant determines the sensitivity of the forecast.

Self-assessment questions

9.8 'All time series follow a simple pattern.' Is this statement true?

9.9 Why do almost all forecasts contain errors?

9.10 How would you compare the results from two forecasting methods?

9.11 Why are simple averages of limited use for forecasting?

9.12 How can a moving average forecast be made more responsive?

9.13 What is the drawback with a responsive forecast?

9.14 How can data be deseasonalized?

9.15 Why is the forecasting method 'exponential smoothing' so called?

9.16 How can exponential smoothing be made more responsive?

9.4 Forecasting with seasonality and trend

9.4.1 Overall approach

The methods described so far give good results for constant time series, but they need adjusting to deal with other patterns. In this section we shall develop a more general model.

There are several ways of forecasting complex time series, but the easiest is to split observations into separate components, and then forecast each component separately. The final forecast is found by recombining the separate components. To be more specific, we shall consider an observation to be made up of four components:

- **trend** (T) is the long-term direction of a time series. It is typically a steady upward or downward movement

- **seasonal factor** (S) is the regular variation around the trend. Typically this reflects a variation in demand over a year

- **cyclical factor** (C) is a longer-term variation that occurs over several seasons. Typically these are business cycles that occur over many years

- **residual** (R) is the random noise whose effects cannot be explained.

Depending on how we define these four components, we can use two different approaches to forecasting. First, we can define them in an **additive model**, so that the observation y is

$$y = T + S + C + R$$

In this model, all the variables are numbers, so the seasonal factor S is an amount added to the trend to allow for the season. Observations in summer may, for example, be 100 units higher than the trend (so S takes a value of 100), while observations in winter are 100 units lower (so S takes a value of -100).

In many situations, particularly when the trend is changing quickly, it is not realistic to add a constant amount over several cycles. Then it may be better to use indices for seasonal and cyclical variations. Summer sales might be defined as, say, 50% higher than the trend, while winter sales are 50% lower than the trend. These indices are used in a **multiplicative model** so that

$$y = T \times S \times C \times R$$

Here T is a number, while S, C and R are ratios.

In general, of course, R is unknown, so we cannot include this in forecasts, which are found from:

---

additive model: $\qquad F = T + S + C$

multiplicative model: $\quad F = T \times S \times C$

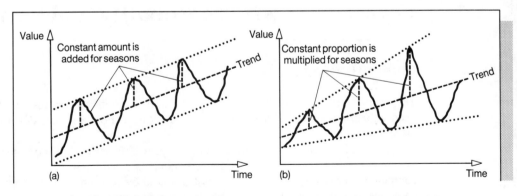

Figure 9.9 Difference between (a) additive and (b) multiplicative models.

WORKED EXAMPLE 9.8

(a) What is the forecast value for an additive model if the trend is 20, seasonal factor is 5 and cyclical factor is 2?

(b) What is the forecast value for a multiplicative model if the trend is 20, seasonal factor is 1.25 and cyclical factor is 1.08?

Solution

(a) With the additive model, $T = 20$, $S = 5$ and $C = 2$, so the forecast is

$$F = T + S + C = 20 + 5 + 2 = 27$$

(b) With the multiplicative model, $T = 20$, $S = 1.25$ and $C = 1.08$, so the forecast is

$$F = T \times S \times C = 20 \times 1.25 \times 1.08 = 27$$

Because it is used more widely, and gives better results for observations with a trend, we shall concentrate on the multiplicative model. The additive model is very similar and the analysis only varies in detail.

In most circumstances there are not really enough data to include cycles in the analysis. Business cycles, for example, may have an effect on an organization's performance, but they are not regular enough to include in an analysis. Several economic cycles have also been proposed with lengths between 2 years and 60 years, but there is not enough evidence or hard data to include these in company forecasting models. In the following analyses we shall assume that there are no usable cyclical factors, so C is fixed at 1.

Now we can start forecasting. The procedure uses historical data to:

- deseasonalize the data and find the underlying trend, T
- find the seasonal indices, S
- use the calculated trend and seasonal indices to forecast $F = T \times S$

This is described in the following sections.

IN SUMMARY

There are many ways of forecasting more complex time series. The easiest is to consider separate components and combine them into a final forecast. We shall use a multiplicative model for this.

9.4.2 | Finding the trend

There are two ways of finding the trend T, both of which we have already met:

- linear regression with time as the independent variable
- moving averages with a period equal to the length of a season

Both of these give generally good results. If the trend is clearly linear, regression is probably the better approach: it gives more information and we have a definite equation for the trend. If the trend is not clearly linear, moving averages are better. The choice is often a matter of individual preference.

WORKED EXAMPLE 9.9

A set of observations has been recorded over the past 12 periods as follows:

Period	1	2	3	4	5	6	7	8	9	10	11	12
Observation	291	320	142	198	389	412	271	305	492	518	363	388

(a) Use linear regression to find the deseasonalized trend.

(b) Use moving averages to find the deseasonalized trend.

Solution

(a) With the values given:

$$n = 12 \qquad \sum x = 78 \qquad \sum y = 4089 \qquad \sum x^2 = 650 \qquad \sum (xy) = 29\,160$$

Substituting these in the standard linear regression equations gives

$$b = \frac{n\sum (xy) - \sum x \sum y}{n\sum x^2 - (\sum x)^2} = \frac{12 \times 29\,160 - 78 \times 4089}{12 \times 650 - 78 \times 78}$$

$$= 18.05$$

$$a = \bar{y} - b \times \bar{x} = 4089/12 - 18.05 \times 78/12$$

$$= 223.41$$

The line of best fit gives the trend as

$$\text{observation} = 223.41 + 18.05 \times \text{period}$$

The deseasonalized trend value for period 1 is $223.41 + 1 \times 18.05 = 241.46$. Substituting other values for the period gives the deseasonalized trend values shown in Table 9.5, and plotted in Figure 9.10. One point about this regression line is that the coefficient of determination is quite low at 0.35. The reason is

Table 9.5

Period	Value	Deseasonalized trend value
1	291	241.46
2	320	259.51
3	142	277.56
4	198	295.61
5	389	313.66
6	412	331.71
7	271	349.76
8	305	367.81
9	492	385.86
10	518	403.91
11	363	421.96
12	388	440.01

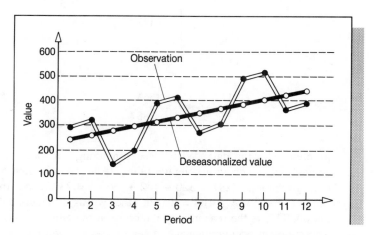

Figure 9.10 Using linear regression to deseasonalize data for Worked Example 9.9.

obviously that a lot of the variation is explained not by the trend, but by the seasonality. When using linear regression to deseasonalize data, a low coefficient of determination does not necessarily mean that the results are unacceptable.

(b) Figure 9.10 shows that the values have a clear season of four periods. Then the data can be deseasonalized by taking a four-period moving average, as shown in Table 9.6. You can see from this table that there is an obvious

Table 9.6

Period	Value	Four-period moving average
1	291	
2	320	
2.5		237.75
3	142	
3.5		262.25
4	198	
4.5		285.25
5	389	
5.5		317.5
6	412	
6.5		344.25
7	271	
7.5		370
8	305	
8.5		396.5
9	492	
9.5		419.5
10	518	
10.5		440.25
11	363	
12	388	

problem with the data. When deseasonalizing data we are suggesting that average values occur at average times. If we take the first four periods, the average value of $(291 + 320 + 142 + 198)/4 = 237.75$ occurs at the average time of $(1 + 2 + 3 + 4)/4 = 2.5$. In other words, it occurs halfway through a period. This is the reason why the entry in the table is shown at period 2.5. This problem occurs whenever a season has an even number of periods (but obviously does not occur when the season has an odd number of periods).

The easiest way to find the deseasonalized value at each period is to take the average of the two values on either side of it. Then the deseasonalized value for period 3 is the average of the deseasonalized values at times 2.5 and 3.5. This is $(237.75 + 262.25)/2 = 250$. This calculation is repeated to give the values shown in Table 9.7, and plotted in Figure 9.11.

Table 9.7

Period	Value	Four period moving average	Deseasonalized values
1	291		
2	320		
2.5		237.75	
3	142		250
3.5		262.25	
4	198		273.75
4.5		285.25	
5	389		301.38
5.5		317.5	
6	412		330.88
6.5		344.25	
7	271		357.13
7.5		370	
8	305		383.25
8.5		396.5	
9	492		408
9.5		419.5	
10	518		429.88
10.5		440.25	
11	363		
12	388		

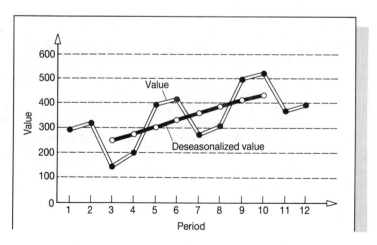

Figure 9.11 Using moving averages to deseasonalize data for Worked Example 9.9.

Another problem with moving averages is that we now only have deseasonalized data for eight periods, rather than the original 12 periods. Here there are enough data to establish patterns, but this is another reason why it is generally better to use regression. It is clear from the results that the two approaches give similar, but not identical, results.

IN SUMMARY

Both linear regression and moving averages can be used to find the deseasonalized trend of a set of data. These methods give similar results, but regression is the more useful approach.

| 9.4.3 | Finding the seasonal indices

In multiplicative models, seasonal variations are measured by seasonal indices (which we have already met in Chapter 6). These are defined as the amounts by which deseasonalized values must be multiplied to get seasonal values:

$$\text{seasonal index} = \frac{\text{seasonal value}}{\text{deseasonalized value}}$$

Suppose a newspaper has average daily sales of 1000 copies in a particular area, but this rises to 2000 copies on Saturday and falls to 500 copies on Monday and Tuesday. The deseasonalized value is 1000; the seasonal index for Saturday is $2000/1000 = 2.0$; the seasonal indices for Monday and Tuesday are $500/1000 = 0.5$; and seasonal indices for other days are $1000/1000 = 1.0$.

In the last section we deseasonalized data and found the trend. Now for every period we have the actual observation and the deseasonalized trend value. If we divide the actual observation by the trend value, we get a value for the seasonal index. This index is affected by noise in the data, so it is only an approximation, but if we take several complete seasons then we can find average indices that are more reliable.

WORKED EXAMPLE 9.10

In Worked Example 9.9, data were deseasonalized using exponential smoothing and moving averages. For each of these, find the seasonal indices.

Solution

Taking a single period, say 4, we have an actual observation of 198. The deseasonalized value using linear regression is 295.61, so the seasonal index is 198/295.61 = 0.67. The deseasonalized value using moving averages is 273.75, so the seasonal index is 198/273.75 = 0.72. As expected, these are similar, but not identical. Repeating these calculations for other periods gives the results shown in Table 9.8.

Table 9.8

		Linear regression		Moving averages	
Period	Observation	Deseasonalized trend value	Seasonal index	Deseasonalized trend value	Seasonal index
1	291	241.46	1.21		
2	320	259.51	1.23		
3	142	277.56	0.51	250	0.57
4	198	295.61	0.67	273.75	0.72
5	389	313.66	1.24	301.38	1.29
6	412	331.71	1.24	330.88	1.25
7	271	349.76	0.77	357.13	0.76
8	305	367.81	0.83	383.25	0.80
9	492	385.86	1.28	408	1.21
10	518	403.91	1.28	429.88	1.20
11	363	421.96	0.86		
12	388	440.01	0.88		

Now we have a seasonal index calculated for each period, so we can take averages to find more accurate values. We know from the graphs in Figures 9.10 and 9.11 that there are four periods in a season, so we need to calculate four seasonal indices.

Taking periods 1, 5 and 9 as the first periods in consecutive seasons has linear regression giving an average seasonal index for the first period in a season as (1.21 + 1.24 + 1.28)/3 = 1.24. Moving averages do not give a value for period 1, but the average index for periods 5 and 9 is (1.29 + 1.21)/2 = 1.25. Similarly, the average indices for other period in a season are:

Using linear regression

- first period in season (1.21 + 1.24 + 1.28)/3 = 1.24
- second period in season (1.23 + 1.24 + 1.28)/3 = 1.24
- third period in season (0.51 + 0.77 + 0.86)/3 = 0.71
- fourth period in season (0.67 + 0.83 + 0.88)/3 = 0.79

Using moving averages

- first period in season (1.29 + 1.21)/2 = 1.25
- second period in season (1.25 + 1.20)/2 = 1.23
- third period in season (0.57 + 0.76)/2 = 0.67
- fourth period in season (0.72 + 0.80)/2 = 0.76

Now that we have found both trend and seasonal index, we can start forecasting for the future. Because it has a specific equation to work with, linear regression is easier to use. The procedure for forecasting is:

- find the deseasonalized value in the future
- multiply this by the appropriate seasonal index

With moving averages we need some method of projecting the trend, and the simplest way is to draw a graph of known values and use extrapolation.

WORKED EXAMPLE 9.11

Forecast values for periods 13 to 17 for the time series in Worked Example 9.9.

Solution

The trend was found by linear regression (in Worked Example 9.9) to be

$$\text{value} = 223.41 + 18.05 \times \text{period}$$

Now we can substitute 13 to 17 for the period and find the deseasonalized trend for these times. Then we multiply these by the appropriate seasonal index (which was found in Worked Example 9.10) to get the forecasts.

Period 13

$$\text{deseasonalized trend} = 223.41 + 18.05 \times 13 = 458.06$$

$$\text{seasonal index} = 1.24 \text{ (first period in season)}$$

$$\text{forecast} = 458.06 \times 1.24 = 568$$

Period 14

>deseasonalized trend = $223.41 + 18.05 \times 14 = 476.11$
>
>seasonal index = 1.24 (second period in season)
>
>forecast = $476.11 \times 1.24 = 590$

Period 15

>deseasonalized trend = $223.41 + 18.05 \times 15 = 494.16$
>
>seasonal index = 0.71 (third period in season)
>
>forecast = $494.16 \times 0.71 = 351$

Period 16

>deseasonalized trend = $223.41 + 18.05 \times 16 = 512.21$
>
>seasonal index = 0.79 (fourth period in season)
>
>forecast = $512.21 \times 0.79 = 405$

Period 17

>deseasonalized trend = $223.41 + 18.05 \times 17 = 530.26$
>
>seasonal index = 1.24 (first period in season)
>
>forecast = $530.26 \times 1.24 = 658$

Notice that the forecasts are quoted to the same number of decimal places as the observations. Although computer packages often give results to several places of decimals, it is misleading to suggest that the forecasts are more accurate than the data from which they were derived.

WORKED EXAMPLE 9.12

Use a multiplicative model to forecast values for the next four periods of the following time series:

t	1	2	3	4	5	6	7	8
y	986	1245	902	704	812	1048	706	514

Solution

Looking at the data, we can see that there is a linear trend with a season of four periods. This observation could be confirmed by drawing a graph, but the pattern is clear enough to make this unnecessary. We can use linear regression to deseasonalize the data, and then calculate four seasonal indices. A spreadsheet is a convenient way of doing these calculations, and Figure 9.12 shows one approach. This finds:

- linear regression equation: $y = 1156.75 - 64.92t$
- average seasonal indices: 0.94, 1.29, 0.97 and 0.80

These can be used to give a forecast for period 9 of

$(1156.75 - 64.92 \times 9) \times 0.94 = 537.82$ (allowing for rounding errors)

Similarly the forecasts for periods 10, 11 and 12 are

$$(1156.75 - 64.92 \times 10) \times 1.29 = 654.35$$

$$(1156.75 - 64.92 \times 11) \times 0.97 = 430.02$$

$$(1156.75 - 64.92 \times 12) \times 0.80 = 300.53$$

	A	B	C	D	E	
1	Period	Value	Regression	Seasonal	Period in	
2			value	index	season	
3	1	986.00	1091.83	0.90	1	
4	2	1245.00	1026.92	1.21	2	
5	3	902.00	962.00	0.94	3	
6	4	704.00	897.08	0.78	4	
7	5	812.00	832.17	0.98	1	
8	6	1048.00	767.25	1.37	2	
9	7	706.00	702.33	1.01	3	
10	8	514.00	637.42	0.81	4	
11						
12		Regression	output			
13	Constant			1156.75		
14	Std error			179.8678		
15	R squared			0.476935		
16	No of observations			8		
17	Degrees of freedom			6		
18						
19	x coefficient		-64.91667			
20	Std error		27.75421			
21						
22		Seasonal	indices			
23	1	2	3	4		
24	0.94	1.29	0.97	0.80		
25						
26		Forecast				
27	9	10	11	12		
28	537.82	654.35	430.02	300.53		
29						

Figure 9.12   Calculations using a spreadsheet for forecasting, for Worked Example 9.12.

WORKED EXAMPLE 9.13

Use an additive model to forecast demand for the time series in Worked Example 9.12.

Solution

The approach of additive models is exactly the same as multiplicative models, except that the seasonal variations are amounts to be added rather than an index to be multiplied. The spreadsheet in Figure 9.13 shows the analysis for this.

	A	B	C	D	E	F
1	Period	Value	Regression	Seasonal	Period in	
2			value	adjustment	season	
3	1	986.00	1091.83	-105.83	1	
4	2	1245.00	1026.92	218.08	2	
5	3	902.00	962.00	-60.00	3	
6	4	704.00	897.08	-193.08	4	
7	5	812.00	832.17	-20.17	1	
8	6	1048.00	767.25	280.75	2	
9	7	706.00	702.33	3.67	3	
10	8	51.00	637.42	-123.42	4	
11						
12		Regression	output			
13	Constant			1156.75		
14	Std error			179.8678		
15	R squared			0.476935		
16	No of observations			8		
17	Degrees of freedom			6		
18						
19	x coefficient		-64.91667			
20	Std error		27.75421			
21						
22		Seasonal adjustments				
23	1	2	3	4		
24	-63.00	249.42	-28.17	-158.25		
25						
26		Forecast				
27	9	10	11	12		
28	509.50	757.00	414.50	219.50		
29						

Figure 9.13   Using an additive model to forecast, for Worked Example 9.13.

The regression equation is $1156.75 - 64.92 \times t$ and the average seasonal adjustments are $-63.00, 249.42, -28.17$ and -158.25. The forecast for period 9 is

$(1156.75 - 64.92 \times 9) - 63.00 = 509.50$ (allowing for rounding errors)

Similarly, the forecasts for periods 10, 11 and 12 are:

$(1156.75 - 64.92 \times 10) + 249.42 = 757.00$

$(1156.75 - 64.92 \times 11) - 28.17 = 414.50$

$(1156.75 - 64.92 \times 12) - 158.25 = 219.50$

As there is a clear trend in the data, the multiplicative model is likely to be more reliable than the additive one.

IN SUMMARY

Seasonal indices are defined as:

$$\text{seasonal index} = \frac{\text{actual value}}{\text{deseasonalized value}}$$

These can be used to adjust the trend and forecast values for any period in the future.

Self-assessment questions

9.17 What is the difference between an additive and a multiplicative forecasting model?

9.18 Why are cyclical data not usually included in forecasting models?

9.19 Does the moving average of deseasonalized data always occur in the middle of a period?

9.20 Would you prefer to use regression or moving averages to deseasonalize a set of data?

CHAPTER REVIEW

This chapter has discussed various aspects of forecasting. It started by considering the need to forecast and then described a variety of ways in which forecasts can be made. In particular it:

- outlined the importance of forecasting in all organizations
- described three basic approaches to forecasting as causal (which was illustrated by linear regression in Chapter 8), judgemental and projective
- discussed the use of judgemental or qualitative methods when there are no relevant quantitative data
- outlined the use of time series, which can be described by an underlying pattern with superimposed random noise
- forecast using simple and moving averages
- forecast using exponential smoothing
- produced forecasts for time series with seasonality and trend

Problems

9.1 Use linear regression to forecast values for periods 11 to 13 with the following time series:

Period	1	2	3	4	5	6	7	8	9	10
Observation	121	133	142	150	159	167	185	187	192	208

9.2 Use simple averages to forecast values for the data in Problem 9.1. Which method gives the better results?

9.3 Use a four-period moving average to forecast values for the data in Problem 9.1.

9.4 Find the two-, three- and four-period moving average for the following time series, and, by calculating the errors, say which gives the best results:

t	1	2	3	4	5	6	7	8
y	280	240	360	340	300	220	200	360

9.5 Use exponential smoothing with $\alpha = 0.1$ and 0.2 to forecast values for the data in Problem 9.4. Which smoothing constant gives better forecasts?

9.6 Use exponential smoothing with smoothing constant equal to 0.1, 0.2, 0.3 and 0.4 to produce one-period-ahead forecasts for the following time series. Use an initial value of $F_1 = 208$ and say which value of α is best.

t	1	2	3	4	5	6	7	8
y	212	216	424	486	212	208	208	204

9.7 Find deseasonalized forecasts for the following time series and hence identify the underlying trend:

t	1	2	3	4	5	6	7	8	9	10
y	75	30	52	88	32	53	90	30	56	96

9.8 Forecast values for the next six periods in Problem 9.7.

9.9 Use an appropriate multiplicative model to forecast values for the next three periods of the following time series:

t	1	2	3	4	5	6
y	100	160	95	140	115	170

9.10 Use an appropriate multiplicative model to forecast values for the next eight periods of the following time series:

t	1	2	3	4	5	6	7	8	9	10
y	101	125	121	110	145	165	160	154	186	210

9.11 Use additive models to forecast values for the time series in Problems 9.9 and 9.10.

Computer Exercises

9.1 Figure 9.14 shows a printout from a specialized forecasting program using moving averages. Make sure you understand what is happening in this printout. Use an equivalent package to check the results.

9.2 Figure 9.15 shows a printout from a specialized forecasting program using exponential smoothing. Make sure you understand what is happening in this printout. Use an equivalent program to check the results.

9.3 Figures 9.12 and 9.13 showed how forecasting with seasonality and trend can be done on a spreadsheet. Make sure you understand what is happening in these printouts. Design a spreadsheet to check the results. Modify your spreadsheets to give improved presentation.

Forecasting with moving averages

Data entered

Number of time periods   : 8
Number of periods in average : 4

Value

Week1	126
Week2	85
Week3	128
Week4	159
Week5	138
Week6	97
Week7	145
Week8	160

Solution

Period	Value	Computed	Difference
Week1	126	126	0
Week2	85	85	0
Week3	128	128	0
Week4	159	159	0
Week5	138	124.50	13.50
Week6	97	127.50	-30.50
Week7	145	130.50	14.50
Week8	160	134.75	25.25

Average value	: 129.7500
Mean square error	: 490.0781
Mean absolute deviation	: 20.9375
Forecast value	: 135

(a)

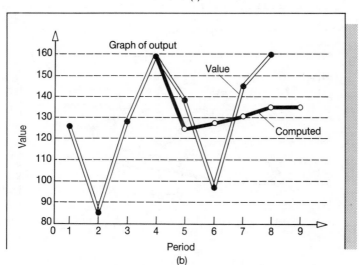

(b)

Figure 9.14   Printout from a forecasting program for moving averages.

Forecasting with simple exponential smoothing

Data entered

Number of time periods	:	8
Data smoothing coefficient	:	0.1000
Initial data value	:	54

Value

P1	55
P2	53
P3	60
P4	61
P5	58
P6	56
P7	62
P8	59

Solution

Period	Y1 (Yp)	Computed (Sp − 1)	Difference (Yp − Sp − 1)
P0	54	0	0
P1	55	54	1
P2	53	54.1000	-1.1000
P3	60	53.9900	6.0100
P4	61	54.5910	6.4090
P5	58	55.2319	2.7681
P6	56	55.5087	0.4931
P7	62	55.5578	6.4422
P8	59	56.2020	2.7980

Average Y1	:	57.5556
Mean square error	:	17.0799
Mean absolute deviation	:	3.3773
Forecast value	:	56.4818

(a)

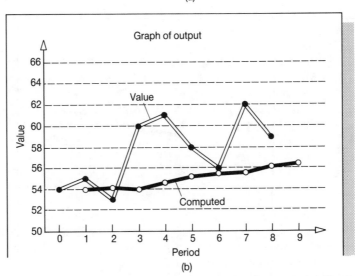

(b)

Figure 9.15 Printout from a forecasting program for exponential smoothing.

9.4 Design a spreadsheet for doing a variety of methods for forecasting. Test your program with the following set of data. These figures show the gross national product (in thousand million pounds) of the United Kingdom between 1949 and 1989 at factor cost.

11.1	11.7	12.9	14.0	15.0	15.9	16.9	18.4	19.5
20.3	21.3	22.8	24.3	25.4	27.1	29.2	31.5	33.4
35.2	37.7	39.9	43.6	49.5	55.4	64.5	74.7	94.4
115.0	129.2	149.5	172.3	199.0	219.0	238.7	262.6	283.5
307.5	327.3	357.8	388.3	411.6				

Use these figures to forecast the GNP for the next ten years. Write a report about your findings, including appropriate graphs and charts.

9.5 Find figures published by the government for the total consumption of electricity in the U.K. over a suitable historic period. Hence forecast the future demand for electricity. Write a report about your findings, emphasizing the methods used and problems met. Assume that your report is to be presented to a group of people for discussion, and that the quality of presentation is therefore important.

Case study

Workload planning

Mary James worked in the purchasing department of a medium-sized construction company. One morning she walked into the office and said, 'The problem with this office is lack of planning. I have been reading a few articles about planning, and it seems to me that forecasting is the key to an efficient business. We never have done any forecasting, but simply rely on experience to guess our future workload. I think that we should start using exponential smoothing to do some forecasting. Then we can foresee problems and schedule our time more efficiently.'

As Mary was in charge of the office, she soon persuaded the others to follow her advice. Unfortunately, they were going through a busy period and nobody in the office had time to develop any plans. A month later nothing had actually happened. Mary was not very pleased and said that their current high workload would be reduced if they did some forecasting and organized their time more effectively. In particular, they would not be overwhelmed by periodic surges in work.

To make some progress with the forecasting, Mary seconded a management trainee to work on some figures. The trainee examined their work, and divided it into seven categories, including searching for business, preparing estimates, submitting tenders, finding suppliers. For each of these categories he added the number of distinct pieces of work that the office had completed in each quarter of the past three years. He took six weeks to collect these figures, and summarized them as shown in Table 9.9.

Table 9.9

Quarter	Work 1	Work 2	Work 3	Work 4	Work 5	Work 6	Work 7
1,1	129	74	1 000	755	1 210	204	24
2,1	138	68	1 230	455	1 520	110	53
3,1	110	99	890	810	1 390	105	42
4,1	118	119	700	475	1 170	185	21
1,2	121	75	790	785	1 640	154	67
2,2	137	93	1 040	460	1 900	127	83
3,2	121	123	710	805	1 860	187	80
4,2	131	182	490	475	1 620	133	59
1,3	115	103	610	775	2 010	166	105
2,3	126	147	840	500	2 340	140	128
3,3	131	141	520	810	2 210	179	126
4,3	131	112	290	450	1 990	197	101

Now the trainee wanted to forecast likely workload for the next two years. He knew a little about forecasting, and felt that exponential smoothing might not be the answer. He was not sure if the results would be reliable enough. He also wanted to link the forecasts to planning, so he converted the different types of work into 'standard work units'. These could be used to determine the office's overall workload. After some discussion he devised a comparison with each piece of work allocated the following work units.

Work 1   2 units   Work 2   1.5 units   Work 3   1 unit

Work 4   0.7 units   Work 5   0.4 units   Work 6   3 units

Work 7   2.5 units

Your job is to prepare a report on the results found by the trainee. This should contain forecasts of future workload, a description of the forecasting methods used, discussion of the reliability of results, patterns of workload in the office, implications for work scheduling and further work to be done.

Using matrices to solve equations

CHAPTER OUTLINE

Chapter 2 described how to solve simultaneous equations. Since then we have come across a number of models that use sets of simultaneous equations. One way of solving these is to use matrices, which provide a convenient notation for describing certain types of problem.

This chapter describes some arithmetic using matrices and shows how this can be used to solve sets of simultaneous equations. After reading the chapter and doing the exercises you should be able to:

● describe problems using matrices
● add and subtract matrices
● multiply matrices
● find the inverse of matrices
● use matrices to solve simultaneous equations

10.1 | What is a matrix?

Imagine that you work for a company that runs two types of shop, wholesale and retail. These shops are in three geographical regions with 20 retail and 2 wholesale shops in the North, 60 retail and 6 wholesale shops in the Midlands and 30 retail and 4 wholesale shops in the South. We can show these figures in a simple table:

	Type of Shop	
Region	Retail	Wholesale
North	20	2
Midlands	60	6
South	30	4

This table gives a useful description of the information, but it becomes awkward if we want to do any calculations. It would be useful to have a similar format for data, but one which allows a range of calculations. This format is provided by a **matrix**. A matrix simply shows the numbers in the body of the table, but ignores all titles and lines. Thus a matrix of the figures above is written:

$$A = \begin{bmatrix} 20 & 2 \\ 60 & 6 \\ 30 & 4 \end{bmatrix}$$

As you can see, a matrix consists of a rectangular array of numbers enclosed in square brackets. The numbers are arranged in rows and columns and each matrix is given an identifying name, which is usually a single capital letter printed in **bold**. The size of a matrix is described as:

(number of rows × number of columns)

As the matrix above has three rows and two columns its size is (3 × 2), which is said '3 by 2'. Then we can say, 'The number of shops is described by the (3 × 2) matrix, **A**'.

In this notation each number in the matrix is called an **element** and is described by a lower case letter with a double subscript to show its row and column. Thus, $a_{i,j}$ is the element in the ith row and jth column of matrix **A**. In the matrix above $a_{1,2}$ is the element in the first row and second column of **A**, which equals 2. So:

$$a_{1,1} = 20 \qquad a_{1,2} = 2 \qquad a_{2,1} = 60 \qquad a_{2,2} = 6$$

and so on.

In some cases a matrix will only have one row, in which case it is called a **row vector**. Similarly, if it only has one column it is called a **column vector**. If

$$C = \begin{bmatrix} 5 & 7 & 3 & 1 & 5 \end{bmatrix}$$

we can say that C is a (1×5) matrix, which is a row vector.

Similarly, if

$$D = \begin{bmatrix} 5 \\ 4 \\ 1 \\ 6 \\ 4 \end{bmatrix}$$

then D is a (5×1) matrix, which is a column vector.

WORKED EXAMPLE 10.1

A company makes three products from four raw materials. The number of units of each raw material needed to make one unit of product 1 are 17, 22, 4 and 7 respectively. The numbers of units of raw material needed to make one unit of the other two products are 12, 5, 22, 6 and 7, 3, 14, 8 respectively. Show this data as a matrix, M. What are the values of $m_{2,3}$ and $m_{3,2}$?

Solution

Describing the problem in a table would give

Product	Raw material 1	Raw material 2	Raw material 3	Raw material 4
1	17	22	4	7
2	12	5	22	6
3	7	3	14	8

Then putting the numbers into a matrix, M, gives

$$M = \begin{bmatrix} 17 & 22 & 4 & 7 \\ 12 & 5 & 22 & 6 \\ 7 & 3 & 14 & 8 \end{bmatrix}$$

Then $m_{2,3}$ is the element in the second row and third column which is 22, while $m_{3,2}$ is the element in the third row and second column which is 3.

In Worked Example 10.1 we showed the products as the rows of the matrix and the raw materials as the columns. There is no special significance in this, so we could equally have shown the products as the columns and the materials as the rows. Then we would have

$$M = \begin{bmatrix} 17 & 12 & 7 \\ 22 & 5 & 3 \\ 4 & 22 & 14 \\ 7 & 6 & 8 \end{bmatrix}$$

This new matrix is described as the **transpose** of the original matrix.

Generally, the transpose of a matrix is defined as follows:

$$A = \begin{bmatrix} a & b & c \\ d & e & f \end{bmatrix} \quad \text{is} \quad A^T = \begin{bmatrix} a & d \\ b & e \\ c & f \end{bmatrix}$$

Matrices give a convenient notation, but the orientation is not significant; we simply use the most convenient. Once chosen, however, you must remember that each row and column has a distinct meaning. Even though the labels are omitted, they are still implicit in the definitions.

By now it should be clear that matrices give a convenient and economical way of describing some problems. They also give a convenient way of organizing the arithmetic, as we shall see in the following section. They do not, however, give any fundamentally new methods of solution.

> Matrices provide a notation but no new methods of solution

IN SUMMARY

Matrices give a useful notation for describing some problems and organizing calculations. They do not give any new means of solutions.

Self-assessment problems

10.1 What is the purpose of a matrix?

10.2 Describe the following matrix. What is the value of $f_{1,3}$? What is the value of $f_{3,1}$?

$$F = \begin{bmatrix} 3 & 1 & 4 \\ 4 & 1 & 1 \\ 6 & 3 & 1 \end{bmatrix}$$

10.3 What is a vector?

10.2 | Matrix arithmetic

Matrix **A** in section 10.1 shows the number of shops operated in different geographical areas. If we know the number of people employed in each type of shop, we can find the total number employed by doing some calculations on the matrix. In this section we shall describe some useful calculations.

10.2.1 | Addition and subtraction

Two matrices can only be added or subtracted if they are the same size. Then to add one matrix to another, the corresponding elements are added:
One consequence of this definition is that matrices are commutative, so that

> $$C = A + B$$
> implies that
> $$c_{ij} = a_{ij} + b_{ij}$$

$A + B = B + A$. When one matrix is subtracted from another, the corresponding elements are subtracted:

> $$C = A - B$$
> implies that
> $$c_{ij} = a_{ij} - b_{ij}$$

WORKED EXAMPLE 10.2

If:

$$A = \begin{bmatrix} 6 & 5 \\ 1 & 8 \end{bmatrix} \quad \text{and} \quad B = \begin{bmatrix} 3 & 5 \\ 6 & 4 \end{bmatrix}$$

What is $A + B$? What is $A - B$?

Solution

Both A and B are (2×2) matrices, so they can be added and subtracted. Then the answers are found by adding and subtracting corresponding elements.

$$A + B = \begin{bmatrix} 6 + 3 & 5 + 5 \\ 1 + 6 & 8 + 4 \end{bmatrix} = \begin{bmatrix} 9 & 10 \\ 7 & 12 \end{bmatrix}$$

$$A - B = \begin{bmatrix} 6 - 3 & 5 - 5 \\ 1 - 6 & 8 - 4 \end{bmatrix} = \begin{bmatrix} 3 & 0 \\ -5 & 4 \end{bmatrix}$$

Two matrices are said to be equal if they are the same size and each corresponding element is the same in both matrices. Then:

$$A = B \quad \text{implies} \quad a_{ij} = b_{ij} \quad \text{for all values of } i \text{ and } j.$$

This leads to a special result when a matrix is subtracted from another equal matrix. Then $A - B$ would define a matrix which is the same size as A and B, but where every element is equal to zero. This is called a **zero matrix**, which performs the same function as a zero in ordinary arithmetic.

WORKED EXAMPLE 10.3

If

$$D = \begin{bmatrix} 10 & 7 \\ 12 & 18 \\ 3 & 16 \end{bmatrix}$$

and $E = D$, what is $e_{2,2}$? What is $D - E$?

Solution

$e_{2,2}$ is the element in the second row and second column of **E**. As **E** = **D**, $e_{2,2} = d_{2,2} = 18$. Similarly $e_{3,1} = d_{3,1} = 3$, $e_{1,2} = d_{1,2} = 7$, and so on.

$$D = \begin{bmatrix} 10 & 7 \\ 12 & 18 \\ 3 & 16 \end{bmatrix} \quad \text{and} \quad E = \begin{bmatrix} 10 & 7 \\ 12 & 18 \\ 3 & 16 \end{bmatrix}$$

so

$$D - E = \begin{bmatrix} 10 - 10 & 7 - 7 \\ 12 - 12 & 18 - 18 \\ 3 - 3 & 16 - 16 \end{bmatrix} = \begin{bmatrix} 0 & 0 \\ 0 & 0 \\ 0 & 0 \end{bmatrix}$$

WORKED EXAMPLE 10.4

A company stocks pots and pans in three different sizes. The numbers in stock are shown in the following table. Describe the present stock by a matrix.

Size	Stock	
	Pots	*Pans*
Large	10	13
Medium	24	16
Small	17	9

A delivery of pots and pans arrives, with the numbers shown in matrix **D** (which has rows showing sizes, and columns showing pots or pans). In the following two weeks the numbers of pots and pans sold are described by the matrices **W1** and **W2**. What are the stocks after the delivery arrives? What stocks remain after each of the following two weeks?

$$D = \begin{bmatrix} 5 & 20 \\ 12 & 7 \\ 3 & 6 \end{bmatrix} \quad W1 = \begin{bmatrix} 3 & 16 \\ 10 & 15 \\ 4 & 2 \end{bmatrix} \quad W2 = \begin{bmatrix} 12 & 17 \\ 26 & 8 \\ 16 & 13 \end{bmatrix}$$

Solution

The current stocks can be described by the (3×2) matrix **S**:

$$S = \begin{bmatrix} 10 & 13 \\ 24 & 16 \\ 17 & 9 \end{bmatrix}$$

Then after the delivery, the stock will rise to $S1$, where:

$$S1 = S + D = \begin{bmatrix} 10 & 13 \\ 24 & 16 \\ 17 & 9 \end{bmatrix} + \begin{bmatrix} 5 & 20 \\ 12 & 7 \\ 3 & 6 \end{bmatrix} = \begin{bmatrix} 15 & 33 \\ 36 & 23 \\ 20 & 15 \end{bmatrix}$$

After week 1 the stock will decline to $S2$, where:

$$S2 = S1 - W1 = \begin{bmatrix} 15 & 33 \\ 36 & 23 \\ 20 & 15 \end{bmatrix} - \begin{bmatrix} 3 & 16 \\ 10 & 15 \\ 4 & 2 \end{bmatrix} = \begin{bmatrix} 12 & 17 \\ 26 & 8 \\ 16 & 13 \end{bmatrix}$$

Then after week 2 the stock will decline to $S3$, where:

$$S3 = S2 - W2 = \begin{bmatrix} 12 & 17 \\ 26 & 8 \\ 16 & 13 \end{bmatrix} - \begin{bmatrix} 12 & 17 \\ 26 & 8 \\ 16 & 13 \end{bmatrix} = \begin{bmatrix} 0 & 0 \\ 0 & 0 \\ 0 & 0 \end{bmatrix}$$

Now all the elements in $S3$ are zero, so this defines a zero matrix.

IN SUMMARY

Matrices of the same size can be added or subtracted according to the rules:

- if $C = A + B$, then $c_{i,j} = a_{i,j} + b_{i,j}$
- if $C = A - B$, then $c_{i,j} = a_{i,j} - b_{i,j}$

10.2.2 | Multiplication of matrices

A matrix can be multiplied by a single number. This is called **scalar multiplication** and it means that every element in the matrix is multiplied by the number.

If $D = f \times E$, where D and E are matrices and f is an ordinary number:

$$d_{i,j} = f \times e_{i,j}$$

WORKED EXAMPLE 10.5

The number of units of different types of product made by a factory is described by the following matrix:

$$P = \begin{bmatrix} 10 & 6 & 20 \\ 4 & 12 & 6 \end{bmatrix}$$

The factory is about to introduce a third shift to increase production by 50%. What is the expected output?

Solution

The new output can be found by multiplying the previous output by 1.5. Then the new output is

$$P = 1.5 \times \begin{bmatrix} 10 & 6 & 20 \\ 4 & 12 & 6 \end{bmatrix}$$

$$= \begin{bmatrix} 1.5 \times 10 & 1.5 \times 6 & 1.5 \times 20 \\ 1.5 \times 4 & 1.5 \times 12 & 1.5 \times 6 \end{bmatrix} = \begin{bmatrix} 15 & 9 & 30 \\ 6 & 18 & 9 \end{bmatrix}$$

There is another type of multiplication called **matrix multiplication**. This occurs when one matrix is multiplied by another. Unfortunately, matrix multiplication is a little more complicated than scalar multiplication. The first thing we have to do is ensure that the matrices are the right size to allow multiplication. The requirement is that the number of columns in the first matrix must equal the number of rows in the second. In other words, a matrix of size $(r \times c)$ can only be multiplied by matrix of size $(c \times n)$. Both r and n can be any numbers, and the result will be a $(r \times n)$ matrix. Thus a (2×4) matrix can be multiplied by a (4×3) matrix and the result will be a (2×3) matrix.

The mechanics of matrix multiplication are as follows. To find D which equals $A \times B$ we calculate each element $d_{i,j}$ separately. Each term $d_{i,j}$ is calculated from the ith row of A and the jth column of B, and is defined as:

$$d_{i,j} = a_{i,1} \times b_{1,j} + a_{i,2} \times b_{2,j} + a_{i,3} \times b_{3,j} + \dots + a_{i,c} \times b_{c,j}$$

where c is the number of columns in A and rows in B.

Thus we start by taking the first element in row i and multiplying it by the first element in column j; then take the second element in row i and multiply this by the second element in column j; then repeat this until we reach the end of the row. Adding these numbers together gives the element $d_{i,j}$. This calculation is then repeated for all rows in matrix A to form the new column in matrix D. Then this whole process is repeated for all columns in matrix B to form the remainder of the columns in D. Thus:

$$d_{1,1} = a_{1,1} \times b_{1,1} + a_{1,2} \times b_{2,1} + a_{1,3} \times b_{3,1} + ... + a_{1,c} \times b_{c,1}$$

$$d_{1,2} = a_{1,1} \times b_{1,2} + a_{1,2} \times b_{2,2} + a_{1,3} \times b_{3,2} + ... + a_{1,c} \times b_{c,2}$$

$$d_{1,3} = a_{1,1} \times b_{1,3} + a_{1,2} \times b_{2,3} + a_{1,3} \times b_{3,3} + ... + a_{1,c} \times b_{c,3}$$

$$d_{2,1} = a_{2,1} \times b_{1,1} + a_{2,2} \times b_{2,1} + a_{2,3} \times b_{3,1} + ... + a_{2,c} \times b_{c,1}$$

$$d_{3,1} = a_{3,1} \times b_{1,1} + a_{3,2} \times b_{2,1} + a_{3,3} \times b_{3,1} + ... + a_{3,c} \times b_{c,1}$$

$$d_{2,2} = a_{2,1} \times b_{1,2} + a_{2,2} \times b_{2,2} + a_{2,3} \times b_{3,2} + ... + a_{2,c} \times b_{c,2}$$

and so on.

At first sight this calculation seems rather complicated. However, with practice it becomes quite easy, and we can always use a computer to save time.

WORKED EXAMPLE 10.6

If

$$A = \begin{bmatrix} 2 & 3 \\ 1 & 6 \\ 5 & 7 \end{bmatrix} \quad \text{and} \quad B = \begin{bmatrix} 4 & 2 & 3 \\ 6 & 1 & 5 \end{bmatrix}$$

what is $A \times B$?

Solution

We start by making sure that A and B are the right size to allow multiplication. A is (3×2) and B is (2×3) so the number of columns in A equals the number of rows in B and the matrices can be multiplied. The result will be a (3×3) matrix.

Suppose we let $C = A \times B$. Then we start by calculating $c_{1,1}$:

$$c_{1,1} = a_{1,1} \times b_{1,1} + a_{1,1} \times b_{1,2} = 2 \times 4 + 3 \times 6 = 26$$

Then:

$$c_{2,1} = a_{2,1} \times b_{1,2} + a_{2,2} \times b_{2,1} = 1 \times 4 + 6 \times 6 = 40$$

$$c_{1,2} = a_{1,1} \times b_{2,1} + a_{1,2} \times b_{2,2} = 2 \times 2 + 3 \times 1 = 7$$

$$c_{2,2} = a_{2,1} \times b_{1,2} + a_{2,2} \times b_{2,2} = 1 \times 2 + 6 \times 1 = 8$$

and so on. These calculations are repeated for all values of $c_{i,j}$, to give

$$C = A \times B$$

$$
= \begin{bmatrix} 2 & 3 \\ 1 & 6 \\ 5 & 7 \end{bmatrix} \times \begin{bmatrix} 4 & 2 & 3 \\ 6 & 1 & 5 \end{bmatrix}
$$

$$
= \begin{bmatrix} 2 \times 4 + 3 \times 6 & 2 \times 2 + 3 \times 1 & 2 \times 3 + 3 \times 5 \\ 1 \times 4 + 6 \times 6 & 1 \times 2 + 6 \times 1 & 1 \times 3 + 6 \times 5 \\ 5 \times 4 + 7 \times 6 & 5 \times 2 + 7 \times 1 & 5 \times 3 + 7 \times 5 \end{bmatrix}
$$

$$
= \begin{bmatrix} 26 & 7 & 21 \\ 40 & 8 & 33 \\ 62 & 17 & 50 \end{bmatrix}
$$

One interesting point is that matrix multiplication is not commutative, so that $A \times B$ does not equal $B \times A$. Suppose, for example, A is a (4×2) matrix, while B is (2×3); then A can be multiplied by B to give a (4×3) matrix $A \times B$. However, B cannot be multiplied by A as their sizes do not match: the number of columns in B would have to be the same as the number of rows in A. In this case the value of $B \times A$ is not defined.

If

$$
A = \begin{bmatrix} 1 & 2 \\ 3 & 4 \\ 5 & 6 \\ 7 & 8 \end{bmatrix} \quad \text{and} \quad B = \begin{bmatrix} 10 & 20 & 30 \\ 40 & 50 & 60 \end{bmatrix}
$$

then

$$
A \times B = \begin{bmatrix} 1 & 2 \\ 3 & 4 \\ 5 & 6 \\ 7 & 8 \end{bmatrix} \times \begin{bmatrix} 10 & 20 & 30 \\ 40 & 50 & 60 \end{bmatrix} = \begin{bmatrix} 90 & 120 & 150 \\ 190 & 260 & 330 \\ 290 & 400 & 510 \\ 390 & 540 & 690 \end{bmatrix}
$$

but

$$
B \times A = \begin{bmatrix} 10 & 20 & 30 \\ 40 & 50 & 60 \end{bmatrix} \times \begin{bmatrix} 1 & 2 \\ 3 & 4 \\ 5 & 6 \\ 7 & 8 \end{bmatrix}
$$

and this is not defined. Even if the matrices are the right size and multiplication is defined, $A \times B$ does not equal $B \times A$, as illustrated in the following example.

WORKED EXAMPLE 10.7

If

$$A = \begin{bmatrix} 2 & 1 \\ 3 & 5 \end{bmatrix} \quad \text{and} \quad B = \begin{bmatrix} 4 & 1 \\ 2 & 7 \end{bmatrix}$$

What is $A \times B$? What is $B \times A$?

Solution

As A and B are both (2×2) then $A \times B$ and $B \times A$ can be calculated, but they are not equal:

$$A \times B = \begin{bmatrix} 2 & 1 \\ 3 & 5 \end{bmatrix} \times \begin{bmatrix} 4 & 1 \\ 2 & 7 \end{bmatrix}$$

$$= \begin{bmatrix} 2 \times 4 + 1 \times 2 & 2 \times 1 + 1 \times 7 \\ 3 \times 4 + 5 \times 2 & 3 \times 1 + 5 \times 7 \end{bmatrix} = \begin{bmatrix} 10 & 9 \\ 22 & 38 \end{bmatrix}$$

$$B \times A = \begin{bmatrix} 4 & 1 \\ 2 & 7 \end{bmatrix} \times \begin{bmatrix} 2 & 1 \\ 3 & 5 \end{bmatrix}$$

$$= \begin{bmatrix} 4 \times 2 + 1 \times 3 & 4 \times 1 + 1 \times 5 \\ 2 \times 2 + 7 \times 3 & 2 \times 1 + 7 \times 5 \end{bmatrix} = \begin{bmatrix} 11 & 9 \\ 25 & 37 \end{bmatrix}$$

WORKED EXAMPLE 10.8

If

$$A = \begin{bmatrix} 2 & 4 & 1 \\ 3 & 5 & 6 \end{bmatrix} \quad \text{and} \quad B = \begin{bmatrix} 1 \\ 1 \\ 1 \end{bmatrix}$$

What is $A \times B$?

Solution

$$A \times B = \begin{bmatrix} 2 + 4 + 1 \\ 3 + 5 + 6 \end{bmatrix} = \begin{bmatrix} 4 \\ 17 \end{bmatrix}$$

This is an interesting result, as the multiplication has the effect of adding the rows. Conversely, if we had multiplied A by a row vector containing only 1s, it would have added the columns.

WORKED EXAMPLE 10.9

A tailor's shop sells two styles of suit called Standard and Super. Each suit contains a jacket, trousers and waistcoat. The selling price of each part of a suit is shown in the following table:

Selling Price	Part		
	Jacket	Trousers	Waistcoat
Standard	20	30	40
Super	60	80	100

Three companies, X, Y and Z, place regular orders for their employees. In one week the number of suits ordered is given in the following table:

Sales	Style	
	Standard	Super
X	1	8
Y	4	3
Z	2	6

Use matrix multiplication to find the income from each customer. Now use matrix arithmetic to find the amount that each customer spent and the total income.

Solution

The income from each customer for each part of a suit is found by multiplying the number of suits by the selling price. For this we need to transform the information into matrices and then multiply them together. We can create a (3×2) matrix, D, for demand and multiply this by the selling price, which must be a (2×3) matrix, P.

$$D = \begin{bmatrix} 1 & 8 \\ 4 & 3 \\ 2 & 6 \end{bmatrix} \quad \text{and} \quad P = \begin{bmatrix} 20 & 30 & 40 \\ 60 & 80 & 100 \end{bmatrix}$$

Then multiplying **D** by **P** gives the information we want. If you look carefully at the arithmetic, you can confirm that we are adding the cost of one standard jacket for X at £20 to the cost of eight super jackets at £60, and so on.

$$\begin{bmatrix} 1 & 8 \\ 4 & 3 \\ 2 & 6 \end{bmatrix} \times \begin{bmatrix} 20 & 30 & 40 \\ 60 & 80 & 100 \end{bmatrix}$$

$$= \begin{bmatrix} 1 \times 20 + 8 \times 60 & 1 \times 30 + 8 \times 80 & 1 \times 40 + 8 \times 100 \\ 4 \times 20 + 3 \times 60 & 4 \times 30 + 3 \times 80 & 4 \times 40 + 3 \times 100 \\ 2 \times 20 + 6 \times 60 & 2 \times 30 + 6 \times 80 & 2 \times 40 + 6 \times 100 \end{bmatrix}$$

$$= \begin{bmatrix} 500 & 670 & 840 \\ 260 & 360 & 460 \\ 400 & 540 & 680 \end{bmatrix}$$

This resulting matrix shows the expenditure of a customer in each row, and purchases in each column. Then customer X spent £500 on jackets, £670 on trousers and £840 on waistcoats. Customer Y spent £260 on jackets, £360 on trousers and £460 on waistcoats, while Z spent £400 on jackets, £540 on trousers and £680 on waistcoats.

The total spent by each customer is found by adding the rows. This addition is done using a matrix notation by multiplying the sales matrix by a column vector consisting of 1s in each of three rows:

$$\begin{bmatrix} 500 & 670 & 840 \\ 260 & 360 & 460 \\ 400 & 540 & 680 \end{bmatrix} \times \begin{bmatrix} 1 \\ 1 \\ 1 \end{bmatrix} = \begin{bmatrix} 2010 \\ 1080 \\ 1620 \end{bmatrix}$$

Customer X spent £2010, Y spent £1080 and Z spent £1620. Adding these gives the total expenditure, and in a matrix notation this is done by multiplying the matrix by a row vector consisting of three 1s:

$$\begin{bmatrix} 1 & 1 & 1 \end{bmatrix} \times \begin{bmatrix} 2010 \\ 1080 \\ 1620 \end{bmatrix} = 4710$$

Then the total expenditure is £4710.

In this last example we saw how the rows or columns of a matrix could be summed by multiplying by a vector consisting of 1s. Another useful result is found when we multiply any matrix by a zero matrix, which has all elements equal to zero. It can easily be seen, for example, that

$$\begin{bmatrix} 2 & 1 \\ 3 & 5 \end{bmatrix} \times \begin{bmatrix} 0 & 0 \\ 0 & 0 \end{bmatrix} = \begin{bmatrix} 0 & 0 \\ 0 & 0 \end{bmatrix}$$

Multiplying by a zero matrix sets all elements in the resulting matrix to zero. Similarly:

$$\begin{bmatrix} 2 & 1 \\ 3 & 5 \end{bmatrix} \times \begin{bmatrix} 1 & 0 \\ 0 & 1 \end{bmatrix} = \begin{bmatrix} 2 & 1 \\ 3 & 5 \end{bmatrix}$$

A matrix which has 1s down the principal diagonal (which goes from the top left corner of the matrix to the bottom right) and all other entries of zero, is called an **identity matrix**. By definition an identity matrix is square (so the number of rows equals the number of columns) and it serves the same purpose as '1' in ordinary arithmetic. When a matrix is multiplied by an identity matrix, the original matrix is unchanged. Thus

$$\boldsymbol{A} \times \boldsymbol{I} = \boldsymbol{A} = \boldsymbol{I} \times \boldsymbol{A}$$

By convention an identity matrix is always called $\boldsymbol{I}$.

IN SUMMARY

Scalar multiplication multiplies all elements in a matrix by a constant. With matrix multiplication a matrix $\boldsymbol{A}$ of size $(r \times c)$ can be multiplied by a matrix $\boldsymbol{B}$ of size $(c \times n)$ to give a matrix of size $(r \times n)$, where:

$$d_{i,j} = a_{i,1} \times b_{1,j} + a_{i,2} \times b_{2,j} + a_{i,3} \times b_{3,j} + \dots + a_{i,c} \times b_{c,j}$$

Matrix multiplication is not commutative, so $\boldsymbol{A} \times \boldsymbol{B}$ does not equal $\boldsymbol{B} \times \boldsymbol{A}$.

10.2.3 | Matrix Inversion

We have now described addition, subtraction and multiplication of matrices, so it would seem logical to discuss division. Unfortunately, division of matrices is not really defined. We can, however, achieve the same effect by multiplying by an **inverse matrix**. If we have a matrix $\boldsymbol{A}$, its inverse is called $\boldsymbol{A}^{-1}$, and is defined so that

$$\boldsymbol{A}^{-1} \times \boldsymbol{A} = \boldsymbol{A} \times \boldsymbol{A}^{-1} = \boldsymbol{I}$$

The inverse of a matrix is equivalent to the reciprocal in ordinary arithmetic. As the identity matrix $\boldsymbol{I}$ is square, it follows that the inverse can only be found for square matrices. In practice, even some square matrices do not have inverses, and in these cases we simply say that an inverse, $\boldsymbol{A}^{-1}$, does not exist and related arithmetic cannot be done.

In effect, then, to divide a matrix A by a matrix B we multiply both matrices by the inverse of B. Obviously, the sizes of the matrices must allow this multiplication.

Matrix division $A\,/\,B$ is not defined but equivalent results are found from $B^{-1} \times A$ where B^{-1} is the inverse of B.

Now we have defined the inverse of a matrix, we need a method of calculating it. If a matrix is (2×2), calculating the inverse is fairly straightforward, using the following standard result:

If $\qquad A = \begin{bmatrix} a_{1,1} & a_{1,2} \\ a_{2,1} & a_{2,2} \end{bmatrix}$

Then $\qquad A^{-1} = \dfrac{1}{a_{1,1}a_{2,2} - a_{1,2}a_{2,1}} \times \begin{bmatrix} a_{2,2} & -a_{1,2} \\ -a_{2,1} & a_{1,1} \end{bmatrix}$

WORKED EXAMPLE 10.10

What is the inverse of the matrix

$$\begin{bmatrix} 1 & 5 \\ 2 & 6 \end{bmatrix}$$

Solution

Substituting in the above equation gives

$$A = \begin{bmatrix} 1 & 5 \\ 2 & 6 \end{bmatrix}$$

So

$$A^{-1} = \frac{1}{1 \times 6 - 2 \times 5} \times \begin{bmatrix} 6 & -5 \\ -2 & 1 \end{bmatrix}$$

$$= \begin{bmatrix} -1.5 & 1.25 \\ 0.5 & -0.25 \end{bmatrix}$$

This result can be checked by calculating $A \times A^{-1} = I$:

$$\begin{bmatrix} 1 & 5 \\ 2 & 6 \end{bmatrix} \times \begin{bmatrix} -1.5 & 1.25 \\ 0.5 & -0.25 \end{bmatrix} = \begin{bmatrix} 1 & 0 \\ 0 & 1 \end{bmatrix}$$

The equation to invert a (2×2) matrix is fairly straightforward, but equivalent results for larger matrices become very complicated. There are, however, several alternative ways of finding inverses. Most matrix inversion is done by computer, and they use a method which manipulates the rows. This method starts by using a **partitioned matrix**, where an identity matrix is put alongside the original matrix. With the matrix in Worked Example 10.10, for example, the partitioned matrix would be

$$\left[\begin{array}{cc|cc} 1 & 5 & 1 & 0 \\ 2 & 6 & 0 & 1 \end{array}\right]$$

To invert the original matrix we have to manipulate the lines of this partitioned matrix so that the left-hand side becomes an identity matrix. Then the right-hand side will show the inverse.

There is already a 1 in the top left-hand corner, so this is a useful start. If we subtract twice the top line from the second line we get

$$\left[\begin{array}{cc|cc} 1 & 5 & 1 & 0 \\ 0 & -4 & -2 & 1 \end{array}\right]$$

Now the first column is correct so we can start work on the second column. Dividing the second row by -4 gives

$$\left[\begin{array}{cc|cc} 1 & 5 & 1 & 0 \\ 0 & 1 & 0.5 & -0.25 \end{array}\right]$$

This almost gives the identity matrix, but we have to remove the 5. This is done by subtracting 5 times the bottom line from the top line, to give

$$\left[\begin{array}{cc|cc} 1 & 0 & -1.5 & 1.25 \\ 0 & 1 & 0.5 & -0.25 \end{array}\right]$$

Now there is an identity matrix on the left-hand side, and the right-hand side shows the inverse. If you look back to Worked Example 10.10 you can see that we get the same result. Although this method may seem a little strange, with some thought you will be able to see why it works.

The main problem with matrix arithmetic is the amount of calculation. It is always better to use a computer for these, and spreadsheets can do almost all matrix arithmetic. An illustration of this is shown in Figure 10.1.

Matrix A				Matrix B	
3	6	1		23	16
2	7	6		31	9
1	4	9		4	22
Inverse of A					
0.85	-1.09	0.63			
-0.26	0.57	-0.35			
0.02	-0.13	0.20			
A*B				**Inverse of A*B**	
259	124			-11.67	17.65
287	227			10.13	-6.74
183	250			-2.76	3.48

Figure 10.1 Matrix calculations using a spreadsheet.

IN SUMMARY

Division of matrices is defined in terms of multiplication by an inverse. Mos
matrices (particularly those which are not square) do not have inverses.

Self-assessment questions

10.4 What size is the resulting matrix when a (4 × 5) matrix is added to a
(3 × 2) matrix?

10.5 What size is the resulting matrix when a (4 × 5) matrix is multiplied by a
(5 × 6) matrix?

10.6 How can the rows of a matrix be added using matrix multiplication?

10.7 'The inverse of any matrix can easily be found using a computer.' Is this
statement true?

10.3 Applications of matrices

In practice, the main use of matrices is to solve sets of simultaneous equations
Suppose we have two known matrices **A** and **B**, which are related to an
unknown matrix **X** by the equation

$$A \times X = B$$

We can use matrix inversion to find the value of X. Multiplying both sides of this equation by the inverse of A gives

$$A^{-1} \times A \times X = A^{-1} \times B$$

But $A \times A^{-1} = I$, an identity matrix, so

$$I \times X = A^{-1} \times B$$

But $I \times X = X$, so

$$X = A^{-1} \times B$$

Thus we can find X by multiplying the inverse of A by B.

WORKED EXAMPLE 10.11

Use matrix inversion to solve the simultaneous equations

$$4x + y = 13$$

$$3x + 2y = 16$$

Solution

These equations can be written in matrix form as

$$\begin{bmatrix} 4 & 1 \\ 3 & 2 \end{bmatrix} \times \begin{bmatrix} x \\ y \end{bmatrix} = \begin{bmatrix} 13 \\ 16 \end{bmatrix}$$

This is in the required form $A \times X = B$, with

$$A = \begin{bmatrix} 4 & 1 \\ 3 & 2 \end{bmatrix} \quad X = \begin{bmatrix} x \\ y \end{bmatrix} \quad B = \begin{bmatrix} 13 \\ 16 \end{bmatrix}$$

Now we need the inverse of A, A^{-1}, which we can calculate either from the formula given, or by manipulating the rows. In this case we shall use the equation to give

$$A^{-1} = \frac{1}{a_{1,1}a_{2,2} - a_{1,2}a_{2,1}} \begin{bmatrix} a_{2,2} & a_{1,2} \\ a_{2,1} & a_{1,1} \end{bmatrix}$$

$$A^{-1} = \frac{1}{4 \times 2 - 3 \times 1} \begin{bmatrix} 2 & -1 \\ -3 & 4 \end{bmatrix}$$

$$A^{-1} = \frac{1}{5} \begin{bmatrix} 2 & -1 \\ -3 & 4 \end{bmatrix}$$

Then substitution gives

$$X = A^{-1} \times B$$

$$X = \frac{1}{5} \begin{bmatrix} 2 & -1 \\ -3 & 4 \end{bmatrix} \times \begin{bmatrix} 13 \\ 16 \end{bmatrix}$$

$$= \frac{1}{5} \begin{bmatrix} 26 & - & 16 \\ -39 & + & 64 \end{bmatrix}$$

$$= \frac{1}{5} \begin{bmatrix} 10 \\ 25 \end{bmatrix}$$

$$= \begin{bmatrix} 2 \\ 5 \end{bmatrix}$$

Thus the solution is $x = 2$ and $y = 5$. This can be checked by substituting in the original equations:

$$4x + y = 13: \qquad 4 \times 2 + 5 = 13$$
$$3x + 2y = 16: \qquad 3 \times 2 + 2 \times 5 = 16$$

WORKED EXAMPLE 10.12

In part of its business, a coffee blender uses two types of beans, T_1 and T_2, to make two blends of coffee, American and Brazilian. The American blend uses 75% of available beans of type T_1 and 10% of available beans of type T_2. The Brazilian blend uses 20% of available beans T_1 and 60% of available beans T_2. One month the blender buys t_1 and t_2 kilograms of beans T_1 and T_2 respectively and makes Q_A and Q_B kilograms respectively of American and Brazilian blends.

(a) Use matrices to describe this problem.

(b) If $t_1 = 200$ kg and $t_2 = 300$ kg, how much of the American and Brazilian blends can the blender produce?

(c) If the blender wants to produce 400 kg of American blend and 600 kg of Brazilian blend, what beans should it buy?

Solution

(a) The equations for production are

$$0.75t_1 + 0.1t_2 = Q_A$$
$$0.2t_1 + 0.6t_2 = Q_B$$

These can be described in matrix notation by

$$\begin{bmatrix} 0.75 & 0.1 \\ 0.2 & 0.6 \end{bmatrix} \times \begin{bmatrix} t_1 \\ t_2 \end{bmatrix} = \begin{bmatrix} Q_A \\ Q_B \end{bmatrix}$$

(b) If $t_1 = 200$ and $t_2 = 300$, the values of Q_A and Q_B can be found by multiplication:

$$\begin{bmatrix} 0.75 & 0.1 \\ 0.2 & 0.6 \end{bmatrix} \times \begin{bmatrix} 200 \\ 300 \end{bmatrix} = \begin{bmatrix} Q_A \\ Q_B \end{bmatrix} = \begin{bmatrix} 180 \\ 220 \end{bmatrix}$$

The beans allow 180 kg of American blend and 220 kg of Brazilian blend.

(c) If $Q_A = 400$ and $Q_B = 600$ we can substitute to give

$$\begin{bmatrix} 0.75 & 0.1 \\ 0.2 & 0.6 \end{bmatrix} \times \begin{bmatrix} t_1 \\ t_2 \end{bmatrix} = \begin{bmatrix} 400 \\ 600 \end{bmatrix}$$

To find the values of t_1 and t_2 we have to multiply both sides of this equation by the inverse of the blend matrix. This inverse is

$$\begin{bmatrix} 1.395 & -0.233 \\ -0.465 & 1.744 \end{bmatrix}$$

Then substitution gives

$$\begin{bmatrix} t_1 \\ t_2 \end{bmatrix} = \begin{bmatrix} 1.395 & -0.233 \\ -0.465 & 1.744 \end{bmatrix} \times \begin{bmatrix} 400 \\ 600 \end{bmatrix} = \begin{bmatrix} 418.2 \\ 860.5 \end{bmatrix}$$

Thus to make these blends the blender needs 418.6 kg of beans T_1 and 860.5 kg of beans T_2.

WORKED EXAMPLE 10.13

A company makes four products (A, B, C and D) using four ingredients (w, x, y and z). Product A consists of 20% w, 30% x, 10% y and 40% z. Product B consists of 10% w, 60% x and 30% z. Product C consists of 30% w, 10% x, 50% y and 10% z. Product D consists of 50% w, 20% x, 10% y and 20% z.

(a) Describe a matrix model of this situation.

(b) If the company want to make 100 tonnes of A, 50 tonnes of B, 40 tonnes of C and 60 tonnes of D, what ingredients should it buy?

(c) If ingredients cost £100, £150, £200 and £160 a tonne respectively, what is the cost for the production plan?

(d) If the company gets a delivery of 60 tonnes of w, 80 tonnes of x, 50 tonnes of y and 90 tonnes of z, what products can it make? What is the total weight of products?

Solution

(a) The first thing to do is build a matrix model of the problem. This will be of the form

$$P \times N = R$$

where:

P = the amounts produced of each product

N = the proportion of ingredients in each product

R = the requirements of each ingredient

We are given the data for N, so we can define

$$N = \begin{bmatrix} 0.2 & 0.3 & 0.1 & 0.4 \\ 0.1 & 0.6 & 0.0 & 0.3 \\ 0.3 & 0.1 & 0.5 & 0.1 \\ 0.5 & 0.2 & 0.1 & 0.2 \end{bmatrix}$$

This shows the proportion of each product (in the rows) which is made up of each ingredient (in the columns). The first row, for example, shows the proportion of ingredients in product A as 0.2 w, 0.3 x, 0.1 y and 0.4 z. The rows should, then, add to 1.

(b) We are given a production plan of the form:

$$P = \begin{bmatrix} 100 & 50 & 40 & 60 \end{bmatrix}$$

so the ingredients required are $P \times N$ (note that we have defined P so that it can be multiplied by N to give the results we want):

$$P \times N = \begin{bmatrix} 100 & 50 & 40 & 60 \end{bmatrix} \times \begin{bmatrix} 0.2 & 0.3 & 0.1 & 0.4 \\ 0.1 & 0.6 & 0.0 & 0.3 \\ 0.3 & 0.1 & 0.5 & 0.1 \\ 0.5 & 0.2 & 0.1 & 0.2 \end{bmatrix}$$

$$= \begin{bmatrix} 67 & 76 & 36 & 71 \end{bmatrix}$$

Hence the production plan needs 67 tonnes of w, 76 tonnes of x, 36 tonnes of y and 71 tonnes of z.

(c) Putting the costs into a matrix C gives the total cost as $R \times C$ (again we have ensured that $R \times C$ is defined):

$$R \times C = \begin{bmatrix} 67 & 76 & 36 & 71 \end{bmatrix} \times \begin{bmatrix} 100 \\ 150 \\ 200 \\ 160 \end{bmatrix} = \begin{bmatrix} 36,660 \end{bmatrix}$$

The cost of ingredients is £36,660.

(d) Here we are told that $R = [60\ 80\ 50\ 90]$ and have to find P. We know that $P \times N = R$, so multiplying by N^{-1} gives $P = R \times N^{-1}$. This means we have to find the inverse of N. It is easy to do this on a computer, and fairly easy to do by hand, giving

$$N^{-1} = \begin{bmatrix} -1 & -0.3333 & -0.3333 & 2.6667 \\ -2.1111 & 2.6296 & 0.4074 & 0.0741 \\ 0.1111 & 0.0370 & 2.2593 & -1.4074 \\ 4.5556 & -1.8148 & -0.7037 & -1.0370 \end{bmatrix}$$

Then

$$R \times N^{-1} = \begin{bmatrix} 60 & 80 & 50 & 90 \end{bmatrix} \times \begin{bmatrix} -1 & -0.3333 & -0.3333 & 2.6667 \\ -2.1111 & 2.6296 & 0.4074 & 0.0741 \\ 0.1111 & 0.0370 & 2.2593 & -1.4074 \\ 4.5556 & -1.8148 & -0.7037 & -1.0370 \end{bmatrix}$$

$$= \begin{bmatrix} 186.6667 & 28.8889 & 62.2222 & 2.2222 \end{bmatrix}$$

This gives the quantities of each product, and the total weight is found by multiplying this by a column vector:

$$\begin{bmatrix} 186.6667 & 28.8889 & 62.2222 & 2.2222 \end{bmatrix} \times \begin{bmatrix} 1 \\ 1 \\ 1 \\ 1 \end{bmatrix} = 280$$

The total production is 280 tonnes.

$\boxed{IN\ SUMMARY}$

The main purpose of matrices is to make the data manipulation of large problems easier. This property can be illustrated by the solution of simultaneous equations.

Self-assessment questions

10.8 In practice, what is the main use of matrices?

10.9 'Matrices can be used to solve all problems in linear algebra.' Is this statement true?

$\boxed{CHAPTER\ REVIEW}$

This chapter has described the use of matrices. These give a convenient format for describing and doing the arithmetic for several types of problems. In particular the chapter:

- defined relevant terms and discussed the use of matrices
- described matrix addition and subtraction
- described scalar and matrix multiplication
- found the inverse of a matrix
- used matrices to solve simultaneous equations

Problems

10.1 Three matrices are:

$$A = \begin{bmatrix} 10 & 4 \\ 3 & 2 \end{bmatrix} \qquad B = \begin{bmatrix} 6 & 10 \\ 7 & 4 \end{bmatrix} \qquad C = \begin{bmatrix} 7 & 7 \\ 1 & 5 \end{bmatrix}$$

What are $A + B, B + A, A - B, B - A$?

Find values for $A + B + C, A + B - C, B + C - A, C - B - A, C + B + A$.

10.2 Using the matrices defined in Problem 10.1, what are $A \times B$ and $B \times A$? What are $A \times B \times C$ and $C \times B \times A$?

10.3 Jane used her last year's annual bonus to buy some shares. She bought 100 shares in company A, 200 shares in company B, 200 shares in company C and 300 shares in company D. The costs of a share in each company were £1.20, £3.15, £0.95 and £2.45 respectively. Use matrix arithmetic to describe the purchases and find how much Jane spent.

10.4 A tailor's shop sells two styles of suit called Standard and Super. Each suit is made up of a jacket, trousers and waistcoat. The selling price of each part of a suit is shown in the following table:

	Part		
Style	Jacket	Trousers	Waistcoat
Standard	35	45	65
Super	95	120	150

Three companies, X, Y and Z, place regular orders for their employees. In one week the number of suits ordered is given in the following table.

	Customer		
Style	X	Y	Z
Standard	2	6	5
Super	4	7	8

Use matrix multiplication to find the income from each style, the amount each customer spent and the total income.

10.5 A company makes three products, A, B and C. To make each unit of A takes 3 units of component X and 2 units of Y. To make each unit of B and C takes 5 and 7 units respectively of X and 4 and 6 units respectively of Y. An order is received for 5 units of A, 10 of B and 4 of C. Use matrix arithmetic to find the components needed for this order. If each unit of X costs £10 and each unit of B costs £20, use matrix arithmetic to find the total cost of the order.

10.6 Invert the following matrices:

$$\begin{bmatrix} 1 & 3 \\ 4 & 3 \end{bmatrix} \quad \text{and} \quad \begin{bmatrix} 7 & 4 \\ 5 & 3 \end{bmatrix}$$

10.7 Use matrices to solve the simultaneous equations:

$$x + y - z = 4$$

$$2x + 3y + z = 13$$

$$3x - y + 2z = 9$$

10.8 A company makes four products (A, B, C and D) using four ingredients (w, x, y and z). Product A consists of 10% w, 20% x, 30% y and 40% z.

Product B consists of 40% w, 20% x, 10% y and 30% z. Product C consists of 10% w, 20% x, 20% y and 50% z. Product D consists of 20% w, 20% x, 10% y and 50% z. If the company want to make 150 tonnes of A, 100 tonnes of B, 80 tonnes of C and 120 tonnes of D, what ingredients should it buy? If ingredients cost £100, £150, £200 and £160 a tonne respectively, what is the cost for the production plan? If the company gets a delivery of 180 tonnes of w, 180 tonnes of x, 250 tonnes of y and 200 tonnes of z, what products can it make?

Computer exercises

10.1 Figure 10.2 shows a printout from a statistics package which can do some matrix manipulation. Make sure you understand what is happening here. Use an equivalent statistics package to check the results. What other results can you get?

```
=> MATRIX
* Ready for matrix arithmetic

=> SET DATA M1
Data => 2 3
Data => 1 5
Data => END
* Matrix M1 formed
         2.00          3.00
         1.00          5.00

=> SET DATA M2
Data => 3 2 4
Data => 1 2 1
Data => END
* Matrix M2 formed
         3.00          2.00          4.00
         1.00          2.00          1.00

=> MULTIPLY M1 BY M2 RESULT M3
* Multiplication completed: M1*M2 = M3 where M3 is
         8.00          9.00         10.00
         8.00         12.00          9.00

=> INVERSE M1 RESULT M4
* Inversion completed: inverse of M1 = M4 where M4 is
       0.714         -0.429
      -0.143          0.286

=> ADD M1 AND M4 RESULT M5
* Addition completed: M1+M4 = M5 where M5 is
       2.714          2.571
       0.857          5.286

=> QUIT
```

Figure 10.2   Printout from a statistics package doing matrix arithmetic.

10.2 Figure 10.3 shows part of a spreadsheet which is doing some matrix manipulation. Design a spreadsheet to check these results. How could the presentation be improved? Design a spreadsheet which will do more matrix calculations and present the results in a reasonable format.

MATRIX ARITHMETRIC					
MATRIX A			**INVERSE A**		
1.0000	4.0000	3.0000	-0.1250	-0.0625	0.2188
3.0000	6.0000	1.0000	0.0000	0.2500	-0.1250
6.0000	4.0000	2.0000	0.3750	-0.3125	0.0938
MATRIX B			**INVERSE B**		
4.0000	1.0000	4.0000	0.2917	0.0417	-0.2083
6.0000	3.0000	2.0000	-0.6667	0.3333	0.3333
2.0000	2.0000	6.0000	0.1250	-0.1250	0.1250
A*B			**B*A**		
34.0000	19.0000	30.0000	31.0000	38.0000	21.0000
50.0000	23.0000	30.0000	27.0000	50.0000	25.0000
52.0000	22.0000	44.0000	44.0000	44.0000	20.0000
A*INVERSE B			**INVERSE B*A**		
-2.0000	1.0000	1.5000	-0.8333	0.5833	0.5000
-3.0000	2.0000	1.5000	2.3333	0.6667	-1.0000
-0.6667	1.3333	0.3333	0.5000	0.2500	0.5000
B*INVERSE A			**INVERSE A*B**		
1.0000	-1.2500	1.1250	-0.4375	0.1250	0.6875
0.0000	-0.2500	1.1250	1.2500	0.5000	-0.2500
2.0000	-1.5000	0.7500	-0.1875	-0.3750	1.4375

Figure 10.3   Part of a spreadsheet doing matrix arithmetic.

10.3 Use appropriate software to find the inverse of the matrix

$$
\begin{bmatrix}
12 & 25 & 12 & 3 & 45 & 15 & 41 \\
52 & 54 & 33 & 16 & 16 & 18 & 15 \\
45 & 2 & 51 & 14 & 37 & 18 & 24 \\
65 & 9 & 57 & 16 & 23 & 33 & 50 \\
21 & 24 & 24 & 26 & 15 & 47 & 15 \\
9 & 11 & 24 & 5 & 8 & 52 & 14 \\
22 & 6 & 7 & 27 & 19 & 48 & 32
\end{bmatrix}
$$

Confirm that your result is correct. Now extend your analysis by generating a number of other matrices with at least seven rows and/or columns and doing a range of arithmetic.

10.4 Describe a situation with which you are familiar, and show how it can be represented by a matrix model. Do any necessary arithmetic to demonstrate your model. Write a report on your findings.

Planning with linear programming | 11

CHAPTER OUTLINE

Many problems in business concern the allocation of scarce resources to achieve stated objectives. There are inevitably constraints on the options available, so these problems are described as 'constrained optimization'. This chapter describes linear programming, which is a widely used method of finding optimal solutions to problems of constrained optimization. Here 'programming' is used in its broad sense of 'planning', and has nothing to do with computer programming.

Linear programming can appear complicated, but this is mainly due to the cumbersome arithmetic. For this reason we shall demonstrate some principles with a simple example, and assume that larger problems will be solved by a computer.

After reading this chapter and doing the exercises you should be able to:

- appreciate the concept of constrained optimization
- formulate linear programmes and recognize the assumptions made
- use graphical methods to solve linear programmes
- calculate the effect of changes in the objective function
- calculate marginal values and the ranges over which these apply
- assess new products
- understand printouts from computer packages for linear programming

11.1 | What is linear programming?

Managers are often faced by problems of achieving some objective when there are constraints on available resources. An operations manager wants to maximize the number of units made using limited production facilities; a marketing manager wants to maximize the impact of an advertising campaign without exceeding a specified budget; a finance manager wants to maximize the return on investment of a limited amount of funds; a construction manager wants to minimize the cost of a project without exceeding the time available. Such problems have:

- an objective of optimizing (i.e. maximizing or minimizing) some function
- a set of constraints which limit the possible solutions

For this reason they are called problems of **constrained optimization.**

Linear programming (LP) is a widely used method of solving problems of constrained optimization. We should say straight away that linear programming was developed in the 1950s, when 'programming' was not used to mean 'computer programming'. The name is derived from the more general meaning of 'planning'. LP is widely used for production planning, and a range of applications in government, oil and chemical industries, agriculture, financial institutions, food industries, and public utilities.

Linear programming, in common with many other methods, uses a number of distinct stages to solve a problem. These stages are:

- **formulation** (getting the problem in the right form)
- **solution** (finding an optimal solution to the problem)
- **sensitivity analysis** (seeing what happens when the problem is changed slightly or the solution is adjusted)

Linear programmes can be quite difficult to formulate, and in practice this is usually the most difficult stage. They need a lot of data (so there may be problems getting reliable information for objectives and constraints) and the formulation is quite unwieldy. However, when a problem is in the right form, getting a solution is quite straightforward because a computer is **always** used. The approach we use here, then, is to demonstrate formulations with simple examples, and show how computers can get optimal solutions. After these are found, a certain amount of sensitivity analysis can be done. We shall illustrate this through the use of marginal values.

| IN SUMMARY |

Many problems in business can be described as constrained optimization. Linear programming is a widely used method of tackling such problems.

Self-assessment questions

11.1 What is constrained optimization?

11.2 What is linear programming?

‖ 11.2 ‖ Getting LP problems in the right form

Linear programming is used to find optimal solutions to some problems of constrained optimization. Before it can be used, however, a problem must be described in a standard format. It is easiest to describe this formulation stage with an example. For this we shall use production planning, which is a typical problem of constrained optimization.

Suppose a small factory produces two types of liquid fertilizer, Growbig and Thrive. These are made by similar processes, using the same equipment for blending raw materials, distilling the mix and finishing (bottling, testing, weighing, etc). Because the factory has a limited amount of equipment, there are constraints on the total time available for each process. In particular, no more than 40 hours of blending are available in a week, 40 hours of distilling and 25 hours of finishing. We shall assume that these are the only constraints operating and that there are none on, say, sales or availability of raw materials.

The fertilizers are made in batches of 1000 litres and each batch requires the following number of hours on each process:

Process	Growbig	Thrive
Blending	1	2
Distilling	2	1
Finishing	1	1

If the factory makes a net profit of £30 on each batch of Growbig and £20 on each batch of Thrive, how many batches of each should it make a week?

This problem is clearly one of optimizing an objective (maximizing profit) subject to constraints (production capacity). Common sense would suggest that the profit on Growbig is higher than the profit on Thrive, so we should make as much of this as possible. Twenty batches of Growbig can be made before all the available distilling time is used, with a resulting profit of £600. As we shall see, this is not a very good solution, and linear programming will suggest an alternative which gives the maximum profit as £650.

In this example we want to find the optimal number of batches of Growbig and Thrive, so these are the **decision variables**, which can be defined as follows:

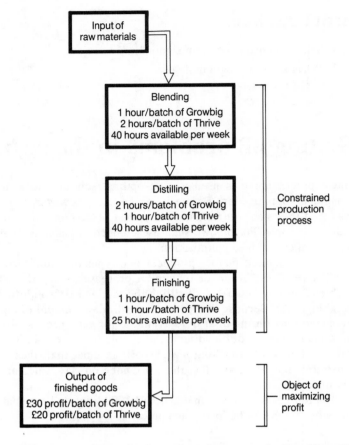

Figure 11.1 Constrained manufacturing process for Growbig and Thrive.

- Let G be the number of batches of Growbig made in a week
- Let T be the number of batches of Thrive made in a week

Now consider the time available for blending. Each batch of Growbig uses 1 hour of blending, so G batches use G hours. Similarly, each batch of Thrive uses 2 hours of blending, so T batches use $2T$ hours. Adding these together gives the total amount of blending time used as $G + 2T$. The maximum amount of blending time available is 40 hours, so the time used must be less than, or at worst equal to, this. Now we have the first constraint:

$$G + 2T \leqslant 40 \qquad \text{blending constraint}$$

(Remember that $\leqslant$ means 'less than or equal to'.)

Turning to the distilling constraint, each batch of Growbig uses 2 hours of distilling, so G batches use $2G$ hours. Each batch of Thrive uses 1 hour of distilling, so T batches use T hours. Adding these together gives the total amount of distilling used and this must be less than, or at worst equal to, the amount of distilling available (40 hours). This gives the second constraint:

$$2G + T \leqslant 40 \qquad \text{distilling constraint}$$

Now the finishing constraint has the total time used for finishing (G for batches of Growbig plus T for batches of Thrive) less than or equal to the time available (25 hours) to give:

$$G + T \leqslant 25 \qquad \text{finishing constraint}$$

These are the three constraints for the process, but there is an additional implicit constraint. The company cannot make a negative number of batches, so both G and T must be positive. This **non-negativity constraint** is a standard feature of linear programmes:

$$G \geqslant 0 \qquad \text{and} \qquad T \geqslant 0 \qquad \text{non-negativity constraints}$$

Now we have all the constraints, and can turn to the objective. In this case the objective is to maximize profit. £30 is made on each batch of Growbig, and G batches are made, so the profit is $30G$; £20 is made on each batch of Thrive, and T batches are made, so the profit is $20T$. Adding these gives the total profit, which is to be maximized. This is called the **objective function**.

$$\text{Maximize} \qquad 30G + 20T \qquad \text{objective function}$$

The linear programming formulation for this problem is now complete with descriptions of:

> - decision variables
> - an objective function
> - a set of constraints
> - a non-negativity constraint

In this example we have:

> Maximize: $30G + 20T$ objective function
> Subject to:
> $$G + 2T \leqslant 40$$
> $$2G + T \leqslant 40$$ constraints
> $$G + T \leqslant 25$$
> with $G \geqslant 0$ and $T \geqslant 0$ non-negativity constraints

This formulation has made a number of assumptions that are implicit in all LPs. Most importantly, the objective function and constraints must all be linear functions of the variables. (There are several extensions to LP, one of which deals with non-linear functions and is, not surprisingly, called non-linear programming.) This means that the use of resources is proportional to the quantity being produced: if production is doubled the use of resources is doubled, and so on. This assumption may not always be valid. Increased production may, for example, use longer production runs which reduce set-up times and running-in problems. Conversely, higher production may mean faster throughput with more units having faults and being scrapped. Linear programming assumes that such effects are included in the data and that the **proportionality assumption** is valid.

A second assumption is that adding the resources used for each product gives the total amount of resources used. Again, this assumption may not always be valid. A craft manufacturer, for example, will use the most skilled craftsmen for more complex jobs. If no complex jobs are available in one period the skilled craftsmen will be used on less complex jobs, which will then be done better or faster than usual. Again, LP assumes that such interactions are included in the data and the **additivity assumption** is valid.

WORKED EXAMPLE 11.1

A political campaign wants to hire photocopying machines to provide leaflets for a local election. There are two suitable machines:

- ACTO costs £120 a month to rent, occupies 2.5 square metres of floor space and can produce 15 000 copies a day

- ZENMAT costs £150 a month to rent, occupies 1.8 square metres of floor space and can produce 18 500 copies a day

The campaign has allowed up to £1200 a month for copying machines, which will be put in a room of 19.2 square metres. What are the problem variables, objective function and constraints for this problem?

Solution

The problem variables are the things we can vary, which are the number of ACTO and ZENMAT machines rented. Let A be the number of ACTO machines rented, and let Z be the number of ZENMAT machines rented.

The objective is to produce as many copies as possible.

Maximize:

$$15\ 000A + 18\ 500Z \qquad \text{objective function}$$

There are constraints on floor space and costs.

Subject to:

$$120A + 150Z \leqslant 1200 \quad \text{cost constraint}$$

$$2.5A + 1.8Z \leqslant 19.2 \quad \text{space constraint}$$

with

$$A \geqslant 0 \text{ and } Z \geqslant 0 \quad \text{non-negativity constraint}$$

WORKED EXAMPLE 11.2

An investment trust has £1 million to invest. After consulting its financial advisers it decides that there are six possible investments with the following characteristics:

Investment	% risk	% dividend	% growth	Rating
1	18	4	22	4
2	6	5	7	10
3	10	9	12	2
4	4	7	8	10
5	12	6	15	4
6	8	8	8	6

The trust wants to invest the £1 million with minimum risk, but with a dividend of at least £70,000 a year, average growth of at least 12% and average rating of at least 7. Formulate this problem as a linear programme.

Solution

The decision variables are the amount of money put into each investment:

Let X_1 be the amount of money put into investment 1

Let X_2 be the amount of money put into investment 2

etc, so X_i is the amount of money put into investment i.

The objective is to minimize risk.

Minimize:

$$0.18X_1 + 0.06X_2 + 0.10X_3 + 0.04X_4 + 0.12X_5 + 0.08X_6$$

Constraints are on the amount of:

money (the total invested must equal £1 million):

$$X_1 + X_2 + X_3 + X_4 + X_5 + X_6 = 1\,000\,000$$

dividend (which must be at least 7% of £1 million):

$$0.04X_1 + 0.05X_2 + 0.09X_3 + 0.07X_4 + 0.06X_5 + 0.08X_6 \geqslant 70\,000$$

average growth (which must be at least 12% of £1 million):

$$0.22X_1 + 0.07X_2 + 0.12X_3 + 0.08X_4 + 0.15X_5 + 0.08X_6 \geqslant 120\,000$$

and rating (the average, weighted by the amount invested, must be at least 7):

$$4X_1 + 10X_2 + 2X_3 + 10X_4 + 4X_5 + 6X_6 \geqslant 7\,000\,000$$

The non-negativity constraints X_1, X_2, X_3, X_4, X_5 and $X_6 \geqslant 0$ complete the formulation.

WORKED EXAMPLE 11.3

An oil company makes two blends of fuel by mixing three oils. The costs and daily availability of the oils are:

Oil	Cost (£/litre)	Amount available (litres)
A	0.25	10 000
B	0.28	15 000
C	0.35	20 000

The requirements of the blends of fuel are:

Blend 1	at most 25% of A
	at least 30% of B
	at most 40% of C
Blend 2	at least 20% of A
	at most 50% of B
	at least 30% of C

Each litre of blend 1 can be sold for £0.60 and each litre of blend 2 can be sold for £0.70. Long-term contracts require at least 10 000 litres of each blend to be produced. Formulate this blending problem as a linear programme.

Solution

The decision variables are the amount of each type of crude oil which is put into each blend:

Let A_1 be the amount of oil A put into blend 1

Let A_2 be the amount of oil A put into blend 2

Let B_1 be the amount of oil B put into blend 1

and so on.

The total quantities of blend 1 and blend 2 produced are

blend 1: $A_1 + B_1 + C_1$

blend 2: $A_2 + B_2 + C_2$

Similarly, the quantities of each oil used are

oil A: $A_1 + A_2$

oil B: $B_1 + B_2$

oil C: $C_1 + C_2$

The objective is to maximize profit. Now the income from selling blends is

$$0.6 \times (A_1 + B_1 + C_1) + 0.7 \times (A_2 + B_2 + C_2)$$

while the cost of buying oil is

$$0.25 \times (A_1 + A_2) + 0.28 \times (B_1 + B_2) + 0.35 \times (C_1 + C_2)$$

The profit is the difference between the income and the cost, which can be rearranged as the objective function:

Maximize:

$$0.35A_1 + 0.45A_2 + 0.32B_1 + 0.42B_2 + 0.25C_1 + 0.35C_2$$

There are constraints on the availability of oils:

$$A_1 + A_2 \leqslant 10\ 000$$

$$B_1 + B_2 \leqslant 15\ 000$$

$$C_1 + C_2 \leqslant 20\ 000$$

There are also six blending constraints. The first of these says that blend 1 must be at most 25% of oil A. In other words:

$$A_1 \leqslant 0.25 \text{ x } (A_1 + B_1 + C_1) \qquad \text{or} \qquad 0.75A_1 - 0.25B_1 - 0.25C_1 \leqslant 0$$

Similarly for the other blends:

$$B_1 \geqslant 0.3 \times (A_1 + B_1 + C_1) \qquad \text{or} \qquad 0.3A_1 - 0.7B_1 + 0.3C_1 \leqslant 0$$

$$C_1 \leqslant 0.4 \times (A_1 + B_1 + C_1) \qquad \text{or} \qquad -0.4A_1 - 0.4B_1 + 0.6C_1 \leqslant 0$$

$$A2 \geqslant 0.2 \times (A_2 + B_2 + C_2) \qquad \text{or} \qquad -0.8A_2 + 0.2B_2 + 0.2C_2 \leqslant 0$$

$$B2 \leqslant 0.5 \times (A_2 + B_2 + C_2) \qquad \text{or} \qquad -0.5A_2 + 0.5B_2 - 0.5C_2 \leqslant 0$$

$$C2 \geqslant 0.3 \times (A_2 + B_2 + C_2) \qquad \text{or} \qquad 0.3A_2 + 0.3B_2 - 0.7C_2 \leqslant 0$$

The long-term contracts impose the conditions that:

$$A_1 + B_1 + C_1 \geqslant 10\ 000$$

$$A_2 + B_2 + C_2 \geqslant 10\ 000$$

The non-negativity conditions that all variables, A_1, A_2, B_1, etc are greater than or equal to 0 completes the formulation.

| IN SUMMARY |

Before linear programming can be used to find an optimal solution, a problem must be put into a standard form. The resulting formulation consists of decision variables, an objective function and constraints.

Self-assessment questions

11.3 What are the main assumptions behind linear programming?

11.4 What is involved in formulating a linear programme?

11.5 What are the components that make up an LP formulation?

11.3 | Using graphs to solve linear programmes

For most real problems the formulation stage is the most difficult. Actually finding the solution to a problem can be relatively straightforward because real LPs are always solved by computer. We shall not go into the details of how these programs work, but will illustrate the general principles. This is not because the method of solving linear programmes is difficult (it is, in fact, rather straightforward), but it relies on a lot of arithmetic that is, at best, tedious. Later in the chapter we shall look at the output from a typical LP package. Here we shall use the previous Growbig and Thrive example to illustrate some general principles.

Returning to the example, the blending constraint is $G + 2T \leqslant 40$. Now we know that the equation $G + 2T = 40$ can be drawn as a straight line on a graph of G against T as shown in Figure 11.2. Remember that the easiest way to draw lines of this type is to take two convenient points and draw a straight line through them. Setting, for example, $G = 0$ gives $2T = 40$ or $T = 20$: similarly, setting $T = 0$ gives $G = 40$. The line of the equation can then be drawn through the points $G = 0$, $T = 20$ and $G = 40$, $T = 0$.

An important observation is that the blending constraint will be broken for any point above this line, while for any point on or below the line the blending constraint will hold. This can be checked by taking any points at random. The

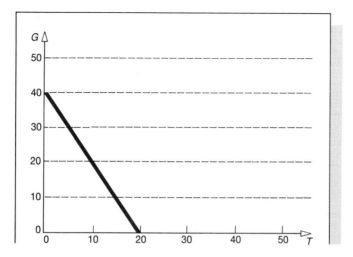

Figure 11.2   Graph of blending constraint.

point $G = 10$, $T = 10$, for example, is below the line and substitution into the constraint gives

$$1 \times 10 + 2 \times 10 \leqslant 40$$

which is true and the constraint is not broken. Conversely, the point $G = 20$, $T = 20$ is above the line and substitution gives

$$1 \times 20 + 2 \times 20 \leqslant 40$$

which is not true and the constraint is broken. Points that are actually on the line satisfy the equality. For example, the point $G = 20$, $T = 10$ is on the line, and substitution gives

$$1 \times 20 + 2 \times 10 \leqslant 40$$

which is true and represents the extreme values allowed by the constraint. The line divides the graph into two areas: all points above the line break the constraint while all points on or below the line do not break the constraint (Figure 11.3).

The other two constraints can be added in the same way. The distilling constraint ($2G + T \leqslant 40$) is the straight line through $G = 20$, $T = 0$ and $G = 0$, $T = 40$. As before, any point above the line breaks the constraint while any point on or below it does not break the constraint and is acceptable for the solution. The finishing constraint ($G + T \leqslant 25$) is the straight line through the points $G = 0$, $T = 25$ to $G = 25$, $T = 0$ and, again, any point above the line will break the constraint and be unacceptable (Figure 11.4).

Any point that is below all three of the constraint lines represents a valid, feasible solution, but if the point is above any of the lines it will break at least one of the constraints and will not represent a feasible solution. Finally, adding the non-negativity constraints limits feasible solutions to the positive quadrant of the graph and defines a **feasible region**, which is the area in which all feasible

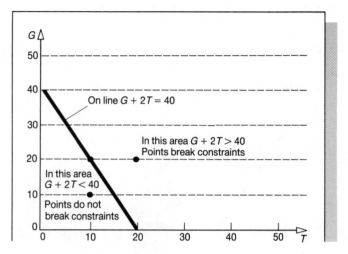

Figure 11.3   Blending constraint divides graph into two areas.

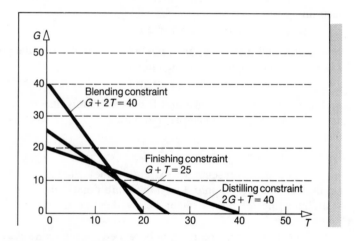

Figure 11.4   Three constraints added to graph.

solutions must lie. Any point inside the feasible region represents a valid solution to the problem while any point outside breaks at least one of the constraints (Figure 11.5).

Now we know the area in which feasible solutions lie, so the next stage is to examine all feasible solutions and identify the optimal one. This is where the objective function is used. For this problem the objective function to be maximized is

$$\text{profit} = 30G + 20T$$

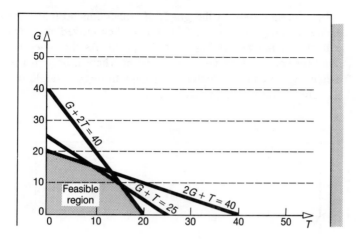

Figure 11.5 Defining the feasible region.

This line can be plotted on the graph of G against T in the same way as the constraints. Although we do not know the optimal value of the profit, we can start looking at an arbitrary, trial value of, say, £600. The graph of $30G + 20T = 600$ can be drawn as before through two convenient points, say $G = 0$, $T = 30$ and $G = 20$, $T = 0$. Similar lines could be drawn for a number of other arbitrary values for profit, with the results shown in Figure 11.6.

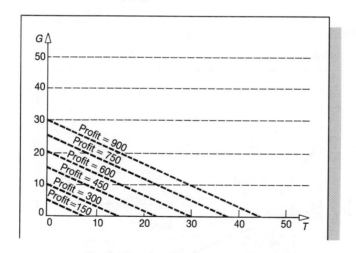

Figure 11.6 Objective function lines for different profits.

The lines for different profits are all parallel and the further they are from the origin the higher is the value of the objective function. This observation shows how we can find an optimal solution for the problem. An objective function line can be superimposed on the graph of constraints so that it passes through the feasible region (Figure 11.7). This line is then moved away from the origin and the further it moves the higher is the profit. As the objective function line is moved further out there will come a point where it only just passes through the feasible region and eventually just passes through a single point (Figure 11.8). This single point is the optimal solution.

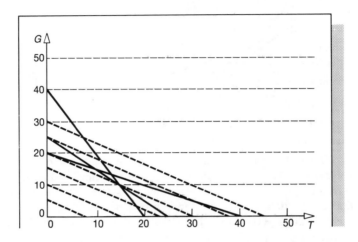

Figure 11.7 Superimposing objective function on constraint lines.

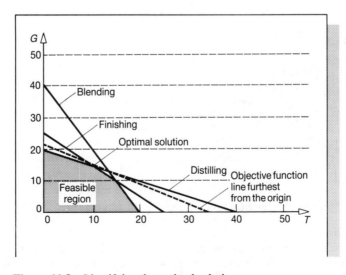

Figure 11.8 Identifying the optimal solution.

The optimal solution can be read from the graph as about the point $G = 15$, $T = 10$. This is the point where the distilling constraint crosses the finishing constraint and these are the active constraints that limit production. There must be spare capacity in blending and this constraint does not limit production. The optimal solution can be found more accurately by solving the simultaneous equations of the limiting constraints.

Limiting constraints are:

$$2G + T = 40 \qquad \text{distilling}$$

$$G + T = 25 \qquad \text{finishing}$$

which can be solved as simultaneous equations to confirm that the optimal solution is

$$G = 15 \qquad \text{and} \qquad T = 10$$

Substituting these values into the objective function gives the maximum profit:

$$30G + 20T = 30 \times 15 + 20 \times 10 = \pounds650$$

Substituting $G = 15$ and $T = 12$ into the constraints gives:

Blending:

> time available = 40 hours
>
> time used = $G + 2T = 15 + 2 \times 10 = 35$
>
> spare capacity = 5 hours

Distilling:

> time available = 40 hours
>
> time used = $2G + T = 2 \times 15 + 10 = 40$
>
> spare capacity = 0

Finishing:

> time available = 25 hours
>
> time used = $G + T = 1 \times 15 + 1 \times 10 = 25$
>
> spare capacity = 0

This gives us the final solution for the linear programme and defines the optimal production plan for the company.

IN SUMMARY

Constraints can be drawn on a graph to identify a feasible region. An objective function line can be superimposed on this graph. Moving the objective function line away from the origin increases its value, and the maximum value is the last point in the feasible region through which the objective function line passes.

WORKED EXAMPLE 11.4

Find the optimal solution to the following linear programme.

Minimize:

$$2X + Y$$

Subject to:

$$X + Y \leqslant 10 \tag{1}$$

$$X - Y \leqslant 2 \tag{2}$$

$$X \geqslant 4 \tag{3}$$

$$Y \leqslant 5 \tag{4}$$

with X and Y greater than or equal to zero.

Solution

The formulation for this problem is already done, so we can immediately draw a graph of the problem, as shown in Figure 11.9. Sometimes it may not be obvious if a constraint restricts solutions to points above the line or below it (constraint 2, for example). In these cases you can take random points on either side of the line and see which ones break the constraint.

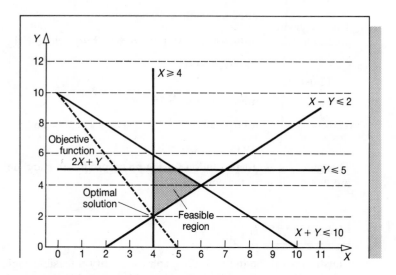

Figure 11.9 Solution for Worked Example 11.4.

This time the objective function is to be minimized, so instead of pushing it as far as possible away from the origin, it should be pulled as close as possible. As the line moves towards the origin the last point it passes through in the feasible region is the point where constraints (2) and (3) cross. Here:

$$X - Y = 2 \tag{2}$$

and

$$X = 4 \tag{3}$$

These can be solved to give the optimal solution of $X = 4$ and $Y = 2$. Substituting these values into the objective function gives a minimum value of $2 \times 4 + 1 \times 2 = 10$.

A useful observation from these examples is that the feasible region is always a polygon without any indentations and the optimal solution always occurs at a corner or **extreme point**. This is not a coincidence but is a fundamental property of all linear programmes.

> If an optimal solution exists for a linear programme it will be at an extreme point of the feasible region.

This is a very useful property as it shows how computers can tackle large problems. Essentially, they search extreme points around the feasible region until an optimal is found.

Self-assessment questions

11.6 What is the feasible region for a problem?

11.7 What is the role of the objective function in a LP model?

11.8 What are the extreme points of a feasible region and what is their significance?

11.9 How can the optimal solution be identified on a graph?

11.4 | Sensitivity of solutions

Linear programming can find an optimal solution to a problem, but managers might want to modify the solution in the light of their experiences, non-quantifiable factors, or assumptions made in the model. It is also clear that LPs use a lot of data and this will include approximations and even errors. We might then ask how sensitive the optimal solution is to such changes and approximations. Sensitivity analysis gives an answer to this question.

11.4.1 | Changes in contribution to profit

Let us have another look at our problem with Growbig and Thrive:

Maximize:

$$30G + 20T$$

Subject to:

$$G + 2T \leqslant 40 \qquad \text{blending}$$

$$2G + T \leqslant 40 \qquad \text{distilling}$$

$$G + T \leqslant 25 \qquad \text{finishing}$$

with $G \geqslant 0$ and $T \geqslant 0$.

Suppose a new accounting convention is used, and this adjusts the profits to £20 for each batch of Growbig and £30 for each batch of Thrive. The objective function is now $20G + 30T$, but how does this affect the optimal solution? The graph of constraints is exactly the same as before and the feasible region is unchanged. However, a new objective function line is used, and when this is moved as far away from the origin as possible a new optimal solution is identified.

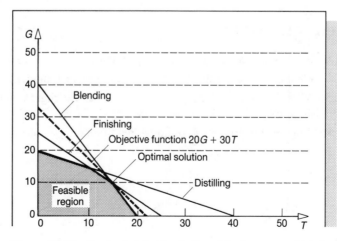

Figure 11.10 Revised optimal solution with changes to objective function.

The revised optimal solution is the point $G = 10$, $T = 15$, where the blending constraint crosses the finishing constraint. These are the active constraints that limit production, and there must be spare capacity in distilling that does not limit production. These results can be confirmed by solving the equations algebraically as before.

Limiting constraints are:

$$G + 2T = 40 \qquad \text{blending}$$

$$G + T = 25 \qquad \text{finishing}$$

which give $G = 10$ and $T = 15$ as the optimal solution. Substituting these values into the objective function gives a profit of $20 \times 10 + 30 \times 15 = £650$.

Suppose the new accounting convention gave the profit on both Growbig and Thrive as £30 a batch. This objective function line can again be super-imposed on the feasible region as shown in Figure 11.11. In this case the line of

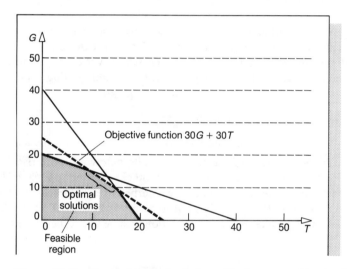

Figure 11.11 Revised optimal solution with changes to objective function.

the objective function does not leave the feasible region at a single point. It is parallel to one of the limiting constraints and leaves the feasible region along one edge. When this happens any point along the edge is optimal and gives the same profit. This can be demonstrated by taking arbitrary points along the edge.

At one extreme point of the edge $G = 15$ and $T = 10$:

$$\text{profit} = 30 \times 15 + 30 \times 10 = £750$$

At the other end of the edge $G = 10$ and $T = 15$:

$$\text{profit} = 30 \times 10 + 30 \times 15 = £750$$

In the middle of the edge $G = 12.5$ and $T = 12.5$:

$$\text{profit} = 30 \times 12.5 + 30 \times 12.5 = £750$$

(assuming there are no disadvantages with part batches).

If you look carefully at the results we are getting, you can see that the important features are the gradient of the objective function, and the gradients of the limiting constraints. We can summarize the main features as follows:

- an optimal solution lies at an extreme point where two constraints cross
- the gradient of the objective function has a value between the gradients of the two limiting constraints
- if the gradient of the objective function changes so that it is no longer between these gradients, the optimal solution moves from one extreme point to another

This observation allows us to find how sensitive the optimal solution is to changes in profit. In general, for equations expressed as $aG + bT = c$ the gradient of the line is $-b/a$ (assuming the G axis is vertical). In the original blending example, the gradients of objective function and limiting constraints are:

$$\text{objective function} = -0.667$$

$$\text{distilling} = -0.5$$

$$\text{finishing} = -1.0$$

If the gradient of the objective falls below -1.0 or rises above -0.5, the optimal solution will move to another extreme point, making two other constraints limiting. Keeping the coefficient of G constant while varying the coefficient of T (so the objective function is $30G + bT$ which has a gradient of $-b/30$) will make the optimal solution change to another vertex when:

either $\quad -b/30 \leqslant -1.0 \quad$ i.e. $\quad b \geqslant 30$

or $\quad -b/30 \geqslant -0.5 \quad$ i.e. $\quad b \leqslant 15$

The optimal solution remains at the original vertex provided the profit on a batch of Thrive remains between £15 and £30.

Similarly, keeping the coefficient of T constant (so the objective function is $aG + 20T$ which has a gradient of $-20/a$) would mean the vertex changes when:

either $\quad -20/a \leqslant -1.0 \quad$ i.e $\quad a \leqslant 20$

or $\quad -20/a \geqslant -0.5 \quad$ i.e $\quad a \geqslant 40$

The optimal solution remains at the original vertex provided the profit on a batch of Growbig remains between £20 and £40.

IN SUMMARY

Changing the profit on each product changes the gradient of the objective function. This can change the location of the optimal solution. The effects of these changes can be calculated.

11.4.2 | Changes in resources available

Returning to the original problem, the limiting constraints were distilling and finishing and the optimal solution was found by solving:

$$2G + T = 40 \qquad \text{distilling constraint}$$

$$G + T = 25 \qquad \text{finishing constraint}$$

If some extra capacity for distilling could be bought, how much would it be worth? The answer can be found by calculating a marginal value for distilling (that is, the value of one additional hour), by replacing the original constraint

$$2G + T \leqslant 40$$

by

$$2G + T \leqslant 41$$

and resolving the problem. In practice, the expansion of the feasible region is so small that it is not worth plotting a new graph. Provided the increase in resources is small, we can be confident that the same constraints will be limiting and the optimal solution will remain at the same extreme point of the feasible region. A revised optimal solution can then be found by solving the equations:

$$2G + T = 41 \qquad \text{distilling constraint}$$

$$G + T = 25 \qquad \text{finishing constraint}$$

to give values of $G = 16$ and $T = 9$. Substitution of these in the objective function gives an maximum profit of $30 \times 16 + 20 \times 9 = £660$. This is a rise of £10 from the previous optimal solution and suggests that distilling has a marginal value of £10 an hour. In other words, an extra hour of distilling will increase profit by £10. In LP this marginal value is usually called a **shadow price**, and this is the maximum amount that should be paid for one extra unit of a resource.

A similar argument shows that the shadow price is also the cost of losing one hour of distilling capacity. The limiting constraints would then be:

$$2G + T = 39 \qquad \text{distilling constraint}$$

$$G + T = 25 \qquad \text{finishing constraint}$$

which can be solved to give $G = 14$, $T = 11$. Then the profit is $30 \times 14 + 20 \times 11 = £640$, which is a reduction of £10. Then if equipment breaks down for a short time the cost of the stoppage is found by multiplying the duration of the breakdown by the shadow price.

The shadow price is only valid for small changes in capacity. We found that an extra hour of distilling is worth £10, but there are limits and an extra 1000 hours would certainly not be worth £10,000. If an extra 20 hours of distilling becomes available the constraint $2G + 1T \leqslant 60$ will replace $2G + T \leqslant 40$, as shown in Figure 11.12.

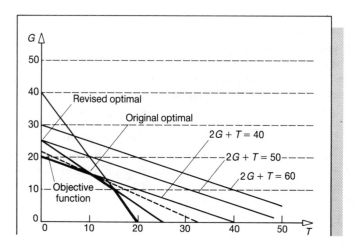

Figure 11.12 Revised optimal solution when distilling is not limiting.

Distilling now has so much capacity that the constraint line has moved up the graph and is no longer limiting, so production is only limited by finishing. The graph shows that distilling ceases to be limiting when the amount available is increased beyond 25 hours. At this point the limiting constraints are finishing, $G + T \leqslant 25$, and the non-negativity constraint, $T \geqslant 0$. Any increase in distilling beyond 25 hours adds spare capacity. Hence it is worth while paying £10 for each extra hour of distilling up to a maximum of 25 hours.

This analysis of shadow prices can be repeated for finishing, where the value of an extra hour is found by replacing the original limiting constraints by:

$$2G + T = 40 \qquad \text{distilling constraint}$$

$$G + T = 26 \qquad \text{new finishing constraint}$$

These equations can be solved to give $G = 14$ and $T = 12$. Then substitution into the objective function gives an optimal value of £660, which is an increase of £10 over the original optimal solution. The shadow price for finishing, i.e. the maximum amount which should be paid for an extra hour of capacity, is £10. (It is simply coincidence that this is the same as the shadow price for distilling.) This value holds for small changes, but if the capacity for finishing were increased markedly the constraint line would move up the graph and would no longer be limiting. The limiting constraints would then be blending, $G + 2T \leqslant 40$, and distilling, $2G + T \leqslant 40$. At this point both G and T equal 13.33, so the maximum useful amount of finishing is $G + T = 26.7$ hours.

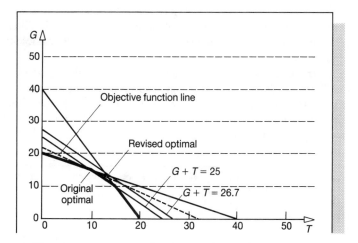

Figure 11.13 Revised optimal solution when finishing is not limiting.

Obviously, if a process already has spare capacity there is no benefit in increasing the capacity further, so the shadow prices of non-limiting resources are zero. In this example there is spare capacity in blending so the shadow price is zero.

The shadow prices for the three processes have now been calculated separately as:

blending	£0 an hour
distilling	£10 an hour
finishing	£10 an hour

It would be useful to see what happens if several resources are increased at the same time. The value of an extra hour of both distilling and finishing, for example, is found by replacing the original constraints by:

$$2G + T = 41 \qquad \text{new distilling constraint}$$

$$G + T = 26 \qquad \text{new finishing constraint}$$

Solving these gives $G = 15$ and $T = 11$ and substitution in the objective function gives a maximum profit of £670. This is £20 more than the original optimal solution and is also the sum of the shadow prices when the increases were considered separately. Thus, for small changes in resources, the total benefit is the sum of the separate benefits of increasing each resource separately.

One application of this principle is the introduction of new products to compete for resources with existing ones. The total cost of reducing the resources available to existing products can be compared with the profit generated by the new product. If the profit generated is greater than the cost, the new product should be introduced.

Suppose a new fertilizer, Vegup, could be made in addition to Growbig and Thrive. Vegup uses 2 hours of blending, 2 hours of distilling and 2 hours of packing for each batch and contributes £50 to profits. Should this new product be introduced?

If one batch of Vegup is made, the cost of reduced production of Growbig and Thrive is found by multiplying the reduction in available capacity for each process by the shadow price. Vegup uses 2 hours of blending with a shadow price of £10 an hour, so this would cost £20. The total cost of producing one batch of Vegup is then:

Process	Hours used	Shadow price	Total cost
Blending	2	0	0
Distilling	2	10	20
Finishing	2	10	20
Total	6		40

The total cost of reducing existing production is £40 while increased profit from a batch of Vegup is £50, so the new product should be manufactured. The next obvious question is how much Vegup should be made. Unfortunately, this cannot be found from the original solution and a revised problem must be solved. As there are now three variables to consider we could try to draw three-dimensional graphs but it is much easier to use a computer.

WORKED EXAMPLE 11.5

An engineering company manufactures two gear boxes, Manual and Automatic. There are four stages in the production of these, with details of required times and weekly availabilities given below. The company makes a profit of £64 on each Manual sold and £100 on each Automatic.

Stage in manufacture	Time required (hours per unit)		Time available (hours per week)
	Manual	Automatic	
Foundry	3	5	7 500
Machine shop	5	4	10 000
Assembly	2	1	3 500
Testing	1	1	2 000

(a) Formulate this profit-maximization problem as a linear programme.

(b) Use a graphical method to find the optimal solution.

(c) Find the spare capacities in each manufacturing stage.

(d) Calculate the shadow prices of each manufacturing stage.

(e) A new semi-automatic gear box is proposed that needs 4, 4, 1 and 1 hour respectively in each manufacturing stage and gives a profit of £80 a unit. Should the company make the semi-automatic gear box?

Solution

(a) Let M be the number of Manual gear boxes made a week and let A be the number of Automatic gear boxes made a week.

The formulation becomes:

Maximize:

$$64M + 100A$$

Subject to:

$$3M + 5A \leqslant 7500 \qquad \text{foundry}$$

$$5M + 4A \leqslant 10\,000 \qquad \text{machine shop}$$

$$2M + A \leqslant 3500 \qquad \text{assembly}$$

$$M + A \leqslant 2000 \qquad \text{testing}$$

$$M, A \geqslant 0 \qquad \text{non-negativity}$$

(b) The graph of this problem is shown in Figure 11.14. The optimal solution

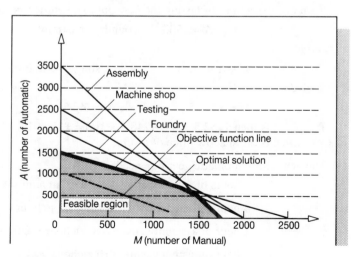

Figure 11.14 Graph for Worked Example 11.5.

occurs where the foundry and testing constraints are limiting, so solving

$$3M + 5A = 7500$$

and

$$M + A = 2000$$

gives the optimal solution of $M = 1250$ and $A = 750$ with a profit of $1250 \times 64 + 750 \times 100 = £155\,000$ a week.

(c) The availability of foundry and testing are limiting so they have no spare capacity. There is spare capacity in both the machine shop and assembly.

- Time used in the machine shop is $1250 \times 5 + 750 \times 4 = 9250$ hours. Time available is 10 000 hours, so there are 750 hours of spare capacity.

- Time used in assembly is $1250 \times 2 + 750 \times 1 = 3250$ hours. Time available is 3500 hours available, so there are 250 hours of spare capacity.

(d) Since both the machine shop and assembly have spare capacity their shadow prices are zero. The shadow prices of the other stages in manufacturing are found by increasing the availability of each by one hour.

With one extra hour of foundry time the new optimal solution is found by solving:

$$3M + 5A = 7501 \qquad \text{new foundry constraint}$$

and

$$M + A = 2000 \qquad \text{testing constraint}$$

to give

$$M = 1249.5 \qquad \text{and} \qquad A = 750.5$$

The profit is then $1249.5 \times 64 + 750.5 \times 100 = £155,018$. This is an increase of £18, which is the shadow price of foundry time.

With one extra hour of testing the new optimal solution is found by solving:

$$3M + 5A = 7500 \qquad \text{foundry constraint}$$

and

$$M + A = 2001 \qquad \text{new testing constraint}$$

to give

$$M = 1252.5 \qquad \text{and} \qquad A = 748.5$$

The profit is then $1252.5 \times 64 + 748.5 \times 100 = £155,010$. This is an increase of £10, which is the shadow price of testing.

(e) The new semi-automatic gear box needs:

4 hours of foundry at a cost of £18 an hour = £72

4 hours of machine shop costing £0 an hour = £ 0

1 hour of assembly costing £0 an hour = £ 0

1 hour of testing costing £10 an hour = £10

The total cost of making one gear box is £82 while the profit is £80. This means there would be a loss of £2 on every unit made and the company should not start making the semi-automatic gear box.

IN SUMMARY

Changing a constraint moves its line across a graph. This can change the position of the optimal solution. The effects of such changes can be calculated fairly easily.

Self-assessment questions

11.10 What is meant by 'sensitivity analysis' in LP problems?

11.11 Within what limits can the coefficients of the objective function vary without affecting the position of the optimal solution?

11.12 What are 'shadow prices' in linear programming?

11.13 Within what limits are the shadow prices valid?

‖ 11.5 ‖ Computer solutions to larger problems

We have seen how problems with two variables can be solved using a graph. If you are good at drawing, this approach can be extended to problems with three variables. However, this is still far too small for any realistic problem and other methods must be used. These are based on matrix manipulation, and involve a large amount of arithmetic. This means that computers are inevitably used to solve real LP problems.

We have already suggested a method by which computers might find solutions to linear programmes. This is based on the observation that the feasible region for LPs is always convex and that an optimal solution will lie at one of the extreme points of the feasible region. The solution procedure is to examine the extreme points and select the best. A formal procedure for this is called the 'simplex method'.

LP packages vary in detail, but they have many common features. We can illustrate these by a typical printout. Throughout this chapter we have done calculations on the production planning problem of Growbig and Thrive. It would be interesting to confirm these calculations by looking at a computer solution to this problem. The formulation is:

Maximize: $30 \times G + 20 \times T$

Subject to:

$$1 \times G + 2 \times T \leqslant 40$$

$$2 \times G + 1 \times T \leqslant 40$$

$$1 \times G + 1 \times T \leqslant 25$$

with $G \geqslant 0$ and $T \geqslant 0$

For many packages the data are presented as a matrix, so we could rewrite this problem as:

	G	T		
Maximize:	30	20		
Subject to:	1	2	$\leqslant$	40
	2	1	$\leqslant$	40
	1	1	$\leqslant$	25

These data were used in a linear programming package to get the results shown in Figure 11.15. This output is fairly straightforward. The first part shows the data, to confirm that they were entered properly. The next part shows the main results, with optimal values, profits, spare resources, shadow prices, and so on. The 'coefficient sensitivity' shows by how much profit would fall if an additional unit of either product were made.

The next part of the printout shows a sensitivity analysis for the objective function, assuming that only one coefficient is changed at a time. Thus the original profit on each batch of Growbig is £30, but this can vary between £20 and £40 without changing the location of the optimal solution (provided the profit on each batch of Thrive remains at £20). Similarly, the profit on each batch of Thrive can vary between £15 and £30 without changing the location of the optimal solution (provided the profit on each batch of Growbig remains at £30).

The final table shows the sensitivity of the right-hand side of constraints. For each constraint the original right-hand side value is given together with the

$-=*=-$ INFORMATION ENTERED $-=*=-$

NUMBER OF VARIABLES : 2
NUMBER OF <= CONSTRAINTS : 3
NUMBER OF = CONSTRAINTS : 0
NUMBER OF >= CONSTRAINTS : 0

MAXIMIZE Profit = 30 G + 20 T

SUBJECT TO:

1	G	+	2	T		<=	40
2	G	+	1	T		<=	40
1	G	+	1	T		<=	25

$-=*=-$ RESULTS $-=*=-$

VARIABLE	VARIABLE VALUE	ORIGINAL COEFFICIENT	COEFFICIENT SENSITIVITY
G	15	30	0
T	10	20	0

CONSTRAINT NUMBER	ORIGINAL RIGHT-HAND VALUE	SLACK OR SURPLUS	SHADOW PRICE
1	40	5	0
2	40	0	10
3	25	0	10

OBJECTIVE FUNCTION VALUE: 650

$--$ SENSITIVITY ANALYSIS $--$

OBJECTIVE FUNCTION COEFFICIENTS

VARIABLE	LOWER LIMIT	ORIGINAL COEFFICIENT	UPPER LIMIT
G	20	30	40
T	15	20	30

RIGHT-HAND-SIDE VALUES

CONSTRAINT NUMBER	LOWER LIMIT	ORIGINAL VALUE	UPPER LIMIT
1	35	40	NO LIMIT
2	35	40	50
3	20	25	26.667

$-------$ END OF ANALYSIS $-------$

Figure 11.15 Printout for Growbig and Thrive.

range in which the shadow costs are valid. Thus constraint 2 (distilling) has a shadow price of 10 provided there are between 35 and 50 hours available. Similarly, the shadow price of blending is zero provided there are more than 35 hours available.

WORKED EXAMPLE 11.6

West Coast Wood Products Ltd make four types of pressed panel from pine and spruce. Each sheet of panel must be cut and pressed. The following table shows the hours needed to produce a batch of each type of panel and the hours available each week:

Panel type	Hours of cutting	Hours of pressing
Classic	1	1
Western	1	4
Nouveau	2	3
East Coast	2	2
Available	80	100

There is a limited amount of suitable wood available. The amounts needed for a batch of each type of panel and maximum weekly availability are given in the following table:

	Classic	Western	Nouveau	East Coast	Availability
Pine	50	40	30	40	2500
Spruce	20	30	50	20	2000

The profit on each batch of panels is estimated to be £40 for Classic, £110 for Western, £75 for Nouveau and £35 for East Coast.

(a) Formulate this as a linear programme.

(b) A computer program gave the results for this problem shown in Figure 11.16. Interpret these results.

Solution

(a) We start by defining the decision variables as the number of batches of each type of panelling made a week (*CLS, WST, NOU* and *EST*). Then the formulation is given by the following matrix:

	CLS	WST	NOU	EST		
Maximize:	40	110	75	35		
Subject to:	50	40	30	40	≤ 2500	pine
	20	30	50	20	≤ 2000	spruce
	1	1	2	2	≤ 80	cutting
	1	4	3	2	≤ 100	pressing

with CLS, WST, NOU and EST ⩾ 0

(b) Putting these figures into a linear programming package gave the results in Figure 11.16. The results show that the optimal solution is to make 37.5 batches of Classic a week, 15.625 batches of Western and none of the others. This gives a profit of £3218.75. If a batch of Nouveau is made it would reduce profit by £7.50 while making a batch of East Coat would reduce profit by £26.25.

The limiting constraints are pine and pressing (numbers 1 and 4), with spare capacity in spruce (781.25) and cutting (26.875 hours). This will remain true while the constraint on spruce remains over 1218.75 and the amount of cutting remains above 53.13 hours. The shadow price of pine is £0.312 (valid for amounts between 1000 and 3933.333) and of pressing is £24.375 (valid for between 50 and 250 hours).

The profit for each batch of Classic could vary between £27.50 and £137.50 without changing the position of the optimal solution (provided the profits on the other panels remained unchanged). Similar ranges are given over which profit can vary on Western, Nouveau and East Coast without affecting the location of the optimal solution (between £100.00 and £160.00, below £82.50 and below £61.25 respectively).

LP formulations can be very large and complex, and it is not uncommon to have tens of thousands of constraints. Such large problems need a considerable effort to ensure that there are no errors. Four particular concerns are found in computer printouts:

- **unbound solution**, which means that the constraints do not limit the solution, and the feasible region effectively extends to infinity
- **infeasible solution**, which means the constraints have left no feasible region
- **degeneracy**, when the objective function is parallel to a limiting constraint and there are many equivalent optimal solutions
- **redundancy**, when some constraints are not needed as there are other, more severe ones

In all of these cases the solution is to check the input data carefully and make sure they are accurate.

−=＊=−   INFORMATION ENTERED   −=＊=−

NUMBER OF VARIABLES   : 4
NUMBER OF <= CONSTRAINTS   : 4
NUMBER OF   = CONSTRAINTS   : 0
NUMBER OF >= CONSTRAINTS   : 0

MAXIMIZE Profit =   40   CLS +   110   WST +   75   NOU +   35   EST

SUBJECT TO:

50	CLS	+	40	WST	+	20	NOU	+	40	EST	<=	2500
20	CLS	+	30	WST	+	50	NOU	+	20	EST	<=	2000
1	CLS	+	1	WST	+	2	NOU	+	2	EST	<=	80
1	CLS	+	4	WST	+	3	NOU	+	2	EST	<=	100

−=＊=−   RESULTS   −=＊=−

VARIABLE	VARIABLE VALUE	ORIGINAL COEFFICIENT	COEFFICIENT SENSITIVITY
CLS	37.5	40	0
WST	15.625	110	0
NOU	0	75	7.5
EST	0	35	26.25

CONSTRAINT NUMBER	ORIGINAL RIGHT-HAND VALUE	SLACK OR SURPLUS	SHADOW PRICE
1	2500	0	0.312
2	2000	781.25	0
3	80	26.875	0
4	100	0	24.375

OBJECTIVE FUNCTION VALUE: 3218.75

−−   SENSITIVITY ANALYSIS   −−

OBJECTIVE FUNCTION COEFFICIENTS

VARIABLE	LOWER LIMIT	ORIGINAL COEFFICIENT	UPPER LIMIT
CLS	27.5	40	137.5
WST	100	110	160
NOU	NO LIMIT	75	82.5
EST	NO LIMIT	35	61.25

RIGHT-HAND-SIDE VALUES

CONSRAINT NUMBER	LOWER LIMIT	ORIGINAL VALUE	UPPER LIMIT
1	1000	2500	3933.333
2	1218.75	2000	NO LIMIT
3	53.125	80	NO LIMIT
4	50	100	250

−−−−−−−−   END OF ANALYSIS   −−−−−−−−

Figure 11.16   Printout for Worked Example 11.6.

IN SUMMARY

Graphs can only solve problems with two (or at most three) variables. For any realistic problem other solution methods must be used. The amount of calculation is so great that this inevitably means that a computer is used.

Self-assessment questions

11.14 Why are computers usually used to solve LPs?

11.15 What information might be given in a computer printout for the solution of an LP?

CHAPTER REVIEW

Many problems in business are types of constrained optimization. This chapter has discussed linear programming, which is a method of tackling such problems. In particular it:

- outlined the characteristics of constrained optimization and linear programmes
- formulated problems as linear programmes
- used a graph to solve linear programmes
- investigated the sensitivity of solutions to changes in objective function and constraints
- looked at computer solutions to larger problems

Problems

11.1 Two additives, X1 and X2, can be used to increase the octane number of petrol. One pound of X1 in 500 gallons of petrol will increase the octane number by 10, while one pound of X2 in 500 gallons will increase the octane number by 20. The total additives must increase the octane number by at least 5, but a total of no more than half a pound can be added to 500 gallons, and the amount of X2 plus twice the amount of X1 must be at least half a pound. If X1 costs £30 a pound and X2 costs £40 a pound, formulate this problem as a linear programme.

11.2 Use a graphical method to solve the formulation in Problem 11.1.

11.3 A local authority is planning a number of blocks of flats. Five types of block have been designed, containing flats of four categories (senior citizens, single person, small family and large family). The number of flats in each block, and other relevant information, is given Table 11.1. The council wants to build a total of 500 flats with at least 40 in category 1 and 125 in each of the other categories. In the past, high-rise flats have proved unpopular and the council wants to limit the number of storeys in the development. In particular, the average number of storeys must be at most five and at least half the flats must be in blocks of three or fewer storeys. An area of 300 units has been set aside for the development and any spare land will be used as a park. Formulate this problem as a linear programme.

Table 11.1

Type of block	No. of flats in each category				No. of storeys	Plan area	Cost per block (£'000)
	1	2	3	4			
A	1	2	4	0	3	5	208
B	0	3	6	0	6	5	320
C	2	2	2	4	2	8	300
D	0	6	0	8	8	6	480
E	0	0	10	5	3	4	480

11.4 Weekly production schedules are needed for the manufacture of two products X and Y. Each unit of X uses one component made in the factory, while each unit of Y uses two of the components, and the factory has a maximum output of 80 components a week. Each unit of X and Y requires 10 hours of subcontracted work and agreements have been signed with subcontractors for a minimum weekly usage of 200 hours and a maximum weekly usage of 600 hours. The marketing department says that all production of Y can be sold but there is a maximum demand of 50 units of X, despite a long-term contract to supply 10 units of X to one customer. The net profit on each unit of X and Y is £200 and £300 respectively.

(a) Formulate this problem as a linear programme.

(b) Use a graphical method to find an optimal solution to the problem.

11.5 Novacook Ltd makes two types of cooker, one electric and one gas. There are four stages in the production of each of these, with details given in Table 11.2. The electric cooker has variable costs of £200 a unit and a selling price of £300 while the gas cooker has variable costs of £160 and a selling price of £240 a unit. Fixed overheads are estimated to be £60,000 a week and the company works a 50-week year. The marketing department suggest maximum sales of 800 electric and 1250 gas cookers a week.

(a) Formulate this as a profit-maximizing linear programme.

(b) Use a graphical method to find an optimal product mix for the company. What is the expected annual profit?

Table 11.2

Manufacturing stage	Time required (hours per unit)		Total time available (hours a week)
	Electric	Gas	
Forming	4	2	3 600
Machine Shop	10	8	12 000
Assembly	6	4	6 000
Testing	2	2	2 800

(c) Find the use and spare capacity of each manufacturing stage.

(d) Calculate the shadow price of each manufacturing stage.

(e) An outside consultant offers his testing services to the company. What price should Novacook be willing to pay for this service and how many hours should they buy a week?

(f) A new cooker is planned, which would use the manufacturing stages for 4, 6, 6, and 2 hours respectively. At what selling price would it be advantageous to make this cooker if the other variable costs are £168 a unit?

11.6 A manufacturer of electrical components produces two types of tester, Standard and Normal. The production time (in hours per hundred units) of each type and the capacity of each production process are given below. All testers made can be sold and the profits on each unit of Standard and Normal are £6 and £8 respectively.

Process	Standard	Normal	Capacity (hours per month)
Pressing	2	4	160
Wiring	6	2	240
Assembly	4	4	200

(a) Formulate the problem of maximizing monthly profit as a linear programme.

(b) Use a graphical method to determine the optimal solution to this problem.

(c) Find the spare capacity in production facilities.

(d) Calculate the shadow prices of production facilities.

(e) It has been suggested that the selling price of the Standard tester should be raised. To what level could the profit be raised without changing the pattern of production found above?

(f) A new tester is planned, which could go through Pressing, Wiring and Assembly at a rate of 200 units an hour on each process. What profit is needed before it becomes advantageous to manufacture the new tester?

11.7 An oil company makes two blends of fuel by mixing three oils. The costs and daily availability of the oils are:

Oil	Cost (£/litre)	Amount available (litres)
A	0.33	5000
B	0.40	10 000
C	0.48	15 000

The requirements of the blends of fuel are:

Blend 1	at least 30% of A
	at most 45% of B
	at least 250% of C
Blend 2	at most 35% of A
	at least 30% of B
	at most 40% of C

Each litre of blend 1 can be sold for £1.00 and each litre of blend 2 can be sold for £1.20. Long-term contracts require at least 10 000 litres of each blend to be produced. Formulate this blending problem as a linear programme.

COMPUTER EXERCISES

11.1 Figure 11.17 shows a printout from a linear programming package. Make sure you can understand all of this and can explain the results. Use an appropriate package to check the results.

11.2 LP packages are often difficult to interpret. Figure 11.18 shows the printout from a typical package. Describe the results given here and say how the printout could be improved.

11.3 Some spreadsheets can solve linear programmes automatically. See if you have access to one of these and find how to use it. Would it be easy to design a spreadsheet for solving linear programmes?

11.4 Use a linear programming package to check the solutions to the problems in Worked Examples 11.1 to 11.5.

−=*=−   INFORMATION ENTERED   −=*=−

NUMBER OF VARIABLES   : 3
NUMBER OF <= CONSTRAINTS : 1
NUMBER OF   = CONSTRAINTS : 0
NUMBER OF >= CONSTRAINTS : 2

MINIMIZE Costs =   10   PrA +   5   PrB +   3   PrC

SUBJECT TO:

120   PrA +   23   PrB + 10   PrC <= 1545

150   PrA +   35   PrB + 10   PrC >=   550

100   PrA +   15   PrB + 55   PrC >=   675

−=*=−   RESULTS   −=*=−

VARIABLE	VARIABLE VALUE	ORIGINAL COEFFICIENT	COEFFICIENT SENSITIVITY
PrA	3.241	10	0
PrB	0	5	3.069
PrC	6.379	3	0

CONSTRAINT NUMBER	ORIGINAL RIGHT-HAND VALUE	SLACK OR SURPLUS	SHADOW PRICE
1	1545	1092.241	0
2	550	0	0.034
3	675	0	0.048

OBJECTIVE FUNCTION VALUE: 51.552

−−   SENSITIVITY ANALYSIS   −−

OBJECTIVE FUNCTION COEFFICIENTS

VARIABLE	LOWER LIMIT	ORIGINAL COEFFICIENT	UPPER LIMIT
PrA	5.455	10	22.535
PrB	1.931	5	NO LIMIT
PrC	0.667	3	5.5

RIGHT-HAND-SIDE VALUES

CONSTRAINT NUMBER	LOWER LIMIT	ORIGINAL VALUE	UPPER LIMIT
1	452.759	1545	NO LIMIT
2	122.727	550	1012.5
3	366.667	675	3025

−−−− END OF ANALYSIS −−−−

Figure 11.17   Printout from a linear programming package.

LINEAR PROGRAMMING SOLUTION

LP OPTIMUM FOUND AT STEP   2

OBJECTIVE FUNCTION VALUE

1)   417.50000

VARIABLE	VALUE	REDUCED COST
X	27.500000	.000000
Y	15.000000	.000000

ROW	SLACK OR SURPLUS	DUAL PRICES
2)	2.500000	.000000
3)	.000000	4.500000
4)	.000000	3.500000

NO. ITERATIONS =   2

RANGES IN WHICH THE BASIS IS UNCHANGED:

OBJ COEFFICIENT RANGES

VARIABLE	CURRENT COEF	ALLOWABLE INCREASE	ALLOWABLE DECREASE
X	7.000000	3.000000	7.000000
Y	15.000000	INFINITY	4.500000

RIGHT-HAND-SIDE RANGES

ROW	CURRENT RHS	ALLOWABLE INCREASE	ALLOWABLE DECREASE
2	30.000000	INFINITY	2.500000
3	15.000000	18.333330	1.666667
4	100.000000	5.000000	55.000000

Figure 11.18   Printout from a linear programming package.

11.5 A manufacturing company has forecast the numbers of a component that it will need each month. Unfortunately, the cost of the component is rising fairly quickly. Table 11.3 shows the forecast requirement and cost. The company can purchase components ahead of time to avoid the price increases, but there is a cost of £2 a unit for carrying stock from one period to the next. Formulate an LP that will determine the best pattern for ordering the component. Use a suitable computer program to find the optimal solution to this problem.

Table 11.3

Month	Jan	Feb	Mar	Apr	May	Jun	Jul	Aug	Sep	Oct	Nov	Dec
Demand	100	90	80	60	50	50	70	90	100	100	110	110
Cost (£)	200	200	205	205	210	210	210	220	220	230	230	240

Case study

Elemental Electronics

Elemental Electronics assemble microcomputers and act as wholesalers for some components. For the manufacturing business, they buy components from a number of suppliers and assemble them in a well-tried design. They do virtually no research and development, and are happy to use designs that have been tested by other manufacturers. They also spend little on advertising, preferring to sell computers through a few specialized retailers. As a result they have very low overheads, and can sell their machines at a much lower cost than major competitors.

a) One component that Elemental buy is a standard board. There are at least six suppliers of this board in America, Europe and the Far East. Elemental act as a wholesaler for two of these suppliers, one in the Far East and one in South America. These boards are delivered in bulk and Elemental test and repackage them to sell to a number of small manufacturers. Each board from the Far East takes 2 hours to test and 2 hours to repackage, while each board from South America takes 3 hours to test and 1 hour to repackage. Elemental has enough facilities to provide up to 8000 hours a week for testing and 4000 hours a week for repackaging. There are maximum sales of 1500 a week for the board from the Far East and each board gives a profit of £10 when sold.

- What is the optimal mix of these boards for Elemental?
- How does this optimal mix vary with changing profits on each board?
- What are the shadow prices on each resource and over what ranges are these valid?
- If another version of the board becomes available from Europe, which takes 2 hours of testing, 1 hour of repackaging and yields a profit of £10, should this new board be imported?

b) Elemental manufacture four models of computer. Each of these has four stages in manufacturing: sub-assembly, main assembly, final assembly and finishing. The times needed for each stage are known approximately, as are the total availabilities each week (Table 11.4).

Table 11.4

Manufacturing stage	Hours needed per unit				Number of machines	Hours available per machine per week
	Model A	Model B	Model C	Model D		
Sub-assembly	2	3	4	4	10	40
Main assembly	1	2	2	3	6	36
Final assembly	3	3	2	4	12	38
Finishing	2	3	3	3	8	40

Fixed costs of production are £3 million a year. Selling prices are £2,500, £2,800, £3,400 and £4,000 for the four models, with direct costs of £1,600, £1,800, £2,200 and £2,500 respectively. On average the sub-assembly machines need 10% of their total time for maintenance, main assembly machines need 16.667%, final assembly machines 25% and finishing machines 10%. The company works a standard 48-hour week.

- Formulate a linear programme describing the assembly.
- What is the best mix of models?
- Write a report explaining your results, highlighting any particularly interesting points.

Using calculus to describe changes | 12

CHAPTER OUTLINE

The average speed of a car is defined as the distance travelled divided by the time taken: any change in speed is described as either acceleration or deceleration. Calculus was originally developed to describe this kind of physical change, but is now widely used for problems which involve any kind of change. This chapter will discuss the application of calculus to business problems, where it looks at the way costs change with production quantities, sales change with price, revenues change with output, and so on.

The first part of the chapter describes differentiation. This analyses the rate of change of a function and allows optimal values to be identified. The use of differentiation is illustrated by marginal analyses and price elasticity of demand.

The rest of the chapter considers integration, which can be viewed as either the reverse of differentiation or as a method of summation.

After reading this chapter and doing the exercises you should be able to:

- understand the concept of differentiation
- differentiate functions of the form $y = ax^n$
- calculate optimal values for continuous functions
- determine whether these optima are minima or maxima
- do partial differentiation of functions of more than one variable
- use differentiation for marginal analyses and price elasticity of demand
- appreciate integration as the reverse of differentiation and as a means of summation

12.1 | Differentiation

12.1.1 | Basis of differentiation

The equation of a straight line is $y = ax + b$, where b is the point at which the line crosses the y axis and a is the gradient. The gradient is defined as the rate of change of y with respect to x, so it is the amount that y changes for every unit change in x.

WORKED EXAMPLE 12.1

The cost of running a family car is £400 a year for fixed costs (road tax, insurance, depreciation, etc) plus a variable cost of 30 pence for every mile travelled (for petrol, oil, maintenance, etc). What is the equation for total annual cost? What is the gradient of this line and what does this mean?

Solution

With y as the total annual cost (in pounds) of running the car, and x as the distance travelled (in miles) in a year, we have

$$y = 0.30x + 400$$

This is in the form $y = ax + b$, and the gradient is clearly the variable cost, with every unit increase in x causing an increase of 0.3 units in y. The total cost y is linear with respect to x, so the gradient is constant and every mile has the same variable cost, whether it is the fifth mile or the five thousandth.

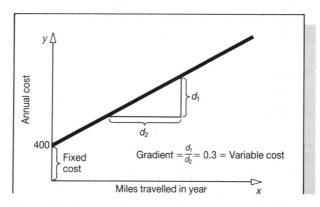

Figure 12.1   Constant gradient of a straight line (for Worked Example 12.1).

Suppose the family in Worked Example 12.1 look at the costs of their car in more detail. They might find that higher annual mileage increases depreciation and insurance costs, so that the variable cost per mile actually rises with distance travelled to give the total cost shown in Figure 12.2 Now it is more difficult to

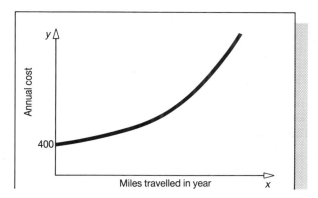

Figure 12.2   Variable cost rising with distance travelled.

calculate the cost of travelling a mile at any particular point. Suppose the car has already travelled 5000 miles this year; what is the cost of travelling the next mile? Worked Example 12.1 reminded us that the graph of total cost against distance travelled has the variable cost equal to the gradient. Unfortunately, in Figure 12.2 the gradient now varies with x, so to find the cost of travelling the 5000th mile we specifically need the gradient of the line when $x = 5000$. We could draw a graph and simply measure the gradient, but this is time-consuming and not very accurate. A more useful approach would calculate the gradient.

For this calculation we could start by approximating the gradient when $x = 5000$ to the average gradient near that point. In general, to find the gradient at a point x, we could take two points, say (x_1, y_1) and (x_2, y_2), so that one point is on either side of x (Figure 12.3). Then:

$$\text{gradient at point } x \text{ is approximately} = \frac{y_2 - y_1}{x_2 - x_1}$$

This gives the average gradient around x, but it is not the gradient **exactly at** x. In other words we have the average gradient, but not the **instantaneous gradient**. If we move x_1 and x_2 closer together we can get closer to the instantaneous gradient. Then, if we make x_1 and x_2 very, very close to x, we can get a value that is very, very close to the instantaneous gradient. In other words, as the distance between x_1 and x_2 approaches zero, we find the instantaneous gradient as the tangent to the curve at x (Figure 12.4)

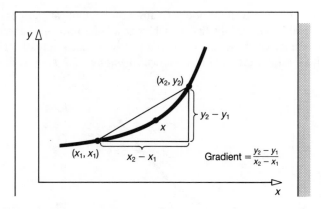

Figure 12.3   Approximate gradient at point x.

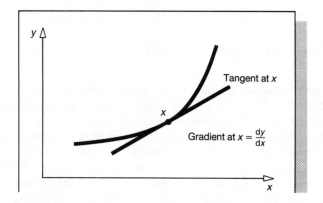

Figure 12.4   The tangent at x gives the instantaneous gradient.

We still need an easy way of calculating the gradient of the tangent at x, and this is where we use **differentiation**. This calculates the instantaneous rate of change of y with respect to x. This instantaneous gradient is referred to as dy/dx (pronounced 'dee y by dee x'), and details of the calculation are described in the following section.

$$\boxed{IN\ SUMMARY}$$

Differentiation finds the instantaneous gradient of a function. This gradient is called dy/dx, and is the rate of change of y with respect to x.

12.1.2 | Rules for differentiation

A lot of differentiation can be done using two simple rules. If you are interested, the derivation of these is outlined at the end of this chapter.

Differentiation rule 1

If
$$y = ax^n$$
where a and n can take any values, then
$$\frac{dy}{dx} = anx^{n-1}$$

WORKED EXAMPLE 12.2

Differentiate $y = 2x^3$. How quickly is y increasing when $x = 5$?

Solution

This has the general form $y = ax^n$ with $a = 2$ and $n = 3$. Substitution into the equation of rule 1 gives

$$\frac{dy}{dx} = anx^{n-1} = 2 \times 3 \times x^{3-1} = 6x^2$$

The instantaneous gradient of $2x^3$ is $6x^2$. When $x = 5$, the gradient is $6 \times 5^2 = 150$.

WORKED EXAMPLE 12.3

The total cost y of a process is related to the daily output x by the equation $y = 7x^2$. How quickly does the cost change when 100 units a day are being produced?

Solution

The rate of change of cost is found by differentiating the total cost. Substituting $a = 7$ and $n = 2$ into the equation of rule 1 gives

$$\frac{dy}{dx} = anx^{n-1} = 7 \times 2 \times x^{2-1} = 14x$$

When $x = 100$ the rate of change of cost is $14 \times 100 = 1400$. In other words, increasing daily output by one unit (to 101 units) will increase processing costs by 1400.

One important result can be found when $y = a$, where a is any constant. We can differentiate this using the fact that anything raised to the power 0 is equal to 1. Then by rewriting the equation as $y = ax^0$ we can use rule 1 with $n = 0$ to give

$$\frac{dy}{dx} = a \times 0 \times x^{0-1} = 0$$

This result is obvious if we realize that the line $y = a$ is a straight line parallel to the x axis, and therefore has a gradient of zero.

A second rule allows us to extend the use of differentiation.

Differentiation rule 2

If
$$y = u + v$$
where both u and v are functions of x, then
$$\frac{dy}{dx} = \frac{du}{dx} + \frac{dv}{dx}$$

This means that a function consisting of several parts, such as a polynomial, is differentiated by applying the first rule to each part separately.

WORKED EXAMPLE 12.4

Differentiate $y = 3x^3 + 14x^2 - x - 12$ with respect to x.

Solution

Rule 2 allows us to apply rule 1 to each part of the equation in turn:

- differentiating the first term, $3x^3$, gives $3 \times 3 \times x^{3-1} = 9x^2$
- differentiating the second term, $14x^2$, gives $14 \times 2 \times x^{2-1} = 28x$
- differentiating the third term, $-x$, gives $-1 \times x^{1-1} = -1$
- differentiating the fourth term, -12, gives zero.

Then adding the separate terms gives the solution as

$$\frac{dy}{dx} = 9x^2 + 28x - 1$$

We can now find the equation of the gradient at any point on a curve, and this is called the **derivative**. Then, if $y = x^3 + x^2$ the derivative is $3x^2 + 2x$. A serious restriction on this method is that both x and y must be continuous in the range considered (so there are no discontinuities in the function such as gaps or sudden jumps).

WORKED EXAMPLE 12.5

The output y from a process over time x is described by $y = 2x^3 - 3x$. How fast is the output changing when (a) $x = 1$, (b) $x = 4$?

Solution

The rate of change of the output is given by the gradient. Differentiating $y = 2x^3 - 3x$ gives the gradient at any point:

$$\frac{dy}{dx} = 3 \times 2 \times x^{3-1} - 1 \times 3 \times x^{1-1} = 6x^2 - 3$$

(a) Substituting $x = 1$ gives the instantaneous gradient when $x = 1$ as

$$6x^2 - 3 = 6 \times 1^2 - 3 = 3.$$

Thus the output is rising by 3 units in each time period.

(b) Substituting $x = 4$ gives the instantaneous gradient when $x = 4$ as

$$6 \times 4^2 - 3 = 93$$

so the output is now rising much faster.

There are several other rules for differentiation, but we need not describe these in detail. If you are interested, some standard results are given in Derivation 12.2 at the end of this chapter.

IN SUMMARY

The two basic rules of differentiation are:

- if $y = ax^n$ then $dy/dx = anx^{n-1}$, for any values of a and n
- if $y = u + v$ where u and v are both functions of x, then $dy/dx = du/dx + dv/dx$

12.1.3 | Maximum and minimum values

In Chapter 11 we saw how linear programming tackled problems of constrained optimization. Differentiation can also be used to find optimal values for certain problems. Specifically, it can find the maximum and minimum values of a continuous function.

Figure 12.5 shows a graph of the equation $y = ax^2 + bx + c$. This is a continuous function with a clear minimum. If we consider the gradient at point

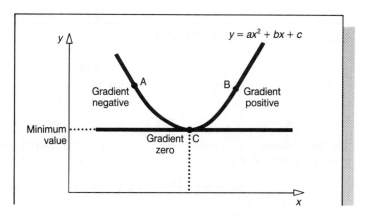

Figure 12.5 The minimum of a function has a gradient of zero.

A, it is clearly negative, implying that y is falling in value with increasing x. Conversely, at point B the gradient is positive, implying that y is increasing in value with increasing x. The most interesting point, however, comes between these at point C, where the gradient is zero; in other words the tangent to the curve is parallel with the x axis. This only happens at one specific point and this is the minimum value of the graph.

Now we can use differentiation to explore this minimum. We can differentiate the function $y = ax^2 + bx + c$ to find the gradient $dy/dx = 2ax + b$. When y is a minimum, this gradient is zero, so we can find the value of x corresponding to the lowest point on the graph. Then substitution back into the equation for y gives the minimal value. This approach is illustrated in the following example.

WORKED EXAMPLE 12.6

What can you say about the minimum of $y = 2x^2 - 4x + 10$?

Solution

We can differentiate $y = 2x^2 - 4x + 10$ to find the gradient at any point. Then

$$\frac{dy}{dx} = 2 \times 2 \times x - 4 = 4x - 4$$

For a minimum value of y this gradient is equal to zero. In other words:

$$4x - 4 = 0 \qquad \text{or} \qquad x = 1$$

Substituting $x = 1$ into the equation for y gives the minimum value:

$$y = 2x^2 - 4x + 10 = 2 \times 1^2 - 4 \times 1 + 10 = 8$$

Thus the minimum value of the graph is $y = 8$, which occurs when $x = 1$.

In the worked example above, the point where the gradient was zero was identified as a minimum. However, if you look at Figure 12.6, you can see that maximum values also have gradients of zero.

Points on a graph where the gradient is zero are generally referred to as **turning points**. They identify optimal values, which may be either maxima or minima. A related problem is that the optimal value may be a **local optimum** rather than a real one, as shown in Figure 12.7. We clearly need to find more information about the shape of the curve, and in particular we need to find if a turning point is a minimum or a maximum. We could do this by drawing a graph of the function, but more information can be found from calculations.

Figure 12.8 shows a curve with a minimum at point A and a maximum at point B. The gradient is clearly zero at these two points, but if we follow the curve we can make some interesting observations. At the left-hand side of the graph the gradient dy/dx is negative. Then at point A it goes through zero and becomes positive. Then at point B it goes through zero and becomes negative

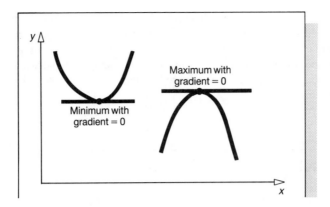

Figure 12.6   Both minima and maxima have gradients of zero.

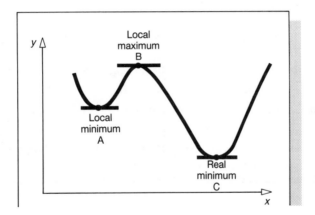

Figure 12.7   Illustrating local and real minima (points A, B and C are turning points).

again. Thus we can draw the graph of dy/dx corresponding to the graph of y, as shown in Figure 12.8.

This graph shows clearly that:

- for a minimum value of the function y, the derivative dy/dx has the value 0 and is increasing

- for a maximum value of the function y, the derivative dy/dx has the value 0 and is decreasing

These observations show how a turning point can be identified as either a maximum or a minimum, without drawing the associated graph. All we need to do is find the rate of change of dy/dx and see if this is positive (implying that dy/dx is increasing and we have a minimum) or negative (implying that dy/dx is decreasing and we have a maximum).

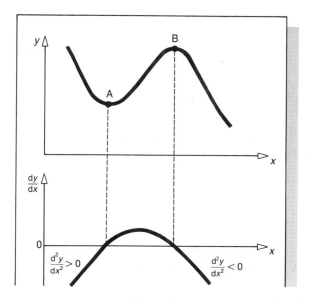

Figure 12.8 For optimal values of y, $dy/dx = 0$, and d^2y/dx^2 identifies maxima and minima.

If we have a function y, its rate of change is found by differentiation to be dy/dx. Now if we have a function dy/dx, its rate of change can be found by differentiation in exactly the same way. In other words, we differentiate dy/dx and the result is the second derivative which is called d^2y/dx^2 (pronounced 'dee two y by dee x squared'). If this is negative the gradient is decreasing and the function has a maximum value; if this is positive the gradient is increasing and the function has a minimum value.

These results can be consolidated into the general rule:

- The maximum of a function occurs when $dy/dx = 0$ and $d^2y/dx^2 < 0$
- The minimum of a function occurs when $dy/dx = 0$ and $d^2y/dx^2 > 0$

WORKED EXAMPLE 12.7

If $y = 4x^2 + 3x - 2$, what are (a) the derivative, (b) the second derivative?

Solution

(a) If $y = 4x^2 + 3x - 2$ then differentiating in the usual way gives the first derivative:

$$\frac{dy}{dx} = 8x + 3$$

(b) If $dy/dx = 8x + 3$ then differentiating in the usual way gives the second derivative:

$$\frac{d^2y}{dx^2} = 8$$

WORKED EXAMPLE 12.8

The total cost of a manufacturing process is found to be $3x^2 - 12x + 30$, where x is the number of units produced (in hundreds) each week. What production level minimizes this total cost?

Solution

We know that $y = 3x^2 - 12x + 30$. This has a gradient given by $dy/dx = 6x - 12$. A turning point occurs when this gradient has a value 0; that is, $6x - 12 = 0$, or $x = 2$. At this point the function has the value

$$y = 3x^2 - 12x + 30 = 3 \times 2^2 - 12 \times 2 + 30 = 18.$$

The second derivative, $d^2y/dx^2 = 6$. This is positive, so the turning point is a minimum. Then the total cost of production is minimized (at 18) when production is 200 units a week.

WORKED EXAMPLE 12.9

The duration of a project can be altered by using varying amounts of resources. Using a quantity x gives a net revenue which is approximated by

$$\text{net revenue} = x^3 - 3x^2$$

This approximation is only valid in the range $x = 0$ to $x = 5$. What does the revenue function look like? What value of x gives the highest net revenue?

Solution

We can differentiate the revenue function to find the turning points. As the equation is a cubic there will generally be two turning points, one a maximum and the other a minimum. Then:

$$y = x^3 - 3x^2 \qquad \text{so} \qquad \frac{dy}{dx} = 3x^2 - 6x$$

The turning points occur when this is equal to zero, so:

$$3x^2 - 6x = 0 \qquad 3x(x - 2) = 0$$

giving

$$x = 0 \qquad \text{and} \qquad x = 2$$

Taking the second derivative:

$$\frac{d^2y}{dx^2} = 6x - 6$$

When $x = 0$, $d^2y/dx^2 = 6x - 6 = -6$, so this point is a maximum, and when $x = 2$, $d^2y/dx^2 = 6x - 6 = 6$, so this point is a minimum.

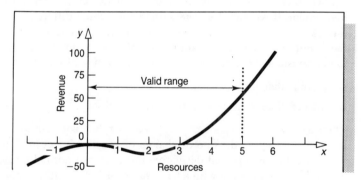

Figure 12.9 Graph of revenue for Worked Example 12.9.

From this information, we might suggest that the revenue is maximized when $x = 0$. However, when we draw a graph of the revenue, as shown in Figure 12.9, we can see that this is only a local maximum. In the valid range of $x = 0$ to $x = 5$ the net revenue is essentially U-shaped and it has a maximum value when $x = 5$, so revenue $= 5^3 - 3 \times 5^2 = 50$.

IN SUMMARY

The optimal value of a function occurs at the point where the gradient is zero, so $dy/dx = 0$. The function has a minimum value when $d^2y/dx^2 > 0$ and a maximum value when $d^2y/dx^2 < 0$. Substitution allows the optimal value of the function to be found.

12.1.4 | Functions of more than one variable

So far we have differentiated functions with only one variable. In other words, we know that $y = f(x)$ and have differentiated y with respect to x to find the gradient dy/dx. Often we are interested in functions that contain several variables. Total revenue, for example, might depend on sales, investment in production, marketing expenditure, and so on. Then we would be interested in changes in the total revenue with respect to all these variables.

Such problems can be examined using an extension to ordinary differentiation, called **partial differentiation**. Suppose that revenue depends on both sales and investment with:

$$y = x^2 + 4x + 6xz + 2z^2$$

where:

y is total revenue

x is a measure of sales

z is a measure of investment.

We want to find how revenue changes with respect to both sales and investment. If we only had one variable we would differentiate y with respect to this. As we have two variables we must differentiate y with respect to both of them. For this we assume that the variable we are not differentiating with respect to is a constant. Then to find the partial derivative of y with respect to x:

● assume that z is a constant

● differentiate with respect to x in the usual way.

Then with $y = x^2 + 4x + 6xz + 2z^2$ we set z as a constant and differentiate with respect to x to give the rate of change of y with respect to x as $2x + 4 + 6z$. To show that this is a partial derivative rather than a normal derivative, we do not call it dy/dx, but use a d with a backwards curl, ∂. Then we define $\partial y/\partial x$, as:

$$\frac{\partial y}{\partial x} = 2x + 4 + 6z$$

Similarly, we can differentiate y with respect to z by setting x as a constant, and differentiating in the usual way. This gives the rate of change of y with respect to z as:

$$\frac{\partial y}{\partial z} = 6x + 4z$$

The turning point can now be found by setting both of these partial derivatives to zero at the same time. Then:

$$2x + 4 + 6z = 0 \quad \text{and} \quad 6x + 4z = 0$$

These two simultaneous equations can be solved to give the values

$$x = 8/14 \quad \text{and} \quad z = -12/14$$

and the optimal value of y is

$$y = x^2 + 4x + 6xz + 2z^2$$
$$= (8/14)^2 + 4 \times 8/14 - 6 \times 8 \times 12/(14 \times 14) + 2 \times (12/14)^2$$
$$= 1.14$$

Although this is a turning point, we still have to find if it is a maximum or a minimum. With ordinary differentiation we take the second derivative and see if this is positive or negative. With partial differentiation, taking the second derivative is slightly more complicated. We could take either y/x or y/z and differentiate with respect to either x or z. This would give the set of four second derivatives:

$$\frac{\partial^2 y}{\partial x^2} \qquad \frac{\partial^2 y}{\partial x^2} \qquad \frac{\partial^2 y}{\partial x \partial z} \qquad \frac{\partial^2 y}{\partial z \partial x}$$

To find each of these we assume that all other variables are held constant, and differentiate in the usual way. Then:

$$\frac{\partial y}{\partial x} = 2x + 4 + 6z$$

so holding z constant and differentiating with respect to x gives

$$\frac{\partial^2 y}{\partial x^2} = 2$$

while holding x constant and differentiating with respect to z gives

$$\frac{\partial^2 y}{\partial x \partial z} = 6$$

Similarly:

$$\frac{\partial y}{\partial z} = 6x + 4z$$

so holding x constant and differentiating with respect to z gives

$$\frac{\partial^2 y}{\partial z^2} = 4$$

while holding z constant and differentiating with respect to x gives

$$\frac{\partial^2 y}{\partial z \partial x} = 6$$

In this case, and in general, $\partial^2 y/\partial x \partial z$ equals $\partial^2 y/\partial z \partial x$. Now we have found all the second derivatives, we can see if we have a maximum or minimum. The rules for this, which we shall simply state, are as follows.

For a **maximum**:

$$\frac{\partial y}{\partial x} = 0 \qquad \text{and} \qquad \frac{\partial y}{\partial z} = 0$$

$$\frac{\partial^2 y}{\partial x^2} < 0 \quad \text{and} \quad \frac{\partial^2 y}{\partial z^2} < 0$$

$$\left[\frac{\partial^2 y}{\partial x^2}\right] \times \left[\frac{\partial^2 y}{\partial z^2}\right] \geq \left[\frac{\partial^2 y}{\partial x \partial z}\right]^2$$

For a **minimum**:

$$\frac{\partial y}{\partial x} = 0 \quad \text{and} \quad \frac{\partial y}{\partial z} = 0$$

$$\frac{\partial^2 y}{\partial x^2} > 0 \quad \text{and} \quad \frac{\partial^2 y}{\partial z^2} > 0$$

$$\left[\frac{\partial^2 y}{\partial x^2}\right] \times \left[\frac{\partial^2 y}{\partial z^2}\right] \geq \left[\frac{\partial^2 y}{\partial x \partial z}\right]^2$$

In the illustration above:

$$\frac{\partial^2 y}{\partial x^2} = 2 \quad \frac{\partial^2 y}{\partial z^2} = 4 \quad \text{and} \quad \frac{\partial^2 y}{\partial x \partial z} = 6$$

This almost appears to be a minimum, but the third condition is not satisfied. To see exactly what is happening we would have to draw a three-dimensional graph to find more details of the function. The answer is that the function does not have a clear maximum or minimum, but there is a **saddle point**. This means that the point we have identified is a minimum with respect to one of the variables, but a maximum with respect to the other. If you can imagine it, a three-dimensional graph of the function would look somewhat like a saddle with a U shape in one direction and an inverted U shape in the other.

WORKED EXAMPLE 12.10

Differentiate

$$y = 3x^3 - 4x^2 z + 2xz - 3xz^2 + z^3$$

with respect to both x and z. What are the second derivatives?

Solution

Treating z as a constant and differentiating in the normal way gives

$$\frac{\partial y}{\partial x} = 9x^2 - 8xz + 2z - 3z^2$$

Treating x as a constant and differentiating in the normal way gives

$$\frac{\partial y}{\partial z} = -4x^2 + 2x - 6xz + 3z^2$$

Then differentiating these partial derivatives gives

$$\frac{\partial^2 y}{\partial x^2} = 18x - 8z \qquad \frac{\partial^2 y}{\partial z \partial x} = -8x + 2 - 6z$$

$$\frac{\partial^2 y}{\partial z^2} = -6x + 6z \qquad \frac{\partial^2 y}{\partial x \partial z} = -8x + 2 - 6z$$

WORKED EXAMPLE 12.11

A cost function is related to two variables by
$$y = 2x^2 + 3xz + 6x + 20 + 10z + 3z^2$$
What is the minimum value of this function?

Solution

Doing the partial differentiations gives

$$\frac{\partial y}{\partial x} = 4x + 3z + 6 \qquad \text{and} \qquad \frac{\partial y}{\partial z} = 3x + 10 + 6z$$

Setting both of these to zero identifies the turning point. This gives two simultaneous equations, which can be solved to give $x = -0.4$ and $z = -1.47$. Substituting these values into the cost equation gives
$$y = 2x^2 + 3xz + 6x + 20 + 10z + 3z^2$$
$$= 2 \times (-0.4)^2 + 3 \times (-0.4) \times (-1.47) + 6 \times (-0.4) + 20 + 10 \times (-1.47) + 3 \times (-1.47)^2$$
$$= 11.47$$

Taking the second derivatives gives

$$\frac{\partial^2 y}{\partial x^2} = 4 \qquad \frac{\partial^2 y}{\partial z^2} = 6 \qquad \frac{\partial^2 y}{\partial x \partial z} = 3$$

These can be compared with the conditions above, where it can be confirmed that a minimum has been found.

Thus the cost function has a minimal value of 11.47 when $x = -0.4$ and $z = -1.47$.

IN SUMMARY

The rates of change of functions with more than one variable can be found by partial differentiation. The second derivatives can be used to see if a maximum or minimum has been found.

12.1.5 | Optimization subject to constraints

So far we have assumed that there are no constraints on an optimal solution. As we found when discussing linear programming, there are many circumstances where a function is to be maximized, but there are constraints on the values which can be used. We might, for example, want to maximize revenue, but find that there are limits on output that constrain the solution.

With continuous functions, the easiest way to find a constrained optimum is to use a **Lagrange multiplier**. This introduces a new variable, which combines the objective function and constraint into a single new function. It is easiest to demonstrate this with an example.

WORKED EXAMPLE 12.12

Suppose we want to find the optimal value of a function of two variables:
$$y(x,z) = -2x^2 + 18x - 8xz + 34z - 10z^2$$
but there is a constraint that $x + z$ must equal 2.

The first thing to do is rewrite the constraint in the form $g(x,z) = 0$. Thus:
$$g(x,z) = x + z - 2 = 0$$
Now we multiply this by a temporarily unknown value λ, which is the Lagrange multiplier:
$$\lambda(x + z - 2) = 0$$
This function has a value of zero, so adding it to the original function $y(x, z)$ will make no difference. This defines the Lagrangian function, $L(x, z, \lambda)$ as
$$L(x, z, \lambda) = y(x, z) + \lambda g(x, z, \lambda)$$
$$= (-2x^2 + 18x - 8xz + 34z - 10z^2) + \lambda(x + z - 2)$$

The constrained optimal value can be found by partially differentiating this Lagrangian function with respect to x, z and λ and setting the results to zero:
$$\frac{\partial L}{\partial x} = -4x + 18 - 8z + \lambda = 0$$

$$\frac{\partial L}{\partial z} = -8x + 34 - 20z + \lambda = 0$$

$$\frac{\partial L}{\partial \lambda} = x + z - 2 = 0$$

This gives three simultaneous equations and three unknowns, so we can solve them to give the solutions $x = 1$, $z = 1$ and $\lambda = -6$. We can check this to ensure that the constraint is not broken:

$$g(x, z) = x + z - 2 = 1 + 1 - 2 = 0$$

This is correct, so now we can substitute into $y(x,z)$ to give the constrained optimal value of

$$y(x, z) = -2x^2 + 18x - 8xz + 34z - 10z^2$$

$$= -2 + 18 - 8 + 34 - 10 = 32$$

Second derivatives can be taken to see if this is a maximum or minimum using the conditions described above:

$$\frac{\partial^2 L}{\partial x^2} = -4 \qquad \frac{\partial^2 L}{\partial z^2} = -20 \qquad \frac{\partial^2 L}{\partial x \partial z} = -8$$

This shows that

$$\frac{\partial^2 y}{\partial x^2} < 0 \qquad \text{and} \qquad \frac{\partial^2 y}{\partial z^2} < 0$$

$$\left[\frac{\partial^2 y}{\partial x^2} \right] \times \left[\frac{\partial^2 y}{\partial z^2} \right] \ge \left[\frac{\partial^2 y}{\partial x \partial z} \right]^2$$

so the result is a maximum.

IN SUMMARY

The general procedure for solving a problem of constrained maximization is:

- write the constraint in the form $g(x, z) = 0$
- multiply this by the Lagrange multiplier λ
- add this to the objective function to form the Lagrangian function $L(x, z, \lambda)$
- partially differentiate the Lagrangian function with respect to x, z and λ
- set these derivatives to zero
- this gives three simultaneous equations, which can be solved to find the constrained optimal solution
- substitute to find the optimal value and then test to see if this is a maximum or minimum

WORKED EXAMPLE 12.13

A cost function is found to be $y(x, z) = x^2 - 8x + 34 - 12z + 2z^2$. This must be minimized subject to the constraint that $x + 2z = 5$. What is the optimal value?

Solution

Following the procedure described above, we start with the constraint

$$g(x, z) = x + 2z - 5 = 0$$

Then we multiply this by the Lagrange multiplier and add it to the cost function to give the Lagrangian function:

$$L(x, z, \lambda) = (x^2 - 8x + 34 - 12z + 2z^2) + \lambda(x + 2z - 5)$$

Differentiating this with respect to x, z and λ and setting the results to zero gives

$$\frac{\partial L}{\partial x} = 2x - 8 + \lambda = 0$$

$$\frac{\partial L}{\partial z} = -12 + 4z + 2\lambda = 0$$

$$\frac{\partial L}{\partial \lambda} = x + 2z - 5 = 0$$

Solving these gives the result $x = 7/3$, $z = 4/3$ and $\lambda = 10/3$. The constraint is not broken:

$$g(x, z) = x + 2z - 5 = 7/3 + 8/3 - 5 = 0$$

and substituting into the cost equation gives the optimal value of

$$y(x, z) = x^2 - 8x + 34 - 12z + 2z^2 = 49/9 - 56/3 + 34 - 48/3 + 32/9 = 8.33$$

Taking second derivatives shows that

$$\frac{\partial^2 L}{\partial x^2} = 2 \qquad \frac{\partial^2 L}{\partial z^2} = 4 \qquad \frac{\partial^2 L}{\partial x \partial z} = 0$$

which confirms the result is a minimum.

Self-assessment questions

12.1 What is the purpose of differentiation?

12.2 What is meant by dy/dx?

12.3 What conditions must be satisfied to identify the minimum point of a curve?

12.4 If $p = q + r$ and both q and r are functions of c, how could you find dp/dc?

12.5 Explain in words what is meant by d^2y/dx^2.

12.6 When is partial differentiation used?

12.7 With partial differentiation, what does it mean if the conditions for a maximum or minimum are not met?

12.8 Is a constrained maximum likely to be higher or lower than an unconstrained maximum?

| 12.2 | Economic applications of differentiation

| 12.2.1 | Marginal analyses

Calculus was originally developed to solve problems in the physical sciences, but it can be used in many management applications. It is particularly useful for calculating the cost of various processes. Suppose, for example, that we know the total cost of producing a number of units of a product. We can divide this total cost by the number of units to get an average cost. However, it is often more useful to look at the **marginal cost**, which is defined as the cost of producing one extra unit. Suppose we have already made 100 units at a total cost of £50,000. The average cost is 50 000/100 = £500. However, the marginal cost is the cost of making the 101st unit. Because all investment in equipment may already have been recovered, and we have considerable experience in making the product, this marginal cost might be considerably lower than the average cost.

The marginal cost, MC, of a product is defined as the additional cost of making one extra unit. In making this extra unit the total cost will increase by MC, so the marginal cost is the rate at which the total cost is changing; in other words it is the gradient of the total cost curve. Now, if we know the equation for the total cost curve, we can differentiate it to get the marginal cost:

$$
\begin{aligned}
&\text{If} &&\text{total cost, } TC = y \\
&\text{then} &&\text{marginal cost, } MC = \frac{dy}{dx}
\end{aligned}
$$

The same argument holds for revenues. If we have a total revenue TR, then the marginal revenue is the additional revenue from the next unit, which is the amount by which the total revenue increases. Then the marginal revenue is the rate of change of total revenue, so we can say:

> If   total revenue, $TR = y$
>
> then   marginal revenue, $MR = \dfrac{dy}{dx}$

WORKED EXAMPLE 12.14

The total cost of producing a quantity x of a product is calculated as $TC = 2x^2 + 4x + 500$. What are the expressions for total, fixed, variable, marginal and average costs? What are these costs if 500 units of the product are made?

Solution

Total cost TC is given in the question as $TC = 2x^2 + 4x + 500$
Fixed cost is the cost that is incurred regardless of production quantity, so this is 500.
Variable cost is the cost that changes with production quantity, so this is $2x^2 + 4x$.
Marginal cost MC is found by differentiating TC, so $MC = 4x + 4$.
Average cost is found from

$$TC/x = (2x^2 + 4x + 500)/x = 2x + 4 + 500/x$$

If x is 500, then

$$TC = 2 \times 500^2 + 4 \times 500 + 500 = 502\,500$$

Fixed cost remains unchanged at 500
Variable cost is $2 \times 500^2 + 4 \times 500 = 502\,000$
Marginal cost $= 4 \times 500 + 4 = 2004$
Average cost $= 2 \times 500 + 4 + 500/500 = 1005$

Similar calculations can be used to find marginal and average revenues. Then the total profit TP is the difference between total revenue TR and total cost TC, so we can use differentiation to find the point of maximum profit. With a little thought, you can see that profit will be maximized when the marginal revenue is equal to the marginal cost. The reasoning behind this is:

- if the marginal cost is higher than the marginal revenue, each additional unit reduces the profit, encouraging fewer units to be made
- conversely, if the marginal revenue is higher than the marginal cost, each additional unit contributes to profit, encouraging still more to be made
- only when the marginal cost is the same as the marginal revenue do we have a point of stability which maximizes profit

WORKED EXAMPLE 12.15

The total cost TC and total revenue TR associated with a product are calculated as

$$TR = 14x - x^2 + 2000$$

$$TC = x^3 - 15x^2 + 1000$$

How many units should the company produce to (a) maximize total revenue, (b) minimize total cost, (c) maximize profit?

Solution

(a) The rate of change of total revenue TR is found by differentiating TR with respect to x. This gives the marginal revenue $MR = 14 - 2x$. A turning point occurs when this is equal to zero, i.e $14 - 2x = 0$ or $x = 7$. The second derivative is constant at -2, which is negative, confirming that the turning point is a maximum. At this point the total revenue is $14 \times 7 - 7 \times 7 + 2000 = 2049$.

(b) The rate of change of total cost TC is found by differentiating TC with respect to x. This gives the marginal cost $MC = 3x^2 - 30x$. Turning points occur when this is equal to zero, i.e. $3x^2 - 30x = 0$, $x(3x - 30) = 0$, so $x = 0$ or 10. Taking the second derivative gives $6x - 30$. This is negative when $x = 0$, indicating a maximum, and positive when $x = 10$, indicating a minimum. Thus the total costs are minimized by making 10 units. At this point the total cost is $10^3 - 15 \times 10^2 + 1000 = 500$. As we have seen before, this may be a local minimum, so a graph should be drawn to check these results.

(c) Total profit TP = total revenue – total cost

$$= TR - TC$$

$$= 14x - x^2 + 2000 - (x^3 - 15x^2 + 1000)$$

$$= -x^3 + 14x^2 + 14x + 1000$$

Differentiating this gives turning points when

$$-3x^2 + 28x + 14 = 0$$

The positive root of this is 9.8. Taking the second derivative gives $-6x + 28$, which is negative when $x = 9.8$, confirming a maximum.

Then the total profit is

$$-x^3 + 14x^2 + 14x + 1000$$

$$= -9.8^3 + 14 \times 9.8^2 + 14 \times 9.8 + 1000 = 1540.6$$

IN SUMMARY

If the equation for the total cost (or revenue) is known, it can be differentiated to give the marginal cost (or revenue). This can be used in a number of associated calculations.

12.2.2 | Price elasticity of demand

Differentiation can also be used to find the **price elasticity of demand**. This is an important concept in economics, and is defined as the response in demand for a product to a change in the price. A formal definition has:

$$\text{elasticity of demand} = \frac{\text{proportional change in demand}}{\text{proportional change in price}}$$

We can add some details to this equation as follows. If the quantity sold is q and the price charged is p, then the definition gives:

$$\text{elasticity of demand} = \frac{\text{change in } q/\text{original } q}{\text{change in } p/\text{original } p}$$

$$= \frac{\text{original } p}{\text{original } q} \times \frac{\text{change in } q}{\text{change in } p}$$

If we look at very small changes in price p and quantity q (so small that they approach zero), then (change in q)/(change in p) is the rate of change of q with respect to p, which is dq/dp.

$$\frac{\text{change in } q}{\text{change in } p} = \text{instantaneous gradient} = \frac{dq}{dp}$$

So:

$$\text{elasticity of demand} = \frac{p}{q} \times \frac{dq}{dp}$$

WORKED EXAMPLE 12.16

Experience suggests that the price and demand for a product are related by

$$p = 200 - q^2$$

What is the price elasticity of demand? What is the value of this when total revenue is maximized?

Solution

Differentiating p with respect to q gives:

$$\frac{dp}{dq} = -2q$$

We want dq/dp, and this can be found from

$$\frac{dq}{dp} = \frac{1}{dp/dq} = -\frac{1}{2q}$$

Then substitution gives

$$\text{elasticity of demand} = \frac{p}{q} \times \frac{dq}{dp}$$

$$= \frac{200 - q^2}{q} \times \frac{(-1)}{2q} = -\frac{(200/q - q)}{2q}$$

Total revenue $TR = qp = 200q - q^3$

A turning point can be found by differentiating this with respect to q and setting the result to zero:

$$200 - 3q^2 = 0$$

or

$$q = 8.2 \qquad \text{(ignoring the negative root)}$$

The second derivative of the revenue function is $-6q$, which is negative and confirms a maximum. Then substituting $q = 8.2$ into the elasticity of demand gives a value of -0.987.

A negative elasticity of demand is the most common result and implies that an increase in price will decrease demand. In this case, every unit increase in price will decrease demand by 0.987 units.

IN SUMMARY

The price elasticity of demand can be calculated from

$$\text{elasticity of demand} = \frac{p}{q} \times \frac{dq}{dp}$$

Self-assessment questions

12.9 How would you define the marginal cost of production?

12.10 Given the total revenue function for a product, how could you find the average revenue and the marginal revenue?

12.11 Explain what is meant by elasticity of demand.

12.12 What would a positive elasticity of demand mean?

12.3 Integration

12.2.1 Reverse of differentiation

Differentiation takes a function and finds the instantaneous gradient at any point. It would be useful to have a reverse process, so that we could start with an equation for the gradient and use this to find the function. This process is known

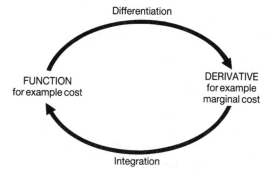

Differentiation

FUNCTION
for example cost

DERIVATIVE
for example
marginal cost

Integration

Figure 12.10   Relationship between differentiation and integration.

as **integration**. Thus integration can be viewed as the reverse of differentiation (Figure 12.10).

Suppose we have a function $y = x^2$. This can be differentiated to give the gradient of $dy/dx = 2x$. Looking at this problem the other way around, if we have a function whose gradient is $2x$, this can be integrated to give the function as x^2. Unfortunately, this intuitive approach to integration immediately meets a problem. If we have a function $y = x^2 + 5$, this can also be differentiated to give a gradient of $2x$. So if we know the derivative is $2x$, we cannot tell whether the function is x^2 or $x^2 + 5$, or $x^2 + c$, where c is any constant.

The standard sign for integration is $\int$, which is an extended 's'. We must also remember that we are integrating with respect to x, so a 'dx' is put at the end of the function being integrated. Then we can write the integration as

$$\int 2x \, dx = x^2 + c$$

This leads to the first rule for integration (which is equivalent to rule 1 for differentiation):

Integration rule 1

> If $\qquad y = ax^n$
>
> Then $\qquad \int y \, dx = \dfrac{ax^{n+1}}{n+1} + c$

You can check this result by differentiating $ax^{n+1}/(n+1) + c$, which will give ax^n. This rule is true for all values of n except -1, which would lead to a division by zero. Then there is an unusual, but standard, result which says that

$$\int x^{-1} \, dx = \int 1/x \, dx = \log_e x + c$$

There is one other rule for integration, which is equivalent to rule 2 for differentiation:

Integration rule 2

> If u and v are both functions of x, then
> $$\int (u + v) \, dx = \int u \, dx + \int v \, dx$$

Now we can use these rules in some examples.

WORKED EXAMPLE 12.17

What is the integral of $12x^5$?

Solution

We want $\int 12x^5 dx$. This is in the form ax^n with $a = 12$ and $n = 5$. Rule 1 tells us that

$$\int ax^n dx = \frac{ax^{n+1}}{n+1} + c$$

so substitution gives

$$\int 12x^5 dx = \frac{12x^6}{6} + c = 2x^6 + c$$

Integration leaves a constant, c, which cannot be evaluated. The only way to find the value is to have more information. If, for example, we know that $dy/dx = 2x$, and when $x = 2$, $y = 20$, we could do a substitution and find the missing constant:

$$\frac{dy}{dx} = 2x \text{ so integration gives } y = x^2 + c$$

But we know that $y = 20$ when $x = 2$, so substitution gives

$$y = x^2 + c \qquad \text{or} \qquad 20 = 2^2 + c \qquad \text{or} \qquad c = 16$$

WORKED EXAMPLE 12.18

What is the value of $\int(x^2 - 2x + 4)dx$? What is the value of the constant of integration if $y = 30$ when $x = 3$?

Solution

From Rule 2:

$$\int(x^2 - 2x + 4)dx = \int x^2 dx - \int 2x \, dx + \int 4 \, dx$$

Applying Rule 1 to each term:

$$\int x^2 dx = \frac{x^3}{3} \qquad \text{(substituting } a = 1 \text{ and } n = 2)$$

$$\int 2x dx = \frac{2x^2}{2} = x^2 \qquad \text{(substituting } a = 2 \text{ and } n = 1\text{)}$$

$$\int 4 \, dx = 4x \qquad \text{(substituting } a = 4 \text{ and } n = 0\text{)}$$

Then adding these terms and the constant of integration gives the solution:

$$\int (x^2 - 2x + 4)dx = \frac{x^3}{3} - x^2 + 4x + c$$

We are told that $y = 30$ when $x = 3$. Substitution gives

$$y = \frac{x^3}{3} - x^2 + 4x + c$$

$$30 = \frac{3^3}{3} - 3^2 + 4 \times 3 + c$$

or

$$c = 18$$

The final solution is

$$y = \frac{x^3}{3} - x^2 + 4x + 18$$

IN SUMMARY

Integration is the reverse process of differentiation and allows a function to be found from its rate of change.

12.3.2 | Definite integrals

The integrals we have described so far are **indefinite integrals,** which means that the result is given as a function. Sometimes we are interested in the **definite integral,** which evaluates this function at two points and finds the difference. The indefinite integral may tell us, for example:

$$\int 2x \, dx = x^2 + c$$

The definite integral evaluates this at two points, say $x = 5$ and $x = 2$ and finds the difference. We use a new notation for this:

$$\int_2^5 2x \, dx = |x^2|_2^5$$

$$= (5^2 - 2^2) = 21$$

In the first part of this, the limits of integration are put around the integral sign. Then the indefinite integral is found and enclosed by vertical lines, with the limits put after the lines. By convention, the value of the integral at the bottom limit is subtracted from the value at the top limit.

This process of finding the definite integral has two distinct advantages:

- It allows a calculation without finding the constant c, which disappears in the subtraction.

- More importantly, it allows us to concentrate on integration as a kind of summation.

We can illustrate the second of these features by looking at the marginal cost. We found earlier that the marginal cost function can be found by differentiating the total cost function; reversing this tells us that the total cost function can be found by integrating the marginal cost function. In other words, integration can be seen as a means of summation. Then we can see more clearly the purpose of the definite integral. The definite integral of the marginal cost function between two points x_1 and x_2 gives the total cost of making the units between x_1 and x_2.

WORKED EXAMPLE 12.19

The marginal cost function of a process is $3x^2 + 6x - 10$. What is the cost of making units 10 to 20?

Solution

To find the total cost, we integrate the marginal cost. In particular, the total cost of producing units 10 to 20 is found by taking the definite integral of the marginal cost function between the limits of 10 and 20:

$$\int_{10}^{20} (3x^2 + 6x - 10)dx$$

$$= |x^3 + 3x^2 - 10x|_{10}^{20}$$

$$= [20^3 + 3 \times 20^2 - 10 \times 20] - [10^3 + 3 \times 10^2 - 10 \times 10]$$

$$= 9000 - 1200$$

$$= 7800$$

IN SUMMARY

Integration can be seen as a form of summation. The definite integral sums values between two limits.

Self-assessment questions

12.13 Explain the meaning of $\int y \, dx = f(x)$

12.14 How can you find the constant of integration?

12.15 What is the purpose of the definite integral?

CHAPTER REVIEW

This chapter has introduced the methods of calculus for describing the way a function changes. In particular it:

- showed how differentiation finds the equation for the instantaneous rate of change of a function at any point
- described two basic rules for differentiation:
    if $y = ax^n$ then $dy/dx = anx^{n-1}$, for any values of a and n
    if $y = u + v$ where u and v are both functions of x,
        then $dy/dx = du/dx + dv/dx$
- showed how optimal values can be identified when $dy/dx = 0$
- extended these analyses to partial differentiation for functions with more than one variable
- considered constrained optimization using a Lagrange multiplier
- outlined the use of differentiation for marginal analysis and price elasticity of demand
- described integration as the reverse of differentiation
- looked at integration as a means of summation

Problems

12.1 Differentiate $y = 12x^7$ with respect to x.

12.2 Differentiate $y = 6.2x^4 + 3.3x^3 - 7.1x^2 - 11.9x + 14.3$ with respect to x and find the turning points. What are the maximum and minimum values?

12.3 Differentiate $x = 2y^2 - 3y + 7$ with respect to y.

12.4 A certain product sells for £10 a unit. The total cost of making and selling x units of the product is given by

$$\text{cost} = x^2 - 20x + 30$$

What is the fixed cost of production? How is the profit related to the number of units produced? What level of production will maximize profit?

12.5 Use the method described in Derivation 12.1 to show that if $y = x^2$, $dy/dx = 2x$.

12.6 What are the first and second derivatives of the following functions:

(a) $7.2x^2 - 3.3x + 7.9$ (b) $2x^7 - 4x^4 - 3x^2$ (c) $x^{24} - 4x^{-1}$

12.7 Does the function $y = 2x^2 + 5x + 10$ have a turning point? Is this a minimum or a maximum? How does this compare with $y = x^3 + 6x^2 - 15x$?

12.8 What are the partial derivatives of $y = 3x^3 + 5x^2z - 4x^2 + 10z + 6xz^2 - 3z^2 - z^3$?

12.9 The cost of a batch of a product is related to the settings x_1 and x_2 on a machine by the equation

$$\text{cost} = 3x_1^2 + 3x_1x_2 + 4x_2^2 - 6x_1 - 3x_2 + 40$$

Determine the settings on the machine that will minimize the cost.

12.10 A company finds that its earnings (in consistent units) are related to its advertising budget x_1 and sales promotions x_2, by:

$$\text{revenue} = -3x_1^2 + 40x_1 + 4x_1x_2 + 30x_2 - 6x_2^2 - 50$$

Find the maximum revenue, and the expenditure on advertising and sales promotion, which give this maximum.

12.11 Find the optimal value of the function $y = -4x^2 + 10x + 4xz + 20z - z^2$ subject to the condition $2x + 4z = 100$.

12.12 What is the minimum value of $2x^2 - 20x + 2xz + z^2 - 14z + 58$, subject to the condition that $x + z = 8$?

12.13 The total cost TC and total revenue TR associated with a product are calculated as

$$TR = 12x - 2x^2 + 5000 \quad \text{and} \quad TC = x^3 - 10x^2 + 3000$$

How many units should the company produce to (a) maximize total revenue, (b) minimize total cost, (c) maximize profit?

12.14 Integrate $9x^3 - 12x^2 + 4x - 6$.

12.15 Integrate $6x^2 - 8$. If the integral is known to have a value of 300 when x equals 5, what is the constant of integration?

12.16 Evaluate the integral of $4x^3 + 12x - 6$ between the limits 5 and 10.

Derivation 12.1: Rule 1 for differentiation

The average gradient of a line is given by $(y_2 - y_1) / (x_2 - x_1)$. Suppose, for convenience, we let $x_1 = x$, and $x_2 = x + h$. We know that y is a function of x, so we can write this as $y = f(x)$. Substitution of $y_1 = f(x)$ and $y_2 = f(x + h)$ gives the average gradient as

$$\frac{y_2 - y_1}{x_2 - x_1} = \frac{f(x + h) - f(x)}{(x + h) - x} = \frac{f(x + h) - f(x)}{h}$$

When h is very small and approaches zero, this gives the instantaneous gradient (or rate of change) which is called dy/dx.

It may seem strange to divide an amount, $f(x + h) - f(x)$, by a number that approaches zero, but let us see what happens when we substitute actual values. If we take a straight line:

$$y = f(x) = ax + b$$

and

$$f(x + h) = a(x + h) + b = ax + ah + b$$

Substitution in the equation above gives

$$\frac{dy}{dx} = \frac{ax + ah + b - ax - b}{h} = \frac{ah}{h} = a$$

This confirms the result that the gradient of a straight line is always constant at a. An extension of this gives the first rule for differentiation, that if $y = ax^n$ then $dy/dx = nax^{n-1}$

Derivation 12.2: Standard results of differentiation

Sometimes, complex functions have to be differentiated, and there are many standard results that can help. Three of these are listed below.

(a) If $y = f(u)$ and $u = f(x)$ then

$$\frac{dy}{dx} = \frac{dy}{du} \times \frac{du}{dx}$$

For example, if

$$y = 2u^2 + u - 2 \qquad \text{and} \qquad u = x^2 + 4x - 7$$

then

$$\frac{dy}{dx} = \frac{dy}{du} \times \frac{du}{dx} = (4u + 1) \times (2x + 4)$$

$$= (4x^2 + 16x - 27) \times (2x + 4)$$

$$= 8x^3 + 48x^2 + 10x - 108$$

(b) If $y = uv$, where both u and v are functions of x, then

$$\frac{dy}{dx} = v \times \frac{du}{dx} + u \times \frac{dv}{dx}$$

For example, if
$$y = (2x^2 + 5x - 3) \times (x^2 - 3x + 2)$$
so
$$u = 2x^2 + 5x - 3 \quad \text{and} \quad v = x^2 - 3x + 2$$
then
$$\frac{dy}{dx} = v \times \frac{du}{dx} + u \times \frac{dv}{dx}$$
$$= (x^2 - 3x + 2) \times (4x + 5) + (2x^2 + 5x - 3) \times (2x - 3)$$
$$= 8x^3 - 3x^2 - 28x + 19$$

(c) If $y = u/v$ where both u and v are functions of x, then
$$\frac{dy}{dx} = \frac{v \times \dfrac{du}{dx} - u \times \dfrac{dv}{dx}}{v^2}$$

For example, if
$$y = \frac{2x^2 - 5x - 3}{4x + 2}$$
so
$$u = 2x^2 - 5x - 3 \quad \text{and} \quad v = 4x + 2$$
then
$$\frac{dy}{dx} = \frac{(4x + 2) \times (4x - 5) - (2x^2 - 5x - 3) \times (4)}{(4x + 2)^2}$$
$$= \frac{8x^2 + 8x + 2}{16x^2 + 16x + 4}$$

Even with such rules, there are many types of differentiation which are difficult to do from scratch. Some of these can use standard results, three of which are stated (but not proved) below:

$$\text{If } y = 1/x \quad \text{then} \quad dy/dx = -1/x^2 \tag{1}$$

This can be confirmed by writing the equation as $y = x^{-1}$ and using the standard equation for differentiation.

$$\text{If } y = e^x \quad \text{then} \quad dy/dx = e^x \tag{2}$$

$$\text{If } y = \log_e x \quad \text{then} \quad dy/dx = 1/x \tag{3}$$

These three standard derivatives could also be written as standard integrals, with:

$$\int -(1/x)^2 \, dx = 1/x \tag{1}$$
$$\int e^x \, dx = e^x \tag{2}$$
$$\int 1/x \, dx = \log_e x \tag{3}$$

We shall not look at more complicated integrals, but many tables of standard results are available.

SECTION FOUR

Business statistics

This book is divided into five sections, each of which covers a different aspect of quantitative methods in business. The first section gave the background and context for the rest of the book. The second section discussed data collection and description. The third section looked at methods of solving specific types of business problem. The problems tackled there were deterministic, which means that they do not involve any probabilities. This is the fourth section, which gives an introduction to probabilities and statistical methods. The final section shows how these ideas can be applied to probabilistic models.

There are four chapters in this section.

Chapter 13 introduces the ideas of probability. In many situations the values taken by variables are not known exactly; there is some uncertainty. Probabilities give a means of measuring this uncertainty and doing associated analyses.

Chapter 14 describes how probability distributions can be used to describe data that contain uncertainty. Many probability distributions follow a standard pattern, and the most important of these are described.

We have already shown how samples are used for collecting data, and this theme is expanded in Chapter 15. The essence of sampling is that some characteristic of a population is inferred from the characteristics of a sample. Here we discuss how confident we are in making such inferences, and how this confidence is related to the sample size.

Chapter 16 introduces the ideas of statistical testing. In particular, it discusses hypothesis testing, which sees if a belief about a population is supported by the evidence from a sample.

Uncertainty and probabilities

13

CHAPTER OUTLINE

Previous chapters in this book have assumed that variables are known with certainty. When considering sales, for example, we assumed that the volume of future sales would be known exactly. In this chapter we are looking at situations where this is not true, and there is some uncertainty. We know roughly what future sales will be, but cannot give exact numbers. This kind of uncertainty is measured by probabilities.

The probability of an event can be viewed as its likelihood or relative frequency. The probability of rolling a six on a dice is 1/6, the probability that Christmas Day is a Monday is 1/7, and so on.

After reviewing some results for independent probabilities, the chapter looks at conditional probabilities. These occur when the probability of one event's occurring is influenced by other events.

The material in this chapter is important, as it lays the foundations for the following chapters. It is important that you thoroughly understand probabilities before moving on.

After reading this chapter and doing the exercises you should be able to:

- appreciate the difference between deterministic and stochastic problems
- calculate probabilities and appreciate their meaning
- know the rules for multiplying and adding probabilities for independent events
- understand dependent events
- use Bayes' theorem to calculate conditional probabilities
- draw probability trees

| 13.1 | Measuring uncertainty

| 13.1.1 | Introduction

So far in this book we have assumed that the value of any variable is fixed and can be known with certainty. When we look at sales we assume that the number of sales and the prices charged are known with certainty, so we can say, 'A company sells 1000 units a year at £20 a unit.' Similarly, when we look at production, the output and costs are known with certainty; when we look at employees, the number of people employed and their hours of work are known with certainty; when we look at a service, we known how many customers there will be and how much each will spend. Such situations are called **deterministic**.

In reality, information about most situations is not so well known. When we spin a coin we do not know whether it will come down heads or tails; a company launching a new product does not know exactly how many sales it will make; someone selling a house does not know exactly how much it will fetch; a manufacturer does not know exactly how much will be made in a period. Each of these has some uncertainty. Such situations are called **stochastic** or **probabilistic**.

Although stochastic problems contain uncertainty, we must emphasize that this is not the same as ignorance. When we spin a coin we know that it will come down either heads or tails, and we know that each of these outcomes is equally likely. When a company launches a new product it will normally do some market research, which suggests that likely sales are, say, around 2000 units a year. Then the company has some information and knows roughly what level of sales to expect, but there is some uncertainty and it does not know the exact figure. In this chapter we are going to discuss ways of measuring this uncertainty. This is done by **probabilities**.

| *IN SUMMARY* |

Many situations are not deterministic (when all values are known exactly) but stochastic (when there is uncertainty). Probabilities are a way of measuring this uncertainty.

| 13.1.2 | Defining probability

Probabilities give a way of measuring uncertainty. To be more precise, the probability of an event is a measure of its likelihood or relative frequency.

Experience leads us to believe that when a fair coin is tossed it will come down heads half the time and tails half the time. This observation allows us to say, 'The probability of a fair coin coming down heads is 0.5.' This statement is based on a definition of the probability of an event as the proportion of times the event occurs:

> probability of an event =
>
> $$\frac{\text{number of ways that the event can occur}}{\text{number of possible outcomes}}$$

When we spin a coin there are two possible outcomes (heads and tails) and one of these is a head, so the probability of a head is 1/2 . Similarly, there are 52 cards in a pack of cards and one ace of hearts, so a card chosen at random has a probability of 1/52 of being the ace of hearts (or any other specified card). In the last 500 days the train to work has broken down 10 times, so the probability of it breaking down on any day is 10/500, or 0.02. For 200 of the last 240 trading days the Toronto Stock Exchange has had more advances than declines, so there is a probability of 200/240, or 0.83, that the Stock Exchange advances on a particular day.

As a probability measures the proportion of times that an event occurs, its values can only be defined in the range 0 to 1:

> - probability = 0 means that the event will **never** occur
> - probability = 1 means that the event will **always** occur
> - probability between 0 and 1 gives relative frequency
> - probabilities outside the range 0 to 1 have no meaning

An event with a probability of 0.8 is quite likely (it will happen eight times out of ten); an event with a probability of 0.5 is equally likely to happen as not; an event with a probability of 0.2 is quite unlikely (it will happen two times out of ten).

Rather than keep saying 'the probability of an event is 0.8' we can abbreviate this to $P(\text{event}) = 0.8$. Then spinning a coin has $P(\text{head}) = 0.5$.

WORKED EXAMPLE 13.1

A magazine advertises a prize draw with one first prize, five second prizes, 100 third prizes and 1000 fourth prizes. The prizes are drawn at random from entries for the competition and after each draw the winning ticket is returned to the draw. By the closing date there are 10 000 entries and at the draw no entry won more than one prize. What is the probability that a given ticket won first prize or that it won any prize?

Solution

There are 10 000 entries and one first prize, so the probability of a given ticket winning first prize is 1/10 000.

Similarly, there are five second prizes, so the probability of winning one of these is 5/10 000. The probabilities of winning third or fourth prizes are 100/10 000 and 1000/10 000 respectively.

There are a total of 1106 prizes so the probability of winning one of these is 1106/10 000 = 0.1106. Conversely, the probability of not winning a prize is 8894/10 000 = 0.8894.

WORKED EXAMPLE 13.2

An office has the following types of employee:

	Female	Male
Administrative	25	15
Operational	35	25

If one person from the office is selected at random, what is the probability that the person is (a) a male administrator, (b) a female operator, (c) male, (d) an operator?

Solution

(a) There are 100 people working in the office. Of these 15 are male administrators, so:

$$P(\text{male administrator}) = 15/100 = 0.15$$

(b) 35 people in the office are female operators, so:

$$P(\text{female operator}) = 35/100 = 0.35$$

(c) A total of 40 people in the office are male, so:

$$P(\text{male}) = 40/100 = 0.4$$

(d) A total of 60 people in the office are operators, so:

$$P(\text{operator}) = 60/100 = 0.6$$

In the worked example above, we calculated the probabilities from observations. Generally, there are two ways in which probabilities can be found:

- Theoretical argument can be used to give **a priori** probabilities:

$$\text{probability of an event} = \frac{\text{number of ways that the event can occur}}{\text{number of possible outcomes}}$$

The probability that a husband and wife share the same birthday is 1/365 (ignoring leap years). This is an a priori probability, calculated by saying that there are 365 days on which the second partner can have a birthday and only one of these corresponds to the birthday of the first partner.

- Historical data can be used to give **empirical** values:

$$\text{probability of an event} = \frac{\text{number of times that the event occurred}}{\text{number of observations}}$$

The last 100 times that a football team has played at home, it has attracted a crowd of more than 20 000 on 62 occasions. This gives an empirical probability of 62/100 = 0.62 that next week's game will have a crowd of more than 20 000 (all other things being equal).

One problem with using empirical values is that the historical data may not be typical. If a coin is tossed five times and comes down heads each time, this does not mean that it will always come down heads. Empirical values must be based on typical values, collected over a sufficiently long period.

There is another method of getting probabilities, which is not generally recommended. This asks people to give their subjective views about likely probabilities. We might, for example, ask knowledgeable people to suggest a probability that a company will make a profit of more than a million pounds next year. This is equivalent to judgemental forecasting, and has the same drawbacks. In particular, subjective probabilities are often little more than guesses and are generally unreliable.

IN SUMMARY :

The probability of an event is the likelihood that the event will occur, or its relative frequency. This is measured on a scale of 0 to 1 with:

probability = 0   meaning that there is no chance of the event happening

probability = 1   meaning that the event is certain to happen

13.1.3 | Calculations with probabilities

An important concept for probabilities is **mutually exclusive** events. Two events are mutually exclusive if one event's happening means that the second event cannot happen. When a coin is tossed, having it come down heads is mutually exclusive with having it come down tails; the event that a company makes a profit in a year is mutually exclusive with the event that it makes a loss in the year; the event that sales increase is mutually exclusive with the event that sales decrease.

With this definition we can do some calculations of probabilities. For mutually exclusive events the probabilities of one **or** another happening is found by adding the separate probabilities:

For mutually exclusive events:
OR means ADD probabilities

$P(a \text{ OR } b) = P(a) + P(b)$

$P(a \text{ OR } b \text{ OR } c) = P(a) + P(b) + P(c)$

$P(a \text{ OR } b \text{ OR } c \text{ OR } d) = P(a) + P(b) + P(c) + P(d)$

and so on.

An illustration of this was given in Worked Example 13.1, where the probability that a particular ticket won a magazine prize draw was calculated as 1106/10 000. The probability that it did not win was 8894/10 000. Each ticket must either win or lose, and these two events are mutually exclusive, so:

$$P(\text{win OR lose}) = 1$$

$$P(\text{win}) + P(\text{lose}) = 0.1106 + 0.8894 = 11$$

or

$$P(\text{lose}) = 1 - P(\text{win})$$

WORKED EXAMPLE 13.3

A company makes 40 000 washing machines a year. Of these, 10 000 are for the home market, 8000 are exported to North America, 7000 to Europe, 5000 to South America, 4000 to the Far East, 3000 to Australasia and 3000 to other markets.

(a) What is the probability that a particular machine is sold on the home market?

(b) What is the probability that a machine is exported?

(c) What is the probability that a machine is exported to either North or South America?

(d) What is the probability that a machine is sold in either the home market or Europe?

Solution

(a) The probability that a machine is sold on the home market is

$$P(\text{home}) = \frac{\text{number sold on home market}}{\text{number sold}} = \frac{10\ 000}{40\ 000} = 0.25$$

(b) All events (that is, areas of sales) are mutually exclusive, so the probability that a machine is exported is found by adding the total number of machines which are exported and dividing this by the total machines made:

$$P(\text{exported}) = 30\ 000/40\ 000 = 0.75$$

Alternatively, we could use the observation that all machines made are sold somewhere, so the probability that a machine is sold is 1.0. It is either sold on the home market or exported, so:

$$P(\text{sold}) = 1 = P(\text{exported}) + P(\text{home})$$

Hence:

$$P(\text{exported}) = 1 - P(\text{home}) = 1 - 0.25 = 0.75$$

(c) $P(\text{North America OR South America}) = P(\text{North America}) + P(\text{South America})$

$$= 8000/40\ 000 + 5000/40\ 000 = 0.2 + 0.125 = 0.325$$

(d) $P(\text{home OR Europe}) = P(\text{home}) + P(\text{Europe})$

$$= 10\ 000/40\ 000 + 7000/40\ 000 = 0.25 + 0.175 = 0.425$$

A useful way of presenting probabilities is given by **Venn diagrams**, which use circles to represent the probabilities of events. If two events are mutually exclusive, the Venn diagram shows separate circles as illustrated in Figure 13.1.

If two events are **not** mutually exclusive, there is a probability that they can both occur, as shown in the Venn diagram of Figure 13.2. The circles now overlap, with the overlap representing the probability that both events occur. If we simply add the probabilities of each event, we effectively add the overlap twice, and to correct this we must subtract the probability of both events.

For events that are not mutually exclusive:

$$P(a \text{ OR } b) = P(a) + P(b) - P(a \text{ AND } b)$$

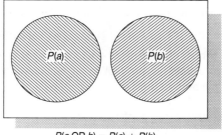

$P(a \text{ OR } b) = P(a) + P(b)$

Figure 13.1   Venn diagram for mutually exclusive events.

Suppose we pick a single card from a pack. What is the probability that it is an ace or a heart? These are not mutually exclusive events, so we say:

$$P(\text{ace OR heart}) = P(\text{ace}) + P(\text{heart}) - P(\text{ace AND heart})$$

$$= 4/52 + 13/52 - 1/52 = 16/52 = 0.31$$

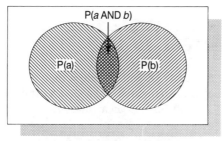

$P(a \text{ OR } b) = P(a) + P(b) - P(a \text{ AND } b)$

Figure 13.2   Venn diagram for non-mutually exclusive events.

Another important concept for events is independence. If the occurrence of one event does not affect the occurrence of a second event, the two events are said to be **independent.** The fact that a person works in a bank is independent of the fact that they are left-handed. The fact that a factory has a shipment of raw materials delayed is independent of the fact that they had problems with machine reliability last year. Using the notation:

$P(a)$ = the probability of event a

$P(a/b)$ = the probability of event a given that b has already occurred

$P(a/\underline{b})$ = the probability of event a given that b has **not** occurred

The two events, a and b, are independent if

$$P(a) = P(a/b) = P(a/\underline{b})$$

The probability that a person buys a particular newspaper is independent of the probability that they suffer from hay fever. Then:

$$P(\text{buys } Times) = P(\text{buys } Times/\text{suffers from hay fever})$$

$$= P(\text{buys } Times/\text{does not suffer from hay fever})$$

A second rule for probabilities is used when a number of separate events all occur. For independent events the probability of one **and** another happening is found by multiplying the probabilities of the separate events:

For independent events:
AND means MULTIPLY probabilities

$P(a \text{ AND } b)$ $= P(a) \times P(b)$

$P(a \text{ AND } b \text{ AND } c)$ $= P(a) \times P(b) \times P(c)$

$P(a \text{ AND } b \text{ AND } c \text{ AND } d) = P(a) \times P(b) \times P(c) \times P(d)$

and so on

WORKED EXAMPLE 13.4

A workshop combines two parts, X and Y, into a final assembly. This is tested and an average of 10% of X are defective and 5% of Y. If defects in X and Y are independent, what is the probability that a final assembly has both X and Y defective?

Solution

For independent events:

$$P(X \text{ defective AND } Y \text{ defective}) = P(X \text{ defective}) \times P(Y \text{ defective})$$

$$= 0.1 \times 0.05$$

$$= 0.005$$

Similarly:

$$P(X \text{ defective AND } Y \text{ not defective}) = 0.095$$

$$P(X \text{ not defective AND } Y \text{ defective}) = 0.045$$

$$P(X \text{ not defective AND } Y \text{ not defective}) = 0.855$$

These are the only four possible combinations, so it is not surprising that the probabilities add to 1.

WORKED EXAMPLE 13.5

A warehouse classifies its stock into three categories: A, B and C. On all category A items it promises a service level of 97% (in other words, there is a probability of 0.97 that the warehouse can meet demand immediately from stock). On category B and C items it promises service levels of 94% and 90% respectively. If service levels are independent, what are the probabilities that the warehouse can immediately supply an order for:

(a) one item of category A and one item of category B

(b) one item from each category

(c) two different items from A, one from B and three from C

(d) three different items from each category?

Solution

(a) As the events are independent the probabilities can be multiplied to give

P(one A AND one B) = P(one A) × P(one B) = 0.97 × 0.94 = 0.912

(b) P(one A AND one B AND one C) = P(one A) × P(one B) × P(one C)

$$= 0.97 \times 0.94 \times 0.90 = 0.821$$

(c) P(two A AND one B AND three C) = P(two A) × P(one B) × P(three C)

This must be broken down further by noting that the probability of two items of category A is the probability that the first is there AND the second is there. In other words:

$$P(\text{two A}) = P(\text{one A AND one A}) = P(\text{one A}) \times P(\text{one A}) = P(\text{one A})^2$$

Similarly:

$$P(\text{three C}) = P(\text{one C})^3$$

Then the answer becomes

$$P(\text{one A})^2 \times P(\text{one B}) \times P(\text{one C})^3 = 0.97^2 \times 0.94 \times 0.9^3$$

$$= 0.645$$

(d) P(three A AND three B AND three C) = P(one A)^3 × P(one B)^3 × P(one C)^3

$$= 0.97^3 \times 0.94^3 \times 0.9^3$$

$$= 0.553$$

WORKED EXAMPLE 13.6

Every year a company bids for an annual contract. The probability that it will win the contract is 0.75. What is the probability that the company will win the contract either this year or next year?

Solution

One thing we **cannot** do with this problem is say

$$P(\text{win this year}) = 0.75$$

$$P(\text{win next year}) = 0.75$$

Then:

$$P(\text{win this year OR win next year}) = P(\text{win this year}) + P(\text{win next year})$$

$$= 0.75 + 0.75 = 1.5$$

The addition rule only works if the two events are mutually exclusive. In this case, the events (winning the contract this year and winning it next year) are not mutually exclusive, and the company could win the contract in both years. A fuller analysis would give:

$$P(\text{win this year AND win next year}) = 0.75 \times 0.75 = 0.5625$$

$$P(\text{win this year AND lose next year}) = 0.75 \times 0.25 = 0.1875$$

$$P(\text{lose this year AND win next year}) = 0.25 \times 0.75 = 0.1875$$

$$P(\text{lose this year AND lose next year}) = 0.25 \times 0.25 = 0.0625$$

The probability that the company wins the contract in at least one year is $1 - 0.0625 = 0.9375$. The probability that the company wins the contract in only one year is $0.1875 + 0.1875 = 0.3750$.

IN SUMMARY

For mutually exclusive events:

OR means ADD probabilities, so $P(a \text{ OR } b) = P(a) + P(b)$

For independent events:

AND means MULTIPLY probabilities, so $P(a \text{ AND } b) = P(a) \times P(b)$

Self-assessment questions

13.1 What is meant by the probability of an event?

13.2 What are independent events?

13.3 What are mutually exclusive events?

13.4 How could you determine the probability that one of several mutually exclusive events occur?

13.5 How could you determine the probability of all of several events occurring?

13.6 If one of events A, B and C is certain to happen, what is $P(A)$?

13.2 | Conditional probability for dependent events

13.2.1 | Bayes' theorem

Most of the analyses described in the last section assume that events are independent. In many circumstances this assumption is not valid, and we should now look at events where the occurrence of one directly effects the occurrence of the other. For example, the fact that a person is employed in one of the professions is not independent of their having higher education; the probability that a machine will break down this week is not independent of its age; the probability that there is a mistake on an invoice is not independent of the company submitting the invoice, and so on.

For dependent events, the fact that one event has occurred or not changes the probability that a second event will occur. Then, if

$P(a)$ = the probability of event a

$P(a/b)$ = the probability of event a given that b has already occurred

$P(a/\underline{b})$ = the probability of event a given that b has **not** occurred

The two events, a and b, are dependent if:

$P(a) \neq P(a/b) \neq P(a/\underline{b})$

(Remember that the symbol $\neq$ means 'is not equal to'.)

The probability that the price of a company's shares rise is dependent on whether the company announces a profit or a loss. Then:

P(share price rises) $\neq P$(share price rises/announce profit)

$\neq P$(share price rises/announce loss)

Probabilities in the form $P(a/b)$ are called **conditional** probabilities. There is one important result that you must understand about conditional probabilities: this is the general rule that the probability of two dependent events' occurring is the probability of the first, multiplied by the conditional probability that the second occurs given that the first has already occurred. This rather clumsy statement can be written as

$$P(a \text{ AND } b) = P(a) \times P(b/a)$$

where:

$P(a \text{ AND } b)$ = probability that both a and b occur

$P(a)$ = probability that a occurs

$P(b/a)$ = probability that b occurs given that a has already occurred

With a little thought this can be extended to give the obvious result

$$P(a \text{ AND } b) = P(a) \times P(b/a) = P(b) \times P(a/b)$$

Taking the second two terms and rearranging them gives:

$$P(a/b) = \frac{P(b/a) \times P(a)}{P(b)}$$

This result is known as **Bayes' theorem**, and is the basis of most calculations of conditional probabilities.

WORKED EXAMPLE 13.7

The students in a class can be classified as follows:

	Home	Overseas
Male	66	29
Female	102	3

(a) If a student is selected at random from the class, what is the probability that the student will be from overseas?

(b) If the student selected is female, what is the probability that she is from overseas?

(c) If the student selected is male, what is the probability that he is from overseas?

(d) If the student is from overseas, what is the probability that he or she is male?

(e) Check that $P(a \text{ AND } b) = P(a) \times P(b/a)$ for several combinations of sex and origin.

Solution

(a) $P(\text{overseas})$ = number from overseas/number of students

$$= 32/200 = 0.16$$

(b) This can be found by considering only the 105 female students, to give:

$$P(\text{overseas/female}) = \text{number of overseas females/number of females}$$

$$= 3/105 = 0.029$$

The same result can be found using Bayes' theorem:

$$P(\text{overseas/female}) = \frac{P(\text{overseas AND female})}{P(\text{female})}$$

Now:

$$P(\text{overseas AND female}) = 3/200 = 0.015$$

$$P(\text{female}) = 105/200 = 0.525$$

so

$$P(\text{overseas/female}) = \frac{P(\text{overseas AND female})}{P(\text{female})}$$

$$= 0.015/0.525 = 0.029$$

(c) $P(\text{overseas/male})$ = number overseas males/number males

$$= 29/95 = 0.305$$

This can also be calculated from Bayes' theorem:

$$P(\text{overseas/male}) = \frac{P(\text{overseas AND male})}{P(\text{male})}$$

Now:

$$P(\text{overseas AND male}) = 29/200 = 0.145$$

$$P(\text{male}) = 95/200 = 0.475$$

so

$$P(\text{overseas/male}) = \frac{P(\text{overseas AND male})}{P(\text{male})} = 0.145/0.475 = 0.305$$

(d) $P(\text{male/overseas})$ = number overseas males/number overseas

$$= 29/32 = 0.906$$

This can also be calculated from Bayes' theorem:

$$P(\text{male/overseas}) = \frac{P(\text{male AND overseas})}{P(\text{overseas})}$$

Now:

$$P(\text{male AND overseas}) = 29/200 = 0.145$$

$$P(\text{overseas}) = 32/200 = 0.16$$

so

$$P(\text{male/overseas}) = \frac{P(\text{male AND overseas})}{P(\text{overseas})} = 0.145/0.16 = 0.906$$

(e) This has already been demonstrated in parts (a) to (d) and can be tested further using any other combinations. For example:

- $P(\text{home AND male}) = P(\text{home}) \times P(\text{male/home}) = 0.84 \times 0.393 = 0.330$
(compare this with 66/200 = 0.33)

- $P(\text{female AND overseas}) = P(\text{female}) \times P(\text{overseas/female}) = 0.525 \times 0.029$
$= 0.015$
(compare this with 3/200 = 0.015)

WORKED EXAMPLE 13.8

Two machines make identical parts, which are combined on a production line. The older machine makes 40% of the units, of which 85% are of satisfactory quality. The newer machine makes 60% of the units, of which 92% are of satisfactory quality. A random check further down the production line shows an unusual fault, which suggests that the machine that made the unit needs adjusting. What is the probability that the older machine made the unit?

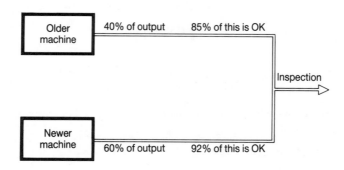

Figure 13.3   Process for Worked Example 13.7.

Solution

This problem is represented in Figure 13.3. Using the abbreviations O for the older machine, N for the newer machine, OK for good units and F for faulty ones, we want $P(O/F)$, and this can be found using Bayes' theorem:

$$P(a/b) = \frac{P(b/a) \times P(a)}{P(b)} \qquad \text{so} \qquad P(O/F) = \frac{P(F/O) \times P(O)}{P(F)}$$

We know that $P(O) = 0.4$ and $P(F/O) = 0.15$, so the remaining value we need is $P(F)$, the probability that a unit is faulty. With a little thought you can see that:

probability that a unit is faulty = probability that it is faulty from the old machine
OR that it is faulty from the new machine

So:

$$P(F) = P(F \text{ AND } O) + P(F \text{ AND } N)$$

or

$$P(F) = P(F/O) \times P(O) + P(F/N) \times P(N)$$

Substitution then gives

$$P(O/F) = \frac{P(F/O) \times P(O)}{P(F)} = \frac{0.15 \times 0 \, 4}{0.15 \times 0.4 + 0.08 \times 0.6} = \frac{0.06}{0.108} = 0.556$$

To check this result we could also calculate:

$$P(N/F) = \frac{P(F/N) \times P(N)}{P(F)} = \frac{0.08 \times 0.6}{0.108} = 0.444$$

As the faulty unit must have come from either the older or newer machine, the fact that $P(O/F) + P(N/F) = 1$ confirms the result.

IN SUMMARY

Conditional probabilities occur when two events are dependent. Associated calculations can be done using Bayes' theorem.

Calculations for Bayes' theorem

13.2.2

The arithmetic for Bayes' theorem is quite straightforward, but it could become tedious for larger problems. An obvious solution is to use a computer, and Figure 13.4 shows a printout for the results of Worked Example 13.8. In this printout you can see a number of values that we calculated. Unfortunately, this package does not label the events, so we must remember

BAYESIAN ANALYSIS MODEL

$- = * = -$ DATA ENTERED $- = * = -$

NUMBER OF STATES   : 2
NUMBER OF ALTERNATIVES : 2

PRIOR PROBABILITIES

1   0.4000
2   0.6000

CONDITIONAL PROBABILITIES

	1	2
1	0.1500	0.8500
2	0.0800	0.9200

$- = * = -$ RESULTS $- = * = -$

PREDICTIONS – JOINT PROBABILITIES

	1	2
1	0.0600	0.3400
2	0.0480	0.5520

PREDICTIONS – MARGINAL PROBABILITIES

1   0.1080
2   0.8920

PREDICTIONS – REVISED PROBABILITIES

	1	2
1	0.5556	0.4444
2	0.3812	0.6188

$- - - - - - - -$ END OF ANALYSIS $- - - - - - - -$

Figure 13.4   Computer printout for Bayesian analysis.

what each means. In practice, there is an easy mechanical procedure that often makes it unnecessary to use a computer. We can demonstrate this with the data from Worked Example 13.8.

The mechanical procedure starts by putting the data in a table:

	Faulty	OK	
Older machine	0.15	0.85	0.4
Newer machine	0.08	0.92	0.6

The left-hand box of figures gives the known conditional probabilities. Thus $0.15 = P(F/O)$, $0.08 = P(F/N)$ etc. The box to the right gives the values of $P(O)$ and $P(N)$, which are called the prior probabilities.

Now we form a third box by multiplying each conditional probability in the left-hand box by the prior probability on the same line. Thus $0.15 \times 0.4 = 0.060$, $0.08 \times 0.06 = 0.048$, etc. These results are called **joint** probabilities.

	Faulty	OK		Faulty	OK
Older machine	0.15	0.85	0.4	0.060	0.340
Newer machine	0.08	0.92	0.6	0.048	0.552
				0.108	0.892

Adding each column of joint probabilities gives a marginal probability. Thus

$0.060 + 0.048 = 0.108$, which is the probability that a unit is faulty;

$0.340 + 0.552 = 0.892$, which is the probability that a unit is OK.

Finally, dividing each of the joint probabilities by the marginal probability in the same column gives the revised probabilities, shown in a bottom box. Thus

$0.060/0.108 = 0.556$, $0.340/0.892 = 0.381$, etc.

These revised probabilities give $P(O/F)$, $P(N/OK)$, and so on.

	Faulty	OK		Faulty	OK
Older machine	0.15	0.85	0.4	0.060	0.340
Newer machine	0.08	0.92	0.6	0.048	0.552
				0.108	0.892
		Older machine		0.556	0.381
		Newer machine		0.444	0.619

Although the description of this procedure may seem a bit strange, comparison with the equation for Bayes' theorem shows that we are simply repeating the calculations described there. The results of this calculation are illustrated in Figure 13.5.

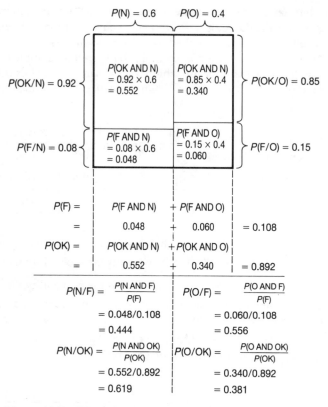

$P(N) = 0.6 \qquad P(O) = 0.4$

$P(OK/N) = 0.92$

$P(OK/O) = 0.85$

$P(F/N) = 0.08$

$P(F/O) = 0.15$

| | P(OK AND N) = 0.92 × 0.6 = 0.552 | P(OK AND N) = 0.85 × 0.4 = 0.340 |
| P(F AND N) = 0.08 × 0.6 = 0.048 | P(F AND O) = 0.15 × 0.4 = 0.060 |

$P(F) = \qquad P(F \text{ AND } N) + P(F \text{ AND } O)$

$= \qquad 0.048 \quad + \quad 0.060 \qquad = 0.108$

$P(OK) = \qquad P(OK \text{ AND } N) + P(OK \text{ AND } O)$

$= \qquad 0.552 \quad + \quad 0.340 \qquad = 0.892$

$P(N/F) = \dfrac{P(N \text{ AND } F)}{P(F)} \qquad P(O/F) = \dfrac{P(O \text{ AND } F)}{P(F)}$

$= 0.048/0.108 \qquad = 0.060/0.108$

$= 0.444 \qquad = 0.556$

$P(N/OK) = \dfrac{P(N \text{ AND } OK)}{P(OK)} \qquad P(O/OK) = \dfrac{P(O \text{ AND } OK)}{P(OK)}$

$= 0.552/0.892 \qquad = 0.340/0.892$

$= 0.619 \qquad = 0.381$

Figure 13.5 Illustrating the calculation of conditional probabilities.

WORKED EXAMPLE 13.9

The probabilities of X and Y are 0.3 and 0.7 respectively. There are three events that can follow X and Y, with conditional probabilities given in the following table. Use Bayes' theorem on these figures.

	A	B	C
X	0.1	0.5	0.4
Y	0.7	0.2	0.1

Solution

The table gives the conditional probabilities of $P(A/X)$, $P(B/X)$, etc. We know that the prior probabilities of $P(X) = 0.3$ and $P(Y) = 0.7$. Then the mechanical procedure for Bayes' theorem is given below:

	Conditional probabilities			Priors	Joint probabilities		
	A	B	C		A	B	C
X	0.1	0.5	0.4	0.3	0.03	0.15	0.12
Y	0.7	0.2	0.1	0.7	0.49	0.14	0.07
					0.52	0.29	0.19
				X	0.058	0.517	0.632
				Y	0.942	0.483	0.368

The marginal probabilities show $P(A) = 0.52$, $P(B) = 0.29$ and $P(C) = 0.19$. The predictions in the bottom boxes show that $P(X/A) = 0.058$, $P(X/B) = 0.517$, and so on.

IN SUMMARY

The calculations for Bayes' theorem are relatively straightforward, particularly if a mechanical procedure is used.

13.2.3 | Probability trees

It is sometimes easier to visualize conditional probabilities on a **probability tree**. These diagrams are drawn from left to right with branches representing a sequence of possible events. Figure 13.6 shows a probability tree for the previous data for faults on two machines. Each branch represents a possible event, and they emerge from nodes, which are represented by circles. Node 1 is the starting point. From here there are two alternatives for a part:

● it comes from the older machine
● it comes from the newer machine

Then at both nodes 2 and 3 there are two possibilities:

● the part is faulty
● the part is all right

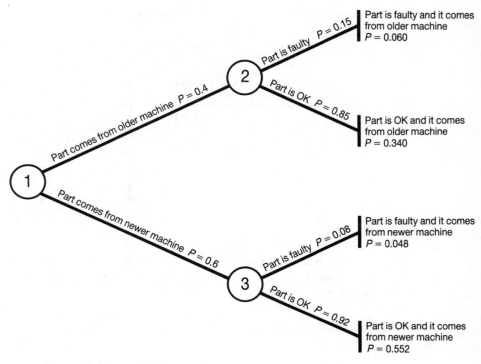

Figure 13.6 A probability tree.

Each branch is labelled with its probability, and as we include all possible events, the sum of probabilities on branches leaving any node should be 1. At the right of the tree are the terminal values, which show the probability of reaching terminal points. Terminal values are found by multiplying the probabilities on all branches taken to reach that point. Thus the first terminal node shows the probability that a part is faulty and that it comes from the older machine, which is $0.4 \times 0.15 = 0.060$. The second terminal node shows the probability that a part is all right and that it comes from the older machine which is $0.4 \times 0.85 = 0.340$. Again, the sum of all terminal values should be 1.

WORKED EXAMPLE 13.10

Second-hand cars can be classified as either good buys or bad buys. Among good buys, 70% have low oil consumption and 20% have medium oil consumption. Among bad buys, 50% have high oil consumption and 30% have medium oil consumption. A test was done on a second-hand car and showed a low oil consumption. If 60% of second-hand cars are good buys, what is the probability that this car is a good buy?

Solution

We can start by defining the abbreviations GB and BB for good buy and bad buy; HOC, MOC and LOC for high, medium and low oil consumption. The known values can be substituted into the equation for Bayes' theorem. Using the mechanical format to ease calculation gives the following results:

	HOC	MOC	LOC		HOC	MOC	LOC
GB	0.1	0.2	0.7	0.6	0.06	0.12	0.42
BB	0.5	0.3	0.2	0.4	0.20	0.12	0.08
					0.26	0.24	0.50
				GB	0.23	0.5	0.84
				BB	0.77	0.5	0.16

From this table, the probability that a car is a good buy, given that it has a low oil consumption, is 0.84. The table also shows that the probability of a low oil consumption is 0.5 (compared with 0.26 for a high oil consumption). The problem can be illustrated in the probability tree in Figure 13.7.

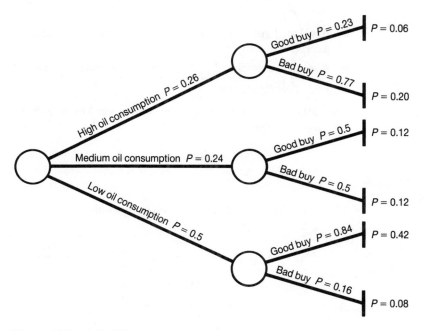

Figure 13.7 Probability tree for Worked Example 13.10.

IN SUMMARY

Sometimes it is easier to visualize a problem with a probability tree. These represent alternative events by branches.

Self-assessment questions

13.7 What are dependent events?

13.8 What are conditional probabilities?

13.9 What is Bayes' theorem and when is it used?

13.10 What is the benefit of a probability tree?

CHAPTER REVIEW

This chapter introduced the ideas of uncertainty and probability. The probability of an event is a measure of its likelihood or relative frequency. The chapter:

- discussed uncertainty and stochastic problems
- defined probabilities and their use
- developed rules for calculating probabilities for independent and mutually exclusive events
- discussed conditional probabilities and calculations using Bayes' theorem
- drew probability trees

The ideas developed in the chapter will be used to build probabilistic models in the following chapters.

Problems

13.1 An office has the following types of employee:

	Female	Male
Administrative	20	21
Managerial	12	10
Operational	42	38

If one person from the office is selected at random what is the probability that the person is: (a) a male administrator, (b) a female manager,

(c) male, (d) an operator, (e) either a manager or an administrator, (f) either a female administrator or a female manager?

13.2 There are five equally likely outcomes to a trial: A, B, C, D and E.

(a) What is the probability of C occurring?

(b) What is the probability of A or B or C occurring?

(c) What is the probability that neither A nor B occurs?

13.3 Four mutually exclusive events A, B, C and D have probabilities of 0.1, 0.2, 0.3 and 0.4 respectively. What are the probabilities of: (a) A and B occurring, (b) A or B, (c) neither A nor B, (d) A and B and C, (e) A or B or C, (f) none of A, B or C?

13.4 If a card is picked from a deck of cards, what is the probability that it is: (a) an ace, (b) a heart, (c) an ace and a heart, (d) an ace or a heart?

13.5 A salesman schedules three calls for a particular day, and each call has a probability of 0.5 of making a sale. What is the probability of making: (a) 3 sales, (b) 2 or more sales, (c) no sales?

13.6 There are 20 people in a room. What is the probability that they all have different birthdays?

13.7 If $P(a) = 0.4$ and $P(b/a) = 0.3$, what is $P(a$ AND $b)$? If $P(b) = 0.6$, what is $P(a/b)$?

13.8 The probabilities of two events X and Y are 0.4 and 0.6 respectively. The conditional probabilities of three other events A, B and C occurring, given that X or Y has already occurred, are given in the following table:

	A	B	C
X	0.2	0.5	0.3
Y	0.6	0.1	0.3

What are the conditional probabilities of X and Y occurring given that A, B or C has already occurred?

13.9 A manufacturer uses three suppliers for a component. X supplies 35% of the component, Y supplies 25% and Z supplies the rest. The quality of each component is described as 'good', 'acceptable' or 'poor', with the proportions from each supplier given below:

	Good	Acceptable	Poor
X	0.2	0.7	0.1
Y	0.3	0.65	0.05
X	0.1	0.8	0.1

What information can you find using Bayes' theorem on these figures?

13.10 Draw probability trees for Worked Examples 13.7 and 13.8.

13.11 Data collected for a major city show that 60% of drivers are above 30 years old. 5% of all the drivers over 30 will be prosecuted for a driving offence during a year, compared with 10% of drivers 30 or younger. If a driver has been prosecuted, what is the probability they are 30 or younger?

13.12 A family have two children. If one of these is a girl, what is the probability the other is a boy?

13.13 It is estimated that 0.5% of the population have a certain type of cancer. A new test for detecting this cancer is said to be 98% accurate. If 10 000 people are tested, how many of them will give a positive response, and how many of these will actually have cancer?

Computer exercises

13.1 Figure 13.8 shows the printout from a computer program that does Bayesian analysis. Make sure you understand what is happening here. Use an equivalent program to check the results.

13.2 Figure 13.9 shows a printout from a spreadsheet that has been used to do a Bayesian analysis. Design a spreadsheet to check these results.

13.3 How could you improve the presentation of the results in Figure 13.9? Design a spreadsheet that will give an improved and more general presentation.

13.4 The number of absentees each day from a factory during a typical period has been recorded as follows:

13 16 24 21 15 23 15 26 25 11 10 24 27 30 15 31 25 19 15 27

A new scheme for payments was introduced without any discussion with the workforce, and the numbers of absentees were recorded as follows:

31 29 27 30 26 28 38 34 40 25 29 34 33 30 28 26 41 45 30 28

After some negotiations, a new, agreed incentive scheme was introduced and the numbers of absentees each day were:

09 12 16 08 24 09 15 16 20 21 09 11 10 10 25 17 16 18 09 08

What do these figures suggest?

BAYESIAN ANALYSIS MODEL

$-=*=-$ DATA ENTERED $-=*=-$

NUMBER OF STATES   : 4
NUMBER OF ALTERNATIVES : 4

PRIOR PROBABILITIES

1	0.15
2	0.25
3	0.3
4	0.3

CONDITIONAL PROBABILITIES

	1	2	3	4
1	0.1000	0.4000	0.2000	0.3000
2	0.2000	0.3000	0.3000	0.2000
3	0.3000	0.3000	0.4000	0.0000
4	0.4000	0.3000	0.2000	0.1000

$-=*=-$ RESULTS $-=*=-$

PREDICTIONS–JOINT PROBABILITIES

	1	2	3	4
1	0.0150	0.0600	0.0300	0.0450
2	0.0500	0.0750	0.0750	0.0500
3	0.0900	0.0900	0.1200	0.0000
4	0.1200	0.0900	0.0600	0.0300

PREDICTIONS – MARGINAL PROBABILITIES

1	0.2750
2	0.3150
3	0.2850
4	0.1250

PREDICTIONS – REVISED PROBABILITIES

1	0.0545	0.1905	0.1053	0.3600
2	0.1818	0.2381	0.2632	0.4000
3	0.3273	0.2857	0.4211	0.0000
4	0.4364	0.2857	0.2105	0.2400

$--------$ END OF ANALYSIS $--------$

Figure 13.8   Computer printout for Bayesian analysis.

	A	B	C	D	E	F	G	
1		**Bayes Theory**						
2								
3		Conditional			Priors	Joint		
4		A	B	C		A	B	
5	P	0.5	0.3	0.2	0.2	0.1	0.06	0.04
6	Q	0.3	0.4	0.3	0.3	0.09	0.12	0.09
7	R	0.2	0.5	0.3	0.5	0.1	0.25	0.15
8					Marginal	0.29	0.43	0.28
9					P	0.344828	0.139535	0.14
10				Prediction	Q	0.310345	0.27907	0.32
11					R	0.344828	0.581395	0.53

Figure 13.9 Spreadsheet for Bayes' theorem.

Case study
The Gamblers' Press

The Gamblers' Press is a weekly paper that publishes large quantities of information that is used by gamblers. Its main contents are detailed sections on horse racing, greyhound racing, football, and other major sporting activities. It also runs regular features on card games, casino games and any other areas that gamblers may find interesting.

The Gamblers' Press was founded in 1897 and now has a regular circulation around 50 000 copies. It is considered a highly respectable paper and has a strict policy of only giving factual information. It never gives tips or advice.

Last year *The Gamblers' Press* decided to run a special feature on misleading or dishonest practices. This idea was suggested when four unconnected reports were passed to the editors.

The first of these reports concerned an 'infallible' way of winning at roulette. Customers were charged £250 for the details of the scheme, which was based on a record of all the numbers that won on the roulette wheel during an evening. Then the customers were advised to bet on two sets of numbers:

- those that had come up more often, because the wheel might be biased in their favour
- those that had come up least often, because the laws of probability say that numbers which appear less frequently on one night, must appear more frequently on another night

The second report showed that a number of illegal chain letters were circulating in the South East. These letters contained a list of eight names. Individuals were asked to send a pound to the name at the top of the list. Then they should delete the name at the top, insert their own name at the bottom, and send a copy of the letter to eight of their friends. As each name moved to the top of the list they would receive payments from people who joined the chain later. The advertising accompanying these letters guaranteed to make respondents millionaires, with frequent claims of 'you cannot lose!!!'. It also said that people not responding would be letting down their friends and would inevitably be plagued by bad luck.

The third report was from a 'horse racing consultant'. This person sent a letter saying which horse would win a race the following week. A week later he sent a second letter saying how the selected horse had won, and giving another tip for the following week. This was repeated for a third week. Then after three wins the consultant said he would send the name of another horse that was guaranteed to win next week, but this time there would be a cost of £1000. This seemed a reasonable price as the horse was certain to win and bets of any size could be placed. Unfortunately, this scheme had a drawback. It was thought that the consultant sent out about 10 000 of the original letters, and randomly tipped each horse in a five-horse race. The second letter was only sent to those people who had been given the winning horse. The next two letters followed the same pattern, with follow-up letters only sent to those who had been given the winning horse.

The fourth report concerned a North American lottery. Here people selected six numbers in the range 00 to 99, and bought a lottery ticket for $1 containing these numbers. At the end of a week a computer would randomly generate a set of six numbers. Anyone with the same six numbers would win the major prize (typically over a million dollars), and people with four or five matching numbers would win smaller prizes. A magazine reported a way of dramatically increasing the chances of winning. This suggested taking your eight favourite numbers and then betting on all possible combinations of six numbers from these eight. The advertisement explained the benefit of this by saying: 'Suppose there is a chance of one in a million of winning the first prize. If one of your lucky numbers is chosen by the computer, you will have this number in over a hundred entries, so your chances of winning are raised by 100 to only one in 10 000.'

The Gamblers' Press was aware of many schemes like these four, and they decided to write a major article on them. Your job is to write this article. You should start by explaining why the four schemes mentioned above do not work, and then expand the study to include other examples of this kind of scheme.

Probability distributions

14

CHAPTER OUTLINE

The last chapter discussed probabilities. In this chapter we are going to extend these ideas by looking at probability distributions, which can be viewed as relative frequency distributions.

Empirical distributions can be drawn for specific problems, but a number of standard distributions are widely applicable. In this chapter we shall discuss the binomial, Poisson and Normal distributions.

The binomial distribution calculates the probability of a number of successes in a series of trials. The Poisson distribution finds the probability of a number of successes in a continuous background of failures. Both the binomial and Poisson distributions are used for discrete data.

The Normal distribution is the most widely used probability distribution. It describes continuous data and can be used in many situations.

After reading this chapter and doing the exercises you should be able to:

● understand the purpose of probability distributions

● draw empirical probability distributions from available data

● do calculations with combinations and permutations

● understand when and how to use the binomial distribution

● understand when and how to use the Poisson distribution

● understand when and how to use the Normal distribution

14.1 | What are probability distributions?

In Chapter 4 we looked at ways of presenting data in diagrams. One useful diagram was a relative frequency distribution, which showed the proportion of observations in different classes. In the last chapter we said that probabilities could be viewed as relative frequencies. Now we are going to combine these two ideas and show how a set of data can be described by a **probability distribution**.

We shall start by building a probability distribution for a set of discrete values. From Chapter 4 you might infer that the three stages in drawing a probability distribution are:

● list all possible events

● calculate the probability of each event

● present these probabilities in a suitable table or diagram

This is demonstrated in the following example.

WORKED EXAMPLE 14.1

Every night a hotel has a number of people who book rooms by telephone, but do not actually turn up. The number of no-shows was recorded over a typical period as follows.

$$2\ 4\ 6\ 7\ 1\ 3\ 3\ 5\ 4\ 1\ 2\ 3\ 4\ 3\ 5\ 6\ 2\ 4\ 3\ 2\ 5\ 5$$

$$0\ 3\ 3\ 2\ 1\ 4\ 4\ 4\ 3\ 1\ 3\ 6\ 3\ 4\ 2\ 5\ 3\ 2\ 4\ 2\ 5\ 3\ 4$$

Draw a probability distribution of this data. What is the probability that there are more than four no-shows?

Solution

Adding the number of nights with various numbers of no-shows gives the following frequency distribution:

No-shows	0	1	2	3	4	5	6	7
Frequency	1	4	8	12	10	6	3	1

If we divide each of the frequencies by the total number of observations (45), we get the following relative frequency or probability distribution:

No-shows	0	1	2	3	4	5	6	7
Probability	0.02	0.09	0.18	0.27	0.22	0.13	0.07	0.02

A histogram can be drawn of this probability distribution, as shown in Figure 14.1. Remember that the **area** of each rectangle in this histogram represents the probability, so the total area under the histogram must equal 1. The probability of more than four no-shows is:

$$P(5) + P(6) + P(7) = 0.13 + 0.07 + 0.02 = 0.22$$

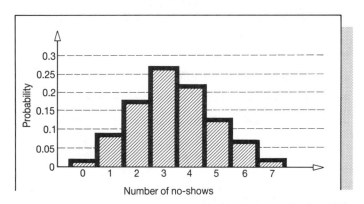

Figure 14.1   Probability distribution for no-shows in Worked Example 14.1.

The probability distribution drawn above is empirical, which means that it was found from actual observations. This approach can be used for any problem where observations are made, but the resulting distribution is specific to that particular problem. It has been found, however, that empirical probability distributions often follow standard patterns. Several of these patterns have been observed, and in the rest of this chapter we shall look at three of them:

● binomial distribution

● Poisson distribution

● Normal (or Gaussian) distribution

The first two describe discrete data, while the Normal distribution describes continuous data.

IN SUMMARY

A probability distribution is a description of the relative frequency of events or classes of observations. Empirical distributions describe specific situations, but several general distributions are widely used.

Self-assessment questions

14.1 What is the purpose of a probability distribution?

14.2 What is the difference between empirical and a priori data?

14.3 What is the total area under a histogram drawn to show a probability distribution?

‖ 14.2 ‖ Combinations and permutations

There are several standard probability distributions, and we shall describe the three most important. The first of these is the binomial distribution, but before we discuss this we need to consider some aspects of sequencing. In particular, we must describe combinations and permutations.

Sequencing problems occur when a number of activities can be performed in different orders. Then the order in which activities are taken can affect the overall performance. The time taken for a bus to travel between a suburb and a city centre, for example, depends on the order in which stops are visited; the time taken to process a number of jobs on a machine depends on the order in which they are taken; the number of people needed to work in a restaurant depends on the order in which they are assigned to shifts, days off and holidays.

The objective with a sequencing problem is to examine all the possible orders in which activities can be taken, and select the best. Although this appears simple it is notoriously difficult, primarily because of the large number of possible sequences that have to be considered. If we look at the sequencing of n activities we can select the first as any one of the n. The second activity selected can be any one of the remaining $(n - 1)$, so there are $n(n - 1)$ possible sequences for the first two activities. The third activity can be any one of the remaining $(n - 2)$, the fourth any of $(n - 3)$, and so on. Then the total number of sequences for n activities is given by:

$$\text{number of sequences} = n(n - 1)(n - 2)(n - 3) \ldots 3 \times 2 \times 1 = n!$$

This means that even a small problem with 15 activities has $15! = 1.3 \times 10^{12}$ possible sequences. Remember that $n!$ (pronounced 'n factorial') is an abbreviation for $n(n - 1)(n - 2) \ldots \times 3 \times 2 \times 1$.

Instead of finding the best sequence of n activities, suppose we only want to find the best sequence of r of the n activities. There are two important calculations for this, which are called **permutations and combinations**.

Suppose we have n things that are distinct (that is, we can tell the difference between them) and we want to select r of these. In how many ways can this be done? If we are not interested in the order in which the r things are selected, the answer is the **combination** of r things from n, which is written as ^nC_r.

> The number of ways in which r things can be selected from n, regardless of the order of selection, is given by:
>
> $$^nC_r = \frac{n!}{r!(n-r)!}$$

If there is a pool of ten cars, and three customers arrive to use them, there are $^{10}C_3$ ways of allocating cars to customers:

$$^{10}C_3 = \frac{10!}{3! \times (10-3)!} = 120$$

If we have n things that are distinct and want to select r of these, but this time we are concerned with the order of selection, then we are interested in the permutation of r things from n, which is written as nPr.

> The number of ways in which r things can be selected from n, when the order of selection is important, is given by:
>
> $$^nP_r = \frac{n!}{(n-r)!}$$

Suppose there are ten applicants for a social club's committee, consisting of a chairman, deputy chairman, secretary and treasurer. We are interested in selecting a group of four from ten, but the order in which they are selected is important (corresponding to the different jobs). Then the number of ways in which the committee of four can be chosen is

$$^nP_r = \frac{n!}{(n-r)!} = \frac{10!}{(10-4)!} = 5040$$

If four ordinary committee members are to be selected (that is, with no differentiation in job description and hence no importance to the order in which they are chosen), we should be interested in the combinations of four from ten. The number of ways of selecting ordinary members is:

$$^nC_r = \frac{n!}{r!(n-r)!} = \frac{10!}{4!(10-4)!} = 210$$

Permutations depend on order of selection and combinations do not, so there are always a lot more permutations than combinations. The number of combinations of four letters of the alphabet is $26!/(4! \times 22!) = 14\,950$. One combination is the letters A, B, C and D, but these can be arranged in 24 different ways (ABCD, ABDC, ACBD, etc). The number of permutations of four letters from the alphabet is $26!/22! = 358\,800$, which is 4! times the number of combinations.

WORKED EXAMPLE 14.2

(a) A company has eight applicants to fill eight different jobs. In how many different ways can it assign applicants to jobs?

(b) There is a sudden reorganization in the company and the number of available jobs falls to six. In how many different ways can the jobs be filled with the eight applicants?

(c) Suppose the reorganization leads to a reclassification of jobs and the six jobs are now identical. In how many different ways can they be filled?

Solution

(a) This essentially asks, 'How many different ways can eight things be sequenced?' and the answer is 8!. The applicants can be assigned to jobs in $8! = 40\,320$ different ways.

(b) This asks the number of ways in which six things can be selected from eight. As the jobs are different we are interested in the order of selection and hence the permutation. The number of ways that six different jobs can be filled from eight applicants is:

$$^{n}P_{r} = \frac{n!}{(n-r)!} = \frac{8!}{(8-6)!} = 20\,160$$

(c) This again asks the number of ways in which six things can be selected from eight, but now the jobs are identical, so the order of selection is not important. The number of ways in which six identical jobs can be filled from eight applicants is:

$$^{n}C_{r} = \frac{n!}{r!(n-r)!} = \frac{8!}{6!(8-6)!} = 28$$

This last problem could be looked at from another viewpoint, of finding how many ways two applicants could be rejected from eight. Then with $r = 2$ we have:

$$^{n}C_{r} = \frac{n!}{r!(n-r)!} = \frac{8!}{2!(8-6)!} = 28$$

WORKED EXAMPLE 14.3

Twelve areas in the North Sea become available for oil exploration, and government policy of encouraging competition limits the allocation of these to at most one area for any exploration company.

(a) If 12 exploration companies bid for the areas, in how many ways can the areas be allocated?

(b) Initial forecasts show that each area is equally likely to produce oil, so they can be considered equally attractive. If 20 exploration companies put in bids for areas, how many ways are there of allocating areas to companies?

(c) A last-minute report shows the probabilities of major oil discoveries in each area. Based on this, four companies withdraw their bid. If the areas are now allocated randomly, in how many ways can this allocation be done?

Solution

(a) There are 12 companies receiving one area each, so the companies can be sequenced in 12! possible ways, or 4.79×10^{8}.

(b) There are 20 companies, only 12 of whom will be selected. As each area is equally attractive, it does not matter in which order the companies are selected, so the number of possible combinations is

$$^{n}C_{r} = \frac{n!}{r!(n-r)!} = \frac{20!}{12!(20-12)!} = 125\,970$$

(c) Now the areas are different, and we are interested in the orders in which the remaining 16 companies can be selected. This is given by

$$^{n}P_{r} = \frac{n!}{(n-r)!} = \frac{16!}{(16-12)!}$$

$$= 8.72 \times 10^{11}$$

IN SUMMARY

- There are $n!$ possible sequences of n different things.
- If the order of selection is **not** important, r things can be selected from n in ^nC_r different ways (these are combinations).
- If the order of selection **is** important, r things can be selected from n in ^nP_r different ways (these are permutations).

$$^nC_r = \frac{n!}{r!(n-r)!} \quad \text{and} \quad {}^nP_r = \frac{n!}{(n-r)!}$$

Self-assessment questions

14.4 In how many ways can n different activities be sequenced?

14.5 What is the difference between a permutation and a combination?

14.6 When selecting r things from n are there more combinations than permutations or vice versa?

| 14.3 | Binomial distribution

Now that we have done the background work, we can return to probability distributions. The first of these is the binomial distribution. This is used when a series of **trials** have the following characteristics:

- each trial has two possible outcomes (conventionally called success and failure)
- the two outcomes are mutually exclusive
- there is a constant probability of success, p, and failure, $q = 1 - p$
- the outcomes of successive trials are independent

Tossing a coin is a standard example of a binomial process. Each toss is a trial; each head, say, is a success with a constant probability of 0.5 and each tail is a failure. Another example of a binomial process occurs when inspecting a batch of a product for defects. Each inspection of a unit is a trial; each fault is a success and each good unit is a failure. Then the binomial distribution gives the probability of any number of faults in the batch. More generally, it considers n trials and finds the probability of r successes. This probability can be found by the following argument.

Suppose the number of trials is n, and we want the probability of r successes. In each trial the probability of a success is constant at p. Then:

$$P(\text{exactly } r \text{ successes}) = P(r \text{ successes AND } n - r \text{ failures})$$

$$= P(r \text{ successes}) \times P(n - r \text{ failures})$$

We know that for independent trials the probability of the first r being successes is p^r, and the probability of the next $n - r$ trials being failures is q^{n-r}. Then the probability of the first r trials being successes **and** the next $n - r$ trials being failures is $p^r q^{n-r}$.

But the sequence of r successes followed by $n - r$ failures is only one way of getting r successes in n trials. We must find how many other possible sequences there are. In the last section we found that the number of sequences of r things chosen from a population of n, when the order of selection does not matter, is $^nC_r = n!/r!(n - r)!$. There must, therefore, be ^nC_r possible sequences of r successes and $n - r$ failures, each with probability $p^r q^{n-r}$. The overall probability of r successes is found by multiplying the number of sequences with r successes by the probability of each sequence. This gives the probability of r successes in n trials as:

$$P(r \text{ success in } n \text{ trials}) = {}^nC_r\, p^r q^{n-r}$$

$$= \frac{n!}{r!(n-r)!}\, p^r q^{n-r}$$

This is the calculation for the binomial probability distribution.

WORKED EXAMPLE 14.4

A salesman knows that in the long term he has a 50% chance of making a sale when calling on a customer. One morning he arranges six calls.
(a) What is the probability of making exactly three sales?
(b) What are the probabilities of making other numbers of sales?
(c) What is the probability of making fewer than three sales?

Solution

The problem is a binomial process with the probability of success (that is, of making a sale) of $p = 0.5$, the probability of failure (not making a sale) $q = 1 - p = 0.5$, and the number of trials $n = 6$.

(a) The probability of making exactly three sales (so $r = 3$) is given by

$$P(r \text{ success in } n \text{ trials}) = {}^{n}C_{r}p^{r}q^{n-r}$$

$$P(3 \text{ success in 6 trials}) = {}^{6}C_{3} \times 0.5^{3} \times 0.5^{(6-3)}$$

$$= \frac{6!}{3!3!} \times 0.125 \times 0.125 = 0.3125$$

(b) Substituting other values for r gives the values

r	0	1	2	3	4	5	6
$P(r$ successes in 6 trials)	0.0156	0.0938	0.2344	0.3125	0.2344	0.0938	0.0156

These values are drawn in the probability distribution in Figure 14.2.

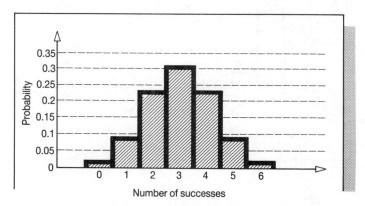

Figure 14.2 Probability distribution for binomial process with $n = 6$ and $P = 0.5$

(c) The probability of making fewer than three sales is the sum of the probabilities of making 0, 1 and 2 sales:

$$P(\text{fewer than 3 sales}) = P(0 \text{ sales}) + P(1 \text{ sale}) + P(2 \text{ sales})$$

$$= 0.0156 + 0.0938 + 0.2344$$

$$= 0.3438$$

The shape of the binomial distribution varies with p and n. For small values of p, the distribution is asymmetrical and the peak is to the left of centre. As p increases the peak moves to the centre of the distribution, and with $p = 0.5$ the distribution is symmetrical. As p increases further the distribution again become asymmetrical but this time the peak is to the right of centre. For larger values of n the distribution is flatter and broader. Some typical binomial distributions are shown in Figure 14.3.

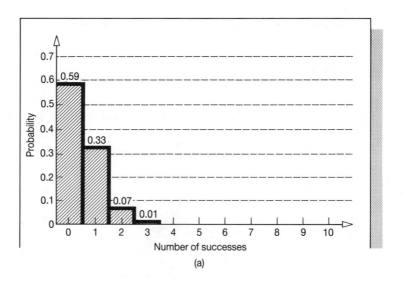

(a)

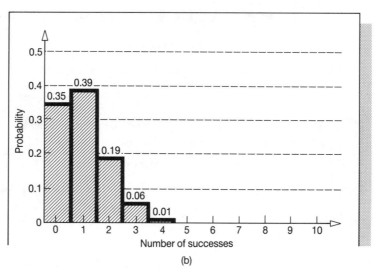

(b)

Figure 14.3 Typical binomial distributions for varying values of n and P: (a) $n = 5$, $p = 0.1$; (b) $n = 10$, $p = 0.1$;

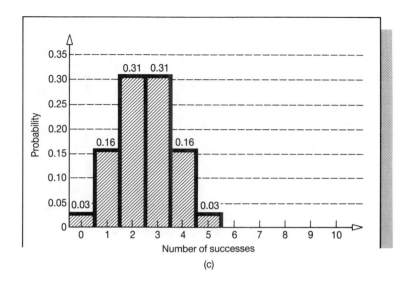

(c)

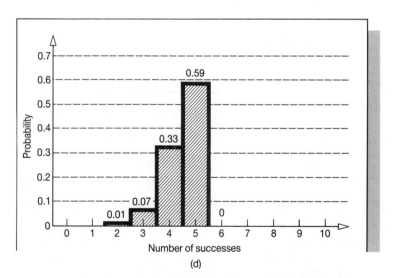

(d)

Figure 14.3 Typical binomial distributions for varying values of *n* and *P*:
(c) *n* = 5, *p* = 0.5; (d) *n* = 5, *p* = 0.9;

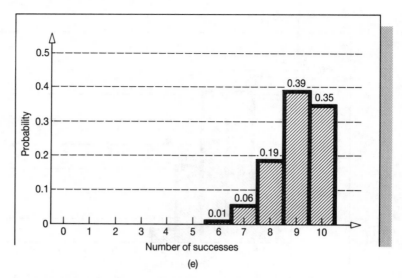

Figure 14.3 Typical binomial distributions for varying values of *n* and *P*:
(e) *n* = 10, *p* = 0.9.

Whatever the values of *n* and *p*, the mean, variance and standard deviation of a binomial distribution are calculated from:

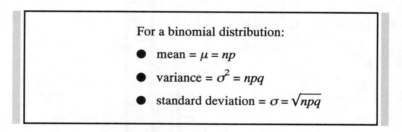

For a binomial distribution:

● mean = $\mu = np$

● variance = $\sigma^2 = npq$

● standard deviation = $\sigma = \sqrt{npq}$

Notice that in these definitions we have used the Greek letter μ (mu) for the mean rather than $\bar{x}$ and the Greek letter σ (sigma) for the standard deviation rather than *s*. This follows a standard notation, where:

● the mean and standard deviation of a sample are called $\bar{x}$ and *s* respectively
● the mean and standard deviation of a population are called μ and σ respectively

We shall use this notation again in the following chapter.

The calculations of probabilities with the binomial distribution are straightforward, and standard tables are available for various combinations of *n* and *p*. Appendix E contains some of these which can be used to confirm the results that we have calculated above.

WORKED EXAMPLE 14.5

A company makes a particularly sensitive electronic component, and 10% of the output is defective. Twenty units of the component are packed into boxes and sold.

(a) Describe the number of defective units in each box.

(b) What is the probability of no defects in a box?

Solution

(a) This is a binomial process, with success being a faulty unit. In each box $n = 20$ and $p = 0.1$. The mean number of faulty units in a box is

$$np = 20 \times 0.1 = 2$$

The variance is

$$npq = 20 \times 0.1 \times 0.9 = 1.8$$

so the standard deviation is

$$\sqrt{1.8} = 1.34$$

(b) The probability of no defects is

$$P(0) = 0.9^{20} = 0.12$$

WORKED EXAMPLE 14.6

A market researcher is asked to visit 12 houses in a given area between 7.30 and 9.30 one evening. Previous calls suggest that there will be someone at home in 85% of houses.

(a) Describe the probability distribution of the number of houses with people at home.

(b) What is the probability that the researcher will find someone at home in exactly nine houses?

(c) What is the probability that there will be someone at home in exactly seven houses?

(d) What is the probability that there will be someone at home in at least ten houses?

Solution

(a) The process is binomial, with visiting a house as a trial and finding someone at home a success. Then we have $n = 12$, $p = 0.85$ and $q = 0.15$. Substituting in the standard values gives

mean number of houses with someone at home $= np = 12 \times 0.85 = 10.2$

variance $= npq = 12 \times 0.85 \times 0.15 = 1.53$

standard deviation $= \sqrt{1.53} = 1.24$

(b) Let $P(9)$ be the probability that there is someone at home in exactly nine houses. Then:

$$P(9) = {}^{12}C_9 \times 0.85^9 \times 0.15^3 = 220 \times 0.2316169 \times 0.003375 = 0.172$$

(c) Similarly:

$$P(7) = {}^{12}C_7 \times 0.85^7 \times 0.15^5 = 792 \times 0.320577 \times 0.000076 = 0.0193$$

These figures can be found in the tables in Appendix E. Values are only given for p up to 0.5, so to use the tables we must redefine 'success' as finding a house with no one at home. Then $p = 0.15$ and $r = 5$. Looking at the entry for $n = 12$, $p = 0.15$ and $r = 3$ (finding nine houses with someone at home is the same as finding three houses with no one at home) confirms the value 0.1720, while $r = 5$ confirms the value 0.0193.

(d) We want:

$$P(\text{at least } 10) = P(10) + P(11) + P(12)$$

If we want to use tables, 'success' must again be defined as finding no one at home. Then

$$P(\text{at least } 10) = 0.2924 + 0.3012 + 0.1422 = 0.7358$$

Sometimes it is more convenient to use a computer to calculate a probability distribution. Figure 14.4 shows a typical result when a statistics package is asked to calculate the binomial probabilities for $n = 20$ and $p = 0.3$. The first command in this Minitab printout asks for the probability distribution function (pdf) and the subcommand specifies the distribution. A spreadsheet would, of course, be equally good for calculating tables of probabilities.

In some circumstances the arithmetic for calculating binomial probabilities becomes difficult, even using tables or computers. Consider the following situation where n is very large. The accounts department of a company sends out 10 000 invoices a month and on average five of these are returned with some error. What is the probability that exactly five invoices will be returned in a given month?

MTB > pdf;
SUBC > binomial n = 20 p = 0.3.

BINOMIAL WITH N = 20 P = 0.300000

K	P(X = K)
0	0.0008
1	0.0068
2	0.0278
3	0.0716
4	0.1304
5	0.1789
6	0.1916
7	0.1643
8	0.1144
9	0.0654
10	0.0308
11	0.0120
12	0.0039
13	0.0010
14	0.0002
15	0.0000

MTB > stop

Figure 14.4   Binomial probabilities from a typical statistics package.

This is a typical application for the binomial distribution, where a trial is sending out an invoice, and a success is having an error. Unfortunately, as soon as we try to do the arithmetic we run into difficulties. Substituting known values gives

$$n = 10\,000 \qquad r = 5 \qquad p = 5/10\,000 \qquad q = 9995/10\,000$$

so:

$$P(r \text{ returns}) = \frac{n!}{r!(n-r)!} \, p^r q^{n-r}$$

$$= \frac{10\,000!}{5! \times 9{,}995!} \times (5/10\,000)^5 \times (9995/10\,000)^{9995}$$

Although this calculation can be done, it does not seem reasonable to raise figures to the power of 9995 or to contemplate 10 000 factorial. Fortunately, there is an alternative. When n, the number of trials, is large and p, the probability of success, is small the binomial distribution can be approximated by a Poisson distribution. This is described in the following section.

IN SUMMARY

The binomial distribution is used when an event has two mutually exclusive outcomes, called success and failure. It calculates the probability of r successes in n trials as

$$P(r \text{ success in } n \text{ trials}) = {}^nC_r p^r q^{n-r}$$

Self-assessment questions

14.7 In what circumstances can a binomial distribution be used?

14.8 Define all the terms in the equation $P(r) = {}^nC_rp^rq^{n-r}$

14.9 How are the mean and variance of a binomial distribution calculated?

14.10 Find, from the tables in Appendix E, the probability of two successes from seven trials, when the probability of success is 0.2.

14.4 | Poisson distribution

The Poisson distribution is a close relative of the binomial distribution and can be used to approximate it when:

- the number of trials, n, is large (say, greater than 20)
- the probability of success, p, is small (so that np is less than 5)

As n gets larger and p gets smaller the approximation becomes better.

The Poisson distribution is also useful in its own right for solving problems where events occur at random. The number of accidents each month in a factory, the number of defects in a metre of cloth, and the number of phone calls received each hour in an office follow Poisson distributions.

The main difference between the binomial and Poisson distributions is that the binomial distribution uses the probabilities of both success and failure, while the Poisson uses only the probability of successes. The reason is that the probability of success is very small, so the number of failures is very large: effectively we are looking for a few successes in a continuous background of failures. When looking at the number of spelling mistakes in a long report, the number of faults in a pipeline, or the number of accidents in a month, we are only interested in the number of successes and are not bothered by the large number of events that are failures.

A Poisson distribution is described by the equation

$$P(r \text{ successes}) = \frac{e^{-\mu}\mu^r}{r!}$$

where:

e = exponential constant = 2.7183

μ = mean number of successes

We can show how the Poisson distribution deals with the binomial example we did not finish above. The accounts department of a company sends out 10 000 invoices a month and on average five of these are returned with some error. What is the probability that exactly five invoices will be returned in a given month?

Here n is large and $np = 5$ (fairly high but the result should still be reasonable), so we can use the Poisson approximation to the binomial. The variables are $r = 5$ and $\mu = 5$.

$$P(r \text{ successes}) = \frac{e^{-\mu} \mu^r}{r!}$$

so

$$P(5 \text{ successes}) = \frac{e^{-5} 5^5}{5!} = \frac{0.0067 \times 3125}{120}$$

$$= 0.1755$$

WORKED EXAMPLE 14.7

In a large office complex there have been 40 accidents that led to absence from work in the past 50 weeks. In what proportion of weeks would you expect 0, 1, 2, 3 and more than 4 accidents?

Solution

A small number of accidents occur, presumably at random, over time. We are not interested in the number of accidents that did **not** occur, so the process can be described by a Poisson distribution:

$$P(r \text{ successes}) = \frac{e^{-\mu} \mu^r}{r!}$$

The mean number of accidents a week is $40/50 = 0.8$, so substituting $\mu = 0.8$ and $r = 0$ gives

$$P(0) = \frac{e^{-0.8} \times 0.8^0}{0!} = 0.4493$$

Similar substitution of $r = 1$ etc gives

$$P(1) = \frac{e^{-0.8} \times 0.8^1}{1!} = 0.3595$$

$$P(2) = \frac{e^{-0.8} \times 0.8^2}{2!} = 0.1438$$

$$P(3) = \frac{e^{-0.8} \times 0.8^3}{3!} = 0.0383$$

$$P(4) = \frac{e^{-0.8} \times 0.8^4}{4} = 0.0077$$

Then:

$$P(>4) = 1 - P(\leq 4)$$

$$= 1 - P(0) - P(1) - P(2) - P(3) - P(4)$$

$$= 1 - 0.4493 - 0.3593 - 0.1438 - 0.0383 - 0.0077$$

$$= 0.0016$$

When events occur at random, a Poisson distribution can often be used, but strictly speaking there are a number of other requirements. In particular a Poisson process needs:

- events that are independent
- the probability of an event happening in an interval is proportional to the length of the interval
- in theory, an infinite number of events should be possible in an interval

Then:

For a Poisson distribution:

- mean, $\mu = np$
- variance, $\sigma^2 = np$
- standard deviation, $\sigma = \sqrt{np}$

The shape and position of the Poisson distribution are determined by the single parameter, μ. For small μ the distribution is asymmetrical with a peak to the left of centre. Then as μ increases the distribution becomes more symmetrical. This is illustrated for some values in Figure 14.5

The arithmetic for calculating probabilities is straightforward, but can become rather tedious if a large number of values are to be found. A computer will help, and a typical printout from a statistics package calculating Poisson probabilities is given in Figure 14.6. Standard tables are also available, and the Poisson tables in Appendix F can be used to check the probabilities calculated in this section.

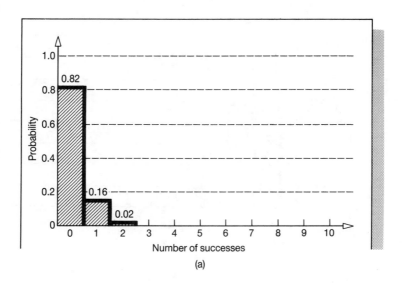

(a)

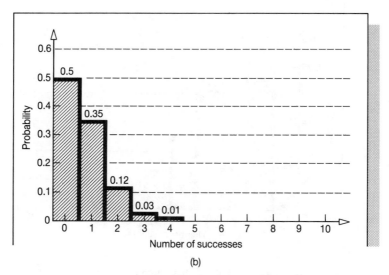

(b)

Figure 14.5   Typical Poisson distribution for varying values of μ:
(a) $\mu = 0.2$;   (b) $\mu = 0.7$;

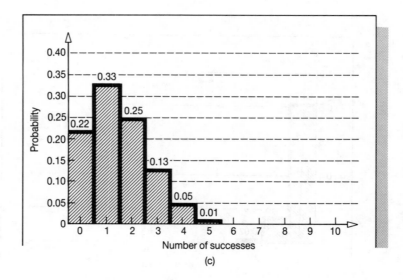

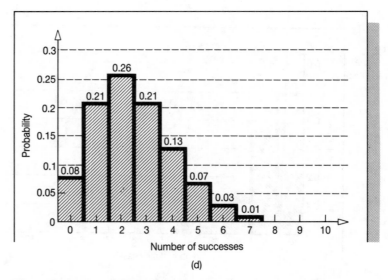

Figure 14.5 Typical Poisson distribution for varying values of μ: (c) $\mu = 1.5$; (d) $\mu = 2.5$;

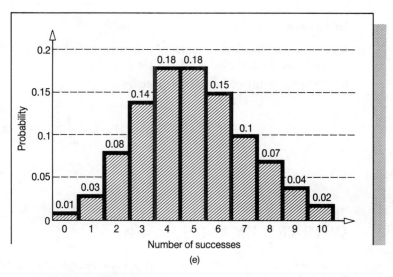

Figure 14.5 Typical Poisson distribution for varying values of μ: (e) $\mu = 5.0$.

```
MTB  > pdf;
SUBC > poisson mu = 6.

POISSON WITH MEAN = 6.000
    K              P(X = K)
    0                0.0025
    1                0.0149
    2                0.0446
    3                0.0892
    4                0.1339
    5                0.1606
    6                0.1606
    7                0.1377
    8                0.1033
    9                0.0688
   10                0.0413
   11                0.0225
   12                0.0113
   13                0.0052
   14                0.0022
   15                0.0009
   16                0.0003
   17                0.0001
   18                0.0000
MTB  > stop
```

Figure 14.6 Poisson probabilities from a typical statistics package.

WORKED EXAMPLE 14.8

A Poisson process has a mean of five events in a period of time
(a) Describe the distribution of events in a period.
(b) What is the probability of two events?

Solution

(a) In this case the mean number of events, μ, is 5. This is also the variance, and the standard deviation is $\sqrt{5} = 2.236$.

(b) The probability of r events is given by:

$$P(r) = \frac{e^{-\mu}\mu^r}{r!} \quad \text{so} \quad P(2) = \frac{e^{-5} \times 5^2}{2!} = 0.0842$$

WORKED EXAMPLE 14.9

A test has been conducted to see if a road intersection should be improved. During this test it was found that cars arrive randomly at the intersection at an average rate of five cars every ten minutes.

(a) What is the probability that during a ten-minute period exactly three cars will arrive?

(b) What is the probability that more than five cars will arrive in a ten-minute period?

Solution

(a) Here random arrivals over time imply a Poisson process. The mean number of successes (that is, cars arriving at the intersection in ten minutes) is $\mu = 5$. Then the probability of exactly three cars arriving can be found from

$$P(r) = \frac{e^{-\mu}\mu^r}{r!} \quad \text{so} \quad P(3) = \frac{e^{-5} \times 5^3}{3!} = 0.1404$$

This value could also be found from the tables in Appendix F. Looking up the value for $\mu = 5$ and $r = 3$ also gives 0.1404.

(b) To find the probability that more than five cars will arrive at the intersection in a ten-minute period we need to calculate

$$P(>5) = 1 - P(5 \text{ or less})$$

$$= 1 - P(0) - P(1) - P(2) - P(3) - P(4) - P(5)$$

These values can either be calculated or looked up in tables to give

$$P(>5) = 1 - 0.0067 - 0.0337 - 0.0842 - 0.1404 - 0.1755 - 0.1755$$

$$= 0.384$$

The probability distribution for this problem is shown in Figure 14.7.

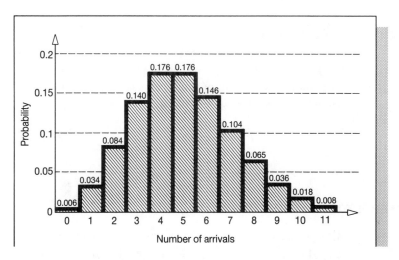

Figure 14.7 Probability distribution of car arrivals for Worked Example 14.9.

Even with appropriate tables and computers there are times when the calculations for Poisson distributions are difficult. This happens particularly when p is high and r is large. Consider the following example. A motor insurance policy is only available to drivers with low risk of accidents. One hundred drivers holding the policy in a certain area would expect an average of 0.2 accidents each a year. What is the probability that less than 15 drivers will have accidents in one year?

This is a binomial process with mean $= np = 100 \times 0.2 = 20$. The probability that exactly r drivers will have accidents in the year is given by

$$^{20}C_r \times 0.2^r \times 0.8^{100-r}$$

Then the probability that less than 15 drivers will have accidents in the year is found by adding this calculation for all values of r from 0 to 14:

$$\sum_{r=0}^{14} {}^{20}C_r \times 0.2^r \times 0.8^{100-r}$$

This is difficult to evaluate, so we would look for a Poisson approximation. Unfortunately np ($= 100 \times 0.2$) $= 20$, which does not meet the requirement that np be less than 5. Another approach is needed, and this time we shall use the most common probability distribution of all. When n is large and np is greater than 5 the binomial distribution can be approximated by the Normal distribution. This is described in the following section.

IN SUMMARY

The Poisson distribution can be used as an approximation to the binomial distribution when the probability of success is small. It can also be used to describe infrequent, random events:

$$P(r \text{ successes}) = \frac{e^{-\mu}\mu^r}{r!}$$

Self-assessment questions

14.11 In what circumstances can a Poisson distribution be used?

14.12 How are the mean and variance of a Poisson distribution calculated?

14.13 The average number of defects per square yard of material is 0.8. Use the tables in Appendix F to find the probability that a square yard has exactly two defects.

14.14 In what circumstances can a Poisson distribution be used as an approximation for a binomial distribution?

| 14.5 || Normal distribution

Both the binomial and Poisson distributions are used with discrete data. Often, however, we want a probability distribution to describe continuous data. Although these two are very similar in principle, there is one fundamental difference. With discrete probabilities we can find the probability of, say, five successes in ten trials. But with continuous data we cannot find the probability that, say, a person weighs exactly 80.456 456 456 kg. If the measurement is made precise enough, the probability of this happening will always be zero. What we really need is the probability that a person weighs, say, between 80.4 kg and 80.5 kg. Thus continuous probability distributions find the probability that a value is within a specified range.

There are a number of distributions for continuous data, including the most widely used distribution of all. The **Normal distribution** (sometimes called Gaussian) is a bell-shaped curve that is used in a wide variety of applications. Many natural phenomena, such as the heights of trees, harvest from an acre of land, weight of horses and daily temperature, follow this distribution. It also describes many business functions, such as daily takings in a shop, number of customers a week, number of employees in particular types of industry, and production in a factory. The distribution is so common that the rule of thumb 'For large numbers of observations use the Normal distribution' is quite defensible.

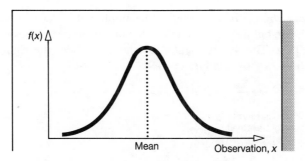

Figure 14.8 Normal probability distribution.

The Normal distribution is illustrated in Figure 14.8. It has the following properties:

> The Normal distribution:
>
> ● is continuous
>
> ● is symmetrical about the mean value, μ
>
> ● has mean, median and mode all equal
>
> ● has the total area under the curve equal to 1
>
> ● in theory the curve extends to plus and minus infinity on the x axis.

The equation for the Normal distribution is rather complicated. The height of the curve at any point is given by

$$f(x) = \frac{1}{\sigma\sqrt{2\pi}}\, e^{-(x-\mu)^2/2\sigma^2}$$

where: x = value of interest

μ = mean value

σ = standard deviation

π, e = constants taking their conventional values of 3.14159 and 2.71828 respectively.

Fortunately, we do not have to worry about this equation as it is hardly ever used. With continuous data the height of the curve at any specific point does not have much meaning, and probabilities are calculated from the area under the curve.

Suppose a factory makes boxes of chocolates with a mean weight of 1000 g. There will be small variations in the weight of each box, and if a large number of boxes are made the weights will follow a Normal distribution. Managers in the factory will not be interested in the number of boxes that weigh, say, exactly 1005.0000 g, but they may be interested in the number of boxes that weigh more than 1005 g. This is represented by the area under the right-hand tail of the distribution, as shown in Figure 14.9.

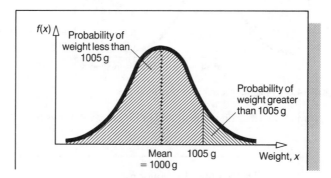

Figure 14.9 Distribution of weights of chocolate boxes.

There are three ways of finding the area under the tail of the distribution:

● We saw in Chapter 12 that integration can be looked at as a summation. Therefore, we could evaluate the definite integral of the curve between 1005.0 and infinity (which would be rather tedious).

● Second,. we could get a computer to do the calculation (which would be easier, but might still present problems).

● We could look up values in standard tables. This third option is frequently the best and is the one we shall use in this chapter.

Normal distribution tables are based on a value, Z, which is calculated from the mean of a distribution and its standard deviation. To be more precise, Z is the number of standard deviations by which a point is away from the mean, and normal tables show the probability that a value greater than this will occur. With the boxes of chocolates mentioned above, the mean weight is 1000 g, and we shall assume that the standard deviation is 3 g. To find the probability that a box has a weight greater than 1005 g, we need the area in the tail of the probability distribution, as shown in Figure 14.9. To find this we calculate the number of standard deviations that the point of interest (1005 g) is away from the mean, and the tables will give the corresponding probability.

$$Z = \text{number of standard deviations from the mean}$$

$$= \frac{\text{value} - \text{mean}}{\text{standard deviation}} = \frac{x - \mu}{\sigma}$$

$$= \frac{1005 - 1000}{3}$$

$$= 1.6$$

A table of areas under the Normal curve is given in Appendix G, and looking up 1.6 in these gives a value of 0.0548. This is the probability that a box will weigh more than 1005 g.

Tables of Normal curves have slight differences, so you must be careful when using them. The tables given in Appendix G show the area under the tail of the distribution.

Because the Normal distribution curve is symmetrical about the mean, we can do some other calculations. For example, the probability that a box of chocolates weighs less than 995 g is the same as the probability that it weighs more than 1005 g and has been calculated as 0.0548 (as shown in Figure 14.10).

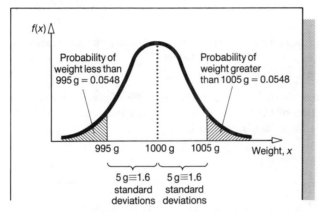

Figure 14.10 Symmetrical distribution of weights of chocolate boxes.

The two factors that affect the position and shape of the Normal curve are the mean and the standard deviation. The distribution is always symmetrical, so these only affect its height and position. The larger the standard deviation the greater is the spread, while the mean determines the position of the distribution on the x axis (as illustrated in Figure 14.11).

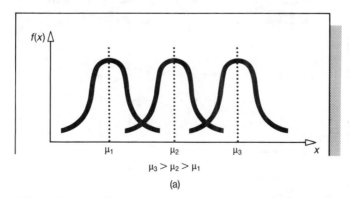

Figure 14.11 Differences in mean and standard deviation for Normal distributions:
(a) normal distributions with same standard deviations but different means

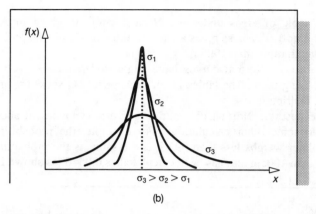

(b)

Figure 14.11 (cont.)   (b) Normal distributions with same means but different standard deviations.

In a Normal distribution, about 68% of observations are within one standard deviation of the mean, 95% are within two standard deviations and 99.7% are within three standard deviations.

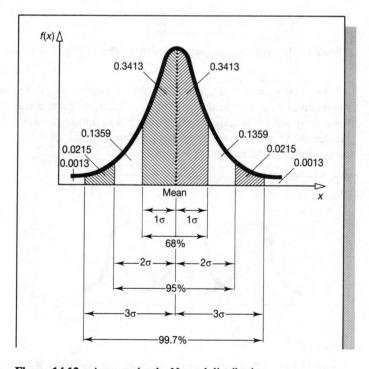

Figure 14.12   Areas under the Normal distribution.

WORKED EXAMPLE 14.10

Figures kept by an auctioneer for the past five years show that the weight of beef cattle brought to market has a mean of 950 kg and a standard deviation of 150 kg. What proportion of these have weights:

(a) more than 1250 kg

(b) less than 850 kg

(c) between 1100 kg and 1250 kg

(d) between 800 kg and 1300 kg?

Solution

In this example there are presumably a large number of cattle brought to market, so we can assume a Normal distribution with $\mu = 950$ and $\sigma = 150$.

(a) The probability of weight greater than 1250 kg is found as follows:

$$Z = \text{number of standard deviations from the mean}$$

$$= \frac{1\,250 - 950}{150}$$

$$= 2.0$$

Looking this up in the normal tables in Appendix G gives a value of 0.0228, which is the required probability.

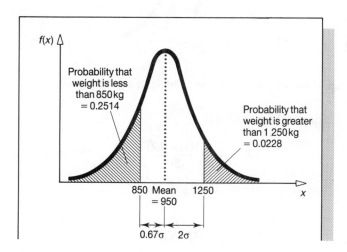

Figure 14.13 Calculations for Worked Example 14.10.

(b) The probability of weight less than 850 kg is found in the same way:

$$Z = \frac{850 - 950}{150}$$

$$= -0.67$$

The table only shows positive values, but as the distribution is symmetrical we can use the value for +0.67, which is 0.2514. This is the area under the tail of the curve and is the required probability.

Because the tables only show probabilities under the tail of the distribution, some juggling of the values is often needed. There are several different ways of doing the following calculations, all of which give the same results.

(c) The calculation that the weight is between 1100 kg and 1250 kg relies on the relationship

$$P(\text{between } 1100 \text{ kg and } 1250 \text{ kg})$$

$$= P(\text{greater than } 1100 \text{ kg}) - P(\text{greater than } 1250 \text{ kg})$$

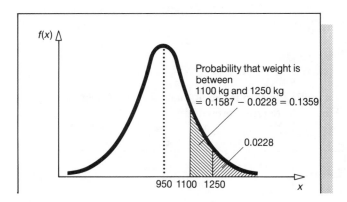

Figure 14.14   Calculations for Worked Example 14.10.

For weight above 1100 kg:

$$Z \quad = \quad \frac{1100 - 950}{150} \quad = 1 \quad \text{probability} = 0.1587$$

For weight above 1,250 kg:

$$Z \quad = \quad \frac{1250 - 950}{150} \quad = 2 \quad \text{probability} = 0.0228$$

Therefore the probability that the weight is between these two is
0.1587 − 0.0228 = 0.1359.

(d) The calculation that the weight is between 800 kg and 1300 kg relies on the relationship

$$P(\text{between 800 kg and 1300 kg})$$

$$= 1 - P(\text{less than 800 kg}) - P(\text{greater than 1300 kg})$$

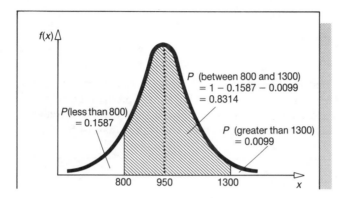

Figure 14.15 Calculations for Worked Example 14.10.

For weight below 800 kg:

$$Z \quad = \quad \frac{800 - 950}{150} \quad = -1 \quad \text{probability} = 0.1587$$

For weight above 1300 kg:

$$Z = \frac{1300 - 950}{150} \quad = 2.33 \quad \text{probability} = 0.0099$$

Therefore the probability that the weight is between these two is

$$1 - 0.1587 - 0.0099 = 0.8314$$

WORKED EXAMPLE 14.11

The Poisson distribution was inappropriate for the example of motor insurance described previously, where a policy is only available to drivers with low risk of accidents. One hundred drivers holding the insurance policy in a certain area would expect an average of 0.2 accidents each a year. Use a Normal distribution to find the probability that less than 15 drivers will have accidents in a year. How might the integer number of accidents be taken into account?

Solution

This is a binomial process with $n = 100$ and $p = 0.2$, so the mean $= np =$ $100 \times 0.2 = 20$. The standard deviation of a binomial distribution is $\sqrt{npq} = \sqrt{16} = 4$. We cannot use a Poisson approximation for the binomial, but we can use a Normal approximation. Then to find the probability of less than 15 drivers having an accident:

$$Z = \frac{15 - 20}{4} \quad = -1.25 \quad \text{probability} = 0.1056$$

Because the number of accidents is discrete, a 'continuity correction' is sometimes used. We are looking for the probability of less than 15 accidents but it is clearly impossible to have **between** 14 and 15 accidents. An allowance can be added to interpret 'less than 15' as 'less than 14.5' (Figure 14.16).

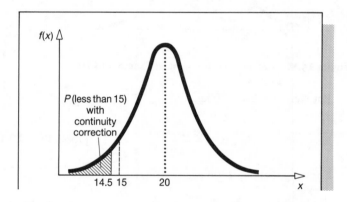

Figure 14.16   Normal distribution with continuity correction for Worked Example

This continuity correction for integer values then gives

$$Z = \frac{14.5 - 20}{4} \quad = -1.375 \quad \text{probability} = 0.0846$$

If the question had asked for '15 or less' accidents the continuity correction might have been applied to interpret this as 'less than 15.5'. Then:

$$Z = \frac{15.5 - 20}{4} \quad = -1.125 \quad \text{probability} = 0.1303$$

WORKED EXAMPLE 14.12

A manufacturer of electric cable finds an average of 20 faults in a week's production. What is the probability of more than 30 faults in a week?

Solution

As this problem looks at random events over time, it is a Poisson process. However, it is clear that the calculations for the Poisson distribution will be somewhat tedious. In these circumstances it is much easier to use a Normal approximation.

We know that for the Poisson distribution:

$$\mu = 20 = \text{variance}$$

so:

$$\sigma = \sqrt{20} = 4.47$$

We shall use a continuity correction and interpret 'more than 30 faults' as '30.5 and more'.

Then:

$$Z = \frac{x - \mu}{\sigma} = \frac{30.5 - 20}{4.47} = 2.35$$

Looking this up in Normal tables gives

$$\text{probability} = 0.0094$$

WORKED EXAMPLE 14.13

On average a supermarket sells 500 pints of milk a day with a standard deviation of 50 pints.

(a) If the supermarket has 600 pints in stock at the beginning of a day, what is the probability that it will sell out of milk?

(b) What is the probability that demand is between 450 and 600 pints in a day?

(c) How many pints should the supermarket stock if it wants the probability of running out to be 0.05?

(d) How many should it stock if it wants the probability of running out to be 0.01?

Solution

(a) The probability of running out of stock with 600 pints is given by

$$Z = \frac{600 - 500}{50} = 2.0 \quad \text{probability} = 0.0228$$

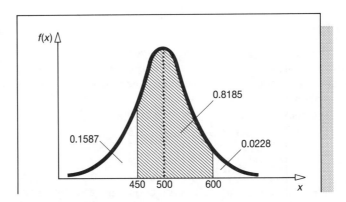

Figure 14.17 Probabilities for Worked Example 14.13.

(b) The probability of demand greater than 600 is 0.0228. The probability of demand less than 450 pints is given by

$$Z = \frac{450 - 500}{50} = -1.0 \quad \text{probability} = 0.1587$$

Therefore the probability of demand between 450 and 600 is
$$1 - 0.0228 - 0.1587 = 0.8185$$

(c) For this problem we know the probability and want to find how far away from the mean this is. For probability = 0.05, $Z = 1.645$ (look up 0.05 in the body of the table and this is midway between 1.64 and 1.65). Thus the point we are interested in is 1.645 standard deviations away from the mean.

1.645 standard deviations is $1.645 \times 50 = 82.25$ pints from the mean. Therefore the supermarket needs to have $500 + 83 = 583$ pints at the beginning of the day (rounding up to ensure a maximum probability of stockouts of 0.05).

(d) For probability 0.01, $Z = 2.33$. This is $2.33 \times 50 = 116.5$ pints from the mean. Therefore the supermarket needs to have $500 + 117 = 617$ pints at the beginning of the day (Figure 14.18).

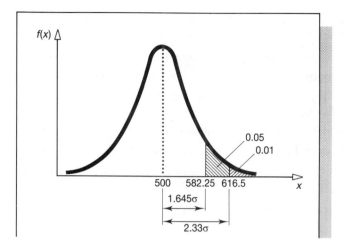

Figure 14.18 Calculations for Worked Example 14.13.

IN SUMMARY

Large numbers of observations often follow a Normal probability distribution. This is a continuous distribution, which gives the probability of observations being within specified ranges. Such probabilities are invariably found from standard tables.

Self-assessment questions

14.15 In what circumstances can a Normal distribution be used?

14.16 What is the most obvious difference between a Normal distribution and a binomial or Poisson distribution?

14.17 What two factors affect the location and shape of a Normal distribution?

14.18 In what circumstances can a Normal distribution be used as an approximation to a binomial distribution?

14.19 If the mean of a set of observations is 100 and the standard deviation is 10, what proportion of observations will be between 90 and 110?

14.20 What is a 'continuity correction' for discrete data?

CHAPTER REVIEW

This chapter has described the use of probability distributions. Empirical distributions can be found for particular problems, but a number of general probability distributions describe a variety of situations. These were illustrated by the binomial, Poisson and normal distributions. In particular the chapter:

● discussed probability distributions in terms of relative frequencies
● discussed sequencing by reference to combinations and permutations
● described the binomial distribution for trials that end in either success or failure
● described the Poisson distribution for random occurrences
● described the Normal distribution for large number of observations

The ideas developed here will be used to build probabilistic models in the following chapters.

Problems

14.1 Find the probability distribution of the following set of observations.

10 14 13 15 16 12 14 15 11 13 17 15 16 14 12 13 11 15 15 14

12 16 14 13 13 14 13 12 14 15 16 14 11 14 12 15 14 16 13 14

14.2 A company calculates its likely profit for next year with the following probabilities.

Profit	− 100 000	− 50 000	0	50 000	100 000	150 000
Probability	0.05	0.15	0.3	0.3	0.15	0.05

What is the probability that the company will make a profit next year? What is the probability that the profit will be at least 100 000?

14.3 Find the value of ^nC_r and ^nP_r when (a) $r = 5$ and $n = 15$, (b) $r = 2$ and $n = 10$, (c) $r = 8$ and $n = 10$.

14.4 An open-plan office has ten desks. If ten clerks work in the area, how many different seating arrangements are there? If two clerks leave, how many seating arrangements are there?

14.5 A salesman wants to visit 12 customers. In how many different ways can he visit them? One day the salesman is only able to visit eight customers. In how many different ways can eight be selected? As the salesman has to travel between customers, the order in which his visits are scheduled is important. How many different schedules are there for eight customers?

14.6 A binomial process has a probability of success of 0.15. If eight trials are run, what is the mean number of successes and the standard deviation? What is the probability of: (a) two successes, (b) seven successes, (c) at least six successes?

14.7 In a town, 60% of families are known to drive British cars. If a sample of ten families is chosen, what is the probability that at least eight will drive British cars? If a sample of 1000 families is chosen, what is the probability that at least 800 will drive British cars?

14.8 An oil company is drilling some exploratory wells on the mainland of Scotland. The results are described as either a dry well or a producer well. Past experience suggests that 10% of such exploratory wells can be classified as producer wells. If 12 wells are drilled, what is the probability that all 12 wells will be producer wells? What is the probability that all 12 wells will be dry wells? What is the probability that exactly one well will be a producer? What is the probability that at least three wells will be producers?

14.9 One hundred trials are run for a Poisson process. If the probability of a success is 0.02, what is the mean number of successes and the standard deviation? What is the probability of: (a) exactly two successes, (b) exactly seven successes, (c) at least six successes?

14.10 During a typical hour an office receives 13 phone calls. What is the expected number of calls in a five-minute period?

14.11 During a busy period at an airport, planes arrive at an average rate of ten an hour. What is the probability that 15 or more planes will arrive in an hour?

14.12 A machine makes a product, with 5% of units having faults. If a sample of 20 units is taken, what is the probability that at least one is defective? If a sample of 200 units is taken, what is the probability that at least ten are defective?

14.13 Some observations follow a Normal distribution with mean 40 and standard deviation 4. What proportion of observations have values: (a) greater than 46, (b) less than 34, (c) between 34 and 46, (d) between 30 and 44, (e) between 43 and 47?

14.14 A large number of observations are found to have a mean of 120 and variance of 100. What proportion of observations is: (a) below 100, (b) above 130, (c) between 100 and 130, (d) between 130 and 140, (e) between 115 and 135?

14.15 A fast-food restaurant finds that the number of meals that it serves in a week is Normally distributed with a mean of 6000 and a standard deviation of 600.

(a) What is the probability that in a given week the number of meals served will be less than 5000?

(b) What is the probability that more than 7500 will be served?

(c) What is the probability that between 5500 and 6500 will be served?

(d) There is a 90% chance that the number of meals served in a week will exceed what value?

14.16 A service consists of two parts. The first part takes an average of 10 minutes with a standard deviation of 2 minutes. The second part takes an average of 5 minutes with a standard deviation of 1 minute. Describe how long it will take to complete the service. What is the probability that a customer can be served in less than 12 minutes? What is the probability that a customer will take more than 20 minutes?

Computer exercises

14.1 Figure 14.19 shows the printout from a statistical package. In this printout the probability distribution function is found for a binomial and Poisson distribution. Then 100 random points are taken from a Poisson distribution with a mean of 6 and are plotted and described. Finally, the cumulative probability distribution (cdf) is used to find the proportion of observations beyond two standard deviations from the mean of the normal distribution with mean 0 and standard deviation 1. Make sure you can understand what is happening in this printout. Use a statistics package to check the results.

```
COMMAND      > pdf;
SUBCOMMAND   > binomial n = 15 p = 0.3.
```

BINOMIAL WITH N = 15 P = 0.300000

K	$P(X = K)$
0	0.0047
1	0.0305
2	0.0916
3	0.1700
4	0.2186
5	0.2061
6	0.1472
7	0.0811
8	0.0348
9	0.0116
10	0.0030
11	0.0006
12	0.0001
13	0.0000

```
COMMAND      > pdf;
SUBCOMMAND   > Poisson mu = 4.
```

POISSON WITH MEAN = 4.000

K	$P(X = K)$
0	0.0183
1	0.0733
2	0.1465
3	0.1954
4	0.1954
5	0.1563
6	0.1042
7	0.0595
8	0.0298

Figure 14.19   Sample printout from a statistical package.

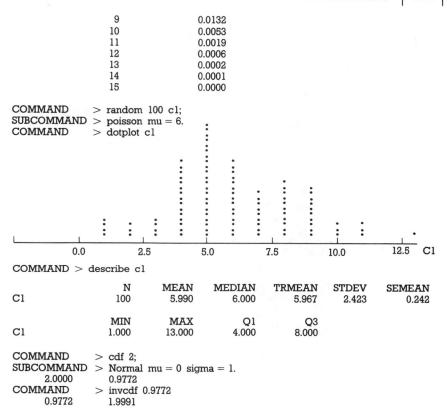

	9	0.0132
	10	0.0053
	11	0.0019
	12	0.0006
	13	0.0002
	14	0.0001
	15	0.0000

COMMAND   > random 100 c1;
SUBCOMMAND > poisson mu = 6.
COMMAND   > dotplot c1

COMMAND > describe c1

	N	MEAN	MEDIAN	TRMEAN	STDEV	SEMEAN
C1	100	5.990	6.000	5.967	2.423	0.242

	MIN	MAX	Q1	Q3
C1	1.000	13.000	4.000	8.000

COMMAND   > cdf 2;
SUBCOMMAND > Normal mu = 0 sigma = 1.
    2.0000   0.9772
COMMAND   > invcdf 0.9772
    0.9772   1.9991

Figure 14.19 (continued)

14.2 Use a spreadsheet to compile your own set of binomial probabilities.

14.3 Use a spreadsheet to compile your own set of Poisson probabilities.

14.3 Plane, bus and train timetables show expected arrival times. Choose a convenient service and collect data to show how actual arrival times compare with expected times. Write a report about your results, including appropriate analyses and diagrams.

14.4 The number of people visiting a shop each working hour for the past week has been recorded as follows:

12 23 45 09 16 74 58 21 31 07 26 22 14 24 50
23 30 35 68 47 17 08 54 11 24 33 55 16 57 27
02 97 54 23 61 82 15 34 46 44 37 26 28 21 07
64 38 71 79 18 24 16 10 60 50 55 34 44 42 47

Use an appropriate package to analyse these figures. What conclusions can you draw? Write a report about your findings.

Case study

Machined components

The operations manager was speaking calmly to the marketing manager: 'I said it usually takes 70 days to make a batch of these components. We have to buy parts and materials, make sub-assemblies, set up machines, schedule operations, make sure everything is ready to start production, then actually make the components, check them and shift them to the finished goods stores, and so on. Actually making the components involves 187 distinct steps taking a total of 20 days. The whole process usually takes 70 days, but there is a lot of variability. This batch you are shouting about is going to take about 95 days because we were busy working on other jobs, and an important machine broke down so we had to wait for parts to be flown in from Tokyo and that took another five days, and so on. It is your fault: you heard my estimate and then assumed I was exaggerating so you promised the customer delivery in 65 days.'

The marketing manager looked worried. 'Why didn't you rush through this important job?' he asked. 'Why is there such variation in time? Why did the breakdown of one machine disrupt production by so much? What am I going to say to our customer?'

The reply was, 'Let me answer your questions in order. Because I was rushing through other important jobs. The variation isn't really that much; our estimates are usually within ten days. It is a central machine that affects the capacity of the whole plant. I can only suggest you apologize and say that you will listen to the operations manager more carefully in the future.'

Despite his apparent calmness, the operations manager was concerned about the variability in production times. He could see why there was some variability, but the total amount for the component they were considering did seem a lot. As an experiment he had once tried to match capacity exactly with expected throughput. Then he found that those operations near the beginning of the process were performing reasonably well, but at the end of the process the variability seemed to have been magnified and the output times seemed to be out of control. At one point he had eight machines in a line, each of which processed a part for 10 minutes before passing it to the next machine. Although this arrangement seemed perfectly balanced, he found that stocks of work-in-progress built up dramatically. Some people suggested that this was because the actual processing time could vary between 5 and 15 minutes. Whatever the reason, the experiment was stopped.

What the operations really need is a study to see why there is variability, how much variability should be expected, what are the effects of this, how can it be reduced, what benefits reduced variability will bring, and so on. Such a study will need some funding, and a proposal will have to be passed by the relevant department. Your job is to write an initial report to this department including a detailed proposal for a larger study.

Using samples in business $\parallel 15 \parallel$

CHAPTER OUTLINE

The last two chapters developed some statistical ideas. In particular, Chapter 13 discussed probabilities, while Chapter 14 described probability distributions. In this chapter we are going to apply these ideas to sampling.

The purpose of sampling is to draw a representative sample from a population. Then the sample is analysed, so that the properties of the population can be estimated from the properties of the sample. This is the basis of statistical inference.

Much statistical inference uses sampling distributions, which show the distribution of values expected in samples. In this chapter we shall use these to estimate the population mean, and do associated calculations.

After reading this chapter and doing the exercises you should be able to:

● understand how and why sampling is used

● appreciate the aims of statistical inference

● use sampling distributions

● find point estimates for population values

● calculate confidence intervals with one- and two-sided distributions

● use t-distributions for small samples

| 15.1 | | Purpose of sampling

All quantitative models need reliable data, and in Chapter 3 we described how these could be collected. We also showed that data collection is often based on sampling. In this chapter we are going to see how statistical analyses can help in selecting and analysing appropriate samples.

The aim of sampling is to get reliable data by looking at a few observations rather than all possible observations; the properties of a population are then estimated by looking at the properties of the sample. Suppose, for example, we want to do a final check on the quality of goods leaving a factory. We might run a test on 10% of the output rather than examine all of it, and the quality of the total output is then judged by the quality of the sample.

This approach is used in public opinion polls. A political party that runs an election campaign will want to know how many votes it can expect in a forthcoming election. There are two ways of finding this:

● it can ask every person eligible to vote in the constituency what their intentions are (this is a census)

● it can take a sample of eligible people, ask them their intentions and use these to estimate the voting intentions of the population as a whole

The second approach has a number of advantages. As information is expensive to collect and analyse, the more people who are surveyed the more it will cost; using a sample will significantly reduce costs. It also reduces the time needed to collect and analyse data. Another important point concerns the amount of effort worth putting into data collection. Even if an entire population of people is surveyed it is unlikely that they will all answer the questions, or that they will tell the truth, or that their views will stay constant over time. It is, therefore, impossible to get completely accurate responses, and we must accept that even the results from a census are approximations. This means that it would be difficult to justify the cost of a census, when results of equal accuracy can be found from a sample.

There are also circumstances in which it is impossible to test all of a population. It would be senseless, for example, to find the mean life of light bulbs produced by a factory by testing the entire output until they failed.

Despite these obvious advantages, sampling has a number of drawbacks. Perhaps the most important is the need to define a reliable sample that represents the whole population fairly. Notice that we are again using the term **population** to refer to all things that could be examined rather than its more general use for populations of people:

> **Population** is used to describe all the things that could be tested
> while **sample** is used to describe those that actually are tested.

The purpose of sampling, then, is to take a sample of units from the population, measure the desired property (quality, weight, length, etc) and hence estimate the value of the property for the population as a whole. This process is called **statistical inference**.

The sample must be representative of the population. One way of ensuring this is to take a random sample. We saw in Chapter 3 how these could be organized, commonly using random numbers. Suppose, for example, that we are interested in the number of people travelling in each car on a particular stretch of road. The cars might be travelling too quickly to count the number of occupants in each, so we would select a sample. A table of random numbers is given in Appendix D, and a section of these gives 836351847101. Using this we could look at the eighth car, then the third after that, then the sixth after that, and so on.

The essence of random sampling is that each member of the population has an equal probability of being selected. This is an important point for statistical analyses. In the following discussion, it is assumed that any sample is a simple random sample drawn from the population. If this condition is not met, many of the analyses are no longer valid.

IN SUMMARY

Data collection often relies on sampling. Using values from samples to estimate values for the population is known as statistical inference. This is generally based on simple random samples.

Self-assessment questions

15.1 What is the purpose of sampling?

15.2 What is statistical inference?

15.2 Estimating the population mean

In this section we are going to look at the most widely used analysis of statistical inference. This finds the mean of some variable in a population by looking at the values in a sample. The first thing we have to do, then, is to examine the distribution of values in a sample.

15.2.1 | Distribution of sample means

If we take any population and take a series of samples from it, we would expect some variation between samples. Suppose, for example, apples are delivered to a jam factory in boxes with a nominal weight of 10 kg. If we take a sample of ten boxes we would expect the mean weight to be about 10 kg, but would not be surprised by small variations about this. Samples of ten boxes taken over consecutive days might have mean weights of 10.2 kg, 9.8 kg, 10.9 kg 10.1 kg, 9.4 kg, and so on. If we continued this over some period we would build a distribution of sample means.

Any distribution that is found from samples is called a sampling distribution. When we build a distribution of sample means it is called the **sampling distribution of the mean**.

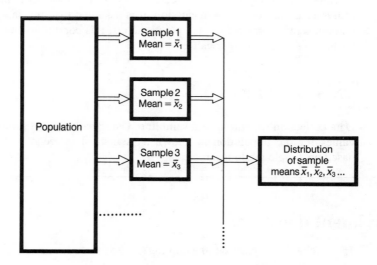

Figure 15.1 Derivation of the sampling distribution of the mean.

Now we can relate the properties of the sampling distribution of the mean back to the original population. To do this we rely on a general result of the **central limit theorem**. This says that if we take large random samples from a population, the sample means are normally distributed. This is true regardless of the distribution of the original population.

The central limit theorem gives us some other information, but for this we need to define a standard notation. This has:

- a population with size of N, mean of μ (the Greek letter mu) and standard deviation of σ (the Greek letter sigma)
- a sample with size n, mean $\bar{x}$ and standard deviation s

Now we can give a fuller statement of the central limit theorem:

> The central limit theorem says:
> if a population is normally distributed, the sampling
> distribution of the mean is also normally distributed. If the
> sample size is large (say more than 30) the sampling
> distribution of the mean is normally distributed regardless
> of the population distribution. The sampling distribution of
> the mean has a mean μ and a standard deviation of $\sigma/\sqrt{n}$.

These observations are given without proof, but if you are interested you can find the derivations in specialized texts on statistics.

Now we can see that the sampling distribution of the mean has three useful properties:

● It is normally distributed if a sample size of more than 30 is used or if the population is normally distributed

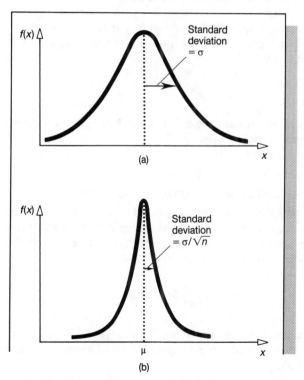

Figure 15.2 Comparison of distributions for (a) population and (b) sampling distribution of the mean.

- The mean of the sampling distribution of the mean equals the mean of the population, μ
- The standard deviation of the sampling distribution of the mean ($\sigma/\sqrt{n}$) is less than the standard deviation of the population (σ) and decreases as the sample size increases. This standard deviation is often called the **standard error**.

This third property confirms the intuitive belief that larger samples give more reliable results.

One obvious problem with discussing statistical inference is the clumsy statements needed to describe, for example, 'the mean of the sampling distribution of the mean'. The ideas behind these phrases are fairly simple, but you must keep a clear mind about what they describe. Remember that the basic distribution is the distribution of sample means. This is the sampling distribution of the mean, which has its own mean and standard deviation.

WORKED EXAMPLE 15.1

A production line makes units with a mean length of 60 cm and standard deviation of 1 cm. What is the probability that a sample of 36 units has a mean length of less than 59.7 cm?

Solution

Samples of 36 units are taken. The mean length of each sample is found, and the distribution of these means is:
- normally distributed
- has mean length = μ = 60 cm
- has standard deviation = $\sigma/\sqrt{n}$ = $1/\sqrt{36}$ = 0.167 cm

The probability that one sample has a mean length less than 59.7 cm is found from the area in the tail of this sampling distribution of the mean. To find this area we need to find the number of standard deviations the point of interest (59.7) is away from the mean:

$$Z = \frac{59.7 - 60}{0.167} = -1.80$$

As normal tables are symmetrical, we look up 1.80, which gives the probability of 0.0359, so we expect 3.59% of samples to have a mean length of less than 59.7 cm.

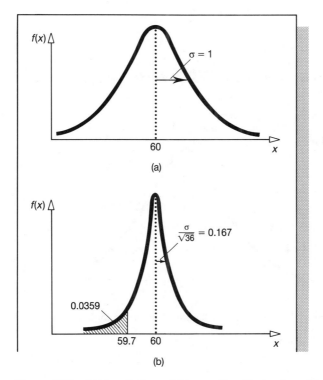

Figure 15.3 (a) Population and (b) sampling distribution of the mean for Worked Example 15.1.

WORKED EXAMPLE 15.2

Soft drinks are put into cans that hold a nominal 200 ml, but the filling machine introduces a standard deviation of 10 ml. These cans are packed into cartons of 25 and exported to a market that requires the mean weight of a carton to be at least the quantity specified by the manufacturer. To ensure that this happens, the canner sets the machine to fill cans to 205 ml. What is the probability that a carton chosen at random will not pass the quantity test?

Solution

The mean volume per can is set at 205 ml and has a standard deviation of 10 ml. Taking a random sample of 25 cans gives a sampling distribution of the mean with mean 205 ml and standard deviation of $10/\sqrt{25} = 2$ ml. The case will fail the quantity test if the average quantity per can is less than 200 ml. That is:

$$Z = \frac{200 - 205}{2} = -2.5$$

$$\text{probability} = 0.0062$$

About six cases in a thousand will fail the test (as shown in Figure 15.4).

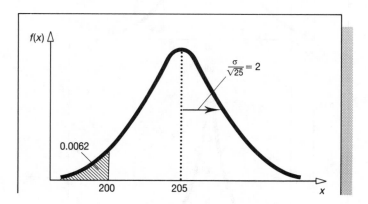

Figure 15.4   Sampling distribution of the mean for Worked Example 15.2.

IN SUMMARY

If samples of size n are taken from a large population with mean μ and standard deviation σ:

- the mean of sample means is equal to μ
- the standard deviation of sample means is equal to $\sigma/\sqrt{n}$
- if the sample size is large the distribution of sample means is normal

15.2.2 | Confidence intervals

The last two worked examples found the characteristics of a sample from the known characteristics of the population. In general, it is much more useful to work the other way round and find the characteristics of a population from a sample. This is the basis of statistical inference.

Suppose we take a sample of 100 parts and find that the mean length is 30 cm. How can we estimate the mean length of the population of parts? The obvious approach suggests that the sample is representative of the population, in which case the population mean can be estimated at 30 cm. This single value is a **point estimate**. Unfortunately, we know that any point estimate comes from a sample and is unlikely to be exactly right. It should be close to the population mean, but is likely to contain some error.

To overcome the problem with point estimates, it is useful to define a range that the population mean is likely to be within. This gives an **interval estimate**. However, for an interval estimate to be useful we need two measures:

● the limits of the interval
● the level of confidence that the mean is within the interval

As the limits of the interval get narrower, we would expect the confidence that the mean is within the limits to decrease. If we have a sample of 100 parts with mean length of 30 cm we might be 99% confident that the population mean is in the interval 20 to 40 cm; we might be 95% confident that the mean is between 25 and 35; cm and we might be 90% confident that the mean is between 27 and 33 cm. This kind of range is called a **confidence interval**, and typically we shall make a statement like, 'We are 95% confident that the population mean lies within a range ...'.

We can calculate the 95% confidence interval using the following argument. The sample mean $\bar{x}$ is the best point estimate for the population mean μ. However, this point estimate is one observation from the sampling distribution of the mean. This sampling distribution is Normal, so 95% of observations lie within 1.96 standard deviations of the mean. Now the standard deviation of the sampling distribution of the mean is $\sigma/\sqrt{n}$. So 95% of samples will be in the range

$$\mu - 1.96\ \sigma/\sqrt{n} \quad \text{to} \quad \mu + 1.96\ \sigma/\sqrt{n}$$

In other words, the probability that the sample mean is within this range is

$$P(\mu - 1.96\ \sigma/\sqrt{n} \leqslant \bar{x} \leqslant \mu + 1.96\ \sigma/\sqrt{n}) = 0.95$$

But this can be rearranged to give the confidence interval for the population:

$$P(\bar{x} - 1.96\ \sigma/\sqrt{n} \leqslant \mu \leqslant \bar{x} + 1.96\ \sigma/\sqrt{n}) = 0.95$$

> The 95% confidence interval for the population mean is:
> $$\bar{x} - 1.96\ \sigma/\sqrt{n} \quad \text{to} \quad \bar{x} + 1.96\ \sigma/\sqrt{n})$$

Similarly, the 90% confidence interval for the population mean is

$$\bar{x} - 1.645\ \sigma/\sqrt{n} \quad \text{to} \quad \bar{x} + 1.645\ \sigma/\sqrt{n}$$

and the 99% confidence interval is

$$\bar{x} - 2.58\ \sigma/\sqrt{n} \quad \text{to} \quad \bar{x} + 2.58\ \sigma/\sqrt{n}$$

WORKED EXAMPLE 15.3

A machine produces parts that have a standard deviation in length of 1.4 cm. A random sample of 100 parts has a mean length of 80 cm. What is the 95% confidence interval for the true mean length of the parts?

Solution

A sample of size 100 is taken from a population with a mean length of 80 cm and a standard deviation of 1.4 cm. The point estimate for population mean is 80 cm.

The sampling distribution of the mean has a mean of 80 cm and standard deviation of $\sigma/\sqrt{n} = 1.4/\sqrt{100} = 0.14$ cm. 95% of observations are within 1.96 standard deviations of the mean, so we expect 95% of observations to be within the range

$$\bar{x} - 1.96\ \sigma/\sqrt{n} \quad \text{to} \quad \bar{x} + 1.96\ \sigma/\sqrt{n}$$

$$80 - 1.96 \times 0.14 \quad \text{to} \quad 80 + 1.96 \times 0.14$$

that is, $\qquad\qquad$ 79.73 cm $\quad$ to $\quad$ 80.27 cm

See Figure 15.5.

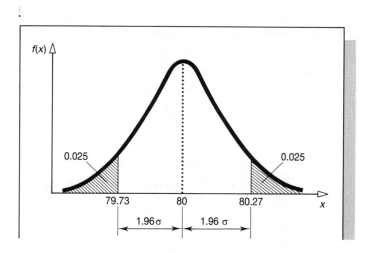

Figure 15.5   Confidence limits for Worked Example 15.3.

In this last worked example we estimated the population mean from a sample mean. However, we assumed that the standard deviation of the population was known. Although possible, it seems unlikely that we would know the standard deviation of a population, but not its mean. It is much more likely that we shall only have information from the sample and will use this to estimate both the population mean and standard deviation.

The obvious estimator of the population standard deviation is the sample standard deviation s. Then the 95% confidence interval becomes:

$$\bar{x} - 1.96 \, s/\sqrt{n} \quad \text{to} \quad \bar{x} + 1.96 \, s/\sqrt{n}$$

WORKED EXAMPLE 15.4

A security company employs night-watchmen to patrol warehouses and they want to find the average time to patrol warehouses of a certain size. On a typical night, records were kept of the time to patrol 40 similar warehouses. These showed the mean time to be 76.4 minutes, with a standard deviation of 17.2 minutes. What are the 95% and 99% confidence intervals on the population mean?

Solution

The point estimate for the population mean is 76.4 minutes.

The standard deviation of the sample is 17.2 minutes, so if we use this as an approximation for the standard deviation of the population, we get a standard error of $\sigma/\sqrt{n} = 17.2/\sqrt{40} = 2.72$ minutes. Then:

● 95% confidence interval:

   $76.4 - 1.96 \times 2.72 \quad \text{to} \quad 76.4 + 1.96 \times 2.72 = 71.07 \quad \text{to} \quad 81.73$

● 99% confidence interval:

   $76.4 - 2.58 \times 2.72 \quad \text{to} \quad 76.4 + 2.58 \times 2.72 = 69.38 \quad \text{to} \quad 83.42$

WORKED EXAMPLE 15.5

A company wants to find the average value of its customer accounts. A large initial sample shows that the standard deviation of the value is £60. What sample size would give a 95% confidence interval for the population mean that is (a) £25 wide, (b) £20 wide, (c) £15 wide? What can you infer from these results?

Solution

The standard deviation of the initial sample is £60, so we can use this as an approximation for the standard deviation of the population and get a standard error of $60/\sqrt{n}$. Then:

(a) A 95% confidence interval is:

$$\text{mean} - 1.96 \times 60/\sqrt{n} \quad \text{to} \quad \text{mean} + 1.96 \times 60/\sqrt{n}$$

giving a range of:

$$2 \times 1.96 \times 60/\sqrt{n}$$

and we want this range to be £25 wide. So:

$$2 \times 1.96 \times 60/\sqrt{n} = 25 \quad \text{or} \quad \sqrt{n} = 9.41 \quad \text{or} \quad n = 88.5$$

In other words, a sample size of 88.5 (rounded to 89) will give a confidence interval for the population mean that is £25 wide.

(b) Repeating this calculation with a confidence interval of £20 has:

$$2 \times 1.96 \times 60/\sqrt{n} = 20 \quad \text{or} \quad n = 11.76 \quad \text{or} \quad n = 138.3$$

(c) Repeating the calculation with a confidence interval of £15 has:

$$2 \times 1.96 \times 60/\sqrt{n} = 15 \quad \text{or} \quad n = 15.68 \quad \text{or} \quad n = 245.9$$

As expected, larger samples give narrower confidence intervals. Decreasing the range from £25 to £20 increased the sample size by (138.3 − 88.5 =) 49.8, however, while decreasing the range from £20 to £15 increased the sample size by (245.9 − 138.3 =) 107.6. There are clearly diminishing returns with increasing sample size. As the standard deviation of the sampling distribution is proportional to $1/\sqrt{n}$, reducing the range to a half would need a sample four times as large, reducing the range to a third would need a sample nine times as large, and so on.

Using the sample standard deviation as an approximation for the population standard deviation works well provided the sample size is large. However, with smaller samples it tends to underestimate the population standard deviation. Then it introduces a bias, which can be removed by a small adjustment. This involves multiplying the sample standard deviation by $\sqrt{n/(n-1)}$. Although it seems strange, there is a sound theoretical reason for using this multiplier.

WORKED EXAMPLE 15.6

A mail order company collects a random sample of 40 customer orders, as shown in the following table. Find the 95% confidence limits on the population mean.

Size of order	Number of customers
£0 – £100	4
£100 – £200	8
£200 – £300	14
£300 – £400	8
£400 – £500	4
£500 – £600	2

Solution

Remember that for grouped data the mean and standard deviation are calculated from:

$$\bar{x} = \frac{\Sigma f x}{\Sigma f}$$

$$s = \sqrt{\frac{\Sigma (x - \bar{x})^2 f}{\Sigma f}}$$

where x is the midpoint of each range and f is the number of observations in each range.

Substituting the data for the sample in these equations gives

$$\bar{x} = 265 \quad \text{and} \quad s = 127.57$$

Now we can use $\bar{x}$ as a point estimator for the population mean and multiply s by $\sqrt{(n/(n-1))}$ to get the unbiased estimator for the population standard deviation, which becomes $127.57 \times \sqrt{(40/39)} = 129.20$. Then the standard error is $129.20/\sqrt{40} = 20.43$

The 95% confidence interval is 1.96 standard deviations from the mean, which is:

$$265 - 1.96 \times 20.43 \quad \text{to} \quad 265 + 1.96 \times 20.43$$

which is $\qquad$ 224.96 to 305.04

This range is relatively wide because of the variance of the data and the relatively small sample size. This example also shows that the multiplier $\sqrt{(n/(n-1))}$ usually makes very little difference to the result.

IN SUMMARY

Point estimates for the population mean are less useful than interval estimates. The sampling distribution of the mean allows confidence intervals to be found for a population mean. Then the 95% confidence interval for the population mean is given by

$$\bar{x} - 1.96 \ s/\sqrt{n} \quad \text{to} \quad \bar{x} + 1.96 \ s/\sqrt{n}$$

15.2.3 | Estimating population proportions

Sometimes, instead of estimating the value of some variable in a population, we want to estimate the proportion of the population that share some characteristic. For quality assurance we might want the proportion of output that is faulty; for finance we might want the proportion of invoices smaller than some amount; or for personal records we might want the proportion of people who work overtime. In these circumstances, statistical inference will take a sample, find the proportion of the sample with the required property, and then estimate the proportion of the population with that property.

This is done using another result of the central limit theorem. Suppose that the proportion of a population with a certain characteristic is π (the Greek letter pi) and a sample is taken that contains a proportion p with the same characteristic. The central limit theorem says that if the sample size is large (say over 30) the sample proportions are:

- normally distributed
- with mean π
- and standard deviation $\sqrt{\left(\dfrac{\pi(1-\pi)}{n}\right)}$

We can use the same approach as before to find the confidence interval for the proportion in the population. We have a sample with a proportion p, and this is the best point estimate for the population proportion π. However, this point estimate is one observation from the sampling distribution, which is Normal. The standard deviation of this sampling distribution is $\sqrt{(\pi(1-\pi)/n)}$, and 95% of observations lie within 1.96 standard deviations of the mean. Then the 95% confidence interval is

$$\pi - 1.96 \times \sqrt{\left(\frac{\pi(1-\pi)}{n}\right)} \quad \text{to} \quad \pi + 1.96 \times \sqrt{\left(\frac{\pi(1-\pi)}{n}\right)}$$

In other words, the probability that the sample proportion is within this range is

$$P\left(\pi - 1.96 \times \sqrt{\left(\frac{\pi(1-\pi)}{n}\right)} \leqslant p \leqslant \pi + 1.96 \times \sqrt{\left(\frac{\pi(1-\pi)}{n}\right)}\right) = 0.95$$

and this can be rearranged to give the confidence interval for the population:

$$P\left(p - 1.96 \times \sqrt{\left(\frac{\pi(1-\pi)}{n}\right)} \leqslant \pi \leqslant p + 1.96 \times \sqrt{\left(\frac{\pi(1-\pi)}{n}\right)}\right) = 0.95$$

This defines the 95% confidence interval for the population as

$$p - 1.96 \times \sqrt{\left(\frac{\pi(1-\pi)}{n}\right)} \quad \text{to} \quad p + 1.96 \times \sqrt{\left(\frac{\pi(1-\pi)}{n}\right)}$$

Unfortunately, this range contains the term π, which is the proportion that we are trying to find. As before, though, we can use the sample value p as an estimator for π.

> The 95% confidence interval for a population proportion is:
>
> $$p - 1.96 \times \sqrt{\left(\frac{p(1-p)}{n}\right)} \quad \text{to} \quad p + 1.96 \times \sqrt{\left(\frac{p(1-p)}{n}\right)}$$

WORKED EXAMPLE 15.7

A random sample of 50 patients is given a new treatment for an illness. 60% of these are cured. Calculate the 95% confidence interval for the proportion of all patients who will be cured by the treatment.

Solution

The proportion of patients in the sample who are cured, p, is 0.6. This is the point estimate for the proportion who will be cured in the population, π.

The 95% confidence interval for the proportion in the population is given by

$$p - 1.96 \times \sqrt{\left(\frac{p(1-p)}{n}\right)} \quad \text{to} \quad p + 1.96 \times \sqrt{\left(\frac{p(1-p)}{n}\right)}$$

$$0.6 - 1.96 \times \sqrt{\left(\frac{0.6 \times 0.4}{50}\right)} \quad \text{to} \quad 0.6 + 1.96 \times \sqrt{\left(\frac{0.6 \times 0.4}{50}\right)}$$

$$0.6 - 0.136 \quad \text{to} \quad 0.6 + 0.136$$

$$0.464 \quad \text{to} \quad 0.736$$

We would be 95% confident that between 46.4% and 73.6% of patients given the new treatment will be cured.

WORKED EXAMPLE 15.8

Last month an opinion poll suggested that 30% of people in a town would vote for a particular political party. This month the poll is being rerun. How many people will have to be interviewed for the poll to be within 2% of actual voting intentions with a 95% level of confidence?

Solution

In polls the proportion of people voting for the party will be Normally distributed with mean p and standard deviation $\sqrt{(\pi(1 - \pi)/n)}$. For the 95% confidence interval we want the error to be within 1.96 standard deviations from the mean. Then:

$$\text{maximum error} = 1.96 \times \text{standard deviation}$$

$$= 1.96 \times \sqrt{\left(\frac{\pi(1-\pi)}{n}\right)}$$

The best estimate we have for the proportion of people in the poll who will vote for the political party is $p = 0.3$, found in last month's poll. This is the point estimate for the proportion in the population, π. The maximum error is 2%, so we get:

$$0.02 = 1.96 \times \sqrt{\left(\frac{0.3 \times 0.7}{n}\right)}$$

or

$$n = 2017$$

In other words, we need to take a poll of 2017 people to get the required accuracy.

| IN SUMMARY |

Point estimates and confidence intervals can be calculated for proportions of the population sharing some characteristic in the same way as point estimates and confidence intervals for the mean.

15.2.4 | One-sided confidence intervals

So far we have assumed that the confidence interval is symmetrical about the mean. Then we use both sides of the sampling distribution to find probabilities. There are many circumstances when we are only interested in one side of the sampling distribution. We might, for example, want to be 95% confident that the mean number of defects is below some maximum, or the weight of goods is above some minimum, or the cost is below some maximum.

In general, one-sided confidence intervals use the same approach as the two-sided intervals discussed previously. A two-sided 95% confidence interval is 1.96 standard deviations away from the mean (with 2.5% of the distribution in each tail); a one-sided 95% confidence interval is 1.645 standard deviations from the mean (with 5% of the distribution in one tail) (Figure 15.6).

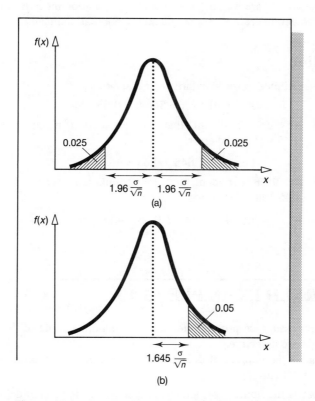

Figure 15.6 Comparison of (a) two-sided and (b) one-sided 95% confidence intervals.

Now we can use the following rules for finding the one-sided 95% confidence interval:

● to find the value that we are 95% confident the population mean is above, use

$$\bar{x} - 1.645 \text{ standard errors}$$

● to find the value that we are 95% confident the population mean is below, use

$$\bar{x} + 1.645 \text{ standard errors}$$

The same arguments would, of course, apply to other levels of confidence, and we are using 95% simply because this is convenient and popular.

WORKED EXAMPLE 15.9

An automated process makes a product, but introduces some variability in the weight of each unit. One day a sample of 60 units is taken and found to have a mean weight of 45 kg and standard deviation of 5 kg.
(a) What weight are we 95% confident the population mean is below?
(b) What weight are we 95% confident the population mean is above?

Solution

The best estimate of the standard error is $s/\sqrt{n}$.

$$\text{standard error} = 5/\sqrt{60} = 0.65$$

(a) We are 95% confident that the population mean will be less than $\bar{x} + 1.645 \times$ standard error:

$$\text{i.e. } 45 + 1.645 \times 0.65 = 46.07 \text{ kg}$$

(b) We are 95% confident that the population mean will be more than $\bar{x} - 1.645 \times$ standard error:

$$\text{i.e. } 45 - 1.645 \times 0.65 = 43.93 \text{ kg}$$

WORKED EXAMPLE 15.10

A quality assurance programme selects a random sample of 40 units, and finds that eight are defective.
(a) What is the number of defectives that we are 95% sure the population mean will fall below?
(b) What is the number of defectives that we are 95% confident the population mean will fall above?
(c) How does this compare with the two-sided 90% confidence interval?
(d) What is the 95% two-sided confidence interval?

Solution

(a) We know that the 95% confidence interval for a one-sided distribution corresponds to 1.645 standard errors.

The proportion of defects in the sample, p, is $8/40 = 0.2$. The best estimate for the standard error of a proportion is $\sqrt{(p(1-p)/n)} = \sqrt{0.2 \times 0.8/40} = 0.063$.

Therefore we can be 95% confident that the population mean is less than

(b) Similarly, we can be 95% confident that the population mean is more than $0.2 - 1.645 \times 0.063 = 0.096$.

(c) The two-sided 90% confidence limits are 1.645 standard errors from the mean, giving an interval of

$$0.2 - 1.645 \times 0.063 \quad \text{to} \quad 0.2 + 1.645 \times 0.063$$

$$0.096 \quad \text{to} \quad 0.304$$

(d) The two-sided 95% confidence limits are 1.96 standard errors from the mean, giving an interval of

$$0.2 - 1.96 \times 0.063 \quad \text{to} \quad 0.2 + 1.96 \times 0.063$$

$$0.077 \quad \text{to} \quad 0.323$$

IN SUMMARY

Sometimes we are only interested in a confidence interval in one tail of a distribution. In these cases the approach is similar to the method with two-sided confidence intervals.

Self-assessment questions

15.3 What is the sampling distribution of the mean?

15.4 Describe the shape of the sampling distribution of the mean.

15.5 Why is a point estimate for the mean unlikely to be exactly right?

15.6 What is the 95% confidence interval for a value?

15.7 Is a 95% confidence interval wider or narrower than a 90% interval?

15.8 When is a one-sided confidence interval used?

15.9 If a sample of size n produces a confidence interval that is w wide, how big a sample would generally be needed to produce a confidence interval that is $w/5$ wide?

15.3 | Using small samples

Early in this chapter we described an important result of the central limit theorem, which said that when the population is Normally distributed or the sample size is large, the sampling distribution of the mean is Normally distributed. What happens, though, when these conditions are not met? Suppose we do not know what the population distribution is, and can only take a small sample (where 'small' is below 30). In these circumstances we cannot assume the sampling distribution is Normal.

The problem is that a small sample must be less representative of the population than a large sample. In particular, experience suggests that small samples show less variation than a population, as fewer outlying results are included. What we need is a distribution that will look at a small sample and take such factors into account. The distribution that does this is called a *t-distribution*.

The *t*-distribution looks similar to the normal, but its shape depends on the **degrees of freedom**. For our purpose, the degrees of freedom are found from the sample size *n*, and are simply defined as *n* − 1. This definition comes about because the degrees of freedom essentially measure the number of independent pieces of information that are used. We might ask, then, 'Why does a sample of size *n* have *n* − 1 pieces of information rather than *n*?' The answer is that we have a value for the mean, so only *n* − 1 values can vary. Suppose, for example, we have four numbers whose mean is 5. The first three numbers can take any value (3, 5 and 7 perhaps) but then the fourth number is fixed (at 5 to get the correct mean).

When the sample size is close to 30, the *t*-distribution looks the same as a Normal distribution. However, as the degrees of freedom get smaller, the distribution gets wider and lower, as shown in Figure 15.7.

t-distributions are used in the same way as Normal distributions, in that values have been tabulated, as shown in Appendix H. However, when using

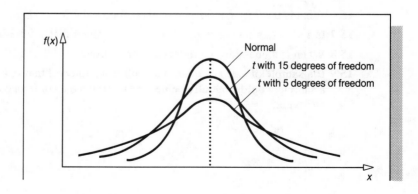

Figure 15.7   Comparison of normal and *t*-distributions.

these tables we have to look up values with the correct number of degrees of freedom. For a two-sided 95% confidence interval we look up the significance level of 0.05 (giving a probability of 0.025 as the area in each tail) and this gives a column of entries for different degrees of freedom. The value is 12.706 with one degree of freedom, 4.303 with two degrees of freedom, 3.182 with three degrees of freedom, and so on. This is the number of standard deviations away from the mean. With a large number of degrees of freedom the value decreases to 1.96, which is the same as the Normal value.

WORKED EXAMPLE 15.11

A survey of ten items in a sales ledger has a mean value of £60 and standard deviation of £8. What is the 95% confidence interval for the population of items?

Solution

The point estimate for the population mean is £60.

If the sample size was large we could calculate the confidence interval by the method used previously. However, with a small sample we can use a similar approach, but substituting a t-distribution for a Normal distribution.

The number of degrees of freedom is $10 - 1 = 9$. Looking up a probability of 0.05 with 9 degrees of freedom in the table in Appendix H gives a value of 2.262. Thus the confidence limits are 2.262 standard errors from the mean.

The best estimate for the standard error is $s/\sqrt{n} = 10/\sqrt{8} = 3.54$. Therefore the confidence interval is

$$60 - 2.262 \times 3.536 \quad \text{to} \quad 60 + 2.262 \times 3.536$$

or $\qquad\qquad\qquad$ 52 to 68

There is a 95% chance that the population mean is within the range £52 to £68.

WORKED EXAMPLE 15.12

The time taken for eight people working in an office to travel to work is found to have a mean of 37 minutes and a standard deviation of 12 minutes.
(a) What is the 90% confidence interval for the mean travel time of everyone in the office?
(b) What is the 95% confidence interval?

(c) If the same results had been found from a sample of 20 what would be the 95% confidence interval?

(d) What would the last result be if a Normal distribution had been used?

Solution

(a) The sample size is 8, so there are 7 degrees of freedom. Looking up the value for a probability of 0.1 (i.e. 5% in each tail) with 7 degrees of freedom in t-distribution tables gives a value of 1.895.

The best estimate of the standard error is $s/\sqrt{n} = 12/\sqrt{8} = 4.24$, so the 90% confidence interval is

$$37 - 1.895 \times 4.24 \quad \text{to} \quad 37 + 1.895 \times 4.24$$

$$28.97 \quad \text{to} \quad 45.03$$

(b) For the 95% confidence interval we look up a probability of 0.05 with 7 degrees of freedom and get a value of 2.365. Then the 95% confidence interval is

$$37 - 2.365 \times 4.24 \quad \text{to} \quad 37 + 2.365 \times 4.24$$

$$26.97 \quad \text{to} \quad 47.03$$

(c) With a sample of 20 the standard error becomes $12/\sqrt{20} = 2.68$. Then the 95% confidence interval is

$$37 - 2.365 \times 2.68 \quad \text{to} \quad 37 + 2.365 \times 2.68$$

$$30.66 \quad \text{to} \quad 43.34$$

(d) 95% confidence limits with a Normal distribution correspond to 1.96 standard errors. Then the interval is

$$37 - 1.96 \times 2.68 \quad \text{to} \quad 37 + 1.96 \times 2.68$$

$$31.75 \quad \text{to} \quad 42.25$$

The small sample has not allowed for the full variability of the data, so the normal distribution has assumed that the data are less spread out than they actually are. This interval, therefore, tends to be too narrow.

| IN SUMMARY |

Sampling distributions are only Normal if the population follows a Normal distribution, or if large samples are taken. If these conditions are not met, a t-distribution should be used. This distribution is similar to the Normal distribution, but its shape is affected by the degrees of freedom, and hence by the sample size.

Self-assessment questions

15.10 Why are sampling distributions not Normal when samples are small?

15.11 What are the 'degrees of freedom'?

CHAPTER REVIEW

A lot of data collection relies on sampling. This chapter has described some statistical analyses that can be used with samples. In particular it:

- outlined the purpose of sampling and statistical inference
- discussed the sampling distribution of the mean
- found point estimates and confidence intervals for population means
- estimated population proportions
- used one-sided confidence intervals
- used *t*-distributions for small samples

Problems

15.1 A production line makes units with a mean weight of 80 g and standard deviation of 5 g. What is the probability that a sample of 100 units has a mean weight of less than 79 g?

15.2 A machine produces parts with a variance of 14.5 cm in length. A random sample of 50 parts is taken and has a mean length of 106.5 cm. What are the 95% and 99% confidence intervals for the length of all parts?

15.3 A food processor specifies the mean weight of a product as 200 g. The output is Normally distributed with a standard deviation of 15 g. A random sample of 20 has a mean of 195 g. Does this evidence suggest that the mean weight is too low?

15.4 During an audit, a random sample of 60 invoices is taken from a large population. The mean value of invoices in this sample was £125.50 and the standard deviation was £10.20. Find the 90% and 95% confidence intervals for the mean value of all invoices.

15.5 A management consultant times 60 people doing a task. The mean time is 6.4 minutes, with a standard deviation of 0.5 minutes. How long would it take the population to do this job?

15.6 During an audit, a random sample of 100 invoices is taken from a large population. Eight of these were found to contain an error. What are the 90% and 95% confidence intervals for the proportion of invoices with faults?

15.7 A company wants to find the weight of its products. A large initial sample shows that the standard deviation of the weight is 20 g. What size of sample would give a 95% confidence interval of the population that is (a) 10 g wide, (b) 8 g wide, (c) 5 g wide?

15.8 Last year a trial survey found that 65% of houses in a town had a telephone. This year a follow-up survey wants to find the actual number of houses with a telephone to within 3% with a 95% confidence interval. How many houses should be surveyed?

15.9 A customer feels that the quantity of chocolates in a particular type of packet seems to have decreased. To test this feeling the customer takes a sample of 40 packets and finds that the mean weight is 228 g with a standard deviation of 11 g.

(a) What weight is the customer 95% confident that the mean falls below?

(b) What are the two-sided confidence limits on this weight?

15.10 A quality assurance programme selects a random sample of 50 units, and finds that 12 are defective.

(a) What is the number of defectives that we are 95% sure the population mean will fall below?

(b) What is the number of defectives that we are 95% confident the population mean will fall above?

(c) How does this compare with the two-sided 90% confidence interval?

15.11 A survey of 20 items in a sales ledger has a mean value of £100 and standard deviation of £20.

(a) What is the 95% confidence interval for the population of items?

(b) What is the 99% confidence interval?

15.12 The time taken for a sample of eight pieces of equipment to do a task has a mean of 52 minutes and a standard deviation of 18 minutes.

(a) What is the 90% confidence interval for the mean time of all equipment to do the task?

(b) What is the 95% confidence interval?

(c) If the same results had been found from a sample of 20 pieces of equipment what would be the 95% confidence interval?

(d) What would be the last result if a Normal distribution had been used?

Computer exercises

15.1 Figure 15.8 shows a printout from a statistics package (Minitab) used for sampling. This printout shows a set of 20 numbers put into a column, C1. These are described by the package. Then a set of six numbers is randomly selected from C1, put into the column C2 and described. Make sure you understand what is happening in this printout. Use a statistics package to get equivalent results.

```
MTB   > set c1
DATA > 3 4 1 6 5 4 4 3 2 3
DATA > 5 3 4 2 2 3 1 4 3 5
DATA > end
MTB   > describe c1
```

	N	MEAN	MEDIAN	TRMEAN	STDEV	SEMEAN
C1	20	3.350	3.000	3.333	1.348	0.302

	MIN	MAX	Q1	Q3
C1	1.000	6.000	2.250	4.000

```
MTB > sample 6 from c1 put into c2
MTB > print c2
```

```
C2
      4    1    4    4    5    2
```

```
MTB > describe c2
```

	N	MEAN	MEDIAN	TRMEAN	STDEV	SEMEAN
C2	6	3.333	4.000	3.333	1.506	0.615

	MIN	MAX	Q1	Q3
C2	1.000	5.000	1.750	4.250

Figure 15.8 Printout from a statistical package used for taking a sample.

15.2 Use a computer to:

- generate a population of random numbers
- draw a frequency distribution of the numbers and confirm that they follow a uniform distribution (which is one in which each number has the same probability)
- take large samples from this population of numbers, and calculate the mean of each sample
- draw a frequency distribution of these means (that is, the sampling distribution of the mean)
- confirm that the result is Normally distributed

Repeat this process for different sample sizes to see what effect this has.

15.3 Take a large population of people's weights (or any other property that is Normally distributed). Use a computer to take random samples from these data and calculate the means. Confirm that, even for small samples, the mean weight of the samples is Normally distributed.

15.4 Repeat the analysis of the last exercise using data that follow different distributions.

Case study
Kings Fruit Farm

In the 1920s Edward Filbert became the tenant of Kings Farm in Cambridgeshire. In 1978 his grandson James Filbert became the latest manager. However, in the intervening years the farm has changed considerably. It has now grown from 195 acres to over 3000 acres and is owned by an agricultural company who own several other farms in the area. Most of Kings Farm is used for growing a variety of vegetables, cereals and fruit. Kings Fruit Farm is a subsidiary of Kings Farm, and manages a range of apples, plum and cherry orchards.

Recently, James has been looking at the sales of plums. These are graded and sold as fruit to local shops and markets, for canning to a local cannery, or for jam to a more distant processor. The plums sold for canning generate about half as much income as those sold for fruit, but twice as much income as those sold for jam.

James is trying to estimate the weight of plums sold each year. This is not currently known, as the plums are sold by the basket rather than by weight. Each basket holds about 25 kg of plums. For a pilot study James set up some scales to see if he could weigh the amount of fruit in a sample of baskets. On the first day he weighed ten baskets, six of which were sold as fruit, three for tinning and one for jam. The weights of fruit, in kg, were as follows:

25.6 20.8 29.4 28.0 22.2 23.1 25.3 26.5 20.7 21.9

This trial seemed to work, so James then weighed a sample of 50 baskets on three consecutive days. The weights of fruit, in kg, were as follows:

- **Day 1** 24.6 23.8 25.1 26.7 22.9 23.6 26.6 25.0 24.6 25.2
          25.7 28.1 23.0 25.9 24.2 21.7 24.9 27.7 24.0 25.6
          26.1 26.0 22.9 21.6 28.2 20.5 25.8 22.6 30.3 28.0
          23.6 25.7 27.1 26.9 24.5 23.9 27.0 26.8 24.3 19.5
          31.2 22.6 29.4 25.3 26.7 25.8 23.5 20.5 18.6 21.5
- **Day2** 26.5 27.4 23.8 24.8 30.2 28.9 23.6 27.5 19.5 23.6
          25.0 24.3 25.3 23.3 24.0 25.1 22.2 20.1 23.6 25.8
          24.9 23.7 25.0 24.9 27.2 28.3 29.1 22.1 25.0 23.8
          18.8 19.9 27.3 25.6 26.4 28.4 20.8 24.9 25.4 25.6
          24.9 25.0 24.1 25.5 25.2 26.8 27.7 20.6 31.3 29.5
- **Day 3** 27.2 21.9 30.1 26.9 23.5 20.7 26.4 25.1 25.7 26.3
          18.0 21.0 21.9 25.7 28.0 26.3 25.9 24.7 24.9 24.3
          23.9 23.0 24.1 23.6 21.0 24.6 25.7 24.7 23.3 22.7
          22.9 24.8 22.5 26.8 27.4 28.3 31.0 29.4 25.5 23.9
          29.5 23.3 18.6 20.6 25.0 25.3 26.0 22.2 23.9 25.7

He also recorded the number of each sample sent to each destination:

	Fruit	Cans	Jam
Day 1	29	14	7
Day 2	25	15	10
Day 3	19	15	16

Pickers are paid by the basket, so the payments book was be used to find the number of baskets picked on the three days as 820, 750 and 700 respectively. During a good harvest, around 6000 baskets are picked.

What information can James find from these figures?

Testing hypotheses

CHAPTER OUTLINE

The last chapter showed how statistical inference could be used to estimate the value of a variable in a population by looking at the value of the variable in a sample. This chapter extends these ideas by describing **hypothesis testing**. This starts by making a statement describing some aspect of the population. This is the hypothesis to be tested. A sample is then taken from the population to see if evidence can be found to support the hypothesis. This general approach can be used in a variety of situations.

We shall generally use a type of statistical test that is called a parametric test. In some circumstances the conditions required by such tests cannot be met, so non-parametric tests must be used. We shall illustrate these by the chi-squared test, which shows how closely actual observations match expected ones.

After reading this chapter and doing the numerical exercises you should be able to:

● appreciate the objectives of hypothesis testing
● understand the function of a significance level and its link with errors
● test hypotheses about population means using data supplied by samples
● extend these ideas to proportions, one-sided tests, differences between means and small samples
● appreciate the use of non-parametric tests
● use the chi-squared test for goodness of fit

|| 16.1 || Hypotheses about population means

| 16.1.1 | Approach to hypothesis testing

In the last chapter we saw how statistical inference used data from a sample to estimate values for a population. In this chapter we are going to extend this idea by testing whether a belief about a population is supported by the evidence from a sample. This is the basis of **hypothesis testing**.

Suppose we have some preconceived idea about the value taken by a population variable. We might, for example, believe that domestic telephone bills have risen by 10% in the past year. This is a hypothesis we want to test. For this test we take a sample from the population and see if the results support our hypothesis or do not support it. The formal procedure for this is as follows:

- define a simple, precise statement about the situation (the hypothesis)
- take a sample from the population
- test this sample to see if it supports the hypothesis, or if it makes the hypothesis highly improbable
- if the hypothesis is highly improbable reject it, otherwise accept it

In practice, statisticians are rather more cautious than this, and they do not often talk about 'accepting' a hypothesis. Instead they say that a hypothesis 'can be rejected' if it is highly unlikely, or it 'cannot be rejected' if it is more likely. We can illustrate the process of hypothesis testing by an example.

WORKED EXAMPLE 16.1

Bottles are filled with a nominal 400 g of fluid. Small deviations occur from this nominal amount and the actual weights are Normally distributed with a standard deviation of 20 g. Periodic samples are taken to ensure that the mean weight is still 400 g. A sample bottle is found to contain 446 g. Are the bottles now being overfilled?

Solution

An initial hypothesis is that the mean weight of bottles is still 400 g. We have a limited sample, which provides data for testing this hypothesis. The distribution of bottle weights should be Normal with mean 400 g and standard deviation 20 g. Assuming that this is correct, we can find the probability of finding a sample containing 446 g. The number of standard deviations from the mean is:

$$Z = \frac{446 - 400}{20} = 2.3$$

Normal tables show that this has probability = 0.01.

If our hypothesis about the population is true, finding a bottle weighing 446 g is highly improbable (1% of occasions). We can, therefore, reject the initial hypothesis that the mean content is 400 g, as we now believe the bottles are being overfilled.

The original statement is called the **null hypothesis**, which is usually called H_0. The name 'null' implies that there has been no change in the value being tested since the hypothesis was formulated. If we reject the null hypothesis then we implicitly accept an alternative. In the worked example above we rejected the hypothesis that the mean weight of bottles is 400 g, so we accept the alternative hypothesis that the mean weight is not 400 g. For each null hypothesis there is always an alternative hypothesis, which is usually called H_1. If the null hypothesis, H_0, is that domestic telephone bills have risen by 10% in the last year, the alternative hypothesis, H_1, is that they have not risen by 10%; if the null hypothesis, H_0, is that first-class letters take two days to deliver, the alternative hypothesis, H_1, is that they do not take two days to deliver, and so on.

Notice that the null hypothesis must be a simple, specific statement, while the alternative hypothesis is more vague and suggests that some statement other than the null hypothesis is true. In practice, this invariably means the null hypothesis is phrased in terms of one thing equalling another. We might have a null hypothesis that the mean weight is 1.5 kg and an alternative hypothesis that the mean weight is not 1.5 kg; a null hypothesis might be that the average salary in an office is £20,000, while the alternative hypothesis is that the average salary is lower than this.

IN SUMMARY

A null hypothesis is a precise statement about a situation. Hypothesis testing uses a sample to see whether the evidence supports this statement, or whether the hypothesis must be rejected.

| 16.1.2 | **Errors in hypothesis testing**

Even a good sample cannot accurately represent an entire population, so sampling always contains some uncertainty. When we use a sample to test a null hypothesis about a population, then we can never be certain of the result. In Worked Example 16.1 we said the result was unlikely and therefore rejected the null hypothesis, but in 1% of samples the result found would occur by chance, and we would be rejecting a perfectly true hypothesis. In general, there are two ways of getting the wrong answer with hypothesis testing, called Type I and Type II errors:

- We may reject a null hypothesis that is true (this is a Type I error)
- We may not reject a null hypothesis that is false (this is a Type II error)

A table of possible outcomes is shown below:

Decision	Null hypothesis is	
	True	*False*
Not reject	Correct decision	Type II error
Reject	Type I error	Correct decision

Ideally, we should like to arrange things so that the probabilities of both Type I and Type II errors are close to zero. The only way to do this is to use a large sample. If we try any other adjustments to reduce the probability of Type I errors, the probability of Type II errors increase, and vice versa. With a limited sample size, we have to accept a compromise between the two errors.

WORKED EXAMPLE 16.2

The mean wage in a certain industry is said to be £300 a week with a standard deviation of £60. There is a feeling that this is no longer true and a random sample of 36 wages is checked. It is decided to reject the null hypothesis if the sample of wages has a mean less than £270 or greater than £330. What are the probabilities of making a Type I error?

Solution

We can start by defining a null hypothesis, H_0, that the mean wage is £300, and the alternative hypothesis, H_1, that the mean wage is not £300.

Hypothesis tests assume that the null hypothesis is true while the tests are being done. Then we assume that the population has a mean of £300 and a standard deviation of £60. With a sample of 36, the standard error (which is the standard deviation of the sampling distribution of the mean) is $s/\sqrt{n} = 60/\sqrt{36} = 10$.

The probability that a sample of 36 wages is greater than £330 is found from Normal tables with $Z = (330 - 300)/10 = 3$. The probability of this is 0.0013. By symmetry, the probability that a sample has a mean of less than £270 is also 0.0013. The null hypothesis is rejected if the sample value is outside the range £270 to £330, so there is a probability of $0.0013 + 0.0013 = 0.0026$ that the hypothesis is rejected even though it is actually true. This is the probability of a Type I error. Unfortunately, the probability of a Type II error cannot be found in this way.

WORKED EXAMPLE 16.3

A city takes a survey of monthly food and shelter costs for a particular type of family. It is suggested that the mean cost is £160 with a standard deviation of £48.90. A sample of 100 families was taken and found to have an average expenditure of £171.25. Is the suggested value of £160 true?

Solution

The null hypothesis, H_0, is that the monthly cost of food and shelter equals £160 while the alternative hypothesis, H_1, is that it does not equal £160.

With a sample of 100 the standard error is $48.90/\sqrt{100} = 4.89$. Then $Z = (171.25 - 160)/4.89 = 2.3$, which corresponds to a probability of 0.0107.

There is a likelihood of 0.0107 that the monthly cost of food and shelter will be £171.25, so we would say that the outcome is extremely unlikely, reject the null hypothesis and accept the alternative hypothesis.

So far in the examples we have rejected the null hypothesis if we considered the result from the sample to be extremely unlikely. However, the judgement of what is 'unlikely' has been purely subjective. In the following section we shall show how to measure this using a significance level.

IN SUMMARY

Results from samples always contain uncertainty. In hypothesis testing this means that there are two types of error:

● Type I error, of rejecting a null hypothesis that is true
● Type II error, of not rejecting a null hypothesis that is false

16.1.3 | Significance levels

In the last example we considered a probability of 0.0107 as unlikely, but this was only an opinion. Such judgements can be formalized into a **significance level**, which is defined as the minimum acceptable probability that an observation is a random sample from the hypothesized population. If we set a 5% significance level, we do not reject a null hypothesis if there is a probability greater than 5% that an observation comes from a population with the specified value. Conversely, if there is a probability of less than 5% that the observation came from such a population, we reject the null hypothesis.

If we take a large sample, the value we are testing will be Normally distributed. If we are working with a 5% significance level, we are concerned with the range that is within 1.96 standard deviations of the mean. In other words, we shall not reject the null hypothesis if the sample result is within 1.96 standard deviations of the mean, and we shall reject it if it is outside this range.

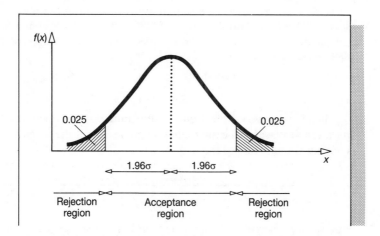

Figure 16.1 Acceptance and rejection regions for 5% significance level.

With a 5% significance level we reject the null hypothesis when an observation falls outside the 95% acceptance range. But if the null hypothesis is true, 5% of observations will fall outside this range anyway. In other words, we are accepting that there is a 5% chance of rejecting a true null hypothesis, which is a Type I error. This means that the significance level can also be viewed as the probability of a Type I error.

Although significance levels can take any value, the most frequently used in business is 5%, followed by 1% and occasionally 0.1%. If a 1% significance level is used, the null hypothesis is not rejected if the observation is within 2.58 standard deviations of the mean. This is a less stringent test, and shows how smaller significance levels need stronger evidence to reject the null hypothesis. With lower significance levels the probability of a Type I error is reduced, but the probability of a Type II error is increased.

WORKED EXAMPLE 16.4

The mean value of accounts received by a firm is thought to be £260. An auditor checks this by taking a sample of 36 accounts, which are found to have a mean of £240 and a standard deviation of £45. Use a 5% significance level to test whether the original view is supported by the evidence of the sample.

Solution

The null hypothesis is that the mean value of all accounts is £260, while the alternative hypothesis is that the mean is not £260. Then the hypotheses are:

$$H_0: \quad \mu = 260 \quad H_1: \quad \mu \neq 260$$

The significance level is 5%, so the null hypothesis is rejected if there is a probability of less than 0.05 that the sample result comes about by chance.

With a sample of 36, the sampling distribution of the mean is Normal with mean 260 and standard deviation $45/\sqrt{36} = 7.5$. For a 5% significance level we look at the points that are within 1.96 standard deviations of the mean. The acceptance range is then

$$260 - 1.96 \times 7.5 \quad \text{to} \quad 260 + 1.96 \times 7.5$$

or $\qquad\qquad\qquad\qquad$ 245.3 $\quad$ to $\quad$ 274.7

The actual observation is outside this range, so we reject the null hypothesis and implicitly accept the alternative hypothesis that the mean value of accounts is not equal to £260.

Now we have seen the detailed steps in hypothesis testing and can list them as follows:

> Steps in hypothesis testing:
>
> ● state the null and alternative hypotheses
> ● specify the level of significance to be used
> ● calculate the acceptance range for the variable tested
> ● find the actual value for the variable tested
> ● decide whether to accept or reject the null hypothesis
> ● state the conclusion reached

This procedure is used, with slight variations, for all types of hypothesis test. In the following sections we shall demonstrate some of these.

WORKED EXAMPLE 16.5

The average income per capita in an area is claimed to be £15,000. A sample of 45 people found their mean income to be £14,300 with a standard deviation of £2,000. Use a 5% significance level to check the original claim. What would be the effect of using a 1% significance level?

Solution

The procedure described above gives the following steps:

● State the null and alternative hypotheses

$$H_0: \quad \mu = 15\ 000 \quad H_1: \quad \mu \neq 15\ 000$$

● Specify the level of significance to be used
This is given as 5%

● Calculate the acceptance range for the variable tested
With a sample of 45, the sampling distribution of the mean is normal with mean 15 000 and standard deviation $2000/\sqrt{45} = 298.14$. For a 5% significance level we look at the points that are within 1.96 standard deviations of the mean. The acceptance range is then

$$15\ 000 - 1.96 \times 298.14 \quad \text{to} \quad 15\ 000 + 1.96 \times 298.14$$

or $\qquad\qquad\qquad$ 14 416 $\quad$ to $\quad$ 15 584

● Find the actual value for the variable tested

$\qquad$ £14,300

● Decide whether to accept or reject the null hypothesis
The actual value is outside the acceptance range, so the null hypothesis must be rejected.

● State the conclusion reached
The evidence from the sample does not support the original claim that the average income per capita in the area is £15,000.

● With a 1% significance level, the acceptance range would be within 2.58 standard deviations of the mean, or

$$15\ 000 - 2.58 \times 298.14 \quad \text{to} \quad 15\ 000 + 2.58 \times 298.14$$

$\qquad\qquad$ 14 231 $\quad$ to $\quad$ 15 769

The actual observation is £14,300, which is within this range, and we cannot reject the null hypothesis.

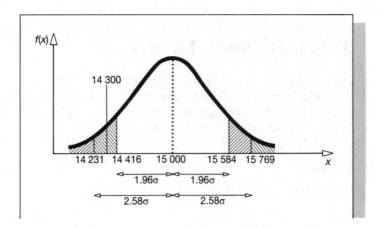

Figure 16.2   Acceptance ranges for Worked Example 16.5.

$\boxed{IN\ SUMMARY}$

A significance level is the minimum acceptable probability that an observation is a random sample from the hypothesized population. It is equivalent to the probability of making a Type I error.

16.1.4 | Population proportions

In the last chapter we showed how sampling could be used to test the proportion of a population that shares some common characteristic. We used the standard result that if the proportion of the population is π, the sampling distribution of the proportion has mean of π and standard deviation of $\sqrt{(\pi\,(1-\pi)/n)}$. Now we can use this to test hypotheses about proportions.

WORKED EXAMPLE 16.6

Last year it was claimed that banks were lending the funds for 20% of all house purchases. To test this, a sample of 100 people with mortgages was interviewed. It was found that 18 of them arranged their loan with a bank. Does this sample support the original claim?

Solution

Hypothesis tests always use the same procedure, and the only difference with this problem is that we are interested in a proportion, π, rather than a mean.

- State the null and alternative hypotheses

  The null hypothesis is that banks lend 20% of funds for mortgages, so using proportions we have

  $$H_0: \quad \pi = 0.2 \quad H_1: \quad \pi \neq 0.2$$

- Specify the level of significance to be used

  This is not given, so we shall assume 5%.

- Calculate the acceptance range for the variable tested

  With a sample of 100, the sampling distribution is Normal with mean 0.2 and standard deviation $\sqrt{(\pi (1 - \pi)/n)} = \sqrt{(0.2 \times 0.8/100)} = 0.04$. For a 5% significance level we look at the points that are within 1.96 standard deviations of the mean. The acceptance range is then

  $$0.2 - 1.96 \times 0.04 \quad \text{to} \quad 0.2 + 1.96 \times 0.04$$

  or $\qquad\qquad\qquad\qquad$ 0.12 $\quad$ to $\quad$ 0.28

- Find the actual value for the variable tested

  The sample had a proportion of $18/100 = 0.18$.

- Decide whether to accept or reject the null hypothesis

  The actual value is within the acceptance range, so the null hypothesis cannot be rejected.

- State the conclusion reached

  The evidence from the sample supports the original claim that banks are lending money for 20% of mortgages.

IN SUMMARY

The standard method of hypothesis testing can be extended to consider the proportion of a population sharing some characteristic.

16.1.5 | One-sided tests

In all the problems we have examined so far we have stated a null hypothesis of the form

$$H_0: \quad \mu = 10$$

and an alternative hypothesis in the form

$$H_1: \quad \mu \neq 10$$

In practice, we are often concerned that an actual value is above (or sometimes below) the claimed value. If we buy boxes of chocolates, we only want to ensure that their weight is not below the specified value; conversely, if we are delivering parcels, we only want to ensure that their weight is not above the claimed value. Problems of this type can be tackled using the standard procedure, but with one adjustment. This adjustment is in the phrasing of the alternative hypothesis and calculation of the acceptance range.

If we are buying boxes of chocolates with a claimed weight of 500 g, and want to ensure that the actual weight is not below this, we can have

$$\text{null hypothesis, } H_0: \quad \mu = 500 \text{ g}$$

$$\text{alternative hypothesis, } H_1: \quad \mu < 500 \text{ g}$$

If we are delivering parcels with a claimed weight of 25 kg, and want to ensure that the actual weight is not above this, we can have

$$\text{null hypothesis, } H_0: \quad \mu = 25 \text{ kg}$$

$$\text{alternative hypothesis, } H_1: \quad \mu > 25 \text{ kg}$$

For this kind of test we only use one tail of the sampling distribution, so the acceptance range is altered. In particular, a 5% significance level has the 5% area of rejection in one tail of the distribution. In a Normal distribution this point is 1.645 standard deviations from the mean, as shown in Figure 16.3.

One-sided tests are said to measure consumers' risk or producers' risk. If a packet of soap powder has a stated weight of 1 kg, consumers will only be concerned if actual quantity is less than this. Consumer groups will, therefore, sample packets using a null hypothesis that the mean weight is 1 kg and an alternative hypothesis that the weight is less than 1 kg. Producers are concerned if the quantity is significantly more than 1 kg. They will sample packets using a null hypothesis that the mean weight is 1 kg and an alternative hypothesis that the mean weight is above 1 kg. In practice, of course, their testing is much more complicated than this.

WORKED EXAMPLE 16.7

A mail order company charges a customer a flat rate for delivery based on a mean weight for packages of 1.75 kg with a standard deviation of 0.5 kg. Postal charges now seem high and it is suggested that the mean weight is greater than 1.75 kg. A random sample of 100 packages has a mean weight of 1.86 kg. Does this support the view that the mean weight is more than 1.75 kg?

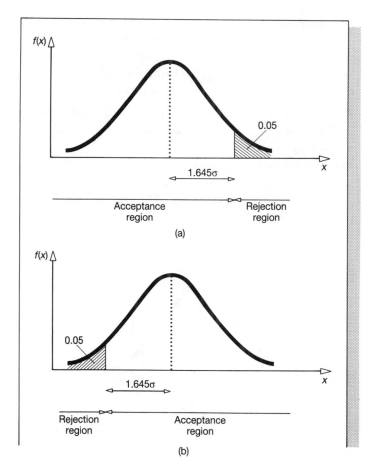

Figure 16.3   One-sided tests for 5% significance level: (a) when concerned with a maximum value; (b) when concerned with a minimum value.

Solution

We can again use the standard procedure.

● State the null and alternative hypotheses
  This time we want to ensure that the mean weight is not above 1.75 kg, so we have

$$H_0: \quad \mu = 1.75 \text{ kg} \quad H_1: \quad \mu > 1.75 \text{ kg}$$

● Specify the level of significance to be used
  This is not given, so we shall assume 5%.

● Calculate the acceptance range for the variable tested
  With a sample of 100, the sampling distribution of the mean is Normal with mean of 1.75 kg standard deviation $0.5/\sqrt{100} = 0.05$ kg. For a 5%

significance level and a one-sided test, we look at the points that are more than 1.645 standard deviations above the mean. The acceptance range is then below $1.75 + 1.645 \times 0.05 = 1.83$ kg.

● Find the actual value for the variable tested

The observed weight of parcels is 1.86 kg.

● Decide whether to accept or reject the null hypothesis

The actual value is outside the acceptance range, so the null hypothesis must be rejected.

● State the conclusion reached

The evidence from the sample does not support the view that the mean weight of packages is 1.75 kg. The evidence suggests that the mean weight is more than this.

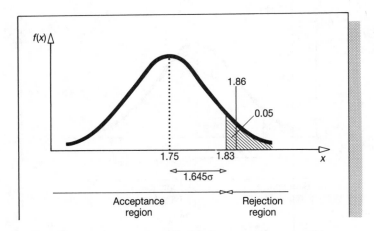

Figure 16.4   Acceptance region for Worked Example 16.7.

WORKED EXAMPLE 16.8

A management consultant has introduced new procedures to a reception office. The receptionist should not do more than 10 minutes of paperwork in each hour, with a standard deviation of 3 minutes. A check is made on 40 random hours of operation and the mean time spent on paperwork is 11.05 minutes. Based on these figures, can the assumption that the new procedures meet specifications be rejected at a 1% level of significance?

Solution

● State the null and alternative hypotheses

This time we are only interested in ensuring that the time spent on paperwork is not above 10 minutes in an hour. Then we have

$$H_0: \quad \mu = 10 \text{ minutes} \qquad H_1: \quad \mu > 10 \text{ minutes}$$

- Specify the level of significance to be used
  This is given as 1%.

- Calculate the acceptance range for the variable tested
  With a sample of 40, the sampling distribution of the mean is Normal with mean of 10 minutes and standard deviation $3/\sqrt{40} = 0.47$ minutes. For a 1% significance level and a one-sided test, we look at the points that are more than 2.33 standard deviations above the mean. Then the acceptance range is below $10 + 2.33 \times 0.47 = 11.10$ minutes.

- Find the actual value for the variable tested
  The observed number of minutes spent on paperwork in each hour is 11.05.

- Decide whether to accept or reject the null hypothesis
  The actual value is inside the acceptance range, so the null hypothesis cannot be rejected.

- State the conclusion reached
  The evidence from the sample supports the view that the mean time spent on paperwork is 10 minutes an hour.

IN SUMMARY

The standard two-sided analysis can be extended to a one-sided analysis when we are only interested in means that are above or below specified levels.

16.1.6 | Testing for differences in means

There are many situations in which we have two different populations and want to know if the means are the same. We might, for example, operate shops in two areas and want to know if the profitability is the same in each area, or we might have two factories and want to know if the productivity is the same, or we might want to check sales before and after an advertising campaign.

To see if the means of two populations are the same, we start by taking a sample from each population. If the sample means are fairly close, we can assume that the population means are the same, but if there is a large difference in the samples we would have to assume that the population means are different. Now we need to define how close the sample means must be to make these decisions. For this we take the means of two samples, $\bar{x}_1$ and $\bar{x}_2$, and find the difference, $\bar{x}_1 - \bar{x}_2$. Then we use the standard result that for large samples the sampling distribution of $\bar{x}_1 - \bar{x}_2$ is Normal with mean 0 and standard deviation:

$$standard\ error = \sqrt{\frac{s_1^2}{n_1} + \frac{s_2^2}{n_2}}$$

where: n_1 = sample size from population 1
          n_2 = sample size from population 2
          s_1 = standard deviation of sample 1
          s_2 = standard deviation of sample 2

With these results we can again use the standard procedure. In this case the null hypothesis is phrased to make the mean of the two populations the same.

WORKED EXAMPLE 16.9

A company uses two machines to fill packets. A sample of 30 packets from the first machine had a mean weight of 180 g and a standard deviation of 40 g. A sample of 40 packets from the second machine had a mean weight of 170 g and a standard deviation of 10 g. Does the evidence from these samples support the view that the two machines produce packets of equal weight?

Solution

Again we can use the standard approach.

● State the null and alternative hypotheses
  We want to see if the two machines put the same mean quantities in packets. Therefore, the null hypothesis is that they do put the same mean in, while the alternative hypothesis is that they do not. This gives

$$\text{null hypothesis, } H_0: \quad \mu_1 = \mu_2$$

$$\text{alternative hypothesis, } H_1: \quad \mu_1 \neq \mu_2$$

● Specify the level of significance to be used
  We can use the standard 5%.

● Calculate the acceptance range for the variable tested
  We are looking at the sampling distribution of $\bar{x}_1 - \bar{x}_2$, with sample sizes $n_1 = 30$ and $n_2 = 40$, and standard deviations $s_1 = 14$ and $s_2 = 10$. This gives a sampling distribution of $\bar{x}_1 - \bar{x}_2$, which is Normal with mean 0 and standard error:

$$standard\ error = \sqrt{\frac{s_1^2}{n_1} + \frac{s_2^2}{n_2}} = \sqrt{\frac{14^2}{30} + \frac{10^2}{40}} = 3.01$$

For a 5% significance level and a two-sided test, the acceptance range is within 1.96 standard deviations of the mean. This defines the range:

$$0 - 1.96 \times 3.01 \quad \text{to} \quad 0 + 1.96 \times 3.01$$

$$-5.90 \quad \text{to} \quad +5.90$$

- Find the actual value for the variable tested
  The observed difference in samples is $\bar{x}_1 - \bar{x}_2 = 180 - 170 = 10$.
- Decide whether to accept or reject the null hypothesis
  The actual value is outside the acceptance range, so the null hypothesis is rejected and the alternative hypothesis is accepted.
- State the conclusion reached
  The evidence from the samples does not support the view that the mean weight put into packets is the same from each machine.

IN SUMMARY

The standard approach to hypothesis testing can be extended to deal with the difference between sample means.

16.1.7 | Tests with small samples

When we looked at confidence intervals we noted that sampling distributions were only Normal when the population is normal or the sample size is more than 30. If this condition is not met the sampling distribution follows a t-distribution. You will remember that the shape of the t-distribution depends on the sample size: with samples greater than 30 the t-distribution is very similar to the Normal, but as the sample size gets smaller the distribution gets lower and wider.

We can use the t-distribution to test hypotheses with small sample sizes.

WORKED EXAMPLE 16.10

A supermarket is getting complaints that its tins of strawberries contain a lot of juice and few strawberries. A team from the supermarket make a surprise visit to the supplier, who is about to deliver another batch. The tins in this batch are claimed to have a minimum of 300 g of fruit in a tin, but when a random sample of 15 tins is taken the mean quantity is only 287 g with a standard deviation of 18 g. What can be said about the tins?

Solution

Again we can use the standard approach for hypothesis testing.

● State the null and alternative hypotheses

The null hypothesis is that the mean weight of the fruit is 300 g, while the alternative hypothesis is that the weight is less than this. Then we have

$$H_0: \quad \mu = 300 \text{ g} \quad H_1: \quad \mu < 300 \text{ g}$$

● Specify the level of significance to be used

We can use the standard 5%.

● Calculate the acceptance range for the variable tested

With a sample of size 15, the sampling distribution of the mean follows a t-distribution with $n - 1 = 15 - 1 = 14$ degrees of freedom, a mean of 300 g and standard deviation $s/\sqrt{n} = 18/\sqrt{15} = 4.65$ g. For a 5% significance level and a one-sided test, we look up a probability of 0.1 (i.e. 0.05 in each tail) with 14 degrees of freedom in t-tables. This gives a value of 1.761. Then the acceptance range is above $300 - 1.761 \times 4.65 = 291.81$ g.

● Find the actual value for the variable tested

The actual mean of the sample was 287 g.

● Decide whether to accept or reject the null hypothesis

The actual value is outside the acceptance range, so the null hypothesis is rejected.

● State the conclusion reached

The evidence from the sample does not support the view that the mean weight is 300 g, but it supports the alternative hypothesis that the mean weight of fruit is less than 300 g.

| IN SUMMARY |

With small samples the sampling distribution of the mean follows a t-distribution. This can be used in the standard procedure for hypothesis testing.

Self-assessment questions

16.1 What is the purpose of hypothesis testing?

16.2 Which is a more precise statement, H_0 or H_1?

16.3 What are Type I and Type II errors?

16.4 What is a significance level?

16.5 Is the probability of a Type II error lower with a 5% significance level or with a 1% significance level?

16.6 If a value is in the acceptance range does this prove that the null hypothesis is true?

16.7 When is a one-sided hypothesis test used?

16.8 Why can the Normal distribution not be used for small samples?

| 16.2 | Non-parametric tests

| 16.2.1 | Introduction

So far in this chapter we have looked at a range of problems where hypothesis testing can be used. In all of these we have proposed a hypothesis about the value of a variable and have then measured the variable in a sample to see if actual observations support the hypothesis. Variables that take a specific value during an investigation are often called parameters, so the hypothesis tests described so far are called **parametric tests**.

There are many situations where we want to test a hypothesis, but there is no appropriate variable to measure. This occurs with nominal data such as the type of industry, value for money, quality, and so on. Then we might suggest a hypothesis that one type of product offers better value for money than another, but there is no measurement to support this view. In these circumstances parametric hypothesis tests cannot be used. They are also inappropriate if the sampling distribution is not known.

When parametric tests cannot be used **non-parametric** or **distribution-free** tests become useful. These have the major benefit of making no assumptions about the distribution of the population. In the next section we shall describe a non-parametric test for hypotheses, and the most important of these is the χ^2 test. χ is the Greek letter chi (pronounced 'ki'); in this context χ is always squared, and the individual value χ has no meaning.

IN SUMMARY

There are situations in which parametric tests cannot be used and distribution-free, or non-parametric tests are needed.

16.2.2 | Chi-squared test for goodness of fit

The chi-squared test is a hypothesis test, so the general approach is the same as with parametric tests. However, the chi-squared test looks at the frequency of observations and sees if these match the expected frequencies.

Suppose we have a series of observed frequencies O_1, O_2, O_3, ... O_n, and were expecting the frequencies E_1, E_2, E_3, ... E_n. The difference between these tells us how closely the observations match expectations. To be specific, we can define χ^2 as

$$\chi^2 = \frac{(O_1 - E_1)^2}{E_1} + \frac{(O_2 - E_2)^2}{E_2} + \frac{(O_3 - E_1)^2}{E_3} \ ... \ \frac{(O_n - E_n)^2}{E_n}$$

or

$$\chi^2 = \sum \frac{(O - E)^2}{E}$$

Squaring the difference between observed and expected values removes any negative values, and then dividing by E_i gives a distribution with a standard shape.

If the hypothesis is true, the observed frequencies will be close to the expected frequencies, and χ^2 will have a value close to zero. Conversely, if the original hypothesis is not true the differences will be large and χ^2 will have a larger value. Now we need to define a test value of χ^2 so that an actual value above this test value leads us to reject the hypothesis, but an actual value below this test value means we cannot reject the hypothesis. This test level is called the **critical value** and can be found from standard tables, shown in Appendix I.

The shape of the χ^2 distribution depends on the degrees of freedom, as shown in Figure 16.5. Notice also that the distribution only has positive values. We met the idea of degrees of freedom when discussing the t-distribution and you will remember that they essentially measure the number of pieces of information that are free to take any value. If we know the mean of n values, $n - 1$ values are free to take any value, but the nth value must then be fixed to give the correct mean. Thus there are $n - 1$ degrees of freedom. With the χ^2 distribution we are looking at the frequency of observations in classes. Then the number of degrees of freedom is calculated from

degrees of freedom = number of classes − number of estimated variables − 1

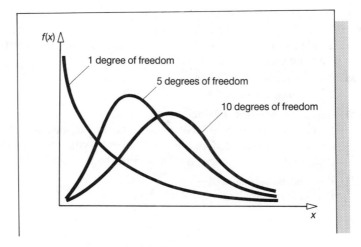

Figure 16.5 Chi-squared distribution with varying degrees of freedom.

This gives all the information we need, and we can now do the test. Even though the χ^2 test is non-parametric, the approach is the same as for the parametric test. There are, however, some small differences. Notably, instead of finding an acceptance range, we find a critical value. If the actual value of χ^2 is above this value we reject the hypothesis, and if it is below this value we accept it.

WORKED EXAMPLE 16.11

Five factories report the following number of minor accidents in a five-year period:

Factory	1	2	3	4	5
Number of accidents	31	42	29	35	38

Does this evidence suggest that some factories have more accidents than others?

Solution

Now we can use the standard procedure.

● State the null and alternative hypotheses
The null hypothesis, H_0, is that each factory expects the same number of accidents. Then the alternative hypothesis, H_1, is that each factory does not have the same number of accidents.

● Specify the level of significance to be used
This can be taken as 5%.

● Calculate the critical value of χ^2
In this problem there are five classes, and no variables have been estimated, so the degrees of freedom are $5 - 0 - 1 = 4$. With a 5% significance level we look up 0.05 in χ^2 tables and find a critical value of 9.4877.

● Find the actual value of χ^2
For this we calculate

$$\chi^2 = \Sigma \frac{(O - E)^2}{E}$$

There are 175 accidents. If each factory expects the same number, the expected number of accidents in each factory, E, is $175/5 = 35$. Then the calculations are as shown in Table 16.1. This tells us that the actual value of χ^2 is 3.143.

Table 16.1

Factory	O	E	$(O - E)$	$(O - E)^2$	$(O - E)^2/E$
1	31	35	-4	16	0.457
2	42	35	7	49	1.400
3	29	35	-6	36	1.029
4	35	35	0	0	0.000
5	38	35	3	9	0.257
Total	175	175			3.143

● Decide whether to accept or reject the null hypothesis
The actual value (3.143) is less than the critical value (9.4877) so we cannot reject the null hypothesis.

● State the conclusion reached
The evidence suggests that each factory can expect the same number of accidents. Any variation is purely by chance.

The above example effectively tested whether there was a uniform distribution of accidents across factories. In other words, we hypothesized that the accident rate was a uniform distribution and saw if the data fitted this. We could use the same approach for other distributions, so we could find whether a distribution fits a binomial, Poisson or any other distribution. This is illustrated in the following examples.

WORKED EXAMPLE 16.12

The quality management function in an office recorded the number of reports that were considered defective each day. The following frequency was obtained:

Defects	0	1	2	3	4	5
Days	26	42	18	10	3	1

Does the number of defects follow a binomial distribution?

Solution

Using the standard procedure:

- State the null and alternative hypotheses
  The null hypothesis, H_0, is that the distribution is binomial. The alternative hypothesis, H_1, is that the distribution is not binomial.
- Specify the level of significance to be used
  This can be taken as 5%.
- Calculate the critical value of χ^2
  In this problem there is going to be some adjustment of the data, so we shall return to this calculation a little later.
- Find the actual value of χ^2
  We have 100 days of data, and the total number of defects is

  $$(26 \times 0) + (42 \times 1) + (18 \times 2) + (10 \times 3) + (3 \times 4) + (1 \times 5) = 125$$

  The mean number of defects is $125/100 = 1.25$ a day and we want to find the probability of 0, 1, 2, 3, 4 and 5 defects occurring in a day. We know from Chapter 14 that the mean of a binomial distribution is np, where n is the number of trials and p is the probability of success. In this case the number of trials is the maximum number of defects, so $n = 5$. Then $1.25 = 5 \times p$ or $p = 0.25$.
  Now we have the probability of a success and can find the expected distribution from the binomial tables in Appendix E. Multiplying these probabilities by the total number of days gives the expected distribution of defects

shown in the following table:

Number of defects	0	1	2	3	4	5
Probability	0.2373	0.3955	0.2637	0.0879	0.0146	0.0010
Expected frequency	23.73	39.55	26.27	8.79	1.46	0.10

One problem here is that the χ^2 distribution does not work well with expected frequencies of less than 5. In these circumstances we have to combine adjacent classes so that the expected number of observations becomes greater than 5. Adding the last three classes gives the modified expected distribution below:

Number of defects	0	1	2	3 or more
Probability	0.2373	0.3955	0.2637	0.1035
Frequency	23.73	39.55	26.37	10.35

Now you can see why we delayed the calculation of the critical value. There are now four classes, and we have estimated one parameter (the probability of success), so the number of degrees of freedom is

number of classes – number of estimated parameters – 1 = 4 – 1 – 1 = 2

Looking up the critical value for a significance level of 5% and two degrees of freedom gives a value of 5.99.

The actual value of χ^2 is calculated in Table 16.5 as 4.313.

Table 16.2

Frequency	O	E	(O – E)	(O – E)²	(O – E)²/E
0	26	23.73	2.27	5.153	0.217
1	42	39.55	2.45	6.003	0.152
2	18	26.37	–8.37	70.057	2.657
3 or more	14	10.35	3.65	13.323	1.287
Total	100	100			4.313

● Decide whether to accept or reject the null hypothesis
The actual value of χ^2 (4.313) is less than the critical value (5.992) so we cannot reject the null hypothesis.

● State the conclusion reached
The evidence suggests that the observations follow a binomial distribution.

WORKED EXAMPLE 16.13

An electrical contractor records the frequency of faults per kilometre of a certain type of cable as follows:

Number of faults	0	1	2	3	4	5	6
Number of kilometres	37	51	23	7	4	2	1

Do these data follow a Poisson distribution?

Solution

- State the null and alternative hypotheses
  The null hypothesis, H_0, is that the distribution is Poisson. The alternative hypothesis, H_1, is that the distribution is not Poisson.
- Specify the level of significance to be used
  This can be taken as 5%.
- Calculate the critical value of χ^2
  Again, there is going to be some adjustment of the data, so we shall return to this calculation a little later.
- Find the actual value of χ^2
  We have 125 km of data, and the total number of defects is

$$(37 \times 0) + (51 \times 1) + (23 \times 2) + (7 \times 3) + (4 \times 4) + (2 \times 5) + (1 \times 6) = 150$$

The mean number of defects is $150/125 = 1.2$ per km. This is the mean of the Poisson distribution, so we can find the expected distribution from the tables in Appendix F (Table 16.3). Again, we need to combine adjacent classes so that each class has more than five observations. Adding the last four classes gives the revised table of expected values shown in Table 16.4.

Now you can see why we delayed the calculation of the critical value. There are now four classes, so the number of degrees of freedom is

number of classes − number of estimated parameters − 1 = 4 − 1 − 1 = 2

Table 16.3

Number of defects	0	1	2	3	4	5	6 or more
Probability	0.3012	0.3614	0.2169	0.0867	0.0260	0.0062	0.0016
Expected frequency	37.65	45.18	27.11	10.84	3.25	0.78	0.20

Here the parameter being estimated is the mean.

Looking up the critical value for a significance level of 5% and two degrees of freedom gives a value of 5.99.

The actual value of χ^2 is calculated in Table 16.5 as 1.459.

Table 16.4

Number of defects	0	1	2	3 or more
Probability	0.3012	0.3614	0.2169	0.1205
Expected frequency	37.65	45.18	27.11	15.06

Table 16.5

Frequency	O	E	$(O-E)$	$(O-E)^2$	$(O-E)^2/E$
0	37	37.65	−0.65	0.42	0.011
1	51	45.18	5.82	33.87	0.750
2	23	27.11	−4.11	16.89	0.623
3 or more	14	15.06	−1.06	1.12	0.075
Total	125	125			1.459

● Decide whether to accept or reject the null hypothesis

The actual value is less than the critical value, so we cannot reject the null hypothesis.

● State the conclusion reached

The evidence suggests that the observations follow a Poisson distribution.

WORKED EXAMPLE 16.14

A factory is about to do some statistical analyses on the mean weight of a product delivered to it, but these analyses are only valid if the weights are normally distributed. The population of parts is known to have a mean weight of 45 g and a standard deviation of 15 g. A sample of 500 units was taken, with weights given in the distribution shown in Table 16.6. Can this be considered normal?

Table 16.6

Weight (g)	Number of observations
less than 10	9
10 to 19.99	31
20 to 29.99	65
30 to 39.99	97
40 to 49.99	115
50 to 59.99	94
60 to 69.99	49
70 to 79.99	24
80 to 89.99	16

Solution

This is an important question, as many statistical analyses are only valid if there is a normal distribution.

● State the null and alternative hypotheses

The null hypothesis, H_0, is that the distribution is Normal. The alternative hypothesis, H_1, is that the distribution is not Normal.

● Specify the level of significance to be used

This can be taken as 5%.

● Calculate the critical value of χ^2

The number of degrees of freedom is $(9 - 0 - 1 =)$ 8. Then Appendix I shows that the critical value for χ^2 with 8 degrees of freedom at a 5% significance level is 15.51.

● Find the actual value of χ^2

The probability that an observation is in the range 10 to 19.99 is

$$P(\text{between 10 and 19.99}) = P(\text{less than 20}) - P(\text{less than 10})$$

Now

20 is $(20 - 45)/15 = -1.67$ standard deviations from the mean, corresponding to a probability of 0.0475

and

10 is $(10 - 45)/15 = -2.33$ standard deviations from the mean, corresponding to a probability of 0.0099

So

$$P(\text{between 10 and 19.99}) = 0.0475 - 0.0099 = 0.0376$$

The expected number of observations in this range is $0.0376 \times 500 = 19$ (to the nearest integer). Repeating this calculation for the other probabilities gives the results in Table 16.7. Adding the values for $(O - E)^2/E$ gives the actual value of χ^2 as 43.41.

Table 16.7

Weight	O	Probability	E	$(O - E)^2/E$
< 10	9	0.0099	4.95	3.31
10 to 19.99	31	0.0376	18.8	7.92
20 to 29.99	65	0.1112	55.6	1.59
30 to 39.99	97	0.2120	106.0	0.76
40 to 49.99	115	0.2586	129.3	1.58
50 to 59.99	94	0.2120	106.0	1.36
60 to 69.99	49	0.1112	55.6	0.78
70 to 79.99	24	0.0376	18.8	1.44
80 to 89.99	16	0.0099	4.95	24.67

● Decide whether to accept or reject the null hypothesis

The actual value (43.41) is greater than the critical value (15.51), so we must reject the hypothesis that the sample is Normally distributed.

● State the conclusion reached

The evidence suggests that the observations do not follow a Normal distribution.

IN SUMMARY

The χ^2 distribution allows a non-parametric test for hypotheses. It is particularly suited to testing the goodness of fit, to see if data follows a specified distribution.

16.2.3 | Tests of association

The χ^2 test is also useful for testing association, which is shown in a **contingency table**. Suppose we are analysing the results of a questionnaire about the source of finance for purchasing a house. We might come across two questions that have the number of responses in the following two tables:

Size of loan	Number of replies
Less than £10,000	65
£10,000 to £30,000	90
More than £30,000	45
Total 200	

Source of loan	Number of replies
Building society	125
Bank	55
Elsewhere	20
Total	200

These answers raise questions about whether there is any relationship or association between the size of a loan and the organization giving it. When we look more closely at the replies to these questions they may break down into the pattern shown in Table 16.8. This is a contingency table. A χ^2 test can tell us if there is any statistical association between the two sets of answers. Not surprisingly, the method for this is the same one we have been using for all hypothesis tests.

Table 16.8

Source of mortgage	Size of loan			Total
	less than £10,000	£10,000 to £30,000	more than £30,000	
Building society	30	55	40	125
Bank	23	29	3	55
Elsewhere	12	6	2	20
Total	65	90	45	200

WORKED EXAMPLE 16.15

Find if there is any association between the two answers described in the contingency table above.

Solution

● State the null and alternative hypotheses

The null hypothesis, H_0, is that there is an association between the size of the mortgage and its source. The alternative hypothesis, H_1, is that there is not an association between the two sets of answers; the two are independent.

● Specify the level of significance to be used

This can be taken as 5%.

● Calculate the critical value of χ^2

For a contingency table the degrees of freedom are calculated from

degrees of freedom = (number of rows – 1) × (number of columns – 1)

Here there are three rows and three columns (ignoring the totals) so there are

$(3 - 1) \times (3 - 1) = 4$ degrees of freedom

Looking up χ^2 tables for a 5% significance level and 4 degrees of freedom gives a critical value of 9.49.

● Find the actual value of χ^2

For this we need to calculate the expected number of replies in each cell of the matrix. Consider the top left-hand cell, which records the number of people who take a loan of less than £10,000 from a building society. A total of 125 loans came from a building society, so the probability that any particular loan came from a building society is 125/200 = 0.625. A total of 65 loans were for less than £10,000, so the probability that any particular loan is for less than £10,000 is 65/200 = 0.325. Then the probability that a loan came from a building society and is for less than £10,000 is 0.625 × 0.325 = 0.203. Since there are 200 loans described in the questionnaire, the expected number of this type is 0.203 × 200 = 40.625.

This calculation has to be repeated for every cell in the matrix. This is simple with a computer spreadsheet, but there is a slight simplification that eases calculation. If you look at the calculation we have just done:

$$125/200 \times 65/200 \times 200 = 40.625$$

and this is

$$\frac{\text{row total}}{\text{overall total}} \times \frac{\text{column total}}{\text{overall total}} \times \text{overall total}$$

which is simplified to:

$$\frac{\text{row total} \times \text{column total}}{\text{overall total}}$$

This gives the numbers of expected loans shown in Table 16.9.

Table 16.9

Source of mortgage	Size of loan			Total
	less than £10,000	£10,000 to £30,000	more than £30,000	
Building society	40.625	56.250	28.125	125
Bank	17.875	24.750	12.375	55
Elsewhere	6.500	9.000	4.500	20
Total	65	90	45	200

Now we have a set of nine observed frequencies, and a corresponding set of nine expected frequencies, so we can calculate the value of χ^2. This is done in Table 16.10 where the actual value of χ^2 is found to be 24.165.

Table 16.10

O	E	$(O-E)$	$(O-E)^2$	$(O-E)^2/E$
30	40.625	−10.625	112.891	2.779
55	56.250	−1.25	1.563	0.028
40	28.125	11.875	141.016	5.014
23	17.875	5.125	26.266	1.469
29	24.750	4.25	18.063	0.730
3	12.375	−9.375	87.891	7.102
12	6.500	5.500	30.250	4.654
6	9.000	−3.000	9.000	1.000
2	4.500	−2.500	6.250	1.389
200	200			24.165

● Decide whether to accept or reject the null hypothesis

The actual value is greater than the critical value, so we reject the null hypothesis and accept the alternative hypothesis.

● State the conclusion reached

The evidence suggests that there is no association between the answer to the two questions, so there is no association between the size of a mortgage and its source.

You should always be careful when doing χ^2 tests, because they do not work well if the number of expected observations in any class falls below five. In this example one cell has an expected frequency of 4.5, so we should really combine this cell with others, perhaps combining the rows for banks and other sources. Here we shall not repeat the calculations, but simply note the adjustment.

One of the obvious problems with χ^2 distributions is the amount of arithmetic that has to be done. Computers will, of course, help but the problems are a little awkward to automate. Figure 16.6 shows the printout from a package that calculates the value of χ^2 for the problem tackled above.

```
001 > read c1 – c3
002 > 30 55 40
003 > 23 29  3
004 > 12  6  2
005 > end
         3 ROWS READ

006 > chisquare c1 – c3
```

Expected counts are printed below observed counts

	C1	C2	C3	Total
1	30	55	40	125
	40.62	56.25	28.12	
2	23	29	3	55
	17.88	24.75	12.37	
3	12	6	2	20
	6.50	9.00	4.50	
Total	65	90	45	200

ChiSq=	2.779	+	0.028	+	5.014	+	
	1.469	+	0.730	+	7.102	+	
	4.654	+	1.000	+	1.389	=	24.165

df=4

* WARNING *
1 cell with expected counts less than 5.0

Figure 16.6   Printout from a statistics package doing a chi-squared test.

IN SUMMARY

Chi-squared distributions can be used for contingency tables. These typically note the association between the answers in a questionnaire.

Self-assessment questions

16.9 What is the main difference between a parametric and a non-parametric test?

16.10 When are non-parametric tests used?

16.11 'When a parametric test cannot be used, a non-parametric test can always be used instead.' Is this statement true?

16.12 Why does a χ^2 test only have a critical value rather than an acceptance range?

16.13 What is χ (the square root of χ^2) used for?

CHAPTER REVIEW

This chapter has discussed hypothesis testing, which is used to see whether a statement about a population is supported by the evidence in a sample. In particular, the chapter:

● described the overall approach of hypothesis testing

● used hypothesis testing on population means

● extended the standard approach to proportions, one-sided tests, differences between means and small samples

● outlined the use of non-parametric tests

● used χ^2 tests for goodness of fit

Problems

16.1 The mean wage of people living in a block of flats is said to be £400 a week with a standard deviation of £100. A random sample of 36 people was examined.

(a) What is the acceptance range for a 5% significance level?

(b) What is the acceptance range for a 1% significance level?

16.2 The weight of packets of biscuits is claimed to be 500 g. A random sample of 50 packets has a mean weight of 495 g and a standard deviation of 10 g. Use a significance level of 5% to see if the data from the sample support the original claim.

16.3 A bus company says that its long-distance coaches take 5 hours for a particular journey. Last week a consumer group tested these figures by timing a sample of 30 journeys. These had a mean time of 5 hours 10 minutes with a standard deviation of 20 minutes. What report can the consumer group make?

16.4 A food processor specifies the mean weight of a product as 200 g. The output is Normally distributed with a standard deviation of 15 g. A random sample of 20 has a mean of 195 g. Does this evidence suggest that the mean weight is too low?

16.5 An emergency breakdown service is suggesting that 50% of all drivers are registered with their service. A random sample of 100 people were interviewed, and 45 of them were registered with the service. Does this sample support the original claim?

16.6 The quality management function in an organization says that 12% of letters posted contain errors. A sample of 200 letters was checked and 31 of them contained errors. What do these results suggest?

16.7 A scheme for doctors should ensure that they do not spend more than 2 hours a day doing paperwork. A sample of 40 doctors had an average of 2 hours 25 minutes a day doing paperwork, with a standard deviation of 55 minutes. Does the sample support the view that doctors spend less than 2 hours a day on paperwork?

16.8 A television has an advertised life of 30 000 hours. A sample of 50 sets had a life of 28 500 hours with a standard deviation of 1000 hours. What can be said about the advertisements?

16.9 A company operate two similar factories. There is some disagreement, because people working in each factory think those in the other factory are getting higher wages. A sample of wages was taken from each factory with the following results:

Sample 1:   size = 45   mean = £250   standard deviation = £45

Sample 2:   size = 35   mean = £230   standard deviation = £40

What can be said about the wages?

16.10 A car manufacturer says its cars cost £100 a year less to maintain than those of its competitors. To test this, a consumer group found the cost of maintaining ten cars for a year, and the mean saving was £79 with a standard deviation of £20. What can be said about the manufacturer's claim?

16.11 Five factories reported the following numbers of minor accidents in a year:

Factory	1	2	3	4	5
Number of accidents	23	45	18	34	28

Does this evidence suggest that some factories have statistically more accidents than others?

16.12 The number of defective components supplied each day by a factory is recorded as follows:

Number of defects	0	1	2	3	4	5
Number of days	8	22	33	29	15	3

Do these data follow a binomial distribution?

16.13 The number of road accidents reporting to a hospital emergency ward is shown in the following table. Do these figures follow a Poisson distribution?

Number of accidents	0	1	2	3	4	5	6
Number of days	17	43	52	37	20	8	4

16.14 Do the figures in Table 16.11 follow a normal distribution?

Table 16.11

Weight (g)	Number of observations
less than 5	5
5 to 19.99	43
20 to 34.99	74
35 to 49.99	103
50 to 64.99	121
65 to 79.99	97
80 to 94.99	43
95 to 109.99	21
110 and more	8

Computer exercises

16.1 It is quite difficult to get statistics packages that automatically do χ^2 goodness of fit tests. Nonetheless, they can give some help. Use a statistics package to see how it tackles these tests. Check the results given in Figure 16.6.

16.2 Design a spreadsheet that will help with χ^2 tests. Use this to check the results given in this chapter.

16.3 Eight observations were taken and a null hypothesis was proposed that these fit a Poisson distribution. Figure 16.7 shows a computer printout from a statistics package used for doing a χ^2 goodness of fit test with these figures. Make sure you can understand what is happening in this printout. Use a statistics package to check the results. Why do you think only four values were tested?

```
001 > name c1 'obs' c2 'expt' c3 'chisqr'

002 > set c1
003 > 34 38 16 7
004 > end

005 > set c2
006 > 36.8 36.8 18.4 8.0
007 > end

008 > let c3=(c1–c2)**2/c2
009 > sum c3 k1
      SUM      =        0.69022

010 > cdf k1 k2;
SUBC > chisquare 3.
011 > let k2=1–k2
012 > print c1–c3 k1 k2
K1           0.690217
K2           0.875502
```

	ROW	obs	expt	chisqr
	1	34	36.8	0.213043
	2	38	36.8	0.039130
	3	16	18.4	0.313043
	4	7	8.0	0.125000

```
013 > stop
```

Figure 16.7   Printout from a statistics package doing a χ^2 test.

16.4 Use a spreadsheet to check the results of Worked Example 16.15. Extend the spreadsheet to deal with larger contingency tables.

Case study
Willingham Consumer Protection Department

Willingham Consumer Protection Department (WCPD) are responsible for administering all weights and measures legislation in their area. A part of their service ensures that packages of food and drink contain the quantities stated.

One week, WCPD decided to test containers of milk. The major part of this work was done at dairies where procedures and historical data were examined. However, they also visited local shops and milk roundsmen to buy random samples of products.

On two consecutive days they bought 50 containers with a nominal content of 4 pints or 2.27 litres. The actual contents of these, in litres, are as follows:

Day 1:
2.274	2.275	2.276	2.270	2.269	2.271	2.265	2.275	2.263	2.278
2.260	2.278	2.280	2.275	2.261	2.280	2.279	2.270	2.275	2.263
2.275	2.781	2.266	2.277	2.271	2.273	2.283	2.260	2.259	2.276
2.286	2.275	2.271	2.273	2.291	2.271	2.269	2.265	2.258	2.283
2.274	2.278	2.276	2.281	2.269	2.259	2.291	2.289	2.276	2.283

Day 2:
2.270	2.276	2.258	2.259	2.281	2.265	2.278	2.270	2.294	2.255
2.271	2.284	2.276	2.293	2.261	2.270	2.271	2.276	2.269	2.268
2.272	2.272	2.273	2.280	2.281	2.276	2.263	2.260	2.295	2.257
2.248	2.276	2.284	2.276	2.270	2.271	2.269	2.278	2.276	2.274
2.291	2.257	2.281	2.276	2.274	2.273	2.273	2.270	2.272	2.278

When they were collecting these figures, WCPD inspectors were convinced that there were no problems with the large dairies, but some small operations were not so reliable. This was because large dairies could afford modern, well-designed equipment and employed special quality assurance staff. Smaller operators used older, less reliable equipment, and could not afford to run a quality assurance department. Two companies, in particular, were identified as needing further checks. Random samples of 15 containers were taken from each of these dairies, with the following results:

Company 1: 2.261 2.273 2.250 2.268 2.268 2.262 2.272 2.269 2.268 2.257
2.260 2.270 2.254 2.249 2.267
Company 2: 2.291 2.265 2.283 2.275 2.248 2.286 2.268 2.271 2.284 2.256
2.284 2.255 2.283 2.275 2.276

What kind of report could the milk inspectors write about their findings?

SECTION FIVE

Business problems with uncertainty

This book is divided into five sections, each of which covers a different aspect of quantitative methods in business. The first section gave the background and context for the rest of the book. The second section discussed data collection and description. The third section looked at methods of solving specific types of business problem. The fourth section gave an introduction to probability and statistical methods, laying the foundations of business statistics. This is the fifth section, which uses some of the ideas developed so far to tackle specific business problems. These problems often contain uncertainty and involve some statistical analysis.

There are four chapters in this section.

Chapter 17 looks at ways of analysing business decisions, particularly those where probabilities can be given to various outcomes. Decisions are often made in an unstructured environment, so an important step is to describe problems in a standard way.

Chapter 18 shows how quantitative models can be used in the control of stocks. Every organization holds stocks of some kind, and the costs can be surprisingly high. Models have been developed that minimize these costs in a range of circumstances.

Chapter 19 describes the use of network analysis for planning projects. A project consists of any self-contained piece of work. Network analysis divides this into a set of activities and shows their relationships using a network. A series of analyses can then be done to organize the timing and resources needed by the project.

Chapter 20 looks at the management of queues. A system will have queues whenever a customer arrives for a service and finds that the server is busy. Many analyses have been done on different queuing problems, but the arithmetic can become tedious. Simulation provides an alternative way of tackling such problems.

Analysing business decisions

CHAPTER OUTLINE

This chapter discusses decision analysis. Its purpose is to show a rational approach to decision making, and to develop methods for improving decisions in a variety of circumstances.

The chapter starts by showing how some structure can be given to decisions. Then it considers decisions in situations of certainty, strict uncertainty (using decision criteria) and risk (using expected values and utilities).

As well as single decisions, series of sequential decisions are considered, emphasizing the use of decision trees.

After reading this chapter and doing the exercises you should be able to:

● draw a map of a decision situation

● construct a payoff matrix

● make decisions under certainty

● describe situations of strict uncertainty and use decision criteria to suggest decisions

● describe situations of risk and use expected values to suggest decisions

● use Bayes' theorem to update conditional probabilities for decisions under risk

● appreciate the use of utilities

● use decision trees to represent sequential decisions

17.1 | Giving structure to decisions

Everybody has to make decisions: which car is the best buy and when should we buy it; where should we eat; should we drive to work or go by train; which play should we go to; should we make tea or coffee; and so on. Such decisions come in a steady stream. Most decisions are fairly unimportant, and are made using a combination of experience, intuition and subjectivity. In business, however, decisions can be important, and managers need a more formal approach to decision making.

Many business decisions are complex and involve a number of interactions. Suppose a company makes an item but finds its profit is too low. Two obvious remedies for this are to reduce costs or increase the price. But if the price is increased the demand may decline. Conversely, if costs are reduced the price may be reduced and demand may increase. If demand changes, the factory may have to reschedule production and change marketing strategies. Changed production schedules could affect production of other items, change employment prospects and so on.

We could continue with these more or less random thoughts for some time, but would soon lose track of the main thrusts of our argument. For this reason it is useful to have a simple diagram that shows the interactions. A **problem map** is useful for this, and part of a map for the discussion above is given in Figure 17.1.

As you can see, the map is an informal way of representing a stream of connected ideas. Such maps are useful for sorting out ideas and clarifying interactions, but they do not help directly in decision making, as they do not identify good policies. There are several ways of identifying good decisions, and these are based on the structure of problems. Any situation where a decision is needed has a number of common characteristics.

Characteristics of decision making:

- a decision maker is responsible for making decisions
- a number of alternatives are available to the decision maker, who must select one of them
- the object of the decision maker is to select the best alternative
- when the decision has been made, events occur over which the decision maker has no control
- each combination of an alternative selected followed by an event happening leads to an outcome that has some measurable value

---

To illustrate these, consider a house owner who is offered fire insurance at a cost of £400 a year. The decision maker is the person who owns the house. They

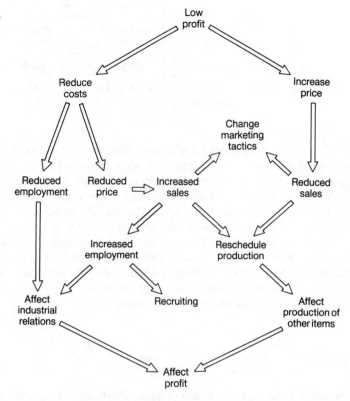

Figure 17.1   Part of a problem map.

have an objective of minimizing costs and must select the best alternative from:

(1) insure the house, or

(2) do not insure the house

Then an event happens, but the decision maker has no control over whether it is:

(1) the house burns down, or

(2) the house does not burn down

This problem has obviously been simplified, and in reality there are a number of alternative insurance companies and policies, the house may be damaged but not destroyed by fire, and so on. If the value of the house is £100,000 and the insurance company pays for all costs and inconvenience if the house burns down, we can summarize the combinations of alternatives, events and outcomes in the following table:

		Events	
		House burns down	House does not burn down
Alternatives	Insure house	£400	£400
	Do not insure house	£100,000	£0

This is called a **payoff matrix;** the entries show the cost to the house owner associated with every combination of alternative and event. It is important to remember that the alternatives (one of which has to be chosen) are listed down the left-hand side; the events (one of which happens and over which the decision maker has no control) are listed across the top. The values of the outcomes given in the body of the matrix are in consistent units and may be either costs or gains.

We have now used two distinct formats to describe the circumstances around decisions: maps and payoff matrices. Both of these are useful in adding a structure to an otherwise unstructured and complex situation. In the following sections we shall describe how these structures can be used to help make decisions in a number of different situations.

IN SUMMARY

Managers make decisions in complex situations. Maps and payoff matrices describe such situations and add structure to problems. This structure is based on the identification of events, alternatives and outcomes.

17.2 Decision making under certainty

The main characteristic of decision making under certainty is that we know, with certainty, which event will occur. We need only consider one event and the method of solution is obvious, in that all possible outcomes are listed and the alternative with the best outcome is selected.

Suppose we have £1,000 to invest for a year. We could list all the alternatives we want to consider and get the following payoff matrix:

		Event Gains interest to give at year end
Alternatives	Bank	£1,065
	Building society	£1,075
	Government stock	£1,085
	Stock market	£1,100
	Others	£1,060

We have obviously simplified the original problem by using 'others' to describe a range of alternatives and using forecast returns from investments in the stock market. There is only one event – 'gains interest' – and by looking down the list of outcomes the best alternative can be identified. The highest value at the end of the year comes from investing in the stock market.

In reality, even decisions under certainty can be difficult, particularly in complex situations. Would it be better, for example, for the Health Service to invest money in providing more kidney dialysis machines, giving nurses higher wages, doing open-heart surgery, funding research into cancer, or providing more parking spaces at hospitals?

WORKED EXAMPLE 17.1

A restaurant manager is given a booking for a large wedding banquet. He has a number of ways of providing staff, each with different associated costs. His most convenient alternatives are to pay full-time staff to work overtime (costing £400), hire current part-time staff for the day (£300), hire new temporary staff (£350) or use an agency (£550). Draw a payoff matrix for this decision and identify the alternative that minimizes cost.

Solution

The payoff matrix for this decision under certainty is shown below. The entries in this are costs, so we want to identify the lowest. This is £300 for hiring current part-time staff for the day.

		Event Pay staff
Alternatives	Pay full-time staff for overtime	400
	Hire current part-time staff	300
	Hire new temporary staff	350
	Use an agency	500

Self-assessment questions

17.1 Why are maps and payoff matrices useful for describing decision-making situations?

17.2 What are the five main characteristics of a decision process?

17.3 What is meant by 'decision making under certainty'?

17.3 | Decision making under strict uncertainty

When making decisions there are usually a number of events that may occur. Sometimes we cannot say which event actually will occur or even assign reasonable probabilities. If, for example, a person decides to change their job a number of events may happen: they may not like the new job and quickly start looking for another; they may get the sack; they may like the job and stay; they may be moved by the company. These events are essentially outside the control of the person taking a new job and it is impossible to assign reliable probabilities to them.

When no probabilities can be given to events we are dealing with **strict uncertainty**. Then simple rules called **decision criteria** are useful in recommending a solution. There are many different criteria, but we shall illustrate their use by three common ones.

17.3.1 | Laplace decision criterion

As no probabilities can be given to events, Laplace suggests that they should all be treated as equally likely and no more importance given to one event than to others. The method of determining the best alternative is:

(1) For each alternative find the mean value of the outcomes (that is, find the average of each row in the payoff matrix)

(2) Select the alternative with the best average outcome (that is, lowest cost or highest gain)

WORKED EXAMPLE 17.2

A restaurateur is going to set up a cream-tea stall at a local gala. On the morning of the gala she visits the wholesale market and has to decide whether to buy a large, medium or small quantity of strawberries. Her profit depends on the number of people attending the gala and this is largely determined by the weather. The matrix of gains (in thousands of pounds) for different weather conditions is given below. The gains in this matrix were found by subtracting the costs of buying strawberries from the net income. What quantity of strawberries should the restaurateur buy?

		Event		
		Weather good	Weather average	Weather poor
Alternatives	Large quantity	10	4	− 2
	Medium quantity	7	6	2
	Small quantity	4	1	4

Solution

(1) Taking the average value of outcomes for each alternative:

- large quantity $(10 + 4 - 2)/3 = 4$
- medium quantity $(7 + 6 + 2)/3 = 5$
- small quantity $(4 + 1 + 4)/3 = 3$

(2) Select the best average outcome. As these figures are profits the best is the highest, which is to buy a medium quantity.

| IN SUMMARY |

Decision criteria are simple rules for helping with decisions under strict uncertainty. The Laplace criterion finds the average outcome for each alternative, and selects the alternative with the best average outcome.

17.3.2 | **Wald decision criterion**

Most organizations have limited resources and cannot afford to risk a large loss. This is the basis of the Wald decision criterion, which assumes that decision makers are cautious (or even pessimistic) and want to avoid large potential losses. The steps are:

(1) For each alternative find the worst outcome.

(2) Select the alternative with the best of these worst outcomes.

With a payoff matrix showing costs, this is sometimes known as the 'minimax cost' criterion, as it looks for the maximum cost of each alternative and then selects the alternative with the minimum of these (that is, the minimum[maximum cost] or minimax cost).

WORKED EXAMPLE 17.3

Use the Wald decision criterion for the example of a cream-tea stall at a local gala described by the following gains matrix:

		Event		
		Weather good	Weather average	Weather poor
Alternatives	Large quantity	10	4	− 2
	Medium quantity	7	6	2
	Small quantity	4	1	4

Solution

Following the procedure described above:

(1) Taking the worst value of outcomes for each alternative:

- large quantity = minimum of $[10, 4, -2] = -2$
- medium quantity = minimum of $[7, 6, 2] = 2$
- small quantity = minimum of $[4, 1, 4] = 1$

(2) Select the best of these worst outcomes. As the figures are profits the best is the highest, which comes from buying a medium quantity.

IN SUMMARY

The Wald decision criterion is pessimistic and assumes that the worst outcome will occur. Then it chooses the alternative with the best of these worst outcomes.

17.3.3 | Savage decision criterion

Sometimes we are judged not by how well we actually did but by how well we could possibly have done. A student who gets 70% in an exam might be judged by the fact that he did not get 100%. An investment broker who recommended a client to invest in platinum may be judged not by the fact that platinum rose 15% in value, but by the fact that gold rose 25%. This happens particularly when performance is judged by someone other than the decision maker.

In such cases there is a **regret,** which is the difference between actual outcome and best possible outcome. A student who gets 70% has a regret of $100 - 70 = 30\%$. An investor who gains 15% when they could have gained 25% has a regret of $25 - 15 = 10\%$. The Savage criterion is based on these regrets. It is essentially pessimistic and minimizes the maximum regret. The steps are:

(1) For each event find the best possible outcome (that is, find the best entry in each column of the payoff matrix).

(2) Find the regret for every other entry in the column, which is the difference between the best in the column and the entry.

(3) Put the regrets found in Step 2 into a 'regret matrix'. There should be at least one zero in each column, and regrets are always positive.

(4) For each alternative find the highest regret (that is, the largest number in each row).

(5) Select the alternative with the lowest value of these highest regrets.

As you can see, steps 4 and 5 apply the Wald criterion to the regret matrix.

WORKED EXAMPLE 17.4

Use the Savage criterion on the example of the cream-tea stall at a local gala described by the following gains matrix:

		Event		
		Weather good	Weather average	Weather poor
Alternatives	Large quantity	**10**	4	− 2
	Medium quantity	7	**6**	2
	Small quantity	4	1	**4**

Solution

Using the steps described above:

(1) The best outcome for each event is shown in bold (that is, with good weather a large quantity, with average weather a medium quantity and with poor weather a small quantity).

(2) The regret for every other entry in the column is the difference between this bold value and the actual entry. Thus if the weather is good and a medium quantity had been bought the regret would be $10 - 7 = 3$. If the weather is good and a small quantity had been bought the regret would be $10 - 4 = 6$, and so on.

(3) Form these regret figures into a regret matrix, replacing the original profit figures:

| | | Event | | |
		Weather good	Weather average	Weather poor
Alternatives	Large quantity	0	2	6
	Medium quantity	3	0	2
	Small quantity	6	5	0

(4) For each alternative find the highest regret:
- large quantity = maximum of [0, 2, 6] = 6
- medium quantity = maximum of [3, 0, 2] = 3
- small quantity = maximum of [6, 5, 0] = 6

(5) Select the alternative with the lowest of these maximum regrets. This is the medium quantity.

IN SUMMARY

The Savage criterion considers regret, which is the difference between the best outcome for an event and the actual outcome. Then it finds the highest regret for each alternative and selects the alternative with the lowest of these highest regrets.

17.3.4 | Selecting the criterion to use

Often different criteria recommend the same alternative, but there is no guarantee of this. When different alternatives are recommended the most relevant criterion should be used. If, for example, the decision maker is working as a consultant and will be held responsible to others for the quality of his decisions, there may be a case for using the Savage criterion. If the decision is made for a small company that cannot afford to risk high losses, then Wald may be best. If there is really nothing to chose between the different events, then Laplace may be useful.

Although it is difficult to go beyond these general guidelines one other factor should be noted. Both the Wald and Savage criteria effectively recommend their decision based on one outcome (the worst for Wald, and the one that leads to the highest regret for Savage). This means that the choice might be dominated by a few atypical results. The Laplace criterion is the only one that uses all values to make its recommendation.

It could be that none of the criteria we have looked at is suitable. Those described are only illustrative and there is a range of others that could be used. An ambitious organization might aim for the highest profit and use a criterion that selects the alternative that gives the highest return (a 'maximax profit' criterion). Alternatively it may try to balance the best and worst outcomes for each event and use a criterion based on selecting the best value for:

$$\alpha \times \text{best outcome} + (1 - \alpha) \times \text{worst outcome}$$

where α is given a value between zero and one.

Different criteria often suggest the same alternative, and this perhaps reduces the importance of selecting the 'right' one for a particular application. Certainly, a major strength of decision criteria is not their ability to recommend good alternatives, but their use in formalizing the structure of a problem and allowing informed discussion.

WORKED EXAMPLE 17.5

The following payoff matrix shows the costs associated with a decision. Use the Laplace, Wald and Savage decision criteria to select the best alternatives.

	1	2	3
A	14	22	6
B	19	18	12
C	12	17	15

Solution

● As the entries are costs, Laplace would select the alternative with the lowest average costs, which is alternative A:

	1	2	3	Mean
A	14	22	6	**14.0***
B	19	18	12	16.3
C	12	17	15	14.7

● Wald would assume that the highest cost would occur for each alternative, and then select the lowest of these. This suggests alternative C:

	1	2	3	Highest
A	14	22	6	22
B	19	18	12	19
C	12	17	15	**17***

● Savage would form the regret matrix, find the highest regret for each alternative and select the alternative with the lowest of these. This is alternative A:

Regret	1	2	3	Highest
A	2	5	0	**5***
B	7	1	6	7
C	0	0	9	9

Self-assessment questions

17.4 What is meant by decision making under strict uncertainty?

17.5 List three useful decision criteria.

17.6 How many of these criteria take into account all outcomes associated with a particular alternative?

17.7 Are the listed criteria the only ones available? If not, suggest others that might be useful.

17.4 | Decision making under risk

In the last section we considered decision making under strict uncertainty, where a number of events could occur but there was no indication of the relative likelihood of each. With decision making under risk there are again a number of events, but now probabilities can be given to each of them. As every event should be included, these probabilities should add to one. A simple example of decision making under risk is a gamble on the outcome of spinning a coin. The events are the coin coming down heads or tails, and probabilities can be put to these (0.5 in each case).

17.4.1 | Expected values

Problems with risk are solved by calculating the **expected value** for each alternative and selecting the alternative with the best expected value. The expected value is defined as the sum of the probability times the value of the outcome:

$$\text{expected value} = \Sigma \text{ probability} \times \text{value of outcome}$$

The expected value for an alternative is the average gain (or cost) that would be expected if the decision were repeated a large number of times. It is not the value that would be returned *every* time but the average value for a large number of repetitions.

Then for decision making under risk there are two steps:

(1) Calculate the expected value for each alternative.

(2) Select the alternative with the best expected value (that is, highest value for gains and lowest value for costs).

WORKED EXAMPLE 17.6

What is the best alternative for the following matrix of gains?

		Events			
		1 $P = 0.1$	2 $P = 0.2$	3 $P = 0.6$	4 $P = 0.1$
Alternatives	A	10	7	5	9
	B	3	20	2	10
	C	3	4	11	1
	D	8	4	2	16

Solution

Calculating the expected value for each alternative as the sum of the probability times the value of the outcome gives:

- alternative A: $0.1 \times 10 + 0.2 \times 7 + 0.6 \times 5 + 0.1 \times 9 = 6.3$
- alternative B: $0.1 \times 3 + 0.2 \times 20 + 0.6 \times 2 + 0.1 \times 10 = 6.5$
- alternative C: $0.1 \times 3 + 0.2 \times 4 + 0.6 \times 11 + 0.1 \times 1 = 7.8$
- alternative D: $0.1 \times 8 + 0.2 \times 4 + 0.6 \times 2 + 0.1 \times 16 = 4.4$

As these are gains, the best alternative is C with an expected value of 7.8. If this decision is made repeatedly the average return in the long run will be 7.8; if the decision is made only once the gain could be any of the four values 3, 4, 11 or 1.

WORKED EXAMPLE 17.7

A transport firm bids for a long-term contract to move newspapers from a printing works to wholesalers. It can submit one of three tenders: a low one based on an assumption of increased newspaper sales and hence reduced unit transport costs; a medium one that would give a satisfactory return if newspaper sales stay the same; or a high one that assumes newspaper sales will decline and unit transport costs will increase. The probabilities of newspaper sales and profits (in thousands of pounds) for the transport firm are shown in the following table. Based on this matrix, which tender should it submit?

	Newspaper sales		
	decrease $P = 0.4$	stay same $P = 0.3$	increase $P = 0.3$
Low tender	10	15	16
Medium tender	5	20	10
High tender	18	10	− 5

Solution

Calculating the expected value for each alternative:

- low tender: $0.4 \times 10 + 0.3 \times 15 + 0.3 \times 16 = 13.3$
- medium tender: $0.4 \times 5 + 0.3 \times 20 + 0.3 \times 10 = 11.0$
- high tender: $0.4 \times 18 + 0.3 \times 10 - 0.3 \times 5 = 8.7$

As these are profits, the best alternative is the one with highest expected value, which is the low tender.

IN SUMMARY

Expected values are defined as Σ probability $\times$ value of outcome. They can be used to suggest the best alternative in situations of risk.

17.4.2 | Using Bayes' theorem to update probabilities

In Chapter 13 we discussed how Bayes' theorem could be used to update conditional probabilities:

$$P(a/b) = \frac{P(b/a) \times P(a)}{P(b)}$$

where:

$P(a/b)$ = probability of event a happening given that b has already happened

$P(b/a)$ = probability of b given that a has already happened

$P(a)$, $P(b)$ = probabilities of a and b respectively

Bayes' theorem can be used for updating conditional probabilities of events, as illustrated in the following worked examples.

WORKED EXAMPLE 17.8

The crowd for a sports event might be small (with a probability of 0.4) or large. To help organize the event, advance sales of tickets can be analysed a week before the event takes place. The advance sales can be classified as high, average or low, with the probability of advance sales conditional on crowd size given by the following table:

		Advance sales		
		High	Average	Low
Crowd size	Large	0.7	0.3	0.0
	Small	0.2	0.2	0.6

The organizers must chose one of two plans in running the event, and the table below gives the net profit in thousands of pounds for each combination of plan and crowd size:

		Plan 1	Plan 2
Crowd size	Large	10	14
	Small	9	5

If the organizers use the information on advance sales, what strategy would maximize their expected profits? How much should they pay for the information on advance sales?

Solution

We can use the abbreviations:

- CL and CS for crowd size large and crowd size small
- ASH, ASA and ASL for advance sales high, average and small.

If the organizers do not use the information on advance sales, the best they can do is use the probabilities of large and small crowds (0.6 and 0.4 respectively) to calculate expected values for the two plans:

- Plan 1: $0.6 \times 10 + 0.4 \times 9 = 9.6$
- Plan 2: $0.6 \times 14 + 0.4 \times 5 = \mathbf{10.4}$ better plan

They would use plan 2 with an expected value of £10,400.

If the organizers do use the information on advance ticket sales they can use the conditional probabilities $P(ASH/CL)$, $P(ASH/CS)$, etc. We should really like these the other way around, $P(CL/ASH)$, $P(CS/ASH)$, etc, and Bayes' theorem will give these. The calculations are shown in the following table (if you have forgotten the details of these calculations you should look them up in Chapter 13):

	ASH	ASA	ASL		ASH	ASA	ASL
CL	0.7	0.3	0.0	0.6	0.42	0.18	0.00
CS	0.2	0.2	0.6	0.4	0.08	0.08	0.24
					0.50	0.26	0.24
				CL	0.84	0.69	0.00
				CS	0.16	0.31	1.00

The probability of advance sales being high is 0.5. If this happens, the probability of a large crowd is 0.84 and that of a small crowd is 0.16. Then, if the organizers choose plan 1 the expected value is $0.84 \times 10 + 0.16 \times 9 = 9.84$; if the organizers choose plan 2 their expected value is $0.84 \times 14 + 0.16 \times 5 = 12.56$. This shows that if advance sales are high they should choose plan 2.

This reasoning can be extended to the other alternatives:

ASH: Plan 1 $0.84 \times 10 + 0.16 \times 9 = 9.84$

Plan 2 $0.84 \times 14 + 0.16 \times 5 = \mathbf{12.56}$

ASA: Plan 1 $0.69 \times 10 + 0.31 \times 9 = 9.69$

Plan 2 $0.69 \times 14 + 0.31 \times 5 = \mathbf{11.21}$

ASL: Plan 1 $0.00 \times 10 + 1.00 \times 9 = \mathbf{9.00}$

Plan 2 $0.00 \times 14 + 1.00 \times 5 = 5.00$

The overall strategy that maximizes the organizer's profit is: if the advance sales are high or average select plan 2; if they are low select plan 1.

We can go a little further with this analysis, as we know the probability of high, average and low advance sales are respectively 0.5, 0.26 and 0.24. Thus we can calculate the overall expected value of following the recommended strategy as:

$$0.5 \times 12.56 + 0.26 \times 11.21 + 0.24 \times 9 = 11.35$$

This can be compared with the expected profit of £10,400 when the advance sales information is not used; using the additional information raises expected profits by 11 350 − 10 400 = £950, or over 9%.

WORKED EXAMPLE 17.9

An oil company drills an exploratory well in deep water off the Irish coast. The company is uncertain of the amount of recoverable oil that it will find, but experience suggests that it could be classified as minor (with a probability of 0.3), significant (with probability 0.5) or major. The company now has to decide how to develop the find and has a choice of either moving quickly to minimize the cost of long-term debt, or moving slowly to ensure continued income. The profits for every combination of size and development speed are given in the following table, where entries are in millions of pounds:

| | Size of find | | |
	Minor	Significant	Major
Develop quickly	100	130	180
Develop slowly	80	150	210

Some further geological tests can be done to give a more accurate picture of the size of the find, but these cost £2.5 million and are not entirely accurate. The tests give results classified as A, B and C with conditional probabilities of results given size of find shown in the following table:

		Test result		
		A	B	C
Find size	Minor	0.3	0.4	0.3
	Significant	0.5	0.0	0.5
	Major	0.25	0.25	0.5

If the oil company wants to maximize its profits, should it do the geological tests?

Solution

Defining the abbreviations:

- MIN, SIG and MAJ for minor, significant and major finds
- QUICK and SLOW for the quick and slow development

then, without using the further geological test, the expected values with each speed of development are:

- QUICK $0.3 \times 100 + 0.5 \times 130 + 0.2 \times 180 = 131$
- SLOW $0.3 \times 80 + 0.5 \times 150 + 0.2 \times 210 = \mathbf{141}$

The company should develop the find slowly with an expected value of £141 million.

From the geological test the company will want information in the form $P(\text{MIN}/A)$, etc, but it is actually presented in the form $P(A/\text{MIN})$, so Bayes' theorem should be used:

	A	B	C		A	B	C
MIN	0.3	0.4	0.3	0.3	0.09	0.12	0.09
SIG	0.5	0.0	0.5	0.5	0.25	0.00	0.25
MAJ	0.25	0.25	0.5	0.2	0.05	0.05	0.10
					0.39	0.17	0.44
				MIN	0.23	0.71	0.20
				SIG	0.64	0.00	0.57
				MAJ	0.13	0.29	0.23

If the test result is A, the probabilities of minor significant and major finds are 0.23, 0.64 and 0.13 respectively. Developing the well quickly will give a profit, which is found by multiplying the profits for each size by the probability to give:

expected profit with test result A and developing quickly

$$= 0.23 \times 100 + 0.64 \times 130 + 0.13 \times 180 = 129.6$$

Repeating this calculation for other results gives the following values:

A: QUICK $0.23 \times 100 + 0.64 \times 130 + 0.13 \times 180 = 129.6$

   SLOW $0.23 \times 80 + 0.64 \times 150 + 0.13 \times 210 =$ **141.7**

B: QUICK $0.71 \times 100 + 0.00 \times 130 + 0.29 \times 180 =$ **123.2**

   SLOW $0.71 \times 80 + 0.00 \times 150 + 0.29 \times 210 = 117.7$

C: QUICK $0.20 \times 100 + 0.57 \times 130 + 0.23 \times 180 = 135.5$

   SLOW $0.20 \times 80 + 0.57 \times 150 + 0.23 \times 210 =$ **149.8**

The best policy would be to develop slowly if test results are A or C and quickly if the test results are B. This policy would have an expected value of

$$0.39 \times 141.7 + 0.17 \times 123.2 + 0.44 \times 149.8 = 142.12$$

Profit without doing the tests is £141 million while doing the test raises it to £142.12 minus the cost of £2.5 million. In these circumstances it is not worth doing the tests, and would not be worth doing them unless their cost was less than £1.12 million.

17.4.3 | Utilities

Expected values are easy to use but they have drawbacks. In particular, they do not always reflect real preferences. Consider the investment in the payoff matrix below, which has a 90% chance of yielding a loss:

		Events	
		Gain $P = 0.1$	Lose $P = 0.9$
Alternatives	Invest	£500,000	– £50,000
	Do not invest	£0	£0

The expected values are:

- invest $0.1 \times 500\,000 - 0.9 \times 50\,000 = £5000$

- do not invest $0.1 \times 0 + 0.9 \times 0 = £0$

Expected values would suggest investing even though there is a 90% chance of losing. The reason is that expected values represent the average value in the long run when the decision is repeated a large number of times. If a decision is made only once expected values may give misleading advice. For this reason **utilities** have been developed, which reflect more accurately the real value of money.

Expected values assume a linear relationship between the amount of money and its value. Then £100 has a value a hundred times as great as £1, and £1,000,000 has a value ten thousand times as great as £100. In practice this strict linear relationship must be doubted. A graph of a more realistic utility function is shown in Figure 17.2.

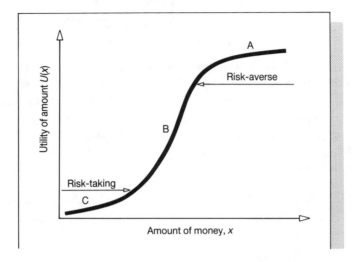

Figure 17.2   Utility curve relating amount of money to its value.

The utility function in Figure 17.2 has three distinct regions. At the top, near point A, the utility is rising slowly with the amount of money. A decision maker in this region already has a lot of money and would not put a high value on even more. However, the decision maker would certainly not like to lose money and move nearer to point B where the utility falls rapidly. Gaining an amount of money is not very attractive but losing it is very unattractive, so this leads to a conservative decision maker who does not like to take risks.

Region B on the graph has the utility of money almost linear, which is the assumption of expected values. A decision maker at point C does not have much money, so losing any would not appreciably affect the utility. Conversely, gaining money and moving nearer to B would have a high value. A decision maker here will be keen to make a gain and not unduly mind a loss, which is characteristic of a risk taker.

Although utilities are useful in principle, defining a reasonable function presents a major problem. Each individual and organization has a different appreciation of the value of money and therefore will work on a different utility function. Moreover, these curves vary over time. This problem is so difficult to overcome that relatively little practical use is made of utility theory. In principle, however, once a utility function is established the process of selecting the best alternative is the same as with expected values, but with expected utilities replacing expected values.

WORKED EXAMPLE 17.10

Suppose a person's utility curve is a reasonable approximation to $\sqrt{x}$. What is their best decision when faced by the following gains matrix?

		Events		
		X $P = 0.7$	Y $P = 0.2$	Z $P = 0.1$
Alternatives	A	14	24	12
	B	6	40	90
	C	1	70	30
	D	12	12	6

Solution

The calculations are similar to those for expected values, except the amount of money, x, is replaced by its utility, $U(x)$, which in this case is the square root, $\sqrt{x}$.

- alternative A: $0.7 \times \sqrt{14} + 0.2 \times \sqrt{24} + 0.1 \times \sqrt{12} = \mathbf{3.95}$
- alternative B: $0.7 \times \sqrt{6} + 0.2 \times \sqrt{40} + 0.1 \times \sqrt{90} = 3.93$
- alternative C: $0.7 \times \sqrt{1} + 0.2 \times \sqrt{70} + 0.1 \times \sqrt{30} = 2.92$
- alternative D: $0.7 \times \sqrt{12} + 0.2 \times \sqrt{12} + 0.1 \times \sqrt{6} = 3.36$

Although the difference is small, the best alternative is A. (If you calculate the results using expected values you will find that alternative B is the best.)

IN SUMMARY

Utilities are designed to reflect the value of different amounts of money. Expected utilities can be used to help decisions in situations of risk, provided a realistic utility function can be defined.

Self-assessment questions

17.8 What is meant by 'decision making under risk'?

17.9 What is the expected value of a course of action?

17.10 Could a subjective probability be assigned to events under risk?

17.11 When could Bayes' theorem be used to calculate expected values?

17.12 Why might expected utilities be a better measure than expected values?

17.5 | Sequential decisions and decision trees

So far we have looked at single decisions. In other words, the problem is finished when the best alternative has been selected. However, there are many situations where one decision leads to a series of other decisions. If, for example, we decide to buy a car the initial decision might be to choose a new or a second-hand one. If a new car is chosen, this opens the choice of British, Japanese, French, German, Italian or others. If the choice here is a British car the choice is Rover, Jaguar, Ford, Rolls Royce, Vauxhall, and so on. Then if a Rover is chosen a range of other decisions have to be made. At each stage in the decision process the selection of one alternative opens up a series of other choices (or sometimes events). These can best be represented by a **decision tree**, in which the alternatives (or events) are represented by the branches of a horizontal tree. This is illustrated in the following example.

WORKED EXAMPLE 17.11

A company approaches a bank manager for a loan to finance an expansion. The bank manager has to decide whether or not to grant the loan. If the bank manager grants the loan the company expansion may be successful or it may not. If the bank manager does not grant the loan, the company may continue banking as before or it may move its account to another bank. Draw a decision tree of this situation.

Solution

A decision tree shows the sequence of alternatives and events. There is a notional timescale going from left to right with early decisions or events on the left followed by later ones towards the right. There is only one decision in this example followed by events over which the bank manager has no control, so the sequence is:

- the manager makes a decision
- one of several possible events happens

These can be represented by the decision tree shown in Figure 17.3.

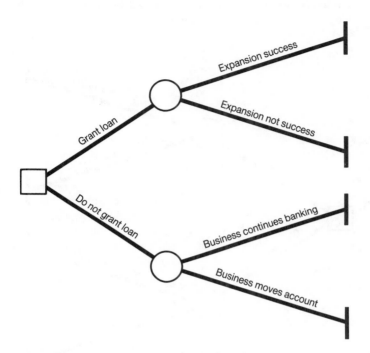

Figure 17.3   Decision tree for Worked Example 17.11.

In the decision tree the alternatives and events have been represented by the branches, so each branch represents a different path (decision or event) that may be followed through the tree. There are also three distinct types of node, which are the points from which branches come:

| **terminal node.** These are at the right-hand side of the tree and show the ends of all sequences of decisions and events.

○ **random node.** These represent points at which things happen, so that all branches leaving random nodes are events with known probabilities.

□ **decision node.** These represent points at which decisions are made, so that all branches leaving a decision node are alternatives, the best of which is selected.

This is the basic structure of the tree, but probabilities and values still have to be added. Suppose the bank currently values its business with the company at £2,000 a year. If the manager grants the loan and the expansion succeeds the value to the bank of increased business and interest charges is £3,000 a year. If the expansion does not succeed the bank will still have business valued at £1,000 a year (reduced because of reduced volume and allowance for writing off bad debt). There is a probability of 0.7 that the expansion plan will prove successful. If the manager does not grant the loan there is a probability of 0.6 that the company will transfer its account to another bank. These figures can be added to the tree as shown in Figure 17.4.

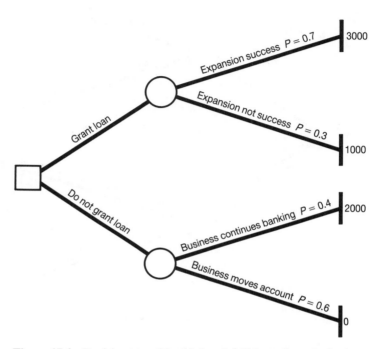

Figure 17.4 Decision tree with added probabilities and terminal values.

The probabilities are now entered on the appropriate event branches (ensuring all events are included and the sum of the probabilities from each random node equals one). Values have been put on terminal nodes, representing the total value of moving through the tree and reaching the terminal node. In this case these values are the annual business expected by the bank.

The next stage of the analysis moves from right to left through the tree and assigns a value to each node in turn. This is done by finding the best decision at each decision node and the expected value at each random node.

- At each decision node the alternative branches leaving are connected to following nodes. The values on these following nodes are compared, the best branch is selected and the node value is transferred.

- At each random node the value is the expected value of the leaving event branches (that is, the sum, for all branches, of the probability of leaving by a branch times the value of the node at the end of the branch).

The value at the left-hand originating node is the overall expected value of following the best policies.

Using this procedure on the tree in Figure 17.4 gives the results shown in Figure 17.5.

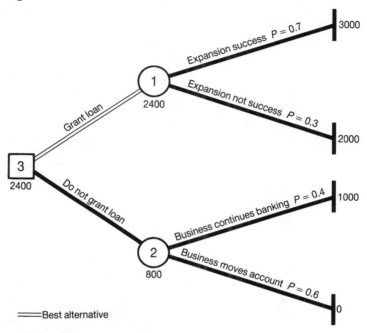

Figure 17.5 Analysing a decision tree.

The calculations are as follows:

At random node 1 calculate expected value:

$$0.7 \times 3000 + 0.3 \times 1000 = 2400$$

At random node 2 calculate expected value:

$$0.4 \times 2000 + 0.6 \times 0 = 800$$

At decision node 3 select the best alternative:

Maximum of $[2400, 800] = 2400$

The best policy is to grant the loan, and this will have an expected value of £2,400.

WORKED EXAMPLE 17.12

Draw a decision tree of the problem of planning a sports event described in Worked Example 17.8.

Solution

This problem has a single decision for which we have already done the calculations. These can be drawn on the tree shown in Figure 17.6. Overall, the expected value is confirmed as £11,350 using the advance sales information.

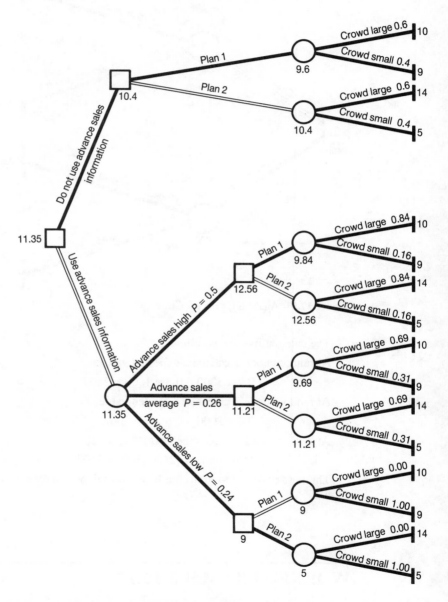

Figure 17.6 Decision tree for Worked Example 17.12 (for problem in Worked Example 17.8).

WORKED EXAMPLE 17.13

A workshop is about to install a new machine for stamping and pressing parts for domestic appliances. Three suppliers have made bids to supply the machine. The first supplier offers the Basicor machine, which automatically produces parts of acceptable, but not outstanding, quality. The output from the machine is variable (depending on material supplied and a variety of settings) but could be 1000 a week (with probability 0.1), 2000 a week (with probability 0.7) or 3000 a week. The notional profit for this machine is £4 a unit. The second supplier offers a Superstamp machine, which makes higher quality parts. The output from this can be 700 a week (with probability 0.4) or 1000 a week, with a notional profit of £10 a unit. The third supplier offers the Switchover machine, which can be set to produce either 1,300 high-quality parts a week at a profit of £6 a unit, or 1600 medium-quality parts a week with a profit of £5 a unit.

If the machine produces 2000 or more units a week, it is possible to export all production as a single bulk order. Then there is a 60% chance of selling for 50% more profit, and a 40% chance of selling for 50% less profit.

What should be done to maximize expected profits?

Solution

The tree for this decision is shown in Figure 17.7. The terminal node values are weekly profit found by multiplying the number produced by the profit per unit. If 1000 are produced on the Basicor machine the value is £4,000, and so on. If the output from Basicor is exported, profit may be increased by 50% (that is, to £6 a unit) or reduced by 50% (that is, to £2 a unit).

Calculations at each node are as follows:

(1) Expected value at random node
$$= 0.6 \times 12\,000 + 0.4 \times 4000 = 8800$$

(2) Expected value at random node
$$= 0.6 \times 18\,000 + 0.4 \times 6000 = 13\,200$$

(3) Best alternative at decision node
$$= MAX[8800, 8000] = 8800$$

(4) Best alternative at decision node
$$= MAX[13\,200, 12\,000] = 13\,200$$

(5) Expected value at random node
$$= 0.1 \times 4000 + 0.7 \times 8800 + 0.2 \times 13\,200 = 9200$$

(6) Expected value at random node
$$= 0.4 \times 7000 + 0.6 \times 10\,000 = 8800$$

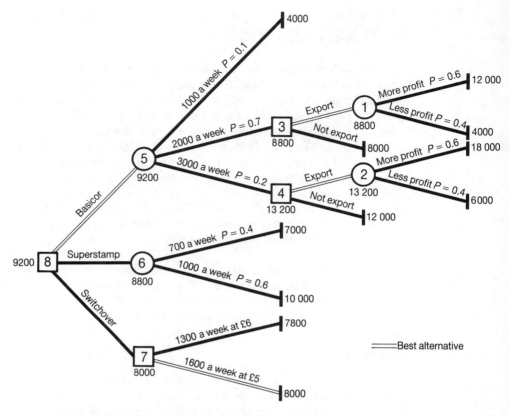

Figure 17.7 Decision tree for Worked Example 17.13

(7) Best alternative at decision node
= MAX[7800, 8000] = 8000
(8) Best alternative at decision node
= MAX[9200, 8800, 8000] = 9200

The best overall policy is to buy the Basicor machine and, if it produces more than 2000 units, export all production. The expected profit from this policy is £9,200 a week.

Decision trees can involve a lot of arithmetic, but they are not easy to draw with a computer. Most software lists tables of results without actually drawing a tree. Figure 17.8 shows a typical printout for Worked Example 17.13. This needs all nodes to be numbered as well as branches from decision nodes, so the tree has to be drawn by hand and then the computer calculates node values. (Notice that the computer assigns different node numbers from the ones used in Figure 17.7.)

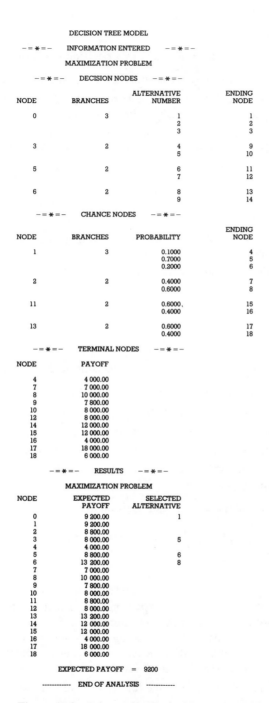

DECISION TREE MODEL

− = * = −   INFORMATION ENTERED   − = * = −

MAXIMIZATION PROBLEM

− = * = −   DECISION NODES   − = * = −

NODE	BRANCHES	ALTERNATIVE NUMBER	ENDING NODE
0	3	1	1
		2	2
		3	3
3	2	4	9
		5	10
5	2	6	11
		7	12
6	2	8	13
		9	14

− = * = −   CHANCE NODES   − = * = −

NODE	BRANCHES	PROBABILITY	ENDING NODE
1	3	0.1000	4
		0.7000	5
		0.2000	6
2	2	0.4000	7
		0.6000	8
11	2	0.6000,	15
		0.4000	16
13	2	0.6000	17
		0.4000	18

− = * = −   TERMINAL NODES   − = * = −

NODE	PAYOFF
4	4 000.00
7	7 000.00
8	10 000.00
9	7 800.00
10	8 000.00
12	8 000.00
14	12 000.00
15	12 000.00
16	4 000.00
17	18 000.00
18	6 000.00

− = * = −   RESULTS   − = * = −

MAXIMIZATION PROBLEM

NODE	EXPECTED PAYOFF	SELECTED ALTERNATIVE
0	9 200.00	1
1	9 200.00	
2	8 800.00	
3	8 000.00	5
4	4 000.00	
5	8 800.00	6
6	13 200.00	8
7	7 000.00	
8	10 000.00	
9	7 800.00	
10	8 000.00	
11	8 800.00	
12	8 000.00	
13	13 200.00	
14	12 000.00	
15	12 000.00	
16	4 000.00	
17	18 000.00	
18	6 000.00	

EXPECTED PAYOFF = 9200

−−−−−−−−−−− END OF ANALYSIS −−−−−−−−−−−

Figure 17.8   Printout for Worked Example 17.13.

| IN SUMMARY |

Sequential decisions can be represented by a decision tree. For this we:

● determine the alternatives, events and their probabilities, outcomes, etc

● draw a tree (moving from left to right) showing the sequences of events and alternatives, and setting the values at terminal nodes

● analyse the tree (moving from right to left) selecting the best alternative at decision nodes and calculating the expected value at random nodes

Self-assessment questions

17.13 How is the node value calculated at a terminal node, a decision node and a random node?

17.14 How is the best policy determined from a decision tree?

| CHAPTER REVIEW |

This chapter has described some aspects of decision analysis. In particular it:

● outlined the characteristics of decision making

● described decision maps and payoff matrices

● mentioned decision making under certainty

● used decision criteria for decision making under strict uncertainty

● calculated expected values for decision making under risk

● mentioned utilities

● discussed sequential decisions and decision trees

Problems

17.1 A pub on the seafront at Blackpool notices that its profits are declining. The landlord has a number of alternatives for increasing his profits (attracting more customers, increasing prices, getting customers to spend more, etc) but each of these leads to a string of effects. Draw a map illustrating interactions for this situation.

17.2 Select the best alternatives in the following matrix of gains:

		Event
Alternatives	a	100
	b	950
	c	− 250
	d	0
	e	950
	f	500

17.3 Use the Laplace, Wald and Savage decision criteria to select alternatives in the following matrices:

(a) Cost matrix

		Events				
		1	2	3	4	5
Alternatives	a	100	70	115	95	60
	b	95	120	120	90	150
	c	180	130	60	160	120
	d	80	75	50	100	95
	e	60	140	100	170	160

(b) Gains matrix

		Events			
		1	2	3	4
Alternatives	a	1	6	3	7
	b	2	5	1	4
	c	8	1	4	2
	d	5	2	7	8

17.4 (a) Which is the best alternative in the following situation of risk described by a gains matrix?

		Events		
		1	2	3
		$P = 0.4$	$P = 0.3$	$P = 0.3$
Alternatives	a	100	90	120
	b	80	102	110

(b) Would this decision change if a utility function $U(x) = \sqrt{x}$ were used?

17.5 A company can launch one of three versions of a new product, X, Y or Z. The profit depends on market reaction and there is a 30% chance that this will be good, a 40% chance that it will be medium and a 30% chance that it will be poor. Which version should the company launch if profits are as given in the following table?

		Market reaction		
		Good	Medium	Poor
Version	X	100	110	80
	Y	70	90	120
	Z	130	100	70

A market survey can be done to give more information on market reaction. Experience suggests that these surveys give results A, B or C with probabilities $P(A/\text{Good})$, etc shown in the following table:

		Result		
		A	B	C
Market reaction	Good	0.2	0.2	0.6
	Medium	0.2	0.5	0.3
	Poor	0.4	0.3	0.3

How much should the company be prepared to pay for this information?

17.6 A road haulage contractor owns a lorry with a one-year-old engine. He has to decide now, and again in one year's time, whether or not to replace the engine. If he decides to replace it, this will cost £500. If he does not replace it there is an increased chance that it will break down during the year, and the cost of replacing an engine then is £800. If an engine is replaced during the year the replacement engine is assumed to be one year old at the time when the next decision is taken. The probability of breakdown of an engine during a year is as follows:

	Age of engine in years		
	0	1	2
Probability of breakdown	0.0	0.2	0.7

Draw a decision tree for this problem and find the decisions that minimize cost over the next two years.

17.7 An organization is considering launching an entirely new service. If the market reaction to this service is good (which has a probability of 0.2) the organization will make £3,000 a week; if market reaction is medium (with probability 0.5) it will make £1,000 a week; but if reaction is poor (with probability 0.3) it will lose £1,500 a week. The organization could run a survey to test market reaction with results A, B or C. Experience suggests that the reliability of such surveys is described by the following matrix of

$P(A/\text{good})$, etc. Use a decision tree to find how much the organization should be prepared to pay for this survey.

		A	Result B	C
Market reaction	Good	0.7	0.2	0.1
	Medium	0.2	0.6	0.2
	Poor	0.1	0.4	0.5

17.8 A television company has an option on a new six-part series. They could sell the rights to this series to the network for £100,000, or they could make the series themselves. If they make the series themselves, advertising profit from each episode is not known exactly but could be £15,000 (with a probability of 0.25), £24,000 (with a probability of 0.45) or £29,000, depending on the success of the series.

A local production company can be hired to run a pilot for the series. For a cost of £30,000 they will give either a favourable or an unfavourable report on the chances of the series being a success. The reliability of their report (phrased in terms of the probability of a favourable report given the likely advertising profit, etc) is given in the following table.

	Advertising profit		
	£15,000	£24,000	£29,000
Unfavourable report	0.85	0.65	0.3
Favourable report	0.15	0.35	0.7

Draw a decision tree of this problem and identify the best course of action and expected profit.

Computer exercises

17.1 Figure 17.9 shows a printout of a program that does the calculations for decision criteria. Describe the criteria that are being used. Use a package to check these results. What other criteria are available? What is the largest problem that you can tackle?

$$-=*=-\quad\text{INFORMATION ENTERED}\quad-=*=-$$

NUMBER OF STATES	: 5
NUMBER OF ALTERNATIVES	: 5
HURWICZ COEFFICIENT	: .3

PAYOFF TABLE

STATES   PAYOFF FROM EACH ALTERNATIVE

STATES	1	2	3	4	5
1	1.00	5.00	9.00	2.00	6.00
2	3.00	7.00	3.00	5.00	1.00
3	6.00	4.00	4.00	6.00	8.00
4	8.00	2.00	7.00	5.00	6.00
5	6.00	9.00	4.00	1.00	2.00

DECISION MAKING UNDER STRICT UNCERTAINTY

$$-=*=-\quad\text{RESULTS}\quad-=*=-$$

CRITERION	ALTERNATIVE	PAYOFF
1. MAXIMAX	A2	9.00
2. MAXIMIN	A3	3.00
3. LIKELIHOOD	A2	5.40
4. MINIMAX REGRET	A3	5.00
5. HURWICZ RULE	A3	4.80

------------ END OF ANALYSIS ------------

Figure 17.9   Computer printout for decision criteria.

17.2 Design a spreadsheet that finds the best alternative when using a variety of decision criteria.

17.3 Figure 17.10 shows a printout for a program that does the calculations for a decision tree. Examine this printout, and make sure you understand what is happening. Draw the tree being described. Use an equivalent package to check the results.

—=＊=—   INFORMATION ENTERED   —=＊=—

MINIMIZATION PROBLEM

—=＊=—   DECISION NODES   —=＊=—

NODE	BRANCHES	ALTERNATIVE NUMBER	ENDING NODE
0	3	1	1
		2	2
		3	3
7	2	4	9
		5	10
8	2	6	11
		7	12

—=＊=—   CHANCE NODES   —=＊=—

NODE	BRANCHES	PROBABILITY	ENDING NODE
2	3	0.3000	4
		0.3000	5
		0.4000	6
3	2	0.5000	7
		0.5000	8
10	3	0.4800	13
		0.3600	14
		0.1600	15
12	3	0.1200	16
		0.2400	17
		0.6400	18

—=＊=—   TERMINAL NODES   —=＊=—

NODE	PAYOFF
1	22 000.00
4	16 000.00
5	22 000.00
6	28 000.00
9	22 300.00
11	22 300.00
13	16 300.00
14	22 300.00
15	28 300.00
16	16 300.00
17	22 300.00
18	28 300.00

—=＊=—   RESULTS   —=＊=—

MINIMIZATION PROBLEM

NODE	EXPECTED PAYOFF	SELECTED ALTERNATIVE
0	21 340.00	3
1	22 000.00	
2	22 600.00	
3	21 340.00	
4	16 000.00	
5	22 000.00	
6	28 000.00	
7	20 380.00	5
8	22 300.00	6
9	22 300.00	
10	20 380.00	
11	22 300.00	
12	25 420.00	
13	16 300.00	
14	22 300.00	
15	28 300.00	
16	16 300.00	
17	22 300.00	
18	28 300.00	

EXPECTED PAYOFF = 21340

——————— END OF ANALYSIS ———————

17.4 Some decision trees use Bayes' theorem for calculating the probabilities. Devise a problem of this type and use appropriate software to calculate all the probabilities and decisions in the tree.

17.5 Some spreadsheet packages can draw decision trees automatically. What would be the benefits of such packages? Design your own spreadsheet for doing such analyses.

Case study
The Newisham Reservoir

Newisham has a population of about 30 000. It had traditionally got its water supply from the nearby River Feltham. Unfortunately, increasing quantities of water were being extracted from the river by industry upstream. When the flow reaching the Newisham water treatment works became too small to supply the town's needs, it was decided to build a reservoir by damming the Feltham and diverting tributaries. This work was finished in the early 1990s and gave a guaranteed supply of water to Newisham.

Unfortunately, the dam reduced the amount of water available to farmers downstream. One of these has recently found that the water supply to his cattle has effectively dried up. He is faced with the option of either connecting to the local mains water supply at a cost of £44,000 or drilling a new well. The cost of the well is not known with certainty but could be £32,000 (with a probability of 0.3), £44,000 (with a probability of 0.3) or £56,000, depending on the underground rock structure and depth of water.

A local water survey company can be hired to do on-site tests. For a cost of £600 they will give either a favourable or an unfavourable report on the chances of easily finding water. The reliability of this report (phrased in terms of the probability of a favourable report given that the drilling cost will be low, etc) is given in the following table:

	Drilling well cost		
	£32,000	£44,000	£56,000
Unfavourable report	0.8	0.6	0.2
Favourable report	0.2	0.4	0.8

Draw a decision tree of the farmer's problem and identify his best course of action and expected costs.

Controlling stocks 18

CHAPTER OUTLINE

This chapter describes some models for controlling stocks. It starts by discussing the reasons why stocks are needed, how much they cost and how these costs can be minimized. The first analysis is the 'economic order quantity', which defines an order quantity to minimize the costs of a simple stock system.

If demand is highly variable, a probabilistic model must be used. The chapter describes a model where demand is Normally distributed, and a policy is defined to give a specified level of customer service.

All stock control systems need some effort, and sometimes the costs involved outweigh the benefits. An ABC analysis shows the amount of effort worth spending on different items.

After reading this chapter and doing the exercises you should be able to:

- appreciate the need for stocks and the associated costs
- calculate economic order quantities
- calculate reorder levels with constant lead times
- calculate the effects of finite production rates
- appreciate the need for safety stock when demand varies
- define 'service level'

- calculate a safety stock when lead time demand is Normally distributed
- describe periodic review systems and calculate target stock levels
- do ABC analyses of inventories

18.1 | Background to stock control

18.1.1 | Why hold stocks?

Stocks are the stores of goods that an organization holds. If you look around any organization you will find stocks of some kind. These always have associated costs (to cover warehouse operations, tied-up capital, deterioration, loss, and so on), so an obvious question is, 'Why do organizations hold stock?' There are several answers to this, but the dominant one is, 'To allow a buffer between supply and demand'.

Think of a supermarket, which obviously has a large stock of goods on its shelves and in its stockroom. This stock is held because large deliveries are made relatively infrequently by lorry, while small demands from customers occur almost continuously. There is a mismatch between supply and demand, and this can only be met by holding stock.

> The main purpose of stocks is to act as a buffer between supply and demand.

The short-term mismatch between supply and demand is only one reason for holding stock, and others include:

- to act as a buffer between different production operations (that is, they 'decouple' operations)
- to allow for demands that are larger than expected, or come at unexpected times
- to allow for deliveries that are delayed or too small
- to take advantage of price discounts on large orders
- to buy items when the price is low and expected to rise
- to buy items that are going out of production or are difficult to find
- to make full loads and reduce transport costs
- to provide cover for emergencies

and so on.

Whatever the reason for holding stocks, there are associated costs, and these are often surprisingly high (as described in the following section). This suggests a purpose of stock control, which is to design policies to ensure the costs of holding stock are as low as possible. In particular it looks for answers to three basic questions:

● What items should be stocked?
● When should an order be placed?
● How much should be ordered?

The following analysis assumes that the item considered is genuinely needed, and then concentrates on the last two questions. Two different policies are commonly used:

● **Fixed order quantity**, in which an order of fixed size is placed whenever stock falls to a certain level. A central heating plant, for example, may order 5000 gallons of oil whenever the amount in the tank falls to 500 gallons. Such systems need continuous monitoring of stock levels and are better suited to systems with low, irregular demand for relatively expensive items.

● **Periodic review**, in which orders of varying size are placed at regular intervals to raise the stock level to a specified value. Supermarket shelves, for example, may be refilled every evening to replace whatever was sold during the previous day. The operating cost of this system is generally lower, so it is better suited to high, regular demand of low-value items.

Later in the chapter we shall describe examples of both of these.

IN SUMMARY

The main purpose of stocks is to act as a buffer between supply and demand. The associated costs can be high, but stock control determines policies that minimize them.

18.1.2 | Costs of holding stock

Typically, the cost of holding stock is around 25% of its value a year. This is a considerable investment for organizations, and it is not surprising that they look for policies that minimize their costs. To show how these policies work, we should look at the costs in more detail, and define a number of distinct types.

Unit cost (U_c)

This is the price of an item charged by the supplier, or the cost to the company of acquiring one unit of an item. It may be fairly easy to find values by looking at quotations or recent invoices from suppliers. Sometimes, however, it is more difficult when there are several suppliers offering alternative products or giving different purchase conditions. If a company makes the item itself, it may be difficult to set a production cost or to calculate a valid transfer price.

Reorder cost (R_c)

This is the cost of placing a repeat order for an item, and might include allowances for drawing up an order (with checking, signing, clearance, distribution and filing), computer time, correspondence and telephone costs, receiving (with unloading, checking and testing), supervision, use of equipment and follow-up. Sometime, costs such as quality control, transport charges, sorting and movement of received goods are included in the reorder cost.

The reorder cost should ideally be for repeat orders and not a first order (which might have additional allowances for searching for suitable suppliers, checking reliability and quality, negotiations with alternative suppliers, and so on). In practice, the best estimate for a reorder cost might be found by dividing the total annual cost of the purchasing department by the number of orders sent out.

A special instance of the reorder cost occurs when the company makes the item itself and is concerned with stocks of finished goods. Here the reorder cost is a batch set-up cost and might include production documentation costs, allowance for production lost while resetting machines, idle time of operators, material spoilt in test runs, time of specialist tool setters, and so on.

Holding cost (H_c)

This is the cost of holding one unit of an item in stock for a period of time (typically a year). The obvious cost is for tied-up money that is either borrowed (with interest payable) or could be put to other use (in which case there are opportunity costs). Other holding costs are due to storage space (supplying a warehouse, rent, rates, heat, light, etc.), loss (due to damage, deterioration, obsolescence and pilferage), handling (including special packaging, refrigeration, putting on pallets, etc.), administration (stock checks, computer updates, etc.) and insurance. Typical annual values for these, as percentages of unit cost, are:

	% of unit cost
Cost of money	10–20
Storage space	2–5
Loss	4–6
Handling	1–2
Administration	1–2
Insurance	1–5
Total	19–40

Shortage cost (S_c)

If an item is needed but cannot be supplied from stock, there is usually a cost associated with this shortage. In the simplest case a retailer may lose direct profit from a sale, but the effects of shortages are usually much more widespread. Goodwill and loss of potential future sales might be added, as well as an element for loss of reputation. Shortages of raw materials for a production process could cause disruption and force rescheduling of production, retiming of maintenance periods, laying off employees, and so on. Also included in shortage costs might be allowances for positive action to counteract the shortage, perhaps sending out emergency orders, paying for special deliveries, storing partly finished goods or using alternative, more expensive suppliers.

Shortage costs are almost invariably difficult to determine. There is general agreement, however, that they can be very high, particularly if production is stopped by a shortage of raw materials. This allows us to look at the purpose of stocks again and rephrase our earlier statement by saying, 'The cost of shortages can be very high and to avoid this organizations are willing to incur the relatively lower costs of carrying stock'.

IN SUMMARY

Holding stocks is expensive, with typical costs amounting to 25% of unit cost a year. The costs of holding stock can be classified as unit, reorder, holding or shortage.

Self-assessment questions

18.1 What is the main reason for holding stock?

18.2 What are the basic questions for stock control systems?

18.3 Name two approaches for determining order quantities in stock control systems.

18.4 List four types of cost associated with stock holdings.

18.2 The economic order quantity

18.2.1 Developing the model

The basis of **scientific stock control** is the economic order quantity. This is a fixed order quantity, which minimizes costs when a number of assumptions are made.

The analysis considers a single item whose demand is known to be continuous and constant at D per unit time. Replenishment of the stock is assumed to be instantaneous, so that when an order arrives it is all available for use immediately. It is also assumed that unit cost U_c, reorder cost R_c and holding cost H_c are all known exactly, while the shortage cost S_c is so large that all demands must be met and no shortages are allowed.

Initially, we shall also assume that the lead time between placing an order and having it arrive is zero. This means that there is no point in placing orders until existing stock is completely exhausted. We are using a fixed order quantity system, so that orders are always placed for the same quantity, Q. Then the stock level alternatively rises with deliveries and falls as units are removed to meet demand, giving the sawtooth pattern shown in Figure 18.1.

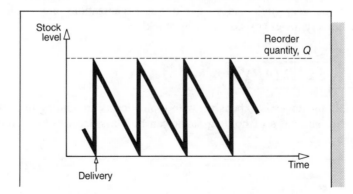

Figure 18.1 Sawtooth stock level over time.

Consider one cycle of this sawtooth pattern (Figure 18.2). At some point an order is placed for a quantity Q, which arrives instantaneously. This is used at a constant rate D until no stock remains, at which point another order is placed.

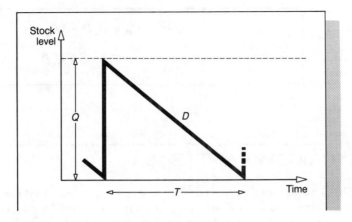

Figure 18.2   A single stock cycle.

The resulting stock cycle has length T, and we know:

$$\text{amount entering stock} = \text{amount leaving stock}$$
$$\text{in the cycle} \qquad \text{in the cycle}$$
$$Q = D \times T$$

The total cost for the cycle is found as follows:

● add the three components of cost (unit, reorder and holding), remembering there are no shortage costs

● divide this cost by the cycle length to give a cost per unit time

● differentiate this cost per unit time with respect to the order quantity

● set this derivative to zero and hence find the order quantity that minimizes the cost per unit time. This is the **economic order quantity**, Q_o.

An outline of this derivation is given at the end of the chapter, but we are primarily interested in the result, which is:

$$\textit{economic order quantity} = Q_0 = \sqrt{\frac{2R_c D}{H_c}}$$

Another result of this derivation is that the equation for minimum total cost contains a 'fixed' element, $U_c D$, which does not vary with order quantity, and a 'variable' element, VC_0, which does. Optimal values for these are:

$$\text{total cost} = TC_O = U_c D + VC_O$$

$$\text{variable cost} = VC_O = \sqrt{2R_c H_c D}$$

WORKED EXAMPLE 18.1

The demand for an item is constant at 20 units a month. Unit cost is £50, cost of processing an order and arranging delivery is £60, and holding cost is estimated to be £18 a unit a year. What are the economic order quantity, corresponding cycle length and costs?

Solution

Listing the values we know in consistent units:

$$D = 20 \times 12 = 240 \text{ units a year}$$

$$U_c = £50 \text{ a unit}$$

$$R_c = £60 \text{ an order}$$

$$H_c = £18 \text{ a unit a year}$$

Then substitution gives

$$Q_0 = \sqrt{\frac{2R_c D}{H_c}} = \sqrt{\frac{2 \times 60 \times 240}{18}} = 40 \text{ units}$$

$$VC_0 = \sqrt{(2R_c H_c D)} = \sqrt{2 \times 60 \times 18 \times 240} = £720 \text{ a year}$$

$$TC_0 = U_c \times D + VC_0 = 50 \times 240 + 720 = £12,720 \text{ a year}$$

The cycle length T_0 is found from $Q_0 = DT_0$, so $40 = 240T_0$ or $T_0 = 1/6$ years or 2 months.

The optimal policy (with total costs of £12,720 a year) is to order 40 units every 2 months.

| IN SUMMARY |

An economic order quantity can be calculated from

$$Q_0 = \sqrt{\frac{2R_cD}{H_c}}$$

This minimizes the total cost of stocking an item and allows several related measures to be calculated.

18.2.2 | Reorder levels with fixed lead times

The economic order quantity answers the question of how much to order, but we still need to know when to place an order. This decision is based on the lead time L between placing an order and having it arrive in stock. For simplicity, we shall assume that this is fixed. The stock level follows the sawtooth pattern shown in Figure 18.3, with stock rising when a delivery is made and falling slowly back to zero. To ensure that a delivery arrives just as stock is running out, an order must be placed a time L earlier. The easiest way of finding this point is to look at the current stock and place an order when there is just enough left to last the lead time. With constant demand of D, an order is placed when the stock level falls to LD, and this point is called the reorder level:

reorder level = lead time demand

ROL = LD

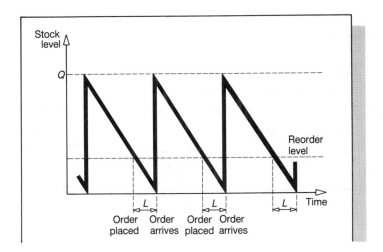

Figure 18.3   Stock level with a fixed lead time, L.

One way of timing orders in practice is called the 'two-bin system'. In this, stock is kept in two bins, one of which holds an amount equal to the reorder level while the second holds all remaining stock. Demand is met from the second bin until this is empty. At this point the stock level has declined to the reorder level and it is time to place an order.

WORKED EXAMPLE 18.2

Demand for an item is constant at 20 units a week, reorder cost is £125 an order and holding cost is £2 a unit a week. If suppliers guarantee delivery within two weeks, what would be the best ordering policy for the item?

Solution

Listing the variables in consistent units:

$$D = 20 \text{ units a week}$$

$$R_c = £125 \text{ an order}$$

$$H_c = £2 \text{ a unit a week}$$

$$L = 2 \text{ weeks}$$

Then substitution gives:

- economic order quantity:

$$Q_0 = \sqrt{\frac{2R_cD}{H_c}} = \sqrt{\frac{2 \times 125 \times 20}{2}} = 50 \text{ units}$$

- reorder level:

$$ROL = LD = 2 \times 20 = 40 \text{ units}$$

The optimal policy is to place an order for 50 units whenever stock declines to 40 units. This will happen every:

$$Q_0 = DT_0 \qquad \text{so} \qquad T_0 = 50/20 = 2.5 \text{ weeks}$$

The variable costs are:

$$VC_0 = \sqrt{2R_cH_cD} = \sqrt{2 \times 125 \times 2 \times 20} = £100 \text{ a week}$$

IN SUMMARY

A convenient way of finding the time to place an order is to define a reorder level.
For constant lead time and demand the reorder level equals lead time demand.

Self-assessment questions

18.5 What is meant by the economic order quantity?

18.6 If small orders are placed frequently (rather than placing large orders infrequently) does this: (a) reduce total costs, (b) increase total costs (c) either increase or decrease total costs?

18.7 What is meant by the reorder level?

18.8 How is the reorder level calculated?

18.3

Stock control with production

The economic order quantity is based on a series of assumptions. Changing these assumptions gives a series of models that are used in a wide range of circumstances. In this section we shall consider one extension of the basic analysis which is relevant to production systems. This assumes that replenishment is done at a finite rate rather than instantaneously.

If a product is manufactured at a rate of 10 an hour, the stock of finished goods will increase at this rate. Then the assumption made for the economic order quantity, that goods arrive in batches, does not hold. However, we can extend the economic order quantity analysis by allowing units to be moved into stock at a finite rate, P.

If the rate of production is less than the rate of demand (P is less than D) there is no problem with stock holding. Supply is not keeping up with demand and as soon as a unit is made it is transferred straight out to customers. Stock problems only arise when the rate of production is higher than the demand (P is greater than D). Then stock builds up at a rate ($P - D$) for as long as production continues.

Production is stopped when a large enough batch of the item has been made, so we shall say that after some time T_P, the production equipment moves on to other items. When production is stopped, demand from customers continues at a rate D and is met from the accumulated stock. After some further time T_D, the stock is exhausted and production must restart. The resulting stock level is shown in Figure 18.4.

We want to find an optimal value for the batch size. This is equivalent to finding the economic order quantity, and the overall method is the same. We find the total cost for a single stock cycle, divide this by the cycle length to give a cost per unit time, and then minimize this cost.

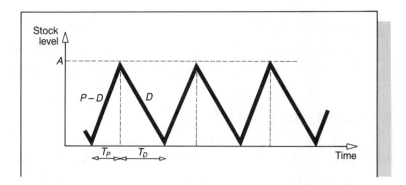

Figure 18.4 Variation in stock level with a finite production rate.

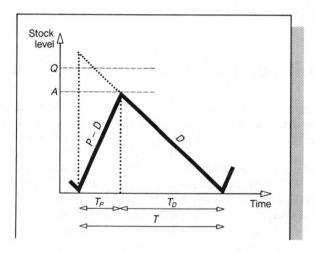

Figure 18.5 One stock cycle with a finite production rate.

Consider one cycle of the stock pattern shown in Figure 18.5. Batches of size Q are made, and if replenishment were instantaneous this would be the highest stock level. As units are actually fed into stock at a finite rate and are continuously being removed to meet demand, the maximum stock level will be lower than Q and will occur at the point where production is stopped. The value for A, the highest actual stock level, can be found in terms of other variables as follows.

Looking at the productive part of the cycle, T_P, we have:

$$A = (P - D) \times T_P$$

We also know that total production during the period is

$$Q = P \times T_P \qquad \text{or} \qquad T_P = Q/P$$

Substituting this value for T_P into the equation for A gives

$$A = \frac{Q(P - D)}{P}$$

We could continue the analysis, remembering that R_c is really a production set-up cost. Again, however, we are more interested in the results than in the derivation (which is given at the end of the chapter). These results only differ from the economic order quantity analysis by the factor $(P-D)/P$.

$$\textit{optimal order quantity} = Q_0 = \sqrt{\frac{2R_cD}{H_c}} \times \sqrt{\frac{P}{P-D}}$$

$$\textit{total cost} = TC_0 = U_cD + VC_0$$
$$\textit{variable cost} = VC_0 = \sqrt{2R_cH_cD} \times \sqrt{\frac{P-D}{P}}$$

With a finite production rate the stock level is somewhat lower than it would be with instantaneous replenishment, so we would expect, all other things being equal, to make larger batches. This is confirmed by the results above, where batch size increases by $\sqrt{P/(P-D)}$.

WORKED EXAMPLE 18.3

Demand for an item is 600 units a month and relevant costs have been estimated as:

- production set-up cost of £64 an order
- shop order preparation of £50 an order
- scheduling of shop order at £11 an order
- insurance of 1% of unit cost a year
- obsolescence, deterioration and depreciation allowance of 2% of unit cost a year
- capital costs of 20% of unit cost a year
- storage space at £5 per unit per annum
- handling costs of £6 per unit per annum
- shortage costs so large that no shortages are allowed

Each unit costs the company £20 and the rate of production is 1200 units a month. Determine the optimal batch quantity and the minimum variable cost a year.

By rescheduling work, the company could reduce its effective rate of production to 900 units a month at an additional cost of £200 a month. Would this be worth while?

Solution

Every cost must be classified as unit, reorder or holding (with no shortage costs). Then:

$$D = 600 \times 12 = 7200 \text{ units a year}$$

$$P = 1200 \times 12 = 14\ 400 \text{ units a year}$$

$$U_c = £20 \text{ a unit}$$

Collecting together all costs that arise per order gives

$$R_c = 64 + 50 + 11 = £125 \text{ per order}$$

Holding costs are of two types: a percentage (1%, 2% and 20%) of unit costs and a fixed amount (£5 + £6) a unit a year. Then:

$$H_c = (5 + 6) + (0.01 + 0.02 + 0.2) \times 20 = £15.60 \text{ a unit a year}$$

Substituting these values gives

$$\sqrt{\frac{P}{P-D}} = \sqrt{\frac{14\ 400}{14\ 400 - 7200}} = 1.414$$

$$Q_0 = \sqrt{\frac{2R_c D}{H_c}} \times \sqrt{\frac{P}{P-D}}$$

$$= \sqrt{\frac{2 \times 125 \times 7200}{15.60}} \times 1.414 = 480 \text{ units}$$

$$VC_0 = \frac{\sqrt{2R_c H_c D}}{\sqrt{P/(P-D)}}$$

$$= \frac{\sqrt{2 \times 125 \times 15.60 \times 7200}}{1.414} = 5299.1/1.414 = £3,748 \text{ a year}$$

The last part of the question reinforces the view that stocks are only needed because of mismatches between supply and demand. If supply could be matched exactly to demand, there would be no need to hold stock. It follows that the smaller this mismatch can be made, the smaller will be the total cost of holding stock. By paying to reduce the production rate we might save money by more closely matching supply and demand.

Reducing P to $900 \times 12 = 8400$ units a year gives

$$VC_0 = \sqrt{\left(\frac{2R_c H_c D}{\sqrt{P/(P-D)}} \right)}$$

$$= =$$

$$= \frac{5299.1}{\sqrt{8400/(8400 - 7200)}} = \text{£2003 a year}$$

The initial saving is (3748 − 2003) = £1745, but if we add the additional rescheduling cost of £200 a month the total cost becomes 2003 + 2400 = £4403 a year and the rescheduling is not worth while.

IN SUMMARY

The economic order quantity analysis can be extended by adding a finite production rate. This makes the analysis more appropriate for production systems, and adds a factor of $\sqrt{(P/(P - D))}$ to the standard results.

Self-assessment questions

18.9 Are finite production rates important for stock control when the production rate is greater than demand, or vice versa?

18.10 Does a finite production rate lead to larger or smaller batches than instantaneous replenishment?

| 18.4 | Probabilistic demand

The analyses we have described so far have assumed that demand is constant and known exactly. In practice this is rarely true and the demand for almost any item varies over time. In addition, there is usually some uncertainty, which is ignored in the analysis of economic order quantity. Fortunately, these effects are generally small and the economic order quantity gives widely used results. Sometimes, however, the variations are too large and another approach must be used. A range of appropriate models have been developed, and we shall start by looking at a model for demand that is Normally distributed.

We can easily show why the results from models that assume constant demand are not appropriate for demand that is Normally distributed. Consider what would happen in a typical stock cycle. Calculations would be based on mean demand, but when demand in the lead time is greater than average, stock will run out and there will be shortages. Unfortunately, the lead time demand will be above the mean value in 50% of cycles, giving a clearly unacceptable performance.

Some other approach is needed for variable demand, and a useful one is based on the balance between shortage costs and holding costs. It is difficult to find accurate costs for shortages, but they are usually high in relation to holding costs. This means that organizations are willing to hold additional stocks, above their perceived needs, to add a margin of safety and avoid the risk of shortages. These **safety stocks** are available if the normal working stock is exhausted (Figure 18.6). The question we can now ask is, 'How much safety stock should be held?'

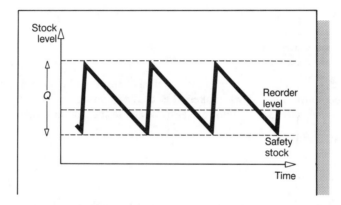

Figure 18.6   Stock levels when a safety stock is added.

In principle, it should be possible to calculate the cost of shortages and balance them with the cost of holding stock. In practice this is rarely possible, as shortage costs are notoriously difficult to find and are often little more than informed guesses. Analyses based on such shortage costs are often unreliable. An alternative approach relies more directly on the judgement of management and allows a **service level** to be used. This involves a positive decision to specify the desired probability that a demand is met directly from stock (or, conversely, the maximum acceptable probability that a demand cannot be met from stock). Typically, a company will specify a service level of 95%, implying a probability of 0.05 that a demand is not met.

There are several different ways of defining service level, including percentage of orders fully met from stock, percentage of units met from stock, percentage of periods without shortages, percentage of stock cycles without shortages, percentage of time for which there is stock available, and so on. In the remainder of this analysis we shall use the probability of not running out of stock in a stock cycle. This is sometimes called the **cycle service level**.

Consider an item whose demand is Normally distributed with a mean of D per unit time and standard deviation of σ. If the lead time is constant at L, the lead time demand is Normally distributed with mean of LD, variance of $\sigma^2 L$ and standard deviation of $\sigma\sqrt{L}$. This result is derived from the fact that variances can be added but standard deviations cannot.

If

- demand in a single period has mean D and variance σ^2
- demand in two periods has mean $2D$ and variance $2\sigma^2$
- demand in three periods has mean $3D$ and variance $3\sigma^2$
- and so on

then

- demand in L periods has mean LD and variance $L\sigma^2$.

With constant demand we used lead time demand ($= LD$) as a reorder level. If lead time demand is Normally distributed, it will be greater than the mean value on half the possible occasions. This means that there will be shortages in 50% of stock cycles. Conversely, the lead time demand will be less than the mean in 50% of stock cycles, and this will give spare stock (as shown in Figure 18.7).

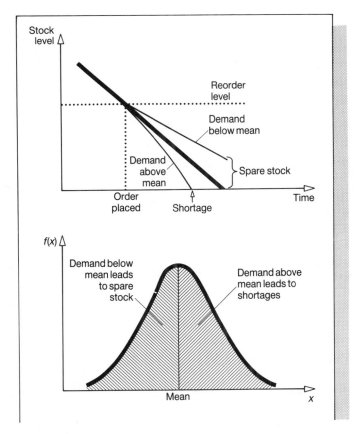

Figure 18.7   When demand is Normally distributed, the probability of a shortage is 0.5.

To give a cycle service level that is greater than 0.5 we need to add a safety stock, so the reorder level becomes:

reorder level = mean lead time demand + safety stock

The size of the safety stock depends on the service level specified. If a high service level is required the safety stock must also be high. Specifically, when lead time demand is Normally distributed the calculation of safety stock becomes:

safety stock = Z × standard deviation of lead time demand

$$= Z\sigma\sqrt{L}$$

Here Z is the number of standard deviations the safety stock is away from the mean, with corresponding probabilities found in Normal tables. To give some examples:

- if $Z = 1$ a shortage will occur in 15.9% of stock cycles
- $Z = 2$ gives shortages in 2.3% of stock cycles,
- $Z = 3$ gives shortages in 0.1% of stock cycles

If demand varies widely, the standard deviation of lead time demand will be high and very high safety stocks would be needed to ensure a service level near to 100%. This may be prohibitively expensive and companies will usually set a lower level, typically around 95%. Sometimes it is convenient to give items different service levels depending on their importance. Very important items may be given levels close to 100%, while less important ones are set around 85%.

WORKED EXAMPLE 18.4

Demand for an item is Normally distributed with a mean of 200 units a week and a standard deviation of 40 units. Reorder cost (including delivery) is £200, holding cost is £6 a unit a year and lead time is fixed at 3 weeks.

(a) Describe an ordering policy that will give a 95% cycle service level.

(b) What is the cost of holding the safety stock in this case?

(c) By how much would the costs rise if the service level is raised to 97%?

Solution

Listing the values we know:

$$D = 200 \text{ units a week}$$

$$\sigma = 40 \text{ units}$$

$$R_c = £200 \text{ an order}$$

$$H_c = £6 \text{ a unit a year}$$

$$L = 3 \text{ weeks}$$

(a) Substituting these gives:

$$\text{order quantity } Q_0 = \sqrt{\frac{2R_cD}{H_c}} = \frac{\sqrt{2 \times 200 \times 200 \times 52}}{6}$$

$$= 833 \text{ (rounded to the nearest integer)}$$

$$\text{reorder level } ROL = LD + \text{safety stock} = 3 \times 200 + \text{safety stock}$$

$$= 600 + \text{safety stock}$$

For a 95% service level,

$$Z = 1.645 \text{ standard deviations from the mean.}$$

Then:

$$\text{safety stock} = Z\sigma\sqrt{L} = 1.645 \times 40 \times \sqrt{3}$$

$$= 114 \text{ (to the nearest integer)}$$

The best policy is to order 833 units whenever stock declines to 600 + 114 = 714 units. On average, orders should arrive when there are 114 units remaining.

(b) The expected cost of the safety stock is given by

$$\text{safety stock} \times \text{holding cost} = 114 \times 6$$

$$= £684 \text{ a year}$$

(c) If the service level is raised to 97%, Z becomes 1.88 and

$$\text{safety stock} = Z\sigma\sqrt{L} = 1.88 \times 40 \times \sqrt{3} = 130$$

The cost of holding this is

$$\text{safety stock} \times \text{holding cost} = 130 \times 6 = £780 \text{ a year}$$

IN SUMMARY

The assumption that demand is constant gives reasonable results as long as actual variations are small. If the variations are large a different model must be used. When the lead time demand is Normally distributed, the reorder level is given by

$$ROL = \text{mean lead time demand} + \text{safety stock}$$

Self-assessment questions

18.11 What is meant by service level and why is it used?

18.12 What is the purpose of safety stock?

18.13 How might the service level be improved?

‖ 18.5 ‖ Periodic review systems

At the beginning of this chapter we said that two different ordering policies could be used:

- **fixed order quantity system**, in which an order of fixed size is placed whenever stock falls to a certain level
- **periodic review system**, in which orders of varying size are placed at regular intervals to raise the stock to a specified level (the target stock level)

If the demand is constant these two systems are identical, so differences only appear when the demand varies, as shown in Figure 18.8.

We can extend the last analysis by considering a periodic review system, in which demand is Normally distributed. Then we look for answers to two basic questions:

- How long should the interval between orders be?
- What should the target stock level be?

The order interval T can really be any convenient period. It might, for example, be convenient to place an order at the end of every week, or every morning, or at the end of a month. If there is no obvious cycle we might aim for a certain number of orders a year or some average order size. One approach would be to calculate an economic order quantity, and then find the period that gives orders of about this size. The final decision is largely a matter for management judgement.

Whatever interval is chosen, we need to find a suitable target stock level, TSL. The system then works by examining the amount of stock on hand when an

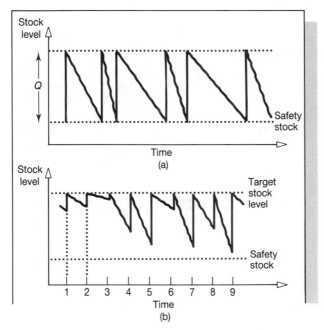

Figure 18.8 Different ways of dealing with varying demand: (a) fixed order quantity; (b) periodic review.

order is placed and ordering the amount that brings this up to the target stock level:

order quantity = target stock level – stock on hand

Suppose the lead time is constant at L. When an order is placed, the stock on hand plus this order must be enough to last until the next order arrives, which is $T + L$ away (as shown in Figure 18.9).

The target stock level should be high enough to cover mean demand over this period, so *TSL* must be at least $(T + L)D$. As demand is Normally distributed, some safety stock is needed to allow for the 50% of cycles when demand is above average. Assuming that both the cycle length and lead time are constant, the demand over $T + L$ is Normally distributed with mean of $(T + L)D$, variance of $\sigma^2(T + L)$ and standard deviation of $\sigma\sqrt{(T + L)}$. A safety stock can then be defined as:

$$\text{safety stock} = Z \times \text{standard deviation of demand over } T + L$$

$$= Z\sigma\sqrt{(T + L)}$$

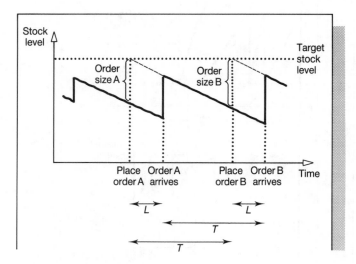

Figure 18.9 Calculating the target stock level.

Then:

$$\text{target stock level} = \text{mean demand over } (T + L) + \text{safety stock}$$
$$= D(T + L) + Z\sigma\sqrt{(T + L)}$$

WORKED EXAMPLE 18.5

Demand for an item has a mean of 200 units a week and standard deviation of 40 units. Stock is checked every four weeks and lead time is constant at two weeks. Describe a policy that gives a 95% service level. If the holding cost is £2 a unit a week, what is the cost of the safety stock with this policy? What would be the effect of a 98% service level?

Solution

The variables are:

$$D = 200 \text{ units}$$

$$\sigma = 40 \text{ units}$$

$$H_c = £2 \text{ a unit a week}$$

$$T = 4 \text{ weeks}$$

$$L = 2 \text{ weeks}$$

For a 95% safety stock Z can be found from normal distribution tables to be 1.645.

Then:

safety stock $= Z\sigma\sqrt{(T + L)} = 1.645 \times 40 \times \sqrt{6} = 161$ (rounded to the nearest integer)

target stock level $= D(T + L) +$ safety stock $= 200 \times (4+2) + 161 = 1361$

When it is time to place an order, the policy is to find the stock on hand, and place an order for

order size $= 1361 -$ stock on hand.

If, for example, there were 200 units in stock the order would be for 1161 units.

The cost of holding the safety stock is $161 \times 2 = £322$ a week.

If the service level is increased to 98%, $Z = 2.05$:

safety stock $= 2.05 \times 40 \times \sqrt{6} = 201$

The target stock level is then $1200 + 201 = 1401$ units and the cost of the safety stock is $201 \times 2 = £402$ a week.

IN SUMMARY

A periodic review system places orders of variable size at regular intervals. The quantity ordered is enough to raise stock on hand to a target level, *TSL*, where:

$$TSL = D(T + L) + Z\sigma\sqrt{(T + L)}$$

Self-assessment questions

18.14 How is the order size calculated for a periodic review system?

18.15 Will the safety stock be higher for a fixed order quantity system or a periodic review system?

18.7 | ABC analysis of stock

A considerable effort is needed to control stocks. Most stock control systems are computerized, but they still need manual effort to input data, check values, update supplier details, and confirm orders. The computer system itself might incur high operating costs. For some items, especially cheap ones, this effort is not worth while. Very few organizations, for example, include routine stationery in their computerized stock system. At the other end of the scale are very expensive items, which require special care above the routine calculations.

An ABC analysis is one way of putting items into categories that reflect the amount of effort worth spending on stock control. This kind of analysis is sometimes called a Pareto analysis or the 'rule of 80/20' (suggesting that 80% of stock items need 20% of the attention, while the remaining 20% of items need 80% of the attention). ABC analyses define:

- A items as expensive and needing special care
- B items as ordinary ones needing standard care
- C items as cheap and needing little care

Typically, an organization might use an automated system to deal with all B items. The computer system might make some suggestions for A items, but final decisions are made by managers after reviewing the circumstances. C items may be left out of the system, with any control left to *ad hoc* procedures.

An ABC analysis starts by calculating the total annual use of each item in terms of value, by multiplying the number of units used in a year by the unit cost. Usually, a few expensive items account for a lot of use, while many cheap ones account for little use. If we list the items in order of decreasing annual use by value, A items are at the top of the list and C items are at the bottom. We might typically find:

Category	% of items	Cumulative % of items	% of use by value	Cumulative % of use by value
A	10	10	70	70
B	30	40	20	90
C	60	100	10	100

Plotting the cumulative percentage of annual use against the cumulative percentage of items gives the graph shown in Figure 18.10.

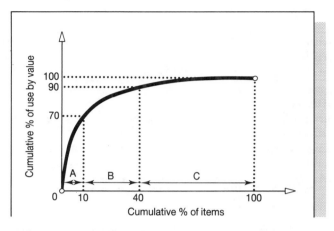

Figure 18.10   ABC analysis of stocks.

WORKED EXAMPLE 18.6

A small store consists of ten categories of product with the following costs and annual demands:

Product	P1	P2	P3	P4	P5	P6	P7	P8	P9	P0
Unit Cost (£)	20	10	20	50	10	50	5	20	100	1
Annual demand ('00s)	2.5	50	20	66	15	6	10	5	1	50

Do an ABC analysis of these items. If resources for stock control are limited, which items should be given least attention?

Solution

The annual use of P1 in terms of value is $20 \times 250 = £5,000$. If this calculation is repeated for the other items and they are sorted into order of decreasing annual use by value we get the results shown in Table 18.1. The boundaries between categories of items are sometimes unclear, but in this case P4 is clearly an A item, P2, P3 and P6 are B items and the rest are C items.

Table 18.1

Product	P4	P2	P3	P6	P5	P8	P9	P1	P7	P0
Cumulative % of items	10	20	30	40	50	60	70	80	90	100
Annual use (£'000s)	330	50	40	30	15	10	10	5	5	5
Cumulative annual use	330	380	420	450	465	475	485	490	495	500
Cumulative % annual use	66	76	84	90	93	95	97	98	99	100
Category	◄─A─►	◄────	B	───►◄	───	───	───	C─	───	───►

The C items account for only 10% of annual use by value and these should be given least attention if resources are limited.

IN SUMMARY

ABC analyses allow items to be categorized according to importance, so that available effort can be shared out appropriately. Typically, 20% of items account for 70% of use by value (A items) while the bulk of items account for very little use by value (C items).

Self-assessment questions

18.16 What is the purpose of doing an ABC analysis of inventories?

18.17 Which items can best be dealt with by routine, automated control procedures?

CHAPTER REVIEW

This chapter described some quantitative models for controlling stocks. In particular, the chapter

- discussed the purpose of holding stocks
- showed how stock control systems minimize the associated costs
- described the economic order quantity

- extended this analysis by adding a reorder level and finite production rate
- discussed service levels and safety stocks
- described periodic review systems
- described ABC analyses

Problems

18.1 The demand for an item is constant at 100 units a year. Unit cost is £50, cost of processing an order is £20 and holding cost is estimated at £10 per unit per annum. What are the economic order quantity, corresponding cycle length and costs?

18.2 A company works 50 weeks a year and has demand for an item that is constant at 100 units a week. The cost of each unit is £20 and the company aims for a return of 20% on capital invested. Annual warehouse costs are estimated to be 5% of the value of goods stored. The purchasing department of the company costs £45,000 a year and sends out an average of 2000 orders. Determine the optimal order quantity for the item, the optimal time between orders and the minimum cost of stocking the item.

18.3 Demand for an item is steady at 20 units a week and the economic order quantity has been calculated at 50 units. What is the reorder level when the lead time is (a) 1 week, (b) 2 weeks?

18.4 How would the results for Problem 18.1 change if the item could only be supplied at a finite rate of 10 units a week?

18.5 A manufacturing company forecasts its demand for components to average 18 a day over a 200-day working year. If there are any shortages, production will be disrupted, with very high costs. The holding cost for the component is £40 a unit a year and the cost of placing an order is estimated to be £80 an order. Determine:

(a) the economic order quantity

(b) the optimal number of orders a year

(c) the total annual cost of operating the system (including the cost of purchases) if the real interest rate is 25% a year.

(d) What would be the effect on the stock system if the components are made internally and can only be supplied at a finite rate of 80 units a day?

18.6 A company advertises a 95% cycle service level for all stock items. Stock is replenished from a single supplier who guarantees a lead time of four weeks.

(a) What reorder level should the company adopt for an item that has a Normally distributed demand with mean 1000 units a week and standard deviation of 100 units?

(b) What would the reorder level be if a 98% cycle service level is used?

18.7 An item of stock has a unit cost of £40, reorder cost of £50 and holding cost of £1 a unit a week. Demand for the item has a mean of 100 a week with standard deviation 10. Lead time is constant at three weeks. Devise a stock policy for the item to give a service level of 95%. How would this be changed to achieve a 90% service level? What are the costs of these two policies?

18.8 Describe a periodic review system with interval of two weeks for the company described in Problem 18.6.

18.9 A small store consists of ten categories of product with the following costs and annual demands:

Product	X1	X2	X3	Y1	Y2	Y3	Z1	Z2	Z3	Z4
Unit cost (£)	20	25	30	1	4	6	10	15	20	22
Annual demand ('00s)	3	2	2	10	8	7	30	20	6	4

Do an ABC analysis of these items.

18.10 Annual demand for an item is 2000 units; each order costs £10 to place and the annual holding cost is 40% of the unit cost. The unit cost depends on the quantity ordered as follows:

- for quantities less than 500, unit cost is £1
- for quantities between 500 and 1000, unit cost is £0.80
- for quantities of 1000 or more, unit cost is £0.60

What is the optimal ordering policy for the item?

Computer exercises

18.1 Figure 18.11 shows the printout from a computer program that has done some calculations for an item held in stock. Examine this printout and make sure you understand what is happening. Use a suitable program to check these results.

18.2 Most stocks are controlled by computer. Describe the functions that you would expect to find in a computerized stock control system.

18.3 A small company wants to control the stocks of 20 items. It seems extravagant to buy an inventory control system for this number of items, and there is no one in the company to write their own software. It has been suggested that a spreadsheet can be used to record weekly sales and do associated calculations. Design a spreadsheet that the company can use.

+++---===   ECONOMIC ORDER QUANTITY CALCULATION   ===---+++

Results for Component

EOQ Input Data:

Demand per year (D)	= 400
Order or setup cost per order (Co)	= 650
Holding cost per unit per year (Ch)	= 20
Shortage cost per unit per year (Cs)	= 1000
Shortage cost per unit, independent of time (π)	= 100
Replenishment or production rate per year (P)	= 500
Lead time for a new order in year (LT)	= .25
Unit cost (C)	= 120

EOQ Output:

EOQ	=	360.555	
Maximum inventory	=	72.111	
Maximum backorder	=	0.000	
Order interval	=	0.901 year	
Reorder point	=	100.000	
Ordering cost	=	721.110	
Holding cost	=	721.110	
Shortage cost	=	0.000	
Subtotal of inventory cost per year	=		1442.220
Material cost per year	=		48000.000
Total cost per year	=		49442.219

Figure 18.11   Printout from inventory control package.

Case study
Templar Manufacturing

Mr Templar founded his own manufacturing company when he was 21 years old. He has continued to run it for the past 35 years and through steady expansion it now employs over 200 people.

A management consultant has recently suggested improving the stock control system, but Mr Templar is not sure that this is necessary. He was talking to a meeting of managers and said: 'I don't know how much the present stock control system costs, if it works as well as it could, or if the proposals would save money or not. I know that we have the things we need in stock, and if we have a shortage enough people complain to make sure we don't have any more. What I want is someone to show me if the proposals are worth looking at.'

When the management consultant asked what kind of demonstration Mr Templar would like, he got the following reply: 'I know you wanted to run a pilot scheme before starting work on a revised stock control system. I still need convincing that it is even worth going ahead with the pilot scheme. I don't want anything fancy. Let me give you an example of one of the components we make and see what you can do.

'This component is basically a flanged orbital hub contact that costs us about £15 to make. We use about 2000 a year. At the moment we can make them at a rate of 70 a week, but only plan one batch every quarter. Each time we set up the production it costs £345 to change the production line and £85 for preparation and scheduling costs. Other stock-holding costs are related to the unit costs, including insurance (1% a year), deterioration and obsolescence (2%) and capital (13%). I think that we could make them a bit faster, say up to 90 a week, and the unit cost could even fall a few per cent. Of course, we could make them a bit slower, but this would raise the cost by a few per cent.'

How would you demonstrate the benefit of a new stock control system to Mr Templar?

Derivation 18.1: Economic order quantity

Consider one cycle of the sawtooth pattern shown in Figure 18.2. We know:

amount entering stock = amount leaving stock in the cycle
in the cycle

$$Q = DT$$

The total cost for the cycle is found by adding the three components of cost (unit, reorder and holding).

Total cost for cycle:

- total unit cost = number of units ordered (Q) × unit cost (U_c) = U_cQ

- total reorder cost = number of orders (1) × reorder cost (R_c) = R_c

- total holding cost = average stock level ($Q/2$) × time held (T) × holding cost (H_c)

$$= \frac{H_cQT}{2}$$

Adding these three gives the total cost per cycle as

$$U_cQ + R_c + \frac{H_cQT}{2}$$

If this is divided by the cycle length T, we find the total cost per unit time, TC:

$$TC = U_cQ/T + R_c/T + H_cQ/2$$

Then substituting $Q = DT$ gives

$$TC = U_c D + R_c D/Q + H_c Q/2$$

We now have an expression for the cost per unit time. The three elements on the right of this equation can be plotted separately against Q, as shown in Figure 18.12.

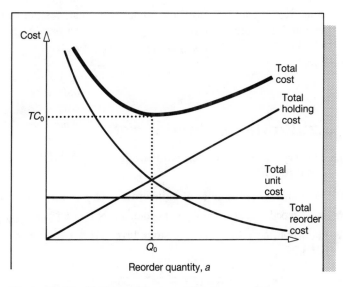

Figure 18.12 Variation of costs with order quantity.

The total unit cost $U_c D$ is independent of Q and can be considered 'fixed'; the total holding cost rises linearly with Q and the total reorder cost falls as Q increases. Clearly, large infrequent orders give high total holding costs and low total reorder costs; small frequent orders give low total holding costs and high total reorder costs. Adding the three contributing costs gives a total cost curve that is an asymmetric 'U' shape with a distinct minimum. This minimum corresponds to the optimal order size, which we shall call Q_0. To find the value Q_0 (which is the economic order quantity), we differentiate the total cost function with respect to Q, and set this to equal zero:

$$0 = \frac{-R_c D}{Q_o^2} + \frac{H_c}{2}$$

or

$$Q_0 = \sqrt{\frac{2R_cD}{H_c}}$$

This result can be substituted back into the cost equations to give the corresponding optimal values:

$$total\ cost = TC_0 = U_cD + VC_0$$

$$variable\ cost = VC_0 = \sqrt{2R_cH_cD}$$

Derivation 18.2: Finite production rate

This is very similar to the derivation of the economic order quantity, so:
Total cost for one cycle:

- total unit cost = number of units ordered (Q) × unit cost (U_c) = U_cQ
- total reorder cost = number of orders (1) × reorder cost (R_c) = R_c
- total holding cost = average stock level ($A/2$) × time held (T) × holding cost (H_c)

$$= \frac{H_cAT}{2} = \frac{H_cQT}{2} \times \frac{P-D}{P}$$

Adding these three gives the total cost per cycle as:

$$U_cQ + R_c + \frac{H_cQT}{2} \times \frac{P-D}{P}$$

If this is divided by the cycle length T, we find the total cost per unit time, TC:

$$TC = U_cQ/T + R_c/T + \frac{H_cQ}{2} \times \frac{P-D}{P}$$

Then substituting $Q = DT$ gives

$$TC = U_cD + R_cD/Q + \frac{H_cQ}{2} \times \frac{P-D}{P}$$

Adding the three contributing costs gives a total cost curve that is an asymmetric 'U' shape with a distinct minimum. This minimum corresponds to the optimal order size which we can find by differentiating the total cost with respect to Q, and setting this to equal zero:

$$0 = \frac{-R_c D}{Q_0^2} + \frac{H_c}{2} \times \frac{P - D}{P}$$

or

$$Q_0 = \sqrt{\frac{2R_c D}{H_c}} \times \sqrt{\frac{P}{P - D}}$$

This result can be substituted back into the cost equations to give the corresponding optimal values:

$$TC_0 = U_c D + VC_0$$
$$VC_0 = \sqrt{2R_c H_c D} \times \sqrt{\frac{P - D}{P}}$$

Planning projects with networks

CHAPTER OUTLINE

A project consists of a set of activities, with a clear start and finish, and with an aim of making a distinct product. In business, projects need detailed planning, and this chapter describes the most widely used method of doing this.

The first part of the chapter discusses the need for project planning. Then it describes the way in which project network analysis identifies the activities that make up a project, builds a dependence table to show their relationships and then transfers this to a network. Having drawn a network, the next stage is to analyse the timing of individual events and activities, and hence the overall duration of the project.

Gantt charts give an alternative view of a project, emphasizing its timing and allowing the resources used at any time to be found.

After reading this chapter and doing the exercises you should be able to:

● appreciate the need for planning complex projects
● represent projects by networks of connected activities and events
● calculate the timing of events and activities
● identify critical paths and hence overall project duration
● extend these analyses to PERT networks
● change the times of activities to achieve stated objectives
● draw Gantt charts
● find the resources needed during a project

19.1 Project network analysis

This chapter describes how projects can be planned with the aid of networks. We should start, then, by defining a **project**:

> A project is a coherent piece of work with a clear start and finish. It consists of a series of activities that result in a distinct product.

This definition is broad enough to mean that each of us does a number of small projects every day, such as preparing a meal, writing a report, building a fence, or organizing a social function. Such projects need planning, and in particular the identification of:

● the activities that make up the project
● the order in which these activities must be done
● the timing of each activity
● the resources needed at each stage

Small projects can be implemented with almost no formal planning, and a little thought is often enough to ensure that they run smoothly. However, business projects can be very large and involve a great deal of money. The installation of a new computer system, building a nuclear power station, organizing the Olympic Games and building a rail tunnel under the English Channel are examples of large projects, and we should only expect them to run smoothly if there had been a considerable amount of planning. **Project network analysis** is the most widely used technique for helping to organize complex projects.

IN SUMMARY

A project is a coherent piece of work that has a clear start and finish, and an aim of making a distinct product. Projects are often very large and rely on detailed planning. Project network analysis is the most widely used technique for doing this planning.

Self-assessment questions

19.1 What is a project?

19.2 What is the purpose of project management?

19.3 'Project management is only concerned with major capital projects.' Is this statement true?

19.2 | Networks for projects

19.2.1 | Drawing networks

A project network consists of a series of nodes connected by arrows. We shall use the convention that each **activity** in a project is represented by an arrow and each node represents a point in time at which activities begin and end. The nodes are called **events**, and a network will consist of alternating activities and events. The arrows show relationships between activities, and there is no significance in their orientation or length.

Figure 19.1 shows part of a project network. This has two activities, A followed by B, and three events. Event 1 is the start of activity A, event 2 is the finish of activity A and the start of activity B, and event 3 is the finish of activity B. We can develop this basic idea to give larger and more complex networks.

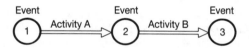

Figure 19.1 Part of a project network.

WORKED EXAMPLE 19.1

A greenhouse is to be built from a kit. The instructions make it clear that this is a project that can be considered in three parts:

- A, preparing the base (which will take 3 days)
- B, building the frame (which will take 2 days)
- C, fixing the glass (which will take 1 day)

Draw a network for the project.

Solution

The project is made up of three activities, which must be done in a fixed order; building the frame must be done after preparing the base and before fixing the glass. This order can be described by a precedence or **dependence table**, in which each activity is listed along with those activities that immediately precede it:

Activity	Duration (days)	Description	Immediate predecessor
A	3	prepare base	-
B	2	build frame	A
C	1	fix glass	B

Labelling the activities A, B and C is a convenient shorthand and allows us to refer to activity B having activity A as immediate predecessor, which is normally stated as 'B depends on A'. In this table only immediate predecessors are entered, so the fact that activity C (fixing the glass) depends on activity A as well as B need not be separately entered, but can be inferred from other dependences. Activity A has no immediate predecessors and can be started whenever convenient.

Now we can draw a network from the dependence table, as shown in Figure 19.2.

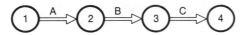

Figure 19.2 Network for Worked Example 19.1.

The directions of arrows in a project network indicate precedence. Each preceding activity must be finished before the following one is started, and following activities can start as soon as preceding ones are finished. In Worked Example 19.1, preparing the base must be done first, and as soon this is finished the frame can be built. The glass can then be fixed as soon as the frame is built.

After drawing the basic network for the project we can consider its timing. It is convenient to assume a notional starting time of 0, and then the start and finish times of each activity can be calculated.

WORKED EXAMPLE 19.2

For the project described in Worked Example 19.1, find the times for each activity. What happens if preparing the base takes more than three days, or building the frame takes less than two days?

Solution

If we take a starting time of 0, preparing the base can be finished by the end of day 3. Then building the frame can start, and as it takes two days it can be finished by the end of day 5. Then fixing the glass can start, and as it takes one day it can be finished by the end of day 6.

If the base takes more than three days the project will be delayed. If the frame take less than two days the project can be finished early.

We now have a timetable for the project showing when each activity starts and finishes. This timetable allows resources to be scheduled, so we can list the major steps in project planning as:

- define the separate activities and their durations
- determine the dependence of activities
- draw a network
- analyse the timing of the project
- schedule resources

IN SUMMARY

Project network analysis starts by dividing the whole project into a number of separate activities. The relationship between these is shown by arrows in a network of alternating activities and events. After the network has been drawn, calculations can be done for timing and resource allocation.

19.2.2 | Larger networks

Large networks can be drawn from a dependence table, and you will find that this becomes much easier with practice. A useful approach is to start drawing the network on the left-hand side with those activities that do not depend on any other. Then activities that only depend on these first activities can be added, then those that only depend on the latest activities can be added, and so on. The network is expanded systematically, working generally from left to right, until all activities have been added and the network is complete.

This procedure relies on some implicit rules, and before continuing, we should state these more formally. The two main rules are:

● before an activity can start all preceding activities must be finished

● the arrows representing activities imply precedence only and neither the length nor orientation is significant

By convention, there are also two other rules:

● a network has only one starting and one finishing event

● any two events can only be connected by one activity

This last rule is for convenience so that we can refer to 'the activity between events i and j' and know exactly which one we are talking about. Using these rules, we can draw networks of almost any size.

WORKED EXAMPLE 19.3

A company is opening a new office and identifies the main activities and dependences as follows:

Activity	Description	Depends on
A	find office location	-
B	recruit new staff	-
C	make office alterations	A
D	order equipment needed	A
E	install new equipment	D
F	train staff	B
G	start operations	C, E, F

Draw a network of this project.

Solution

Activities A and B have no predecessors and can be started as soon as convenient. As soon as activity A is finished both C and D can start: E can start as soon as D is finished and F can start as soon as B is finished. G can only start when C, E and F have all finished. This gives the network shown in Figure 19.3.

The network conforms to the rules above, and in particular has a single starting and finishing event, and only one activity between any pair of events.

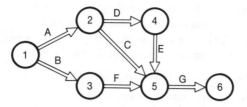

Figure 19.3 Network for worked example 19.3.

The network shows the project starting with activities A and B, but this does not imply that these must start at the same time, only that they can start as soon as convenient and must be finished before any following activity can start. Similarly, event 2 marks the point at which both C and D can start, but this does not mean that they must start at the same time. Conversely, event 5 is the point at which C, E and F are finished, but this does not mean that they must finish at the same time, only that they must all be finished before G can start.

IN SUMMARY

Networks of almost any size can be drawn from a dependence table. The general approach is to draw the first activities, and then systematically add all following ones.

19.2.3 | Dummy activities

There are two circumstances that complicate networks. The first of these is illustrated by the following dependence table:

Activity	Depends on
A	-
B	A
C	A
D	B, C

We may be tempted to draw this as shown in Figure 19.4(a), but this would break one of the rules above, which says, 'Any two events can only be connected by one activity.' The conventional way round this is to define a **dummy activity**. This is not a part of the project, has zero duration and requires no resources, but is simply there to allow a sensible network. In this case the dummy ensures that only one activity goes between two events and is called a **uniqueness dummy**. In Figure 19.4(b) the dummy activity is shown as the broken line, X.

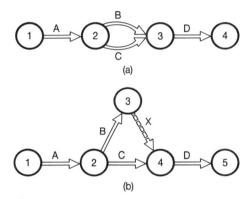

Figure 19.4 Network with a uniqueness dummy: (a) incorrect network; (b) correct network using dummy activity X.

A second situation that needs a dummy activity is illustrated by the part of a dependence table shown below:

Activity	Depends on
D	not given
E	not given
F	D, E
G	D

We may be tempted to draw this part of the network as shown in Figure 19.5(a), but the dependence would clearly be wrong. Activity F is shown as depending on D and E, which is correct, but G is shown as having the same dependence. The dependence table shows that G can start as soon as D is finished but the network shows it waiting for E to finish as well. The way to avoid this relies on separating the dependences by introducing a dummy activity, as shown in Figure 19.5(b). The dependence of F on D is shown through the dummy activity X. In effect, the dummy cannot start until D has finished, and then F cannot start until the dummy and E are finished. As the dummy activity has zero duration this does not add any time to the project. This type of dummy is called a **logical dummy**.

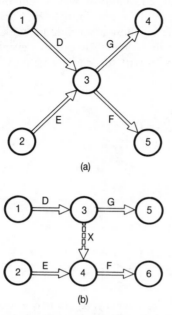

(a)

(b)

Figure 19.5 Network with a logical dummy: (a) incorrect network; (b) correct network using dummy activity X.

These are the only two circumstances (ensuring that only one activity goes between two events and ensuring that the logic is correct) in which dummies are used.

WORKED EXAMPLE 19.4

A project is described by the following dependence table. Draw a network of the project.

Activity	Depends on	Activity	Depends on
A	J	I	J
B	C, G	J	-
C	A	K	B
D	F, K, N	L	I
E	J	M	I
F	B, H, L	N	M
G	A, E, I	O	M
H	G	P	O

Solution

This seems a difficult network, but the steps are fairly straightforward. Activity J is the only one that does not depend on anything else, so this starts the network. Then activities A, E and I, which only depend on J, can be added. Then activities that depend on A, E and I can be added. Continuing this systematic addition of activities leads to the network shown in Figure 19.6, which includes four dummy activities: W, X, Y and Z.

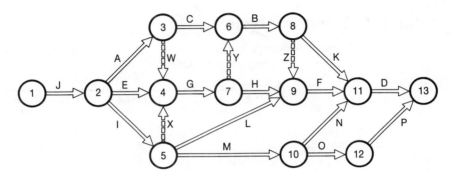

Figure 19.6 Network for Worked Example 19.4

IN SUMMARY

Two types of dummy activity may be needed to draw a network. Uniqueness dummies ensure that only one activity starts and finishes with the same events, and logical dummies ensure that the logic of the network is accurate.

Self-assessment questions

19.4 In the networks we have drawn, what are represented by: (a) nodes, (b) arrows?

19.5 What information is needed to draw a project network?

19.6 What are the main rules for drawing a project network?

19.7 When are dummy activities used?

19.3 | Timing of projects

The timing of events and activities is a major part of project planning. In particular, it is important to find the earliest time that an activity can start and the latest time by which it must be finished. It would be difficult to find these intuitively for a project of any size, and a more systematic approach must be used. This is described in the next two sections.

19.3.1 | Event analysis

Suppose a project is represented by the following dependence table, where a duration (in weeks) has been added:

Activity	Duration	Depends on
A	3	-
B	2	-
C	2	A
D	4	A
E	1	C
F	3	D
G	3	B
H	4	G
I	5	E, F

This network for this project is shown in Figure 19.7, where durations have been noted under the activities.

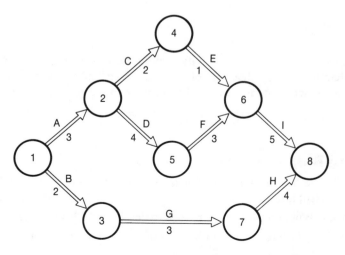

Figure 19.7   Network for event timing.

The analysis of times starts by finding the earliest possible time for each event, assuming a notional start time of zero for the project as a whole. The earliest time for event 1 is clearly 0. The earliest time for event 2 is when A finishes, which is three weeks after its earliest start at 0; the earliest time for event 4 is the time when C finishes, which is two weeks after its earliest start at 3 (week 5). Similarly, the earliest time for event 5 is $4 + 3 = 7$, for event 3 is 2 and for event 7 is $2 + 3 = 5$ (as shown in Figure 19.8).

When several activities have to finish before an event, the earliest time for the event is the earliest time by which **all** preceding activities can be finished. The earliest time for event 6 is when both E and F are finished. E can finish one week after its earliest start at 5 (week 6), F can finish three weeks after its earliest start at 7 (week 10). Then the earliest time when both of these can be finished is week 10. Similarly, event 8 must wait until both activities H and I are finished. Activity H can be finished by week $5 + 4 = 9$ while activity I can be finished by week $10 + 5 = 15$. The earliest time for event 8 is the later of these which is week 15. This gives the overall duration of the project as 15 weeks. Figure 19.8 shows the earliest times for each event added to the network.

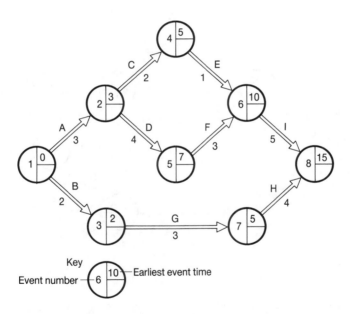

Figure 19.8 Earliest event times added to network.

Having gone through the network and found the earliest time for each event we can do a similar analysis to find the latest time for each. The procedure for this is almost the reverse of that used to find the earliest times. Starting at the end of the project with event 8, this has a latest time for completion of week 15. To allow activity I to be finished by week 15 it must be started five weeks before this, so the latest time for event 6 is week $15 - 5 = 10$. The latest that H can finish is week 15, so the latest time it can start is 4 weeks before this, so the latest time for event 7 is week $15 - 4 = 11$. Similarly, the latest time for event 3 is $11 - 3 = 8$, for event 5 is $10 - 3 = 7$ and for event 4 is $10 - 1 = 9$ (as shown in Figure 19.9).

For events that have more than one following activity, the latest time must allow all following activities to be completed on time. Event 2 is followed by activities C and D; C must be finished by week 9 so it must be started 2 weeks before this (week 7), while D must be finished by week 7 so it must be started 4 weeks before this (week 3). The latest time for event 2 that allows both C and D to start on time is the earlier of these, which is week 3.

Similarly, the latest time for event 1 must allow both A and B to finish on time. The latest start time for B is $8 - 2 = 6$ and the latest start time for A is $3 - 3 = 0$. The latest time for event 1 must allow both of these to start on time and this means a latest time of 0. Figure 19.9 shows the network with latest times added for each event.

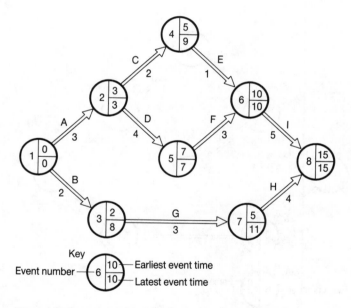

Figure 19.9 Latest event times added to network.

$\boxed{\textbf{\textit{IN SUMMARY}}}$

Finding the times for events and activities is an important part of project planning. An earliest and latest time can be found for each event.

19.3.2 | Activity analysis

The analysis of project times can be extended to activities, where earliest and latest start times (and corresponding earliest and latest finish times) can be found.

The earliest start time for an activity is the earliest time of the preceding event; the earliest finish time is the earliest start time plus the duration. Looking at one activity in Figure 19.9, say G, the earliest start time is week 2 and the earliest finish time is, therefore, week 2 + 3 = 5.

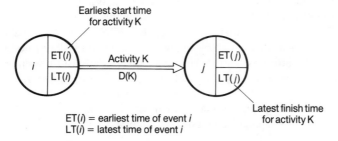

Figure 19.10   Earliest and latest activity times.

The latest start and finish time for an activity can be found using similar reasoning, but working backwards. The latest finish time for each activity is the latest time of the following event; the latest start time is the latest finish time minus the duration. For activity G the latest finish is week 11 and the latest start is week 11 − 3 = 8.

Table 19.1

Activity	Duration	Earliest start	Earliest finish	Latest start	Latest finish
A	3	0	3	0	3
B	2	0	2	6	8
C	2	3	5	7	9
D	4	3	7	3	7
E	1	5	6	9	10
F	3	7	10	7	10
G	3	2	5	8	11
H	4	5	9	11	15
I	5	10	15	10	15

Repeating these calculations for all activities in the project gives the results in Table 19.1. In this table there are some activities that have flexibility in time:

activity G, as we have seen, can start as early as week 2 or as late as week 8, while activity C can start as early as week 3 or as late as week 7. Conversely, there are others activities that have no flexibility at all: activities A, D, F, and I have no freedom and their latest start time is the same as their earliest start time. The activities that have to be done at fixed times are called the **critical activities**, and they form a continuous path through the network, called the **critical path**. The length of this path determines the overall project duration. If one of the critical activities is extended by a certain amount the overall project duration is also extended by this amount; if one of the critical activities is delayed by some time the overall project duration is extended by the time of the delay. Conversely, if one of the critical activities is reduced in duration the overall project duration may be reduced by this amount.

Those activities that have some flexibility in timing are the **non-critical activities**, and these may be delayed or extended without necessarily affecting the overall project duration. However, there is a limit to the possible expansion, and this is measured by the **float**. The total float of an activity is defined as the difference between the maximum amount of time available for it and the time actually used. It follows that critical activities have zero total float, while non-critical activities have some positive amount:

> Total float = latest finish − earliest start − duration

Calculating the total float for activity G in the example above has:

> latest finish = latest time of following event (7) = 11
>
> earliest start = earliest time of preceding event (3) = 2
>
> duration of activity G = 3

So:

> total float = latest finish − earliest start − duration
>
> = 11 − 2 − 3 = 6

Repeating the calculations for other activities in the example gives the results in Table 19.2.

The total float measures the amount by which an activity can expand without affecting the duration of the project. Activity E, for example, can expand by up to four weeks without affecting the duration of the project, as can activity C. However, these expansions are not independent, and only one of them can occur without delaying the project.

Table 19.2

Activity	Duration	Earliest start	Earliest finish	Latest start	Latest finish	Total float
A	3	0	3	0	3	0 *
B	2	0	2	6	8	6
C	2	3	5	7	9	4
D	4	3	7	3	7	0 *
E	1	5	6	9	10	4
F	3	7	10	7	10	0
G	3	2	5	8	11	6
H	4	5	9	11	15	6
I	5	10	15	10	15	0 *

WORKED EXAMPLE 19.5

A small telephone exchange is planned as a project with ten main activities. Estimated durations (in weeks) and dependences are shown in Table 19.3. Draw the network for this project, find its duration and calculate the total float of each activity.

Table 19.3

Activity	Description	Duration	Depends on
A	design internal equipment	10	–
B	design exchange building	5	A
C	order parts for equipment	3	A
D	order material for building	2	B
E	wait for equipment parts	15	C
F	wait for building material	10	D
G	employ equipment assemblers	5	A
H	employ building workers	4	B
I	install equipment	20	E, G, J
J	complete building	30	F, H

Solution

The network for this is shown in Figure 19.11; repeating the calculations described above gives the results listed in Table 19.4. The duration of the project is 77 days, defined by the critical path A, B, D, F, I and J.

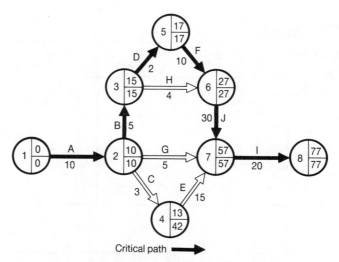

Figure 19.11 Network for Worked Example 19.5.

Table 19.4

Activity	Duration	Earliest		Latest		Total float
		start	finish	start	finish	
A	10	0	10	0	10	0 *
B	5	10	15	10	15	0 *
C	3	10	13	39	42	29
D	2	15	17	15	17	0 *
E	15	13	28	42	57	29
F	10	17	27	17	27	0 *
G	5	10	15	52	57	42
H	4	15	19	23	27	8
I	20	57	77	57	77	0 *
J	30	27	57	27	57	0 *

IN SUMMARY

An earliest and latest start and finish time can be found for each activity. The amount of flexibility that is available can be measured by the total float. Critical activities have no float and form the critical path, which determines the overall project duration.

Self-assessment questions

19.8   How are the earliest and latest times for an event calculated?

19.9   What is meant by the total float of an activity?

19.10 How big is the total float of a critical activity?

19.11 What is the significance of the critical path?

‖ 19.4 ‖ Project evaluation and review technique

The approach we have described so far is the **critical path method** (CPM), in which each activity is given a single, fixed duration. A useful extension to this adds some uncertainty to activity durations. This extension is the main difference between CPM and PERT (project evaluation and review technique).

Experience suggests that activity durations can often be described by a beta distribution. This looks like a skewed Normal distribution, and has one very useful property: the mean and variance can be found from three estimates of duration. In particular it needs:

- an optimistic duration O, which is the shortest time that an activity will take if everything goes smoothly and without any difficulties
- a most likely duration M, which is the duration of the activity under normal conditions
- a pessimistic duration P, which is the time needed if there are significant problems and delays

Expected activity duration and variance are then calculated from the **rule of sixths**:

$$\text{Expected duration} = \frac{O + 4M + P}{6}$$

$$\text{Variance} = \frac{(P - O)^2}{36}$$

Suppose the duration of a particular activity is uncertain but can be assigned an optimistic duration of four days, a most likely duration of five days and a pessimistic duration of 12 days. Assuming a beta distribution for duration:

$$\text{Expected duration} = \frac{O + 4M + P}{6} = \frac{4 + 4 \times 5 + 12}{6} = 6$$

$$\text{Variance} = \frac{(P - O)^2}{36} = \frac{(12 - 4)^2}{36} = 1.78$$

The expected durations from these calculations can be used for analysing project timing in the same way as the single estimate of CPM.

WORKED EXAMPLE 19.6

A network consists of nine activities with dependences and estimated activity durations shown in Table 19.5. Draw the network, identify the critical path and estimate the overall duration of the project.

Table 19.5

Solution

Using the rule of sixths for activity A:

			Duration	
Activity	*Depends on*	*Optimistic*	*Most likely*	*Pessimistic*
A	-	2	3	10
B	-	4	5	12
C	-	8	10	12
D	A, G	4	4	4
E	B	3	6	15
F	B	2	5	8
G	B	6	6	6
H	C, F	5	7	15
I	D, E	6	8	10

$$\text{expected duration} = \frac{O + 4M + P}{6} = \frac{2 + 4 \times 3 + 10}{6} = 4$$

$$\text{variance} = \frac{(P - O)^2}{36} = \frac{(10 - 2)^2}{36} = 1.78$$

Repeating these calculations for other activities gives the results listed in Table 19.6. The network for this problem is drawn in Figure 19.12. The analysis of activity times gives the results listed in Table 19.7. The critical path for the project is B, G, D and I which has an expected duration of 24.

Table 19.6

Activity	*Expected duration*	*Variance*
A	43	1.78
B	6	1.78
C	10	0.44
D	4	0
E	7	4.00
F	5	1.00
G	6	0
H	8	2.78
I	8	0.44

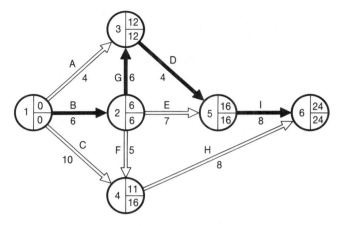

Figure 19.12 Network for Worked Example 19.6.

Table 19.7

Activity	Expected duration	Earliest start	Earliest finish	Latest start	Latest finish	Total float
A	4	0	4	8	12	8
B	6	0	6	0	6	0 *
C	10	0	10	6	16	6
D	4	12	16	12	16	0 *
E	7	6	13	9	16	3
F	5	6	11	11	16	5
G	6	6	12	6	12	0 *
H	8	11	19	16	24	5
I	8	16	24	16	24	0 *

The duration of the critical path is the sum of the durations of activities making up that path. If there are a large number of activities on the path, and if the duration of each activity is independent of the others, then the overall duration of the project will follow a Normal distribution. This distribution has:

- a mean equal to the sum of the expected durations of activities on the critical path

- a variance equal to the sum of the variances of activities on the critical path

These values can be used to find the probability that a project will be completed by any particular time.

WORKED EXAMPLE 19.7

What are the probabilities that the project described in Worked Example 19.6 will be finished before: (a) day 26,   (b) day 20?

Solution

The critical path has been identified as activities B, G, D and I with expected durations of 6, 6, 4 and 8 respectively and variances of 1.78, 0, 0 and 0.44 respectively. Although the number of activities on the critical path is small, we can reasonably assume that the overall duration of the project is Normally distributed (at least to illustrate the process) as shown in Figure 19.13. The expected duration then has mean 6 + 6 + 4 + 8 = 24. The variance in project duration is 1.78 + 0 + 0 + 0.44 = 2.22, so the standard deviation is $\sqrt{2.22}$ = 1.49.

(a) The probability that it will not be finished before 26 can be found using normal distribution tables with Z as the number of standard deviations by which the point of interest is away from the mean:

$$Z = \frac{26 - 24}{1.49} = 1.34 \text{ standard deviations}$$

Normal tables (in Appendix G) show that this corresponds to a probability of = 0.0901.

(b) Similarly, the probability that it will be finished before 20 is:

$$Z = \frac{24 - 20}{1.49} = 2.68 \text{ standard deviations}$$

probability = 0.0037

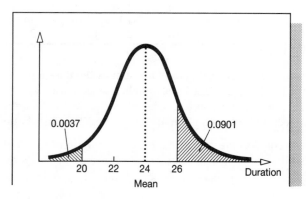

Figure 19.13   Normal distribution of project duration in Worked Example 19.7.

IN SUMMARY

When there is uncertainty in an activity's duration, an expected duration and variance can be found using the rule of sixths. The timing analysis is then the same as for CPM networks. The overall project duration is Normally distributed with mean and variance found by adding values for activities on the critical path.

Self-assessment questions

19.12 What is the difference between CPM and PERT?

19.13 What is the 'rule of sixths' and when is it used?

19.14 How could you calculate the expected duration of a project and its variance?

‖ 19.5 ‖ Resource planning

‖ 19.5.1 ‖ Changing project durations

There are two main reasons why project durations may need changing:

● when a network is analysed the timing is found to be unacceptable (it may, for example, take longer than the organization has available)

● during the execution of a project an activity might take a different time from that originally planned

Taking the first of these, the initial length of a project may be excessive and need reducing. To do this we must remember that the duration of a project is set by the critical path. Then any reductions in the overall duration can only be achieved by reducing the durations of critical activities. Reducing the duration of non-critical activities will have no effect on the overall project duration.

We must also consider what happens when a critical path is shortened. Small reductions may have little effect, but if we keep reducing the time of the critical path there must come a point when some other path through the network becomes critical. This point can be found from the total float on paths parallel to the critical path. Each activity on a parallel path has the same total float, and when the critical path is reduced by more than this, the parallel path becomes critical.

WORKED EXAMPLE 19.8

The project network shown in Figure 19.14 has a duration of 14 with A, B and C as the critical path. If each activity can be reduced by up to 50% of the original duration, how would you reduce the overall duration to: (a) 13 weeks, (b) 11 weeks, (c) 9 weeks? If reductions cost an average of £1,000 per week what would be the cost of finishing the project by week 9?

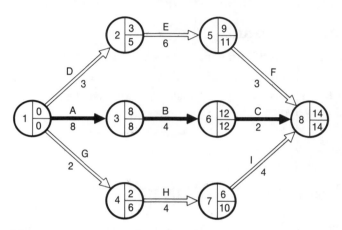

Figure 19.14   Network for Worked Example 19.8.

Solution

The analysis of activity times for this project is shown in Table 19.8. The amount by which the critical path can be reduced without affecting any parallel path is found from the total float in parallel paths. In this network there are three parallel paths: A–B–C, D–E–F and G–H–I. The total floats of activities on these paths are 0, 2 and 4 respectively. This means that the critical path A–B–C can be reduced by up to 2, but if it is reduced by more than this the path D–E–F

Table 19.8

Activity	Duration	Earliest		Latest		Total float
		start	*finish*	*start*	*finish*	
A	8	0	8	0	8	0 *
B	4	8	12	8	12	0 *
C	2	12	14	12	14	0 *
D	3	0	3	2	5	2
E	6	3	9	5	11	2
F	3	9	12	11	14	2
G	2	0	2	4	6	4
H	4	2	6	6	10	4
I	4	6	10	10	14	4

becomes critical. If the critical path is reduced by more than 4, the path G–H–I becomes critical.

(a) A reduction of 1 week is needed in the critical path, so reducing the longest activity (as it is usually easier to find savings in longer activities) would give activity A a duration of 7 weeks and the project could be finished by week 13.

(b) To finish in 11 weeks requires a further reduction of 2 weeks in the critical path, and this can again be removed from A. Unfortunately, the path D–E–F now becomes critical with a duration of 12 weeks, and a week must be removed from E (again chosen as the longest activity in the critical path).

(c) To finish in 9 weeks would need 5 weeks removed from the path A–B–C (say 4 from A and 1 from B), 3 weeks removed from the path D–E–F (say from E) and 1 week removed from the path G–H–I (say from H).

To achieve a 5-week reduction in project duration has meant a total reduction of $5 + 3 + 1 = 9$ weeks from individual activities, at a total cost of £9,000.

The duration of a project can often be reduced by using more resources and hence increasing costs. Then a compromise is needed between time and costs, and some useful calculations for this are based on two figures:

● **normal time** is the expected time to complete the activity, and this has an associated **normal cost**

● **crashed time** is the shortest possible time to complete the activity, and this has a higher **crashed cost**

To simplify the analysis, it is usually assumed that the cost of completing an activity in any particular time is a linear combination of these costs. Then the cost of crashing an activity by a unit of time is:

$$\text{cost of crashing by one time unit} = \frac{\text{crashed cost} - \text{normal cost}}{\text{normal time} - \text{crashed time}}$$

IN SUMMARY

A critical path can only be reduced by a certain amount before another path becomes critical. This limit is the total float of each activity on the parallel path. The cost of a project varies with its duration.

19.5.2 | Gantt charts and resource levelling

When a project is being executed, there should be constant monitoring of progress to ensure that activities are performed at the required times. These required times are not always clear from a network, but a **Gantt chart** shows them much more clearly. A Gantt chart is simply another way of representing a project, which emphasizes the timing of activities. The chart has a timescale across the bottom; activities are listed down the left-hand side, and times when activities should be done are blocked off in the body of the chart.

WORKED EXAMPLE 19.9

Draw a Gantt chart for the original data in Worked Example 19.8, assuming that each activity starts as early as possible.

Solution

The activity analysis for this example was listed in Table 19.8. If each activity

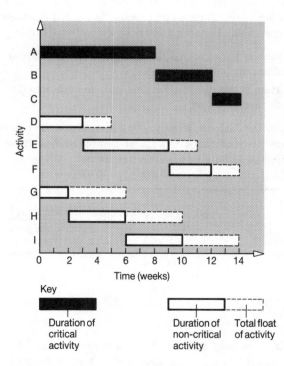

Figure 19.15 Gantt chart for Worked Example 19.9.

starts as early as possible, the time needed is shown by the blocked-off areas in Figure 19.15. The total float of each activity is added afterwards as a broken line. The total float is the maximum expansion that can still allow the project to finish on time, so provided an activity is completed before the end of the broken line there should be no problem keeping to the planned project duration.

The main benefit of Gantt charts is that they show clearly the state of each activity at any point in the project. They show which activities should be in hand, as well as those that should be finished, and those about to start. Gantt charts are also useful for planning the allocation of resources.

Consider the Gantt chart shown in Figure 19.15 and assume, for simplicity, that each activity uses one unit of a particular resource (perhaps one team of workers). If all activities start as soon as possible, we can draw a vertical bar chart to show the resources in use at any time. The project starts with activities

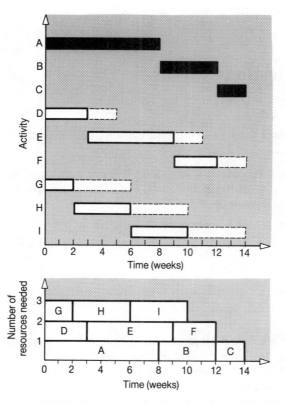

Figure 19.16   Resources used during project of Worked Example 19.9.

A, D and G so three teams will be used. At the end of week 2 one team can move from G to H, but three teams will still be needed. Continuing this allocation gives the graph of resources shown in Figure 19.16.

In this example, the use of resources is steady for most of the project and only begins to fall near the end. It is rare to get such a smooth pattern of resource use, and usually there are a series of peaks and troughs, which should be levelled. As critical activities are at fixed times, this levelling must be done by rescheduling non-critical activities, and in particular by delaying those activities with relatively large total floats.

Adjusting and monitoring schedules, workloads, times and costs needs a lot of arithmetic and is best done using a computer. Unfortunately, the quality of software for project network analysis is variable. Some programs need details of the network to be specified as input data and simply do the timing calculations.

IN SUMMARY

Gantt charts give another representation of projects, emphasizing the timing. They are primarily used in the planning of resources, and to monitor progress through the execution phase of a project.

Self-assessment questions

19.15 Which activities must be shortened to reduce the overall duration of a project?

19.16 By how much can a critical path usefully be shortened?

19.17 What is the crashed time of an activity?

19.18 'The total cost of a project declines with its duration, as penalty costs, labour costs, financing costs, etc are all reduced with shorter times.' Is this statement true?

19.19 What are the main benefits of Gantt charts?

19.20 How can the use of resources be smoothed during a project?

CHAPTER REVIEW

A project is a coherent piece of work with a clear start and finish. It consists of the activities needed to make a distinct product. This chapter has described the way in which project network analysis can help with the planning and control of projects. In particular it:

- showed how the relationship between activities in a project can be shown in a dependence table
- showed how a project can be represented by a network of alternating activities and events
- calculated the timing of events and activities
- found the critical path
- described PERT for activities of uncertain length
- changed the duration of a project
- used Gantt charts to monitor progress and plan resources.

Problems

19.1 A project consists of the activities described by the following dependence table. Draw the network for this project.

Activity	Depends on	Activity	Depends on
A	-	G	B
B	-	H	G
C	A	I	E, F
D	A	J	H, I
E	C	K	E, F
F	B, D	L	K

19.2 (a) An amateur dramatic society is planning its annual production and is interested in using a network to coordinate the various activities. What activities do you think should be included in the network?

(b) If discussions lead to the following activities, what would the network look like?

- assess resources and select play
- select actors and cast parts
- design and organize advertisements
- prepare stage, lights and sound
- final arrangements for opening
- prepare scripts
- rehearse
- build scenery
- sell tickets

19.3 Draw a network for the dependence table shown in Table 19.9.

Table 19.9

Activity	Depends on	Activity	Depends on
A	H	I	F
B	H	J	I
C	K	K	L
D	I, M, N	L	F
E	F	M	O
F	–	N	H
G	E, L	O	A, B
H	E	P	N

19.4 If each activity in problem 19.3 has a duration of one week, find the earliest and latest times for each event. Calculate the earliest and latest start and finish times for each activity and the corresponding total floats.

19.5 Draw the network represented by the dependence table given in Table 19.10, and calculate the total float for each activity. If each activity can be reduced by up to two weeks, what is the shortest duration of the project and which activities are reduced?

Table 19.10

Activity	Duration (weeks)	Depends on
A	5	-
B	3	-
C	3	B
D	7	A
E	10	B
F	14	A, C
G	7	D, E
H	4	E
I	5	D

19.6 A project is represented by the data in Table 19.11, which shows the dependence of activities and three estimates of durations.

(a) What is the probability that the project will be completed before time 17?

(b) By what time is there a probability of 0.95 that the project will be finished?

Table 19.11

Activity	Depends on	Duration		
		Optimistic	Most likely	Pessimistic
A	-	1	2	3
B	A	1	3	6
C	B	4	6	10
D	A	1	1	1
E	D	1	2	2
F	E	3	4	8
G	F	2	3	5
H	D	7	9	11
I	A	0	1	4
J	I	2	3	4
K	H, J	3	4	7
L	C, G, K	1	2	7

19.7 A project consists of ten activities with estimated durations (in weeks) and dependences shown in Table 19.12.

(a) What are the estimated duration of the project and the earliest and latest times for activities?

(b) If activity B requires special equipment to be hired, when should this be scheduled?

(c) A check on the project at week 12 shows that activity F is running 2 weeks late, that activity J will now take 6 weeks, and that the equipment for B will not arrive until week 18. What affect does this have on the overall project duration?

Table 19.12

Activity	Depends	Duration	Activity	Depends	Duration
A	-	8	F	C, D	10
B	A	6	G	B, E, F	5
C	-	10	H	F	8
D	-	6	I	G, H, J	6
E	C	2	J	A	4

19.8 Draw a Gantt chart for the project described in Problem 19.7. If each activity uses one team of men, draw a graph of manpower requirements assuming each activity starts as soon as possible. How might these requirements be smoothed?

19.9 Analyse the times and resource requirements of the project described by the data in Table 19.13.

Table 19.13

Activity	Depends on	Duration	Resources
A	-	4	1
B	A	4	2
C	A	3	4
D	B	5	4
E	C	2	2
F	D, E	6	3
G	-	3	3
H	G	7	1
I	G	6	5
J	H	2	3
K	I	4	4
L	J, K	8	2

19.10 In the project described in Problem 19.9 it costs £1,000 to reduce the duration of an activity by 1. If there is £12,000 available to reduce the overall duration of the project, how should this be allocated and what is the shortest time in which the project can be completed? What are the minimum resources needed by the revised schedule?

Computer exercises

19.1 Figure 19.17 shows a printout from a program that is set to do a PERT analysis. Make sure you understand what is happening in this printout. Draw the network described. Use appropriate software to check the results.

PROJECT PLANNING AND CONTROL
Three Time Estimates
DATA ENTERED

Activity	Times		# pred	<− −predecessor activities −>	
1 Plan	Optimistic	12	0		
	Modal	14			
	Pessimistic	18			
2 Searc	Optimistic	2	0		
	Modal	3			
	Pessimistic	5			
3 Order	Optimistic	10	1	1–Plan	
	Modal	12			
	Pessimistic	14			
4 Emplo	Optimistic	2	1	2–Searc	
	Modal	5			
	Pessimistic	8			
5 Buy	Optimistic	3	1	1–Plan	
	Modal	4			
	Pessimistic	4			
6 Cost	Optimistic	3	1	2–Searc	
	Modal	5			
	Pessimistic	6			
7 Build	Optimistic	12	2	4–Emplo	5–Buy
	Modal	15			
	Pessimistic	20			
8 Setup	Optimistic	2	2	4–Emplo	5–Buy
	Modal	5			
	Pessimistic	8			
9 Check	Optimistic	2	2	3–Order	8–Setup
	Modal	5			
	Pessimistic	8			
10 Contr	Optimistic	6	1	6–Cost	
	Modal	7			
	Pessimistic	9			

SOLUTION

Activity		Start	Finish	Expected Duration	Total Float	Critical Path
1 Plan	Earliest:	0	14.333	14.333	0	yes
	Latest:	0	14.333			
2 Searc	Earliest:	0	3.167	3.167	10	no
	Latest:	10	13.167			
3 Order	Earliest:	14.333	26.333	12	2.167	no
	Latest:	16.500	28.500			

Figure 19.17 Printout for PERT analysis.

4 Emplo	Earliest:	3.167	8.167	5	10	no
	Latest:	13.167	18.167			
5 Buy	Earliest:	14.333	18.167	3.833	0	yes
	Latest:	14.333	18.167			
6 Cost	Earliest:	3.167	8	4.833	18.333	no
	Latest:	21.500	26.333			
7 Build	Earliest:	18.167	33.500	15.333	0	yes
	Latest:	18.167	33.500			
8 Setup	Earliest:	18.167	23.167	5	5.333	no
	Latest:	23.500	28.500			
9 Check	Earliest:	26.333	31.333	5	2.167	no
	Latest:	28.500	33.500			
10 Contr	Earliest:	8	15.167	7.167	18.333	no
	Latest:	26.333	33.500			

Project Summary

Expected Completion Time	:	33.500		
Variance on Critical Path	:	2.806		
Standard Deviation	:	1.675		
Critical Path =	1-Plan	5-Buy	7-Build	

PROBABILITY ANALYSIS

Project Due Date	:	30
Expected Completion Time	:	33.500
Variance on Critical Path	:	2.806
Standard Deviation	:	1.675
Z (number of standard deviations)	:	-2.090
Probability of Completion by Due Date	:	0.018
Revised Due Date	:	31
Expected Completion time	:	33.500
Variance on Critical Path	:	2.806
Standard Deviation	:	1.675
Z (number of standard deviations)	:	-1.493
Probability of Completion by Due Date	:	0.068

Figure 19.17   Printout for PERT analysis (continued).

19.2   Figure 19.18 shows a printout from a program that crashes networks. Make sure you understand what is happening. Draw a network of the problem. Use appropriate software to check the calculations and give a full analysis of results. Notice that this part of the program only analyses the timing of a network. This has to be drawn by some other means, so that the input data includes the start and end events for each activity.

Input Data for the Problem – CPM Demonstration   Page 1

Activity number	Activity name	Start event	End event	Normal duration	Crash duration	Normal cost	Crash cost
1	Start 1	1	2	15.000	12.000	4500	5500
2	Start 2	1	3	10.000	8.000	3000	4500
3	Check	2	3	7.000	5.000	1500	1800
4	Build	2	4	8.000	6.000	800	1200
5	Employ	3	4	15.000	10.000	4000	5000
6	Purchase	3	5	12.000	10.000	3500	4000
7	Install	4	6	16.000	12.000	6000	8000
8	Operate	5	6	12.000	8.000	6000	8000

CPM Analysis for the problem – CPM Demonstration

Activity number	Activity name	Earliest Start	Latest Start	Earliest Finish	Latest Finish	Slack LS–ES
1	Start 1	0	0	15.000	15.000	Critical
2	Start 2	0	12.000	10.000	22.000	12.000
3	Check	15.000	15.000	22.000	22.000	Critical
4	Build	15.000	29.000	23.000	37.000	14.000
5	Employ	22.000	22.000	37.000	37.000	Critical
6	Purchase	22.000	29.000	34.000	41.000	7.000
7	Install	37.000	37.000	53.000	53.000	Critical
8	Operate	34.000	41.000	46.000	53.000	7.000

Completion time = 53   Total cost = 29300

Critical paths for CPM Analysis for the problem – CPM Demonstration

Critical Path Number 1   :
Activities   Start 1   Check   Employ   Install
Events   1 =====> 2 =====> 3 ======> 4   ======> 6

Crash Analysis for the Problem – CPM Demonstration   Page 2

Target Crashed Duration is 40

Activity number	Activity name	Earliest Start	Latest Start	Earliest Finish	Latest Finish	Slack LS–ES
1	Start 1	0	0	12.000	12.000	Critical
2	Start 2	0	7.000	10.000	17.000	7.000
3	Check	12.000	12.000	17.000	17.000	Critical
4	Build	12.000	19.000	20.000	27.000	7.000
5	Employ	17.000	17.000	27.000	27.000	Critical
6	Purchase	17.000	17.000	28.000	28.000	Critical
7	Install	27.000	27.000	40.000	40.000	Critical
8	Operate	28.000	28.000	40.000	40.000	Critical

Completion time =40   Total cost = 33350

Critical Paths for CPM Analysis for the Problem – CPM Demonstration

Critical Path Number 1   :
Activities   Start 1   Check   Employ   Install
Events   1 ======> 2 ======> 3 ======> 4 ======> 6

Figure 19.18   Printout for an analysis of crashed costs.

```
Critical Path Number 2   :
Activities            Start 1            Check          Purchase          Operate
Events          1  ======>  2  ======>  3  ======>  5  ======>  6
```

Analysis of Crashed Activities for the Problem – CPM Demonstration

```
Crash activity Start 1
     by 3 time units:  new duration = 12:   incremental cost = 1000
Crash activity Check
     by 2 time units:  new duration =  5:   incremental cost =  300;
Crash activity Employ
     by 5 time units:  new duration = 10:   incremental cost = 1000
Crash activity Purchase
     by 1 time units:  new duration = 11:   incremental cost =  250
Crash activity Install
     by 3 time units:  new duration = 13:   incremental cost = 1500
```

Crashed duration = 40:   new duration = 4050:   Crashed cost = 33350

Figure 19.18   Printout for an analysis of crashed costs (continued).

19.3 Design a spreadsheet that will do the calculations to analyse CPM and PERT networks. Use this to check the results obtained in this chapter.

19.4 Find a project with which you are familiar and break it into about 50 activities. Draw the network for the project, and do the relevant analyses. Write a detailed report on your findings.

Case study
Westin Contractors

William Purvis looked across his desk at the company's latest recruit and said: 'Welcome to Westin Contractors. This is a good company to work for, and I hope you settle in and will be very happy here. Everyone working for Westin has to be familiar with our basic tools, so you should start by looking at network analysis. Here is a small project we have just costed, and I have to give the customer some details about times, workloads and costs by the end of the week. I would like a couple of alternative views, with your recommendation of the best. Everything you need is available in the office, so don't be afraid to ask for help and advice.'

William Purvis supplied the data listed in Table 19.14. There is a penalty cost of £3,500 for every week the project finished after week 28. Prepare a suitable report for the company.

Table 19.14

Activity	Depends on	Normal time	cost	Crashed time	cost	Number of teams
A	-	3	13	2	15	3
B	A	7	25	4	28	4
C	B, E	5	16	4	19	4
D	C	5	12	3	24	2
E	-	8	32	5	38	6
F	E	6	20	4	30	1
G	F	8	30	6	35	5
H	-	12	41	7	45	6
I	H	6	25	3	30	4
J	E	4	18	3	26	6
K	I, J	12	52	10	60	4
L	I, J	6	20	3	30	1
M	D, G, I	2	7	1	14	1
N	B, E	6	18	5	24	5

Queues and simulation

CHAPTER OUTLINE

This chapter looks at the management of queues. We are all familiar with queues of people, but there are many other types of queue, such as programs queuing to be processed in a computer system, faulty machines queuing to be repaired, or aeroplanes queuing to land

Models of queuing systems often have the objective of balancing the number of servers with the length of the queue. Unfortunately, analytical solutions can only be found for small problems.

Simulation offers a more robust method of tackling queuing problems by imitating the operations of the system over a typical period. It is widely used and can tackle problems that are too complex to be solved by other means. Unfortunately, the models involve large amounts of arithmetic, so computers are always used in practice.

After reading this chapter and doing the exercise you should be able to:

- appreciate the scope of queuing problems
- calculate the characteristics of queues at a single server where both arrival and service times are random
- describe the characteristic approach of simulation
- do manual simulations of queuing systems
- appreciate the use of computers in simulation

20.1 | Background to queuing

Queues form when customers want a particular service but must wait to be served. This situation is familiar to us all; it happens when buying a ticket for a train, getting money from a bank, at the checkout of a supermarket, waiting for traffic lights to change, and in many other circumstances. Not all queues involve people, so we may also have a queue of jobs waiting to be processed on a computer, items waiting to move along an assembly line, telephone calls waiting for equipment to become free, faulty equipment waiting for maintenance engineers, or ships waiting for a berth.

All queues have features in common, so we can describe some general characteristics. By convention a **customer** is anyone or anything wanting a service and a **server** is the person or thing providing that service. Then queues are formed when a customer wants a service, but arrives to find that the server is busy. The customer may decide not to use the service, particularly if other customers are already waiting, but more usually they decide to wait and line up in the queue (Figure 20.1).

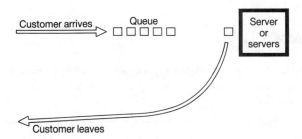

Figure 20.1 A single server queuing system.

The queue formed can take many forms:

- customers may form a single queue or they may form separate queues for each server
- customers may arrive singly or in batches (when, for example, a train arrives)
- arrivals may be at random or spread out by an appointment system
- customers may be served individually or in batches (at a bus stop, for example)
- servers may be in parallel (where each does the same job) or in series (where each provides part of the service and then passes the customer on to the next stage)
- service time may be constant or variable
- customers may be served in order of arrival or some other order (hospitals may admit patients in order of urgency, and so on)

As you know from experience, the service provided is, in part, judged by the time that customers have to wait. The length of the queue depends on three factors:

- the rate at which customers arrive to be served
- the time taken for a server to deal with a customer
- the number of servers available

In a given situation, providing a lot of servers gives a short queue, but the cost of providing the service is high; providing a few servers reduces the cost of the service, but potential customers might see the length of the queues and go elsewhere. A balance is needed that seems reasonable to all parties. This will differ according to circumstances. When visiting a doctor's surgery it is common to wait a long time. This is because doctors' time is considered expensive while patients' time is cheap. To ensure that the doctor does not wait for patients, appointments are made close together and patients are expected to wait. Conversely, in petrol stations the cost of servers (petrol pumps) is low and customers will generally drive to a competitor if there is a queue. Then a large number of servers is provided and, although the utilization of each server is low, customers wait a short time in any queue.

IN SUMMARY

Queues arise in many situations, not all of which involve people. When managing queues, a balance is needed between large numbers of servers and reasonable costs.

Self-assessment questions

20.1 What causes a queue?

20.2 'It is undesirable to make customers wait, so enough servers should be provided to eliminate queues.' Is this statement true?

20.2 Single-server queues

The simplest type of queue consists of a single server dealing with a queue of customers who arrive at random and use random service times. If we make some more assumptions we can build a model with the following features:

- a single server
- random arrivals
- random service time
- service is in the order 'first come first served'
- the system has reached its steady state
- there is no limit to the number of customers allowed in the queue
- there is no limit on the number of customers who use the service
- all arrivals wait to be served

In Chapter 14 we said that random occurrences could be described by a Poisson distribution. Now we can use this to describe customer arrivals. If the average number of customers arriving per unit time is λ the probability of r arrivals in unit time is:

$$P(r) = \frac{e^{-\lambda} \times \lambda^{r}}{r!}$$

where:

r = number of arrivals

λ = mean number of arrivals

e = exponential constant (2.71828...)

Service time is a continuous variable, which experience suggests often follows a negative exponential distribution (Figure 20.2). This is related to the Poisson distribution and has the useful property that the probability of service time not exceeding some specified value T is given by

$$P(t \leqslant T) = 1 - e^{-\mu T}$$

where:

μ = mean service rate

= the average number of customers served per unit of time

so the probability that service is not completed by time T is

$$P(t > T) = 1 - P(t \leqslant T) = e^{-\mu T}$$

We have now described a random arrival rate of customers in terms of λ (the mean arrival rate) and a random service time in terms of μ (the mean service rate). If the mean arrival rate is greater than the mean service rate, the system will never settle down to a steady state but the queue will increase in length continuously. Any analysis of queues must, then, assume that a steady state has been reached and that μ is greater than λ.

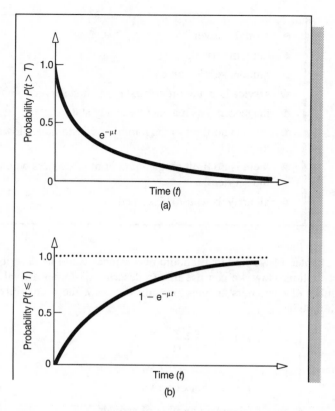

Figure 20.2 Random service times follow a negative expotential distribution:
(a) probability that service is not completed within a time T;
(b) probability that service is completed within a time T.

The following set of results describe the **operating characteristics** of a single-server queue. Some of these results are not obvious and will need some thinking about. Here they are quoted as standard results without a detailed derivation.

On average, the system is busy for a proportion of time λ/μ. Here 'busy' is defined as having at least one customer either being served or in the queue. This is also the average number of customers being served at any time. If, for example, the mean arrival rate is two an hour and the mean service rate is four an hour, we have $\lambda/\mu = 2/4 = 0.5$. This means that the system is busy for half the time or there is an average of half a customer in the system.

The probability that there is no customer in the system is

$$P_0 = 1 - \lambda/\mu$$

This is the probability that a new customer can be served without any wait.

The probability that there are n customers in the system is given by

$$P_n = P_0(\lambda/\mu)^n$$

This result (which may not be obvious but can be accepted as generally true) allows us to calculate some other characteristics of the queue. To start with, the average number of customers in the system is given by

$$L = \sum_{n=0}^{\infty} nP_n = \frac{\lambda}{\mu - \lambda}$$

The average number of customers in the queue is equal to the average number in the system minus the average number being served:

$$L_q = L - \frac{\lambda}{\mu} = \frac{\lambda}{\mu - \lambda} - \frac{\lambda}{\mu} = \frac{\lambda^2}{\mu(\mu - \lambda)}$$

If L is the average number of customers in the system and λ is the mean arrival rate, the average time that any arriving customer has to spend in the system is given by

$$W = \frac{L}{\lambda} = \frac{1}{\mu - \lambda}$$

The average time spent in the queue is the average time in the system minus the average service time:

$$W_q = W - \frac{1}{\mu} = \frac{\lambda}{\mu(\mu - \lambda)}$$

WORKED EXAMPLE 20.1

People arrive randomly at a bank teller at an average rate of 30 an hour. What are the average numbers of customer in the queue if the teller takes an average of 0.5 minutes to serve each customer? What happens if the average service time changes to 1.0, 1.5 or 2.0 minutes? What are the average times in the queue for each service time?

Solution

The average arrival rate is $\lambda = 30$. If the teller takes an average of 0.5 minutes to serve each customer, this is equivalent to a service rate of 120 an hour. Then the average number of customers in the queue (excluding anyone being served) is L_q:

$$L_q = \frac{\lambda^2}{\mu(\mu - \lambda)} = \frac{30^2}{120 \times (120 - 30)} = 0.083$$

The average time in the queue is W_q:

$$W_q = \frac{\lambda}{\mu(\mu - \lambda)} = \frac{30}{120 \times (120 - 30)} = 0.003 \text{ hours}$$

Similarly, substituting $\mu = 60$ and 40 (corresponding to average service times of one minute and 1.5 minutes respectively) gives

$$\mu = 60: \; L_q = 0.5 \qquad W_q = 0.017 \text{ hours}$$

$$\mu = 40: \; L_q = 2.25 \qquad W_q = 0.075 \text{ hours}$$

If the average service time is raised to 2 minutes, the service rate is $\mu = 30$. This does not satisfy the condition that $\mu > \lambda$, so the system will not settle down to a steady state and the queue will continue to grow.

To find the average number of people in the system rather than the queue:

$$L = L_q + \lambda/\mu$$

Similarly, the average time in the system is

$$W = W_q + 1/\mu$$

Then:

$\mu = 120$: $L = 0.083 + 30/120 = 0.333$

                $W = 0.003 + 1/120 = 0.011 \text{ hours} = 0.66 \text{ minutes}$

$\mu = 60$: $L = 0.5 + 30/60 = 1.0$

                $W = 0.017 + 1/60 = 0.034 \text{ hours} = 2.04 \text{ minutes}$

$\mu = 40$: $L = 2.25 + 30/40 = 3.0$

                $W = 0.075 + 1/40 = 0.1 \text{ hours} = 6.0 \text{ minutes}$

WORKED EXAMPLE 20.2

Customers arrive randomly at a railway information desk at a mean rate of 20 an hour. The single server manning the desk takes an average of two minutes with each customer. Calculate the characteristics of the queuing system.

Solution

The mean arrival rate λ is 20 an hour and the mean service rate μ is 30 an hour.

The probability that there is no one in the system is

$$P_0 = 1 - \lambda/\mu = 1 - 20/30 = 0.33$$

Conversely, there is a probability of 0.67 that a customer has to wait to be served.

The probability of n customers in the system is

$$P_n = P_0 \times (\lambda/\mu)^n = 0.33 \times (0.67)^n$$

That is, $P_1 = 0.22, P_2 = 0.15, P_3 = 0.10, P_4 = 0.07$, etc

The average number of customers in the system is

$$L = \frac{\lambda}{\mu - \lambda} = \frac{20}{30 - 20} = 2$$

The average number of customers in the queue is

$$L_q = \frac{\lambda^2}{\mu(\mu - \lambda)} = \frac{20^2}{30 \times 10} = 1.33$$

The average time that a customer spends in the system is

$$W = \frac{1}{\mu - \lambda} = \frac{1}{30 - 20} = 0.1 \text{ hours} = 6 \text{ minutes}$$

The average time that a customer spends in the queue is

$$W_q = \frac{\mu}{\mu(\mu - \lambda)} = \frac{20}{30 \times 10} = 0.0667 \text{ hours} = 4 \text{ minutes}$$

We could now go on to describe multiserver or other types of queue, but unfortunately the calculations for these become even more complicated. There are two ways of avoiding this:

- use a computer to do the arithmetic
- use some other method of solution

We shall deal with the second of these in the remainder of the chapter. First, though, we should say that it is fairly easy to develop computer software for queuing models and there are a number of standard packages available. Figure 20.3 shows a straightforward printout from a package working with (a) a single-server queue and (b) multiservers. This package, like most others, finds the operating characteristics and then calculates some cost figures.

IN SUMMARY

After making a number of assumptions, the operating characteristics of a single-server queue can be calculated. More complex queuing problems become very difficult to solve. Alternative ways of dealing with these are to use computers or to find a different type of solution procedure.

Self-assessment questions

20.3 Define the variables λ and μ in a queuing system.

20.4 What happens in a queue if $\lambda \geqslant \mu$?

20.5 What are the assumptions of the single-server queue model?

```
SUMMARY OF A 1 CHANNEL WAITING LINE WITH
*************************************************
```
    MEAN NUMBER OF ARRIVALS = 25
    MEAN NUMBER OF SERVICES = 30
    COST FOR UNITS IN THE SYSTEM = £ 20 PER TIME PERIOD
    COST FOR A CHANNEL = £ 35 PER TIME PERIOD

THE PROBABILITY THAT THE CHANNEL IS IDLE	0.1667
THE AVERAGE NUMBER OF UNITS WAITING FOR SERVICE	4.1667
THE AVERAGE NUMBER OF UNITS IN THE SYSTEM	5.0000
THE AVERAGE TIME A UNIT SPENDS WAITING FOR SERVICE	0.1667
THE AVERAGE TIME A UNIT SPENDS IN THE SYSTEM	0.2000
THE PROBABILITY THAT AN ARRIVING UNIT HAS TO WAIT	0.8333
THE TOTAL COST PER TIME PERIOD	£135.00

(a)

```
SUMMARY OF A 4 CHANNEL WAITING LINE WITH
*************************************************
```
    MEAN NUMBER OF ARRIVALS = 100
    MEAN NUMBER OF SERVICES PER CHANNEL = 30
    COST FOR UNITS IN THE SYSTEM = £ 20 PER TIME PERIOD
    COST FOR A CHANNEL = £ 35 PER TIME PERIOD

THE PROBABILITY THAT ALL 4 CHANNELS ARE IDLE	0.0213
THE AVERAGE NUMBER OF UNITS WAITING FOR SERVICE	3.2886
THE AVERAGE NUMBER OF UNITS IN THE SYSTEM	6.6219
THE AVERAGE TIME A UNIT SPENDS WAITING FOR SERVICE	0.0329
THE AVERAGE TIME A UNIT SPENDS IN THE SYSTEM	0.0662
THE PROBABILITY THAT AN ARRIVING UNIT HAS TO WAIT	0.6577
THE TOTAL COST PER TIME PERIOD	£272.44

(b)

Figure 20.3 Printout from a package for analysing queues.

| 20.3 | Simulation models

| 20.3.1 | Overall approach

In this section we are going to describe an alternative way of solving problems. This does not rely on finding the solution to an equation, but on simulating the operations.

The term **simulate** is used quite widely (simulated anger, simulated leather, etc). Here we are going to use it in the same general sense, but specifically referring to the imitation of real situations by quantitative models. In these circumstances, the essential characteristic of simulation is that it is dynamic and duplicates the continuous operation of a system. An ordinary model for, say, stock control looks at the system, collects data for some fixed point of time and draws conclusions: a simulation follows the operations of the system and sees exactly what happens over time. A simple analogy would be an ordinary model providing a snapshot of the system at some fixed point, while a simulation model takes a movie of the system.

We can demonstrate this approach with the following illustration. An item is made on a production line at a rate of one every two minutes. At some point there is an inspection, which takes virtually no time. At this inspection 50% of units are rejected and the remaining 50% continue along the line to the next process which takes three minutes per unit (Figure 20.4).

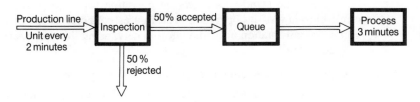

Figure 20.4 An illustration of a simulation.

We might be interested in answering a number of questions about this system, such as:

● How much space should be left for the queue between the inspection and the next process?

● How long will each unit stay in the system?

● What is the utilization of the processor?

● Are there any bottlenecks?

The system is essentially a single-server queue in which all data are known, so a queuing theory model could be used, but we want to develop an alternative approach. One practical alternative would be to stand and watch the system operating over a typical period and see what happens. We could follow a few units through the system and record information, perhaps using a table like that shown in Table 20.1.

Table 20.1

Unit no.	Arrival time	Accept or reject	Time joins queue	No in queue	Time process starts	Time in queue	Time process finish	Time in system
1	0	A	0	0	0	0	3	3
2	2	A	2	0	3	1	6	4
3	4	A	4	0	6	2	9	5
4	6	R	–	–	–	–	–	–
5	8	R	–	–	–	–	–	–
6	10	A	10	0	10	0	13	3

Here the first unit arrived for inspection at some time, which was arbitrarily set to 0. The unit was accepted and moved straight to processing which took 3 minutes. The total time the unit was in the system (consisting of inspection, queue and processing) was 3 minutes.

The second unit arrived at time 2 from the arbitrary start time, was accepted and joined the queue (the fifth column shows the number already in the queue when the next customer joins it). Processing could only start on unit 2 when unit 1 was finished at time 3. This processing then took 3 minutes and unit 2 left the system at time 6.

We could stand and watch the operation for as long as necessary to get a reliable view of its operation. The figures collected could then be analysed to give the information needed. Unfortunately, using this approach has a number of disadvantages:

- it is time-consuming to stand and watch the process
- it might take a large number of observations to get reliable figures
- only one method of operating the production line was observed; comparisons of different methods would need each to be implemented and the observations repeated
- watching a system is unpopular with people working on it (as well as those doing the observation)
- observing a system might change its characteristics (to return to normal when the observer has left)

These disadvantages are eliminated by using simulation to imitate the actual process. In the illustration above we know all the characteristics of the process, so a simulation would duplicate the sheet of observations without our actually having to stand and watch the process.

There is one element of uncertainty in the system: whether a unit is going to be accepted or rejected. We need some method of randomly assigning these decisions to a unit, giving a 50% chance of acceptance and a 50% chance of rejection. An obvious way of doing this would be to spin a coin. If it comes down heads the unit is rejected and if it comes down tails it is accepted (or vice versa). A more formal way of doing the same thing would be to use random numbers, as described in Chapter 3. Given the following string of random digits:

$$5284778016941356756454793017714943179046 5825$$

we could use even digits (including 0) for acceptance and odd digits for rejection. Thus the first unit would be rejected (based on 5), the second would be accepted (based on 2), the third accepted (based on 8), and so on. We could then develop a typical set of results for the process without actually watching it. Table 20.2 shows one set of results using the random numbers above. In this table each unit arriving is given a unique identifying number (in column 1). Then we know that one unit arrives for inspection every 2 minutes, so column 2 can be completed. Column 3 shows the sequence of random numbers and the corresponding decision is given in column 4.

Table 20.2

1	2	3	4	5	6	7	8	9	10
Unit no.	Arrival time	Random number	Accept or reject	Time joins queue	No in queue	Time process starts	Time in queue	Time process finishes	Time in system
1	0	5	R	–	–	–	–	–	0
2	2	2	A	2	0	2	0	5	3
3	4	8	A	4	0	5	1	8	4
4	6	4	A	6	0	8	2	11	5
5	8	7	R	–	–	–	–	–	0
6	10	7	R	–	–	–	–	–	0
7	12	8	A	12	0	12	0	15	3
8	14	0	A	14	0	15	1	18	4
9	16	1	R	–	–	–	–	–	0
10	18	6	A	18	0	18	0	21	3

Units that are rejected leave the system, while those that are accepted join the queue at their arrival time (assuming that the inspection takes no time). This completes column 5. Column 6 shows the number already in the queue, while column 7 shows the time at which processing starts. If there is already a unit being processed, a queue is formed until the processor becomes free (shown in column 9); if there is no unit being processed, work can start immediately (at the time shown in column 5).

Processing finishes three minutes after it starts (shown in column 9) and the time spent in the queue (column 8) is the difference between arrival time and the time that processing starts. Column 10 shows the total time in the system, which is the difference between arrival time and the time that processing is finished.

This gives the rules for calculating each column in the table as:

- column 1: number increases by 1 for each unit entering
- column 2: arrival time increases by 2 for each unit entering
- column 3: from the given string of random numbers
- column 4: a unit is accepted if the corresponding random number is even and is rejected if it is odd
- column 5: accepted units join the queue straight away (that is, at arrival time) while rejected ones leave the system
- column 6: the number already in the queue is 1 more than it was for the last arrival, minus the number that have left since the last arrival
- column 7: processing starts at the arrival time if the equipment is already free, or when the equipment next becomes free (the previous entry in column 9)

- column 8: the time in the queue is the difference between the arrival time in the queue and the time that processing starts (column 7 – column 5)
- column 9: processing finishes three minutes after it starts (column 7 + 3)
- column 10: the time in the system is the difference between the arrival time and the finish of the processing (column 9 – column 2)

The simulation has been run for ten units arriving, and the figures obtained can be used to give a number of results. We can, for example, note that there was at most one unit in the queue for the processor. We could also find:

- number accepted = 6 (in the long run this would be 50% of units)
- number rejected = 4 (again this would be 50% in the long run)
- maximum time in queue = 2 minutes
- average time in queue = 4/6 minutes = 40 seconds
- maximum time in system = 5 minutes
- average time in system = 22/6 = 3.67 minutes
- average time in system including rejects = 22/10 = 2.2 minutes
- processor was busy for 18 minutes
- utilization of processor = 18/21 = 86%

It is important to ask how reliable these figures are. The simulation certainly demonstrates the working of the system through a typical period of 10 units, but this is a very small number of observations. The current results are not likely to be very accurate, so the next step would be to extend this simulation for a much larger number of observations. When information has been collected about several hundred arrivals we can be fairly confident that the results are reliable. As the process includes a random element, we can never be positive that the results are accurate, but large numbers of repetitions should give a reasonable picture. Unfortunately, to repeat the simulation over a large number of observations involves a lot of simple, repetitive arithmetic. This is the kind of process that is ideally suited to computers, so real simulations are never done by hand.

WORKED EXAMPLE 20.3

One customer has an appointment at a reception desk (A) every eight minutes. After answering some standard questions, which takes two minutes, customers are passed on to one of two areas (B or C). 50% of customers are passed to B for five minutes each and 50% are passed to C for ten minutes each. Finally all customers go to area D, where they fill in forms for six minutes before leaving. Simulate this system for ten arrivals and find the utilization of each area.

Solution

This system is shown in Figure 20.5. We are only interested in the times spent in each area so we can do the analysis using the form in Table 20.3. Column 1 gives the unit number arriving, while column 2 shows an arrival every eight minutes starting from a notional time of zero. Column 3 adds 2 minutes for processing at A before each customer is ready to move to B or C. The random numbers in column 4 are from the sequence given previously, starting at an arbitrary point about halfway along. Units corresponding to odd random digits are sent to area B while those corresponding to even digits are sent to area C. After leaving A, a customer can start immediately in areas B or C (if empty) or must wait until the next time their area will become empty (shown in columns 5 or 7). Columns 6 and 8 show the finishing times in areas B and C,

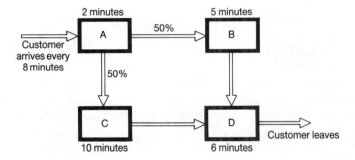

Figure 20.5 Process for Worked Example 20.3.

Table 20.3

1	2	3	4	5	6	7	8	9	10
Arrival number	Start A	Leave A	Random number	Start B	Leave B	Start C	Leave C	Start D	Leave D
1	0	2	6	–	–	2	12	12	18
2	8	10	4	–	–	12	22	22	28
3	16	18	5	18	23	–	–	28	34
4	24	26	4	–	–	26	36	36	42
5	32	34	7	34	39	–	–	42	48
6	40	42	9	42	47	–	–	48	54
7	48	50	3	50	55	–	–	55	61
8	56	58	0	–	–	58	68	68	74
9	64	66	1	66	71	–	–	74	80
10	72	74	7	74	79	–	–	80	86

found by adding 5 and 10 minutes respectively to the starting times. Column 9 shows the starting time in area D, which is either the finishing time in B or C (if D is empty) or the next time D will be empty (if it is busy). Column 10 shows the finish time in area D by adding 6 to the start time.

The utilization of each area can be found from the proportion of time that each is busy. We should ignore unusual effects, so taking the period between, say, minutes 20 and 80 gives:

$$A: \ 14/60 = 23\% \qquad B: \ 28/60 = 47\%$$

$$C: \ 22/60 = 37\% \qquad D: \ 48/60 = 80\%$$

These figures are approximations and many more results would be needed to get reliable figures (actually 25%, 31%, 63% and 75% respectively).

IN SUMMARY

Simulation provides a way of dynamically modelling problems. The purpose of simulation is to reproduce a typical set of results from operations without actually running the operation. It produces realistic, but artificial results.

| 20.3.2 | Random sampling

In the last section we used random numbers in simulation, but only looked at situations where a variable could take two values, each with a probability of 0.5. With more complex problems we need more sophisticated ways of giving values to variables. How, for example, could a probability of acceptance of 0.6 be dealt with?

One way of generating a probability of acceptance of 0.6 is to use random digits 0 to 5 to represent acceptance and 6 to 9 to represent rejection. Then the string:

5284778016941356756454793017714943179046582 5

would represent accept, accept, reject, accept, reject and so on. This approach can be extended to sampling from more complex patterns. If 50% of units are accepted, 15% sent for reworking, 20% for reinspection and 15% rejected we might use the following approach.

Split the stream of random digits into pairs:

52 84 77 80 16 94 13 56 75 64 54 79 30 17 71 etc

Then let

00 to 49 (i.e. 50% of pairs) represent acceptance

50 to 64 (i.e. 15% of pairs) represent reworking

65 to 84 (i.e. 20% of pairs) represent reinspection

and   85 to 99 (i.e. 15% of pairs) represent rejection.

The stream of random digits would then represent rework, reinspect, reinspect, reinspect, accept and so on. In the long term the proportion of outcomes will be as required, but in the short term there will obviously be random variations. Here three units out of the first four need reinspecting, and while there is a temptation to 'adjust' such figures this should not be done. Simulation is based on the principle that a large number of repetitions is needed to show typical figures and these will include fairly unlikely occurrences from time to time.

Such sampling could be extended to more complex forms, including sampling from probability distributions. If the process we are simulating has a Poisson distribution with mean 1.0, the probability of no event is 0.3679 (found from tables in Appendix F). To represent this we could split the stream of random digits into groups of four:

5284 7780 1694 1356 7564 5479 3017 7149 4317 9046 etc

Then:

0000 to 3678 represent 0 events (probability = 0.3679)

3679 to 7358 represent 1 event (probability = 0.3679)

7359 to 9196 represent 2 events (probability = 0.1839)

9197 to 9809 represent 3 events (probability = 0.0613)

9810 to 9962 represent 4 events (probability = 0.0153)

9963 to 9993 represent 5 events (probability = 0.0031)

9994 to 9998 represent 6 events (probability = 0.0005)

9999 represents 7 events (probability = 0.0001)

Then our random number string would give 2, 3, 1, 1, 3 events and so on.

WORKED EXAMPLE 20.4

The stock of an item is checked at the beginning of each month and an order is placed so that:

order size = 100 – initial stock

The order is equally likely to arrive at the end of the month in which it is placed or one month later. Demand follows the pattern:

Monthly demand	10	20	30	40	50	60	70
Probability	0.1	0.15	0.25	0.25	0.15	0.05	0.05

Assuming that there are 40 units in stock at the beginning of the first month, simulate the system for 10 months and say what values can be calculated from the results.

Solution

The variables are delivery time and demand. Samples for these can be found using the following schemes.

Delivery time:
- even random number means delivery in current month
- odd random number means delivery in next month

Demand:

Demand	10	20	30	40	50	60	70
Probability	0.1	0.15	0.25	0.25	0.15	0.05	0.05
Random number	00-09	10-24	25-49	50-74	75-89	90-94	95-99

Two streams of random digits were found from tables:

delivery time: 2 5 9 1 0 7 3 8 7 6

demand: 83 50 56 49 37 15 84 52 66 41

Table 20.4

Month	1	2	3	4	5	6	7	8	9	10
Initial stock	40	50	10	20	80	150	130	80	60	20
Order	60	50	90	80	20	0	0	20	40	80
Arrival RN	2	5	9	1	0	7	3	8	7	6
Arrival month	1	3	4	5	5	7	8	8	10	10
Demand RN	83	50	56	49	37	15	84	52	66	41
Demand size	50	40	40	30	30	20	50	40	40	30
Arrival	60	0	50	90	100	0	0	20	0	120
Closing stock	50	10	20	80	150	130	80	60	20	110
Shortages	0	0	0	0	0	0	0	0	0	0

Following the system through ten months gives the results in Table 20.4. In this, the stock at the end of a month is found from the initial stock plus arrivals minus demand. In month 1 the initial stock is 40, so 60 are ordered. The arrival random number determines that this will arrive in the same month. The demand random number determines a demand of 50 in the month, so the closing stock is closing stock = initial stock + arrivals − demand

$$= 40 + 60 - 50 = 50$$

There are no shortages and the closing stock is transferred to the opening stock for month 2. These calculations are repeated for the following ten months.

The conclusions from this very limited simulation are not at all reliable. If, however, the simulation is continued for longer, reliable figures could be found for measures such as distribution of opening and closing stock levels (including mean, maximum and minimum), distribution of orders (mean, minimum and maximum), mean demand, shortages and mean lead time. Adding costs to the model would allow a range of other calculations.

IN SUMMARY

Random numbers can be used to generate samples with a range of characteristics. These can then be used in more sophisticated simulation models.

Self-assessment questions

20.6 What is meant when simulation is described as a 'dynamic' representation?

20.7 'Simulation can be used to model complex situations.' Is this statement true?

20.8 Why are random numbers used in simulation?

20.9 'Random numbers can only be used to give sample values from certain distributions.' Is this statement true?

CHAPTER REVIEW

Queues occur in a number of circumstances. This chapter described some aspects of the management of queues. In particular it:

- discussed the characteristics of queues and the need to balance the quality of service offered with its cost
- developed a model for a single-server queue where both arrivals and service times were random
- mentioned the difficulty of solving realistic queuing problems

- described the general approach of simulation
- illustrated the use of simulation in queuing problems

Problems

20.1 Describe the operating characteristics of a single-server queue where arrivals are random at an average rate of 100 an hour and service time is random at an average rate of 120 an hour.

20.2 A single-server queue has random arrivals at a rate of 30 an hour and random service time at a rate of 40 an hour. If it costs £20 for each hour a customer spends in the system and £40 for each hour of service time, how much does the queue cost?

20.3 A self-employed plumber offers a 24-hour emergency service to deal with burst pipes. For most of the year, calls arrive randomly at a rate of six a day. The time he takes to travel to a call and do the repair is randomly distributed with a mean of 90 minutes. Forecasts for February suggest that the weather will be cold; the last time this happened, emergency calls came in at a rate of 18 a day. Because of repeat business, the plumber is anxious not to lose a customer and wants average waiting time to be no longer in February than during a normal month. How many assistants should he employ to achieve this?

20.4 Use random digits to take samples from:

(a) a binomial distribution for samples of size eight and probability of success equal to 0.3

(b) a Poisson distribution with mean 2.0

Computer exercises

20.1 Figure 20.6 shows the printout from a program that analyses queues. The title 'M/M/3' is an abbreviation that shows the queue has random arrivals, random service time and three servers. Make sure you understand what is happening here. Use a suitable package to check these results.

Input Data of the Problem Queueing

M/M/3

Customer arrival rate (lambda)	=	20.000
Distribution	:	Poisson
Number of servers	=	3
Service rate per server	=	8.000
Distribution	:	Poisson
Mean service time	=	0.125 hour
Standard deviation	=	0.125 hour
Queue limit	=	Infinity
Customer population	=	Infinity

Final Solution for The Problem Queueing

M/M/3

With lamda = 20 customers per hour   and μ = 8 customers per hour

Utilization factor (p)	=	.8333333
Average number of customers in the system (L)	=	6.011236
Average number of customers in the queue (Lq)	=	3.511236
Average time a customer in the system (W)	=	.3005618
Average time a customer in the queue (Wq)	=	.1755618
The probability that all servers are idle (Po)	=	4.494328E−02
The probability an arriving customer waits (Pw)	=	.7022472

P(1) = 0.11236   P(2) = 0.14045   P(3) = 0.11704   P(4) = 0.09753
P(5) = 0.08128   P(6) = 0.06773   P(7) = 0.05644   P(8) = 0.04704
P(9) = 0.03920   P(10) = 0.03266

$$\sum_{i=1}^{10} P(i) = 0.791736$$

Figure 20.6   Printout from a queue analysis program.

20.2 Figure 20.7 shows the printout from a program that analyses the cost of queues. Make sure you can understand what is happening. Check the results with your own software.

MULTIPLE SERVER QUEUES

−=✱=−   INFORMATION ENTERED   −=✱=−

ALTERNATIVE CHOSEN   :   MULTIPLE SERVER – FINITE QUEUE

Arrival Rate   :   30.000
Service Rate   :   12.000

Number of Servers   :   1   –   5
Maximum in System   :   20

Service Cost Rate   :   150.000
Waiting Cost Rate   :   25.000

−=✱=−   RESULTS – NUMBER OF SERVERS   −=✱=−

NUMBER OF SERVERS	SYSTEMS WAIT	SYSTEMS LENGTH	TOTAL COSTS
1	arrival rate exceeds system capacity		
2	arrival rate exceeds system capacity		
3	0.183	5.470	586.743
4	0.101	3.031	675.774
5	0.088	2.630	815.758

OPTIMAL NUMBER OF SERVERS IS 3

−=✱=−   RESULTS – WITH 3 SERVERS   −=✱=−

BALKING RATE (PERCENT)	:	0.542
SERVER IDLE (PERCENT)	:	17.118
EXPECTED NUMBER IN SYSTEM	:	5.470
EXPECTED NUMBER IN QUEUE	:	2.983
EXPECTED TIME IN SYSTEM	:	0.183
EXPECTED TIME IN QUEUE	:	0.100
COST OF SERVICE	:	450.000
COST OF WAITING	:	136.743
TOTAL COST	:	586.743

−=✱=−   END OF ANALYSIS   −=✱=−

Figure 20.7   Analysis of a queue with costs.

20.3 Figure 20.8 shows the printout from a program that is simulating a six-server queue. Make sure you understand what is happening. Use appropriate software to check the results. Write a report about the findings.

I ——————————————————————————————————— I
Input Data of The Problem Simulation   Page 1
I ——————————————————————————————————— I

Server # 1	Mean time: 10.00 Distribution: Exponential
Server # 2	Mean time: 12.00 Distribution: Exponential
Server # 3	Mean time: 8.00 Distribution: Exponential
Server # 4	Mean time: 7.00 Distribution: Uniform
Server # 5	Mean time: 10.00 Distribution: Normal
Server # 6	Mean time: 12.00 Distribution: Normal

I ——————————————————————————————————— I
Qu. # 1 Qu. limit: 20   Dispatch: FIFO
I ——————————————————————————————————— I
Customer mean interarrival time = 2.00   Distribution: Exponential
Random seed = 113
I ——————————————————————————————————— I

I ——————————————————————————————————— I
Summary Results for Servers in Simulation   Page : 1
I ——————————————————————————————————— I

Servers	Util.	Wq.	Var.(Wq)	W.	Var.(W)	Obsvtn.
1	0.8291	1.0455	1.1254	11.43	152.43	8
2	0.8698	0	0	18.37	171.95	5
3	0.5565	0.0641	0.0329	6.2593	36.24	9
4	0.6164	0.0359	0.0090	7.7561	1.3795	8
5	0.7726	0.5496	0.9087	10.23	6.3880	8
6	0.7260	0	0	12.12	5.4677	6

I ——————————————————————————————————— I
Data collection period: 0 to 100.1996 (in minutes)
I ——————————————————————————————————— I

I ——————————————————————————————————— I
Summary Results for Queues in Simulation   Page : 2
I ——————————————————————————————————— I

Queues	Qmax	Qmin	Current Q	Lq.	Var.(Lq)	L.
1	3	0	0	0.1360	0.2419	0.9651

I ——————————————————————————————————— I
Data collection period: 0 to 100.1996 (in minutes)
I ——————————————————————————————————— I

I ——————————————————————————————————— I
Combined Results for Simulation   Page : 3
I ——————————————————————————————————— I
Util. = 4.37039   Lq. = 0.1360   V.(Lq) = 0.2419   L. = 4.5064
Wq. = 0.3097   V.(Wq) = 0.5371   W. = 10.37   V.(W) = 69.43
I ——————————————————————————————————— I
Data collection period: 0 to 100.1996 (in minutes)
I ——————————————————————————————————— I

Figure 20.8   Simulation of a six-server queue.

20.4 In practice, the easiest way to generate random samples is to use a computer. Figure 20.9 shows the printout from a statistical program that is generating a sample of ten random numbers from a Normal distribution with mean 10 and standard deviation 2. See what programs you have to get equivalent results.

```
MTB  > random 10 c1;
SUBC > normal mean 10 standev 2.
MTB  > print c1

C1
  11.3160      9.3408      8.7069     10.1302      9.4253
  10.8556     10.5541     11.2570      8.9433     11.9657

MTB > stop
```

Figure 20.9 Using a computer to generate random numbers.

20.5 Customers arrive at a server at a rate of 100 an hour and each server can serve at a rate of 15 an hour. If customer time is valued at £20 an hour and server time costs £50 an hour, use a suitable program to identify the optimal number of servers.

Appendix A

References for further reading

Many books discuss quantitative methods for business. Some of these are general and cover a range of topics, while others are more specialized. The following list shows a number of books you may find useful.

Books giving a general introduction

Bamcroft G. and O'Sullivan G. (1988)
Maths and Statistics 2nd edn. Maidenhead: McGraw-Hill
Cooke S. and Slack N. (1991)
Making Management Decisions 2nd edn. Hemel Hempstead: Prentice-Hall
Curwin J. and Slater R. (1991)
Quantitative Methods for Business Decisions 3rd edn. London: Chapman & Hall
Johnson D. (1986)
Quantitative Business Analysis. London: Butterworth & Co.
Mabbett A.J. (1986)
Workout Mathematics for Economists. London: Macmillan
Morris C. (1989)
Quantitative Approaches in Business Studies 2nd edn. London: Pitman Publishing
Pearson J.M. (1982)
Mathematics for Economists. London: Longman
Rowe R.N. (1986)
Refresher in Basic Mathematics. London: DP Publications
Slater R. and Ashcroft P. (1990)
Quantitative Techniques in a Business Context. London: Chapman & Hall
Stafford L.W.T (1979)
Business Mathematics. London: Macdonald & Evans
Weber J.E. (1976)
Mathematical Analysis – Business and Economic Applications. New York: Harper & Row

Books which are a bit more technical

Anderson D.R., Sweeney D.J. and Williams T.A. (1991)
An Introduction to Management Science 6th edn. St Paul: West Publishing Co.
Anderson D.R., Sweeney D.J. and Williams T.A. (1992)
Quantitative Methods for Business 5th edn. St Paul: West Publishing Co.
Bierman H, Bonini C.P. and Hausman W.H. (1986)
Quantitative Analysis for Business Decisions 7th edn. Homewood, IL: Irwin
Davis K.R., McKeown P.G. and Rakes T.R. (1986)
Management Science: an Introduction. Boston: Kent Publishing

Gordon G., Pressman I. and Cohen S. (1990)
Quantitative Decision Making for Business 3rd edn. Englewood Cliffs, NJ: Prentice-Hall
Johnson D. (1986)
Quantitative Business Analysis. London: Butterworth & Co.
Levin R.I., Rubin D.S., Stinson J.P. and Gardner E.S. (1989)
Quantitative Approaches to Management 7th edn. McGraw-Hill International
Waters C.D.J. (1989)
A Practical Introduction to Management Science. Wokingham: Addison-Wesley

Sources of statistics

The UK government publish regular statistics prepared by the Central Statistical Office including:
Annual Abstract of Statistics
Monthly Digest of Statistics
Financial Statistics
Economic Trends
Social Trends

A list of available publications is given in
Guide to Official Statistics
or *Government Statistics - A Brief Guide to Sources*

These are all published by Her Majesty's Stationery Office.

Wider International Statistics are published by the United Nations (particularly the Statistical Yearbook), European Community, Organization of Economic Cooperation and Development, International Monetary Fund, and many other sources.

Regression and forecasting

Bowerman B.L. and O'Connell R.T. (1979)
Forecasting and Time Series. Massachusetts: Duxbury Press
Granger C.W.J. (1980)
Forecasting in Business and Economics. New York: Academic Press
Hanke J.E. and Reitsch A.G. (1986)
Business Forecasting 2nd edn. Boston: Allyn & Bacon
Makridakis S., Wheelwright S.C. and McGee V.E. (1983)
Forecasting: Methods and Applications 2nd edn. New York: John Wiley
Thomopoulos N.T. (1980)
Applied Forecasting Methods. Englewood Cliffs, NJ: Prentice-Hall
Wheelwright S.C. and Makridakis (1985)
Forecasting Models for Management 4th edn. New York: John Wiley
Willis R.E. (1987)
A Guide to Forecasting for Planners and Managers. Englewood Cliffs, NJ: Prentice-Hall
Younger M.S. (1979)
A Handbook for Linear Regression. Massachusetts: Duxbury Press

Linear programming

Anderson D.R., Sweeney D.J. and Williams T.A (1974)
Linear Programming for Decision Making. St Paul: West Publishing
Bradley S.P, Hax A.C. and Magnanti T.L. (1977)
Applied Mathematical Programming. Reading: Addison-Wesley
Bunday B. (1984)
Basic Linear Programming. London: Edward Arnold
Hayhurst G. (1976)
Mathematical Programming for Management and Business. London: Edward Arnold
Kolman B. and Beck R. (1980)
Elementary Linear Programming with Applications. New York: Academic Press
Schrage L. (1991)
LINDO: An Optimization Modelling System 4th edn. San Francisco: Scientific Press
Shapiro R.O. (1984)
Optimization for Planning and Allocation. New York: John Wiley
Wu N. and Coppins R. (1981)
Linear Programming and Extensions. New York: McGraw-Hill

Calculus

Mabbett A.J. (1986)
Workout Mathematics for Economists. London: Macmillan
Mendelson E. (1985)
Beginning Calculus. New York: McGraw-Hill
Pearson J.M. (1982)
Mathematics for Economists. London: Longman
Praserk C. (1987)
Calculus with Applications to Management, Economics and the Social and Natural Sciences. New York: Merrill

Statistics

Daniel W.W. and Terrell J.C. (1986)
Business Statistics. Boston: Houghton Mifflin Company
Freund J.E. and Williams F.J. (1984)
Elementary Business Statistics: The Modern Approach 4th edn. Englewood Cliffs, NJ: Prentice-Hall
Greensted C.S., Jardine A.K.S. and Macfarlane J .D. (1978)
Essentials of Statistics in Marketing 2nd edn. London: Heinemann
Harper W.M. (1982)
Statistics 4th edn. London: Macdonald & Evans
Huff D. (1973)
How to Lie with Statistics. Middlesex: Penguin Books
Kennedy G. (1983)
Invitation to Statistics. Oxford: Martin Robertson
McClave J.T. and Benson P.G. (1988)
Statistics for Business and Economics 4th edn. San Francisco: Dellen-Macmillan
Rowntree D. (1981)
Statistics Without Tears: A Primer for Non-Mathematicians. Middlesex: Penguin Books

Spiegel M.R. (1972)
Schaum's Outline of Theory and Problems of Statistics. McGraw-Hill
Walpole W. (1982)
Introduction to Statistics 3rd edn. Collier Macmillan
Wonnacott T.H. and Wonnacott R.J. (1977)
Introductory Statistics 3rd edn. New York: John Wiley

Sampling

Duncan A.J. (1974)
Quality Control and Industrial Statistics 4th edn. Homewood: Irwin
Grant E.L. and Leavensworth R.S. (1980)
Statistical Quality Control 5th edn. New York: McGraw-Hill
Jardine A.K.S., Macfarlane J.D. and Greensted C.S. (1975)
Statistical Methods for Quality Control. London: Heinemann
Rendall F.J. and Wolf D.M. (1983)
Statistical Sources and Techniques. Maidenhead: McGraw-Hill

Decision analysis

Brown R.V., Kahr A.S. and Peterson C. (1974)
Decision Analysis for the Manager. New York: Holt, Rinehart & Winston
Buchanan J.T. (1982)
Discrete and Dynamic Decision Analysis. Chichester: John Wiley & Sons
Bunn D. (1984)
Applied Decision Analysis. New York: McGraw-Hill
Holloway C.A. (1979)
Decision Making Under Uncertainty. Englewood Cliffs, NJ: Prentice-Hall
Lindley D.V. (1971)
Making Decisions. London: John Wiley & Sons
Moore P.G., Thomas H., Bunn D.W. and Hampton J. (1976)
Case Studies in Decision Analysis. Middlesex: Penguin Books
Newman J.W. (1971)
Management Applications of Decision Theory. New York: Harper & Row

Inventory Control

Buffa E.S. and Miller J.G. (1979)
Production-Inventory Systems: Planning and Control 3rd edn. Homewood, IL: Irwin
Lewis C.D. (1975)
Demand Analysis and Inventory Control. London: Saxon-House
Love S.F. (1979)
Inventory Control. New York: McGraw-Hill
Plossl G. and Welch W.E. (1979)
The Role of Top Management in the Control of Inventory. Reston: Reston Publishing
Silver E.A. and Peterson·R. (1985)
Decision Systems for Inventory Management and Production Planning 2nd edn. New York: John Wiley

Tersine R.J. (1987)
Principles of Inventory and Materials Management 3rd edn. New York: Elsevier North-Holland
Waters C.D.J. (1992)
Inventory Control and Management. Chichester: John Wiley

Project network analysis

Cleland D.I. and King W.R. (1983)
Project Management Handbook. New York: Van Nostrand Reinhold
Goodman L.J. and Love R.N. (1980)
Project Planning and Management: An Integrated Approach. New York: Pergamon Press
Harrison F.L. (1981)
Advanced Project Management. New York: Halsted
Kerzher H. (1984)
Project Management for Executives. New York: Van Nostrand Reinhold
Kerzner H. and Thamhain H. (1984)
Project Management for Small and Medium-Sized Business. New York: Van Nostrand Reinhold
Meredith J.R. and Mantel S.J. (1985)
Project Management. New York: John Wiley
Modder J.J., Phillips C.K. and Davis E.W. (1983)
Project Management with CPM and PERT 3rd edn. New York: Van Nostrand Reinhold
Weist J.D. and Levy F.K. (1977)
A Management Guide to PERT/CPM 2nd edn. Englewood Cliffs, NJ: Prentice-Hall

Queues and simulation

Banks J. and Carson J.S. (1984)
Discrete-Event Simulation. Englewood Cliffs, NJ: Prentice-Hall
Cooper R.B. (1972)
Introduction to Queueing Theory. New York: Macmillan
Gross D. and Harris C.M. (1974)
Fundamentals of Queueing Theory. New York: John Wiley & Sons
Law A.M. and Kelton W.D. (1982)
Simulation Modelling and Analysis. New York: McGraw Hill
Payne J.A. (1982)
Introduction to Simulation: Programming Techniques and Methods Of Analysis. New York: McGraw-Hill
Pidd M. (1988)
Computer Simulation in Management Science 2nd edn. Chichester: John Wiley & Sons
Solomon S.L. (1983)
Simulation of Waiting-Line Systems. Englewood Cliffs, NJ: Prentice-Hall
Watson H.J. (1981)
Computer Simulation in Business. New York: John Wiley

Appendix B

Solutions to self-assessment questions

Chapter 1
Numbers and managers

1.1 They allow rational analyses of problems, measurement of various factors, and decisions based on a sound, logical footing.

1.2 No, but most analyses include quantitative elements.

1.3 No; managers make decisions.

1.4 There are several reasons for this, including increased availability of computers, fiercer competition requiring better decisions, development of new quantitative methods, good experiences with earlier analyses encouraging managers to expand their use, and better education of managers making available techniques more widely known.

1.5 A simplified representation of reality.

1.6 They are used to develop solutions for real problems, allow experimentation without risk to actual operations, allow experiments that would not be possible in reality, assess the consequences of decisions, see how sensitive operations are to change, and so on.

1.7 Symbolic models.

1.8 Observation, modelling, experimentation and implementation.

1.9 No. Any approach that efficiently gets a good answer can be used.

Chapter 2
Tools for quantitative methods

2.1 Yes.

2.2 (a) 4, (b) 168/15 or 11.2, (c) 3.

2.3 There is no difference. None is always the best, so the choice depends on circumstances.

2.4 1745, 800.362 and 1 750 000.

2.5 Because it provides a precise method of describing and solving quantitative problems.

2.6 Yes.

2.7 No. Two equations are needed to find two unknowns.

2.8 There is no best format for all occasions. You should use the format that is best suited to your needs.

2.9 0.

2.10 By rearranging them to (a) $11 - 8pr/3q$ and (b) $q/4 + 7pq/2r$

2.11 7.

2.12 $27/32 = 0.84$.

2.13 1.

2.14 1.23×10^9 and 2.53×10^{-7}

2.15 They are imaginary.

2.16 Because (with odd exceptions) there are no other formulae.

2.17 The cost must be positive, so $x^{22} + 50x - 1000$ must be greater than zero, so x must be greater than 15.3.

2.18 Each term in an arithmetic series is a fixed amount larger than the previous term, while each term in a geometric series is found by multiplying the previous term by a fixed amount.

2.19 5.

2.20 One whose value is set by the value taken by the independent variable.

2.21 y is a function of both x and z (so the value of the dependent variable y is determined by the values of two independent variables x and z).

2.22 (0,0).

2.23 It is a straight line that crosses the y axis at 4 and has a gradient of 2.

2.24 (a) 0, (b) 1, (c) infinite.

2.25 At the points where the curve crosses the x axis.

2.26 A point where the gradient changes from positive to negative (or vice versa), often corresponding to a maximum or minimum value.

2.27 Because graphs are difficult to draw exactly and it is difficult to read accurate results from them.

2.28 At the point where the graphs cross, equations for both lines are true.

Chapter 3
Collecting data

3.1 Data are the raw numbers, measurements, opinions, etc that are processed to give useful information.

3.2 Because managers need reliable information to make their decisions, and this is provided by data collection (and subsequent analysis).

3.3 False.

3.4 Because data of different types are collected, analysed and presented in different ways.

3.5 There are several ways, including quantitative/qualitative, nominal/cardinal /ordinal, discrete/continuous, primary/secondary.

3.6 Discrete data can only take integer values, while continuous data can take any values.

3.7 There are many possible examples, such as: nominal – industrial sectors of companies: ordinal – social class: cardinal – weight of products.

3.8 Because it would be too expensive, time-consuming or impractical to collect data from the population.

3.9 Because the wrong population would give misleading survey results.

3.10 One classification has census, random, systematic, quota, stratified, multistage and cluster samples.

3.11 Every member of the population has an equal chance of being selected.

3.12 Stratified sampling is random and ensures that all groups within the population are represented: quota sampling is not truly random but it ensures that the sample has the same properties as the population.

3.13 Relevant figures are published in many government statistics (as well as by international organizations such as the United Nations) so they should be available in any reasonable library.

3.14 Different views are valid, but suggestions are: (a) telephone survey, (b) personal interview, (c) longitudinal survey, (d) observation.

3.15 (a) Leading question. (b) Vague – what is 'too much'? (c) Several questions in one. (d) Speculative.

3.16 Non-respondents should be contacted and encouraged to reply. If this gets no response they should be examined for common characteristics to ensure that no bias is introduced.

3.17 Because interviewers will keep asking people until they fill the required quotas.

Chapter 4
Using diagrams to present data

4.1 Data are the raw numbers, measurements, opinions, etc that are processed to give useful information.

4.2 Many of these can be found in advertisements, political campaigns, company reports, newspapers, etc.

4.3 To simplify raw data, remove the detail, and hence show underlying patterns.

4.4 Unfortunately not.

4.5 Graphical and numerical methods.

4.6 They can display lots of information, show varying attributes and highlight specific results.

4.7 Graphs show patterns well, but if the axes are not scaled properly they can give a misleading impression. Labelling the axes shows that they are properly drawn and the meaning is clear.

4.8 Probably tables.

4.9 No. There are many variations in bar charts and the most appropriate is largely a matter of choice. This is also true of other presentation methods.

4.10 They are not very accurate and can be misleading.

4.11 A diagram showing the number of observations in a set of data falling into each class.

4.12 A frequency distribution shows the number of observations in each class; a percentage frequency distribution shows the percentage of observations in each class; a cumulative frequency distribution shows the total number of observations up to (and including) the class; the cumulative percentage frequency distribution shows the percentage of observations up to (and including) the class.

4.13 No. It is true for bar charts, but in histograms the area shows the number of observations.

4.14 The average height of the two separate bars.

4.15 To show the cumulative frequency against class.

4.16 No. The diagonal line shows an equally distributed population, but this may not be fair.

Chapter 5
Using numbers to describedata

5.1 They give an overall impression of data, but are not so good at giving objective measures.

5.2 Where the centre of the data is (when drawn on, say, a frequency diagram). This is generally some form of average.

5.3 No. These only partially describe a set of data.

5.4 No.

5.5 The most common measures are: arithmetic mean = $\Sigma x/n$; median = middle observation; mode = most frequent observation.

5.6 There are a number of reasons, including its ease of calculation, use in further analysis, and general acceptance.

5.7 $(10 \times 34 + 5 \times 37)/15 = 35$

5.8 Because the calculations will usually be done by a computer.

5.9 Range, mean absolute deviation, variance, standard deviation. Yes.

5.10 Because positive and negative deviations cancel each other.

5.11 Metres^2.

5.12 Because it is very useful in other analyses.

5.13 The coefficients of variation are 0.203 and 0.128 respectively, which suggests that the first set of data is more widely dispersed than the second.

Chapter 6
Describing changes with index numbers

6.1 To measure the changes in a variable over time.

6.2 False. Any suitable base value can be used, but 100 is the most common.

6.3 When circumstances change significantly or when the old index gets too high.

6.4 A percentage rise of 10% increases the value by 10% of the previous value; a percentage point rise of 10 increases the value by 10% of the base value.

6.5 364.32

6.6 Mean price relative index for period n

$$= \frac{\text{sum of all price relatives for period } n}{\text{number of indices}} \times 100$$

Simple aggregate index for period n

$$= \frac{\text{sum of prices in period } n}{\text{sum of prices in base period}} \times 100$$

6.7 They are sensitive to the units used and do not take into account the relative importance of variables.

6.8 Base-period weighting assumes that the basket of items used in the base period is always used; current-period weighting considers price changes based on the current basket of items.

6.9 Because the basket of items actually used will be affected by prices. In particular, any items with rapidly rising prices are replaced by ones with lower price rises.

6.10 Yes.

6.11 Not really. The RPI considers only purchases by a 'typical' family, it omits expenses that may be significant (such as income tax and life insurance), it does not mention the quality of goods, and so on.

Chapter 7
Calculations with money

7.1 No.

7.2 Return on assets =

$$\frac{income}{assets} = \frac{income}{sales} \times \frac{sales}{assets}$$

7.3 The number of units processed (made, sold, served, etc).

7.4 The number of units that must be sold before a profit is made.

7.5 The product is making a loss, as revenue does not cover all costs.

7.6 False. Economies of scale mean that it is **usually** better to have a single large factory than a number of smaller ones, but there may also be diseconomies of scale.

7.7 (a) More than £1, 000 in five years' time.

7.8 No. £100 invested for a year at 12% will have a value of $100 \times (1+0.12) = £112$; £100 invested for 12 months at 1% will have a value of $100 \times (1+0.01)^{12} = £112.68$.

7.9 By reducing all costs and revenues to present values, and calculating the net present value for each project.

7.10 An estimate of the proportional increase or decrease in the value of money in each time period.

7.11 Straight-line depreciation reduces the value by a fixed amount each period; the reducing-balance method reduces the value by a fixed percentage each period.

7.12 Discounting where values are assumed to decline continuously over time rather than in discrete steps.

7.13 A fund that receives regular payments so that a specified sum is available at some time in the future.

7.14 By using the equation $A_n = A_0 \times (1 + i)^n + [F \times (1 + i)^n - F]/i$, to find A_0 when $A_n = 0$ and F is the regular payment received.

7.15 No; other factors can be included.

Chapter 8
Relating variables by regression

8.1 The errors, or deviations from expected values.

8.2 Mathematical relationships look at underlying patterns, but they cannot deal with short-term, random noise. Errors are introduced by noise, incorrectly identifying the underlying pattern and changes in the system being modelled.

8.3 The mean error is defined as $1/n \times \Sigma E_i$. Positive and negative errors cancel each other, so the mean error should have a value around zero unless there is bias in the model.

8.4 Mean absolute deviation = $1/n \times \Sigma |E_i|$ and mean squared error = $1/n \times \Sigma [E_i]^2$.

8.5 By using each equation to calculate values for the dependent variable for a range of values of the independent variable. These will give the individual errors, which can be used to give mean errors, mean absolute deviations, and mean squared errors for each relationship. All things being equal, the stronger relationship is the one with smaller errors.

8.6 To find the line of best fit relating a dependent variable to an independent one, and hence predict values for the dependent variable.

8.7 x_i and y_i are the ith values of independent and dependent variables respectively; a is the point where the line crosses the y axis, b is the gradient of the line; $E(i)$ is the error introduced by random noise.

8.8 This finds the regression line with y as the independent variable and x as the dependent variable. No.

8.9 The proportion of the total sum of squared error that is explained by the regression.

8.10 −1 to +1. The coefficient of determination is the square of the coefficient of correlation.

8.11 They are essentially the same, but Pearson's coefficient is used for cardinal data, while Spearman's is used for ordinal data.

8.12 No. Variation in the dependent variable is explained by, but not necessarily caused by, variation in the independent variable.

8.13 Non-linear and multiple linear regression.

8.14 No.

8.15 No.

8.16 Yes.

Chapter 9
Business forecasting

9.1 Because all decisions become effective at some point in the future, they should take into account future circumstances, and these must inevitably be forecast.

9.2 No.

9.3 Judgemental, projective and causal forecasting.

9.4 Relevant factors include: What is to be forecast? Why is this being forecast? Are quantitative data available? How does the forecast affect other parts of the organization? How far into the future are forecasts needed?: Are reliable data available and how frequently are they updated? What external factors are relevant? How much will the forecast cost and how much will errors cost? How much detail is required? How much time is available?

9.5 Forecasts that are subjective views based on opinions and intuition rather than quantitative analysis.

9.6 Personal insight, panel consensus, market surveys, historical analogy and Delphi method.

9.7 They can be unreliable, experts may give conflicting views, cost of data collection is high, there may be no available expertise, and so on.

9.8 No.

9.9 Because observations contain random noise, which cannot be forecast.

9.10 By using both forecasts for a typical period of time and comparing the errors.

9.11 Because older data tend to swamp more recent (and more relevant) data.

9.12 By using a lower value of n.

9.13 It can be influenced by random fluctuations.

9.14 By using a moving average with n equal to the length of the season.

9.15 Because the weight given to the data declines exponentially with age, and the method smooths the effects of noise.

9.16 By using a higher value for the smoothing constant a.

9.17 An additive model adds separate numbers for T, S and C to give a value. A multiplicative model uses a number, T, and multiplies this by ratios for S and C.

9.18 Because it is very difficult to get reliable data for long-term cycles.

9.19 No; only when there is an even number of periods in a season.

9.20 Regression is generally preferred.

Chapter 10
Using matrices to solve equations

10.1 They provide a convenient and efficient way of describing some problems and doing associated arithmetic.

10.2 **F** is a (3×3) matrix with $f_{1,3} = 4$ and $f_{3,1} = 6$.

10.3 A matrix with only one row or column.

10.4 Matrices can only be added if they are the same size, so this calculation cannot be done.

10.5 (4×6).

10.6 By multiplying by a column vector containing 1s.

10.7 No; most matrices do not have inverses.

10.8 Solving sets of simultaneous equations.

10.9 No.

Chapter 11
Planning with linear programming

11.1 A situation where an optimal solution is needed for a problem, but there are constraints that limit the solution.

11.2 A method of tackling problems of constrained optimization.

11.3 The main assumptions are: the problem is constrained optimization, both constraints and objective function are linear with respect to decision variables, proportionality and additivity assumptions are valid, problem variables are non-negative and reliable data are available.

11.4 Formulation involves putting a problem in a standard form.

11.5 The components are decision variables, constraints (including non-negativity) and an objective function.

11.6 The area representing solutions that satisfy all constraints, including the non-negativity conditions.

11.7 To supply the measure by which solutions are judged and hence allow an optimal solution to be identified.

11.8 The feasible region is always surrounded by straight lines; the vertices of the feasible region are the extreme points. An optimal solution will always be at an extreme point.

11.9 As the objective function line moves away from the origin its value increases and the maximum value is at the last point that it passes through in the feasible region. As the line moves in towards the origin its value decreases and the minimum value is at the last point that it passes through in the feasible region.

11.10 This looks at the way that an optimal solution varies with changes to the constraints and objective function.

11.11 The gradient of the objective function line is between the gradients of the two limiting constraints. If the gradient of the objective function rises or falls until it is no longer between the gradients of these two constraints, the optimal solution moves to another extreme point.

11.12 These measure the rate of change of the objective function with changes in resource levels; they are equivalent to the marginal values of resources.

11.13 Until so many resources become available that the constraint is no longer limiting (or resources are reduced until a new constraint becomes limiting).

11.14 The solution needs a lot of simple arithmetic on matrices which can be done easily and reliably on computers.

11.15 Many kinds of information can be given, but the most usual are: a copy of the problem solved; details of the optimal solution; limiting constraints and unused resources; shadow prices and ranges over which these are valid; variations in the objective function that will not change the position of the optimal solution.

Chapter 12
Using calculus to describe changes

12.1 It finds the instantaneous rate of change (or gradient) of a function at any point.

12.2 This is the notation used to describe the derivative of y with respect to x. It is the equation of the gradient at any point.

12.3 The function is continuous in the region considered, $dy/dx = 0$ and $d^2y/dx^2 > 0$.

12.4 The variable names have no significance, so $dp/dc = dq/dc + dr/dc$.

12.5 The gradient of a function is found from dy/dx. This gradient itself changes with x, and the rate of change is given by d^2y/dx^2.

12.6 To find the rates of change of a function of more than one variable.

12.7 That the function does not have a true maximum or minimum, but there is a saddle point, so the function has a minimum with respect to one variable and a maximum with respect to the other.

12.8 Lower.

12.9 As the additional cost of producing one more unit of a product.

12.10 The average revenue is the total revenue divided by the number produced, while the marginal revenue is found by differentiating the total revenue function.

12.11 It is the ratio of change in demand for a product to change in price.

12.12 Demand would rise with increasing price.

12.13 The integral of y with respect to x equals a function of x. Then y is the gradient of $f(x)$ at any point.

12.14 By knowing some other information that allows substitution to find c.

12.15 It finds the sum of a function between two limits.

Chapter 13
Uncertainty and probabilities

13.1 A measure of its likelihood or its relative frequency.

13.2 Two events are independent if the probability of one occurring is not affected by whether or not the other occurs.

13.3 Two events are mutually exclusive if they cannot both occur.

13.4 For mutually exclusive events the rule 'OR means ADD' can be used and the separate probabilities are added.

13.5 For independent events the rule 'AND means MULTIPLY' can be used and the separate probabilities are multiplied together.

13.6 $P(A) = 1 - P(B) - P(C)$

13.7 Two (or more) events are dependent if they are not independent. This obvious statement means that $P(a) \neq P(a/b) \neq P(a/b)$.

13.8 Conditional probabilities take the form $P(a/b)$ and represent the probability of event a occurring given that event b has already occurred.

13.9 Bayes' Theorem is used for calculating conditional probabilities. It states:

$$P(a/b) = \frac{P(b/a) \times P(a)}{P(b)}$$

13.10 It gives a diagrammatic view of a problem and organizes some calculations.

Chapter 14
Probability distributions

14.1 To describe the probability or relative frequencies of events or classes of observations.

14.2 Empirical data show historical values that actually happened; a priori data are found from theoretical reasoning.

14.3 1

14.4 $n!$

14.5 The order of selection is not important for a combination, but it is important for a permutation.

14.6 There are more permutations.

14.7 When a series of trials is conducted; each trial has two possible outcomes; the two outcomes are mutually exclusive; there is a constant probability of success, p, and failure, $q = 1 - p$; the outcomes of successive trials are independent.

14.8 $P(r)$ is the probability of r successes, n is the number of trials, p is the probability of success in each trial, q is the probability of failure in each trial, ^nC_r is the number of ways of combining r items from n.

14.9 Mean = np; variance = npq; standard deviation = $\sqrt{npq}$.

14.10 0.2753.

14.11 When events occur infrequently and at random. Other requirements include: independent events; the probability of an event happening in an interval is proportional to the length of the interval; in theory an infinite number of events should be possible in an interval.

14.12 Mean = variance = np.

14.13 0.1438.

14.14 When the number of events, n, in the binomial process is large and the probability of success is small, so np is less than 5.

14.15 In a wide range of applications when there is a large number of observations.

14.16 Binomial and Poisson distributions describe discrete data, while the Normal distribution describes continuous data.

14.17 The mean determines the location of the distribution and the standard deviation determines its spread.

14.18 When the number of events n is large and the probability of success is relatively large (with np greater than 5).

14.19 About 68% of observations are within one standard deviation of the mean.

14.20 The Normal distribution describes continuous data, so a small continuity correction can be used for discrete data ('between 3 and 6 people', for example, can be adjusted to 'between 2.5 and 6.5 people'). This correction is usually small.

Chapter 15
Using samples in business

15.1 To take a sample of observations that fairly represent the whole population.

15.2 A process in which the value of a property (quality, weight, length, etc) in a sample is used to estimate the value of the property in the population.

15.3 If a series of samples are taken from a population and a mean value of some variable is found for each sample, these means form the sampling distribution of the mean.

15.4 If the sample size is greater than about 30, or the population is Normally distributed, the sampling distribution of the mean is Normally distributed with mean μ and standard deviation $\sigma/\sqrt{n}$.

15.5 Because it comes from a sample that is unlikely to be perfectly representative of the population.

15.6 The range within which we are 95% confident the actual value lies.

15.7 Wider.

15.8 When we want to be confident that a value is either above or below a certain point.

15.9 $25n$.

15.10 Because the samples are not representative of the population, and tend to underestimate variability.

15.11 The number of independent pieces of data.

Chapter 16
Testing hypotheses

16.1 To test whether a statement about a population is supported by the evidence collected in a sample.

16.2 The null hypothesis, H_0.

16.3

	Null hypothesis is	
Decision	*True*	*False*
Not reject	Correct decision	Type II error
Reject	Type I error	Correct decision

16.4 The minimum acceptable probability that an observation is a random sample from the hypothesized population.

16.5 5% significance.

16.6 No; but the evidence does support the null hypothesis and means it cannot be rejected.

16.7 When we want to ensure that a variable is above or below a specified value.

16.8 Because a small sample is not truly representative of the population, and it underestimates the variability.

16.9 A parametric test makes assumptions about the distribution of variables, and only works with quantitative data.

16.10 When the conditions needed by parametric tests are not met.

16.11 No; there may be no appropriate test.

16.12 Because the distribution only takes positive values, so the acceptance range is 0 to the critical value.

16.13 Nothing.

Chapter 17
Analysing business decisions

17.1 Because they give structure to the situation and clearly show alternatives, events and consequences.

17.2 A decision maker, a number of alternatives, a number of events, a set of measurable outcomes, and an objective of selecting the best alternative.

17.3 There is only one event, so the method of solution is to list the outcomes and select the alternative that leads to the best.

17.4 One of several events may occur, but there is no way of telling which events are more likely. Probabilities cannot be given to events.

17.5 The three criteria described are due to Laplace, Wald and Savage.

17.6 Only the Laplace criterion.

17.7 No. There are many criteria that could be devised to fit a particular situation. Ones mentioned are maximax profit and a ¥ best outcome + $(1 - a)$ ¥ worst outcome.

17.8 There are several events that may occur and probabilities can be given to each of these.

17.9 The expected value is the sum of the probabilities multiplied by the values of the outcomes: expected value = $\Sigma P \times V$.

17.10 Yes, but care should be taken as the results may be unreliable.

17.11 When the conditional probabilities are available in situations of risk.

17.12 Expected values assume that the value of money rises linearly with the amount. A utility function describes a more realistic relationship.

17.13 The value of a terminal node is the total cost or gain of reaching that node. The value of a decision node is the best value of nodes reached by leaving alternative branches. The value of a random node is the expected value of the leaving branches (that is, the sum, for all branches, of the probability times the value of the node at which the branch ends).

17.14 At each decision node the best alternative is selected. The value given at the left-hand, originating node is the overall expected value of following the best policy.

Chapter 18
Controlling stocks

18.1 To act as a buffer between supply and demand.

18.2 What items to stock, when to place orders, how much to order?

18.3 Fixed order quantity and periodic review system.

18.4 Unit cost, reorder cost, holding cost and shortage cost.

18.5 The fixed order quantity that minimizes costs (with the assumptions made).

18.6 (c) Either increase or decrease total costs, depending on the economic order quantity.

18.7 The amount of an item that is in stock when an order for replenishment should be made.

18.8 From the lead time demand

18.9 When the production rate is greater than demand.

18.10 Larger batches (all other things being equal).

18.11 The service level gives the probability that a demand can be satisfied. We have used cycle service level, which is the probability that an item remains in stock during a cycle. It is used because alternative analyses are based on shortage costs, which are very difficult to determine.

18.12 Without safety stock there would be shortages in 50% of cycles. Safety stock reduces the probability of shortages and increases service levels.

18.13 By increasing the amount of safety stock.

18.14 Order size is equal to the difference between current stock and target stock level. Target stock level equals expected demand over $T + L$ plus safety stock.

18.15 A periodic review system.

18.16 To determine which items are most important so that appropriate effort can be spent on controlling their stocks.

18.17 B items.

Chapter 19
Planning projects with networks

19.1 A coherent piece of work with a clear start and finish, consisting of the set of activities that make a distinct product.

19.2 Project management is concerned with the planning, scheduling and controlling of activities in a project and hence the management of resources.

19.3 No.

19.4 (a) Events (that is, the start and finish of activities), (b) activities.

19.5 A list of all activities in the project and the immediate predecessors of each activity. Durations, resources needed and other factors can be added but these are not essential for drawing the network.

19.6 The two main rules are:
- before an activity can begin all preceding activities must be finished
- the arrows representing activities imply precedence only and neither the length nor orientation is significant

19.7 There are two uses of dummy activities:
- uniqueness dummies ensure that only one activity is directly between any two events

● logical dummies ensure that the logic of the dependence table is maintained in the network

19.8 The earliest time of an event is the earliest time by which **all** preceding activities can be finished. The latest time of an event is the latest time that allows **all** following activities to be started on time.

19.9 Total float is the difference between the maximum amount of time available for an activity and the time actually used.

19.10 Zero.

19.11 The critical path is the chain of activities that determine the project duration. If any critical activity is extended or delayed the whole project is delayed.

19.12 CPM assumes a fixed activity duration, while PERT assumes that activity durations follow a known distribution.

19.13 The rule of sixths assumes that the duration of an activity follows a beta distribution, in which case: expected duration = $(O + 4M + P)/6$; variance = $(P - O)^2/36$.

19.14 The project duration is assumed to be Normally distributed with mean equal to the sum of the expected durations of activities on the critical path, and variance equal to the sum of the variances of activities on the critical path.

19.15 The critical activities.

19.16 By the amount of total float of activities on a parallel path. Reductions beyond this make the parallel path critical.

19.17 The minimum time in which an activity can be completed.

19.18 No.

19.19 They show what stage each activity in a project should have reached at any time.

19.20 By delaying non-critical activities to times when fewer resources are needed.

Chapter 20
Queues and simulation

20.1 Customers who want a service but find the server is busy, so they have to wait.

20.2 No. A balance is needed between large numbers of servers and high costs.

20.3 λ is the average arrival rate and μ is the average service rate.

20.4 Customers arrive faster than they are served and the queue continues to grow.

20.5 Assumptions include: a single server; random arrivals; random service time; first come first served service discipline; the system has reached its steady state; there is no limit to the number of customers allowed in the queue; there is no limit on the number of customers who use the service and all customers wait until they are served.

20.6 Ordinary quantitative analyses describe a problem at some point of time and build a model accordingly. Simulation models follow the operation of a process over time.

20.7 Yes. Simulation can be used to model very complex situations that could not be tackled by other means.

20.8 To give typical (that is, random) values to variables.

20.9 No.

Appendix C

Solutions to numerical problems

This Appendix lists the answers to the numerical problems at the end of each chapter.

Chapter 1
Numbers and Managers

1.1 1946

1.2 7

1.3 30 minutes

1.4 £40

Chapter 2
Tools for Quantitative Methods

2.1 −96, 5, 144, 2, −10

2.2 11/10, 1/8, 5/8, −15, 35/96

2.3 1.1,0.125, 0.625, −15, 0.365

2.4 57.5%, 65/100 = 13/20, 0.17

2.5 a) 74.071 b) 74.1 c) 74 d) 70

2.6 The first exam.

2.7 60 miles/hour   speed = distance/time

2.8 $n \times$ (selling price - purchase price)

2.9 15 match balls and 45 practice balls

2.10 Direct labour costs £7500, raw materials cost £16,000 and overheads cost £1500.

2.11 (a) $a = 4, b = -1$ (b) $x = 3, y = 7$ (c) $x = 3, y = -1, z = 2$ (d) $r = -1, s = -2, t = 4$

2.12 $n = 3, e = 5$

2.13 $x^{3/4}$, x, 3, 32, 506.19, 288

2.14 (a) 2, 4 (b) 10/6, −1 (c) roots are imaginary

2.15 6.18

2.16 a. 295 b. 88,572

2.17 11.5 months

2.18 0.176   The same.

2.19 7.27

2.21 53

2.24 $y = 300,000$ when $x = 250$

2.25 cost = 1600 when $x = 40$

2.26 (−0.557, 3.86) and (12.557, 266.14)

2.27 (3.372, 15.370) and (−2.372, 9.626)

Chapter 3 Collecting Data

3.6

		16–25	26–35	36–45	46–55	56–65	66–75	≥76
Female	A	22	40	44	33	22	15	7
	B	33	60	66	49	33	22	11
	C1	22	40	44	33	22	15	7
	C2	11	20	22	16	11	7	4
	D	4	7	7	5	4	2	1
Male	A	36	65	71	54	36	24	12
	B	54	98	107	80	54	36	18
	C1	36	65	71	54	36	24	12
	C2	18	33	36	27	18	12	6
	D	6	11	12	9	6	4	2

Chapter 4
Using Diagrams to Present Data

4.7

	Frequency	Cumulative frequency	Percentage
less than 100	3	3	6.67
100–149	4	7	8.89
150–199	3	10	6.67
200–249	5	15	11.11
250–299	7	22	15.56
300–349	5	27	11.11
350–399	8	35	17.78
400–449	4	39	8.89
450 or greater	6	45	13.33

Chapter 5
Using Numbers to Describe Data

5.1 3, 2, 1
5.2 24.77, 24.50, 24
5.3 13.94, 14, 13.86
5.4 7.57, 6.73, 7.82
5.5 39.93, 30.83, 34.13
5.6 2.67, 8.67, 2.94
5.7 624.72, 24.99
5.8 ● range = 1–7, variance = 5.2, standard deviation = 2.28
  ● range = 21–29, variance = 3.71, standard deviation = 1.93
5.9 ● variance = 23.54, standard deviation = 4.85
  ● variance = 5.39, standard deviation = 2.32
  ● variance = 297.85, standard deviation = 17.26
5.10 mean = 150, standard deviation = 32.13
5.11 mean = 3.36, standard deviation = 1.54

Chapter 6
Describing Changes with Index Numbers

6.1 100, 101.9, 104.7, 105.7, 111.3, 117.9, 122.6, 124.5
  80.3, 81.8, 84.1, 84.8, 89.4, 94.7, 98.5, 100
6.2 100, 98.8, 97.2, 90.5, 80.9, 74.2, 60.6, 45.5, 31.4, 21.5

464.3, 458.6, 451.4, 420.0, 375.7, 344.3, 281.4, 211.4, 145.7, 100.0
6.3 100, 95.0, 80.2, 92.6, 105, 111.6, 125.6, 128.1, 133.1, 121.5, 109.9, 108.3
6.4 19,080, 23,850, 29,192, 31,864, 34,737, 39,830, 44,609, 52,575: 25%, 22%, 9%, 9%, 15%, 12%, 18%
6.5 261, 291, 353, 397: 45.9, 55.8, 66.7, 74.9, 84.4:395, 481, 574, 645, 727, 861, 973, 1085, 1317, 1481
6.6 Base weighted indices = 106.1, 114.2: current period indices = 106.3, 114.8
6.7 100, 109, 115, 124
6.8 106.65, 106.78
6.9 110.6, 126.7, 144.8

Chapter 7
Calculations with Money

7.1 45,000, £48,000, £11,500
7.2 300 No (greater than plane capacity)
7.4 £4661
7.5 £20,000 now
7.6 (a) 6133   (b) 18,540   (c) 29,856
7.7 (a) 24.95%   (b) 27.24%   (c) 37.52%
7.8 −5.39%
7.9 2167, 2670, 49.2%
7.10 a. 5699   b. 17,302   c. 28,440
7.11 £15,741
7.12 £263.31
7.13 7% loan, £1288

Chapter 8
Relating Variables by Regression

8.1 Manager's forecast: mean error = −1.0, MAD = 2.0, MSE = 5.6
  Foreman's forecast: mean error = −2.0, MAD = 2.0, MSE = 5.6
  Management Services: mean error = 0, MAD = 1.0, MSE = 1.4
8.2 $y = 16.59 + 4.98x$, $r = 0.9976$
8.3 £493
8.4 $2.16 + 2.96 \times$ bonus. Coefficient of determination = 0.99.
8.5 265.9, 293.0, 320.1, 347.2, 374.3, 401.4
8.7 $r_s = 0.741$
8.8 $r_s = 0.952$

Chapter 9
Business Forecasting

9.1 $y = 113.27 + 9.30 \times$ time $r^2 = 0.989$
9.2 164.4
9.3 193
9.4 2 period: MAD = 83.33, MSE = 8366.67
3 period: MAD = 76, MSE = 7422.22
4 period: MAD = 73.75, MSE = 7043.75
9.5 280, 276, 284.4, 290, 291, 283.9, 275.5, 283.9
280, 272, 289.6, 299.7, 299.7, 283.8, 267, 285.6
9.6 208, 208.4, 209.2, 230.6, 256.2, 251.8, 247.4, 243.5
208, 208.8, 210.2, 253, 299.6, 282.1, 267.3, 255.4
208, 209.2, 211.2, 275.1, 338.4, 300.4, 272.7, 253.3
208, 209.6, 212.2, 296.9, 372.5, 308.3, 268.2, 244.1
9.7 $y = 50.6 + 1.75t$
9.8 36.3, 63.0, 106.3, 39.0, 67.6, 113.9
9.9 133.7, 199.9, 146.4
9.10 203.3, 185.9, 229.5, 259.9, 245.1, 222.3, 272.2, 306.2
9.11 133.0, 186.4, 147.0
203.9, 195.4, 228.5, 251.2, 246.1, 237.6, 270.8, 293.4

Chapter 10
Using Matrices to Solve Equations

10.1
$\begin{bmatrix} 16 & 14 \\ 10 & 6 \end{bmatrix}, \begin{bmatrix} 16 & 14 \\ 10 & 6 \end{bmatrix}, \begin{bmatrix} 4 & -6 \\ -4 & -2 \end{bmatrix}, \begin{bmatrix} -4 & 6 \\ 4 & 2 \end{bmatrix}$

$\begin{bmatrix} 23 & 21 \\ 11 & 11 \end{bmatrix}, \begin{bmatrix} 9 & 7 \\ 9 & 1 \end{bmatrix}, \begin{bmatrix} 10 & 13 \\ 5 & 7 \end{bmatrix}, \begin{bmatrix} -9 & -7 \\ -9 & 1 \end{bmatrix}, \begin{bmatrix} 23 & 21 \\ 11 & 11 \end{bmatrix}$

10.2
$\begin{bmatrix} 88 & 116 \\ 32 & 38 \end{bmatrix}, \begin{bmatrix} 90 & 44 \\ 82 & 36 \end{bmatrix}, \begin{bmatrix} 732 & 1196 \\ 262 & 414 \end{bmatrix}, \begin{bmatrix} 1204 & 560 \\ 500 & 224 \end{bmatrix}$

10.3 £1675
10.4 1750, 3425, 3645, 8820
10.5 $x = 930, y = 1480$, £2410

10.6
$\begin{bmatrix} -0.33 & 0.33 \\ 0.44 & -0.11 \end{bmatrix}, \begin{bmatrix} 3 & -4 \\ -5 & 7 \end{bmatrix}$

10.7 $x = 3, y = 2, z = 1$
10.8 $w = 87, x = 90, y = 83, z = 190$.
There is no inverse.

Chapter 11
Planning with Linear Programming

11.2 X1 = 0.167, X2 = 0.167, cost = £11.67
11.4 $X = 40, Y = 20$, profit = £14,000
11.5 E = 200, G = 1200, income = £116,000, annual profit = £2.8m.
Spare capacity in forming (400), machine shop (400), market for E (600) and market for G (50). Shadow prices for assembly (£10) and testing (£10). £20 for up to 33.34 hours a week. £268.
11.6 S = 20, N = 30, profit = £36,000.
Spare capacity in wiring (60); shadow prices for pressing (£100) and assembly (£100). £8, £1.

Chapter 12
Using Calculus to Describe Changes

12.1 $84x^6$
12.2 $24.8x^3 + 9.9x^2 - 14.2x - 11.9$
Easiest to find is minimum when $x = 0.9$.
12.3 $6y - 3$
12.4 $30, -x^2 + 30x - 30, x = 15$
12.6 (a) $14.4x - 3.3$, 14.4
(b) $14x^6 - 16x^3 - 6x, 84x^5 - 48x^2 - 6$
(c) $24x^{23} + 4x^{-2}, 552x^{22} - 8x^{-3}$
12.7 Minimum of 19.4 when $x = 1.25$.
Minimum of -8 when $x = 1$, maximum of 100 when $x = -5$.
12.8 $9x^2 + 10xz - 8x + 6z^2, 5x^2 + 10 + 12xz - 6z - 3z^2$
12.9 $x_1 = 1, x_2 = 0$
12.10 255.4, $x_1 = 10.7, x_2 = 6.1$
12.11 500 (when $x = 10$ and $z = 20$)

12.12 7.25 (when $x = 5.5$ and $z = 2.5$)
12.13 (a) 3 (b) 6.67 (c) 6
12.14 $2.25x^4 - 4x^3 + 2x^2 - 6x + c$
12.15 90
12.16 9795

Chapter 13
Uncertainty and Probabilities

13.1 (a) 0.15 (b) 0.08 (c) 0.48 (d) 0.56
(e) 0.44 (f) 0.22
13.2 0.2, 0.6, 0.6
13.3 (a) 0 (b) 0.3 (c) 0.7 (d) 0 (e) 0.6
(f) 0.4
13.4 (a) 1/13 (b) 1/4 (c) 1/52 (d) 16/52
13.5 (a) 0.125 (b) 0.5 (c) 0.125
13.6 0.589
13.7 0.12, 0.2
13.8

	A	B	C
X	0.18	0.77	0.4
Y	0.82	0.23	0.6

13.9

	G	A	P
X	0.38	0.34	0.40
Y	0.41	0.22	0.15
Z	0.22	0.44	0.45

13.11 0.57
13.12 0.67
13.13 248, 49

Chapter 14
Probability Distributions

14.1

1	2	3	4	5	6	7	8
0.025	0.075	0.125	0.175	0.275	0.175	0.125	0.025

14.2 0.5, 0.2
14.3 (a) 3003, 360,360 (b) 45, 90
(c) 45, 1,814,400
14.4 3,628,800
14.5 479,001,600, 495, 19,958,400
14.6 1.2, 1.01 (a) 0.2376 (b) 0 (c) 0.0002
14.7 0.1672
14.8 0.1×10^{-11}, 0.2824, 0.3766, 0.1109

14.9 2, 1.414 (a) 0.2707 (b) 0.0034
(c) 0.0165
14.10 1.08 $P(0) = 0.3329, P(1) = 0.3662,$
$P(2) = 0.2014, P(3) = 0.0738,$
$P(4) = 0.0203, P(5) = 0.0045$, etc
14.11 0.0778
14.12 0.632, 0.564
14.13 (a) 0.0668 (b) 0.0668 (c) 0.8664
(d) 0.8351 (e) 0.1865
14.14 (a) 0.0228 (b) 0.1587 (c) 0.8185
(d) 0.1359 (e) 0.6247
14.15 0.0475, 0.0062, 0.5934, 5232
14.16 Mean = 15 minutes, variance = 7 minutes
(reasonably). 0.1292, 0.0294

Chapter 15
Using Samples in Business

15.1 0.0228
15.2 105.44 – 107.56, 105.11 – 107.89
15.3 0.0681
15.4 123.92 – 127.67, 122.92 – 128.08
15.5 mean = 6.4 minutes, standard deviation = 3.87 minutes
15.6 0.035 – 0.125, 0.027 – 0.133
15.7 61.5, 96.0, 245.9
15.8 971
15.9 230.86, 224.59 - 231.41
15.10 0.339, 0.141, 0.141 – 0.339
15.11 90.64 – 109.36, 87.21 – 112.79
15.12 39.94 – 64.04, 36.95 – 67.05, 43.58 – 60.42, 44.11 – 59.89

Chapter 16
Testing Hypotheses

16.1 367.33 – 432.67, 357 – 443
16.2 No.
16.4 No.
16.5 No.
16.7 No.
16.8 The claim can be rejected.
16.9 The claim can not be rejected at 1% significance level.
16.10 Reject the manufacturer's claim.
16.11 Yes.
16.12 Can not reject hypothesis.
16.13 Can not reject hypothesis.
16.14 Can not reject hypothesis.

Chapter 17
Analysing Business Decisions

17.2 *b* or *e*
17.3 (a) *d, d, d*   (b) *d, d, d*
17.4 (a) a   (b) a
17.5 2.66
17.6 £592
17.7 70.35
17.8 139,500

Chapter 18
Controlling Stocks

18.1 20, 0.2, £5200
18.2 212, 0.045, £101,060
18.3 20, 40
18.4 24.7, 0.24, £5162
18.5 120, 30, £580,800, 136, 26.7, £580,224
18.6 4328, 4410
18.7 Q = 100, ROL = 328.4, cost = £4128 a
      week, ROL = 322.2, cost = £4122 a week
18.8 TSLs = 6402, 6502
18.10 Q = 1000

Chapter 19
Planning Projects with Networks

19.4

Activity	Duration	Earliest Start	Earliest Finish	Latest Start	Latest Finish	Total float
A	1	3	4	3	4	0
B	1	3	4	3	4	0
C	1	3	4	6	7	3
D	1	6	7	6	7	0
E	1	1	2	1	2	0
F	1	0	1	0	1	0
G	1	2	3	6	7	4
H	1	2	3	2	3	0
I	1	1	2	5	6	4
J	1	2	3	6	7	4
K	1	2	3	5	6	3
L	1	1	2	4	5	3
M	1	5	6	5	6	0
N	1	3	4	5	6	2
O	1	4	5	4	5	0
P	1	4	5	6	7	2

19.5 14 weeks, B, C, E, F
19.6 0.079, 21.3
19.7 34 weeks, any convenient time starting
      between weeks 8 and 17, 2 weeks delay
19.9 75

Chapter 20
Queues and Simulation

20.1 $P(0) = 0.167$, $P(n) = 0.167 \times (0.833)n$,
      $L = 5$, $L_q = 4.167$, $W = 0.05$, $W_q = 0.04$
20.2 £100 an hour
20.3 2

Appendix D

Table of random numbers

83635	18471	01664	97316	13751	22904	46465	55782	13047	64812
66791	25482	48893	34611	07709	24016	81064	00876	11197	35664
46879	05246	13006	17669	16587	25597	24106	67913	05438	97013
98520	97410	96305	57421	23489	67492	31647	85500	69477	55523
68227	06488	52064	30027	66988	20333	47881	20944	67822	01668
20034	17909	14246	28346	10972	38106	20079	99555	24768	25009
03504	71668	64982	34679	97643	18164	28640	27913	64820	57913
59731	12389	60071	04587	32881	66749	12400	64478	94613	00457
00456	67910	17219	89404	62840	37898	74613	01346	78994	00657
98015	67623	15678	01541	34613	26546	51255	25245	53345	42031
19994	64313	43100	32065	40324	60354	60106	14659	01346	43213
79844	57645	00247	61683	09830	98401	87410	01964	30687	46280
19601	68163	54387	46338	46324	57621	05151	23544	57987	98037
69771	02344	00168	98884	23467	90120	34970	35668	76137	90173
14865	05576	58425	97031	26459	73156	87109	01348	76218	40245
83116	77102	00886	01134	46905	58766	41003	28979	84341	28752
46103	25571	93826	40319	73150	46283	79134	67229	87766	35441
90087	51685	24641	35794	58525	81000	17991	77851	00356	48440
16624	00975	11300	24687	12665	78941	12265	02399	54613	87291
03154	67913	83739	19726	48505	64213	58467	91349	72344	31164

Appendix E

Probabilities for the binomial distribution

n	r	.05	.10	.15	.20	.25	p .30	.35	.40	.45	.50
1	0	.9500	.9000	.8500	.8000	.7500	.7000	.6500	.6000	.5500	.5000
	1	.0500	.1000	.1500	.2000	.2500	.3000	.3500	.4000	.4500	.5000
2	0	.9025	.8100	.7225	.6400	.5625	.4900	.4225	.3600	.3025	.2500
	1	.0950	.1800	.2550	.3200	.3750	.4200	.4550	.4800	.4950	.5000
	2	.0025	.0100	.0225	.0400	.0625	.0900	.1225	.1600	.2025	.2500
3	0	.8574	.7290	.6141	.5120	.4219	.3430	.2746	.2160	.1664	.1250
	1	.1354	.2430	.3251	.3840	.4219	.4410	.4436	.4320	.4084	.3750
	2	.0071	.0270	.0574	.0960	.1406	.1890	.2389	.2880	.3341	.3750
	3	.0001	.0010	.0034	.0080	.0156	.0270	.0429	.0640	.0911	.1250
4	0	.8145	.6561	.5220	.4096	.3164	.2401	.1785	.1296	.0915	.0625
	1	.1715	.2916	.3685	.4096	.4219	.4116	.3845	.3456	.2995	.2500
	2	.0135	.4086	.0975	.1536	.2109	.2646	.3105	.3456	.3675	.3750
	3	.0005	.0036	.0115	.0256	.0469	.0756	.1115	.1536	.2005	.2500
	4	.0000	.0001	.0005	.0016	.0039	.0081	.0150	.0256	.0410	.0625
5	0	.7738	.5905	.4437	.3277	.2373	.1681	.1160	.0778	.0503	.0312
	1	.2036	.3280	.3915	.4096	.3955	.3602	.3124	.2592	.2059	.1562
	2	.0214	.0729	.1382	.2048	.2637	.3087	.3364	.3456	.3369	.3125
	3	.0011	.0081	.0244	.0512	.0879	.1323	.1811	.2304	.2757	.3125
	4	.0000	.0004	.0022	.0064	.0146	.0284	.0488	.0768	.1128	.1562
	5	.0000	.0000	.0001	.0003	.0010	.0024	.0053	.0102	.0185	.0312
6	0	.7351	.5314	.3771	.2621	.1780	.1176	.0754	.0467	.0277	.0156
	1	.2321	.3543	.3993	.3932	.3560	.3025	.2437	.1866	.1359	.0938
	2	.0305	.0984	.1762	.2458	.2966	.3241	.3280	.3110	.2780	.2344
	3	.0021	.0146	.0415	.0819	.1318	.1852	.2355	.2765	.3032	.3125
	4	.0001	.0012	.0055	.0154	.0330	.0595	.0951	.1382	.1861	.2344
	5	.0000	.0001	.0004	.0015	.0044	.0102	.0205	.0369	.0609	.0938
	6	.0000	.0000	.0000	.0001	.0002	.0007	.0018	.0041	.0083	.0516

p

n	r	.05	.10	.15	.20	.25	.30	.35	.40	.45	.50
7	0	.6983	.4783	.3206	.2097	.1335	.0824	.0490	.0280	0152	.0078
	1	.2573	.3720	.3960	.3670	.3115	.2471	.1848	.1306	.0872	.0547
	2	.0406	.1240	.2097	.2753	.3115	.3177	.2985	.2613	.2140	.1641
	3	.0036	.0230	.0617	.1147	.1730	.2269	.2679	.2903	.2918	.2734
	4	.0002	.0026	.0109	.0287	.0577	.0972	.01442	.1935	.2388	.2734
	5	.0009	.0002	.0012	.0043	.0115	.0250	.0466	.0774	.1172	.1641
	6	.0000	.0000	.0001	.0004	.0013	.0036	.0084	.0172	.0320	.0547
	7	.0000	.0000	.0000	.0000	.0001	.0002	.0006	.0016	.0037	.0078
8	0	.6634	.4305	.2725	.1678	.1001	.0576	.0319	.0168	.0084	.0039
	1	.2793	.3826	.3847	.3355	.2670	.1977	.1373	.0896	.0548	.0312
	2	.0515	.1488	.2376	.2936	.3115	.2965	.2587	.2090	.1569	.1094
	3	.0054	.0331	.0839	.1468	.2076	.2541	.2786	.2787	.2568	.2188
	4	.0004	.0046	.0815	.0459	.0865	.1361	.1875	.2322	.2627	.2734
	5	.0000	.0004	.0026	.0092	.0231	.0467	.0808	.1239	.1719	.2188
	6	.0000	.0000	.0002	.0011	.0038	.0100	.0217	.0413	.0703	.1094
	7	.0000	.0000	.0000	.0001	.0004	.0012	.0033	.0079	.0164	.0312
	8	.0000	.0000	.0000	.0000	.0000	.0001	.0002	.0007	.0017	.0039
9	0	.6302	.3874	.2316	.1342	.0751	.0404	.0207	.0101	.0046	.0020
	1	.2985	.3874	.3679	.3020	.2253	.1556	.1004	.0605	.0339	.0176
	2	.0629	.1722	.2597	.3020	.3003	.2668	.2162	.1612	.1110	.0703
	3	.0077	.0446	.1069	.1762	.2336	.2668	.2716	.2508	.2119	.1641
	4	.0006	.0074	.0283	.0661	.1168	.1715	.2194	.2508	.2600	.2461
	5	.0000	.0008	.0050	.0165	.0389	.0735	.1181	.1672	.2128	.2461
	6	.0000	.0001	.0006	.0028	.0087	.0210	.0424	.0743	.1160	.1641
	7	.0000	.0000	.0000	.0003	.0012	.0039	.0098	.0212	.0407	.0703
	8	.0000	.0000	.0000	.0000	.0001	.0004	.0013	.0035	.0083	.0716
	9	.0000	.0000	.0000	.0000	.0000	.0000	.0001	.0003	.0008	.0020
10	0	.5987	.3487	.1969	.1074	.0563	.0282	.0135	.0060	.0025	.0010
	1	.3151	.3874	3474	.2684	.1877	.21211	.0725	.0403	.0207	.0098
	2	.0746	.1937	.2759	.3020	.2816	.2335	.1757	.1209	.0763	.0439
	3	.0105	.0574	.1298	.2013	.2503	.2668	.2522	.2150	.1665	.1172
	4	.0010	.0112	.0401	.0881	.1460	.2001	.2377	.2508	.2384	.2051
	5	.0001	.0015	.0085	.0264	.0584	.1029	.1563	.2007	.2340	.2461
	6	.0000	.0001	.0012	.0055	.0162	.0368	.0689	.1115	.1596	.2051
	7	.0000	.0000	.0001	.0008	.0031	.0090	.0212	.0425	.0746	.1172
	8	.0000	.0000	.0000	.0001	.0004	.0014	.0043	.0106	.0229	.0439
	9	.0000	.0000	.0000	.0000	.0000	.0001	.0005	.0016	.0042	.0098
	10	.0000	.0000	.0000	.0000	.0000	.0000	.0000	.0001	.0003	.0010

n	r	.05	.10	.15	.20	.25	.30	.35	.40	.45	.50
							p				
11	0	.5688	.3138	.1673	.0859	.0422	.0198	.0088	.0036	.0014	.0005
	1	.3293	.3835	.3248	.2362	.1549	.0932	.0518	.0266	.0125	.0054
	2	.0867	.2131	.2866	.2953	.2581	.1998	.1395	.0887	.0513	.0269
	3	.0137	.0710	.1517	.2215	.2581	.2568	.2254	.1774	.1259	0806
	4	.0014	.0158	.0536	.1107	.1721	.2201	.2428	.2365	.2060	.1611
	5	.0001	.0025	.0132	.0388	.0803	.1321	.1830	.2207	.2360	.2256
	6	.0000	.0003	.0023	.0097	.0268	.0566	.0985	.1471	.1931	.2256
	7	.0000	.0000	.0003	.0017	.0064	.0173	.0379	.0701	.1128	.1611
	8	.0000	.0000	.0000	.0002	.0011	.0037	.0102	.0234	.0462	.0806
	9	.0000	.0000	.0000	.0000	.0001	.0005	.0018	.0052	.0126	.0269
	10	.0000	.0000	.0000	.0000	.0000	.0000	.0002	.0007	.0021	.0054
	11	.0000	.0000	.0000	.0000	.0000	.0000	.0000	.0000	.0002	.0005
12	0	.5404	.2824	.1422	.0687	.0317	.0138	.0057	.0022	.0008	.0002
	1	.3413	.3766	.3012	.2062	.1267	.0712	.0368	.0174	.0075	.0029
	2	.0988	.2301	.2924	.2835	.2323	.1678	.1088	.0639	.0339	.0161
	3	.0173	.0852	.1720	.2362	.2581	.2397	.1954	.1419	.0923	.0537
	4	.0021	.0213	.0683	.1329	.1936	.2311	.2367	.2128	.17090	.1208
	5	.0002	.0038	.0193	.0532	.1032	.1585	.2039	.2270	.2225	.1934
	6	.0000	.0005	.0040	.0155	.0401	.0792	.1281	.1766	.2124	.2256
	7	.0000	.0000	.0006	.0033	.0115	.0291	.0591	.1009	.1489	.1934
	8	.0000	.0000	.0001	.0005	.0024	.0078	.0199	.0420	.0762	.1208
	9	.0000	.0000	.0000	.0001	.0004	.0015	.0048	.0125	.0277	.0537
	10	.0000	.0000	.0000	.0000	.0000	.0002	.0008	.0025	.0068	.0161
	11	.0000	.0000	.0000	.0000	.0000	.0000	.0001	.0003	.0010	.0029
	12	.0000	.0000	.0000	.0000	.0000	.0000	.0000	.0000	.0001	.0002
13	0	.5133	.2542	.1209	.0550	.0238	.0097	.0037	.0013	.0004	.0001
	1	.3512	.3672	.2774	.1787	.1029	.0540	.0259	.0113	.0045	.0016
	2	.1109	.2448	.2937	.2680	.2059	.1388	.0836	.0453	.0220	.0095
	3	.0214	.0997	.1900	.2457	.2517	.2181	.1651	.1107	.0660	.0349
	4	.0028	.0277	.0838	.1535	.2097	.2337	.2222	.1845	.1350	.0873
	5	.0003	.0055	.0266	.0691	.1258	.1803	.2154	.2214	.1989	.1571
	6	.0000	.0008	.0063	.0230	.0559	.1030	.1546	.1968	.2169	.2095
	7	.0000	.0001	.0011	.0058	.0186	.0442	.0833	.1312	.1775	.2095
	8	.0000	.0000	.0001	.0011	.0047	.0142	.0336	.0656	.1089	.1571
	9	.0000	.0000	.0000	.0001	.0009	.0034	.0101	.0243	.0495	.0873
	10	.0000	.0000	.0000	.0000	.0001	.0006	.0022	.0065	.0162	.0349
	11	.0000	.0000	.0000	.0000	.0000	.0001	.0003	.0012	.0036	.0095
	12	.0000	.0000	.0000	.0000	.0000	.0000	.0000	.0001	.0005	.0016
	13	.0000	.0000	.0000	.0000	.0000	.0000	.0000	.0000	.0000	.0001

		p									
n	*r*	.05	.10	.15	.20	.25	.30	.35	.40	.45	.50
14	0	.4877	.2288	.1028	.0440	.0178	.0068	.0024	.0008	.0002	.0001
	1	.3593	.3559	.2539	.1539	.0832	.0407	.0181	.0073	.0270	.0009
	2	.1229	.2570	.2912	.2501	.1802	.1134	.0634	.0317	.0141	.0056
	3	.0259	.1142	.2056	.2501	.2402	.1943	.1366	.0845	.0462	.0222
	4	.0037	.0348	.0998	.1720	.2202	.2290	.2022	.1549	.1040	.0611
	5	.0004	.0078	.0352	.0860	.1468	.1963	.2178	.2066	.1701	.1222
	6	.0000	.0013	.0093	.0322	.0734	.1262	.1759	.2066	.2088	.1833
	7	.0000	.0002	.0019	.0092	.0280	.0618	.1082	.1574	.1952	.2095
	8	.0000	.0000	.0003	.0020	.0082	.0232	.0510	.0918	.1398	.1833
	9	.0000	.0000	.0000	.0003	.0018	.0066	.0183	.0408	.0762	.1222
	10	.0000	.0000	.0000	.0000	.0003	.0014	.0049	.0136	.0312	.0611
	11	.0000	.0000	.0000	.0000	.0000	.0002	.0010	.0033	.0093	.0222
	12	.0000	.0000	.0000	.0000	.0000	.0000	.0001	.0005	.0019	.0056
	13	.0000	.0000	.0000	.0000	.0000	.0000	.0000	.0001	.0002	.0009
	14	.0000	.0000	.0000	.0000	.0000	.0000	.0000	.0000	.0000	.0001
15	0	.4633	.2059	.0874	.0352	.0134	.0047	.0016	.0005	.0001	.0000
	1	.3658	.3432	.2312	.1319	.0668	.0305	.0126	.0047	.0016	.0005
	2	.1348	.2669	.2856	.2309	.1559	.0916	.0476	.0219	.0090	.0032
	3	.0307	.1285	.2184	.2501	.2252	.1700	.1110	.0634	.0318	.0139
	4	.0049	.0428	.1156	.1876	.2252	.2186	.1792	.1268	.0780	.0417
	5	.0006	.0105	.0449	.1032	.1651	.2061	.2123	.1859	.1404	.0916
	6	.0000	.0019	.0132	.0430	.0917	.1472	.1906	.2066	.1914	.1527
	7	.0000	.0003	.0030	.0138	.0393	.0811	.1319	.1771	.2013	.1964
	8	.0000	.0000	.0005	.0035	.0131	.0348	.0710	.1181	.1647	.1964
	9	.0000	.0000	.0001	.0007	.0034	.0116	.0298	.0612	.1048	.1527
	10	.0000	.0000	.0000	.0001	.0007	.0030	.0096	.0245	.0515	.0916
	11	.0000	.0000	.0000	.0000	.0001	.0006	.0024	.0074	.0191	.0417
	12	.0000	.0000	.0000	.0000	.0000	.0001	.0004	.0016	.0052	.0139
	13	.0000	.0000	.0000	.0000	.0000	.0000	.0001	.0003	.0010	.0032
	14	.0000	.0000	.0000	.0000	.0000	.0000	.0000	.0000	.0001	.0005
	15	.0000	.0000	.0000	.0000	.0000	.0000	.0000	.0000	.0000	.0000

							p				
n	r	.05	.10	.15	.20	.25	.30	.35	.40	.45	.50
16	0	.4401	1853	.0743	.0281	.0100	.0033	.0010	.0003	.0001	.0000
	1	.3706	.3294	.2097	.1126	.0535	.0228	.0087	.0030	.0009	.0002
	2	.1463	.2745	.2775	.2111	.1336	.0732	.0353	.0150	.0056	.0018
	3	.0359	.1423	.2285	.2463	.2079	.1465	.0888	.0468	.0215	.0085
	4	.0061	.0514	.1311	.2001	.2252	.2040	.1553	.1014	.0572	.0278
	5	.0008	.0137	.0555	.1201	.1802	.2099	.2008	.1623	.1123	.0667
	6	.0001	.0028	.0180	.0550	.1101	.1649	.1982	.1983	.1684	.1222
	7	.0000	.0004	.0045	.0197	.0524	.1010	.1524	.1889	.1969	.1746
	8	.0000	.0001	.0009	.0055	.0197	.0487	.0923	.1417	.1812	.1964
	9	.0000	.0000	.0001	.0012	.0058	.0185	.0442	.0840	.1318	.1746
	10	.0000	.0000	.0000	.0002	.0014	.0056	.0167	.0392	.0755	.1222
	11	.0000	.0000	.0000	.0000	.0002	.0013	.0049	.0142	.0337	.0667
	12	.0000	.0000	.0000	.0000	.0000	.0002	.0011	.0040	.0115	.0278
	13	.0000	.0000	.0000	.0000	.0000	.0000	.0002	.0008	.0029	.0085
	14	.0000	.0000	.0000	.0000	.0000	.0000	.0000	.0001	.0005	.0018
	15	.0000	.0000	.0000	.0000	.0000	.0000	.0000	.0000	.0001	.0002
	16	.0000	.0000	.0000	.0000	.0000	.0000	.0000	.0000	.0000	.0000
17	0	.4181	.1668	.0631	.0225	.0075	.0023	.0007	.0002	.0000	.0000
	1	.3741	.3150	.1893	.0957	.0426	.0169	.0060	.0019	.0005	.0001
	2	.1575	.2800	.2673	.1914	.1136	.0581	.0260	.0102	.0035	.0010
	3	.0415	.1556	.2359	.2393	.1893	.1245	.0701	.0341	.0144	.0052
	4	.0076	.0605	1457	.2093	.2209	.1868	.1320	.0796	.0411	.0182
	5	.0010	.0175	.0668	.1361	.1914	.2081	.1849	.1379	.0875	.0472
	6	.0001	.0039	.0236	.0680	.1276	.1784	.1991	.1839	.1432	.0944
	7	.0000	.0007	.0065	.0267	.0668	.1201	.1685	.1927	.1841	.1484
	8	.0000	.0001	.0014	.0084	.0279	.0644	.1134	.1606	.1883	.1855
	9	.0000	.0000	.0003	.0021	.0093	.0276	.0611	.1070	.1540	.1855
	10	.0000	.0000	.0000	.0004	.0025	.0095	.0263	.0571	.1008	.1484
	11	.0000	.0000	.0000	.0001	.0005	.0026	.0090	.0242	.0525	.0944
	12	.0000	.0000	.0000	.0000	.0001	.0006	.0024	.0021	.0215	.0472
	13	.0000	.0000	.0000	.0000	.0000	.0001	.0005	.0021	.0068	.0182
	14	.0000	.0000	.0000	.0000	.000	.0000	.0001	.0004	.0016	.0052
	15	.0000	.0000	.0000	.0000	.0000	.0000	.0000	.0001	.0003	.0010
	16	.0000	.0000	.0000	.0000	.0000	.0000	.0000	.0000	.0000	.0001
	17	.0000	.0000	.0000	.0000	.0000	.0000	.0000	.0000	.0000	.0000

Appendix F

Probabilities for the Poisson distribution

r	.005	.01	.02	.03	.04	μ .05	.06	.07	.08	.09
0	.9950	.9900	.9802	.9704	.9608	.9512	.9418	.9324	.9231	.9139
1	.0050	.0099	.0192	.0291	.0384	.0476	.0565	.0653	.0738	.0823
2	.0000	.0000	.0002	.0004	.0008	.0012	.0017	.0023	.0030	.0037
3	.0000	.0000	.0000	.0000	.0000	.0000	.0000	.0001	.0001	.0001

r	0.1	0.2	0.3	0.4	0.5	μ 0.6	0.7	0.8	0.9	1.0
0	.9048	.8187	.7408	.6703	.6065	.5488	.4966	.4493	.4066	.3679
1	.0905	.1637	.2222	.2681	.3033	.3293	.3476	.3595	.3659	.3679
2	.0045	.0164	.0333	.0536	.0758	.0988	.1217	.1438	.1647	.1839
3	.0002	.0011	.0033	.0072	.0126	.0198	.0284	.0383	.0494	.0613
4	.0000	.0001	.0002	.0007	.0016	.0030	.0050	.0077	.0111	.0153
5	.0000	.0000	.0000	.0001	.0002	.0004	.0007	.0012	.0020	.0031
6	.0000	.0000	.0000	.0000	.0000	.0000	.0001	.0002	.0003	.0005
7	.0000	.0000	.0000	.0000	.0000	.0000	.0000	.0000	.0000	.0001

r	1.1	1.2	1.3	1.4	1.5	μ 1.6	1.7	1.8	1.9	2.0
0	.3329	.3012	.2725	.2466	.2231	.2019	.1827	.1653	.1496	.1353
1	.3662	.3614	.3543	.3452	.3347	.3230	.3106	.2975	.2842	.2707
2	.2014	.2169	.2303	.2417	.2510	.2584	.2640	.2678	.2700	.2707
3	.0738	.0867	.0998	.1128	.1255	.1378	.1496	.1607	.1710	.1804
4	.0203	.0260	.0324	.0395	.0471	.0551	.0636	.0723	.0812	.0902
5	.0045	.0062	.0084	.0111	.0141	.0176	.0216	.0260	.0309	.0361
6	.0008	.0012	.0018	.0026	.0035	.0047	.0061	.0078	.0098	.0120
7	.0001	.0002	.0003	.0005	.0008	.0011	.0015	.0020	.0027	.0034
8	.0000	.0000	.0001	.0001	.0001	.0002	.0003	.0005	.0006	.0009
9	.0000	.0000	.0000	.0000	.0000	.0000	.0001	.0001	.0001	.0002

					μ					
r	2.1	2.2	2.3	2.4	2.5	2.6	2.7	2.8	2.9	2.0
0	.1225	.1108	.1003	.0907	.0821	.0743	.0672	.0608	.0550	.0498
1	.2527	.2438	.2306	.2177	.2052	.1931	.1815	.1703	.1596	.1494
2	.2700	.2681	.2652	.2613	.2565	.2510	.2450	.2384	.2314	.2240
3	.1890	.1966	.2033	.2090	.2138	.2176	.2205	.2225	.2237	.2240
4	.0992	.1082	.1196	.1254	.1336	.1414	.1488	.1557	.1662	.1680
5	.0417	.0476	.0538	.0602	.0668	.0735	.0804	.0872	.0940	.1008
6	.0146	.0174	.0206	.0241	.0278	.0319	.0362	.0407	.0455	.0504
7	.0044	.0055	.0068	.0083	.0099	.0118	.0139	.0163	.0188	.0216
8	.0011	.0015	.0019	.0025	.0031	.0038	.0047	.0057	.0068	.0081
9	.0003	.0004	.0005	.0007	.0009	.0011	.0014	.0018	.0002	.0027
10	.0001	.0001	.0001	.0002	.0002	.0003	.0004	.0005	.0006	.0008
11	.0000	.0000	.0000	.0000	.0000	.0001	.0001	.0001	.0002	.0002
12	.0000	.0000	.0000	.0000	.0000	.0000	.0000	.0000	.0000	.0001

					μ					
r	3.1	3.2	3.3	3.4	3.5	3.6	3.7	3.8	3.9	4.0
0	.0450	.0408	.0369	.0334	.0302	.0273	.0247	.0224	.0202	.0183
1	.1397	.1304	.1217	.1135	.1057	.0984	.0915	.0850	.0789	.0733
2	.2165	.2087	.2008	.1929	.1850	.1771	.1692	.1615	.1539	.1465
3	.2237	.2226	.2209	.2186	.2158	.2125	.2087	.2046	.2001	.1954
4	.1734	.1781	.1823	.1858	.1888	.1912	.1931	.1944	.1951	.1954
5	.1075	.1140	.1203	.1264	.1322	.1377	.1429	.1477	.1522	.1563
6	.0555	.0608	.0662	.0716	.0771	.0826	.0881	.0936	.0989	.1042
7	.0246	.0278	.0312	.0348	.0385	.0425	.0466	.0508	.0551	.0595
8	.0095	.0111	.0129	.0148	.0169	.0191	.0215	.0241	.0269	.0298
9	.0033	.0040	.0047	.0056	.0066	.0076	.0089	.0102	.0116	.0132
10	.0010	.0013	.0016	.0019	.0023	.0028	.0033	.0039	.0045	.0053
11	.0003	.0004	.0005	.0006	.0007	.0009	.0011	.0013	.0016	.0019
12	.0001	.0001	.0001	.0002	.0002	.0003	.0003	.0004	.0005	.0006
13	.0000	.0000	.0000	.0000	.0001	.0001	.0001	.0001	.0002	.0002
14	.0000	.0000	.0000	.0000	.0000	.0000	.0000	.0000	.0000	.0001

					μ					
r	4.1	4.2	4.3	4.4	4.5	4.6	4.7	4.8	4.9	5.0
0	.0166	.0150	.0136	.0123	.0111	.0101	.0091	.0082	.0074	.0067
1	.0679	.0630	.0583	.0540	.0500	.0462	.0427	.0395	.0365	.0337
2	.1393	.1323	.1254	.1188	.1125	.1063	.1005	.0948	.0894	.0842
3	.1904	.1852	.1798	.1743	.1687	.1631	.1574	.1517	.1460	.1404
4	.1951	.1944	.1933	.1917	.1898	.1875	.1849	.1820	.1789	.1755
5	.1600	.1633	.1662	.1687	.1708	.1725	.1738	.1747	.1753	.1755
6	.1093	.1143	.1191	.1237	.1281	.1323	.1362	.1398	.1432	.1462
7	.0640	.0686	.0732	.0778	.0824	.0869	.0914	.0959	.1002	.1044
8	.0328	.0360	.0393	.0428	.0463	.0500	.0537	.0575	.0614	.0653
9	.0150	.0168	.0188	.0209	.0232	.0255	.0280	.0307	.0334	.0363
10	.0061	.0071	.0081	.0092	.0104	.0118	.0132	.0147	.0164	.0181
11	.0023	.0027	.0032	.0037	.0043	.0049	.0056	.0064	.0073	.0082
12	.0008	.0009	.0011	.0014	.0016	.0019	.0022	.0026	.0030	.0034
13	.0002	.0003	.0004	.0005	.0006	.0007	.0008	.0009	.0011	.0013
14	.0001	.0001	.0001	.0001	.0002	.0002	.0003	.0004	.0004	.0005
15	.0000	.0000	.0000	.0000	0001	.0001	.0001	.0001	.0001	.0002

μ										
r	5.1	5.2	5.3	5.4	5.5	5.6	5.7	5.8	5.9	6.0
0	.0061	.0055	.0050	.0045	.0041	.0037	.0033	.0030	.0027	.0025
1	.0311	.0287	.0265	.0244	.0225	.0207	.0191	.0176	.0162	.0149
2	.0793	.0746	.0701	.0659	.0618	.0580	.0544	.0509	.0477	.0446
3	.1348	.1293	.1239	.1185	.1133	.1082	.1033	.0985	.0938	.0892
4	.1719	.1681	.1641	.1600	.1558	.1515	.1472	.1428	.1383	.1339
5	.1753	.1748	.1740	.1728	.1714	.1697	.1678	.1656	.1632	.1606
6	.1490	.1515	.1537	.1555	.1571	.1584	.1594	.1601	.1605	.1606
7	.1086	.1125	.1163	.1200	.1234	.1267	.1298	.1326	.1353	.1377
8	.0692	.0731	.0771	.0810	.0849	.0887	.0925	.0962	.0998	.1033
9	.0392	.0423	.0454	.0486	.0519	.0552	.0586	.0620	.0654	.0668
10	.0200	.0220	.0241	.0262	.0285	.0309	.0334	.0359	.0386	.0413
11	.0093	.0104	.0116	.0129	.0143	.0157	.0173	.0190	.0207	.0225
12	.0039	.0045	.0051.	0058	.0065	.0073	.0082	.0092	.0102	.0113
13	.0015	.0018	.0021	.0024	.0028	.0032	.0036	.0041	.0046	.0052
14	.0006	.0007	.0008	.0009	.0011	.0013	.0015	.0017	.0019	.0022
15	.0002	.0002	.0003	.0003	.0004	.0005	.0006	.0007	.0008	.0009
16	.0001	.0001	.0001	.0001	.0001	.0002	.0002	.0002	.0003	.0003
17	.0000	.0000	.0000	.0000	.0000	.0001	.0001	.0001	.0001	.0001

μ										
r	6.1	6.2	6.3	6.4	6.5	6.6	6.7	6.8	6.9	7.0
0	.0022	.0020	.0018	.0017	.0015	.0014	.0012	.0011	.0010	.0009
1	.0137	.0126	.0116	.0106	.0098	.0090	.0082	.0076	.0070	.0064
2	.0417	.0390	.0364	.0340	.0318	.0296	.0276	.0258	.0240	.0223
3	.0848	.0806	.0765	.0726	.0688	.0652	.0617	.0584	.0552	.0521
4	.1294	.1249	.1205	.1162	.1118	.1076	.1034	.0992	.0952	.0912
5	.1579	.1549	.1519	.1487	.1454	.1420	.1385	.1349	.1314	.1277
6	.1605	.1601	.1595	.1586	.1575	.1562	.1546	.1529	.1511	.1490
7	.1399	.1418	.1435	.1450	.1462	.1472	.1480	.1486	.1489	.1490
8	.1066	.1099	.1130	.1160	.1188	.1215	.1240	.1263	.1284	.1304
9	.0723	.0757	.0791	.0825	.0858	.0891	.0923	.0954	.0985	.1014
10	.0441	.0469	.0498	.0528	.0558	.0588	.0618	.0649	.0679	.0710
11	.0245	.0265	.0285	.0307	.0330	.0353	.0377	.0401	.0426	.0452
12	.0124	.0137	.0150	.0164	.0179	.0194	.0210	.0227	.0245	.0264
13	.0058	.0065	.0073	.0081	.0089	.0098	.0108	.0119	.0130	.0142
14	.0025	.0029	.0033	.0037	.0041	.0046	.0052	.0058	.0064	.0071
15	.0010	.0012	.0014	.0016	.0018	.0020	.0023	.0026	.0029	.0033
16	.0004	.0005	.0005	.0006	.0007	.0008	.0010	.0011	.0013	.0014
17	0001	.0002	.0002	.0002	.0003	.0003	.0004	.0004	.0005	.0006
18	.0000	.0001	.0001	.0001	.0001	.0001	.0001	.0002	.0002	.0002
19	.0000	.0000	.0000	.0000	.0000	.0000	.0000	.0001	.0001	.0001

Appendix G

Probabilities for the normal distribution

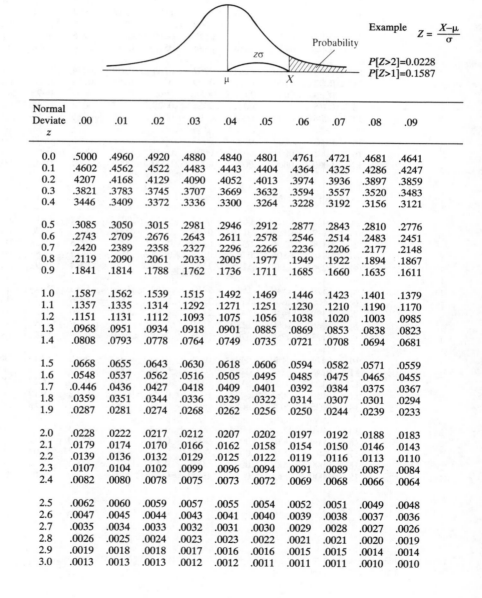

Example $Z = \dfrac{X-\mu}{\sigma}$

$P[Z>2]=0.0228$
$P[Z>1]=0.1587$

Normal Deviate z	.00	.01	.02	.03	.04	.05	.06	.07	.08	.09
0.0	.5000	.4960	.4920	.4880	.4840	.4801	.4761	.4721	.4681	.4641
0.1	.4602	.4562	.4522	.4483	.4443	.4404	.4364	.4325	.4286	.4247
0.2	4207	.4168	.4129	.4090	.4052	.4013	.3974	.3936	.3897	.3859
0.3	.3821	.3783	.3745	.3707	.3669	.3632	.3594	.3557	.3520	.3483
0.4	3446	.3409	.3372	.3336	.3300	.3264	.3228	.3192	.3156	.3121
0.5	.3085	.3050	.3015	.2981	.2946	.2912	.2877	.2843	.2810	.2776
0.6	.2743	.2709	.2676	.2643	.2611	.2578	.2546	.2514	.2483	.2451
0.7	.2420	.2389	.2358	.2327	.2296	.2266	.2236	.2206	.2177	.2148
0.8	.2119	.2090	.2061	.2033	.2005	.1977	.1949	.1922	.1894	.1867
0.9	.1841	.1814	.1788	.1762	.1736	.1711	.1685	.1660	.1635	.1611
1.0	.1587	.1562	.1539	.1515	.1492	.1469	.1446	.1423	.1401	.1379
1.1	.1357	.1335	.1314	.1292	.1271	.1251	.1230	.1210	.1190	.1170
1.2	.1151	.1131	.1112	.1093	.1075	.1056	.1038	.1020	.1003	.0985
1.3	.0968	.0951	.0934	.0918	.0901	.0885	.0869	.0853	.0838	.0823
1.4	.0808	.0793	.0778	.0764	.0749	.0735	.0721	.0708	.0694	.0681
1.5	.0668	.0655	.0643	.0630	.0618	.0606	.0594	.0582	.0571	.0559
1.6	.0548	.0537	.0562	.0516	.0505	.0495	.0485	.0475	.0465	.0455
1.7	.0.446	.0436	.0427	.0418	.0409	.0401	.0392	.0384	.0375	.0367
1.8	.0359	.0351	.0344	.0336	.0329	.0322	.0314	.0307	.0301	.0294
1.9	.0287	.0281	.0274	.0268	.0262	.0256	.0250	.0244	.0239	.0233
2.0	.0228	.0222	.0217	.0212	.0207	.0202	.0197	.0192	.0188	.0183
2.1	.0179	.0174	.0170	.0166	.0162	.0158	.0154	.0150	.0146	.0143
2.2	.0139	.0136	.0132	.0129	.0125	.0122	.0119	.0116	.0113	.0110
2.3	.0107	.0104	.0102	.0099	.0096	.0094	.0091	.0089	.0087	.0084
2.4	.0082	.0080	.0078	.0075	.0073	.0072	.0069	.0068	.0066	.0064
2.5	.0062	.0060	.0059	.0057	.0055	.0054	.0052	.0051	.0049	.0048
2.6	.0047	.0045	.0044	.0043	.0041	.0040	.0039	.0038	.0037	.0036
2.7	.0035	.0034	.0033	.0032	.0031	.0030	.0029	.0028	.0027	.0026
2.8	.0026	.0025	.0024	.0023	.0023	.0022	.0021	.0021	.0020	.0019
2.9	.0019	.0018	.0018	.0017	.0016	.0016	.0015	.0015	.0014	.0014
3.0	.0013	.0013	.0013	.0012	.0012	.0011	.0011	.0011	.0010	.0010

Appendix H

Probabilities for the *t* distribution (two-tail)

Degree of freedom	Student's t distribution												
	Level of significance (α)												
	.9	.8	.7	.6	.5	.4	.3	.2	.1	.05	.02	.01	.001
1	.158	.325	.510	.727	1.000	1.376	1.963	3.078	6.314	12.706	31.821	63.657	636.619
2	.142	.289	.445	.617	.816	1.061	1.386	1.886	2.910	4.303	6.965	9.925	31.598
3	.137	.277	.424	.584	.765	.978	1.250	1.638	2.353	3.182	4.541	5.841	12.941
4	.134	.271	.414	.569	.741	.941	1.190	1.533	2.132	2.776	3.747	4.604	8.610
5	.132	.267	.408	.559	.727	.920	1.156	1.476	2.015	2.571	3.365	4.032	6.859
6	.131	.265	.404	.553	.718	.906	1.134	1.440	1.943	2.447	3.143	3.707	5.959
7	.130	.263	.402	.549	.711	.896	1.119	1.415	1.895	2.365	2.998	3.499	5.405
8	.130	.262	.399	.546	.706	.889	1.108	1.397	1.860	2.306	2.896	3.355	5.041
9	.129	.261	.398	.543	.703	.883	1.100	1.383	1.833	2.262	2.821	3.250	4.781
10	.129	.260	.397	.542	.700	.879	1.093	1.372	1.812	2.228	2.764	3.169	4.587
11	.129	.260	.396	.540	.697	.876	1.088	1.363	1.796	2.201	2.718	3.106	4.437
12	.128	.259	.395	.539	.695	.873	1.083	1.356	1.782	2.179	2.681	3.055	4.318
13	.128	.259	.394	.538	.694	.870	1.079	1.350	1.771	2.160	2.650	3.012	4.221
14	.128	.258	.393	.537	.692	.868	1.076	1.345	1.761	2.145	2.624	2.977	4.140
15	.128	.258	.393	.536	.691	.866	1.074	1.341	1.753	2.131	2.602	2.947	4.073
16	.128	.258	.392	.535	.690	.865	1.071	1.337	1.746	2.120	2.583	2.921	4.015
17	.128	.257	.392	.534	.689	.863	1.069	1.333	1.740	2.110	2.567	2.898	3.965
18	.127	.257	.392	.534	.688	.862	1.067	1.330	1.734	2.101	2.552	2.878	3.922
19	.127	.257	.391	.533	.688	.861	1.066	1.328	1.729	2.093	2.539	2.861	3.883
20	.127	.257	.391	.533	.687	.860	1.064	1.325	1.725	2.086	2.528	2.845	3.850
21	.127	.257	.391	.532	.686	.859	1.063	1.323	1.721	2.080	2.518	2.831	3.819
22	.127	.256	.390	.532	.686	.858	1.061	1.321	1.717	2.074	2.508	2.819	3.792
23	.127	.256	.390	.532	.685	.858	1.060	1.319	1.714	2.069	2.500	2.807	3.767
24	.127	.256	.390	.531	.685	.857	1.059	1.318	1.711	2.064	2.492	2.797	3.745
25	.127	.256	.390	.531	.684	.856	1.058	1.316	1.708	2.060	2.485	2.787	3.725
26	.127	.256	.390	.531	.684	.856	1.058	1.315	1.706	2.056	2.479	2.779	3.707
27	.127	.256	.389	.531	.684	.855	1.057	1.314	1.703	2.052	2.473	2.771	3.690
28	.127	.256	.389	.530	.683	.855	1.056	1.313	1.701	2.048	2.467	2.763	3.674
29	.127	.256	.389	.530	.683	.854	1.055	1.311	1.699	2.045	2.462	2.756	3.659
30	.127	.256	.389	.530	.683	.854	1.055	1.310	1.697	2.042	2.457	2.750	3.646
40	.126	.255	.388	.529	.681	.851	1.050	1.303	1.684	2.021	2.423	2.704	3.551
60	.126	.254	.367	.527	.679	.848	1.046	1.296	1.671	2.000	2.390	2.660	3.460
120	.126	.254	.386	.526	.677	.845	1.041	1.289	1.658	1.980	2.358	2.617	3.373
∞	.126	.253	.385	.524	.674	.842	1.036	1.282	1.645	1.960	2.326	2.576	3.291

Appendix I

Critical values for the χ^2 distribution

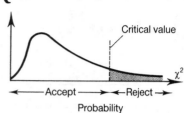

Critical value

←— Accept —→ ←Reject→

Probability

Degree of freedom	0.250	0.100	0.050	0.025	0.010	0.005	0.001
1	1.32	2.71	3.84	5.02	6.63	7.88	10.8
2	2.77	4.61	5.99	7.38	9.21	10.6	13.8
3	4.11	6.25	7.81	9.35	11.3	12.8	16.3
4	5.39	7.78	9.49	11.1	13.3	14.9	18.5
5	6.63	9.24	11.1	12.8	15.1	16.7	20.5
6	7.84	10.6	12.6	14.4	16.8	18.5	22.5
7	9.04	12.0	14.1	16.0	18.5	20.3	24.3
8	10.2	13.4	15.5	17.5	20.3	22.0	26.1
9	11.4	14.7	16.9	19.0	21.7	23.6	27.9
10	12.5	16.0	18.3	20.5	23.2	25.2	29.6
11	13.7	17.3	19.7	21.9	24.7	26.8	31.3
12	14.8	18.5	21.0	23.3	26.2	28.3	32.9
13	16.0	19.8	22.4	24.7	27.7	29.8	34.5
14	17.1	21.1	23.7	26.1	29.1	31.3	36.1
15	18.2	22.3	25.0	27.5	30.6	32.8	37.7
16	19.4	23.5	26.3	28.8	32.0	34.3	39.3
17	20.5	24.8	27.6	30.2	33.4	35.7	40.8
18	21.6	26.0	28.9	31.5	34.8	37.2	42.3
19	22.7	27.2	30.1	32.9	36.2	38.6	43.8
20	23.8	28.4	31.4	34.2	37.6	40.0	45.3
21	24.9	29.6	32.7	35.5	38.9	41.4	46.8
22	26.0	30.8	33.9	36.8	40.3	42.8	48.3
23	27.1	32.0	35.2	38.1	41.6	44.2	49.7
24	28.2	33.2	36.4	39.4	43.0	45.6	51.2
25	29.3	34.4	37.7	40.6	44.3	46.9	52.6
26	30.4	35.6	38.9	41.9	45.6	48.3	54.1
27	31.5	36.7	40.1	43.2	47.0	49.6	55.5
28	32.6	37.9	41.3	44.5	48.3	51.0	56.9
29	33.7	39.1	42.6	45.7	49.6	52.3	58.3

Degree of freedom	0.250	0.100	0.050	0.025	0.010	0.005	0.001
30	34.8	40.3	43.8	47.0	50.9	53.7	59.7
40	45.6	51.8	55.8	59.3	63.7	66.8	73.4
50	56.3	63.2	67.5	71.4	76.2	79.5	86.7
60	67.0	74.4	79.1	83.3	88.4	92.0	99.6
70	77.6	85.5	90.5	95.0	100	104	112
80	88.1	96.6	102	107	112	116	125
90	98.6	108	113	118	123	128	137
100	109	118	124	130	136	140	149

Index

729